Technical Challenges and Design Issues in Bangla Language Processing

M. A. Karim
Old Dominion University, USA

M. Kaykobad
Bangladesh University of Engineering and Technology, Bangladesh

M. Murshed
Monash University, Australia

An Imprint of IGI Global

Managing Director:	Lindsay Johnston
Editorial Director:	Joel Gamon
Production Manager:	Jennifer Yoder
Publishing Systems Analyst:	Adrienne Freeland
Development Editor:	Monica Speca
Assistant Acquisitions Editor:	Kayla Wolfe
Typesetter:	Alyson Zerbe
Cover Design:	Jason Mull

Published in the United States of America by
Information Science Reference (an imprint of IGI Global)
701 E. Chocolate Avenue
Hershey PA 17033
Tel: 717-533-8845
Fax: 717-533-8661
E-mail: cust@igi-global.com
Web site: http://www.igi-global.com

Library of Congress Cataloging-in-Publication Data

Technical challenges and design issues in Bangla language processing / M.A. Karim, M. Kaykobad, and M. Murshed, editors.
pages cm
Includes bibliographical references and index.
Summary: This book addresses the difficulties as well as the overwhelming benefits associated with creating programs and devices that are accessible to the speakers of the Bangla language -- Provided by publisher.
ISBN 978-1-4666-3970-6 (hardcover) -- ISBN 978-1-4666-3971-3 (ebook) -- ISBN 978-1-4666-3972-0 (print & perpetual access) 1. Bengali language--Data processing. 2. Computational linguistics. I. Karim, M. A., 1953- editor of compilation. II. Kaykobad, M., 1954- editor of compilation. III. Murshed, M., 1970- editor of compilation.
PK1658.5.T43 2013
491.4'40285--dc23

2012051564

British Cataloguing in Publication Data
A Cataloguing in Publication record for this book is available from the British Library.

All work contributed to this book is new, previously-unpublished material. The views expressed in this book are those of the authors, but not necessarily of the publisher.

Editorial Advisory Board

Table of Contents

Preface xiv

Chapter 1
Digital Typeface Design and Font Development for Twenty-First Century Bangla Language Processing 1
Fiona G. E. Ross, University of Reading, UK

Chapter 2
Bangla Braille Adaptation 16
Syed Akhter Hossain, Daffodil International University, Bangladesh
Fakhruddin Muhammad Mahbub-ul-Islam, Military Institute of Science and Technology, Bangladesh
Samiul Azam, Military Institute of Science and Technology, Bangladesh
Ahamad Imtiaz Khan, Military Institute of Science and Technology, Bangladesh

Chapter 3
UNL-Based Bangla Machine Translation Framework 35
Nawab Yousuf Ali, East West University, Bangladesh
Shamim H. Ripon, East West University, Bangladesh

Chapter 4
Machine Learning Approaches for Bangla Statistical Machine Translation 79
Maxim Roy, Simon Fraser University, Canada

Chapter 5
Selection of an Optimal Set of Features for Bengali Character Recognition 96
Hasan Sarwar, United International University, Bangladesh
Mizanur Rahman, Institute of Science and Technology (IST), Bangladesh
Nasreen Akter, St. Francis Xavier University, Canada
Saima Hossain, LEADS Corporation Limited, Bangladesh
Sabrina Ahmed, Local Government Engineering Department (LGED), Bangladesh
Chowdhury Mofizur Rahman, United International University, Bangladesh

Detailed Table of Contents

Typeface and font design are fundamental to textual communication, and therefore, such communication, whether for use in print or on screen, is greatly enhanced and facilitated by the development and application of high-quality designs. The chapter discusses the key issues that underpin best practice in Bengali digital type design—from a design's conception to its implementation, that is, the design concept and brief, the character set, the design dimensions, character fitting, and also the considerations for harmonious multi-script setting. The design methodology described is founded on research-based practice in non-Latin type design and font development. It considers how past practices in type-making and typesetting affected current Bengali typeforms and how an evaluation of these practices, in conjunction with the use of the existing and emerging font technologies, can inform the practitioner in the design of high-quality cross-platform OpenType Bengali fonts.

Braille, a tactile writing system, is used by visually impaired and partially sighted people for reading and writing in everyday life. Visually impaired persons in Bangladesh are deprived of basic education due to inadequate textbooks and sufficient reading materials written in Bangla Braille. This is widening the knowledge gap and disparity within the society with progress of time. In order to improve this scenario, an automated information system for facilitating machine translation of Bangla text to readable and recognizable Braille code is essential. In this book chapter, a detailed research on Bangla Braille has been accomplished and necessary grammatical rules as well as conventions are identified for rule-based Bangla Braille translation. Through the analysis of investigations, a computational model is proposed using Deterministic Finite Automata (DFA) for the machine translation. The proposed DFA demonstrated very acceptable conversion, which is validated by the visually impaired community. Based on the computational model, another software architecture is also proposed for the implementation of machine translation of Bangla to Braille using open source technology. The translator is tested with Bangla Unicode-based text contents, and the generated Braille code is validated after printing in the Braille printer. The performance of the conversion of Bangla to Braille code has been found accurate and also free from grammatical errors.

The usage of native language through Internet is highly demanding due to the rapid increase of Internet-based applications in daily life. As information is available in the Internet in different languages, it is impossible to retrieve the information in other languages. Universal Networking Language (UNL) addresses this issue by converting the requested information from other languages to UNL expressions followed by UNL expressions to respective native languages. Even though Bangla is the sixth most popular language in the world, there is no system developed so far to convert Bangla text into UNL expressions and vice versa. For this purpose, the authors develop a framework. The framework has two constituent parts: 1) EnConverter: converts Bangla native sentences into UNL expressions considering UNL compatible Bangla word dictionary and analysis rules, and 2) DeConverter: converts UNL expressions into respective Bangla sentences considering Bangla word dictionary and generations rules. In both cases, case structure analysis, Bangla parts of speech, and different forms of verbs along with their prefixes, suffixes, and inflections are taken into consideration. This chapter describes the complete theoretical analyses of the EnConversion and DeConversion frameworks. The experimental results confirm that the proposed framework can successfully convert Bangla sentences into UNL expressions, and also can convert UNL expressions into corresponding Bangla sentences.

Machine Translation (MT) from Bangla to English has recently become a priority task for the Bangla Natural Language Processing (NLP) community. Statistical Machine Translation (SMT) systems require a significant amount of bilingual data between language pairs to achieve significant translation accuracy. However, being a low-density language, such resources are not available in Bangla. In this chapter, the authors discuss how machine learning approaches can help to improve translation quality within as SMT system without requiring a huge increase in resources. They provide a novel semi-supervised learning and active learning framework for SMT, which utilizes both labeled and unlabeled data. The authors discuss sentence selection strategies in detail and perform detailed experimental evaluations on the sentence selection methods. In semi-supervised settings, reversed model approach outperformed all other approaches for Bangla-English SMT, and in active learning setting, geometric 4-gram and geometric phrase sentence selection strategies proved most useful based on BLEU score results over baseline approaches. Overall, in this chapter, the authors demonstrate that for low-density language like Bangla, these machine-learning approaches can improve translation quality.

Feature extraction is an essential step of Optical Character Recognition. Accurate and distinguishable feature plays a significant role to leverage the performance of a classifier. The complexity level of feature identification algorithm differs for alphabet sets of different languages. Apart from generic algorithms to find features of different alphabet sets, these algorithms take care of individual characteristic common for a particular alphabet set. Dominant features of one alphabet set might completely differ from that of another set. Since there always remains the chance that inaccurate features may cause inefficient recognition, special attention should be given to identify the set of optimal features of a character set. Bengali characters also have some specific issues apart from the existing issues of other character sets. For example, there are about 300 basic, modified, and compound character shapes in the script, the characters in a word are topologically connected, and Bengali is an inflectional language. Literature survey shows that several authors have used different features and classification algorithms. The authors have extensively reviewed all these feature sets. In order to identify an optimal feature set, variability analysis has been proposed here. They focus on the specific peculiarities of Bengali alphabet sets, its different usage as vowel and consonant signs, compound, complex, and touching characters. The authors also took care to generate easily computable features that take less time for generation. However, more attention needs to be given in order to choose an efficient classifier.

Automatic Bangla character recognition has been a great challenge for research and development because of the huge number of characters, change of shape in a word and in conjunctive characters, and other similar reasons. An optical joint transform correlation-based technique is developed for Bangla character recognition which involves a simple architecture, but can operate at a very high speed because of optics, and offer a very high level of accuracy with negligible false alarms. The proposed correlation technique can successfully identify a target character in a given input scene by producing a single correlation peak per target at the target location. The discrimination between target and non-target correlation peaks is found to be very high even in noisy conditions. The recognition performance of the proposed technique is observed to be insensitive to the type and number of targets. Further improvement of the technique is made by incorporating a synthetic discriminant function, which is created from distorted images of the target character and hence can make the system efficiently recognize Bangla characters in different practical scenarios.

Chapter 7

Al-Mahmud, Khulna University of Engineering and Technology (KUET), Bangladesh
Bishnu Sarker, Khulna University of Engineering and Technology (KUET), Bangladesh
K. M. Azharul Hasan, Khulna University of Engineering and Technology (KUET), Bangladesh

Parsing plays a very prominent role in computational linguistics. Parsing a Bangla sentence is a primary need in Bangla language processing. This chapter describes the Context Free Grammar (CFG) for parsing Bangla language, and hence, a Bangla parser is proposed based on the Bangla grammar. This approach is very simple to apply in Bangla sentences, and the method is well accepted for parsing grammar. This chapter introduces a parser for Bangla language, which is, by nature, a predictive parser, and the parse table is constructed for recognizing Bangla grammar. Parse table is an important tool to recognize syntactical mistakes of Bangla sentences when there is no entry for a terminal in the parse table. If a natural language can be successfully parsed then grammar checking of this language becomes possible. The parsing scheme in this chapter works based on a top-down parsing method. CFG suffers from a major problem called left recursion. The technique of left factoring is applied to avoid the problem.

Chapter 8

Utpal Garain, Indian Statistical Institute, India
Sankar De, Gupta College of Technological Sciences, India

A grammar-driven dependency parsing has been attempted for Bangla (Bengali). The free-word order nature of the language makes the development of an accurate parser very difficult. The Paninian grammatical model has been used to tackle the free-word order problem. The approach is to simplify complex and compound sentences and then to parse simple sentences by satisfying the Karaka demands of the Demand Groups (Verb Groups). Finally, parsed structures are rejoined with appropriate links and Karaka labels. The parser has been trained with a Treebank of 1000 annotated sentences and then evaluated with un-annotated test data of 150 sentences. The evaluation shows that the proposed approach achieves 90.32% and 79.81% accuracies for unlabeled and labeled attachments, respectively.

Chapter 9

Mohammed Rokibul Alam Kotwal, United International University, Bangladesh
Foyzul Hassan, United International University, Bangladesh
Mohammad Nurul Huda, United International University, Bangladesh

This chapter presents Bangla (widely known as Bengali) Automatic Speech Recognition (ASR) techniques by evaluating the different speech features, such as Mel Frequency Cepstral Coefficients (MFCCs), Local Features (LFs), phoneme probabilities extracted by time delay artificial neural networks of different architectures. Moreover, canonicalization of speech features is also performed for Gender-Independent (GI) ASR. In the canonicalization process, the authors have designed three classifiers by male, female, and GI speakers, and extracted the output probabilities from these classifiers for measuring the maximum. The maximization of output probabilities for each speech file provides higher correctness and accuracies for GI speech recognition. Besides, dynamic parameters (velocity and acceleration coefficients) are also used in the experiments for obtaining higher accuracy in phoneme recognition. From the experiments, it is also shown that dynamic parameters with hybrid features also increase the phoneme recognition performance in a certain extent. These parameters not only increase the accuracy of the ASR system, but also reduce the computation complexity of Hidden Markov Model (HMM)-based classifiers with fewer mixture components.

The chapter provides an overview of the theory of speech production, analysis, and synthesis, and status of Bangla speech processing. As nasality is a distinctive feature of Bangla and all the vowels have their nasal counterpart, both Bangla vowels and nasality are also considered. The chapter reviews the state-of-the-art of nasal vowel research, cross language perception of vowel nasality, and vowel nasality transformation to be used in a speech synthesizer.

The aim of this chapter is to clearly understand the salient features of Bangla vowels and the sources of acoustic variability in Bangla vowels, and to suggest classification of vowels based on normalized acoustic parameters. Possible applications in automatic speech recognition and speech enhancement have made the classification of vowels an important problem to study. However, Bangla vowels spoken by different native speakers show great variations in their respective formant values. This brings further complications in the acoustic comparison of vowels due to different dialect and language backgrounds of the speakers. This variation necessitates the use of normalization procedures to remove the effect of non-linguistic factors. Although several researchers found a number of acoustical and perceptual correlates of vowels, acoustic parameters that work well in a speaker-independent manner are yet to be found. Besides, study of acoustic features of Bangla dental consonants to identify the spectral differences between different consonants and to parameterize them for the synthesis of the segments is another problem area for study. The extracted features for both Bangla vowels and dental consonants are tested and found with good synthetic representations that demonstrate the quality of acoustic features.

This chapter introduces Bengali Information Retrieval (IR) to students by explaining the fundamental concepts of IR such as indexing, retrieval, and evaluation metrics. This chapter also provides a survey of and comparisons between various Bengali language-specific methodologies, and hence can serve researchers particularly interested in the state-of-the-art developments in Bengali IR. It can also act as a guideline for application developers on how to set up an information retrieval system for the Bengali language. All steps for creating and evaluating an information retrieval system are introduced, including content processing, indexing, retrieval models, and evaluation. Special attention is given to language-specific aspects of Bengali information retrieval. In addition, the chapter discusses cross-lingual information retrieval, where queries are entered in English with an objective to retrieving Bengali documents.

Chapter 13
The Bengali Literary Collection of Rabindranath Tagore: Search and Study of Lexical Richness.... 302
Suprabhat Das, Indian Institute of Technology Kharagpur, India
Anupam Basu, Indian Institute of Technology Kharagpur, India
Pabitra Mitra, Indian Institute of Technology Kharagpur, India

Rabindranath Tagore is one of the most prolific authors of Bengali literature. He has added a vast amount of richness in style and language to the Bengali text. The present study aims at a quantitative study of vocabulary size and lexical richness as well as effective search engine for his works. Several statistical measures of term distribution have been used to measure lexical richness. An initial attempt has been made to build a search engine, Anwesan, for Rabindra Rachanabali collection. The first complete digital Rabindra Rachanabali released by Society for Natural Language Technology Research, Kolkata, in 2010, has been used in the study. It was observed that a high lexical richness value was characteristics of most of Rabindranath Tagore's work.

Chapter 14
Sentiment Recognition from Bangla Text 315
K. M. Azharul Hasan, Khulna University of Engineering and Technology (KUET), Bangladesh
Sajidul Islam, Khulna University of Engineering and Technology (KUET), Bangladesh
G. M. Mashrur-E-Elahi, Khulna University of Engineering and Technology (KUET), Bangladesh
Mohammad Navid Izhar, Khulna University of Engineering and Technology (KUET), Bangladesh

Sentiment analysis is a very important area of the natural language processing. In general, sentiment classification means the analysis to determine the expression of a speaker whether he or she holds positive or negative opinion to a specific subject. With the rapid growth of e-commerce, sentiment analysis can greatly influence everyone in their real life. For example, product reviews on the Web have become an important source of information for customers' decision making when they want to buy any product. As the reviews are often too many for customers to go through, how to automatically classify and detect the sentiment from them has become an important research problem. In this chapter, the authors present a Sentiment Analyzer that recognizes the Bangla sentiment or opinion about a subject from Bangla text. They construct some phrase patterns and calculate their sentiment orientation. They add tags to words in the Bangla text to construct the phrase pattern for positive and negative sentiment. Then the authors match the phrase pattern in Bangla text with their predefined phrase pattern and cumulate the sentiment orientation of each sentence.

Chapter 15
(*Jantra-Na*: Not-Machine) Can Only Feel (*Jantrana*: Pain)! 328
Amitava Das, Norwegian University of Science and Technology, Norway
Björn Gambäck, Norwegian University of Science and Technology, Norway

Arguably, the most important difference between machines and humans is that humans have feelings. For several decades researchers have been trying to create methods to simulate sentimentality for machines, and currently Sentiment Analysis is the hottest, most demanding, and rapidly growing task in the language processing field. Sentiment analysis or opinion mining refers to the application of Natural Language Processing, Computational Linguistics, and text analytics to identify and extract sentimental (opinionated, emotional) information in a text. The basic task in sentiment analysis is to classify the polarity of a given text at the document, sentence, or feature/aspect level, that is, to decide whether the expressed sentiment in a document, a sentence, or a feature/aspect is positive (happy), negative (sad), neutral (memorable), and so forth. In this chapter, the authors discuss various challenges and solution strategies for Sentiment Analysis with a particular view to texts in Bangla (Bengali).

Chapter 16
Building Language Resources for Emotion Analysis in Bengali 346
Dipankar Das, National Institute of Technology (NIT), India
Sivaji Bandyopadhyay, Jadavpur University, India

Rapidly growing Web users from multilingual communities focus the attention to improve the multilingual search engines on the basis of sentiment or emotion and provide the opportunities to build resources for languages other than English. At present, there is no such corpus or lexicon available for emotion analysis in Indian languages, especially for Bengali, the sixth most popular language in the world, second in India, and the national language of Bangladesh. Thus, in the chapter, the authors describe the preparation of an emotion corpus and lexicon in Bengali. The emotion lexicon, termed Bengali WordNet Affect has been developed from its equivalent version in English by traversing the steps of expansion, translation, and sense disambiguation. In addition to emotion lexicon, a Bengali blog corpus for emotion analysis has also been developed by manual annotators with detailed linguistic expressions such as emotional phrases, intensities, emotion holder, emotion topic and target span, and sentential emotion tags.

Compilation of References 369

About the Contributors 396

Index 404

Preface

Over 250 million people speak Bangla (or Bengali), an Indo-Iranian language. The overwhelming majority of this population lives in the eastern flank of South Asia that surrounds the Bay of Bengal. They are geographically distributed as follows: over 95% of those living in Bangladesh, and from amongst the Indian states about 26% of those in Andaman and Nicobar Islands, 28% of those in Assam, 67% of those in Tripura, and 85% those in West Bengal. A large Bangla-speaking population is now in diaspora in Canada, Malawi, Nepal, Pakistan, Saudi Arabia, Singapore, United Arab Emirates, United Kingdom, and United States. Although it is the sixth most spoken language in the world, it is not necessarily as highly ranked in terms of the most read, or the most wired, or the most archived, or the most used on the Internet.

Despite significant progress in Information and Communication Technology (ICT) and the availability of a huge, enriched English knowledge database around the globe, the potential ICT benefit continues to elude a large majority of the Bangla-speaking population who are not equipped with either English or the language of their own diaspora. This is complicated by the fact that Bangla is not without its own peculiar nuances and structural issues. It has a relatively large alphabet set that also includes many compound letters, two acceptable forms with varying pronouns and verb conjugations, many regional dialects, and variant spellings for too many of its words. Additionally, there are at least two non-standard dialects of Bangla – Chittagonian and Sylheti, respectively, with 47% and 30% lexical dissimilarity. Bangla Language Processing (BLP) is an evolving computer science discipline that is cognizant of these language realities and seeks to create a robust digital platform for use by a large majority of the Bangla-speaking population who are being bypassed currently by the ICT revolution. The success of BLP is envisioned to have a positive impact for many of the common people and their socio-economic life.

This book had its origins in a major IEEE-sponsored international conference, namely the International Conference in Computer and Information Technology (ICCIT), now in its 16th year, which continues to highlight the latest works in BLP. While there continues to be progress in BLP research, lack of enough archived material outside of that already included in IEEE xPlore continues to force not only the students of computer science and engineering but also the researchers and technologists to fall often in the trap of re-inventing the wheel. We hope that this milestone source book will fill a serious void in both teaching and research, facilitate further BLP research and development, and, consequently, preserve Bangla as a vibrant digitization-ready language for a long time to come.

The 16 chapters of *Technical Challenges and Design Issues in Bangla Language Processing,* selected from 27 initially proposed papers, are authored by 41 researchers from Bangladesh, Canada, India, Ireland, Norway, United Kingdom, and United States. These chapters span seven BLP topical areas – font design, machine translation, character recognition, parsing, speech processing, information retrieval, and sentiment analysis. Additional acceptable chapters on word processing, spell checking, database management, digital displays, and wireless applications would have made this a much stronger resource book.

In chapter 1, Fiona Ross discusses the key issues that underpin best practices in Bengali digital type design – from a design's conception to its implementation. Aspects of the character set such as dimensions, character fitting, and harmonious multi-script setting are considered from a perspective of non-Latin type design and font development. The chapter elaborates on how past practices in type-making and typesetting has affected current Bengali type forms and how the existing and emerging font technologies can be used effectively to support high-quality cross-platform Open Type Bengali fonts. The next chapter by Hossain, Mahbub-ul-Islam, Azam, Ahamad, and Khan reviews Bangla Braille development and identifies necessary grammatical rules as well as conventions for rule-based Braille translation. A computational model that uses Deterministic Finite Automata (DFA) for machine translation is introduced and studied for its acceptability by the visually impaired community. Architecture for the implementation of machine translation of Bangla to Braille using open source technology is demonstrated and is tested with Bangla Unicode-based text contents, and the generated Braille code is validated after printing in a Braille printer.

Machine Translation (MT) by creating lexical resources allows computers to translate texts from one natural language to another; its importance has become ever more significant with increasing use of the Internet. While the MT for English-Chinese, English-Arabic, and English-French, for example, are already advanced, developing Bangla MT hasn't progressed as much. In chapter three, Ali and Ripon develop a framework for Bangla MT that consists of an EnConverter to convert Bangla native sentences to UNL expressions and a DeConverter, which converts UNL expressions to respective Bangla sentences. In both, the authors consider case structure analysis, Bangla parts of speech, and different forms of verbs along with their prefixes, suffixes, and inflexions. Experimental results confirm that the proposed framework can successfully convert Bangla sentences to UNL expressions, and vice versa. This is followed by chapter four in which Maxim Roy considers the ideas behind Statistical Machine Translation (SMT) systems, which depend otherwise on the availability of bilingual data between language pairs to improve accuracy. The author considers machine-learning approaches such as sentence selection strategies that can improve accuracy without requiring a huge increase in resources. In semi-supervised settings, it is shown that the reversed model approach outperformed all other approaches for Bangla-English SMT and in active learning settings.

Optical Character Recognition (OCR) will play a significant role in the digitization of both printed and handwritten documents and texts. It depends on the performance of classifiers, which in turn relies on the feature extraction methodology used. For Bangla OCR, there are additional challenges to overcome since it is an inflectional language; there are about 300 *basic*, *modified,* and *compound* character shapes in the script, and the characters in a word are often topologically connected. In chapter five, Sarwar, Rahman, Akter, Hossain, Ahmed, and Rahman provide a review of various feature sets and a variability analysis for an optimal feature set by focusing on the specific peculiarities of Bangla such as its different usage as vowel and consonant signs, as well as compound, complex, and connected characters. Islam and Karim then follow up with chapter six, which provides for coverage of optical techniques/system for recognition of Bangla characters. The authors review phase-only filter-based hybrid electro-optical systems but then build upon them to elaborate on the use of joint Fourier transform optical correlators in recognition of Bangla characters.

Morphological information is integral to parsing, lemmatization, and in applications such as text generation, machine translation, and document retrieval. The next two chapters (7 and 8) focus on parsing that plays a prominent role in computational linguistics. Words consist of individually meaningful root elements known otherwise as morphemes. Since combining morphemes forms a large number of words, the capacity to produce and understand new words depends often on knowing which morphemes are involved. Morphological analysis of simple and compound Bangla words can be used to make a Universal Natural Language (UNL)-Bangla dictionary for converting the natural Bangla sentences to UNL documents and vice versa. In chapter seven, Al-Mahmud, Sarker, and Hasan review the Context-Free Grammar (CFG) for parsing Bangla language processing. It involves a predictive parser, and the parse table is constructed for recognizing Bangla grammar and overcoming possible syntactical errors when there is no entry for a terminal in the parse table. The top-down CFG parsing suffers often from left recursion issues that are overcome by considering a left-factoring technique. Garain and De, in chapter eight, next consider a constraint-based Dependency Parsing, in general, and a Paninian grammatical model, in particular. The authors attempt to simplify complex and compound sentential structures first, then parse the simple structures so obtained by satisfying the Karaka demands of the verb groups and finally rejoin the parsed structures with the appropriate links and Karaka labels. The trained parser is shown to achieve very high accuracy.

The understanding of human speech by computers is limited in part because it interfaces usually through a keyboard and mouse. Speech recognition as a concept has multiple application possibilities including for user authentication and for use by those who are disabled. The next three chapters focus on varying aspects of speech recognition.

In chapter 9, Kotwal, Hassan, and Huda review Bangla Automatic Speech Recognition (ASR) techniques by evaluating different speech features, such as Mel frequency cepstral coefficients, local features, and phoneme probabilities for different artificial neural networks. The authors have designed three classifiers by male, female, and gender-independent speakers and explored the use of dynamic parameters in their experiments for obtaining higher accuracy in phoneme recognition. Haque follows up in chapter ten and provides an overview of the theory of speech production and analysis and synthesis of Bangla ASR. The author explores nasality, which is a distinctive feature of Bangla vowels, in particular. The chapter provides a review of nasal vowel research, cross-language perception of Bangla vowel nasality and vowel nasality transformation for use in a speech synthesizer. Finally, chapter eleven by Hossain, Rahman, Ahmed, and Sobhan reviews the salient features of Bangla vowels and the sources of acoustic variability in Bangla vowels, and suggests the classification of vowels based on normalized acoustic parameters. The normalization is necessary to remove the effect of non-linguistic factors given that Bangla vowels are spoken differently by different native speakers and by different regions. The authors also consider the study of acoustic features of Bangla dental consonants to identify the spectral differences and parameterize them for the purposes of synthesis.

Ganguly, Leveling, and Jones, in chapter 12, provide an introduction to Bangla information retrieval by reviewing its latest state-of-the-art and identifying the guidelines for application developers on how to set up an information retrieval system, with special attention given to language-specific aspects. The chapter identifies steps for creating and evaluating an information retrieval system including content processing, indexing, retrieval models, and evaluation. They also explore cross-lingual information retrieval, in which queries are entered in English with an objective to retrieve documents in Bangla. Chapter thirteen, by Das, Basu, and Mitra, next explores the specific case of Bangla information retrieval by considering the literary work of Rabindranath Tagore. Tagore's work happens to also provide for richness in both style and language. This work includes a quantitative study of vocabulary size and lexical richness in terms of statistical measures as well as an effective search engine for his works.

The final three chapters of the book are devoted to sentiment analysis, which is turning out to be an important area of natural language processing. The effort to determine whether the expression of a speaker or writer is positive or negative toward a specific subject is becoming relevant given the rapid growth of e-commerce and e-governance. In chapter fourteen, Hasan, Islam, Masur-E-Elahi, and Izhar present a *Sentiment Analyzer* that recognizes Bangla sentiment or opinion about a subject from Bangla text. It relies on specific phrase patterns and their sentiment orientations. Next in chapter fifteen, Amitava and Gambäck explore a particular sentiment analysis to determine if the opinion in question is positive (happy), negative (sad), or neutral (memorable). Finally, in chapter sixteen, Das and Bandyopadhyay consider improving multilingual search engines on the basis of sentiment or emotion and in an effort to build resources for languages other than English. The authors describe the preparation of an emotion corpus and lexicon, termed the Bengali *WordNet Affect*, by considering expansion, translation, and sense disambiguation. Manual annotators develop a Bangla blog corpus for emotion analysis with considerations given to emotional expressions and intensities, emotion holders, and sentential emotion tags.

From a scan of the chapters and topics included in this book, it is clear that there is an effort at exploring research on vital BLP topics. Few of the serious challenges, as we see, remain to be addressed. There still seems to be a lack of detailed morphological analysis of the Bangla language, which is going to impact software framework for the purposes of spell checker, OCR, grammar checker, speech generation, and machine translation. Developing a reliable machine translation system is key to benefitting from the huge English knowledge database of the Internet as well as journals. The need to build a larger and elaborate lexicon as well as a fully Unicode-compatible Bangla operating system in Windows and Linux platforms remain serious issues. Except for newspapers, there exists hardly much of any archived Bangla corpus. Most importantly, there is a lack of coordination and integration not only among the BLP research groups but also between how it is being pursued often differently in Bangladesh and India.

Mohammad A. Karim
Old Dominion University, USA

Mohammad Kaykobad
Bangladesh University of Engineering and Technology, Bangladesh

Manzur Murshed
Monash University, Australia

November 2012

Chapter 1
Digital Typeface Design and Font Development for Twenty-First Century Bangla Language Processing

Fiona G. E. Ross
University of Reading, UK

ABSTRACT

Typeface and font design are fundamental to textual communication, and therefore, such communication, whether for use in print or on screen, is greatly enhanced and facilitated by the development and application of high-quality designs. The chapter discusses the key issues that underpin best practice in Bengali digital type design—from a design's conception to its implementation, that is, the design concept and brief, the character set, the design dimensions, character fitting, and also the considerations for harmonious multi-script setting. The design methodology described is founded on research-based practice in non-Latin type design and font development. It considers how past practices in type-making and typesetting affected current Bengali typeforms and how an evaluation of these practices, in conjunction with the use of the existing and emerging font technologies, can inform the practitioner in the design of high-quality cross-platform OpenType Bengali fonts.

INTRODUCTION

Typeface design is a multi-disciplinary activity that sees the practical application of artistic, technical and, often, linguistic skills. Its outcomes, in the form of fonts, provide the bedrock for effective textual communication in the many and diverse writing-systems of the world that represent an even greater range of languages. The existing and emerging font technologies now allow for the accurate rendering of complex scripts[1], hitherto unattainable for many writing-systems, and so make this an apposite time in typographic history to redress the recognized dearth of high-quality non-Latin typeface designs. The recent availability of reliable yet relatively low-cost font-making tools,

DOI: 10.4018/978-1-4666-3970-6.ch001

that are no longer limited to proprietary systems, enable the generation of Unicode[2] compliant cross-platform OpenType[3] fonts by independent designers as well as by design studios or software companies.

This chapter describes a design methodology which is founded on research-based practice in non-Latin typeface design (Ross, 2002) to achieve optimum readability in typographic compositions, whether in print or on screen. It considers the key issues of Bengali type design that arise from a design's conception to its implementation that come under the broader categories of the design brief, the character set, the design dimensions, and character fitting. Consideration is also given to the increasing requirement for multi-script setting. The chapter describes how the evaluation of past practices of type-making and typesetting, and the anticipation of further technological developments, can inform today's practitioners in order to achieve best practice in this field to answer the needs of over 250 million Bangla-language speakers.

BACKGROUND

This chapter is written from a type designer's and font developer's point of view based on the premise that typeface and font design are fundamental to visual communication. The focus here is primarily on designing text typefaces since these are the workhorses of textual communication by means of pre-fabricated letterforms, and are the most challenging to execute. The current repertoire of Bengali typeface designs is noticeably limited[4], and fonts often exist in incompatible formats. Furthermore, the quality in terms of readability and appropriateness of the design for its purpose is poor in comparison to Latin typefaces and in comparison to the early Bengali foundry types.

The urgency of addressing this subject for the Bengali language is underlined by the continued apparent ubiquitous use of the Linotype Bengali digital typeface[5] in the majority of publications in the Bengali script although fonts of this typeface have not been available for purchase by legitimate means for over two decades. Furthermore, the typeface was originally designed for setting newspaper text on newsprint, yet it is nowadays used to answer a multiplicity of functions, however inappropriate its design, including for display purposes on billboard posters, and for text passages on Web pages[6], albeit in a cloned form (see Figure 1).

Hitherto, little has been written on the subject, except by the author, and particularly in relation to the visual representation of the Bengali language. The focus has been on printing histories, publishing history in Kolkata (Khan, 1976; Shaw, 1981; Kesavan, 1985) and not on the design of Bengali typeforms for current technology. This chapter therefore develops further the new chapter in the author's re-published book (Ross, 2009), which highlights some of the issues that are covered here in greater depth. For want of other reference texts that are based on original research[7], this work and other writings by the author are necessarily cited in order to provide further information that is helpful in substantiating particular assertions within the essay. In the field of Latin typeface design, Walter Tracy's work (Tracy, 1986), based on his many years of experience whilst working at Linotype-Paul Limited, provides useful insights into good practice that is applicable to Bengali and other non-Latin scripts, and is cited where appropriate.

Terminology

Currently there is no standard terminology for discussing typeforms in non-Latin scripts and those used for the Latin are at times inappropriate (e.g. x-height) or fail to describe aspects peculiar to the Bengali script. For the purpose of this essay, the use of the terminology developed by the

Figure 1. Overview of four Bengali newspapers published in Kolkata, 14 April 2010. All four use the Linotype Bengali digital typeface design.

author (Ross, 1999) will be used in conjunction with the key terms and definitions defined at the end of this chapter (see Figure 2).

DIGITAL TYPEFACE DESIGN AND FONT DEVELOPMENT IN THE BENGALI SCRIPT

The Design Brief

As in many other areas of visual communication, in the specific field of typeface design, the design brief, which here is the intended function of a typeface, is crucial to the initial design concept. The considerations regarding the designing of a newspaper text typeface are quite different from those that are required for, say, a display typeface or a screen font for mobile devices (Tracy, 1986). Newspaper text fonts are designed for providing readable continuous texts at small point sizes that fit as many as words as possible to each text column, which is usually of a narrow measure, has little interlinear spacing and is set justified. This requires a compact typeface of relatively narrow characters that are not too widely spaced, and whose height and depth do not compromise the interlinear spacing, by causing clashes between lines, and do not produce irregular dark spots within the text by compacting deep or tall type-forms. Large, open counters assist in increasing the apparent size of body copy, and adherence to perceived acceptable proportions optimise readability. With this in mind, the Linotype Bengali digital typeface, whose design comprising two weights was conceived in 1978, was intended to achieve economic use of space whilst maintaining clarity and regularity of image at small sizes. It possessed a sufficiently light stroke weight in the Light font to cater for anticipated ink-gain that the variable quality of the newsprint and the printing processes of the time were likely to incur. The overall design was intended to overcome the aesthetic deficiencies of Linotype's hot-metal

Figure 2. Typeface nomenclature for the Bengali script (Ross, 1999)

Bengali fonts and to incorporate the elegance and vibrancy visible in manuscripts that pre-date printed Bengali typeforms.

In contrast to the Linotype Bengali Light digital font, which was designed to form an invisible interface between the reader and the textual content, the Bold weight was designed with sufficiently bold strokes and greater stroke contrast to attract attention for use in headlines and to create differentiation from the body text, but again with a view to economies of space. Book text faces, not being constrained by the narrow measure of newspaper columns and the concomitant tightness of leading, have different criteria for their design. Accordingly, the brief for the Bengali typeface design for the Murty Classical Library of India requires a typeface that is classical in its proportions and yet contemporary to appeal to a new generation of readers. It is more relaxed in its spacing and in its height and depth than the newspaper typeface in order to allow comfortable immersive reading. Yet again, the typographic requirements for typefaces used in reference texts such as dictionaries would produce quite a different brief, where lax spacing would not be a preference, and differentiation is achieved by means of variations in typestyles and in type sizes to create the visual hierarchy essential to assisting the reader in navigating efficiently to the desired content.

Furthermore, whereas previously the type designer needed to consider the use of fonts on a wide range of paper surfaces with different printing and, therefore, inking techniques, now there is an additional and increasing demand for digital fonts that can be read on a variety of screens with different resolutions. These fonts are also expected to function in a range of sizes as the user may 'zoom' in and out of the reading matter at will. Moreover, the designer may also need to contend with the demand from a newspaper that the same presence be evident in its printed editions and its electronic versions, even though the latter would ideally require quite different design treatments for its typefaces and its typography. The design of Web-fonts or, more commonly, the adaptation of existing fonts for better rendering on the Web, now forms an important part of a type foundry's activity. The listing of over 50 Bengali newspapers available on-line alone testifies to the value of designing for this environment, and one in which different browsers and rendering engines may produce quite different results; and Web designers need to be aware that reading fatigue may permanently deter readers from re-visiting a Website.

All of these considerations highlight the continued requirement for a broader typographic palette[8] to answer the needs of Bengali-speaking communities. As intimated above, determining the style for a new typeface is often intimately connected with its primary function. Whilst reader conservatism (the preference to read shapes that are familiar) can inhibit the creation of original designs, there are many models of letterform practice both historical and contemporary that can inspire new designs. Familiarity with type history, the typefaces, and the technological influences on them, occasioned by type-making and typesetting methods, is an excellent and indeed essential means of informing good practice. Much can be learnt from researching the clear, elegant Bengali typeforms that were skillfully produced by foundries from the nineteenth century onwards. Although typeface design can be regarded as an abstraction of hand-written letterforms, the relationship between the formal Bengali penned hand and its printed counterpart are not too distant despite a period during the twentieth century when the ungainly hot-metal linear forms dominated the most widely disseminated publications. Therefore, examining manuscripts from different periods as well as the works of calligraphers, sign-writers, and even contemporary graffiti artists can apprise the designer of the wide range of possibilities available for the development of new designs to produce aesthetically pleasing, cohesive and readable typefaces that are fit for purpose.

These rich and varied sources can impart information regarding the execution of particular observable characteristics such as the sizing of enclosed counters relative to the stroke weight; the degree of stroke modulation at particular sizes; the junction of diagonal strokes to the verticals; the treatment of ascending flourishes; the relative widths and spacing; the placement of superscripts or subscripts, and the like. It is immeasurably useful for the designer to observe and evaluate such characteristics, whose styling may have been determined by their intended function and by the cultural influences of their period, and whose shaping and resulting image would have been formed by different tools and substrates, and in certain cases by technical and economic restrictions, or even by an inexperienced or misinformed author. Such research and analysis can aid the designer in conscious, informed decision-making in the formulation of pre-fabricated letterforms for the relatively unconstrained font technology of OpenType.

There is sometimes a misconception that digital type design is related to software programming and requires high-level mathematical skills, but it is a discipline that has its roots firmly in the creative design field. Yet there are practical technical considerations that need to be observed throughout the design process.

The Character Set

One of the first considerations is determining the extent of the character set. Historically, restrictions have almost always been placed on the number of typeforms in a font either due to cost or technical limitations; and the legacy of these limitations are evident in non-Latin fonts even today. There is no finite character set for the majority of Indian scripts since the combination of different consonantal clusters (conjuncts) can introduce new ligated forms. Neologisms and the transliteration of foreign names and loan words continually add to the desired character count and require, if possible, the flexibility to add or create new forms. In metal type, when each type size required an entire new font of type, economic considerations were primarily focussed on the cost of the metal and the manufacture and storage of type; this was radically altered in the era of hot-metal when setting speeds and technical limitations prescribed the number of sorts available. These limitations eased in filmsetting and digital type, but even with the advent of DeskTop publishing the expected limit was 256 characters. In OpenType there are Latin fonts that number thousands of glyphs to provide extensive language coverage and alternative forms; but the design and production costs, in terms of the time needed to design and produce high-quality fonts, have become natural limitations to extensive character sets.

A concise history of Bengali character-set sizes provides a useful indication of the variability of non-Latin font repertoires. The first fully functional font of Bengali types was produced by Charles Wilkins in 1778 for N.B. Halhed's *A Grammar of the Bengal Language*. Wilkins was able to employ what can be regarded as a relatively small font of circa 170 sorts by the means of using '*phalas*' (character components) to create many of the required conjuncts[9]. The Bengali font repertoire was later extended to 370 sorts by Vincent Figgins in his neat and eminently readable Pica Bengali font that appeared in 1826 and which was used regularly for over a century. An undated listing of the font repertoire shows the inclusion of special sorts to generate particular character combinations, the successful use of which depended much upon the skills of the compositor and the printer. These sorts obviated the need to extend the character set to the standard number of just over 500 sorts that indigenous Bengali foundries employed from the mid-nineteenth century onwards; a period which witnessed some exemplary typography in Bengali book production (see Figure 3).

However, the implementation of the Bengali script on the Linotype line-casting machine for newspaper production drastically reduced the number of sorts, or rather, in this case, matrices. Thus in 1935 the Linotype Bengali matrix listing shows 90 sorts in the main magazine for the requisite speedy typesetting of newspaper copy, augmented by one auxiliary and one Pi magazine. The reduced character set, which depended on often ill-fitting components, compounded by other technological constraints of the linecaster, produced very poor results but the outcome was functional in that it enabled newspaper production in the Bengali language. Hot-metal fonts by Monotype initially provided a set of 225 sorts, which was later increased due to an adapted keyboard arrangement, and which was converted to film fonts with some improvements in 1970. In

Figure 3. Foundry typeface no. 6 used by Ananda Bazar Patrika Ltd before 1982

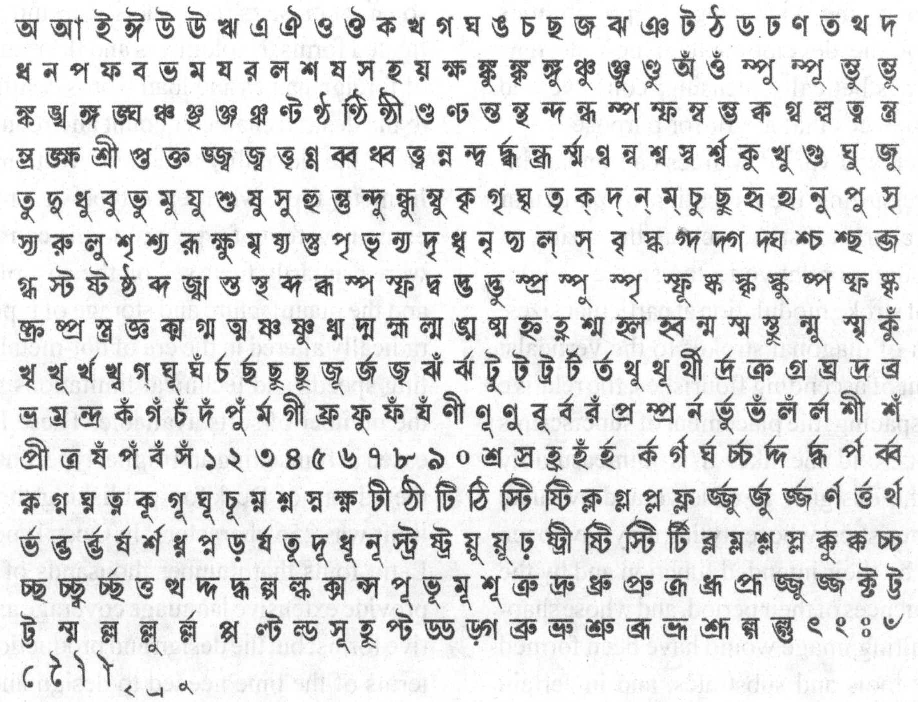

1982, the publication of the first digital Bengali font used proprietary software for the Linotron 202 typesetter to overcome the 256-glyph set limitation adhered to by most font manufacturers. This enabled the design of fully integrated conjuncts inspired by manuscript forms in an initial font of approximately 300 glyphs, which was only made possible by the invention of the *phonetic keyboard* for Indian scripts by Linotype initially for Bengali typesetting in 1978[10]. Over thirty years later, it is anticipated that the new OpenType font planned for setting classical and contemporary Bengali texts will contain around 500 glyphs.

Defining the required character set for a digital typeface forms an essential initial part of the design process. Observing the contents of past font repertoires is a useful starting point for planning the final glyph set, i.e. for determining the full character set coverage required to answer the design brief and how this is effected: whether by means of complete designs or by components, or a combination of methods. However, these earlier Bengali font listings also reflect the shortcomings of previous technologies; and there continues to be an economically convenient predilection in the field of typeface design to convert earlier designs and the conventions of past practices wholesale into new font formats. Yet, OpenType digital font technology is an opportunity for reflection. In the case of the Bengali script, it is no longer necessary to split conjuncts in order to reduce the character set; on the other hand, there is now no need to include sorts which are merely combinations of base characters or conjuncts with subscripts or superscripts as these can be generated by precise glyph positioning, which hitherto had only been achievable in digital fonts by means of proprietary software that is now embedded in the font. The inclusion of ligatures that adopt a particular shape, such as in the case of শু *shu*, (see Figure 2) are commonplace in many text fonts and those such as ধ্রু *dhru*, and similar contextual alternative glyphs, can be a choice of styling. Yet the inclusion of all such ligatures might seem too traditional and hard to read at small sizes for, say, mobile phone screens. The fact that ligatures and conjuncts are not covered by Unicode, which is only concerned with key codes as it facilitates the portability of documents, is advantageous to the designer, who can tailor the design appropriate to its expected function.

The final glyph set, devised by the designer in conjunction with a client and any project collaborators, usually takes the form of a spreadsheet sometimes termed the master glyph list. This document necessarily contains all the required glyphs including punctuation, numerals (proportional and tabular) and any typographic symbols. Unicode numbers may then be allocated as appropriate as well as alternative simple development names (usually a form of transliteration) to facilitate the design development. As encoding files can be generated from this master glyph list, and further information pertinent to font production processes may be entered, for example character look-ups for conjuncts, this spreadsheet becomes an invaluable design and production tool (see Figure 4).

Typeface Dimensions

Once the style of the font and the character set are defined, then the dimensions of the typeface can be determined. A survey of the characters to be included will quickly show which are the tallest and the deepest glyphs, and the design of these needs to be essayed along with the first few base characters that represent the key features of the typeface.

A decision will need to be made whether the deepest character would take subscripts and whether the typeface is expected to be set 'solid,' that is, without leading. In practice, for Bengali script setting it would seem unduly limiting to reduce the overall size of a typeface to fit within its digital 'bounding box' for the rare occasion when the deepest conjunct may take a subscribed vowel sign. It is also unrealistic, other than in specific environments, to expect that the script not be

Figure 4. Section from Bengali master glyph list spreadsheet

Index	Unicode	DevName	PostName	ABP	Name composition
146		bKKa	uni099509CD0995	ক্ক	bKa bVirama bKa
147		bKTta	uni099509CD099F	ক্ট	bKa bVirama bTta
148		bKTa	uni099509CD09A4	ক্ত	bKa bVirama bTa
149		bKNa	uni099509CD09A8	ক্ন	bKa bVirama bNa
150		bKVa	uni099509CD09AC	ক্ব	bKa bVirama bVa
151		bKMa	uni099509CD09AE	ক্ম	bKa bVirama bMa
152		bKLa	uni099509CD09B2	ক্ল	bKa bVirama bLa

permitted to enjoy reasonably generous interlinear spacing, so that the ascenders on characters such as ট *ta,* or the *ikars* ি and ী and *candrabindu* ঁ do not appear too dense and do not collide with deep characters or subscripts from a preceding line of text.

It is perhaps surprising to the novice designer, that low-contrast fonts, often conceived to work alongside Latin sans serif fonts, occupy more room to describe the intricate features that characterize Indian scripts, for instance the ব *ba (va)* element in such conjuncts a দ্ধ্ব as *ddhva*. The careful design of these elements can be a great challenge in a bold weight when trying to ensure that they are not too pronounced or dark in relation to the rest of the typeface and to ensure, as is often required, compatibility of scale with an existing high-contrast font. Indeed, another consideration is whether there is a requirement for compatibility with regard to the overall size of the typeface in relation to other fonts that the typeface may work with, be it a Bengali, a Devanagari or a Latin font. For this reason, the deepest, tallest and most complex designs of the heaviest weight are best drafted and tested before the dimensions of a new typeface design are finally established. The lighter weights, which a client often requests be delivered first, can then be undertaken in the full knowledge that no future re-scaling will be required (see Figure 5).

Of the base glyphs, ক *ka* is perhaps the natural first choice with which to begin the design. This frequently occurring character will be crucial to determining the prevalent typeface characteristics, viz. the body height; the weights of the various strokes; the method of joining the diagonal to the vertical stroke at the neck and at the base of the glyph; the degree of stroke contrast; etc. Next might come a rounded-shaped glyph, for instance the vowel sign ে *e*, as decisions need to be made as to how pronounced the curve will be, and how it will fit with an adjacent 'host' character, here the ক *ka*. Then perhaps the vowel sign া *ā* would be undertaken in order to consider whether the individual vertical stroke is tapered, whether the glyph carries a spike at the headline, and whether the headline and the base of the stroke are sheared diagonally in accordance with Bengali penmanship and, if so, to what angle. Similar considerations are tried, tested, revised, and re-tested as the character set is slowly built up into a fully functioning coherent typeface design.

Decisions regarding key aspects of the design need to be made by the well-informed eye. Visual perceptual skills are essential for the designer to develop and to hone when designing type. The designer becomes cognisant of visual effects that can disturb the regular texture of a typeface; this has mainly to do with proportions, for instance, where a stroke may appear stronger than another

Figure 5. Establishing the dimensions by means of a deep glyph with superscript and subscript

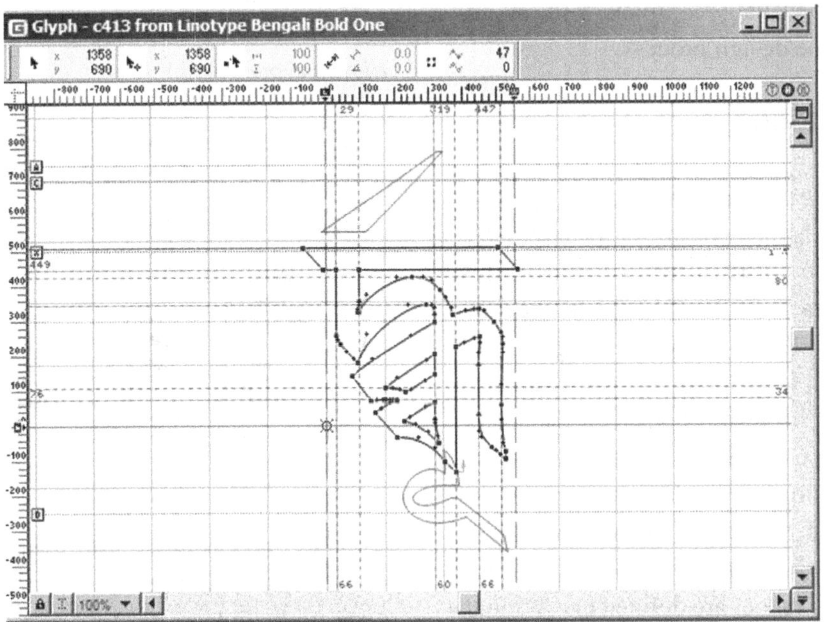

of the same measured width due to a difference in its length or angle. In Bengali characters and conjuncts that are composed of seemingly identical elements, these elements need to differ in actuality to harmonize and maintain an even color in text setting. In other words, in order to appear to be the same, and thereby create a cohesive typeface, they need to be different. On the other hand, it is vital that each typeform is distinctive and unambiguous to the reader, for example in cases where either স *sa* or ম *ma* form the initial parts of conjuncts. A designer needs to develop the ability to perceive how letterforms drawn at a comparatively large size will function in the range of sizes for which the typeface is intended to function optimally (see Figure 6).

Whether the designer works from sketches on paper, which are then scanned, or directly on a computer, is immaterial and not specific to OpenType font production. However, current technology allows fonts to be generated and tested with ease during different stages of development. Frequent testing is immensely beneficial to making sound visual judgements, and where possible outputting the tests to different printers on a range of papers further assist in decision-making regarding the image quality of the emerging typeface. Similarly, testing new Web or user-interface designs on screens that are, or can, approximate their target environment is important; particularly when unexpected visual effects, such as those described above, can be exacerbated by the rendering technology, but which can be improved by 'hinting'[11]. Type design is a singular field in that the designer has no control over how a typeface will be used, and clearly not in what sequence any of the letterforms might appear. Therefore

Figure 6. An example of Bengali typeforms in two weights that need show affiliation and differentiation

tests that anticipate the most frequent words, as well as the most visually complex, form an important part of the design process.

Character Fitting

Irrespective of the medium for which a typeface is being designed, character fitting, or spacing, needs to be done at the outset. There is no algorithm for spacing characters; it cannot be mathematically calculated (Tracy, 1986). Here again good visual judgement is required. The importance of spacing, or the fitting of characters, cannot be overestimated. In this day when solid type has dematerialized into binary code, typeforms depend on the black and the white, or two contrasting colours, to describe them or they simply do not exist. Letterform shapes are defined just as much by the space that encompasses them as by the space they encompass in open or closed counters. Character fitting consequently has a huge impact on the readability of the texts in any environment.

In the case of a joining script as in Bengali, there is no real room for spacing errors: a user has little opportunity to adjust the character fit, particularly if it is too tight. It is important to ensure that the degree of overlap in a connecting headline is sufficient so that is does not separate in some formats, for instance in PDF forms on certain screens. The useful but comparatively restrictive 18-unit system for character fitting introduced by Monotype hot-metal composition has over the years and through different technologies relaxed to provide a relatively flexible means of defining character widths to a choice of finer resolutions of 1000 or 2048 units to the em square, or even higher. This means that the designer has fine gradations within which to adjust and fine-tune the spacing. It also permits the specifying of x-y co-ordinates for precise positioning of superscripts and subscripts, which is essential to readable Bengali text, and which was notably missing in the newspaper composition produced by the Linotype line-casting machine (see Figure 7).

Figure 7. Top two lines: newspaper clipping showing hot-metal linear setting; bottom line: correct kerning and subscript positioning in digital typesetting

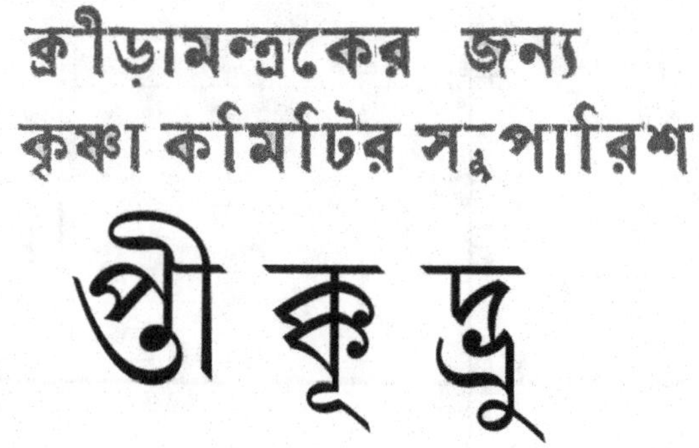

The line-caster's poor positioning of any vowel sign, which peppered Bengali newspaper texts with 'holes' or rather gaps within words, notwithstanding the continuity of the headline, highlighted the necessity of kerning typeforms for good Bengali typography. This deficiency in line-casting composition that characterised Indian vernacular newspapers for many years has long been rectified. However, the question now posited by OpenType technology is whether a Bengali font would benefit from incorporating kerning vowel signs of variable lengths to be selected according to the varying widths of the base characters and conjuncts[12]. This could be achieved by making use of the OpenType facility to have contextual alternates. It seems that there is indeed a benefit of having alternative forms of some vowel signs to handle problems when there are potential clashes with ascenders, *reph* and *candrabindu* marks. However, great variations in the length of kern of *ikars* can be distracting, especially in connection with very wide characters; perhaps providing a small range of alternates and a width limit would be a preferable solution. As suggested above with regard to Bengali ligatures, stylistic alternates available to the designer, and therefore the user, in OpenType fonts, provide choices according to different preferences. Furthermore, language tags can address specific requirements of languages which share the same script within the same font, for instance Bengali and Assamese.

There is now also the possibility of having different scripts within the same OpenType font, which can be designed to work harmoniously together. The concept of compatible designs across a range of scripts does not mean that any one script need lose its integrity. Observation of traditional stroke modulation, which in Bengali and Devanagari, for instance, is the reverse of that in Latin, assists readability and should not be jettisoned in favour of attempting a closer match. Rather, well-balanced multi-script typography is achieved by focusing on scale, style and colour on the page, so that a similar voice and regular texture is created, and there is no apparent dominance of one script over another. In order to achieve an even density across scripts, it may require that the principal stroke weight of glyphs differ as the various scripts and languages create very different textual patterns. The character fit of one script, may need to be more open with physically larger counters and greater space between characters. Generally, joining scripts tend to look denser than those that do not join; having a lighter headline than the vertical strokes can diminish this effect when Bengali text is mixed with English.

Tools

Some of the points discussed above constitute design issues that depend upon production processes for their realization. There are a small number of design and production tools available; and improvements to these and the development of new tools have emerged very recently. The choice of tools can depend on the preferred working method of the designer, or the required method of delivery by the type foundry. At times the decision is machine dependent: for instance, at present the VOLT[13] tools that are the usual means of generating Bengali fonts with the required OpenType features function only in a Windows environment. The Adobe Font Development Kit[14] for OpenType presents a possible alternative means that is cross-platform but is as yet unproven for Bengali font production.

The correct rendition of the script to create good typography is still dependent on the facilities available for correctly shaping Bengali text in word processing and page layout applications. Unfortunately, the correct processing of many Indian scripts including Bengali is not supported in many applications, and therefore the OpenType features, which include contextual forms, character re-ordering, kerning tables, glyph positioning, etc. that may be embedded in the fonts, are not implemented in the typographic output. However, driven by the demands of globalization, there appears to be a real commitment by major software

Figure 8. 'Bangla digital type design' set in Linotype Bengali Light and Bold

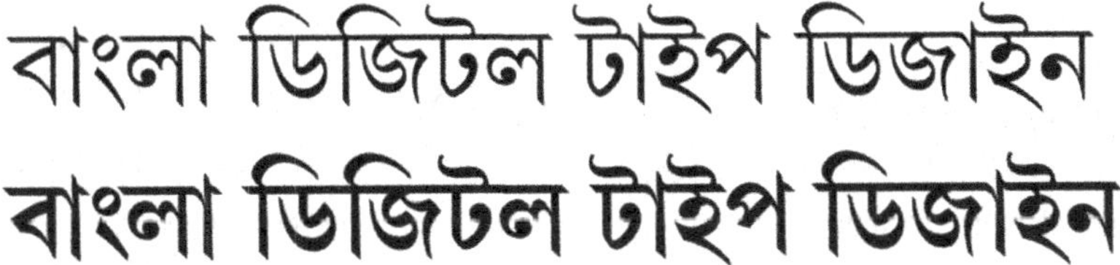

developer companies to rectify the situation in the very near future, as is testified by constant software updates that include or promise further support for non-Latin typography.

FUTURE RESEARCH DIRECTIONS

It is evident that in contrast to the production of typographic tools and applications prior to the digital era, recent technological developments in this field have benefited from tools developed in research-led environments. For instance, the results of legibility studies conducted for the Advanced Reading Technology group at Microsoft have informed the development of ClearType and other reading technologies (Larson, 2004); scholarly outputs from the Typography Department at the University of Reading in the field of non-Latin typeface design (e.g. De Baerdemaeker, 2009, and Kshetrimayum, 2011) are regularly consulted by companies like Adobe Inc. and Dalton Maag in preparation for providing and supporting writing-systems that do not use the Latin script in a variety of products, including the developing technology of small screen devices. There remains much to be done that is research-dependent in this multi-disciplinary area in order to realize the desired provision of cross-platform Bengali fonts that deliver optimally readable text for print and for the screen that can be indexed, searched, tagged and digitally transmitted[15].

CONCLUSION

The application of today's technologies to produce well-designed OpenType fonts can indubitably enrich the, at present, very limited typographic expression available in the Bengali script. However, irrespective of current or impending technological developments, the creation of new high-quality digital typefaces still depends upon the skilful execution of the design by the informed designer who has addressed the key issues described in this chapter. Type design remains a creative process: it relies upon the visual perceptual skills of the designer that have been developed through research, by evaluating the products of past practices, assessing current typeforms and anticipating future typographic needs, and refined through the practice of typeface design. The longevity of the Linotype Bengali typeface, which at the time of its publication in 1982 was considered both retrogressive and highly innovative, testifies to the validity of a research-based design methodology underpinning the conception and development of original designs of enduring quality (see Figure 8).

REFERENCES

Adobe. (2008). *OpenType user guide for Adobe fonts*. Retrieved July 16, 2012, from http://www.adobe.com/type/browser/pdfs/OTGuide.pdf

De Baerdemaeker, J. (2009). *Tibetan typeforms: An historical and visual evaluation of Tibetan typefaces from their inception in 1738 up to 2009*. (Unpublished Doctoral Thesis). University of Reading. Reading, UK.

Halhed, N. B. (1778). *A grammar of the Bengal language*. Hoogly.

Kesavan, B. S. (1985). *History of printing and publishing in India*. New Delhi: National Book Trust.

Khan, M. H. (1976). *Printing in Bengali characters up to 1866*. (Unpublished Doctoral Thesis). University of London. London.

Kshetrimayum, N. (2010). *A comparative study of Meetei Mayek: From the inscribed letterform to the digital typeface*. (Unpublished Masters Dissertation). University of Reading. Reading, UK.

Larson, K. (2004). *The science of word recognition*. Retrieved July 17, 2012 from http://www.microsoft.com/typography/ctfonts/wordrecognition.aspx

Ross, F. (1998). Translating non-Latin scripts into type. *Typography Papers, 3*, 75–86.

Ross, F. (1999). *The printed Bengali character and its evolution*. Richmond, UK: Curzon Press.

Ross, F. (2002). An approach to non-Latin type design. In J. Berry (Ed.), Language culture type (pp. 65–75). New York: Association Typographique Internationale (ATypI).

Ross, F. (2009). *The printed Bengali character and its evolution* (2nd ed.). Kolkata, India: Sishu Sahitya Samsad.

Shaw, G. (1981). *Printing in Calcutta to 1800*. London: Bibliographical Society.

Tracy, W. (1986). *Letters of credit*. London: Gordon Fraser.

ADDITIONAL READING

Bandhyopadhyaya, C. (Ed.). (1981). *Dui satakera bamla mudrana o prakasana*. Calcutta, India: Ananda Bazar Publishers.

Chakravorty, S., & Gupta, A. (Eds.). (2004). *Print areas, book history in India*. Delhi: Permanent Black.

Gaur, A. (1979). *Writing materials of the East*. London: The British Library.

Hatcher, B. A. (2001). How the girisa vidyaratna press acquired its font: A supplement to the work of Fiona G.E. Ross. *Journal of the American Oriental Society. American Oriental Society, 1*(4), 637–663. doi:10.2307/606504.

Hudson, J. (2002). Unicode, from text to type. In J. Berry (Ed.), Language culture type (pp. 24–44). New York: Association Typographique Internationale (ATypI).

India, B. R. C. (2012). *Bengali manuscripts*. Retrieved from http://brcindia.com/manuscripts

Lambert, H. M. (1953). *Introduction to the Devanagari script*. London: Oxford University Press.

Losty, J. P. (1982). *The art of the book in India*. London: The British Library.

McLean, R. (1980). *The Thames and Hudson manual of typography*. London: Thames and Hudson.

Naik, B.S. (1971). *Typography of devanagari*. Bombay: Directorate of Languages.

Ogborn, M. (2007). *Indian ink: Script and print in the making of the east india company*. Chicago: The University of Chicago Press. doi:10.7208/chicago/9780226620428.001.0001.

Ross, F. (1989). From metal type to digital letterforms – A straightforward transition for Indian scripts? *Matrix (Stuttgart, Germany), 9*, 129–136.

Ross, F. (1993). The Bengali types of Vincent Figgins. *Matrix (Andoversford: Whittington Press), 13*, 205–212.

Ross, F. (2002). *Non-Latin type design at linotype*. Paper presented at St Bride Printing Library Conference, 2002, Twentieth Century Graphic Communication: Technology, Society and Culture. London, UK.

Ross, F. (2002). Non-Latin typesetting in the digital age. In Sassoon, R. (Ed.), *Computers and Typography 2* (pp. 42–53). Bristol, UK: Intellect Books.

Ross, F. (2008). The linotype non-Latin collection, University of Reading. In Banham, R., & Ross, F. (Eds.), *Non-Latin typefaces: At St Bride Library, London and Department of Typography & Graphic Communication, University of Reading* (pp. 32–62). London: St Bride Library.

Ross, F., & Shaw, G. (2003). An unexpected legacy and its contribution to early Indian typography. *Matrix (Andoversford: Whittington Press)*, 7.

Southall, R. (2005). *Printer's type in the twentieth century*. London: The British Library and Oak Knoll Press.

KEY TERMS AND DEFINITIONS

Conjunct: The combination of a consonant with another consonant or consonants, whereby another shape is produced, i.e. a consonantal cluster.

Glyph: Specific form or shape that a character can take in a digital font.

Kern: The art of a movable type projecting beyond the body; the term continues to be used in current typesetting technologies (see Figure 2).

Justified Text: The even and equal spacing of words or blocks of text to a given measure.

Ligature: (In Indian scripts) The combination of a consonant with a vowel, whereby another shape is produced.

Reph: A superscript denoting a preceding র.

Sort: Any particular matrices or types as distinct from a complete font.

Typography: The design of printed matter.

ENDNOTES

1 Complex scripts, like Bengali, are those that are keyed in a different sequence to that in which they appear or there is not a one-to-one relationship between encoded characters and displayed forms. It is the 're-ordering', rather than the presence of conjuncts, that causes difficulties for OCR processing of texts.

2 A font format introduced in the late 1990s by Adobe and Microsoft that functions on Macs and Windows and has particular typographic features that can be embedded in the font. http://www.adobe.com/type/opentype/.

3 Unicode is an 'international multi-byte character encoding that covers virtually all of the world's languages' and assists in the portability of documents (Adobe, 2008, p. 2).

4 An example of this is in the font library of Linotype Library GmbH, which has 10500 fonts but only one Bengali font, viz. the Microsoft UI font Vrinda; it no longer sells or supports the Linotype Bengali font. http://www.linotype.com/.

5 Linotype Bengali was designed by the author and Tim Holloway for the newspaper *Ananda Bazar Patrika* (Kolkata) at Linotype-Paul Ltd; the design was begun in 1978 and it was published in 1982. Close copies of the design are prevalent worldwide; many copies are of inferior quality.

6 The Web editions of the two Bangladeshi newspapers also use a version of this typeface; again, these are not in Unicode format; see http://www.bangladeshnews24.com/ittefaq/2012/11/04/79492.htm and http://www.eprothomalo.com/index.php?opt=view&page=1&date=2012-11-04. Further examples of Bengali newspapers are listed here: http://www.allbanglanewspaper.com/.

7 There have been a few works published in Bengali and English, but these have drawn heavily on the author's work and used her images as unauthorized reference material.

8 This paucity of high-quality non-Latin fonts, including Bengali, was already noted over a decade ago (Ross, 1998).

9 Sometimes called *half-forms*, although these differ from the Devanagari *half-forms* (Ross, 1999).

10 *The phonetic keyboard*, invented by the author and Dr Mike Fellows permit flexibility in the character-set size and formation of contextual forms since there no longer needed to be a direct correspondence between key-codes and character output; i.e. direct entry keyboarding was not longer essential. This type of keyboarding, that accelerated keying speeds and enabled Bengali and other scripts to use standard hardware, has become an industry standard. For full description (see Ross, 1999, 2002).

11 For an explanation of 'hinting', see http://www.microsoft.com/typography/TrueType-HintingWhat.mspx.

12 These were first introduced in digital fonts with the Adobe Devanagari typeface but were first published with the Vodafone Hindi typeface design; both designs by Timothy Holloway and the author (Ross, 2009; http://store1.adobe.com/cfusion/store/html/ index.cfm?store=OLS-US&event=displayFontPackage&code=1940).

13 Visual OpenType layout tool (VOLT) http://www.microsoft.com/typography/volt.mspx.

14 http://www.adobe.com/devnet/opentype/afdko.html.

15 Unicode is essential for this as it is a means of mapping Bengali glyphs irrespective of the typeface as long as the fonts are Unicode compliant. The ability to search and index depends on the development of applications that handle complex scripts. This differs from OCR that is outwith the author's expertise (but see note 1) and which considers such issues as recognizing handwritten or differently encoded typeforms; see, for example, http://pdf.aminer.org/000/368/586/on_recognition_of_handwritten_bangla_characters.pdf.

Chapter 2
Bangla Braille Adaptation

Syed Akhter Hossain
Daffodil International University, Bangladesh

Fakhruddin Muhammad Mahbub-ul-Islam
Military Institute of Science and Technology, Bangladesh

Samiul Azam
Military Institute of Science and Technology, Bangladesh

Ahamad Imtiaz Khan
Military Institute of Science and Technology, Bangladesh

ABSTRACT

Braille, a tactile writing system, is used by visually impaired and partially sighted people for reading and writing in everyday life. Visually impaired persons in Bangladesh are deprived of basic education due to inadequate textbooks and sufficient reading materials written in Bangla Braille. This is widening the knowledge gap and disparity within the society with progress of time. In order to improve this scenario, an automated information system for facilitating machine translation of Bangla text to readable and recognizable Braille code is essential. In this book chapter, a detailed research on Bangla Braille has been accomplished and necessary grammatical rules as well as conventions are identified for rule-based Bangla Braille translation. Through the analysis of investigations, a computational model is proposed using Deterministic Finite Automata (DFA) for the machine translation. The proposed DFA demonstrated very acceptable conversion, which is validated by the visually impaired community. Based on the computational model, another software architecture is also proposed for the implementation of machine translation of Bangla to Braille using open source technology. The translator is tested with Bangla Unicode-based text contents, and the generated Braille code is validated after printing in the Braille printer. The performance of the conversion of Bangla to Braille code has been found accurate and also free from grammatical errors.

DOI: 10.4018/978-1-4666-3970-6.ch002

INTRODUCTION

Bangla (or Bengali), one of the more important Indo-Iranian languages, is the sixth-most popular in the world and spoken by a population that now exceeds 250 million. Geographical Bangla-speaking population percentages are as follows: Bangladesh (over 95%), and the Indian States of Andaman & Nicobar Islands (26%), Assam (28%), Tripura (67%), and West Bengal (85%). The global total includes those who are now in diaspora in Canada, Malawi, Nepal, Pakistan, Saudi Arabia, Singapore, United Arab Emirates, United Kingdom, and United States.

It is one of the most spoken languages (ranking sixth) in the world, with nearly 300 million total speakers (Bangla, 2009). According to Titumir (Titumir & Hossain, 2005) about 0.75 million people are blind in Bangladesh. Blind person cannot read text written on a plain paper and use Braille system in their reading and writing. Braille is a universal code for mapping character sets of various languages to Braille cells. Series of Braille cells are embossed on paper so that visually impaired persons can read them by touching the raised dots of the cells using their fingers. Like other languages Bangla has its own representation for Braille system.

There are few schools, institutes and organizations for blind people in Bangladesh where they can get their education. But they always face problem with inadequate reading materials, books and notes available in the form of Braille. Rewriting of books into Braille code is accomplished by certified Braille experts. But this process takes time and cost of translation is also higher. For this reason books written in Braille code are insufficient. This is a potential constraint in the education for visually impaired. This constraint can be overcome by an automated translation system which will be able to convert Bangla text to Bangla Braille code with all grammatical considerations and standards without any error.

This book chapter elaborates on the adaptation of Braille for Bangla. The discussion includes detail literature review on Braille and related works. The chapter also discusses the coding convention, the grammatical rule devised from a standard based on Unicode which is elaborated in detail for the purpose of design and implementation of the machine translation system. The chapter also includes implementation of the proposed model and thereafter the development of a software solution based on proposed model. The chapter concludes with the future research issues and challenges.

LITERATURE REVIEW

Generally, the communication between two people for writing becomes an easy task since both can read and write the same language. However if this communication takes place between a sighted and a visually impaired person, then this will cause problems since the sighted person really does not understand the language of the visually impaired which is called Braille. In this case, a translator of any sort is needed to convert the print message into Braille, which works as a mediator for a blind person in order to read as well as produce expressions.

The Braille system is a method that is widely used by blind people to read and write. Braille was devised in 1821 by Louis Braille, a blind Frenchman. Each Braille character or cell is made up of six dot positions, arranged in a rectangle containing two columns of three dots each. A dot may be raised at any of the six positions to form sixty-four (2^6) permutations, including the arrangement in which no dots are raised. For reference purposes, a particular permutation may be described by naming the positions where dots are raised, the positions being universally numbered 1 to 3, from top to bottom, on the left, and 4 to 6, from top to bottom, on the right. For example, dots 1-3-4 would describe a cell with three dots raised, at the top and bottom in the left column and on top of the right column, i.e., the letter *m*. The lines of horizontal Braille text are separated by a space, much like visible printed text, so that the dots of one line can be differentiated from the Braille text above and below. Punctuation is represented by its own unique set of characters.

At the advent of modern digital computers, several new approaches to computerised Braille translation have been developed and as a result, computerized Braille became very popular. This further resulted into many software systems for translation of text into Braille. Despite these developments, there is a felt need of an efficient machine translator to be designed for the use of allowing multiple translation grades within one given conversion area. Besides, there is a shortage of a software system which allows translation from Braille to printed form except for some proprietary systems. Also, multiple languages within a single document are yet to have Braille translation through one efficient software system and have the resultant Braille output as the translation of their respective translation rules based on language context.

In one work, Yousuf (Yousuf & Shams, 2007) illustrated some ideas on translation of Bangla text into Braille but without specific formation on model or rules based on finite automata. In another work Belousov (Belousov & Teves, 2011) in a project with Young Power in Social Action (YPSA) worked with the customization of the TechBridge World Braille Writing Tutor to facilitate an enhanced learning system for the new Braille learners. Another primary objective of the study was to adapt TechBridge World Braille Writing Tutor for Bangla along with the audio instruction with contextual matching.

There are different innovations for Braille software solution. Liblouis is an open source text to Braille and Braille Back translator (Liblouis, 2008). It supports contracted and uncontracted Braille for many languages such as: Arabic, Armenian, Bulgarian, Chinese, Croatian, Czech, Danish, Dutch, English, Esperanto, Estonian, Finish, French, Gaelic, German, Greek, Icelandic, Italian, Lithuanian, Norwegian, Polish, Portuguese, Romanian, Russian, Slovakian, Spanish, Swedish, Turkish, Vietnamese and Welsh. New languages can be easily added through tables that support a rule or dictionary based approach. It also supports tools for testing and debugging tables.

Another software solution, "BrailleTrans for Java," is also an open source solution for text to Braille translation implemented in Java (King, 2001). It is built on an existing software system which was implemented using C and includes a finite state machine with left and right context matching and a set of translation rules. It supports different languages to different grades of Braille contraction. It also allows both the forward and backward translation i.e. text to Braille and Braille to text translation.

There is also a hardware-based text-to-Braille translation system which performs faster and is able to generate greater throughput than software-based text-to-Braille translation system (Zhang & Murray, 2007). This system is based on Field Programmable Gate Arrays (FPGAs) for fast text to Braille translation.

Another automated system for English and Hindi text to Braille representation is implemented in Java (Singh & Vatia, 2010). It uses a chart as the database. This database is used for mapping corresponding Braille representation through implementation of the mapping for translation. It can translate both English and Hindi into corresponding Braille (Lahiri, 2005).

Quranic Braille system translates Quranic verse into Braille symbol. It is implemented using Visual Basic (Abualkishik & Omar, 2009). It can translate special vibration for the Quran. But it is limited for the noun and scoon vibrations. Sparsha is another comprehensive Indian language toolset for the blind. The contribution made by this research has enabled the visually impaired to read and write in Indian vernaculars with the help of a computer. It can handle various languages of Indian sub-continent (Rajasenathipathi & Sivakumar, 2010).

TextBraille is another user-friendly Braille transcription software for Indian languages in Windows platform. The software transcribes the text files into the Braille format and display the text file as well as the Braille converted code side by side. It can translate various Indian languages into Braille such as Hindi, Bengali, Assamese, Oriya, Marathi, Gujarati, Tamil, Telegu, Kannada, Malayalam, Punjabi (Ono & Takagi, 2000). It can translate Bangla to Braille but this software does not fulfill the purpose because Bangla to Braille conversion rules for Indian Bangla and Bangladeshi Bangla is different. There are also others research works related to text to Braille conversion in different languages (Khan & Shet, 2005; Pramait, 2002; Hopcroft, 2007).

In another work Hossain (Hossain & Shams, 2005) took a project to design and implement Bangla Braille embosser, a Braille keyboard interface with the computer, to help visually impaired using the computer with ease. In a similar type of another software based work, Dasgupta (Dasgupta & Basu, 2009) developed a system called *Sparsha* to facilitate speech enabled bidirectional automatic Braille transliteration system for Indian languages. Another interesting work by Bhattachrya (Bhattachrya & Basu, 2007) on speech enabled communication system called *Sanyog* proposed a computer based speech enabled another form of communication system for speech and motor impairment kind of disabilities in India.

BRAILLE AND BANGLA

The Braille system comprises of a 6-dot cell for each character and these six embossed or raised dots arranged as shown below. All these dots are raised as per the meaning or character and in grade one Braille, each cell has the meaning of only one letter or character, number or simple punctuation mark.

The numbering system for the dots in the Braille cell is shown in Figure 1 and this shows that the Braille cell contains six dots in two rows of three. For example, Figure 2 has the dots 1, 2 and 5 raised which give the letter 'h.' These six cells allow $2^6 = 64$ characters to be represented, being split up into 26 letters.

There is also an 8-dot cell (2 dots wide by 4 dots high) for Braille which gives a total of 256 combinations and is encoded using the Unicode standard. The advantage of this system is outweighed by that fact that it is more difficult for people to remember 256 characters, as opposed to 64 in 6-dot representation. As a result the usage of this system is not widespread.

A dot position can have two states. It may be raised or not raised. So depending on these two states of six dot positions, 64 permutations are possible (Pramait, 2001). Figure 3 shows all 64 Braille cells. An example can be given by nam-

Figure 1. Braille cell numbering

Figure 2. Braille cell representing 'h'

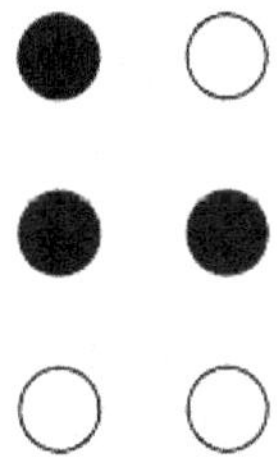

Figure 3. 64 Braille cells

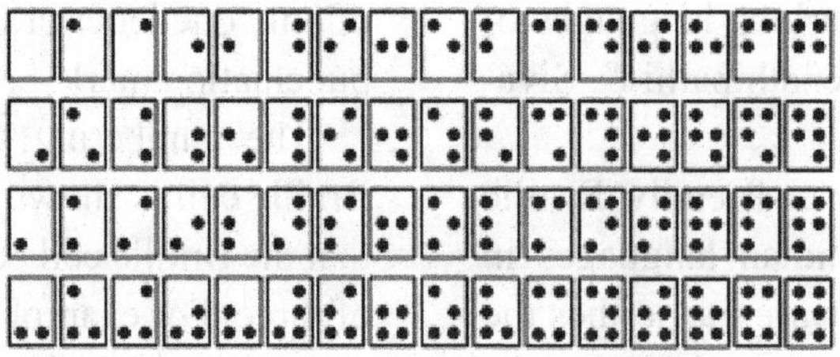

ing the raised dot positions. For example if it is said like dots 1-2-3-5, it describes dots 1, 2 and 3 are raised in first column and dot 5 is raised in second column. This particular permutation indicates English letter *R*.

In Bangla there are 11 independent vowels, 10 amongst them can also be used as dependent vowels and 39 consonants. Independent vowels are অ, আ, ই, ঈ, উ, ঊ, ঋ, এ, ঐ, ও, ঔ; dependent vowels are া, ি, ী, ু, ূ, ৃ, ে, ৈ, ো, ৌ, and different consonants are ক, খ, গ, ঘ, ঙ, চ, ছ, জ, ঝ, ঞ, ট, ঠ, ড, ঢ, ণ, ত, থ, দ, ধ, ন, প, ফ, ব, ভ, ম, য, র, ল, শ, ষ, স, হ, ড়, ঢ়, য়, ৎ, ং, ঃ, ঁ.

Each letter of Bangla alphabet has corresponding Braille representation. Bangla letters and their corresponding Braille code representation are given in the following Table 1.

MAPPING BANGLA CHARACTER INTO BRAILLE

Braille is not a language and it is a code for mapping character sets of various languages to its 64 fixed permutations. Mapping of character sets of a language to Braille symbols is called character mapping. Different countries developed their own

Table 1. Bangla and English Braille representation (only vowels)

Braille	DOTS	Braille Unicode Entity	English	Bangla
Vowels				
A	1	10241	A 1	অ ১
⠜	345	10268	Aa	আ
⠊	24	10250	I 9	ই ৯
⠔	35	10260	In	ঈ
⠥	136	10277	U	উ
⠳	1256	10291	Ou	ঊ
⠐⠗	5,1235	10256, 10263		ঋ
⠑	15	10257	E 5	এ ৫
⠌	34	10252	Oi	ঐ
⠕	135	10261	O	ও
⠪	246	10282	Ou	ঔ

standard character mapping for their language. This character mapping is not necessarily one-to-one because some languages may have more than 64 letters in their alphabet. So possible character mapping can be one-to-one and many-to-one. For example:

Bangla letter 'ক' ⟶ : (One-to-one)

Bangla letter 'হ' & digit '৮' ⟶ :. (Many-to-one)

Each letter of Bangla alphabet, numeric and punctuation has corresponding Braille representation. Bangla letters and their corresponding Braille representations are given in Tables 2, 3, and 4.

As seen in the Table 2 for one to one character mapping, each Bangla character is represented through a unique Braille code with proper cell position. In case of two to one character mapping shown in Table 3, two different Bangla characters are represented using one unique Braille code which is further differentiated in the next occurrence of corresponding Bangla character. The other representation of three to one character mapping is shown in Table 4.

The different character mapping shown in the tables indicates a system of conversion based on each corresponding Bangla character. In this case of mapping, due to the required conversion of entire Bangla text into Braille, frequency of letters is not used in the design of the mapping table.

Grammatical Conversion and Mapping Rules

In conversion of Bangla text to the corresponding Braille code, this is necessary to deal with the conjunctions, consonants, dependent and independent vowels, punctuations and numbers. The different grammatical conversion rules are discussed with examples below.

Replacing Rule: In replacing rule, each Bangla character is replaced by its corresponding Braille cell(s)(Pramait, 2001). Some uses of consonants, vowels (dependent and independent) and punctuations are given in Table 5.

Inserting Rule: In inserting rule, a Braille cell is inserted as prefix. Other characters are replaced according to replace rule (Pramait, 2001). If there

Table 2. One to one character mapping

Bangla	Braille	Bangla	Braille	Bangla	Braille
ক	[illegible]	ধ	[illegible]	ড়	[illegible]
খ	[illegible]	ন	[illegible]	ঢ়	[illegible]
ঘ	[illegible]	প	[illegible]	য়	[illegible]
ঙ	[illegible]	ম	[illegible]	ৎ	[illegible] [illegible]
ঞ	[illegible]	য	[illegible]	ঁ	[illegible]
ঝ	[illegible]	র	[illegible]	ং	[illegible]
ট	[illegible]	ল	[illegible]	ঃ	[illegible]
ঠ	[illegible]	শ	[illegible]	ক্ষ	[illegible]
ড	[illegible]	ষ	[illegible]	জ্ঞ	[illegible]
ঢ	[illegible]	স	[illegible]	;	[illegible]
ত	[illegible]	।	[illegible]	!	[illegible]
থ	[illegible]	‘	[illegible] [illegible]	=	[illegible] [illegible]
ভ	[illegible]	’	[illegible] [illegible]	*	[illegible] [illegible]
-	[illegible]	[	[illegible] [illegible]	]	[illegible] [illegible]

Table 3. Two to one character mapping

Bangla		Braille	Bangla		Braille
অ	১		চ	৩	
আ	া		জ	০	
ঈ	ী		ঞ	:	
উ	ু		ণ	Number prefix	
ঊ	ূ		দ	৪	
ঋ	ৃ		ফ	৬	
ও	ো		ব	২	
ঔ	ৌ		হ	৮	
গ	৭		়	”	
(	)		?	“	

Table 4. Three to one character mapping

Bangla			Braille
ই	ি	৯	
এ	ে	৫	
ঐ	ৈ	/	
,	.	'(lop)	

is “ই”, “উ”, or “ও” after consonant and if “অ” is pronounced, then Bangla “অ” equivalent Braille cell dot 1 is inserted after consonant in Braille. Examples are shown in Table 6.

Braille cell dot 4 is inserted before conjunctions having combination of two letters (Pramait, 2001). Examples are shown in Table 7.

Braille cells dot 4, 6 are inserted before conjunctions having combination of three letters or four letters (Pramait, 2001). Examples are shown in Table 8.

Two Bangla conjunctions have direct representation in Bangla Braille. So there is no need to use Braille cell dot 4 before them (Pramait, 2001). They are given in Table 9.

Braille cell dots 3,4,5,6 are inserted before first digit of a number (Pramait, 2001). Examples are shown in Table 10.

Table 5. Uses of consonants, vowels, and punctuations

Bangla Word	Distribution	Braille Representation
বল	ব ল	
উৎস	উ ৎ স	
কাঠ	ক া ঠ	
দৃঢ়	দ ৃ ঢ়	
কমা	,	
সেমি কোলন	;	

Table 6. Insertion of "অ"

Bangla Word	Distribution	Braille Representation
বই	ব ই	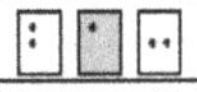
রওনা	র ও না	

Table 7. Conjunction of 2 letters

Bangla Word	Conjunct	Distribution	Braille Representation
গ্রাম	গ্র	গ ্ র	
পূর্ব	র্ব	র ্ ব	

Table 8. Conjunction of 3 and 4 letters

Bangla Word	Conjunct	Distribution	Braille Representation
রাষ্ট্র	ষ্ট্র	ষ ্ ট ্ র	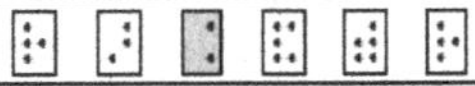
স্বাতন্ত্র্য	ন্ত্র্য	ন ্ ত ্ র ্ য	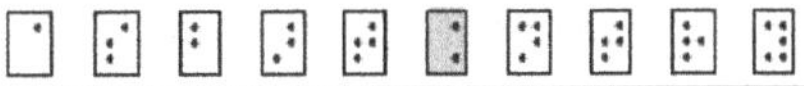

Table 9. Two conjunctions without prefix

Bangla Word	Conjunct	Distribution	Braille Representation
কক্ষ	ক্ষ	ক ্ ষ	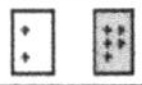
জ্ঞান	জ্ঞ	জ ্ ঞ	

COMPUTATIONAL MODEL FOR BANGLA TEXT TO BRAILLE

Based on study of Bangla language, Braille system and conversion rules a computational model is proposed to translate Bangla text to Braille using computer. The proposed computational model consists of four modules. Each module contributes to the whole translation process. The computational model is shown in Figure 4.

Table 10. Number rule

Bangla Number	Braille Representation
১২৩৪	
১২.৩৪	

Figure 4. Computational model for Bangla text to Braille

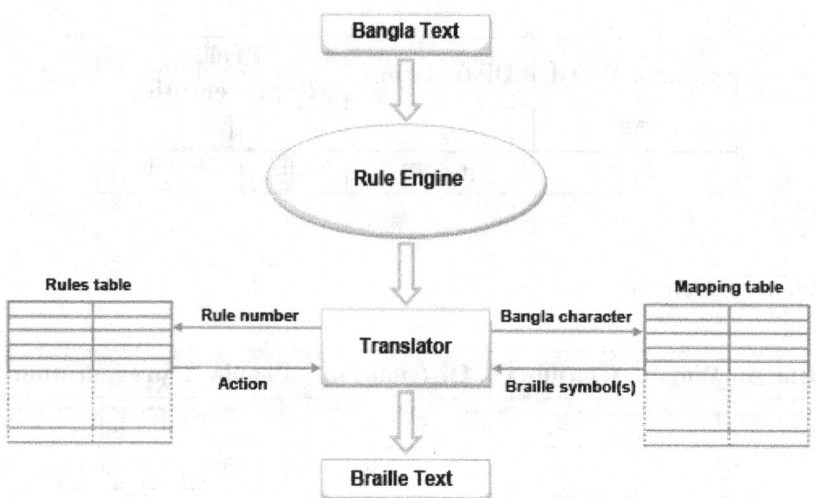

In the model shown in Figure 4, Bangla text consists of Bangla alphabets, digits, punctuations, spaces and formatting characters. Later part of the computational model is applied on this Bangla text in an iterative manner. Bangla text will be in the form of Unicode and font independent.

Introduction to Rule Engine

The rule engine is the core of the computational model in this work. The Rule engine generates token from the parsed characters and apply corresponding rules based on the character from the Unicode Bangla text. A Deterministic Finite Automata (DFA) is proposed for developing the rule engine. The term 'deterministic' refers to the fact that on each input there is one and only one state to which the automaton can transition from its current state. It is convenient to represent automata by a graph in which the nodes are the states and arcs are labeled by input symbols indicating the transitions of that automaton. The start state is designated by an arrow and the accepting states by double circles (Hopcroft, 2007).

Translation and DFA

The proposed DFA is constructed according to Bangla text to Braille conversion grammar for tokenizing Bangla characters. Each accepting states indicates that a token has been found with applicable rules. The constructed DFA in "five tuple" notation is DFA, $A = (Q, \sum, \delta, q_0, F)$ (see Table 11).

- Here A is the name of the DFA.
- Q is the set of states. It contains 26 states. $Q = \{0, 1, 2, 3, 4, 5, 6, 7, 8, 9, 10, 11, 12, 13, 14, 15, 16, 17, 18, 19, 20, 21, 22, 23, 24, 25\}$.
- $\sum$ is input symbols. We have seven input symbols which are shown in Table 10. Each of them represents set of Bangla characters.
- q_0 is the start state of the DFA, q_0 = state 0.
- F is the set of accepting states. It contains 12 accepting states. F = {2, 4, 10, 11, 12, 13, 14, 15, 19, 22, 24, 25}.

Each accepting state indicates that a token has been found and also represents different rules or combination of rules applicable on that token.

Table 11. Input symbols and characters

Input Symbols	Description	Bangla Characters
Vol_spe	Set of three independent vowels ই, উ, ও	ই, উ, ও
Vol	Set of independent vowels except ই, উ, ও and all dependent vowels	অ, আ, ঈ, ঊ, ঋ, এ, ঐ, ঔ, া, ি, ী, ু, ূ, ৃ, ে, ৈ, ো, ৌ
Con	Set of all Bangla consonants	ক, খ, গ, ঘ, ঙ, চ, ছ, জ, ঝ, ঞ, ট, ঠ, ড, ঢ, ণ, ত, থ, দ, ধ, ন, প, ফ, ব, ভ, ম, য, র, ল, শ, ষ, স, হ, ড়, ঢ়, য়, ৎ, ং, ঃ, ঁ
Num	Set of all Bangla digits	০, ১, ২, ৩, ৪, ৫, ৬, ৭, ৮, ৯
Pun	Set of all punctuation signs	, । ? ; : ' ' " " - ! ( ) [ ]
Hos	Represents Bangla hasanta symbol	্
Dot	Represents decimal sign (.)	.

As a result when it reaches to an accepting state a token is generated and decide which rule or combination of rules are applicable on this token. The applicable rules for the accepting states are given in Table 12.

As shown in Figure 2, the Translator maintains a look up table of characters mapping and rules. The mapping table contains mapping between Bangla and Braille character. The rules table contains rule number and corresponding actions. In this case translator receives token and rules number from rule engine. Then it looks up rules table by using rule number and find out corresponding action. Finally it executes this action using Braille and Bangla character mapping Table and generates Braille symbols of the corresponding Bangla text. Braille text consists of equivalent Bangla Braille symbols of Bangla alphabets, digits, punctuations and formatting characters. This Braille text must be in ASCII and can be printed through Braille Embosser.

δ is the transition function that takes a state and an input symbol as arguments and returns a state. In a transition diagram each transition from one state to another or same state for a specific input symbol also represents a transition function. It means transition function $\delta(a,x) = b$ is a transition from state a to state b for input symbol x in transition diagram where state a and b can be same or different state. In the proposed DFA, there are 182 (7 input symbols X 26 states) transition functions. All these transition functions are represented as transition diagram as shown in Figure 5.

Implementation Architecture

The implementation architecture of the proposed computational model shows how the model translates Bangla text to Braille. Here is an example illustration on how to translate a Bangla word ভ্রম into its corresponding Braille representation. At first the word is passed to the rule engine. The Rule engine is actually a Deterministic Finite Automata that generates a token (ভ্‌র) and an accepting state number (12) which represents the particular rule number. After determining the states, the token and the rule number are passed to the Translator. Using the rule number, translator looks up for the corresponding action for the rule number. Here the action is

Table 12. Accepting states and corresponding description

Accepting States	Description
2	Single Bangla character is replaced by equivalent Braille cell.
4	A consonant is replaced and then Braille cell dot 1 is inserted.
10	All Bangla characters are replaced by equivalent Braille cells.
11	Braille cell dot 4, 6 is inserted and three Bangla characters are replaced by equivalent Braille cells.
12	Braille cell dot 4 is inserted and then two Bangla characters are replaced by equivalent Braille cells.
13	Single character ending with hasanta are replaced.
14	Braille cell dot 4 is inserted and then two Bangla characters ending with hasanta are replaced by equivalent Braille cells.
15	Braille cell dot 4, 6 is inserted and three Bangla characters ending with hasanta are replaced by equivalent Braille cells.
19	Numbers are replaced in equivalent Braille cells with number prefix inserted at first.
22	Braille cell dot 4 is inserted and then two Bangla characters are replaced by equivalent Braille cells and Braille cell 1 is inserted at last.
24	Braille cell dot 4, 6 is inserted and then three Bangla characters are replaced by equivalent Braille cells and Braille cell 1 is inserted at last.
25	Braille cell dot 4, 6 is inserted and then four Bangla characters are replaced by equivalent Braille cells.

insert dot 4 (˙) and replace two characters (ভ, র). Then translator inserts dot 4 and looks up the Braille symbols of "ভ" and "র" in Mapping Table for replacing. Finally Braille symbols for ভ্র is generated. Similarly, using iterative way the Bangla text ভ্রম is translated into its Braille representation. This view model based on the proposed DFA is shown in Figure 6.

Buffer and Rule Engine Implementation

In the proposed implementation architecture shown in Figure 7, there are six modules whose function is described as follows.

Input Module

The purpose of input module is to read electronic Bangla text from the archive. The archive may contain books in file formats like Portable Document Format (pdf), Microsoft Office Word (doc, docx), Open Office (doc), Text Documents (txt) and Rich Text Format (rtf). This module automatically detects format of the input file and according to the file format it translates file data structure to a suitable ones. Bangla text will be in the form of Unicode and font independent.

Input Buffer

The input buffer is the data structure where data and related information are stored. It contains a *head*, which primarily points to the initial position of the buffer. Based on the request it sends character from current *head* position and points the *head* to next position. When it reaches at end of the buffer it generates a signal indicating there is no more data to be processed.

Rule Engine

Bengali text to Braille translation follows some rules (Pramait, 2001). A sequence of characters which satisfies any of the translation rules is called token. This module reads character from Input Buffer module and depending on translation rules it determines whether a sequence of characters leads to a token or not. If it forms a token then the token and rules it follows is sent to the next module. If not then it sends a request to Input Buffer module for the next character and checks again.

Figure 5. Transition diagram for proposed DFA

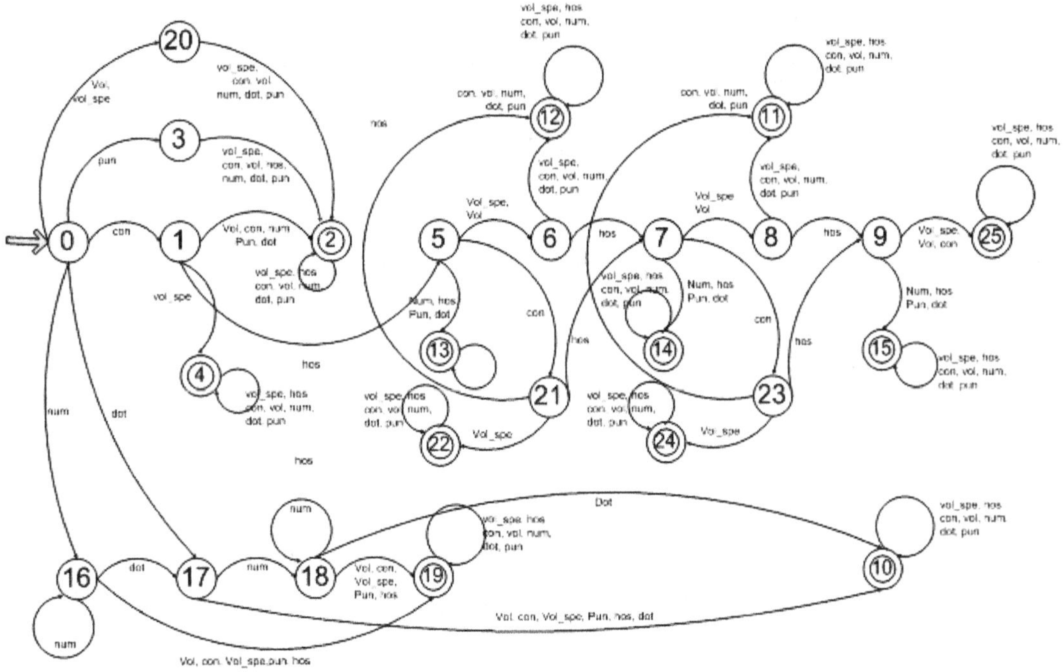

Figure 6. View model of the proposed computational model

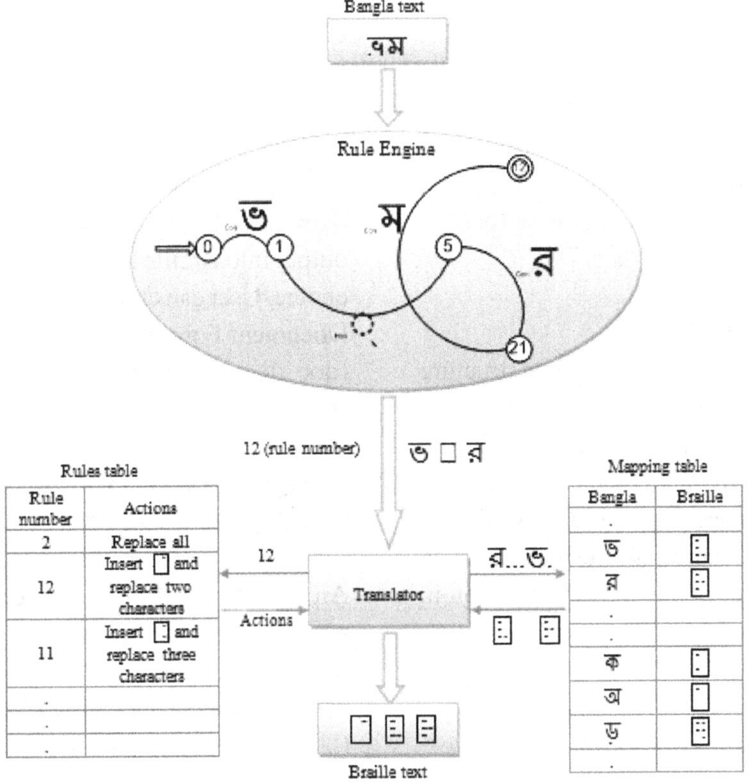

Figure 7. Architecture of Bangla text to Braille system

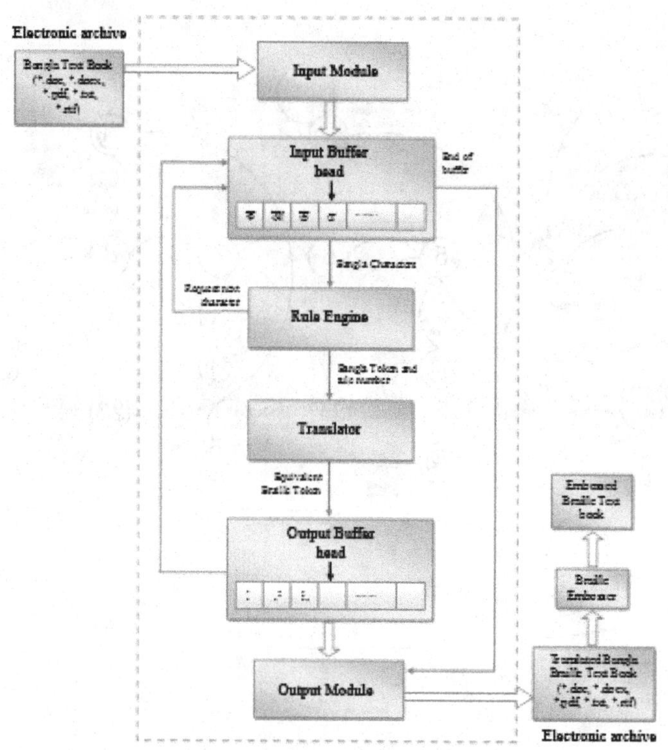

Translator

This module maintains a look up Table of character mapping and rules. Mapping Table contains mapping between Bangla and Braille character and performing the same task as discussed earlier.

Output Buffer

The output buffer maintains similar data structure as of Input Buffer. It receives and stores translated Braille tokens from Translator. It also contains a *head,* which primarily points the initial position of the buffer and changes its position when it gets Braille tokens from Translator. After getting token form Translator *head* points the next position in the buffer where the last token was placed.

Output Module

Task of this module is to collect all translated Braille symbols from Output Buffer when it gets an indication of the end of Buffer form Input Buffer. Now its task is to generate the translated Braille output into Braille text document based on user's choice. User can choose file formats like Portable Document Format (pdf), Microsoft Office Word (doc, docx), Open Office (doc), Text Documents (txt), and Rich Text Format (rtf).

Bangla Text to Braille Object and Dynamic Model

An object model of the system is designed and represented using class diagram and sequence diagram to implement the above architecture. The class diagram in the Unified Modeling Language (UML) is a type of static structure diagram that describes the structure of a system by showing the system's classes, their attributes and the relationships between the classes (Booch, 1993). Figure 8 demonstrates the object model of the proposed Bangla Text to Braille translation system with classes and relationships between them. In this object model, we have several classes each of which is responsible for specific purpose.

The *Main* class controls conversion process by interacting with *Input*, *Output* and *RuleEngine* class. *Input* class reads Bangla text files and keeps it to an input buffer using *InBuffer* class. Relation between *Main* class and *Input* class is one-to-many and between *Input* class and *InBuffer* class is many to one. The *RuleEngine* class accesses input buffer by using *InBuffer* class for generating token. They have one to one relationship. Generated token is translated into Braille text by interacting with *Translator* class and using *Queue* class. Relation between *RuleEngine* class and *Queue* class is one to one and between *RuleEngine* and *Translator* class is one to many. *Translator* class writes Braille text into the output buffer through *OutBuffer* class. Accessing *OutBuffer* class, *Output* class writes translated Braille text into output file.

Sequence diagram in Unified Modeling Language (UML) is a kind of interaction diagram that

Figure 8. Object model of Bangla text to Braille system

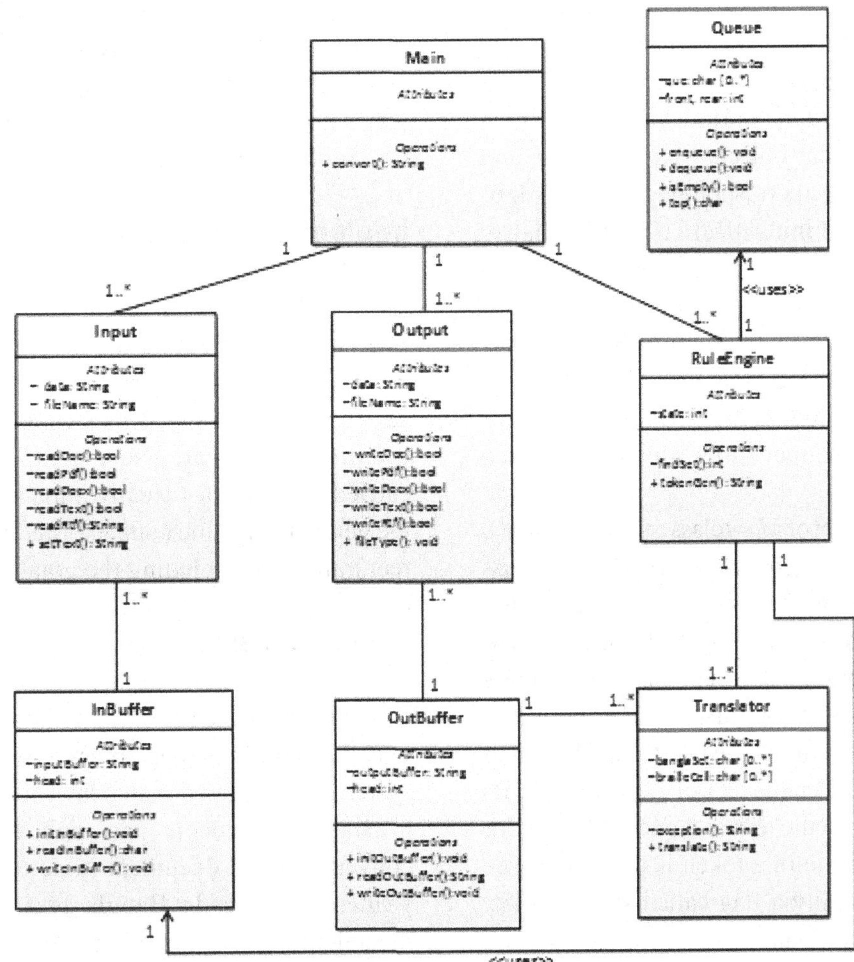

shows how processes operate with one another and in what order (Booch, 1993). The sequence diagram is used primarily to show the interactions between objects in the sequential order that those interactions occur (Booch, 1993). In a sequence diagram time is shown in vertical dimension. Objects involved in interaction appear horizontally across the page and represented by life lines. Solid horizontal arrow indicates messages and returns are shown with a dashed arrow. The execution of an operation is shown by activation. The interaction between the instances of different classes is shown in the Figure 8. The message that is sent to the receiving object represents an operation/method that the receiving object's class implements. The main focus is on the order of occurrence of messages rather than messages themselves. Initially the user starts the interface. Then a message named convert() is called by an object of *Main* class. The object of *Main* class then calls initInBuffer() and initOutBuffer() which are methods of the objects of *InputBuffer* and *OutputBuffer* class correspondingly. The task of initInBuffer() and initOutBuffer() is to initialize input and output buffer. *Input* class detects and fetches the Bangla text given by user. Object of *Main* class calls a method called setText() for setting the text. At the same time object of *Input* class calls a method named writeInBuffer() for writing the text in input buffer which will be used for conversion.

After that object of *Main* class calls tokenGen(), a method of *RuleEngine* class. *RuleEngine* class implements this method. The task of the method tokenGen() is to generate token from input text saved in input buffer. Object of class *RuleEngine* then calls a method readInBuffer() of InputBuffer class's object to fetch text. After fetching text it calls a method enqueue() of *Queue* class. Its task is to enqueue the text to a queue. This work is done in a loop until a token is generated (see Figure 9). Normally a flag called state is false. When a token is found state becomes true and loop is terminated. After finding a token method of *Queue* class's object dequeue() is called for collecting that token. Object of *RuleEngine* then calls Translate class's method translate(). The work of this method is to map the generated token to its corresponding Braille symbol. After that object of *Translate* class calls a method writeOutBuffer() for storing translated Braille symbol in output Buffer. The process of translation is done in a loop until input buffer is empty. Finally object of *Main* class calls a method of *Output* class called writeText(). After this method is being called, object of *Output* class calls method of *OutputBuffer* class named readOutputBuffer(). The task of this method is to collect all Braille symbols written in output Buffer. Finally the translated Braille symbols are written in a document of preferred format.

The above models are implemented using open source technology platform Java and all different modules of the proposed Bangla Braille system architecture is implemented using Java. The system is implemented using Java to take the advantage of the cross platform supports.

Implementation and Experimental Results

The proposed DFA and the system architecture along with the rule engine is implemented using Java and XML to support necessary parsing and determination of states. Several experiments were carried out with the visually impaired to validate the generated Braille code in order to ensure correct translation including the grammar.

Experimental Results

Based on the proposed system architecture along with the class and object interaction diagram, the system is developed using Java for Bangla text to Braille conversion. The application program converts a word document (.doc extension) file written in Unicode Bangla text into another document file containing translated ASCII Braille symbols. Alternatively Bangla text can be typed

Figure 9. Object interaction model of Bangla text to Braille system

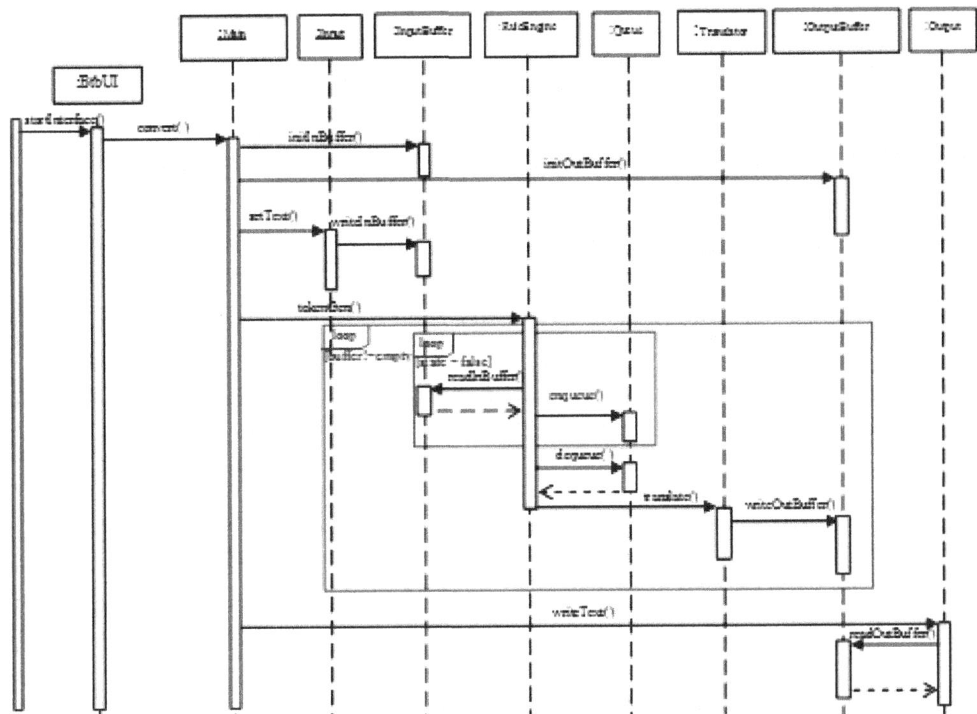

on the text area of application interface and the translated Braille symbols are shown in another text area of the same application interface. Some of the screenshot of Bangla-2-Braille system is shown in Figure 10.

The system is tested with translation of some Bangla text from Bangla news paper with words containing almost all type of Bangla conjunct characters. The result is 100% accurate. Some test results are shown in Table 13.

A popular historical book on liberation war written in Bangla titled *Muktizudher Itihash*, by Iqbal (Iqbal, 2008) which upon agreement was converted into Bangla Braille book for the first time appearance in a popular month long book fair. This machine translated Braille book was printed on index printer with support from Blind Education and Rehabilitation Development Organization (BERDO) at Bangladesh. Besides, Bangladesh Organization for Disabled Advancement (BODA) and Bangladesh Visually Impaired People's Society (BVIPS) supported enormously at different stage of testing. As part of the usability testing, speed of reading machine translated Braille book is considered as the metrics. Several visually impaired readers expressed satisfaction with the correctness of the grammar while reading and specially reading Braille code of Bangla conjunct letters that appear within different paragraph of the book.

FUTURE RESEARCH DIRECTIONS

This research work and the successful implementation of the model created new scope for future developments. In order to operate the machine translator by the visually impaired, the software system needs to be more flexible with the support of assistive keys and other hot commands. From this

Figure 10. Screen shots of the Bangla Braille system

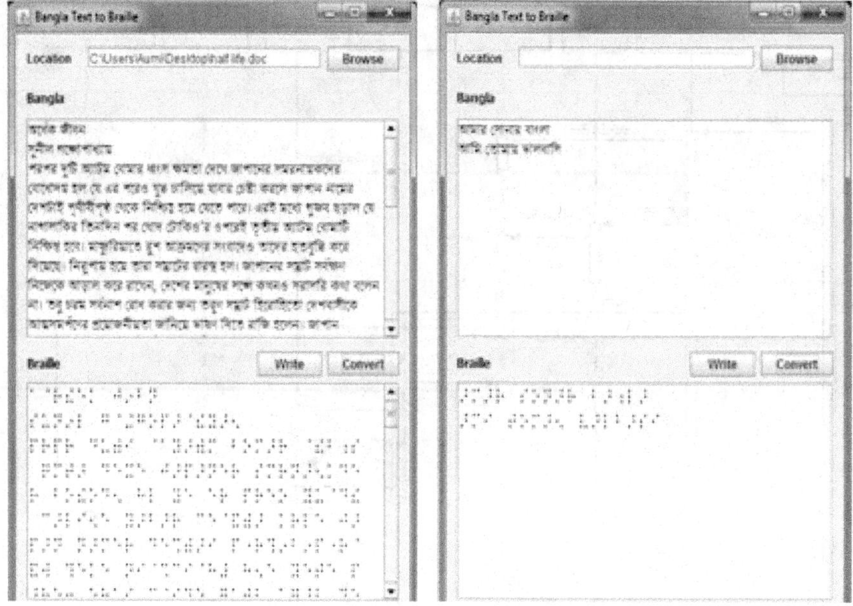

Table 13. Test results of Bangla Braille system

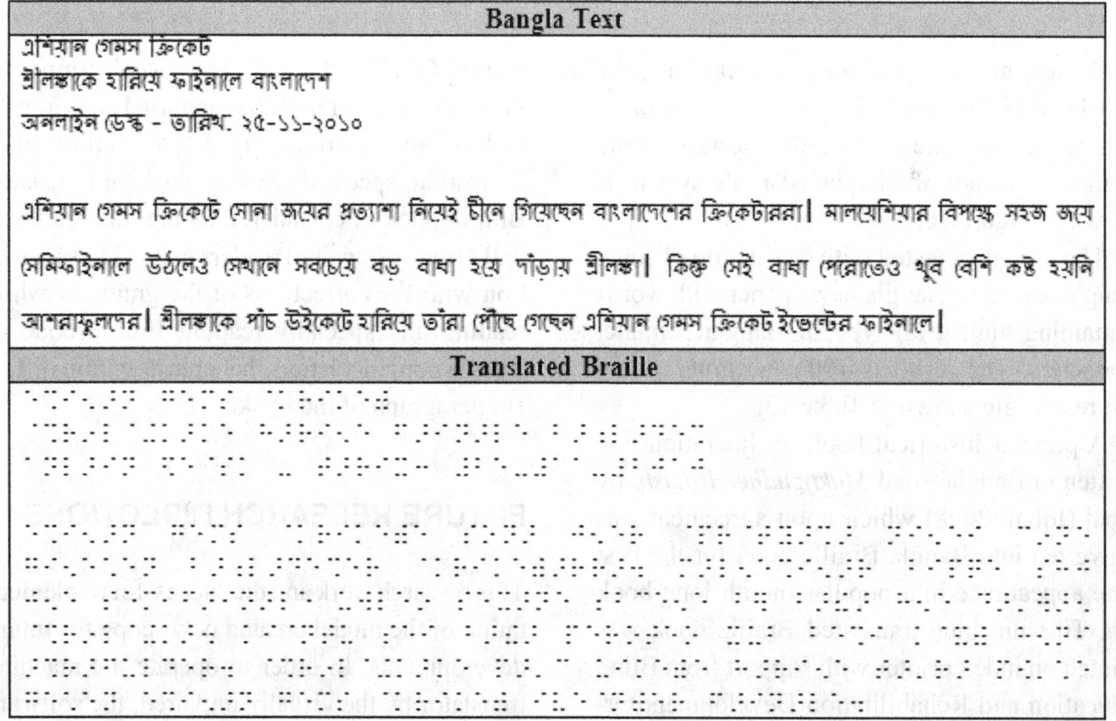

Bangla Text
এশিয়ান গেমস ক্রিকেট শ্রীলঙ্কাকে হারিয়ে ফাইনালে বাংলাদেশ অনলাইন ডেস্ক - তারিখ: ২৫-১১-২০১০ এশিয়ান গেমস ক্রিকেটে সোনা জয়ের প্রত্যাশা নিয়েই চীনে গিয়েছেন বাংলাদেশের ক্রিকেটাররা। মালয়েশিয়ার বিপক্ষে সহজ জয়ে সেমিফাইনালে উঠলেও সেখানে সবচেয়ে বড় বাধা হয়ে দাঁড়ায় শ্রীলঙ্কা। কিন্তু সেই বাধা পেরোতেও খুব বেশি কষ্ট হয়নি আশরাফুলদের। শ্রীলঙ্কাকে পাঁচ উইকেটে হারিয়ে তাঁরা পৌঁছে গেছেন এশিয়ান গেমস ক্রিকেট ইভেন্টের ফাইনালে।
Translated Braille

perspective, the proposed Bangla Braille translator will incorporate Bangla voice synthesis tool to assist for keyboard command operation and reading of the translated Braille codes after conversion. Besides, the keyboard based operational flow will be improved further to simplify the usage of the translator along with the incorporation of Braille embosser to provide independent platform for both the Braille translation and printing.

CONCLUSION

Bangla Braille system is designed based on the analysis and understanding of the Braille grammar and developing necessary mapping between Bangla and Braille. In the process, DFA is designed to comply with the rules and assist translation. Using the proposed system, Bangla text written in Unicode format can be translated to Braille without any expertise on Braille codes with greater speed and accuracy. The generated Braille code is tested for grammatical accuracy and found satisfactory.

REFERENCES

Abualkishik, A. M., & Omar, K. (2009). Quran vibrations in Braille code. In *Proceedings of the International Conference on Electrical Engineering and Informatics*, (pp. 12-17). Selangor, Malaysia: IEEE.

Belousov, S., & Coopery, M. Yonina, Dias, B., Dias, M., Horwitz, F., ... Teves, E. A. (2011). *Study report on disabilities: iSTEP Bangladesh* (Tech. Report CMU-RI-TR-35). Pittsburgh, PA: Carnegie Melon University.

Bhattachrya, S., Sarker, S., & Basu, A. (2007). Sanyog: A speech enabled communication system for the speech impaired and people with multiple disorders. *Journal of Technology in Human Services, 25*(1/2).

Booch, G. (1993). *Object oriented analysisa and design with applications* (3rd ed.). Boston: Addison-Wesley.

Dasgupta, T., & Basu, A. (2009). Automatic transliteration of indian language text to Braille for the visually challenged in India. *Information Technology in Developing Countries, 19.*

Hopcroft, J. E. (2007). Introduction to automata theory, languages and computation (2nd ed). New York: Prentice Hall.

Hossain, G., & Asaduzzaman, M.A., Ullah, & Saif Shams, S. M. (2005). Bangla Braille embosser: A tool for Bengali speaking visually impaired people. *Bangladesh Education Journal, 4*(1), 49–55.

Iqbal, Z. (2008). *Muktizudher itihash.* Dhaka, Bangladesh: Protity Publisher.

Khan, D. O., & Shet, K. C. (2005). A new Architecture for Braille transcription from optically recognized Indian languages. In *Proceedings of International Conference.* London: Academic Press.

King, A. (2001). *Text and Braille computer translation.* (Dissertation). University of Manchester Institute of Science and Technology. Manchester, UK.

Lahiri, A., Chattopadhyay, S. J., & Basu, A. (2005). A comprehensive Indian languages tool set for the blind. In *Proceedings of the 7th International Conference Conference on Computers and Accessibility*. ACM.

Language, B. (2009). *Wikipedia.* Retrieved May 10, 2009, from http://en.wikipedia.org/wiki/Bengali_language

Liblouis. (2008). *Google.* Retrieved February 10, 2009, from http://code.google.com/p/liblouis

Ono, S., Hamada, Y., & Takagi, Y. (2000). Interactive Japanese-to-Braille translation using case-based knowledge on the web. *PRICAI 2000 Topics in Artificial Intelligence, 1886*, 638-646.

Pramait & Bangla Braille. (2001). *By blind education and rehabilitation development organisation (BERDO) and Bangladesh blind mission (BBM)*. Dhaka, Bangladesh: Bangla Braille.

Rajasenathipathi, M., Arthanari, M., & Sivakumar, M. (2010). Conversion of English text to Braille code vibration signal for visually impaired people. *International Journal of Computer Science and Information Security Publication*, *8*(5), 59–63.

Singh, M., & Vatia, P. (2010). Automated conversion of English and Hindi text to Braille representation. *International Journal of Computers and Applications*, *4*(5), 18–24.

Titumir, R. A. M., & Hossain, J. (2005). *Disability in Bangladesh: Prevalence, knowledge, attitudes and practices*. Dhaka, Bangladesh: Unnayan Onneshan.

Yousuf, M. A., & Shams, S. M. S. (2007). Bangla Braille information system: An affordable system for the sightless population. *Asian Journal of Information Technology*, *6*(6), 696–699.

Zhang, X., Ortega-Sanchez, C., & Murray, L. (2007). A hardware based Braille note taker. In *Proceedings of the 3rd Southern Conference on Programmable Logic,* (pp. 125-130). Mar del Plata, Argentina.

Chapter 3
UNL-Based Bangla Machine Translation Framework

Nawab Yousuf Ali
East West University, Bangladesh

Shamim H. Ripon
East West University, Bangladesh

ABSTRACT

The usage of native language through Internet is highly demanding due to the rapid increase of Internet-based applications in daily life. As information is available in the Internet in different languages, it is impossible to retrieve the information in other languages. Universal Networking Language (UNL) addresses this issue by converting the requested information from other languages to UNL expressions followed by UNL expressions to respective native languages. Even though Bangla is the sixth most popular language in the world, there is no system developed so far to convert Bangla text into UNL expressions and vice versa. For this purpose, the authors develop a framework. The framework has two constituent parts: 1) EnConverter: converts Bangla native sentences into UNL expressions considering UNL compatible Bangla word dictionary and analysis rules, and 2) DeConverter: converts UNL expressions into respective Bangla sentences considering Bangla word dictionary and generations rules. In both cases, case structure analysis, Bangla parts of speech, and different forms of verbs along with their prefixes, suffixes, and inflections are taken into consideration. This chapter describes the complete theoretical analyses of the EnConversion and DeConversion frameworks. The experimental results confirm that the proposed framework can successfully convert Bangla sentences into UNL expressions, and also can convert UNL expressions into corresponding Bangla sentences.

DOI: 10.4018/978-1-4666-3970-6.ch003

1. INTRODUCTION

Universal Networking Language (UNL) is a project under the auspices of the United Nations University (UNU), Tokyo, Japan. The mission of the UNL project is to allow people across nations to access information in the Internet in their own languages (Uchida, Zhu & Senta, 2005). Hundreds of millions of people of almost all levels of education and attitudes of different jobs all over the world use the Internet for different purposes (Ali, Das, Mamun & Nurannabi, 2008). The last decade of the 20th century witnessed an unimaginary acceleration in the development of information technology in all fields of life. The decade also witnessed a great increase in the spread and popularity of the Internet. English is the main language of the Internet. Understandably not all people know English. Teeming millions are deprived to access the information repositories directly in native language. On the other hand, vast information resources in different languages could not be shared. Knowledge and information are scattered all over the world and remain mostly inaccessible due to non-machine representation and language barrier (Ali, Das, Mamun & Choudhury, 2008). Translation is the only means to disseminate information but only with much effort and involving direct and indirect cost. Language barrier hinders progress at individual level, institutionally and nationally although nations are becoming more interdependent and need to exchange information. Knowledge sources are to be shared globally as much as possible to advance civilization.

Among those who did their best to tackle this problem was the United Nations University/Institute of Advanced Studies (UNU/IAS). The institute conducted a review of all internationally available machine translation programs and finally decided to start devising a better, more efficient and more workable technique to develop a human language neutral meta-language for Internet. The result of the project is Universal Networking Language (UNL) (Chudhury, Ali, Sarkar & Ahsan, 2005).

The UNL project is a large scale international cooperation with the goal to provide information in the Internet in all national languages of the members of the United Nations. The goal is to eliminate the massive task of translation between two languages and reduce language to language translation to a one time conversion to UNL. Once information written in one language is "enconverted" into UNL it will be able to be shared by anyone in the world (Ali, Das, Mamun & Choudhury, 2008). That means the UNL is based on developing an intermediary language system whereby any written text can be converted to many languages and simultaneously, all texts written in different languages can be converted to that particular language. For example, Bangla corpora, once converted to UNL, can be translated to any other language given UNL system built for that language shown in Figure 1.

The UNL system does this by representing only the semantics of a native language sentence in a hypergraph. The hypergraph is composed of nodes connected by semantic relations. Nodes or Universal Words (UWs) are words loaned from English and disambiguated by their positioning in a knowledge base (KB) of conceptual hierarchies. Function words, such as determiners and auxiliaries are represented as attributes to UWs or nodes to provide additional information. English is used for UW, attributes and relations. Enconverter (Enconverter, 2002) converts each native language sentence to a UNL hypergraph and Deconverter (Deconverter, 2002) translates from hypergraph to any native language. The hypergraph has formal English text realization termed as UNL document (like HTML or XML). The development of the language specific components - dictionary and analysis rules - is carried out by researchers across the world.

The difficulty in these translation systems lies in the language analysis process to be performed by the computer in analyzing a sentence in its semantic representation. The computer has to discriminate the lexical and syntactic ambiguities, and

Figure 1. The UNL system

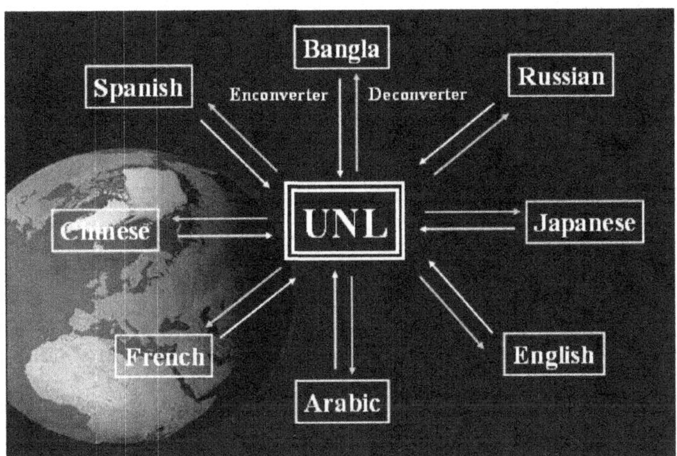

then, derive the correct semantic representation. There are many problems to be solved in these processes. This situation will change dramatically with the UNL. UNL will provide a common educational environment to different languages (UNDL, 2003). Furthermore, UNL will expand business opportunities immensely around the world. As Bangla is the 4th widely spoken language it is highly demanding to develop a framework that will be used to build up a converter, which will convert Bangla text to UNL expressions and UNL expressions to Bangla texts so that a great number of people can access and share a vast repository of knowledge from Internet.

This chapter addresses the following key points to develop a interlingua framework:

1. Analysis of case structures have been carried out meticulously for all kinds of Bangla cases regarding UNL that reflect all kinds of relations between the words and morphemes in the sentences and also describes the development of different rules for converting case sentences.
2. Development of Bangla Word Dictionary for Bangla roots, verbal inflexions, primary suffixes have been carried out by dividing them into different groups and set grammatical attributes for them.
3. Morphological analysis of Bangla words for nouns, pronouns, verbs, adjective have been performed regourously and the development of morphological rules have been discussed for performing accurate morphological analysis of the words for correct translation.
4. A complete computational analysis for the proposed framework have been extended by developing analysis and generation rules for performing conversions, i.e., Bangla texts to UNL expressions and UNL expressins to Bangla texts by introducing new algorithms.

The rest of the chapter is organized as follows. Section 2 describes the structure of UNL along with its analyzer systems: Enconverter and Deconverter. Analysis of Bangla grammar is presented in section 3 that explains all parts of speeches along with their inflexions. It also describes the case structure analysis of Bangla sentences. Section 4 focuses our main work where we explain how Bangla text is converted into UNL expressions where we develop Bangla Word Dictionary along with their grammatical attributes. We also perform morphological analysis of Bangla words along with their prefixes and suffixes and develop morphological rules. After analyzing semantics of Bangla sentences we develop a set of semantic rules. Generation rules are also presented in this section. Section 5 reviews the existing works of Bangla Machine Translation. Finally, in Section 6 we summarize our work and outline our future plans.

2. UNIVERSAL NETWORKING LANGUAGE

The UNL (Uchida, Zhu & Senta, 2005) has been defined as a digital meta language for describing, summarizing, refining, storing and disseminating information in a machine independent and human language neutral form. It represents information, i.e. meaning, sentence by sentence. Each sentence is represented as a hypergraph, where nodes represent concepts and arcs represent relation between concepts. This hypergraph is also represented as a set of directed binary relations between the pair of concepts present in the sentence. Concepts are represented as character-strings called Universal Words (UWs). Knowledge within a UNL document is expressed in three dimensions:

1. **Universal Words (UWs):** Word knowledge is expressed by Universal Words which are language independent. UWs constitute the UNL vocabulary and the syntactic and semantic units that are combined according to the UNL laws to form UNL expressions. They are tagged using restrictions describing the sense of the word in the current context. For example, *drink(icl>liquor)* denotes the noun sense of drink restricting the sense to a type of liquor. Here *icl* stands for inclusion and form an *is-a* relation as in semantic nets (Chudhury, Ali, Sarkar & Ahsan, 2005)[4].
2. **Relation Labels:** Conceptual knowledge is captured by the relationship between Universal Words (UWs) through a set of UNL relations. For example, *Human affects the environment* is described in the UNL expression as:

```
{unl}
agt (affect(icl>do).@present.@en-
try:01,
                  human(icl>animal).@pl)
obj(affect(icl>do).@present.@en-
try:01,
        environment (icl>abstract
thing).@pl)
{/unl}
```

where *agt* means the agent and *obj* means object. The terms *affect(icl>do)*, *human(icl>animal)* and *environment(icl>abstract thing)* are the UWs denoting concepts.

3. **Attribute Labels:** Speaker's view, aspect, time of event, etc. are captured by UNL attributes. For instance, in the above example, the attribute *@entry* denotes the main predicate of the sentence, *@present* denotes the present tense, *@pl* is for the plural number and *:01* represents the scope ID.

A UNL expression can also be represented as a graph. For example, the UNL expressions and the UNL graph for the sentence, *I went to Malaysia from Bangladesh by aeroplane to attend a conference,* are shown in Figure 2.

In the Figure 2 *agt* denotes the agent relation, *obj* the object relation, *plt* the place relation denoting the place to go, *plf* is also a place relation that

Figure 2. UNL expression and UNL graph

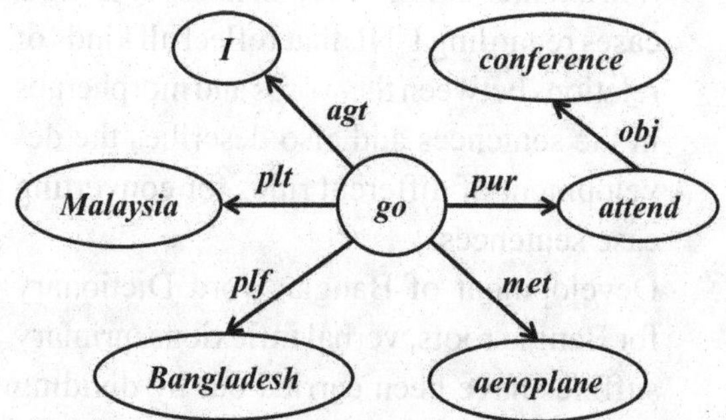

denotes the place from, *pur* states the purpose relation, whereas *met* is for method relation.

UNL expressions provide the *meaning content* of the text. Hence, search could be carried out on the meaning rather than on the text. This of course means developing a novel kind of search engine technology. The merit of such a system is that the information in one language can be stored in multiple languages. See Box 1.

2.1. The Analyzer System: Enconverter

The EnConverter (EnCo) (Enconverter, 2002) is a language independent parser provided by the UNL project, a multi-headed Turing Machine (Pairkh, Khot, Dave & Bhattacharyya, 2004) providing synchronously a framework for morphological, syntactic and semantic analysis. The machine has two types of windows namely *Analysis Windows (AW)* and *Condition Windows (CW)* shown in Figure 3. The machine traverses the input sentence back and forth, retrieves the relevant dictionary entry (UW) from the Word Dictionary (Lexicon) and depending on the *attributes* of the nodes under the AWs and those under the surrounding CWs and finally generates the semantic relations between the UWs and/or attaches speech act attributes to them. As a result a set of UNL expressions is made equivalent of UNL graph.

EnCo is driven by analysis rules to analyze a sentence using Word Dictionary and Knowledge Base. These rules are condition-action structure that can be looked upon as program written in a specialized language to process various complex phenomena of a natural language sentences. The enconversion rules have the following format (Enconverter, 2002):

```
<TYPE>
[ "(" <PRE> ")" ["*"] ]...
"{"|"""" [<COND1>] ":" [<ACTION1>]
":"[<RELATION1>] ":" [<ROLE1>]
"}"|""""
[ "(" <MID> ")" ["*"] ]...
"{"|"""" [<COND2>] ":" [<ACTION2>]
":"[<RELATION2>] ":" [<ROLE2>]
"}"|""""
[ "(" <SUF> ")" ["*"] ]...
"P(" <PRIORITY> ");"
```

where characters between double quotes are predefined delimiters of the rule. The rule means that IF, under the Left Analysis Window (LAW) there is a node that satisfies <COND1> attributes and under the Right Analysis Widow (RAW) a

Box 1.

```
{unl}
  agt(go (icl>move>do,plt>place,plf>place,  agt>thing). @entry.@past,
i(icl>person))
  plt(go (icl>move>do, plt>place, plf>place, agt>thing) .@entry.@past,
  Malaysia (iof>asian_country>thing)) plf(go (icl>move>do, plt>place, plf>place,
  agt>thing) .@entry.@past,  Bangladesh (iof> asian_country> thing))
  met(go (icl>move>do, plt>place, plf>place,  agt>thing) .@entry .@past,
  aeroplane (icl> heavier-than-air_ craft>thing,  equ> airplane))
  obj:01 (attend (icl>go_to>do, agt>person, obj>place) .@entry,
  conference (icl>meeting>thing) .@indef) pur(go (icl>move>do, plt>place,
plf>place,
  agt>thing) .@entry .@past, :01)
{/unl}
```

Figure 3. Structure of EnConverter ("A" indicates an Analysis Window, "C" indicates a Condition Window, and "n_n" indicates an Analysis Node)

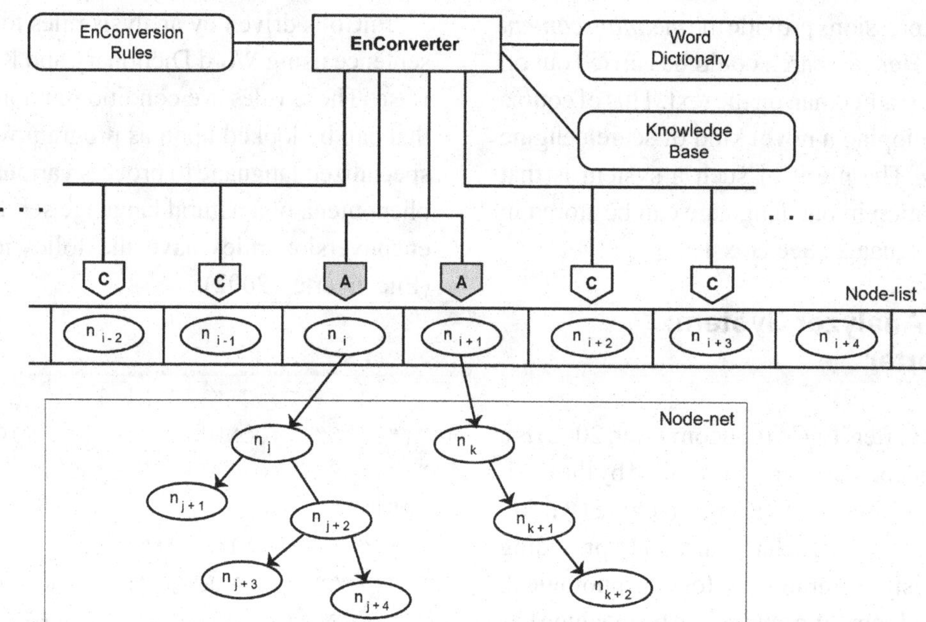

node that satisfies <COND2> attributes and there are nodes to the left of the LAW, between the LAW and the RAW and to the RAW that fulfill the conditions in <PRE>, <MID> and <SUF> respectively, THEN the lexical attributes in the nodes under the AWs are rewritten according to the <ACTION1> and <ACTION2> as specified in rule and new attributes are added if necessary. The operations are done on the node-list depending on the type of the rule shown in the field <TYPE>. <RELATION1> describes the semantic relation of the node on the RAW to the node on the LAW and <RELATION2> describes the reverse (Enconverter, 2002). <PRIORITY> describes the interpretation order of the rules, which is in the range of 0-255. Larger number indicates higher priority. Matching rule with the highest priority is selected for multiple matching rules (Enconverter, 2002). A sequence of such rules get activated depending on the sentence situation i.e. the conditions of the nodes under the AWs. The main task is to creating the UNL expressions of natural language sentences using EnCo by providing a rich lexicon and a comprehensive set of analysis rules. There are 15 types of enconversion rules and each type is represented by the symbols: '+", '-', '<', '>', 'L', 'R', ':', '?', '?L', '?R', 'C', 'G', 'X', 'DL', and 'DR'. These symbols are used in the <TYPE> field of rules. The '+' and '-' types of rules can also have extensional functions by attaching certain operators (Uchida, Zhu & Senta, 2005/2006). Among these 15 analysis rules the following four rules are mostly used. Those are left and right composition rules, and left and right modification rules. The former two rules are used to perform morphological analysis of the words in a sentence whereas the latter two rules are used for semantic analysis.

2.2. The Generation System: DeConverter

DeConverter is a language independent generator. DeConverter operates on the nodes of the Node-list, and inserts nodes from the Node-net into the Node-list through its windows. There are two types of window, namely Generation Window and Condition Window. Two current focused windows are called Generation Windows (GW), circumscribed by the Condition Windows (CW) shown in Figure 4. DeConverter generates a sentence using the Word Dictionary, Deconversion Rules, and Co-occurrence Dictionary. The use of the Co-occurrence Dictionary is optional. Figure 4 shows the structure of DeConverter. It retrieves relevant dictionary entries from the Word Dictionary, operates or inserts nodes by applying Deconversion Rules, and makes word selection for natural wording by referring to the Co-occurrence Dictionary. DeConverter uses the Condition Windows (CW) for checking the neighbouring nodes on both sides of the Generation Windows (GW) in order to determine whether the neighbouring nodes satisfy the conditions for applying a deconversion rule.

The deconversion rule has the syntax below (Deconverter, 2002):

```
<TYPE>
["("<PRE>")" ["*"]]...
"{" | """" [ <COND1> ] ":" [ <AC-
TION1> ] ":" [ <RELATION1> ] ":" [
<ROLE1>] "}" | """"
["("<MID>")" ["*"]]...
"{" | """" [ <COND2> ] ":" [ <AC-
TION2> ] ":" [ <RELATION2> ] ":" [
<ROLE2> ] "}" | """"
["("<SUF>")" ["*"]]...
"P(" <PRIORITY> ");"
```

Each part of the rule expresses the conditions of, or actions on, the adjacent nodes in the node-list in the order of the Left Condition Windows (LCW or PRE), the Left Generation Window (LGW), the Middle Condition Windows (MCW or MID), the Right Generation Window (RGW), and the Right Condition Windows (RCW or SUF). When the node on the left Generation Window satisfies <COND1> attributes, the node on the right Generation Window satisfies <COND2> attributes, and the two words of the two nodes satisfy the Co-occurrence Relation of <ROLE1> or <ROLE2>; and as relevant, when the nodes in the left, middle and right sides of the Generation Windows fulfill the conditions described in <PRE>, <MID> and <SUF> of the Condition Windows, the grammatical attributes of the nodes in the Generation Windows are rewritten according to <ACTION1> and <ACTION2> respectively. If either node in the Generation Windows is indicated as "Insertion", the node linked to the other node by <RELATION1> or <RELATION2> in

Figure 4. Structure of DeConverter ("G" indicates a Generation Window, "C" indicates a Condition Window, and "n_n" indicates a Generation Node)

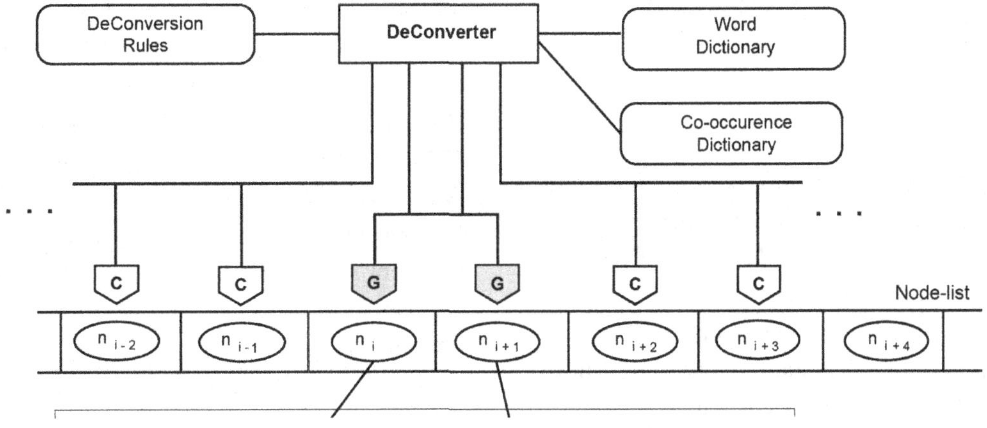

the Node-net is inserted into the Node-list. And the operations are carried out on the Node-list depending on the type of rule shown in field <TYPE> (Enconverter, 2002).

There are 10 types of generation rules. Each type is represented by the following symbols: ':', 'R', 'L', '?', '?L', '?R', 'C', 'CR', 'DL' and 'DR'. These symbols are used in the type field of the rules. Attribute changing rule (:) is the most widely used generation rule.

Attribute Changing Rule ":": This type of rule is used basically to rewrite the attributes of the nodes in both Generation Windows. If any rewriting actions occur in the node of the Left Generation Window, the position of the Generation Window moves to the left so that the Right Generation Window will always be placed on the rewritten node. Node insertion also uses this type of rule. In this case, either node in the Generation Windows must be indicated as being an inserted node. If the left node is an inserted node, the Right Generation Window will move so that it is placed on it after the rule application.

3. ANALYSIS OF BANGLA GRAMMAR

There are around 550,000 words (Bondopoddaye, 2001) in Bangla language including their prefixes and suffixes. All these forms are to be morphologically analyzed and UW (Bangla word/prefix/suffix) for these Bangla head words are to be prepared.

3.1. Nouns (বিশেষ্য)

Learning the Bangla nouns is very important, because its structure is used in every day conversation. We have analyzed the role of nouns in the structure of the grammar in Bangla. Bangla nouns are words used to name a person, animal, place, thing, or abstract ideas. Nouns are usually the most important part of vocabulary.

There are around 700000 nouns found in Bangla language (Bondopoddaye, 2001). We consider six different types of nouns in Bangla shown below.

- **Proper Noun (নামবাচক):** The name of specific things, e.g., দুলাল, *dulal* (Dulal),- the name of a person, পদ্মা, *padma* (Padma), the name of a river etc.
- **Common Noun (জাতিবাচক):** Common names of particular things, e.g., মানুষ, *manush* (Man), গরু, *goru* (Cow), গাছ, *gachh* (Tree), মাছ, *machh* (Fish) etc. Common nouns can be singular or plural.
- **Material Noun (দ্রব্যবাচক):** The names of the materials, for example, জল, *jol* (water), বাতাস, *batash* (air), আকাশ, *akash* (sky), লোহা, *loha* (iron) etc.
- **Abstract Noun (গুণবাচক):** This type of nouns represents names of quality, e.g., সুখ, *shukh* (happiness), দুঃখ, *dukh* (sadness) etc.
- **Verbal Noun (ক্রিয়াবাচক):** This type of nouns indicates the names of verbs. For example, যাওয়া, *jawa* (go), করা, *kora* (do), etc.
- **Collective Noun (সমষ্টিবাচক):** This type of nouns indicates the collective names of people or things, e.g., জনতা, *jonota* (people), শ্রেণী, *sreni* (class), সমাজ, *shomaj* (society), সেনা, *shena* (soldier) etc.

A lot of other issues come in front for analyzing nouns in Bangla. These are quantifiers such as এক (*ek*), দুই (*dui*), বহু (*bohu*), অনেক (*onek*), determiners such as টি (*ti*), টা (*ta*), খানা (*khana*), খানি (*khani*), inflexions, বিভক্তি (*bibhokti*) such as জন (*jon*), কে (*ke*), in plural, দের (*der*), দিগকে (*digoke*), রা (*ra*), এরা (*era*), গুলো (*gulo*), গণ (*gon*) (Asaduzzaman & Ali, 2003) [21] etc. We have analyzed all these forms to define appropriate grammatical attributes for them for correct translation. Some examples of analysis of nouns are shown in Table 1. based on numbers.

3.2. Adjectives (বিশেষণ)

There are more than 50,000 adjectives (Bondopoddaye, 2001) found in Bangla language. Inflectional suffixes are also present in Bangla adjectives. Some examples of analysis of adjectives are given in Table 2.

Here, we consider Bangla words "mvnm" pronounce as *shahosh* and "ভালো" pronounce as *valo* meaning "bravery" and "good", respectively. From the first word, we get "সাহসী" (*shahoshi*), "সাহসের" (*sahosher*), etc. and from the second word we get "ভালোকে" (*valoke*), "ভালোটা" (*valota*), "ভালোর" (*valor*), etc. are adjectives.

3.3. Pronouns (সর্বনাম)

Bangla pronouns, unlike their English counterparts, do not differentiate for gender; that is, the same pronoun may be used for "he" or "she." In the following tables, the abbreviations used are as follows: VF=very familiar (neglect), F=familiar, and P=polite (honor); H=here, T=there, and E=elsewhere (proximity). The nominative case is used for pronouns that are the subject of the sentence, such as "*I* already did that" or "Will *you* please stop making that noise?" Table 3 shows the personal pronouns for nominative case.

Table 1. Examples of noun morphology

Number	Root Word	Word as Appears in a Sentence	Inflexional Suffix
Singular	ছেলে, chhele (boy)	ছেলেকে (to the boy)	কে(ke)
		ছেলের (of the boy)	র (r)
		ছেলেটি (the boy)	টি (ti)
		ছেলেটির (the boy's)	টির (tir)
Plural	ছেলে, chhele (boy)	ছেলেদের (of the boys)	দের (der)
		ছেলেরা (boys)	রা (ra)
		ছেলেদেরকে (to the boys)	দেরকে (derke)
	কবি, kobi (poet)	কবিকুল (poets)	কুল (kul)
	শিক্ষক, shikkhok (teacher)	শিক্ষকবৃন্দ (teachers)	বৃন্দ (brindo)
	পর্বত, porbot (mountain)	পর্বতসকল (mountains)	সকল (shokol)

Table 2. Examples of adjective morphology

Root Word (Adjective)	Word as Appears in a Sentence with inflexion	Inflectional Suffix
সাহস, shahosh (brave)	সাহসী, shahoshi	ঈ(ee)
	সাহসের, shahosher	এর (er)
সুখ, shukh (happy)	সুখি, shukhi	ই (i)
	সুখের, shukher	এর (er)
মন্দ, mondo (bad)	মন্দটা, mondota	টা (ta)
	মন্দকে, mondoke	কে (ke)
	মন্দর, mondor	র (r)
বড়, boro (big)	বড়টি, boroti	টি (ti)
সুন্দর, shundhor (beautiful)	সুন্দরী, shundhori	ঈ(ee)

Table 3. Personal pronouns for nominative case

Subject	Proximity	Honor	Singular	Plural
1			আমি, *ami* (I)	আমরা, *amra* (we)
2		VF	তুই, *tui* (you)	তোরা, *tora* (you)
		F	তুমি, *tumi* (you)	তোমরা, *tomra* (you)
		P	আপনি, *apni* (you)	আপনারা, *apnara* (you)
3	H	F	এ, *e* (he/she)	এরা, *era* (they)
		P	ইনি, *ini* (he/she)	এঁরা, *ẽra* (they)
	T	F	ও, *o* (he/she)	ওরা, *ora* (they)
		P	উনি, *uni* (he/she)	ওঁরা, *õra* (they)
	E	F	সে, *she* (he/she)	তারা, *tara* (they)
		P	তিনি, *tini* (he/she)	তাঁরা, *tãra* (they)

The objective case is used for pronouns serving as the direct or indirect objects, such as "I told *him* to wash the dishes" or "The teacher gave *me* the homework assignment." Table 4 shows the personal pronouns for objective case.

The *possessive case* is used to show possession, such as "Where is *your* coat?" or "Let's go to *our* house." Note that the plural forms are identical to those for the objective case. Table 5 shows the personal pronouns for possessive case.

3.4. Verbs (ক্রিয়া)

Bangla verbs are highly inflected and are regular with only a few exceptions. They consist of a stem and an ending; which is usually formed by adding –*a*(আ) to the stem, for instance, রাখা (*rakha)* = "to put or place." The stem can end in either a vowel or a consonant. Verbs are conjugated for tense and person by changing the endings, which are largely the same for all verbs. An example would

Table 4. Personal pronouns for objective case

Subject	Proximity	Honor	Singular	Plural
1			আমাকে, *amake* (me)	আমাদের, *amader* (us)
2		VF	তোকে, *toke* (you)	তোদের, *toder* (you)
		F	তোমাকে, *tomake* (you)	তোমাদের, *tomader* (you)
		P	আপনাকে, *apnake* (you)	আপনাদের, *apnader* (you)
3	H	F	একে, *eke* (him/her)	এদের, *eder* (them)
		P	এঁকে, *ẽke* (him/her)	এঁদের, *ẽder* (them)
	T	F	ওকে, *oke* (him/her)	ওদের, *oder* (them)
		P	ওঁকে, *õke* (him/her)	ওঁদের, *õder* (them)
	E	F	তাকে, *take* (him/her)	তাদের, *tader* (them)
		P	তাঁকে, *tãke* (him/her)	তাঁদের, *tãder* (them)

Table 5. Personal pronouns for possessive case

Subject	Proximity	Honor	Singular	Plural
1			আমার, *amar* (my)	আমাদের, *amader* (our)
2		VF	তোর, *tor* (your)	তোদের, *toder* (your)
		F	তোমার, *tomar* (your)	তোমদের, *tomader* (your)
		P	আপনার, *apnar* (your)	আপনাদের, *apnader* (your)
3	H	F	এর, *er* (his/her)	এদের, *eder* (their)
		P	এঁর, *ẽr* (his/her)	এঁদের, *ẽder* (their)
	T	F	ওর, *or* (his/her)	ওদের, *oder* (their)
		P	ওঁর, *õr* (his/her)	ওঁদের, *õder* (their)
	E	F	তার, *tar* (his/her)	তাদের, *tader* (their)
		P	তাঁর, *tãr* (his/her)	তাঁদের, *tãder* (their)

be the verb "to write," with stem *lekh-*: তোমরা লিখ *(tomra likho)* meaning "you (pl.) write" but আমরা লিখি *(amra likhi)* meaning "we write." A prototype verb from each of these classes will be used to demonstrate conjugation for that class.

- **Non-Finite Forms:** The Bangla verb can occur in six non-finite forms. By definition, they do not offer any information on tense (present, past, or future) or person (one or more subjects). They do, however, indicate other information - these are shown below using the verbal root আঁক *(aak)*, "draw":
  - **আঁকা (*aka*):** Verbal noun ("act of drawing").
  - **আঁকতে (*akte*):** Verbal infinitive ("to draw").
  - **আঁকতে-আঁকতে (*akte-akte*):** Progressive participle ("while drawing").
  - **আঁকলে (*akle*):** Conditional participle ("if X draws").
  - **এঁকে (*eke*):** Perfect participle ("having drawn").
  - **এঁকে-এঁকে (*eke-eke*):** Iterative participle ("having drawn many times").
- **Person:** Verbs are inflected for person and honor but not for number. There are five forms: first person, second person (very familiar), second person (familiar), third person (familiar), and second/third person (polite). The same sample subject pronouns will be used for all the example conjugation paradigms: আমি (*ami*), তুই (*tui),* তুমি *(tumi)*, সে *(she)* and আপনি *(apni)*. These have the following plurals respectively আমরা *(amra)*, তোরা *(tora)*, তোমরা *(tomra)*, তারা *(tara)*, and আপনারা *(apnara)*.
- **Mood:** There are two moods for Bangla verbs: the indicative and the imperative. The imperative mood is used to give commands. The indicative mood is used for statements of fact.
- **Tense:** Bangla has four simple tenses: the present tense, the past tense, the conditional or habitual past tense, and the future tense. These combine with mood and aspect to form more complex conjugations, such as the past progressive, or the present perfect.
  - **Simple Present Tense:** The present tense in Bangla is similar to that of English: I eat, you run, he reads. Some examples of verbs for present tense of different persons are shown in Table 6.
  - **Simple Past Tense:** The (simple) past tense differs from its use in English in that it is usually reserved for events that

Table 6. Examples of verbs for present tense in different persons

Verb	1	2 (VF)	2 (F)	3 (F)	2/3 (P)
বলা	আমি বলি	তুই বলিস	তুমি বলো	সে বলে	আপনি বলেন
bola	*ami boli*	*tui bolish*	*tumi bôlo*	*she bôle*	*apni bôlen*
খোলা	আমি খুলি	তুই খুলিস	তুমি খোলো	সে খোলে	আপনি খোলেন
Kholo	*Ami khuli*	*tui khulish*	*tumi kholo*	*she khole*	*apni kholen*

have occurred recently; for instance, less than a day ago. It would be translated into the English simple past tense: I ate, you ran, he read. The endings are লাম *(-lam)*, লি *(-li)*, লে *-(le)*, ল *(-lo)*, লেন *(-len)*. For example: আমি দেখলাম *(ami dekhlam)*, তুই দেখলি *(tui dekhli)*, তুমি দেখলে *(tumi dekhle)*, সে দেখল *(se dekhlo)*, আপনি দেখলেন *(apni dekhlen)*. Some examples are shown in Table 7.

- **Future Tense:** In less standard varieties of Bangla, "a" is substituted for "e" in second-person familiar forms; thus তুমি বলবা, খুলবা, খেলবা *(tumi bolba, khulba, khelba), etc*. Table 8 shows some examples of verbs for future tense.

Bangla language has more than 30000 (Bondopoddaye, 2001) verbs. Diversity of verb morphology in Bangla is very significant (Asaduzzaman & Ali, 2003). For example, if we consider "লিখ্" (*likh* means 'write') as a root word then after adding verbal inflexion "ইতেছি" (*itechhi*), we get a word "লিখিতেছি" (*likhitechhi* means 'am writing') which means a work is being doing in present (for first person). Similarly, after adding inflexion "ইতেছিলাম" (*itechhilam*) we get the word "লিখিতেছিলাম"(*likhitechhilam* means 'was writing') which means a work was being done in past. Here, one word represents present continuous tense of the root word "লিখ্" (*likh*) and another represents past continuous tense. Therefore, by morphological analysis we get the grammatical attributes of the main word and other attributes. For this

Table 7. Examples of verbs for past tense in different person

Verb	1	2 (VF)	2 (F)	3 (F)	2/3 (P)
বলা	আমি বললাম	তুই বললি	তুমি বললে	সে বললো	আপনি বললেন
bôla	*ami bollam*	*tui bolli*	*tumi bolle*	*she bollo*	*apni bollen*
খোলা	আমি খুললাম	তুই খুললি	তুমি খুললে	সে খুললো	আপনি খুললেন
khola	*ami khullam*	*tui khulli*	*tumi khulle*	*she khullo*	*apni khullen*

Table 8. Examples of verbs for future tense in different persons

Verb	1	2 (VF)	2 (F)	3 (F)	2/3 (P)
বলা	আমি বলব	তুই বলবি	তুমি বলবে	সে বলবে	আপনি বলবেন
bôla	*ami bolbo*	*tui bolbi*	*tumi bolbe*	*she bolbe*	*apni bolben*
খোলা	আমি খুলবো	তুই খুলবি	তুমি খুলবে	সে খুলবে	আপনি খুলবেন
khola	*ami khulbo*	*tui khulbi*	*tumi khulbe*	*she khulbe*	*apni khulben*

reason we have applied morphological analysis for different persons with different transformations to find out the actual meaning of the word. Morphological analysis of Bangla verbs has been considered in different works (Ali et al., 2008; Choudhury et al., 2005; Choudhury & Ali, 2008). We show some data for root verbs যা (go) shown in Table 9.

As verbs come from roots and verbal inflexios, for appropriate morphological analysis, there are two categories of verb roots:

- **Vowel Ended Roots:** In Bangla there are around 25 vowel ended roots e.g পা (*pa*), খা (*kha*), গা (*ga*), চা (*cha*), ছা (*chha*), নি (*ni*), দি (*di*), যা (*ja*), ছুঁ (*chhu*), থু (*thu*), শু (*shu*), ধু (*ddhu*), ন (*n*), দু (*dhu*), নু (*chha*), রু (*ru*), হ (*h*), ধা (*dha*), না (*na*), বা (*ba*), ক (*ko*), ব (*bo*), র (*ro*) and স (*sho*).
- **Consonant Ended Roots:** There are around around 1500 consonant ended roots in Bangla Language. For examples, কর্ (*kor*), খেল্ (*khel*), গড়্ (*gor*), ঘষ্ (*gosh*), বথ্ (*bokh*), কহ্ (*koh*), গিল্ (*gil*), পিষ্ (*pish*), etc. are consonant ended roots.

Table 9. Morphology of root verb যা (go)

Person/Tense	Verb as Appears in a Sentence	Verbal Inflection
First		
Present	যাই (jai)	ই (i)
Past	গেলাম (gelam)	লাম (lam)
Past Perfect	গিয়েছিলাম (giechhilam)	য়েছিলাম (echhilam)
Second		
Present	যান (jan)	ন (n)
Present Continuous	যাচ্ছেন (jachhen)	চ্ছেন (chhen)
Third		
Present	যায় (jae)	য় (e)
Past Habitual	যেত (jeto)	ত (to)
Future	যাবে (jabe)	বে (be)

3.5. Postpositions (অব্যয়)

Postpositions in Bangla are like prepositions in English but they are placed behind the noun or pronoun. The noun or pronoun is often in the possessive case. Some prepositions are shown in Table 10.

Example: আপনার সামনে (*apnar samne*), 'in front of you,' বাবার কাছে (*babar kachhe*), 'near father.' Around 300 prepositions are found in Bangla language. They do not undergo any morphological change.

3.6. Inflexions

Inflexions are used with Bangla words or root words to make thousands of meaningful words (Shahidullah, 2003; Kumar, 1999). Two types of inflexions are available in Bangla language (Kumar, 1999; Azad, 1994).

- **Prefixes (উপসর্গ)**

Prefixes are the words that are used before word roots to express various meanings of the same word roots. There are around fifty (50) prefixes used in Bangla sentences. In Shangskrit Bangla we use twenty (20) prefixes (Shahidullah, 2003) say, প্র (প্রকর্ষ) [pro (prokorsho)], পরা (বৈপরীত্য) [pora (boiporitto)], অপ (বৈপরীত্য) [opp (boiporitto)], etc., in Bangla we use thirteen prefixes (13) prefixes (Shahidullah, 2003) such as বে (be), গর (gor), অন (on) etc, five (5) foreign prefixes (Kumar, 1999) such as গর (না) [gor (na)], দর [dor (nimnoshoho)], বদ (খারাপ) [bod (kharap)] etc., four English prefixes

Table 10. Examples of Bangla prepositions

in	(-o / -e) ও/এ
on / to	(-e) এ
at	(-te) তে
for	(-jonno) জন্য
and	(-ebong) এবং

(Ali, Das, Mamun & Choudhury, 2008) such as সাব (অধীন) [sub (odhin)], হেড (প্রধান) [hed (prodhan)], ফুল (পুরা) [ful (pura)], হাফ (অধ) [half(ordho)] etc. and other prefixes (Ramesuar, 1996; Kumar, 1999) say পুরঃ (দৃষ্টিগোচর) [puro(dristgochor)], প্রাদু (দৃষ্টিগোচর) [pradu (dristigochor)], বহিঃ (বাহিরে) [bohi (bahire)], etc.

- **Affix (উপসর্গ):** A good number of affixes are combined with words or word roots or roots. There are two types of affixes used with Bangla words.
- **Suffix (প্রত্যয়):** The suffixes that are used after words/roots to form new meaningful words called suffixes (Choudhury, Ali, Sarkar & Ahsan, 2005). Two types of suffixes are:
    - **Primary Suffix: (কৃৎ প্রত্যয়):** Used after verb roots to form meaningful words. For example, অন (বাঁধ + অন = বাঁধন, নাচ+ অন = নাচন), etc.
    - **Secondary Suffix: (তদ্ধিত প্রত্যয়):** Used after words to form meaningful new words called secondary suffixes. For example, some secondary suffixes are, অই (পাঁচ + অই = পাঁচই, আই (মিঠা+আই), etc.
- **Verbal Inflexion (ক্রিয়া বিভক্তি):** The inflexions that are added after roots to make only verbs called verbal inflexions (Kumar, 1999). For example, ই (*i*), ইতেছি (*itechhi*), ইতেছিলেন (*itechhilen*), বে (*be*), এলাম (*elam*), ইলাম (*ilam*), লাম (*lam*), ছিলাম (*chhilam*), ইতেছিলাম (*itechhilam*), তেছিলাম (*techhilam*), যেছিলাম (*echilam*), ইয়েছিলাম (*iechhilam*), etc.

3.7. Case Structure Analysis of Bangla Sentence

Case (in Bangla Kaarok) in Bangla denotes the relationship of the nominal with the main verb of the clause. The cases are broadly classified into six categories (Shahidullah, 2003), each having a finer categorization into sub-types. The traditional cases with their inflexions are shown in Table 11.

- **Nominative Case (কর্তৃ কারক)**

This case is the form of a noun or pronoun used in the subject or predicate nominative. It denotes the agent of the action stated by the verb. For example, "করিম পড়িতেছে", pronounced *Karim Poritechhe*, means "Karim is reading." To convert this sentence into UNL expressions one morphological and one semantic analysis will be held. Morphological analysis will be between "পড়" (*por*) and "ইতেছে" (*itechhi*). As subject *Karim* initiates an action, agent (agt) relation is made between subject "করিম" (*karim*) and "পড়িতেছে" (*poritechhe*).

- **Accusative Case (কর্ম কারক)**

Accusative case is a noun or pronoun or thing on which the subject executes the verb. For example: "আমি ভাত খাই" pronounce as *Aami vat khai* means "I eat rice." In this sentence, one morphological and two semantic relations are made. Morphological analysis will be between "খা" (*kha*) and "ই" (*i*). One semantic relation is agent (agt) relation to be held between "আমি" (*aami*) and "খাই" (*khai*) and another relation is between "ভাত" (rice) and "খাই" (eat). Here, rice is an *object* and relation between rice and eat is the accusative case.

- **Instrumental Case (করণ কারক)**

Instrumental case is the thing, tool or method by which the subject of the sentence executes the specified action. Say, "সে কলম দিয়ে একটি নোট লিখেছিল" pronounced *Se kolom die ekti note likhechhilo,* means "He wrote a note with a pen." Here, two morphological and three semantic analyses are taken place. Morphological analyses to be held between "কলম" (*kolom*) and "দিয়ে" (*die*) and between "লিখ্" (*likh*) and "এছিল" (*echhilo*), whereas first semantic relation is object (obj) relation

Table 11. Bangla cases and their inflexions

Classical Case vs. Bangla Kaarok	Inflexions (Case Maker)	
	Singular	Plural
Nominative case (কর্তৃ কারক)	0 (null), এ (e), য় (oy), তে (te)	রা (ra), এরা (era)
Accusative case (কর্ম কারক)	0 (null), কে (ke), রে (re), এরে (ere)	দিগকে (digoke)
Instrumental case (করণ কারক)	দ্বারা (dara), দিয়া (dia), কর্তৃক (kortik)	দের দ্বারা (der dara), দিগের দ্বারা (diger dara)
Dative case (সম্প্রদান কারক)	0 (null), কে (ke), রে (re), এরে (ere), এ (e), য় (oy), তে (et)	দিগকে (digoke)
Ablative case (অপাদান কারক)	হইতে (hoite), থেকে (theke)	দের হইতে (der hoite), দিগের হইতে (diger hoite)
Genitive case (সম্বন্ধ পদ)	র (r), এর (er)	দের (der), দিগের (diger)
Case of time-place (অধিকরণ কারক)	এ (e), য় (oy), তে (te)	সকলে (sokole), দের মধ্যে (der modde)

which is made between "নোট" (note) and "লিখেছিল" (*likhechhilo*) and the second semantic relation is made between "কলম" (pen) which is instrument and "লিখেছিল" (wrote) is instrumental case. Third semantic relation is object (obj) relation to be held between "সে" (he) and "লিখেছিল" (wrote).

- **Dative Case (সম্প্রদান কারক)**

In dative case, subject of a sentence does or gives something for or to someone. For example: "রাজা তাহার পুত্রকে মুকুট দিবে" pronounced *Raja tahar putroke mukut dibe*, means "The king will give crown to his son." In this sentence, three morphological and four semantic analyses are made to convert the sentence into UNL expressions. First, second and third morphological analyses to be held between "দি" (*di*) and "বে" (*be*), "পুত্র" (*putro*) and "কে" (*ke*) and "তাহা"(*taha*) and "র" (*r*) to complete the meaning of the words "দিবে" (*dibe*), "পুত্রকে"(*putroke*) and "তাহার"(*tahar*) respectively. First semantic relation is object (obj) relation which is made between "মুকুট" (crown) "দিবে" (will give). Second semantic relation is made between "পুত্রকে" (to son), which is beneficiary and "দিবে" (will give) is dative case. Third semantic relation is possessive (pos) relation to be held between "তাহার" (his) and "পুত্রকে" (to son) and the fourth semantic relation is agent (agt) relation to be held between "রাজা" (king) and "দিবে" (give) respectively.

- **Ablative Case (অপাদান কারক)**

It describes the concept of sources of creation, location, position etc. All types of relations having the concept of source are eligible to come into this category.

For example, "পাখিটি খাচা থেকে উড়ে যায়" pronounced *Pakhiti khacha theke ure jae*, means "The bird flies from the nest." In the sentence, four morphological and three semantic analyses are made to convert the sentence into UNL expressions. First, second and third morphological analyses to be held between "যা" (*ja*) and "য়" (*ye*), "উড়" (*ur*) and "এ"(*e*), "খাচা" (*khacha*) and "থেকে" (*theke*) and "পাখি" (*pakhi*) and "টি"(*ti*) to complete the meaning of the words "যায়" (*jae*), "উড়ে" (*ure*), "খাচা থেকে" (*khacha theke*) and "পাখিটি" (*pakhiti*) respectively.

First semantic relation is object (obj) relation which is made between "খাচা" (nest) and থেকে" (from). Second semantic relation is from (frm) relation which is made between "খাচা থেকে" (from nest) and "উড়ে যায়" (fly) and third semantic relation is agent (agt) relation, made between "পাখিটি" (the bird), and "উড়ে যায়" (fly) respectively.

- **Case of Time-Place (অধিকরণ কারক)**

This case describes the place, time and topic of the action performed by the sentence. For example, "আমরা ঢাকায় থাকি" pronounced *Aamra dhakae thaki* means "We live in Dhaka." To convert this sentence into UNL expressions two morphological and two semantic analyses to be held. Morphological analyses between root 'থাক' (*thak* means 'live') and inflexion 'ই' (*i*) and noun "ঢাকা" (*Dhaka*) and inflexion "য়"(*e*) to be held and first semantic relation is *things with attribute* (aoj) relation to be held between "আমরা" (*Aamra* means 'we') and "থাকি" (*thaki* means live in present form) and another semantic relation is place (plc) relation to be held between "ঢাকায়" (*Dhakae* means in Dhaka and "থাকি" (*thaki*). Here, "ঢাকা" (*Dhaka*) is a *place* and relation between "ঢাকা" (*Dhaka*) and "থাকি" (*thaki*) is the case of time-place.

Using the above discussions about nouns, adjectives, pronouns, verbs, prepsoitions, inflexions and case structure analysis of Bangla sentences we extort huge ideas about Bangla grammar for morphological, syntactic and semantic analysis. These are required to prepare Bangla word dictionary (for roots, root words prefixes, suffixes, etc) along with their grammatical attributes, morphological rules, analysis rules and generation rules in the UNL format provided by the UNL center of the UNDL Foundation (Uchida, Zhu & Senta, 2005/2006). These Word Dictionary and rules will be required for converting a Bangla sentence to UNL expression and vice versa.

4. BANGLA AND UNL CONVERSION PORCEDURES

In conversion procedure Word Dictionary is an essential part. The Word Dictionary is a collection of the word dictionary entries. Each entry of the Word Dictionary is composed of three kinds of elements: the Headword (HW), the Universal Word (UW) and the Grammatical Attributes (GA). A headword is a notation/surface of a word of a natural language that composing the input sentence and it is to be used as a trigger for obtaining equivalent UWs from the Word Dictionary during EnConversion. An UW expresses the meaning of the word and is to be used in creating UNL networks (UNL expressions) of output. Grammatical Attributes are the information on how the word behaves in a sentence and they are to be used in enconversion rules. Each Dictionary entry has the format shown in Box 2 (UNDL, 2003; Choudhury & Ali, 2008).

The format of an element of Bangla-UNL Dictionary is shown in Figure 5.

4.1. Development of Grammatical Attributes

To represent Universal Words (UWs) of each of the Bangla Head Words it is required to develop grammatical attributes. They play very important roles for writing Enconversion and Deconversion rules because a rule uses GA in morphological and syntactic analysis, to connect or analyze one morpheme with another to build a meaningful word and to examine or define the position of a word in a sentence. We define all the possible specifications of the HWs as grammatical attributes, so that they can be used in the dictionary for making rules (EnCo and DeCo). For example, if we consider "পাখি (*pakhi*) meaning 'bird' as a head word, then we can use attributes N (as it is noun), ANI (as bird is an animal), SG for singular number and CONCRETE (as it a concrete thing

Box 2. Dictionary entry format

[HW]{ID} "UW" (Attribute1, Attribute2,...) <FLG, FRE, PRI>

where:
HW ← Head Word (Bangla word)
ID ← Identification of Head Word (optional)
UW ← Universal Word
ATTRIBUTE ← Attribute of the HW
FLG ← Language Flag
FRE ← Frequency of Head Word
PRI ←Priority of Head Word

Figure 5. Format of a Bangla word dictionary

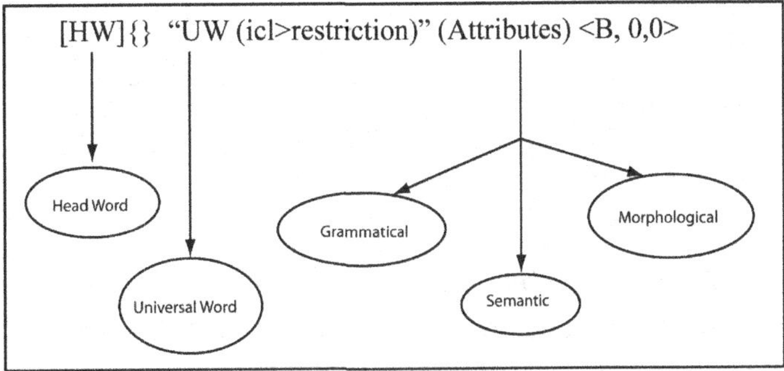

which is touchable). So, this word can be represented in the dictionary as in Box 3.

Some proposed grammatical attributes for developing Word Dictionary of Bangla words and morphemes are shown in Table 12.

4.2. Template for Bangla Verb Root

In Bangla language, 25 vowel ended roots have been found so far (Bondopoddaye, 2001). After analyzing these roots we have categorized them into 10 groups based on how verbal inflexions are added with them to form verbs. Duing this categorization, we have considered the behavior of verbal inflexions with various kinds of persons (1st, 2nd and 3rd) and tenses (present, past and future). For example:

আমি বিশ্ববিদ্যালয়ে যাই, *aami bishabiddaloye jai*

Here, verb is 'যাই', *jai*. In this verb, root 'যা' is a vowel ended root and 'ই' is verbal inflexion. If we write the present continuous form of the above sentence, we get, আমি বিশ্ববিদ্যালয়ে যাচ্ছি, *aami bishabiddaloye jachhi*. Although the root is same as previous sentence due to change of tense the verbal inflexion for this sentence is 'চ্ছি'. Whereas the present perfect form of this sentence is, আমি

Box 3.

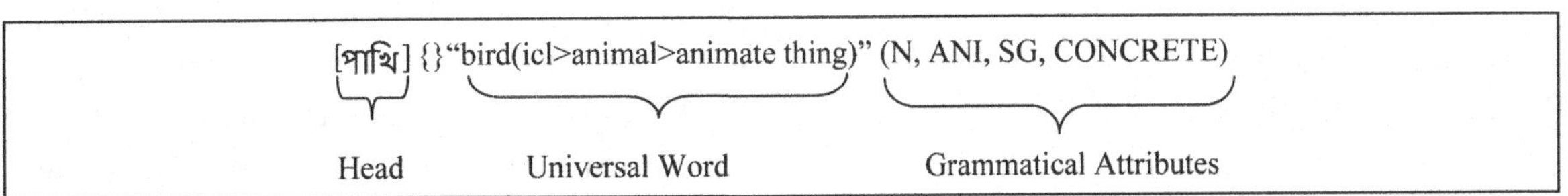

Table 12. Proposed grammatical attributes

Grammatical Attributes	Descriptions of Attributes	Examples (Bangla/English Words)
ADJ	adjective	ভাল (good), সুন্দর (beautiful), etc.
ALT	alternative root	গি (gi), যে (je), etc.
CEND	verb roots or nouns that are ended with consonant	পড় (read), ধর্ (catch), লন্ডন (London), etc.
CHL	inflexions that are used for cholti language	তাম (tam), লাম (lam), etc.
CONCRETE	solid thing	জমি (land), ঘর (house), etc.
FUT	verbal inflexions that make future tense with root	বে (be) etc.
HON	respected pronouns	আপনি (you), তিনি (he), etc.
HPRON	human pronoun	আমি (ami), সে (she), etc.
MAL	male person	সে (পুরুষ), he (male), etc.
N	any noun	কলম (pen), আম (mango), etc.
NP	noun phrase	কলম দিয়ে (by pen), etc.
PL	plural number	আমরা (amra), তাহারা (tahara), etc.
PRON	pronoun	আমি (I), আমরা (we), etc.

বিশ্ববিদ্যালয়ে গিয়েছি, *Ammi bishabiddaloye giechhi*. In this sentence, the original root 'যা' is changing its form to 'গি', *gi*' for making verb গিয়েছি, '*giechhi*', where য়েছি, '*echhi*' is the verbal inflexion. Similar changes have been observed in different roots for different tenses.

For appropriate morphological analysis and to design verb root templates, verb roots have been divided into two broad categories according to tenses and persons namely Vowel Ended Group (VEG) and Consonant Ended Group (CEG). Each of them again divided into sub-groups. Some examples of Vowel Ended Groups are shown in the following tables (Table 13, 14 and 15).

There are around 1,500 consonant ended roots. Among them we have analyzed around 200 roots. We have done similar analysis as vowel ended roots and divided them into 7 groups. Table 16, 17, 18 show some of the variations of Consonant Ended Roots (CERs) and their Verbal Inflexion (Vis) for first, second and third person respectively.

Template [23] that has been developed for Bangla roots is depicted in Box 4.

For first two entries the relation *plf* (place from) indicates from where agent go/goes, plt (place to) means to where go/goes, agt(agent) for who go/goes and attribute ALT indicates that root "গি "(*gi*) is the first alternative of root "যা "(*ja*) discussed in Table 13. Attributes #PLF, #PLT and #AGT indicate that relations *plf, plt* and *agt* can be made with roots "গি" (*gi*) and "যা" (*ja*). Similarly, other entries have been developed according to the format discussed above.

4.3. Template for Verbal Inflexion

Verbal inflexions do not have any universal word and they have only grammatical attributes and differ from each other with the attributes they use. See Box 5.

Like verb roots, some attributes like VI, V are fixed for all Verbal Inflexions, but a person can be either attributes P1 (for first person), P2 (for second person) or P3 (for third person) and a tense can be any tense such as attributes PRS (present indefinite), PRG (progress for present continuous), CMPL (complete for perfect tense), etc. If the tense is past continuous then two attributes are

Table 13. *Variations of vowel ended roots and their verbal inflexions of VEG1, VEG1.1, VEG2, and VEG3 for first person*

Tense		পা (pa)	খা (kha)	গা (ga)	চা (cha)	ছা (ccha)	নি (ni)	দি (ni)	যা (ja)
Present	Indefinite	ই	ই	ই	ই	ই	ই	ই	ই
	Cont.	চ্ছি	চ্ছি	চ্ছি	চ্ছি	চ্ছি	চ্ছি	চ্ছি	চ্ছি
	Perfect	পা > পে য়েছি	খা > খে য়েছি	গা > গে য়েছি	চা > চে য়েছি	ছা > ছে য়েছি	য়েছি	য়েছি	যা > গি য়েছি
Past	Indefinite	পা > পে লাম	খা > খে লাম	গা > গাই লাম	চা > চাই লাম	ছা > ছাই লাম	লাম	লাম	যা > গে লাম
	Habitual	পা > পে তাম	খা > খে তাম	গা > গাই তাম	চা > চাই তাম	ছা > ছাই তাম	তাম	তাম	যা > যে তাম
	Cont.	চ্ছিলাম	চ্ছিলাম	চ্ছিলাম	চ্ছিলাম	চ্ছিলাম	চ্ছিলাম	চ্ছিলাম	চ্ছিলাম
	Perfect	পা > পে য়েছিলাম	খা > খে য়েছিলাম	গা > গে য়েছিলাম	চা > চে য়েছিলাম	ছা > ছে য়েছিলাম	য়েছিলাম	য়েছিলাম	যা > গি য়েছিলাম
Future	Indefinite	বো, ব	বো, ব	বো, ব	বো, ব	বো, ব	বো, ব	বো, ব	বো, ব
		VEG1		**VEG1.1**			**VEG2**		**VEG3**

Table 14. *Variations of vowel ended roots and their verbal inflexions of VEG4 for second person*

Tense		ছুঁ (chhu)			থু (thu)			শু (shu)			ধু (dhu)		
		তুমি (Gen)	তুই (Neg)	আপনি (Res)	তুমি (Gen)	তুই (Neg)	আপনি (Res)	তুমি (Gen)	তুই (Neg)	আপনি (Res)	তুমি (Gen)	তুই (Neg)	আপনি (Res)
Present	Indefinite	ছুঁ > ছো ও	ছুঁ > ছো স	ছুঁ > ছো ন	থু > থো ও	থু > থো স	থু > থো ন	শু > শো ও	শু > শো স	শু > শো ন	ধু > ধো ও	ধু > ধো স	ধু > ধো ন
	Cont.	চ্ছ	চ্ছিস	চ্ছেন	চ্ছ	চ্ছিস	চ্ছেন	চ্ছ	চ্ছিস	চ্ছেন	চ্ছ	চ্ছিস	চ্ছেন
	Perfect	য়েছ	য়েছিস	য়েছেণ	য়েছ	য়েছিস	য়েছেণ	য়েছ	য়েছিস	য়েছেণ	য়েছ	য়েছিস	য়েছেণ
	Imperative	ও	*	ন	ও	*	ন	ও	*	ন	ও	*	ন
Past	Indefinite	লে	লি	লেন	লে	লি	লেন	লে	লি	লেন	লে	লি	লেন
	Habitual	তে	তি	তেন	তে	তি	তেন	তে	তি	তেন	তে	তি	তেন
	Cont.	চ্ছিলে	চ্ছিলি	চ্ছিলেন	চ্ছিলে	চ্ছিলি	চ্ছিলেন	চ্ছিলে	চ্ছিলি	চ্ছিলেন	চ্ছিলে	চ্ছিলি	চ্ছিলেন
	Perfect	য়েছিলে	য়েছিলি	য়েছিলেন	য়েছিলে	য়েছিলি	য়েছিলেন	য়েছিলে	য়েছিলি	য়েছিলেন	য়েছিলে	য়েছিলি	য়েছিলেন
Future	Indefinite	বে	বি	বেন	বে	বি	বেন	বে	বি	বেন	বে	বি	বেন
	Imperative	য়ো	স	*	য়ো	স	*	য়ো	স	*	য়ো	স	*
		VEG4											

Table 15. Variations of vowel ended roots and their verbal inflexions of VEG5 and VEG6 for third person

Tense		ন		দু		নু		রু	
		সে (Gen)	তিনি (Res)	সে (Gen)	তিনি (Res)	সে (Gen)	তিনি (Res)	সে (Gen)	তিনি (Res)
Present	Indefinite	য়	ন	দু > দো য়	দু > দো ন	নু > নো য়	নু > নো ন	রু > রো য়	রু > রো ন
	Cont.			চ্ছে	চ্ছেন	চ্ছে	চ্ছেন	চ্ছে	চ্ছেন
	Perfect			যেছে	যেছেন	যেছে	যেছেন	যেছে	যেছেন
	Imperative			ক	ন	ক	ন	ক	ন
Past	Indefinite			দু > দুই ল	দু > দুই লেন	নু > নুই ল	নু > নুই লেন	রু > রুই ল	রু > রুই লেন
	Habitual			ইত	ইতেন	ইত	ইতেন	ইত	ইতেন
	Cont.			চ্ছিল	চ্ছিলেন	চ্ছিল	চ্ছিলেন	চ্ছিল	চ্ছিলেন
	Perfect			যেছিল	যেছিলেন	যেছিল	যেছিলেন	যেছিল	যেছিলেন
Future	Indefinite			ইবে	ইবেন	ইবে	ইবেন	ইবে	ইবেন
	Imperative			*	*	*	*	*	*
		VEG5		VEG6					

Table 16. Variations of consonant ended roots and their verbal inflexions of CEG1 for first person

Tense		কম্, কর্, কশ্, কষ্, খেঁচ্, খেপ্, খেল্, গড়্, গল্, ঘট্, ঘষ্, ঘেঁষ্, চট্, চড়্, চর্, চল্, চষ্, চেত্, ছড়্, ছল্, ছেঁক্, ছেঁচ্, জপ্, জম্, জর্, জ্বল্, ঝর্, টক্, টল্, ঠক্, ঠেক্, ঠেল্, ঠেস্, ডল্, ঢল্, দম্, দল্, দেখ্, ধর্, ধস্, পড়্, পর্, ফল্, ফেল্, বক্, বথ্, বন্, বল্, বস্, বেচ্, বেড়্, বেল্, ভজ্, ভর্, মজ্, মল্, মেল্, রট্, রস্, রোপ্, লড়্, লেপ্, সঁপ, সর্, সেঁক, সেক, সেচ, হট্, হর্, হের্, হেল্, হ্রেস, থস্, ঘোষ্
Present	Indefinite	ই
	Cont.	ছি
	Perfect	এছি
	Imperative	*
Past	Indef inite	লাম
	Habitual	তাম
	Cont.	ছিলাম
	Perfect	এছিলাম
Future	Indefinite	বো, ব
	Imperative	*
		CEG1

Table 17. Variations of consonant ended roots and their verbal inflexions of CEG5 and CEG6 for second person

Tense		কিন্, খিঁচ্, গিল্, ঘির্, চিন্, চির্, ছিঁড়্, জিত্, জিন্, টিক্, টিপ্, নিব্, পিজ্, পিট্, পিষ্, ফির্, বিধ্, ভিজ্, ভিড়্, মিট্, মিল্, মিশ্, লিখ্, শিখ্, সিচ্			আছ্		
		তুমি (Gen)	তুই (Neg)	আপনি (Res)	তুমি (Gen)	তুই (Neg)	আপনি (Res)
Present	Indefinite	কিন্ > কেন্চলতি); অ(সাধু) অ(	ইস	কিন্ > কেন্চলতি); এন(সাধু)এন(	অ	ইস	এন
	Cont.	ছ	ছিস	ছেন	আছ্ > থাক্ ছ	আছ্ > থাক্ ছিস	আছ্ > থাক্ ছেন
	Perfect	এছ	এছিস	এছেন	আছ্ > থেক্ এছ	আছ্ > থেক্ এছিস	আছ্ > থেক্ এছেন
	Imperative	কিন্ > কেন্ অ	*	উন	আছ্ > থাক্ অ	আছ্ > থাক্	উন
Past	Indefinite	লে	লি	লেন	আছ্ > ছ্ ইলে	আছ্ > ছ্ ইলি	আছ্ > ছ্ ইলেন
	Habitual	তে	তি	তেন	আছ্ > থাক্ তে	আছ্ > থাক্ তি	আছ্ > থাক্ তেন
	Cont.	ছিলে	ছিলি	ছিলেন	আছ্ > থাক্ ছিলে	আছ্ > থাক্ ছিলি	আছ্>থাক্ ছিলেন
	Perfect	এছিলে	এছিলি	এছিলেন	আছ্ > থেক্ এছিলে	আছ্ > থেক্ এছিলি	আছ্ > থেক্ এছিলেন
Future	Indefinite	বে	বি	বেন	আছ্ > থাক্ বে	আছ্ > থাক্ বি	আছ্ > থাক্ বেন
	Imperative	ইও	ইস	*	আছ্ > থাক্ ইও	আছ্ > থাক্	উন
		CEG5			CEG6		

Table 18. Variations of consonant ended roots and their verbal inflexions of CEG7 for third person

Tense		উঠ্, উড়্, উব্, কুঁদ্, কুদ্, কুট্, কুর্, খুঁজ্, খুঁট্, খুঁড়্, খুদ্, খুল্, গুঁজ্, গুণ্, গুল্, ঘুঁট্, ঘুচ্, ঘুর্, চুক্, চুন্, চুষ্, ছুঁড়্, ছুট্, ছুড়্, ছুল্, জুট্, জুড়্, ঝুল্, টুক্, টুট্, ঠুক্, ঠুস্, ডুব্, ঢুক্, ঢুঁড়্, ঢুল্, তুল্, তুষ্, দুল্, দুষ্, ধুঁক্, ধুন্, পুঁছ্, পুঁত্, পুছ্, পুড়্, পুর্, পুষ্, ফুঁক্, ফুঁড়্, ফুট্, ফুল্, বুঁজ্, বুজ্, বুঝ্, বুন্, বুল্, ভুগ্, ভুল্, মুছ্, মুড়্, মুত্, মুদ্, রুখ্, রুধ্, লুট্, লুফ্, শুঁক্, শুধ্, শুন্, শুষ্	
		সে (Gen)	তিনি (Res)
Present	Indefinite	এ	এন
	Cont.	ছে	ছেন
	Perfect	এছে	এছেন
	Imperative	উক	উন
Past	Indefinite	ল	লেন
	Habitual	ত	তেন
	Cont.	ছিল	ছিলেন
	Perfect	এছিল	এছিলেন
Future	Indefinite	বে	বেন
	Imperative	*	*
		CEG7	

Box 4. Bangla verb root template

[HW] {} "UW(icl/iof…>concept1>concept2…, REL1>…,REL2>…," (ROOT, VEND/ CEND [,ALT/ ALT1/ALT2..] VEG_n/CEG_n, #REL1, #REL2, … <FLG, FRE, PRI>

where:
HW← Head Word (Bangla Word; in this case it is Bangla root);
UW← Universal Word (English word from knowledge base);
icl/iof/… means *inclusion/instance of*… to represent the concept of universal word
REL1/REL2.., indicates the related relations regarding the corresponding word.
ROOT ← It is an attribute for Bangla roots. This attribute is immutable for all Bangla roots.
CEND and VEND are the attributes for consonant ended and vowel ended roots respectively.
VEG_n ← attribute for the group number of vowel ended roots
CEG_n ← attribute for the group number of consonant ended roots

ALT, ALT1, ALT2 etc. are the attributes for the first, second and third alternatives of the vowel or consonant ended roots respectively. If the root is default, then no alternative is used.
#REF1, #REF2 etc. are the possible corresponding relations regarding the root word.
Here, attributes, ROOT, CEND/VEND are fixed for all Bangla roots whereas ALT or ALT1 or ALT2 etc. is not necessary for all roots, they are used only for alternative roots.
In the following examples we are constructing the dictionary entries for some sample verb roots using our designed template:

[যা]{}"go(icl>move>do, plf>place, plt>place, agt>thing)" (ROOT, VEND, VEG3, #PLF, #PLT, #AGT)<B, 0, 0>
[গি]{}"go(icl>move>do, plf>place, plt>place, agt>thing)" (ROOT, VEND, ALT, VEG3, #PLF, #PLT, #AGT) <B,0,0>
[খা]{}"eat(icl>consume>do,agt>living_thing, ins>thing, obj>concrete_thing, plf>thing, tim>abstract_thing)" (ROOT, VEND, VEG1, #PLF, #PLT, #AGT)<B, 0, 0>

Box 5. Verbal inflexion template

[HW]{} “” (VI, V, Aperson [,ALT/ALT1,ALT2...], GEN/RES/NEG, Atense, SD/CH, VEG_n/ CEG_n/^VEG_n/ ^CEG_n.) <FLG, FRE, PRI>

where:
HW ← Head Word (Verbal Inflexion of Bangla Verb Root); UW← Universal Word (In case of Verbal Inflexion, UW is null); VI ← is an attribute of Verbal Inflexion, V← Verb, since Verbal Inflexions form verb when it is added with Bangla verb root as Suffixes so we keep the ‘V’ as an attribute.
Aperson ← Attribute person; this is an important attribute because verb varies according to Bangla Person.
ALT/ALT1/ALT2 ← Attributes for alternative roots. These attributes are used as attributes of verbal inflexions when they are combined with respective verb roots.
GEN/RES/NEG ← Attributes for verbal inflexions when they are combined with verb roots to form general (GEN), respective (RES) and neglect (NEG) verbs in respect to person. They are used as attributes with the VIs that are combined with verb roots to form verb for second and third persons.
Atense ← Attribute of tense, This is also an important attribute because verb varies according to Bangla tense.
SD/CH ← Attribute for types of languages. SD for ‘shadhu’, which is literature language and CH for ‘cholti’, which is conversation language. They are used as attributes with the VIs as they form SD or CH types of verbs.
VEG_n/CEG_n/^VEG_n/^CEG_n ← Attributes indicate vowel ended group number or consonant ended group number or not vowel or not consonant ended group. They are used as attributes of VIs as they are combined with respective groups or not.

used consecutively such PST (for past) and PRG (for continuous) and for future tense FUT are used.

Some examples of dictionary entries of Verbal Inflexions according to the proposed template are given below:

[য়েচ্ছিলাম] “ ”{}(VI, P1, PST, CMPL, ALT, CH, VEG1, VEG1.1, VEG9)

[চ্ছিলাম] “ ”{}(VI, P1, PST, PRG, CH)

[বি] “ ”{}(VI, P2, NEG, FUT, CH)

[চ্ছেন] “ ”{}(VI, P2, RES, PRT, PRG, CH)

Here, VI, ‘য়েচ্ছিলাম’ can be combined with first alternative roots (as ALT is used to define attribute) with verb roots of *vowel ended group 1* or *vowel ended group 1.1* for past perfect tense (attribute PST for past and CMPL for perfect) to create the verbs of conversation language (CH attribute for conversation language) for first person (attribute is P1).

4.4. Template for Primary Suffix

Like Bangla root and verbal inflexion, the primary suffix also has some attributes. The template for primary suffix is defined as in Box 6.

Using the primary suffix template we are building here some sample dictionary entries of primary suffix:

[আ] {} “” (KPROT, CEND, NOUN, AA);

[ওয়া] {} “” (KPROT, VEND, NOUN, OWA)

Dictionary entries for other primary suffixes can be built in a similar fashion.

4.5. Morphological Analysis of Bangla Words

Morphological analysis is found to be centered on analysis and generation of word forms. It deals with the internal structure of words and how words can be formed (Asaduzzaman & Ali, 2003). It is applied to identify the actual meaning of the words (Ali, Das, Mamun & Choudhury, 2008; Choudhury, Ali, Sarkar & Ahsan, 2005) by identifying the prefixes and suffixes.

Box 6. Primary suffix template

[HW] {} "UW" (PSUF, CEND/VEND, N/ADJ, Gname…..) <FLG, FRE, PRI>

HW← Head Word (primary suffix).
UW← Universal Word (In case of primary suffix, UW is null).
PSUF ← primary suffix.
CEND/VEND ← This is an important attribute since we need to know whether the primary suffix will be added with Consonant ended or Vowel ended roots or both of them.
N/ADJ← Noun/Adjective, the primary suffix adding with Root as suffix can form either Noun or Adjective. So, this is another vital attribute.
Gname ← Group Name of primary suffix.

Noun Morphology

Bangla Nouns have very strong and structural inflectional morphology base on case. Case of noun may be nominative (ছেলে", boy), accusative ("ছেলে-কে", to the boy) and genitive ("ছেলে-র", of the boy) and so on. Gender and number are also important for identifying proper categories of nouns. Number may be singular ("ছেলে", boy or "ছেলেটি", the boy, "বই", book, "বইটি", the book) plural ("ছেলেরা", boys "ছেলেগুলি", the boys, "e বইগুলো", the books etc.). So, from the word "ছেলে" we get "ছেলের", "ছেলেকে", "ছেলেরা", "ছেলেটি", "ছেলেগুলিj" etc. and from the word "বই" we get "বইটি", "বইগুলো" etc. Some dictionary entries are as follows:

[ছেলে]{}"boy(icl>person)"(N,HN,C,ANI)<B,0,0>

[র] {} "" (P3, SUF, N)<B,0,0>

[কে] {}""(P3, SUF, N, HUMN, SG)<B,0,0>

[রা] {}"" (P3, PL, SUF, N, HUMN)<B,0,0>

[টি] {}"" (N, SG, SUF, P3) <B,0,0>

[গুলি] {}"" (N, PL, SUF, P3) (<B,0,0>

[গুলো] {}""(N, SG, SUF, P3) <B,0,0>

Here we use P3, SUF and N as grammatical attributes with "রা", because "রা" is used for third person say "ছেলেরা", N for noun and SUF as "রা" is a suffix. We have to put meticulous attention while defining the grammatical attributes. Because we use HUMN for human noun as "কে", "রা" are used with human being only, say ছেলেক, তাহাকে, ছেলেরা, তাহারা. But we can not use HUMN with "রা", "টি", "গুলি" and "গুলো" because they are used with both human and non human, say, ছেলের, পাখির, ছেলেটি, পাখিটি, গরুগুলো, বইগুলো, etc. In morphological analysis we will combine the word "ছেলে" with suffix "র", "কে", "রা", "টি", "গুলি" to get the meanings of complete words "ছেলের", "ছেলেকে", "ছেলেরা", "ছেলেটি", "ছেলেগুলি", respectively using the morphological rules discussed in the next section.

Adjective Morphology

As adjectives, we can consider Bangla words "সাহস", "সুন্দর" and "ভালো" meaning "bravery", "beautiful" and "good" in English respectively. From the first word we get সাহসী (সাহস + ই), সাহসের (সাহস + এর). And from the second and third words we get সুন্দরী, ভালোর, ভালোটা, etc. Some dictionary entries for words mvnm, "সাহস", "সুন্দর", "ভালো" and morphemes ই, রা, এর, টা are given below to make the meaningful words সাহসী, সাহসের, সুন্দরী, ভালোর and ভালোটা etc. Say, if we consider a Bangla sentence, "সাহসীরা সাহসের সাথে অন্যায়ের প্রতিবাদ করে," we can represent the sentence as "সাহসী-রা সাহস-এর সাথে অন্যায়-এর প্রতিবাদ কর-এ." Here, ই, রা, এর, টা etc. are morphemes. So, we can see that a number of morphemes are added with the root words to make the full meaning of the new words as well as the sentence.

Some dictionary entries are given:

[সাহস]{}"bervary(iof>quality)"(N)<B,0,0>

[সুন্দর] {}"beautiful(iof>quality)(N)<B,0,0)>

[ভালো]{}"good(iof>quality)" (N)<B,0,0)>

[ই]{}(SUF, ADJ) <B,0,0)>

[এর]{}(SUF,ADJ) <B,0,0)>

[র]{} (SUF, ADJ) <B,0,0)>

[টা]{} (SUF, ADJ) <B,0,0)>

Pronoun Morphology

Here we can consider the word root "তাহা," (he/she). From this we get তাহা-রা, তাহা-কে, তাহা-দের, তাহা-দের-কে, তাহা-দিগকে etc. So, we have to consider these morphemes রা, কে, দের, দিগকে for dictionary entries to form words with "তাহা." Some dictionary entries along with grammatical attributes of pronouns are given below:

[সে (পুরুষ)] {} "he(icl>person)"

[সে (মহিলা)] {} "she(icl>person)"

[আপনাকে]{} "you(icl>person)" (PRON, HPRON, HON,SG,P2)

[আপনাদিগকে]{} "you(icl>person)" (PRON, HPRON,HON,PL,P2,,SHD)

[আপনি]{} "you(icl>person)" (PRON, HPRON,HON,SG,P2)

[আমা]{} "me(icl>person)" (PRON, HPRON, SG, P1, SHD)

[উহারা]{} "they(icl>person)" (PRON, HPRON,PL, P3, SHD)

[ও]{} "he(icl>person)" (PRON,HPRON, SG, GEN, P3, CHL)

[ওরা]{} "they(icl>person)" (PRON, HPRON, PL, GEN, P3,CHL)

[তাঁরা]{} "they(icl>person)" (PRON, HPRON, PL, HON, P3, CHL)

[তুই]{} "you(icl>person)" (PRON, HPRON, SG, NEG, P2)

where, PRON for Pronoun, HPRON for Human Pronoun, GEN for General, NEG for Neglect, HON for Respect, SG for singular, PL for plural,CH for conversation language, SD for literature language, P1 foo first person, P2 for second person and P3 for third person respectively.

Verb Morphology

Diversity of verbs in Bangla is very significant (Choudhury, Ali, Sarkar & Ahsan, 2005). Morphological analysis is applied to verbs to get roots and suffixes. For morphological analysis we are now providing some examples of dictionary entries of roots and verbal inflexions.

For example:

[যা] {}"go(icl> move>do, plt>place, plf>place, agt>thing)" (ROOT, VEND, VEG3, #AGT, #PLF, #PLT)

[গি] {}" go(icl>move>do, plt>place, plf>place, agt>thing)" (ROOT, VEND, VEG3, ALT1, #AGT, #PLF, #PLT)

[গে] {}" go(icl>move>do, plt>place, plf>place, agt>thing)" (ROOT, VEND, VEG3, ALT2, #AGT, #PLF, #PLT)

[যে] {}" go(icl>move>do, plt>place, plf>place, agt>thing)" (ROOT, VEND, VEG3, ALT3 #AGT, #PLF, #PLT)

[ই] “ ”{}(VI, P1, PRT)

[য়েছি] “ ”{} (VI, P1, PRT, PER, ALT1, CHL, VEG1, VEG1.1, VEG3, VEG9)

[লাম] “ ”{} (VI, P1, PST, ALT2, CHL, VEG1, VEG1.1, VEG3, VEG9)

[তাম] “ ”{} (VI, P1, PST, DEF, SHD, VEG3)

In dictionary entries, there are four entries for ‘go.’ One is root ‘যা’ (*ja*), which is default, that combines with inflexion ‘ই’(*i*) to make verb ‘যাই’ (*jai*), root ‘গি’ (*gi*) which is *first alternative* (we use attribute ALT1) combines with inflexion ‘য়েছি’ (*echhi*) to make verb ‘গিয়েছি’ (*giechhi*), root ‘গে’ (*ge*), is *second alternative* (attribute ALT2) and it will combine with inflexions ‘লাম’ (*lam*) to make verb ‘গেলাম’ (*gelam*). Root ‘যে’ (*je*), which is *third alternative* (attribute ALT3) that is combined with inflexions ‘তাম’ (*tam*) to make verb ‘যেতাম’ (*jetam*) to complete the morphological analysis. Using the same procedure, Dictionary entries for different transformations of other verbs such as Ki& (do), wjL& (write), ‡` (give) etc. have been prepared.

Many different words (nouns, adjectives or verbs) can be derived from a single root. For example, the verb “করিতেছি” (*koritechhi*), is analyzed into root ‘কর’ (*kor*) and suffix ‘ইতেছি’ (*itechi*). In Bangla there is a significant number of roots. A good number of suffixes are combined with these roots to form verbs or nouns or adjectives (Shahidullah, 2003; Kumar, 1999; Rameswar, 1996). The suffixes, roots and their classifications are given below:

1. **Verbal Inflexions (ক্রিয়া বিভক্তি, pronounced ‘*kria bivokti*’):** The suffixes that are combined with roots to form verbs are known as Verbal Inflexions (VIs). For instance, the VIs ‘ই’(*e*), ‘বেন’(*ben*), ‘চ্ছে’(*chhe*) and ‘ছিলেন’ (*chhilen*) make verbs যাই (*jai*), যাবেন (*jaben*) and যাচ্ছে (*jachhe*) respectively, combining with verb root ‘যা’(*ja*) means ‘go’ in English.

2. **Primary Suffixes (কৃৎ প্রত্যয় pronounced ‘*krit prottoy*’):** These types of suffixes are combined with roots to form nouns or adjectives. For example, see Box 7.

In this chapter, we focus on first type of suffixes named Verbal Inflexions that are combined with roots to form verbs.

Verb = Root + Verbal Inflexion

3. **Roles of root and verbal inflexion in the formation and meaning of a verb:** A root contains the core meaning, which relates with the action or state of the verb, whereas verbal inflexion (VI) defines the formation of the verb and reflects person, tense (in case of finite verb) and other properties. For instance, the root ‘খা’(*kha*) means ‘eat’ indicates the action of the verb খাইতেছি (*khaitechi*), to get food through mouth where as the VI ইতেছি (*itechi*) indicates the person (1st person) and tense (present continuous) of that verb. In UNL, person of an inflexion plays role in morphological and syntactic analyses of the verb but has no importance in semantic analysis of the verbs. That means it does not add or change any semantic relation and attribute. On the other hand, tense of an inflexion plays a significant role in semantic field. It adds or changes semantic attributes in the UNL expressions but does not affect on the relation.
GAs for root: ROOT
GAs for VI: V, VI

Box 7.

চল্ (*chol*)	+ অন্ত (*onto*)	=	চলন্ত (*cholonto*)
Root	Primary Suffix		Adjective
ধর্ (*dhor*)	+ আ (*aa*)	=	ধরা (*dhora*)
Root	Primary Suffix		Noun

4. **Classification of Verbs:** Verbs can be divided into finite and infinite verbs (Kumar, 1999; Shahidullah, 2003).
   a. **Finite Verb (সমাপিকা ক্রিয়া pronounced '*shomapika kria*'):** Finite verbs are verb forms, which carry the characteristics of subjects and tenses of those verbs. Finite verbs can be used to complete a sentence independently with other verbs. In many other languages gender and number influence in formation of verbs. But in Bangla they have no affect in verb formation. Say, আমি লিখিতেছি (*Aami likhitechi*) means 'I am writing,' সে লিখিয়াছে (*Se likhiache*) means 'He has written,' তুমি লিখিবে (*Tumi likhibe*) means 'You will write.' In these examples লিখিতেছি (*likhitechi*), লিখিয়াছে (*likhiache*) and লিখিবে (*likhibe*) are finite verbs. Here, Inflexions 'ইতেছি' (*itechi*), 'ইয়াছ' (*iacho*) and 'ইবে' (*ibe*) are combined with root 'লিখ' (*likh*) means 'write' to form finite verbs.
   For finite verbs:
   Grammatical attributes (GAs) for verbs are: ROOT, FINITE
   Grammatical attributes (GAs) for VIs are: P1/P2/P3, PRS/PST/FUT/ PRGR/ CMPL/IMPR
   b. **Infinite Verb (অসমাপিকা ক্রিয়া, pronounced '*oshomapika kria*'):** Infinite verb does not reflect the person and tense and can not use independently with other verbs to complete a sentence. It indicates an indifinite time span. There are three VIs of this type- ইয়া (*ia*), ইলে (*ile*) and ইতে (*ite*). For example, combining with these VIs the root খা (*kha*) means 'eat' makes verbs like খাইয়া (*khaia*), খাইলে (*khaile*) and খাইতে (*khaite*). The infinite verbs combining with finite verbs make various complex verbal concepts.
   GAs for infinite verb is INFINITE
5. **Classification of Roots:** There are three types of roots in Bangla languge (Kumar, 1999; Shahidullah, 2003).
   a. **Primary Root (মৌলিক ধাতু):** The roots that are not possible to anlyzed further or that can not be divided into smaller meaningful units. Say, খা (*kha*) means 'eat', কর (*kor*) means 'do' etc. GAs for primary roots are: ROOT, PROOT
   b. **Secondary Root (সাধিত ধাতু):** A root that is derived from a primary root (নাম শব্দ pronounced *Nam Shobdo*) and combined with a primary suffix. For example, primary suffix আ (*aa*) makes the secondary root করা (*kora*).

কর্ (kor)+আ (*aa*) = করা (*kora*)

(Primary root) + (Primary suffix) = (Secondary root)

   GAs for secondary roots are: ROOT, SROOT
   c. **Compounded Root (যৌগিক ধাতু):** Different types of nouns, adjectives and other words are used with roots to form compound roots. Compound roots are formed using two roots or one root and one word, but they mean one work. Say, 'গান কর্' (*gan kor*) means 'to sing', 'খেলা কর্ (*khela kor*) means 'to play' etc. In morphological analysis this type of roots does not play any role.
   Another kind of root is also available in Bangla:
   d. **Causative Root:** A suffix 'আ'(*aa*), or 'ওয়া' (*oa*) combining with some primary roots constructs secondary roots, which further create causative verbs (প্রযোজক ক্রিয়া pronounced *projojok kria*) added with VIs. For example, with primary root 'কর্'(*kor*), means 'do', suffix 'আ'(*aa*) creates secondary root

'করা' (*kora*) means 'to do'. The secondary root 'করা' (*kora*) forms causative verbs 'করাই' (*korai*) 'করাইতছি' (*koraitechi*) 'করাও' (*korao*), etc. combining with VIs 'ই' (*i*), 'ইতেছি' (*itechi*) and 'ও' (*oo*) respectively. Suffix 'আ' (*aa*) always combines with consonant ended primary roots. If the primary root is vowel ended then 'আ' (*aa*) will be replaced by 'ওয়া' (*oa*).
GAs for আ are: SROOT, INFLEX, CAUSATIVE, CEND
GAs for ওয়া are: SROOT, INFLEX, CAUSATIVE, VEND
where, SROOT denotes Secondary root, INFLEX for inflexion, CAUSITIVE for causative root, CEND for consonant ended and VEND for vowel ended word/morpheme.

7. **Classification of Verbal Inflexions:** Verbal inflexions can be classified according to tenses and persons. They define attributes related with tense and person of a verb. Table 19, Table 20 and Table 21 show the verbal inflexions for present, past and future tenses respectively. In these tables, the rows indicate types of tenses and the columns indicate persons. In the tables: P1=1st Person, P2=2nd Person, P3=3rd Person, GEN=General, NEG=Negligible and HON= Respect.

There is no dictionary entry for verbal inflexions of imperative tense for first person. A rule will be applied, which will add *&imperative* as UNL attribute. Some dictionary entries are as follows:

[ইতেছি] {} "" (V, INFLX, P1, PRS, PRGR, FINITE)

[লেন] {}" " (V, INFLX, P2, PST, INDEF, HON, FINITE)

[ইবে] {} "" (V, INFLX, P3, FUT, INDEF, FINITE)

Here, attributes "V" indicates that all the suffixes are added with roots to form verbs, KBIV for Verbal Inflexions, P1, P2 and P3 denotes that the Inflexions are added with first, second and third persons respectively. The attributes PRS, PST, FUT, CONT, INDEF denote that the Inflexions are added with roots to form different forms of verbs of tenses while PRG for present continuous, HON for respect form of Inflexions and FINITE indicates that the suffixes are forming finite verbs. According to the above examples, the grammatical attributes for all others Verbal Inflexions are formed.

Table 19. Verbal inflexions in present tense

বতমান কাল (Present Tense)	P1 (উত্তম পুরুষ) আমি (I)	P2 (মধ্যম পুরুষ)			P3 (নাম পুরুষ)	
		তুমি you GEN	তুই you NEG	আপনি you HON	সে he GEN	তিনি he HON
সাধারণ বতমান (Indefinite)	-ই i	-অ o	-ইস্ ish	-এন en	-এ e	-এন en
ঘটমান বতমান (Cont.)	-ইতেছি itechhi	-ইতেছ itechho	-ইতেছিস itechhish	-ছেন chhen	-ইতেছে itechhe	-ইতেছেন itechhen
পুরাঘটিত বতমান (Perfect)	-ইয়াছি iachhi	-ইয়াছ iachho	-ইয়াছিস iachhish	-এছেন echhen	-ইয়াছে iachhe	-ইয়াছেন iachhen
অনুজ্ঞা (Imperative)		-অ, -ও o, oo	মুলধাতু muldhatu	-উন un	-উক uk	-উন un

Table 20. Verbal inflexions in past tense

অতীত কাল (Past Tense)	P1 (উত্তম পুরুষ) আমি (I)	P2 (মধ্যম পুরুষ)			P3 (নাম পুরুষ)	
		তুমি you GEN	তুই you NEG	আপনি you HON	সে he GEN	তিনি he HON
সাধারণ অতীত (Indefinite)	-ইলাম ilam	-ইলে ile	-ইলি ili	-লেন len	-ইল lio	-ইলেন ilen
নিত্যবৃত্ত অতীত (Habitual)	-ইতাম itam	-ইতে ite	-ইতিস্ itish	-তেন ten	-ইত ite	-ইতেন iten
ঘটমান অতীত (Cont.)	ইতেছিলাম (itechilam)	-ইতেছিলে itechile	-ইতেছিলি itechili	-ছিলেন chilen	-ইতেছিল itechilo	-ইতেছিলেন itechilen
পুরাঘটিত অতীত (Perfect)	-ইয়াছিলাম iachilam	-ইয়াছিলে iachile	-ইয়াছিলি iachili	-এছিলেন echilen	-ইয়াছিল iachilo	-ইয়াছিলেন iachilen

Table 21. Verbal inflexions in future tense

ভবিষৎত কাল (Future Tense)	P1 উত্তম পুরুষ আমি (I)	P2 (মধ্যম পুরুষ)			P3 (নাম পুরুষ)	
		তুমি you GEN	তুই you NEG	আপনি you HOH	সে he GEN	তিনি he RES
সাধারণ ভবিষ্য (Indefinite)	-ইব (ibo), -ব (b), বো (bo)	-ইবে ibe	-ইবি ibi	-বেন ben	-ইবে ibe	-ইবেন iben
ভবিষ্য অনুজ্ঞা Imperative		-ইও io	-ইস ish	-বেন ben	-ইবে ibe	-ইবেন iben

4.6. Morphology of Words Combined with Inflexions

The inflexions of Bangla language are divided into two groups according to the formation of the words.

Morphology of Words Combined with Prefixes

In our work, we will make separate Word Dictionary entries for all of these prefixes and roots, so that they can combinely make meaningful words by applying rules. For example, if we consider prefix প্রতি (*proti*) (Asaduzzaman, 2008) (means like/ similar/ every/ opposite/against, etc.) we can make প্রতিদিন (*protidin*) means 'everyday,' প্রতিশব্দ (*protishobdo*) means *echo*, প্রতিপক্ষ (*protipokhho*) means 'respondent,' etc. Now we can make the word "প্রতি" for dictionary entry. But the word "প্রতি" has two or more meanings so that we have to prepare two or more dictionary entries for the word as follows:

[প্রতি]{}"every (icl>thing)" (ABSTRACT THING) <B,0,0>

[প্রতি]{}"opposite (icl>thing)" (ABSTRACT THING) <B,0,0>

[প্রতি]{}"against (icl>thing)" (ABSTRACT THING) <B,0,0>

Now, if we want to represent the concepts of the words say প্রতিদিন, প্রতিশব্দ, প্রতিপক্ষ etc., we need not represent the whole words. We have to represent only the root words দিন (*day*) means 'day,' শব্দ (*shobdo*) means 'sound' and পক্ষ (*pokhho*) means 'group' in the dictionary entry as per the following format:

[দিন] {} "day(icl>period>time)"(N, ABSTRACT THING, LIGHT)<B,0,0>

[শব্দ] {} "sound(icl>occure>thing)"(N, ABSTRACT THING)<B,0,0>

[পক্ষ] {} "group(icl>person)"(N,)<B,0,0>

If we have the concepts of the prefix "প্রতি" and the root words "দিন", "শব্দ", and "পক্ষ" with their grammatical attributes in the Word Dictionary as above format, the conversion rule will make the concepts of the whole words "প্রতিদিন", "প্রতিশব্দ" and "প্রতিপক্ষ", combining the first, second and third concepts of "প্রতি" respectively. By applying the same rule the EnCo can make all other words used with "প্রতি", which have the concepts of the root words in the word dictionary.

Similarly, if we consider Bangla prefix "রাম" (*ram*) means *big* we can make "রামছাগল" (*ramchhagol*) means *big sized goat*, "রামদা" (*ramda*) means *big sized knife* etc. We can separately represent the concepts of "রাম", "ছাগল" and "দা" in the dictionary entry according to the following format:

[রাম] {} "big (icl>large>thing)" (ADJ, C) <B,0,0>

[ছাগল] {} "goat (icl>animal>animate thing)" (N, C, ANI) <B,0,0>

[দা] {} "knife (icl>edge_tool>thing)" (N,C) <B,0,0>

Therefore, if we have the concepts of all the root words in the dictionary we can make the dictionary entry of all the complete words combined with "ivg" (ram). Finally, we can infer that conversion rules can be applied to prepare thousands of complete Bangla words combining with prefixes and roots to represent their concepts in the Bangla Word Dictionary.

Morphology of Words Combined with Affixes

The suffixes that are combined with *root words* or *roots* to make noun, adjective or verb are called affix. Two types of affixes are

- **Suffix (প্রত্যয়):** Some suffixes, namely primary suffixes say, অন্ (*on*), আ (*a*), অন্ত (*onto*), উনি (*uni*), etc. are combined with verb roots বাঁধ্ (*bad*), পড় (*por*), চল্ (*chol*), রাঁধ্ (*rad*), etc, to make complete words বাঁধন (*badhon*), পড়া (*pora*), চলন্ত (*cholonto*), রাঁধুনী (*radhuni*), etc. respectively. Again some other suffixes namely secondary suffixes say, অই (*oi*), আই (*aai*), ইক (*ik*) etc. are combined with words সাত (*saat*), মিঠা (*mitha*), ইক (*ik*) etc. to make meaningful words সাতই (*saatoi*), মিঠাই (*mithai*), মাসিক (*mashik*) etc. respectively. We have developed dictionary entries for both roots/words and suffixes, and use analysis rules to combine them to complete morphological analyses for making thousands of meaningful Bangla words.
- **Verbal Inflexion (ক্রিয়াবিভক্তি):** Verb roots are combined with verbal inflexions to make only verbs.

4.7. Morphological Rules

Left and right composition rules are used to perform morphological analysis. By applying these rules the two headwords of the left and right nodes are combined into a composite node, the original left and right nodes are replaced by the composite node in the node-list. Some proposed morphological rules are given below.

Format 1: Format of morphological rule for primary and secondary roots:

**-:C{<COND1>:::}
{<COND2>:<ACTION>::}**

where COND1::=ROOT
COND2::= V, INFLEX
ACTION::=@, -ROOT, -INFLEX, -PROOT, -SROOT

For example:

-:C{ROOT:::} {V, INFLEX:@, -ROOT, -INFLEX, -PROOT, -SROOT::}

Here, ROOT denotes verb root, PROOT for primary root, CEND for consonant ended root, SROOT for secondary root, INFLEX for inflexion and CAUSITIVE for causative root respectively. Rules of above format can be applied to complete the morphological analyses of the verbs that can be formed using roots (primary and secondary) combined with their inflexions.

Format 2: Format of morphological rule for causative root with suffix 'আ' (*aa*)):

**+:C {<COND1>: <ACTION>::}
{<COND2>:::}**

where COND1::= ROOT, PROOT, CEND
COND2::= [আ], SROOT, INFLEX, CAUSATIVE
ACTION::=@, -CEND, -PROOT

For example:

+:C {ROOT, PROOT, CEND:::=@, -CEND, -PROOT::} { [আ], SROOT, INFLEX, CAUSATIVE:::}

Rules of above format can be applied to complete the morphological analysis of the causative verbs that can be formed using causative roots combined with their suffixes.

Format 3: Format of morphological rule for causative root with suffix "ওয়া" (*wa*):

**+:C {<COND1>:<ACTION>::}
{<COND2>:::}**

where COND1::= ROOT, PROOT, VEND
COND2::= [ওয়া], SROOT, INFLEX, CAUSATIVE
ACTION::=@, -VEND, -PROOT,

For example:

+:C ROOT, PROOT, CEND:::=@, -CEND, -PSUF::}{ [ওয়া], SROOT, INFLEX, CAUSATIVE:::}

Format 4: Format of morphological rule for Bangla root and primary suffix:

**+:C{<COND1>:<ACTION>::}
{<COND2>:::}**

where COND1::=ROOT, VER/CER, GROUP NAME
COND2::= PSUF, SROOT, INFLEX, CAUSATIVE
ACTION2::= +VERB, -PSUF

For example:

-: C {ROOT:::} {PSUF:+VERB, -PSUF, -VER/CER, -GROUP NAME::}

For example, Bangla word, 'খাওয়া' (pronounced as "khawa", meaning "to eat") is divided into two morphological parts, 'খা' (pronounced *kha*, meaning "eat") and 'ওয়া' (pronounced *wa*), where 'খা' is verb root and 'ওয়া' is primary suffix. The corresponding dictionary entries are as follows:

[খা] {} "eat(icl>consume>do)" (ROOT, VEND) <B,0,0>

[ওয়া] {} "" (PROT, KPROT, WA, VNOUN) <B, 0, 0>

Some morphological rules under format 4 are given below according to their groups,

Rule 4.1: For WA(ওয়া) group and the root ended with vowel:

-:C{ROOT, VEND, WA:::} {KPROT, VEND, WA: -KPROT, -VEND, -WA, +VNOUN`::}

Example from the dictionary entry:

[চা] {} "want(icl>do)" (ROOT, VEND, WA) <B,0,0>

[ওয়া] {} "" (PROT, KPROT, WA, VNOUN) <B,0,0>

Using this rule, the root "চা" (when it is in the LAW) is added with suffix "ওয়া" (when it is in the RAW) to form a verbal noun "চাওয়া" (pronounced *chaowa*). It describes if there is a vowel ended root of group WA (ওয়া) is in LAW and a vowel ended suffix in group WA (ওয়া) is in RAW, then two head words will be added to make "চাওয়া." This rule also describes that all the attributes of the node of RAW (attributes for "ওয়া") are added with the attributes of new word and the following attributes KPROT, VEND and WA are deleted, and attribute VNOUN is added denoting the new word "চাওয়া" is a verbal noun.

Similarly, we can write the following rules for other groups as follows:

Rule 4.2: For AA(আ) group and the root ended with consonant:

-:C{ROOT, CEND, AA:::} {KPROT, CEND, AA: -KPROTOY, - CEND, - AA, +MNOUN::}

Rule 4.3: For EI(ই) group and the root ended with vowel:

-:C{ROOT, VEND, EI:::} {KPROT, VEND, EI: -KPROT, -VEND, -EI, +MNOUN::}

Rule 4.4: For EI(ই) group and the root ended with consonant:

-:C{ROOT, CEND,EI:::} {KPROT, CEND,EI: -KPROT,- CEND,-EI,+MNOUN::}

Rule 4.5: For AOW(আও) group and the root ended with vowel:

-:C{ROOT,VEND,AOW:::} {KPROT,VEND,AOW:-KPROT,-VEND,-AOW,+ MNOUN::}

Rule 4.6: For AOW (আও) group and the root ended with consonant:

-:C{ROOT,CEND,AOW:::} {KPROT,CEND,AOW:-PROTOY,-CEND,-AOW, +MNOUN::}

Rule 4.7: For ANOW(আনো) group and the root ended with vowel:

-:C{ROOT,VEND,ANOW:::} {KPROT,VEND,ANOW:-KPROT,-VEND,-ANOW, +MNOUN::}

Rule 4.8: For ANOW (আনো) group and the root ended with consonant:

-:C{ROOT,CEND,ANOW:::} {KPROT,CEND,ANOW:-KPROT,-CEND, -ANOW, +MNOUN::}

Rule 4.9: For ANTO(অন্ত) group and the root ended with consonant:

-:C{ROOT,CEND,ANTO:::} {KPROT, CEND, ANTO: -KPROT, -CEND, -ANTO, +MADJ::}

Rule 4.10: For OAN(অন্) group and the root ended with consonant:

-:C{ROOT, CEND,OAN:::} {KPROT, CEND, OAN: -KPROT, -CEND,-OAN, +MNOUN::}

Rule 4.11: For OAN (অন) group, the root ended with vowel:

-:C{ROOT, VEND,OAN:::} {KPROT, CEND,OAN: -KPROT, - CEND,-OAN::}

Rule 4.12: For TI(তি) group and the root ended with consonant only:

-:C{ROOT, CEND,TI} {KPROT, CEND,TI: -KPROT,- CEND,-TI,+MADJ::}

Rule 4.13: For YEA(ইয়ে) group and the root ended with vowel only:

-:C{ROOT, VEND,YEA} {KPROT,VEND,YEA: -KPROT, -VEND,-YEA, +MADJ::}

Rule 4.14: For YEA(ইয়ে) group and the root ended with consonant only:

-:C{ROOT, CEND,YEA:::} {KPROT, CEND, YEA: -KPROT, - CEND, -YEA, +MADJ::}

Rule 4.15: For OO(ও) group and the root ended with vowel only:

-:C {ROOT, VEND, OO:::}{KPROT, VEND, OO: -KPROT, -VEND,-OO, + MADJ::}

Rule 4.16: For OO(ও) group and the root ended with consonant only:

-:C{ROOT,CEND,OO:::}{KPROT, CEND, OO: -KPROTOY, - CEND, -OO+ MADJ::}

Rule 4.17: For UAW (উয়া) group and the root ended with consonant:

-:C {ROOT, CEND, UWA:::}{KPROT, CEND, UWA: - KPROTOY,- CEND,-UWA, +MADJ::}

4.8. Semantic Analyses of Bangla Sentence

The purpose of syntactic analysis is to determine the structure of the input sentence and the purpose of semantic analysis is to determine how the relations between the words of the sentence are made. This structure consists of a hierarchy of *phrases*, the smallest of which are the *basic symbols* and the largest of which is the *sentence*. It can be described by a tree with one node for each phrase. Basic symbols are represented by leaf nodes and other phrases by interior nodes. The root of the tree represents the sentence. Computations based on the input can be written with attribute, grammar specifications that are based on an abstract syntax. The abstract syntax describes the structure of an abstract syntax tree, in the same way the concrete syntax describes the phrase structure of the input. An example of Bangla sentence to UNL conversion is given below where we can see the semantic relations between the words in the sentence:

অধ্যাপক আলী গতকাল সকালে (সকাল-এ) গরীবদের (গরীব-দের) অর্থ দিয়েছেন (দি-য়েছেন), pronounced *oddhapok Ali gotokal shokal-e gorib-der ortho diechhen*, meaning, "Professor Ali gave money to poor people yesterday morning."

To convert this sentence into UNL expressions we need the following dictionary entries:

[অধ্যাপক] {}"professor (icl> academician> thing)" (N, TITLE)

[আলী] {}"ali (iof>person>thing)" (N)

[গতকাল] {} "yesterday (icl>how>thing)" (N, TIME)

[সকাল] {} "morning(icl> time_period>thing)" (N, TIME)

[গরীব] {}"poor(icl>adj, ant>rich)" (ADJ)

[অর্থ] {}“money (icl>medium_of_exchange>thing)” (N)

[দি]{}“give(icl>do, equ>hand_over, agt>thing, obj>thing,rec>person)” (ROOT, VER, VEG3)

[এ] {}“”(SUF, N)

[দের] {}“”(SUF, PLURAL, N)

[য়েছেন] {}“”(VI, P3, RES, PRT, PER, CH, VEG2, VEG4, VEG6, VEG8, VEG10)

The UNL semantic relations among the UWs of the given sentence is shown as UNL hypergraph in Figure 6.

From UNL Hypergraph we can conclude that the following semantic relations (UNDL, 2003) can be made between the words of the sentence shown in Table 22.

After conversion the given sentence we get the following UNL expressions that consists of a group of semantic relations between the words shown in Box 8.

There is a wide variety of classifications of semantic relations in Bangla case. We take into account all of them for appropriate conversion of sentences into UNL expessons and vice versa. In the next section, we discuss about the semantic rules for sentence conversion.

Figure 6. The UNL hypergraph

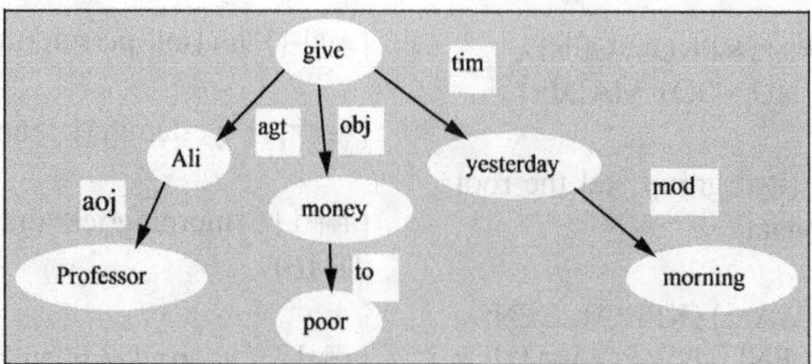

4.9. Semantic Rules

Left and right modification rules are applied to perform semantic relations between the words in a sentence. By applying these rules, a semantic relation according to the designation of the relation in the <RELATION> field, with the node, where the relation is described in the <RELATION> field as the to-node and the partner node as the form-node of the semantic relation. We propose some semantic rules for different Bangla cases to perform semantic analysis in order to convert Bangla sentences to UNL expressions.

Format 1: Format of semantic rules for nominative case:

>{<COND1>::<RELATION>:}
{<COND2>:<ACTION>::} ·

where COND1::= N/PRON, SUBJ
RELATION::= agt/cag/ptn/aoj/cao

Table 22. UNL relations of the given sentence

Relations Name	Relations Label	Relations Between Words
Agent	agt	Ali and give
Thing with attribute	aoj	Ali and professor
Object	obj	money and give
Destination	to	money and poor
Time	tim	yesterday and give
Modification	mod	morning and yesterday

Box 8. Semantic relations of given sentence

```
agt(give (icl>do, equ>hand_over, agt>thing, obj>thing, rec>person). @entry.@
past, professor(icl> academician>thing))
aoj (professor(icl>academician>thing), ali(iof>person>thing))
obj(give(icl>do, equ>hand_over, agt>thing, obj>thing, rec>person).@entry.@
past, money(icl>medium_of_exchange>thing))
to(money(icl>medium_of_exchange>thing) .@pl,poor(icl>adj,ant>rich))
tim(give(icl>do, equ>hand_over, agt>thing, obj>thing, rec>person) .@entry.@
past, yesterday(icl>how))
mod(yesterday(icl>how), morning(icl>time_period>thing)
```

COND2::= VERB
ACTION::= @, +&TENSE,+&@entry

For example: "করিম পড়িতেছে", pronounced *Karim Poritechhe*, means "Karim is reading." Here subject *Karim* initiates an action. So, agent (*agt*) relation is made between subject "Karim" and verb "read."

The following dictionary entries are needed for converting the sentence (Giri, 2001):

[করিম] {} "karim (icl>name, iof>person, com>male) (N)

[পড়] {} "read (icl>see>do,agt>person,obj>infor mation) (ROOT, CEND, ^ALT)

[ইতেছে] {} ""(VI, CEND, CEG1, PRS, PRG, P3)

where N denotes noun, ROOT for verb root, CEND for Consonant Ended Root, ^ALT for not alternative, VI for verbal inflexion, CEG1 for Consonant Ended Group 1, PRS for present tense, PRG for progress means continuous tense and 3P for third person. To convert this sentence into UNL expression a semantic analysis is made between "করিম" (*karim*) and "পড়িতেছে" (*poritechhe*).

Rule of Semantic Analysis: After morphological analysis when noun "করিম" (*karim*) appears in the LAW and verb "পড়িতেছে" (*poritechhe*) appears in the RAW the following agent (agt) relation is made between "করিম" (*karim*) and "পড়িতেছে" (*poritechhe*) to complete the semantic analysis.

>{N,SUBJ::agt:} {VERB,#AGT:+ &@present, +&@progress::} P1;

Format 2: Format of semantic rules for accusative case:

**>{<COND1>::<RELATION>:}
{<COND2>:<ACTION2>::}**

where COND1::=N/PRON,SUBJ

RELATION::=obj/cob
COND2::= VERB
ACTION2::=@, +&TENSE,+&@entry

For example, "আমি ভাত খাই" pronounced *Aami vat kha*, means "I eat rice." The following dictionary entries are needed for the sentence:

[আমি]{}"i(icl>person)"(PRON, HPRON, P1, SG, SUBJ) <B,1,1>

[ভাত]{}"{}"rice(icl>food)"(N)<B,0,0>

[খা]{}"eat(icl>consume>do,agt>living_thing,obj>concrete_thing)"(ROOT,VEND,#AGT,#OBJ,VEG1)<B,0,2>

[ই]{}"" (VI,VERB,VEND, P1,PRS)<B,0,0>

where PRON denotes pronoun, HPRON for human pronoun, P1 for first person, SG for singular number and SUBJ for subject of the sentence.

To convert this sentence into UNL expressions two semantic analyses to be held (Shachi & Bhattacharyya, 2001).

Rules for Semantic Analysis: Two semantic relations are made for the given sentence. One semantic relation is agent (agt) relation to be held between "আমি" (*aami*) and "খাই" (*khai*) using the following rule.

> {PRON, HPRON, SUBJ::agt:}
{VERB,#AGT:::} P10;

Another relation is between "ভাত" (rice) and "খাই" (eat).

Here, rice is an object and the relation between rice and eat is the accusative case. Semantic rule for accusative case to perform semantic analysis is

>{N::obj:} {VERB, #OBJ: +&@present.& @ entry::} P10;

Format 3: Format of semantic rules for instrumental case:

>{<COND1>::<RELATION>:}
{<COND2>:<ACTION2>::}

where COND1::=N/PRON, SUBJ

RELATION::=ins/met
COND2::= VERB
ACTION2::=@, +&TENSE,+&@entry

For example:

সে কলম দিয়ে একটি নোট লিখেছিল, pronounced *Se kolom die ekti note likhechhilo*, means "He wrote a note with a pen."

The following dictionary entries are needed for converting the sentence into UNL expression:

[সে] {} "he(icl>person)"(PRON,HPRON,1P, SUBJ, MAL)

[কলম] {} "pen(icl>writing_implement>thing"(N)

[দিয়ে] {} "" (INF, 3RD, PRON)

[নোট] {} "note(icl>personal_letter)>thing)"(N)

[লিখ্] {}"write(icl>do, agt>person, obj>abstract_thing plc>thing, ins>functional_thing)" (ROOT, CEND)

[এছিল]{} "" (VI, VERB,CEND, 3P, PST)

where MAL denotes male, INF is the attribute for inflexion, 3RD for third types of inflexion and PST for past tense.

In this sentence, semantic relation for instrumental case is made between "কলম" (pen) which is instrument and "লিখেছিল" (wrote).

The rule for the instrumental case to perform semantic analysis is:

>{PRON, HPRON, INS::ins:} {VERB:+&@ past::}

Format 4: Format of semantic rules for dative case:

>{<COND1>::<RELATION>:}
{<COND2>:<ACTION2>::}

where COND1::=N/PRON,SUBJ

RELATION::=ben/pur/rsn
COND2::= VERB
ACTION2::=@, +&TENSE.&@entry

For example, "রাজা তাহার পুত্রকে মুকুট দিবে" pronounced *Raja tahar putroke mukut dibe* means "The king will give crown to his son."

The following dictionary entries are needed for converting the sentence into UNL expression.

[রাজা]{} "king (icl>sovereign>thing, ant>queen)" (N,3P)

[তাহা]{}"he(icl>person)" (PRON, HPRON, 3P)

[র]{} ""(INF, 6TH, OBJ, POS)

[পুত্র]{}"son (icl>male_offspring>thing, ant>daughter)" (N)

[কে]{} ""(INF, 2ND, NOM, OBJ, BEN)

[মুকুট]{} "crown(icl>jewelled_headdress > thing)"(N)

[দি]{}"give(icl>do, equ>hand_over, agt>thing, obj>thing, ben>person)" (ROOT, VEND, VEG1, #AGT, #OBJ)

[বে]{} ""(VI, VERB, 3P, FUT)

where FUT denotes future tense.

In the above sentence, the semantic analysis is made between "পুত্রকে" (to son), which is beneficiary and "দিবে" (will give) is dative case.

The rule for the dative case to perform semantic analysis is:

>{N,BEN::ben:}{VERB:+&@future.@entry::}

Format 5: Format of semantic rules for ablative case:

>{<COND1>::<RELATION>:}{<COND2>:<ACTION2>::}

where COND1::=N/PRON,SUBJ
RELATION::=frm/scr/plf/tmf
COND2::= VERB
ACTION2::=@, +&TENSE.&@entry

For example, "পাখিটি খাচা থেকে উড়ে যায়" pronounced *Pakhiti khacha theke ure jae*, means "The bird flies from the nest." The following dictionary entries are needed for converting the sentence into UNL expression:

[পাখি]{} "bird(icl>vertebrate>thing)" (N)

[টি]{} ""(ART)

[খাচা]{} "nest(icl>retreat>thing)" (N,CONCRETE)

[থেকে]{} "from (icl>how,obj>thing,plc>uw)" (FRM)

[উড়]{} "fly(icl>do)"(ROOT, CEND, CEG, #FRM, #TO)

[এ]{} ""(INF, 7TH,CEND)

[যা]{} "go(icl>move>do)" (ROOT, VEND, VEG1, #AGT, #PLC)

[য়]{} ""(VI,VEND,3P,PRS)

In the above sentence, the semantic relation for ablative case is made between between "খাচা থেকে" (from nest) and "উড়ে যায়" (fly) using the following rule.

> {N, FRM::frm:} { VERB, #FRM:+&@present::}

Format 6: Format of semantic rules for case of time-place:

>{<COND1>::<RELATION>:}{<COND2>:<ACTION2>::}

where COND1::=N/PRON,SUBJ
RELATION::=plc/plt/tim/tmt/to/gol/scn/opl
COND2::= VERB
ACTION2::=@, +&TENSE.&@entry

For example, "আমরা ঢাকায় থাকি" pronounced *Amra dhakae thaki*, means "We live in Dhaka."

The following dictionary entries are needed for the sentence:

[আমরা]{}" we(icl>group)"(PRON,HPRON,1P,SG,SUBJ) <B,1,1>

[ঢাকা]{}" dhaka(iof>city)"(N)<B,0,0>

[য়]{}"" (7TH,N)<B,0,2>

[থাক]{}" (live(icl>inhabit>be,aoj>living_thing,plc>place)"(ROOT, CEND, #AGT, VEG1) <B,0,2>

[ি]{}""(VI, VERB,CEND,1P,PRS)<B,0,0>

In the above sentence, the semantic relation for *case of time-place* is held between "ঢাকায়" (in Dhaka) and "থাকি"(live). Here, Dhaka is a *place* and relation between *place* and *live* is the case of time-place.

UNL rule for case of time-place to perform semantic analysis is:

> {N, PLACE::plc:}{ VERB:+&@present.&@entry::}

Format 7: Format of semantic rules for possessive case:

>{<COND1>::<RELATION>:} {<COND2>:<ACTION2>::}

where COND1::=N/PRON,SUBJ
RELATION::=pos/mod/pof
COND2::= VERB
ACTION2::=@, +&TENSE.&@entry

For example, রাজার বাড়ি, pronounced *Rajar bari*, means "King's house."

The following dictionary entries are needed for the sentence:

[রাজা]{} "king(icl>sovereign>thing,ant>queen)" (N)

[র]{} " "(INF, INF6TH, N,PRON, POSS)

[বাড়ি]{}"house(icl>dwelling>thing)"

In the above sentence, the semantic relation is possessive (pos) relation to be held between "রাজার" (King's) and "বাড়ি"(house)).

UNL semantic rule for possive case to perform semantic analysis is:

> {N::pos:} { N:+&@present.&@entry::}

4.10. Generation Rules

In this section we have proposed the formats of some generation rules that are to be used for converting UNL expressions to Bangla sentence.

Format 1: Format of rules to insert subjective pronouns of not alternative roots for agent (*agt*) relation:

:"HPRON, P(x), SUBJ::agt:" {ROOT, VEND, ^ALT, #AGT, ^(x)p:(x)p::} P9;

where grammatical attributes *HPRON* denotes human pronoun, *SUBJ* for subject of a sentence, agt for agent relation, ROOT for verb root, VEND for vowel ended root, ^ALT for not alternative root, #AGT indicates that the corresponding root involves with agent relation, P indicates person and when the value of x=1, 2 and 3 then P1 denotes first person, P2 second person and P3 third person respectively and p is the temporary attribute for person to prevent recursive operations. Some examples of rules for not alternative roots are as follows:

- :"HPRON, P1, SUBJ::agt:" {ROOT, VEND, ^ALT, #AGT, ^1p:1p::} P9;

- :"HPRON, P2, SUBJ::agt:" {ROOT, VEND, ^ALT, #AGT, ^2p:2p::} P9;
- :"HPRON, P2, SUBJ, @respect, ^@contempt, HON, ^NGL::agt:" {ROOT, VEND, ^ALT, #AGT, ^2p:2p::} P9;
- :"HPRON, P2, SUBJ, ^@respect, @contempt, ^HON, NGL::agt:" {ROOT, VEND, ^ALT, #AGT, ^2p:2p::} P9;
- :"HPRON, P3, SUBJ::agt:" {ROOT, VEND, ^ALT, #AGT, ^3p:3p::} P9;

Format 2: Format of rules to insert subjective pronouns alternative roots for agent (*agt*) relation:

:"HPRON,(x)P,SUBJ, [^] @respect, | [^]@contempt, | [^]HON,[^]NGL::agt:" {ROOT,VEND,[^]@present|@progress|@complete,VEG(y),ALT,#AGT,^(x)p:(x)p::}P10;

where UNL attributes @respect, @contempt, @present, @past, @future, @progress, and @complete denotes for respected person, neglected person, present tense, past tense, future tense, continuous tense and perfect tense respectively. *ALT* indicates alternative roots and when the value of y=1 then VEG1 is to be used for vowel ended group 1 and when y=2 then VEG2 for vowel ended group 2 and so on. '^' expresses negation of the following value. Some examples of rules for not alternative roots are as follows:

- :"HPRON, P1, SUBJ::agt:" {ROOT, VEND, @present, ^@progress, @complete, VEG1, ALT, #AGT, ^1p:1p::} P10;
- :"HPRON, P1, SUBJ::agt:" {ROOT, VEND, @past, ^@progress, ^@complete, VEG1, ALT, #AGT, ^1p:1p::} P10;
- :"HPRON, P2, SUBJ, ^@respect, ^@contempt, ^HON, ^NGL, ^PL::agt:" {ROOT, VEND, @present, ^@progress, ^@complete, VEG4, ALT, #AGT, ^2p:2p::} P10;
- :"HPRON, P2, SUBJ, @respect, HON::agt:" {ROOT, VEND, @present, ^@progress, ^@complete, VEG4, ALT, #AGT, ^2p, ^hon:2p,hon::} P10;
- :"HPRON, P2, SUBJ, @contempt, NGL::agt:" {ROOT, VEND, @present, ^@progress, ^@complete, VEG4, ALT, #AGT, ^2p, ^ngl:2p,ngl::} P10;
- :"HPRON, P3, SUBJ::agt:" {ROOT, VEND, @present, ^@progress, ^@complete, VEG2, ALT, #AGT, ^3p:3p::} P10;
- :"HPRON, P3, SUBJ::agt:" {ROOT, VEND, @past, ^@progress, ^@complete, VEG1, ALT, #AGT, ^3p:3p::} P10;

Format 3: Format of rules to insert subjective pronouns of not alternative roots for thing with attribute (*aoj*) relation:

:"HPRON, (x)P, SUBJ::aoj:" {ROOT, VEND, ^ALT, #AOJ, ^(x)p:(x)p::} P9

Some examples are:

- :"HPRON, P1, SUBJ::aoj:" {ROOT, VEND, ^ALT, #AOJ, ^1p:1p::} P9;
- :"HPRON, P2, SUBJ::aoj:" {ROOT, VEND, ^ALT, #AOJ, ^2p:2p::} P9;
- :"HPRON, P3, SUBJ::aoj:" {ROOT, VEND, ^ALT, #AOJ, ^3p:3p::} P9;

Format 4: Format of rules to insert subjective pronouns alternative roots for agent (*agt*) relation:

:"HPRON, (x)P, SUBJ, [^]@respect, [^]@contempt, [^]HON, [^]NGL::aoj:" {ROOT, VEND, [^]@present, @progress, @complete, VEG(y), ALT, #AOJ, ^(x)p:(x)p::} P10;

Examples are:

- :"HPRON, P1, SUBJ::aoj:" {ROOT, VEND, @present, ^@progress, @complete, VEG1, ALT, #AOJ, ^1p:1p::} P10;

- :"HPRON, P1, SUBJ::aoj:" {ROOT, VEND, @past, ^@progress, ^@complete, VEG1, ALT, #AOJ, ^1p:1p::} P10;
- :"HPRON, P2, SUBJ, ^@respect, ^@contempt, ^HON, ^NGL, ^PL::aoj:" {ROOT, VEND, @present, ^@progress, ^@complete, VEG4, ALT, #AOJ, ^2p:2p::} P10;
- :"HPRON, P2, SUBJ, @respect, HON::aoj:" {ROOT, VEND, @present, ^@progress, ^@complete, VEG4, ALT, #AOJ, ^2p, ^hon:2p,hon::} P10;
- :"HPRON, P2, SUBJ::aoj:" {ROOT, VEND, @past, ^@progress, @complete, VEG1, ALT, #AOJ, ^2p:2p::} P10;

Format 5: Format of rules for backtracking:

Rule 5.1: ?{:::} {PRON, SG, @pl:::} P8;
Rule 5.2: ?{:::} {PRON, PL, ^@pl:::} P8;
Rule 5.3: ?{:::} {HPRON, SUBJ, HON, ^@respect:::} P8;
Rule 5.4: ?{:::} {HPRON, SUBJ, ^HON, @respect:::} P8;
Rule 5.5: ?{:::} {HPRON, SUBJ, NGL, ^@contempt:::} P8;
Rule 5.6: ?{:::} {HPRON, SUBJ, ^NGL, @contempt:::} P8;

Format 6: Format of rules to insert verbal inflexions at the end of roots for first person:

:{ROOT, VEND, (x)p, [^]@present, [^]@progress, [^]@complete, ^kbiv:kbiv::}" [[KBIV]], KBIV, VEND, P(x), PRS|PST|FUT, [^]PRGR, [^]CMPL:::" P10;

Examples are:

- :{ROOT, VEND, 1p, @present, ^@progress, ^@complete, ^kbiv:kbiv::}" [[KBIV]], KBIV, VEND, P1, PRS, ^PRGR, ^CMPL:::" P10;
- :{ROOT, VEND, 1p, @present, @progress, ^@complete, ^kbiv:kbiv::}" [[KBIV]], KBIV, VEND, P1, PRS, PRGR, ^CMPL:::" P10;

Format 7: Format of rules to insert verbal inflexions at the end of roots for second person:

:{ROOT, VEND, (x)p, [^]@present, [^]@progress, [^]@complete, [^]hon, [^]ngl, ^kbiv:kbiv::}" [[KBIV]], KBIV, VEND, P(x), PRS|PST|FUT, [^]PRGR, [^]CMPL, [^]HON, [^]NGL:::" P10;

Examples are:

- :{ROOT, VEND, 2p, @present, ^@progress, ^@complete, ^hon, ^ngl, ^kbiv:kbiv::}" [[KBIV]], KBIV, VEND, P2, PRS, ^PRGR, ^CMPL, ^HON, ^NGL:::" P10;
- :{ROOT, VEND, 2p, @present, ^@progress, ^@complete, ^hon, ngl, ^kbiv:kbiv::}" [[KBIV]], KBIV, VEND, P2, PRS, ^PRGR, ^CMPL, ^HON, NGL:::" P10;

Format 8: Format of rules to insert verbal inflexions at the end of roots for third person:

:{ROOT, VEND, (x)p, [^]@present, [^]@progress, [^]@complete, ^hon,|^ngl, ^kbiv:kbiv::}" [[KBIV]], KBIV, VEND, (x)P, PRS|PST|FUT, [^]PRGR, [^]CMPL, ^HON, ^NGL:::" P10;

Examples are:

- :{ROOT, VEND, 3p, @present, ^@progress, ^@complete, ^hon, ^kbiv:kbiv::}" [[KBIV]], KBIV, VEND, P3, PRS, ^PRGR, ^CMPL, ^HON:::" P10;
- :{ROOT, VEND, 3p, @present, @progress, ^@complete, ^ngl, ^kbiv:kbiv::}" [[KBIV]], KBIV, VEND, P3, PRS, PRGR, ^CMPL, ^NGL:::" P10;

Format 9: Format of rules to insert noun before root:

:"N,[^]@pl, ^SUBJ:SUBJ:agt:" {ROOT, VEND, #AGT, ^3p, [^]sg|pl:3p,sg|pl::} P10;

Examples are:

- :"N,^@pl, ^SUBJ:SUBJ:agt:" {ROOT, VEND, #AGT, ^3p, ^sg:3p,sg::} P10;
- :"N,@pl, ^SUBJ:SUBJ:agt:" {ROOT, VEND, #AGT, ^3p, ^pl:3p,pl::} P10;

Format 10: Format of rules to insert article:

Rule 10.1 (for singular):

:{N,^@pl, @def, ^boch:boch::}" [[BIV]], BIV, BOCH, DEF, ^PL:::" P10;

Rule 10.2 (for plural):

:{N,[^] HUMN,@pl, @def,^boch:boch::}" [[BIV]], BIV,BOCH, DEF, PL, [^]HUMN:::" P10;

Examples are:

- :{N,^HUMN, @pl,@def, ^boch:boch::} "[[BIV]], BIV, BOCH, DEF, PL, ^HUMN:::" P10;
- :{N, HUMN, VEND, @pl, @def, ^boch:boch::}" [[BIV]], BIV, BOCH, DEF, PL, HUMN, VEND:::" P10;

5. RELATED WORK

Morphological rules have been developed in (Parteek & Sharma, 2009) only for noun and verb for Punjabi EnConverter. They have also developed semantic rules only for agent (*agt*) and conjunction (and) relation. An implementation of Punjabi EnConverter has also been presented in this paper. Whereas we have developed morphological rules for most of the parts of speeches and semantic rules for most of the relations.

Hindi DeConverter has been developed to generate Hindi from UNL representation (Singh et al.). The system has been tested on agricultural corpora and it produced average BLEU score of 0.34 which correlates well with the human evaluators' scores. We have only developed generation rules which is able to successfully generate Bangla sentences from UNL expressions using DeConverter provided by the UNDL Foundation (Deconverter, 2002).

Computational analysis for Bangla case structures have been described (Kuntal & Bhattacharyya, 2003) for the purpose of interlingua based MT using UNL. The complementary generator system has also been implemented that provides the platform for inter system verification. We have also analyzed Bangla case structure in iccit 2010 and found UNL relation for respective cases and finally developed semantic rules for different Bangla cases to convert Bangla texts into UNL expressions.

Dictionary development procedure for Bangla nouns and verbs has been outlined in for Bangla language. They have divided nouns in different forms based on numbers, case and gender and also presented morphological rules for different forms of nouns. Some rules to constructs feminine nouns from masculine nouns are also presented in this paper. They have also analyzed verbs into five categories according to how their stems are formed and how they are conjugated. Morphological rules have also been discussed here.

These morphological analyzing help us a lot to analyze parts of speech of Bangla language to analyze them into a computational approach for UNL. But for building Bangla Word Dictionary we have extremely followed the standard format of Word Dictionary provided by the UNDL Foundation, Tokyo, Japan. According to their format we have prepared Bangla Word Dictionary for UNL.

There are 25 vowel ended roots in Bangla literature. Development of dictionary entries for vowel ended roots are presented in (Sarker, Ali & Das, 2012). The vowel ended roots are added with verbal inflexions to form verbs based on different tenses and persons considering their groups.

The structure of Bangla word dictionary for Bangla suffixes, prefixes and verbal inflexions are explained in (Mridha, Huda, Rahman & Rahman, 2010) considering the format provided by UNDL foundation. It also focuses on the structure of Bangla roots based on all the possible specifications and grammatical attributes.

In (Islam, 2009) a survey has been conducted on the existing works of Bangla machine translation. After detailed analysis of existing works a lot of changes has been listed leading to comprehensive use of Bangla in ICT. One of the major chalenges identified that there is a lack of morphological analysis of Bangla language. Our major work focuses on this issues and we have developed a set of morphological rules for most of the parts of speech to be able to UNL base machine translation.

6. FUTURE RESEARCH DIRECTIONS

In this chapter, we have developed a framework for converting Bangla texts into UNL expressions and UNL expressions to Bangla texts. But UNL system is not yet well developed to convert any poetic texts. A good number of researchers have already started analyzing poetic texts to convert into UNL.

To accommodate the full Bangla texts into UNL expressions we need to develop a comprehensive UNL compatible Bangla Word Dictionary for about 1,000,000 words along with their prefixes and affixes and around 200000 Enconversion and Deconversion rules (Pairkh, Khot, Dave & Bhattacharyya, 2004).

An observation appears in possessive case (in Bangla Shambondh Pad), where the sentence রাজার বাড়ি, is pronounced *Rajar Bari*, and means "King's house;" and sentence, কাঠের বাড়ি, pronounced *Kather Bari*, means "Wooden house," not "Wood's house," unlike the previous sentence. First type of sentences can be converted according to the possessive case constructs into UNL expressions and second type of sentences has to be analyzed further for proper conversion. Some observations emerge on reduplication of words (দ্বৈত শব্দ). If we consider a sentence, ঘরে ঘরে কলেরা লেগেছে, pronounced "*Ghore ghore kolera legechhe*," here ঘরে ঘরে indicates every or all. Another sentence, পাথরে পাথরে ঘষনে আগুন লেগেছে pronounced "*Pathore pathore ghorshone aagun lagechhe*," পাথরে পাথরে indicates পরস্পর pronounced "*porospor*." In the sentence সে আমার দিকে ফিরে ফিরে চায়, pronounced "*Se aamar dike fire fire chai*," here ফিরে ফিরে indicates repeatedly. There is a good number of *reduplication* of words in Bangla. They vary in meanings and concepts. All these concepts have to be analyzed properly for correct translation. More research is needed on annotated texts by clarifying semantic structures of sentences in order to generate their proper representations.

Therefore, we have to give more efforts on analyzing poetic texts so that we can convert any poem written by the famous poets into UNL expressions and vice versa. We will work on some sentences of possessive case to overcome the problems we face to convert. And also give more labor on reduplication of words by dividing them into different groups and resolve the conceptual problems between them and present them into computational approach for UNL conversion.

We have already mentioned some discrepancies of UNL expressions of annotated texts in the above. Therefore, one of the future concentrations will be on analysis of semantic structures of sentences in order to generate the target meaning representations. We would analyze annotated text by clarifying semantic structures of sentences in order to generate the target meaning representations of sentences.

We have outlined only the templates of dictionary entries of Bangla word dictionary and formats of Enconversion and Econversion rules. Now we need to prepare a UNL comprehensive Bangla

Word Dictionary for all the necessary Bangla words, prefixes, suffixes and inflexions, and a good number of EnConversion and DeConversion rules so that we can convert most of the texts in daily needs.

7. CONCLUSION

Machine translation of any native language requires a detailed analysis of language and its syntactic and semantic structures. While there are various machine translation scheme available, most of them are able to keep the semantics of the original texts during translation. UNL provides a platform which acts as an interlingua during machine translations and keeps the semantics of the native language in an interoperable way allowing the meaning of the native language to be conveyed to the target translstion.

This chapter presented a framework for bridging Bangla to Universal Networking Language considering Bangla parts of speech, case structure analysis, prefixes, affixes, UNL compatible Bangla Word Dictionary, Analysis and Generation rules respectively. In parts of speech we have analyzed nouns, adjectives, pronouns especially different kinds of verbs, verb roots and their inflexions.

We have presented UNL compatible formats of dictionary entries of Word Dictionary of Bangla words and inflexions along with their constraint lists and grammatical attributes by integrating their types, properties and other characteristics. Using these formats we can prepare any types of dictionary entries for words that are fully workable. We have also presented UNL companionable formats of some morphological and semantic rules taking into consideration the design of enconversion rules, morphological, syntactic, semantic and grammatical analyses of the Bangla words and sentences respectively. Models of some generation rules in view of the layout of deconversion rules, morphological and syntactic generation and word selection of natural collection have also been presented.

The dictionary entries, morphological and semantic rules are practically implemented by means of the dictionary builder and EnConverter files (provided by the UNDL Foundation of UNL Center) to convert Bangla text to UNL expressions. We have also tested generation rules with DeConverter (provided by the UNDL Foundation) to convert UNL expressions from other languages into respective Bangla text.

Both theoretical and practical analyses have shown that our framework is working well for converting Bangla sentence into UNL expressions and vice versa. Bangla spoken people will be highly benefited through this work by entering into the knowledge source of the multilingual Internet.

REFERENCES

Ali, M. N. Y., Das, J. K., Mamun, S. M. A. A., & Choudhury, M. E. H. (2008). Specific features of a converter of web documents from Bengali to universal networking language. In *Proceedings of the International Conference on Computer and Communication Engineering 2008 (ICCCE'08),* (pp. 726-731). Kuala Lumpur, Malaysia. ICCCE. DOI:10.1109/ICCCE.2008.4580700

Ali, M. N. Y., Das, J. K., Mamun, S. M. A. A., & Nurannabi, A. M. (2008). Morphological analysis of Bangla words for universal networking language. In *Proceedings of the Third International Conference on Digital Information Management (ICDIM 2008),* (pp. 532-537). London, UK: ICDIM. DOI:10.1109/ICDIM.2008.4746734

Asaduzzaman, M. (2008). Bangla shdhito prottoy: Punorbuchar. *The Dhaka University Journal of Linguistic, 1*(1), 79–92.

Asaduzzaman, M. M., & Ali, M. M. (2003). Morphological analysis of Bangla words for automatic machine translation. In *Proceedings of the International Conference on Computer and Information Technology (ICCIT),* (pp.271-276). ICCIT.

Azad, H. (1994). Bakkotottoy (2nd ed). Dhaka.

Bondopoddaye, H. (2001). *Bongioi shobdokosh.* Calcutta, India: Shahitto Okademy.

Choudhury, M. E. H., & Ali, M. N. Y. (2008). Framework for synthesis of universal networking language. *East West University Journal, 1*(2), 28–43.

Choudhury, M. E. H., Ali, M. N. Y., Sarkar, M. Z. H., & Ahsan, R. (2005). Bridging Bangla to universal networking language- A human language neutral meta- language. In *Proceedings of the International Conference on Computer and Information Technology (ICCIT)*, (pp.104-109). ICCIT.

DeConverter. (2002). *DeConverter specification, Version 2.7.* Tokyo, Japan: UNL Center, UNDL Foundation.

EnConverter. (2002). *EnConverter specification, Version 3.3.* Tokyo, Japan: UNL Center/UNDL Foundation.

Giri, L. (2001). *Semantic net like knowledge structure generation from natural languages.* (Unpublished B Tech Dissertation). IIT Bombay. Bombay, India.

Islam, M. S. (2009). Research on Bangla language processing in Bangladesh: Progress and challenges. In *Proceedings of the 8th International Language & Development Conference*. Dhaka, Bangladesh: IEEE.

Kumar, D. C. S. (1999). *Vasha-prokash Bangla vyakaran.* Calcutta, India: Rupa and Company Prokashoni.

Kuntal, D., & Bhattacharyya, P. (2003). Universal networking language based analysis and generation for bengali case structure constructs. In *Proceedings of the International Conference of the Convergence of Knowledge, Culture, Language and Information Technologies*. Alexandria, Egypt: IEEE.

Mridha, M. F., Huda, M. N., Rahman, M. S., & Rahman, C. M. (2010). Structure of dictionary entries of Bangla morphemes for morphological rule generation for universal networking language. In *Proceedings of the International Conference on Computer Information Systems & Industrial Management Applications*. doi:10.1109/CISIM.2010.5643498

Pairkh, J., Khot, J., Dave, S., & Bhattacharyya, P. (2004). *Predicate preserving parsing.* Bombay, India: Department of Computer Science and Engineering, Indian Institute of Technology.

Parteek, B., & Sharma, R. K. (2009). Role of punjabi morphology in designing punjabi-UNL enconverter. In *Proceedings of the International Conference on Advances in Computing, Communication and Control (ICAC3'09)*, (pp. 562-566). ICAC3.

Rameswar, D. S. (1996, November). Shadharan vasha biggan and bangla vasha. *Pustok Biponi Prokashoni*, 358-377.

Sarker, M. Z. H., Ali, M. N. Y., & Das, J. K. (2012). Development of dictionary entries for the Bangla vowel ended roots for universal networking language. *International Journal of Computers and Applications, 52*(19). doi:doi:10.5120/8313-1958.

Shachi, D., & Bhattacharyya, P. (2001). Knowledge extraction from Hindi text. *Journal of the Institution of Electronics and Telecommunication Engineers, 18*(4).

Shahidullah, D. M. (2003). *Bangala vyakaran.* Dhaka: Maola Brothers Prokashoni.

Uchida, H., Zhu, M., & Senta, T. C. D. (2005). *Universal networking language*. Geneva, Switzerland: UNDL.

UNDL. (2003). *UNDL foundation: The universal networking language (UNL) specifications version 3.2.* Geneva: UNDL.

Chapter 4
Machine Learning Approaches for Bangla Statistical Machine Translation

Maxim Roy
Simon Fraser University, Canada

ABSTRACT

Machine Translation (MT) from Bangla to English has recently become a priority task for the Bangla Natural Language Processing (NLP) community. Statistical Machine Translation (SMT) systems require a significant amount of bilingual data between language pairs to achieve significant translation accuracy. However, being a low-density language, such resources are not available in Bangla. In this chapter, the authors discuss how machine learning approaches can help to improve translation quality within as SMT system without requiring a huge increase in resources. They provide a novel semi-supervised learning and active learning framework for SMT, which utilizes both labeled and unlabeled data. The authors discuss sentence selection strategies in detail and perform detailed experimental evaluations on the sentence selection methods. In semi-supervised settings, reversed model approach outperformed all other approaches for Bangla-English SMT, and in active learning setting, geometric 4-gram and geometric phrase sentence selection strategies proved most useful based on BLEU score results over baseline approaches. Overall, in this chapter, the authors demonstrate that for low-density language like Bangla, these machine-learning approaches can improve translation quality.

INTRODUCTION

Machine Translation (MT) from Bangla to English has recently become a priority task for the Bangla Natural Language Processing (NLP) community. MT is a hard problem because of the highly complex, irregular and diverse nature of natural language. MT refers to computerized systems that utilize software to translate text from one natural language into another with or without human assistance. It is impossible to accurately model all the linguistic rules and relationships that shape the translation process, and therefore MT has to make decisions based on incomplete data.

DOI: 10.4018/978-1-4666-3970-6.ch004

In order to handle this incomplete data, a principled approach is to use statistical methods to make optimum decisions given incomplete data. Statistical Machine Translation (SMT) uses a probabilistic framework to automatically translate text from one language to another. Using the co-occurrence counts of words and phrases from the bilingual parallel corpora where sentences are aligned with their translation, SMT learns the translation of words and phrases. From the initial word-based translation models, research on SMT has seen dramatic improvement. At the end of the last decade the use of context in the translation model, which is known as a phrase-based SMT approach, led to a clear improvement in translation quality.

In SMT massive amounts of parallel text in the source and target language are required to achieve high quality translation. However, there are a large number of languages that are considered "low-density," either because the population speaking the language is not very large, or if insufficient amounts of bilingual text are available involving that language. Bangla is one such language. Bangla, one of the more important Indo-Iranian languages, is the sixth-most popular in the world and spoken by a population that now exceeds 250 million. Geographical Bangla-speaking population percentages are as follows: Bangladesh (over 95%), and the Indian States of Andaman and Nicobar Islands (26%), Assam (28%), Tripura (67%), and West Bengal (85%). The global total includes those who are now in diaspora in Canada, Malawi, Nepal, Pakistan, Saudi Arabia, Singapore, United Arab Emirates, United Kingdom, and United States. Although being among the top ten most widely spoken languages around the world, the Bangla language still lacks significant research in the area of NLP specifically in SMT.

SMT systems require a significant amount of bilingual data between language pairs to achieve significant translation accuracy. However, being a low-density language, such resources are not available in Bangla. In this chapter we discuss how machine learning approaches can help to improve translation quality within as SMT system without requiring a huge increase in resources.

We provide a novel semi-supervised learning and active learning framework for SMT, which utilizes both, labeled and unlabeled data. We propose two semi-supervised learning techniques for sentence selection within a Bangla-English phrase-based SMT System. We also propose several effective active learning techniques for sentence selection from a pool of untranslated sentences, for which we ask human experts to provide translations. We perform detailed experimental evaluations on the sentence selection methods and demonstrate that these sentence selection techniques can help to improve translation quality in SMT.

Overall, in this chapter we demonstrate that for low-density language like Bangla, these machine-learning approaches can improve translation quality.

BACKGROUND

Semi-Supervised Learning

Semi-supervised learning refers to the use of both labeled and unlabeled data for training. Semi-supervised learning techniques can be applied to SMT when a large amount of bilingual parallel data is not available for language pairs. Sarkar, Haffari, and Ueffing (2007) explore the use of semi-supervised model adaptation methods for the effective use of monolingual data from the source language in order to improve translation accuracy.

Self-training is a commonly used technique for semi-supervised learning. In self-training a classifier is first trained with a small amount of labeled data. The classifier is then used to classify the unlabeled data. Typically, the most confident unlabeled points, together with their predicted labels, are added to the training set. The classifier is retrained and the procedure repeated. Note the classifier uses its own predictions to teach itself. The procedure is also called self-teaching or bootstrapping.

Semi-Supervised Learning Approaches

Recently the availability of monolingual corpora in the source language has been shown to improve the translation quality in SMT. It has been also shown that adding large amounts of target language text can improve translation quality because the decoder can benefit from the improved language model estimates concerning potential output translations. Many researchers have studied language model adaptation as well as translation model adaptation. Translation model and language model adaptation are usually used in domain adaptation for SMT.

Language model adaptation has been widely used in speech recognition. In recent years, language model adaptation has also been studied for SMT. Bulyko, Matsoukas, Schwartz, Nguyen, and Makhoul (2007) explored discriminative estimation of language model weights by directly optimizing MT performance measures such as BLEU (Papineni, Roukos, Ward & Zhu 2002). Their experiments indicated about a 0.4 BLEU score improvement.

Eck, Vogel, and Waibel (2003) developed a method to adapt language models using information retrieval methods for SMT. In their approach, they first translated input sentences with a general language model, then used these translated sentences to retrieve the most similar documents from the Web applying cross language information retrieval techniques. Later these documents extracted from the Web were used to build an adapted language model and then the documents were re-translated with the adapted language model.

Hildebrand, Eck, Vogel, and Waibel (2005) also applied information retrieval techniques to select sentence pairs from the training corpus that are relevant to the test sentences. Both the language and the translation models are retrained on the extracted data.

Several studies investigated mixture model adaptation for both translation models and language models in SMT. Foster and Kuhn (2007) investigated two basic settings: cross-domain adaptation and dynamic adaptation. In cross-domain adaptation a small sample of parallel in-domain text is assumed and in dynamic adaptation only the current input source text is considered. Adaptation relies on mixture models estimated on the training data through some unsupervised clustering methods. Given available adaptation data, mixture weights are re-estimated *ad hoc*.

Semi-supervised learning has been previously applied to improve word alignments. Callison-Burch, Talbot, and Osborne (2004) trained a generative model for word alignment using unsupervised learning on parallel text. Also another model is trained on a small amount of hand-annotated word alignment data. A mixture model provides a probability for word alignment. Their experimental results indicate that assigning a large weight on the model trained with labeled data performs best.

Koehn and Schroeder (2007) investigated different adaptation methods for SMT. They applied cross-domain adaptation techniques in a phrase-based SMT system trained on the Europarl task, in order to translate news commentaries, from French to English. They used linear interpolation techniques to exploit a small portion of in-domain bilingual data to adapt the Europarl language model and translation models. Their experiments indicate an absolute improvement of more than 1 point on their BLEU score.

Munteanu and Marcu (2005) automatically extracted in-domain bilingual sentence pairs from comparable corpora in order to enlarge the in-domain bilingual corpus. They presented a novel method that uses a maximum entropy classifier that, given a pair of sentences, can reliably determine whether or not they are translations of each other in order to extract parallel data from large Chinese, Arabic, and English non-parallel newspaper corpora. They evaluated the quality of the extracted data by showing that it improves the performance of a state-of-the-art SMT system.

Callison-Burch (2002) applied co-training to MT. This approach requires several source languages which are sentence-aligned with each other and all translate into the same target language. One language pair creates data for another language pair and can be naturally used in a Blum and Mitchell (1998)-style co-training algorithm. Experiments on the EuroParl corpus show a decrease in WER.

Self-training for SMT was proposed in (Ueffing, 2006). Sarkar, Haffari and Ueffing (2007) proposed several elaborate adaptation methods relying on additional bilingual data synthesized from the development or test sets. They explored transductive learning for SMT, where source language corpora are used to train the models. They repeatedly translated source sentences from the development set and test set. Then the generated translations were used to improve the performance of the SMT system. They presented detailed experimental evaluations on the French-English EuroParl data set and on data from the NIST Chinese–English large data track which showed a significant improvement in translation quality on both datasets.

Active Learning

Active Learning (AL) is an emerging area in machine learning that explores methods that rely on actively participating in the collection of training examples rather than random sampling. In AL, a learner selects as few instances as possible to be labelled by a labeller and iteratively trains itself with the new examples selected. One of the goals of active learning is to reduce the number of supervised training examples needed to achieve a given level of performance. Also in the case where limited amount of training examples are available, to add most useful examples to the training data which can improve the performance.

Supervised learning strategies require a large set of labeled instances to perform well. In many applications, unlabeled instances may be abundant but obtaining labels for these instances could be expensive and time-consuming. AL was introduced to reduce the total cost of labeling. The process of collecting the most useful examples for training an MT system is an active learning task, as a learner can be used to select these examples.

Active Learning Techniques

AL systems may construct their own examples, request certain types of examples, or determine which unsupervised examples are most useful for labeling. Due to the availability of an abundant amount of text and the need to annotate only the most informative sentences, the AL approach known as selective sampling, is particularly attractive in natural-language learning.

In selective sampling, learning begins with a small pool of annotated examples and a large pool of unannotated examples, and the learner attempts to choose the most informative additional examples for annotation. Existing work in this area has emphasized on two approaches:

1. Certainty-based methods
2. Committee-based methods

Certainty-Based Methods: In the certainty-based paradigm, a system is trained on a small number of annotated examples to learn an initial classifier. Then, the system examines the unannotated examples, and attaches certainties to the predicted annotation of those examples. A predefined amount of examples with the lowest certainties are then presented to the user for annotation and retraining. Many methods for attaching certainties have been used, but the methods typically estimate the probability that a classifier consistent with the prior training data will classify a new example correctly.

Committee-Based Methods: In the committee-based paradigm, a diverse committee of classifiers is created, again from a small number of annotated examples. Then, each committee member labels additional examples. The examples whose annotation results in the most disagreement amongst the committee members are presented to the user for annotation and retraining. A diverse committee, consistent with the prior training data, will produce the highest disagreement on examples whose label is most un- certain with respect to the possible classifiers that could be obtained by training on that data. The density-weighted sampling strategy is also very common and is based on the idea that informative instances are those that are uncertain and representative of the input distribution.

For many language learning tasks, annotation is particularly time-consuming since it re- quires specifying a complex output rather than just a category label, so reducing the number of training examples required can greatly increase the utility of learning. An increasing number of researchers are successfully applying machine learning to natural language processing. However, only a few have utilized active learning techniques. Active learning, as a standard method has been applied to a variety of problems in natural language processing such as parsing, automatic speech recognition, part of speech tagging, text categorization, named-entity recognition, and word-sense disambiguation. However, little work has been done in using these techniques to improve machine translation.

There has been very little work published on active learning for SMT for low-density/low-resource languages. Callison-Burch (2003) in his Ph.D. proposal lays out the promise of AL for SMT and proposes some algorithms. However, no experimental results were reported for his approaches.

There is work on sampling sentence pairs for SMT but the goal has been to limit the amount of training data in order to reduce the memory footprint of the SMT decoder. Eck, Vogel, and Waibel (2005) used a weighting scheme to sort sentences based on the frequency of unseen n-grams. After sorting they selected smaller training corpora and showed that systems trained on much less training data achieve a very competitive performance compared to baseline systems, which were trained on all available training data. They also proposed a second approach to rank sentences based on TF-IDF (term frequency–inverse document frequency) which is a widely used similarity measure in information retrieval. The TF-IDF approach did not show improvements over the other approach. They evaluated the system against a weak baseline that selected sentences based on the original order of sentences in the training corpus. Usually in such a baseline, adjacent sentences tend to be related in topic and only a few new words are added in every iteration. A random selector might have been a better baseline.

Gangadharaiah, Brown, and Carbonell (2009) proposed using AL strategies to sample the most informative sentence pairs. While more data is always useful, a large training corpus can slow down an MT system. They used a pool based strategy to selectively sample the huge corpus to obtain a sub-corpus of most informative sentence pairs. Their approach outperformed a random selector and also a previously used sampling strategy (Eck, Vogel &Waibel, 2005) in an EBMT framework by about one BLEU point.

Kato and Barnard (2007) implement an AL system for SMT for language pairs with limited resources (En-Xhosa, En-Zulu, En-Setswana and En-Afrikaans), but the experiments are on a very small simulated data set. The only feature used is the confidence score for sentence selection in the SMT system.

Haffari and Sarkar (2009) introduced an AL task of adding a new language to an existing multilingual set of parallel text and constructing high quality MT systems, from each language in the collection into this new target language. They showed that adding a new language using

AL to the EuroParl corpus provides a significant improvement in translation quality compared to a random sentence selection baseline.

Dataset

The corpus we used for training the system was provided by the Linguistic Data Consortium (LDC Catalog No.: LDC2008E29) containing around 11,000 sentences of newswire text taken from the BBC Asian Network and some other South Asian news Websites. For our language model we used data from the English section of EuroParl combined with LDC training set. The development set used to optimize the model weights in the decoder, and test set used for evaluation was taken from the same LDC corpus mentioned above. We also have a large monolingual Bangla dataset which contains more than one million sentences. The monolingual corpus was provided by the Center for Research on Bangla Language Processing, BRAC University, Bangladesh. The corpus was built by collecting text from the Prothom Alo newspaper Website and contains all the news available for the year of 2005 (from 1st January to 31st December), including magazines and periodicals. There are 18,067,470 word tokens and 386,639 distinct word types in this corpus. The resource statistics are shown in Table 1.

Table 1. Dataset statistics

Resources	Used for	Sentences
LDC training set (Bangla-English)	Phrase table + LM	11226
Europarl (English)	LM	182234
LDC dev. set (Bangla - English)	Development	600
LDC test set (1 ref. Bangla-English)	Test	1000
Prothom-Alo monolingual data (Bangla)	ML approaches	1000000

OUR SEMI-SUPERVISED APPROACHES TO BANGLA

Since sufficient amount of bilingual parallel data between Bangla and English for SMT is not publicly available, we are exploring the use of semi-supervised techniques like self-training in SMT. We are proposing several self-training techniques to effectively use this large monolingual corpus (from the source language) in our experiments in order to improve translation accuracy. We propose several sentence selection strategies to select sentences from a large monolingual Bangla corpus, which are briefly discussed below along with the baseline system where sentences are chosen randomly.

Baseline Approach

In our baseline system the initial MT system is trained on a bilingual corpus L and we randomly select k sentences from a large monolingual corpus U. We translate these randomly selected sentences with our initial MT system $M_{B\rightarrow E}$ and denote these sentences along with their translation as U^+. Then we retrain the SMT system on $L\cup U^+$ and use the resulting model to decode the test set. We also remove these k randomly selected sentences from U. This process is continued iteratively until a certain level of translation quality, which in our case is measured by the BLEU score, is met. In Algorithm 1 we describe the baseline algorithm.

Figure 1 illustrates our overall baseline system. The baseline SMT system consists of a translation model, language model and the decoder. The translation model is used for initial training of the bilingual corpus and retraining with additional new sentences in each iterative step. The decoder is used to translate randomly selected sentences from the monolingual data in each iterative step and translate test data for evaluation.

Algorithm 1. Baseline algorithm semi-supervised SMT

Given bilingual corpus L, and monolingual corpus U.
$M_{B\rightarrow E}$ =train(L,∅)
for t = 1, 2, ... till certain level of translation quality is reached do
    Randomly select k sentence pairs from U
    U^{+} = **translate**(k, $M_{B\rightarrow E}$)
    $M_{B\rightarrow E}$ = **train**(L, U^{+})
    Remove the k sentences from U
    Evaluate the performance on the test set T
end for

Figure 1. Baseline

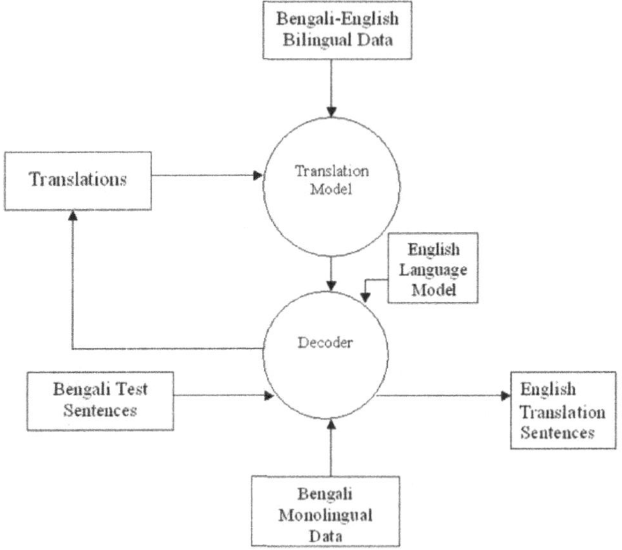

Reverse Model Approach

Our first sentence selection approach uses the reverse translation model to rank all sentences in the monolingual corpus U based on their BLEU score and only select sentences, which have higher BLEU score. Mainly we want to select those sentences from the monolingual corpus U for which our MT system can generate good translations. In order to obtain a BLEU score for sentences in the monolingual corpus U we used the reverse translation model. While a translation system $M_{B\rightarrow E}$ is built from language B to language E, we also build a translation system in the reverse direction $M_{E\rightarrow B}$. To measure the BLEU score of all monolingual sentences B from monolingual corpus U, we translate them to English sentences E by $M_{B\rightarrow E}$ and then project the translation back to Bangla using $M_{E\rightarrow B}$. We denote this reconstructed version of the original Bangla sentences by B'. We then use B as the reference translation to obtain the BLEU score for sentences B'. In Algorithm 2, we describe the reverse model sentence selection algorithm.

Figure 2 illustrates the reverse model approach. Here the MT system consists of two translation models- one for translation in the original direction (Bangla to English) and other in the reverse

Algorithm 2. Reverse model sentence selection algorithm

Given bilingual corpus L, and monolingual corpus U.

$M_{B\rightarrow E}$ = **train**(L,∅)

$M_{E\rightarrow B}$ = **train**(L,∅)

for t = 1, 2, ... till certain level of translation quality is reached **do**

  U^+ : (B,E) = **translate**(U, $M_{B\rightarrow E}$)

  U^* : (B , E) = **translate**(E, $M_{E\rightarrow B}$)

  Use B and B' to rank all sentences in U^+ based on the BLEU score

  Select k sentences and their translations k' from ranked U^+

  $M_{B\rightarrow E}$ = **train**(L, $k \cup k'$)

  $M_{E\rightarrow B}$ = **train**(L, $k \cup k'$)

  Remove the k sentences from U

  Evaluate the performance on the test set T

end for

Figure 2. Reverse model

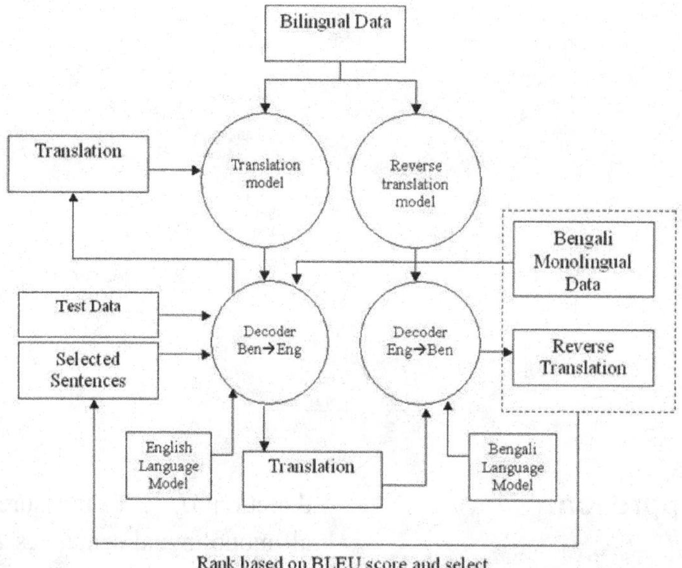

direction (English to Bangla). Both translation model are initially trained with bilingual training data and retrained with new data in each iterative step. In each iteration the monolingual data is first translated with the Bangla to English decoder and the output of the decoder is used as input for the English to Bangla decoder which basically regenerates the monolingual corpus known as reverse translation. Then the quality of the reverse translation can be evaluated using monolingual data as the reference. The sentences with higher BLEU score are translated and added with bilingual training data to retrain both translation models.

Frequent Word Model Approach

Our next sentence selection approach uses statistics from the training corpus L for sentence selection from the monolingual corpus U. In this approach we first find the most frequent words in the training corpus L. We call them seed words. Then we filter the seed words based on their confidence score, which reflects how confidently we can predict their translation. Seed words with confidence scores lower than a certain threshold values are removed. Then we use these remaining seed words to select sentences from the monolingual corpus U and remove selected sentences from U. Next we look for the most frequent words other than the initial seed words in the selected sentences to be used for the next iteration as new seed words. We translate these selected sentences and add them to the training corpus L. After that we re-train the system with the new training data. In the next iteration we select new sentences from the monolingual corpus U using the new seed words and repeat the steps. We keep on repeating the steps until no more new seed words are available. In each iteration we monitor the performance on the test set T. In Algorithm 3, we describe the frequent word sentence selection procedure.

Algorithm 3. Frequent word sentence selection algorithm

Given bilingual corpus L, and monolingual corpus U.
$M_{B \rightarrow E}$ = **train**(L,∅)
S = **select_seed**(L)
for all s in S **do**
    if score(s) > threshold **then**
        $S^+ = S^+ \cup s$
    end if
end for
while $S^+ \neq \{\}$ **do**
    Select k sentences from U based on S^+
    U=U-K
    U^+ =**translate**(k, $M_{B \rightarrow E}$)
    S = **select_seed**(U^+)
    for all s in S **do**
        if score(s) > threshold then
            $S^+ = S^+ \cup s$
        end if
    end for
    $M_{B \rightarrow E}$ = **train**(L, U^+)
    Evaluate the performance on the test set T
end while

Figure 3 illustrates the frequent word model approach. The MT system consists of a translation model, decoder and language model. The translation model is initially trained on the bilingual training data and retrained with new data in each iterative step. Frequent words also known as seed words are selected from bilingual training data and are used to select sentences from the monolingual data. The decoder is used to translate the selected sentences from monolingual data and output of the decoder is used to retrain the translation model again. The decoder is also used to translate test data from evaluation purposes.

Semi-Supervised Learning Setup

We conducted semi-supervised learning experiments for Bangla SMT using the Portage (Ueffing, Simard, Larkin, & Johnson, 2007) SMT system. Similar to Moses (Koehn et al., 2007), another popular SMT system, the models (or features) which are employed by the decoder in Portage are: (a) several phrase table(s), which model the translation direction $p(f|e)$, (b) one or several n-gram language model(s) trained with the SRILM toolkit (Stolcke, 2002); in the experiments reported here, we used a trigram model on EuroParl, (c) a distortion model which assigns a penalty based on the number of source words which are skipped when generating a new target phrase, and (d) a word penalty. These different models are combined log-linearly. Their weights are optimized with respect to BLEU score using the algorithm described in (Och, 2003) using the same development corpus provided by the LDC.

Initially we trained the translation model on the training set of 11000 sentences provided by the Linguistic Data Consortium. Then we select sentences for a Bangla monolingual dataset using one of our three approaches either random, reverse or frequent word model. In the random approach we just randomly select sentences from the monolingual dataset. In the frequent word

Figure 3. Frequent word model

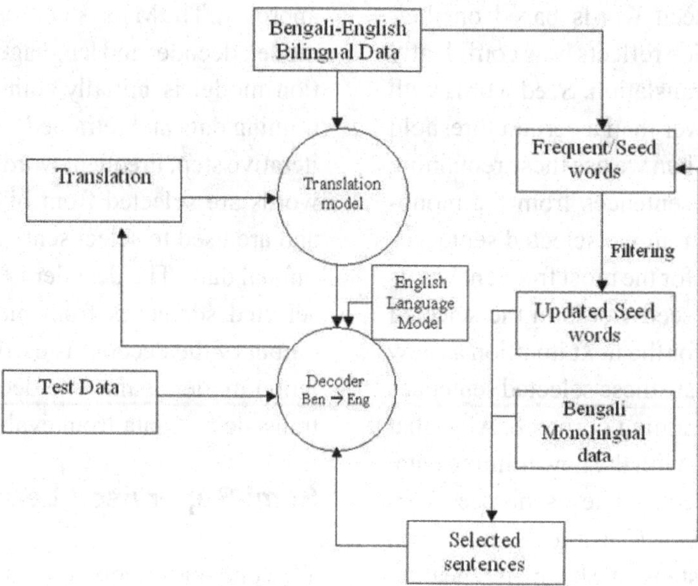

model approach, we select sentences from the monolingual dataset based on the most frequent words in the training data. In the reversed model approach we select sentences from the monolingual dataset that have the highest BLEU score obtained using the reversed translation model. We select 500 sentences in each iteration of the semi-supervised loop using these approaches. Then we translate selected sentences using our initial translation model and add these sentences together with their translation to our training data and retrain the system using the new dataset. Then in the next iteration, we again select sentences from our monolingual dataset using one of our approaches and add them to training data after translating them with the new translation model. We continue this iterative process for a certain number of iterations and monitor the translation performance in each iteration.

Semi-Supervised Learning Results

We applied the semi-supervised learning framework to the problem of Bangla-English SMT. In order to evaluate the effectiveness of our sentence selection strategies we tested our approaches on English-French language pair. The main reason for applying our approaches to a different language pair (English-French) is to demonstrate that our approaches are language independent and can be applied to any language pair with limited resources. Our results in Table 2 indicate that our reverse model approach and frequent word model out performs strong random baseline approach. For the semi-supervised learning framework,

Table 2. Impact of semi-supervised learning approaches on Bangla-English SMT in BLEU score

Iteration	Random Baseline	Reverse Model	Frequent-Word Model
1	5.47	5.47	5.47
2	5.57	5.63	5.61
3	5.79	5.69	5.70
4	5.66	5.67	5.63
5	5.73	5.82	5.82
6	5.76	5.89	5.81
7	5.74	6.05	5.88
8	5.75	6.08	5.89

we conducted experiments on Portage on both language pairs.

The reverse model approach outperformed all other approaches for Bangla-English SMT however, in the case of French-English SMT, the frequent word model outperformed all other approaches. The reverse model performs better than the frequent word model for Bangla because Bangla has a rich morphology (a lot of words are inflected) so a frequent word model which is based on word frequency does not perform that well. This is not the case when translating from French to English since French and English are quite similar in their structure and grammar (see Table 3).

The two graphs in Figures 4 and 5 show the BLEU score for all the approaches for semi-supervised learning for both language pairs. We presented the results in graphs too because for iterative approaches graphs are better than tables to demonstrate how each approach performs in each iterative step.

Table 3. Impact of semi-supervised approaches on French-English SMT in BLEU score

Iteration	Random Baseline	Reverse Model	Frequent-Word Model
1	13.60	13.60	13.60
2	13.61	13.61	13.63
3	13.75	13.71	13.70
4	13.82	13.80	13.93
5	13.85	13.91	13.99
6	13.90	13.94	14.01
7	13.92	14.01	14.07
8	13.93	14.03	14.17

OUR ACTIVE LEARNING APPROACHES TO BANGLA SMT

In this section we provide an experimental study of AL for Bangla-English SMT. Specifically, we use AL to improve quality of a phrase-based Bangla-English SMT system since a limited amount of bilingual data is available for the language pair.

In order to improve or adapt an SMT system an obvious strategy is to create or add more new bilingual data to the existing bilingual corpora. However, just randomly translating text and adding to the bilingual corpora might not always benefit SMT systems since new translated sentences might be similar to the existing bilingual corpora and might not contribute a lot of new phrases to the SMT system. Selective sampling of sentences for AL will lead to a parallel corpus where each sentence does not share any phrase pairs with the existing bilingual corpora and the SMT system will benefit for the new phrase pairs.

We use a novel framework for AL. We assume a small amount of parallel text and a large amount of monolingual source language text. Using these resources, we create a large noisy parallel text which we then iteratively improve using small injections of human translations.

Starting from an SMT model trained initially on bilingual data, the problem is to minimize the human effort involved with translating new sentences which will be added to the training data to make the *retrained* SMT model achieve a certain level of performance. Thus, given a bitext $L := \{(f_i, e_i)\}$ and a monolingual source text $U := \{f_j\}$, the goal is to select a subset of highly informative sentences from U to present to a human expert for translation. Highly informative sentences are those which, together with their translations, help the retrained SMT system quickly reach a certain level of translation quality.

Algorithm 4 describes the experimental setup we propose for AL. We train our initial MT system on the bilingual corpus L, and use it to translate all monolingual sentences in U. We denote sentences in U together with their translations as U^+ (line 4 of Algorithm 4). Then we retrain the SMT system on $L \cup U^+$ and use the resulting model to decode

Figure 4. Impact of semi-supervised approaches on Bangla-English SMT

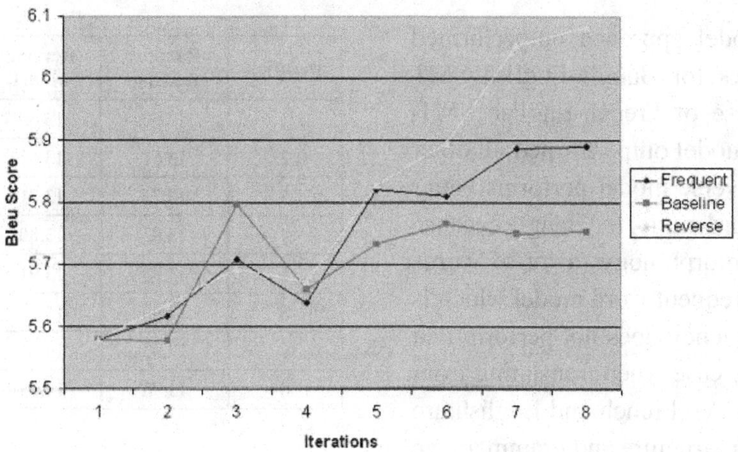

Figure 5. Impact of semi-supervised approaches on French-English SMT

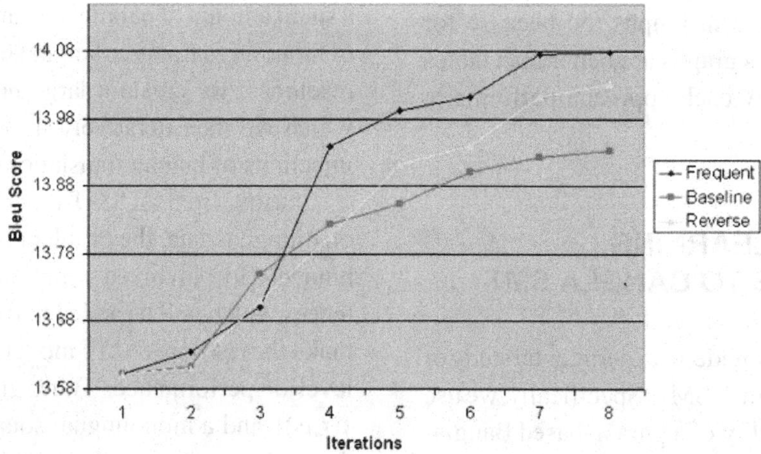

Algorithm 4. Active learning in SMT

Given bilingual corpus L, and monolingual corpus U.
$M_{F \to E}$ = **train**(L,∅)
for t = 1,2,... **do**
  U^+ = **translate**(U, $M_{F \to E}$)
  Select k sentence pairs from U^+, and ask a human for their *true* translations.
  Remove the k sentences from U, and add the k sentence pairs (translated by human) to L
  $M_{F \to E}$ = **train**(L, U^+)
  Evaluate the performance on the test set T
end for

the test set. Afterwards, we select and remove a subset of highly informative sentences from *U*, and add those sentences together with their human-provided translations to *L*. This process is continued iteratively until a certain level of translation quality, which in our case is measured by the BLEU score, is met. In the baseline, against which we compare the sentence selection methods, the sentences are chosen randomly. When (re-) training the model, two phrase tables are learned: one from *L* and the other one from U^+.

The setup in Algorithm 4 helps us to investigate how to maximally take advantage of human effort (for sentence translation) when learning an SMT model from the available data, that includes bilingual and monolingual text. $M_{F \to E}$ in Algorithm 4 denotes a MT system that translates from language *F* to *E*. Figure 6 illustrates the overall AL setting.

SENTENCE SELECTION STRATEGIES

Below we discuss several sentence selection strategies proposed by Haffari, Roy and Sarkar (2009) and used in our AL scenario for Bangla-English SMT.

Geometric-Phrase and Arithmetic-Phrase

The more frequent a phrase is in the unlabeled data, the more important it is to know its translation; since it is more likely to occur in the test data (especially when the test data is in-domain with respect to unlabeled data). The more frequent a phrase is in the labeled data, the more unimportant it is; since probably we have observed most of its translations.

Figure 6. Active learning setting

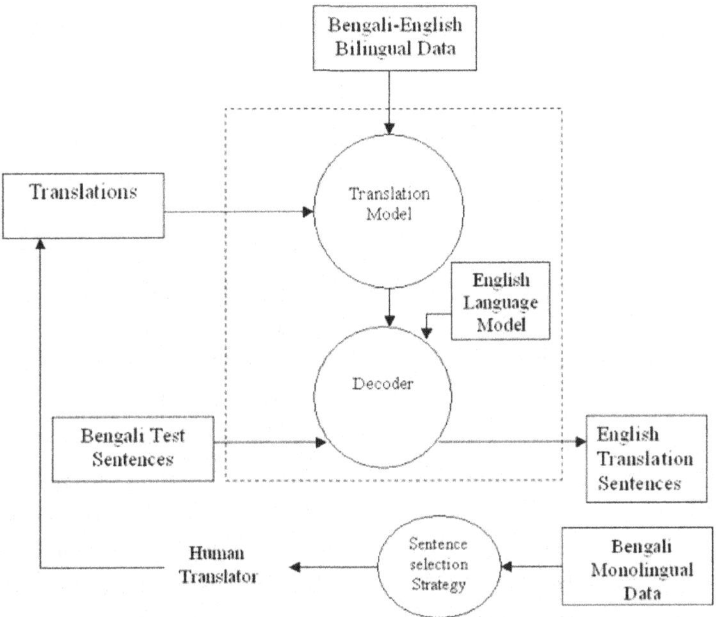

Based on the above observations, we measure the importance score of a sentence as:

$$\phi_g^p(s) = [\prod_{x \in X_s^p} \frac{P(x \mid U)}{P(x \mid L)}]^{\frac{1}{|X_s^p|}} \tag{1}$$

where X_s^p is the set of possible phrases that sentence s can offer, and $P(x|D)$ is the probability of observing x in the data D:

$$P(x \mid D) = \frac{Count(x) + \varepsilon}{\sum_{x \in X_D^p} Count(x) + \varepsilon}$$

Equation 1 is the averaged probability ratio of the set of candidate phrases, i.e. the probability of the candidate phrases under a probabilistic phrase model based on U divided by that based on L. In addition to the geometric average in (1), we may also consider the arithmetic average score:

$$\phi_a^p(s) = \frac{1}{|X_s^p|} \sum_{x \in X_s^p} \frac{P(x \mid U)}{P(x \mid L)} \tag{2}$$

Note that (1) can be re-written as:

$$\frac{1}{|X_s^p|} \sum_{x \in X_s^p} \log \frac{P(x \mid U)}{P(x \mid L)}$$

in the logarithm space, which is similar to (2) with the difference of additional log.

Geometric *n*-Gram and Arithmetic *n*-Gram

As an alternative to phrases, we consider *n*-grams as basic units of generalization. The resulting score is the weighted combination of the *n*-gram based scores:

$$\phi_g^N(s) = \sum_{n=1}^{N} \frac{w_n}{|X_s^n|} \sum_{x \in X_s^n} \log \frac{P(x \mid U, n)}{P(x \mid L, n)} \tag{3}$$

where X_s^n denotes *n*-grams in the sentence *s*, and $P(x|D,n)$ is the probability of *x* in the set of *n*-grams in *D*. The weights w_n adjust the importance of the scores of *n*-grams with different lengths. In addition to taking geometric average, we also consider the arithmetic average:

$$\phi_a^N(s) = \sum_{n=1}^{N} \frac{w_n}{|X_s^n|} \sum_{x \in X_s^n} \frac{P(x \mid U, n)}{P(x \mid L, n)} \tag{4}$$

As a special case when $N = 1$, the score motivates selecting sentences which increase the number of unique words with new words appearing with higher frequency in *U* than *L*.

Active Learning Setup

We applied active learning to the Bangla-English SMT task to create a larger Bangla-English parallel text resource. Similar to the semi-supervised learning approach, we train our initial translation model on the training set of 11000 sentence provided by the Linguistic Data Consortium. Then we select sentences for a Bangla monolingual dataset using one of the four sentence selection strategies, which are Geometric-Phrase, Arithmetic-Phrase, Geometric *n*-gram and Arithmetic *n*-gram. A user participated in the AL loop, translating 100 sentences in each iteration. In each iteration we added the selected sentences and their translation to our training data and retrained the model. We continued this iterative process for 6 iterations and monitored the translation perform in each iteration. Also as part of active learning loop we created a small parallel corpora of 3000 new sentences between Bangla and English. Since each iteration in AL loop is very time consuming due to the manual translation we only translated 100 sentences in each iteration.

Active Learning Results

Our experimental results show that adding more human translation does not always result in better translation performance. This is likely due to the fact that the translator in the AL loop was not the same as the original translator for the labeled data. The results are shown in Table 4. Geometric 4-gram and Geometric phrase are the features that prove most useful in extracting useful sentences for the human expert to translate.

Figure 7 also represents the BLEU score for random, geometric 4-gram and geometric phrase sentence selection strategy in the AL setting for Bangla-English SMT. WE see that two of the graphs have leveled off after 5 iterations. All dropped significantly in the initial iterations before recovering.

Table 4. Impact of active learning approaches on Bangla-English SMT in BLEU score

Iteration	Random Baseline	Geometric 4-Gram	Geometric Phrase
1	5.42	5.42	5.42
2	5.17	5.34	5.14
3	5.25	5.42	5.07
4	5.40	5.58	5.23
5	5.49	5.65	5.40
6	5.46	5.66	5.62

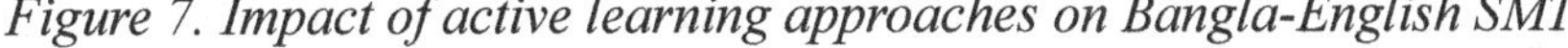

Figure 7. Impact of active learning approaches on Bangla-English SMT

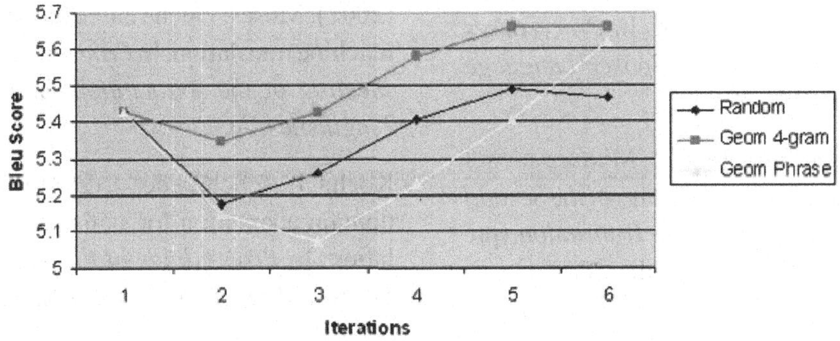

FUTURE RESEARCH DIRECTIONS AND CONCLUSION

In this chapter, we provided a novel semi-supervised learning and active learning framework for SMT that utilizes both labeled and unlabeled data. Similar machine learning approaches can be applied to other language pairs specially languages with limited resources. Several sentence selection strategies were discussed and detailed experimental evaluations were performed on the sentence selection method. In semi-supervised settings, reversed model approach outperformed all other approaches for Bangla-English SMT and in active learning setting, geometric 4-gram and geometric phrase sentence selection strategies proved most useful.

ACKNOWLEDGMENT

We would like to acknowledge and extend our heartfelt gratitude to Dr. Fred Popowich and Dr. Anoop Sarkar from Simon Fraser University and Dr. Gholamreza Haffari from Monash University for their advice and support in the research project.

REFERENCES

Blum, A., & Mitchell, T. (1998). Combining labeled and unlabeled data with co-training. In *Proceedings of the Workshop on Computational Learning Theory*. COLT.

Bulyko, I., Matsoukas, S., Schwartz, R., Nguyen, L., & Makhoul, J. (2007). Language model adaptation in machine translation from speech. In *Proceedings of the 32nd IEEE International Conference on Acoustics, Speech, and Signal Processing (ICASSP)*. IEEE.

Callison-Burch, C. (2002). *Co-training for statistical machine translation.* (Master's Thesis). University of Edinburgh. Edinburgh, UK.

Callison-Burch, C. (2003). *Active learning for statistical machine translation*. (PhD Dissertation). Edinburgh University. Edinburgh, UK.

Callison-Burch, C., Talbot, D., & Osborne, M. (2004). Statistical machine translation with word and sentence-aligned parallel corpora. In *Proceedings of the 42nd Annual Meeting on Association for Computational Linguistics*. Barcelona, Spain: ACL.

Eck, M., Vogel, S., & Waibel, A. (2003). Language model adaptation for statistical machine translation based on information retrieval. In *Proceedings of the International Conference on Language Resources and Evaluation (LREC)*, (pp. 327-330). Lisbon, Portugal: LREC.

Eck, M., Vogel, S., & Waibel, A. (2005). Low cost portability for statistical machine translation based in n-gram frequency and tf-idf. In *Proceedings of International Workshop on Spoken Language Translation (IWSLT)*. IWSLT.

Foster, G., & Kuhn, R. (2007). Mixture model adaptation for SMT. In *Proceedings of the Second Workshop on Statistical Machine Translation*, (pp. 128-135). Prague, Czech Republic: SMT.

Gangadharaiah, R., Brown, R. D., & Carbonell, J. (2009). Active learning in example-based machine translation. In *Proceedings of the 17th Nordic Conference of Computational Linguistics, NODALIDA*. NODALIDA.

Haffari, G., Roy, M., & Sarkar, A. (2009). Active learning for statistical phrase-based machine translation. In *Proceedings of the North American Chapter of the Association for Computational Linguistics - Human Language Technologies (NAACL-HLT)*. NAACL-HLT.

Haffari, G., & Sarkar, A. (2009). Active learning for multilingual statistical phrase based machine translation. In *Proceedings of the Joint Conference of the 47th Annual Meeting of the Association for Computational Linguistics and the 4th International Joint Conference on Natural Language Processing of the Asian Federation of Natural Language Processing (ACL-IJCNLP)*. ACL-IJCNLP.

Hildebrand, M. S., Eck, M., Vogel, S., & Waibel, A. (2005). Adaptation of the translation model for statistical machine translation based on information retrieval. In *Proceedings of the 10th EAMT Conference Practical Applications of Machine Translation*, (pp. 133-142). EAMT.

Kato, R. S. M., & Barnard, E. (2007). Statistical translation with scarce resources: A South African case study. *SAIEE Africa Research Journal*, *98*(4), 136–140.

Koehn, P., Hoang, H., Birch, A., Callison-Burch, C., Federico, M., & Bertoldi, N. … Herbst, E. (2007). Moses: Open source toolkit for statistical machine translation. In *Proceedings of the Annual Meeting of the Association for Computational Linguistics*. ACL.

Koehn, P., & Schroeder, J. (2007). Experiments in domain adaptation for statistical machine translation. In *Proceedings of the ACL Workshop on Statistical Machine Translation*. ACL.

Munteanu, D., & Marcu, D. (2005). Improving machine translation performance by exploiting comparable corpora. *Computational Linguistics*, *31*(4), 477–504. doi:10.1162/089120105775299168.

Och, F. J. (2003). Minimum error rate training in statistical machine translation. In *Proceedings of the 41st Annual Meeting of the ACL*, (pp. 160-167). ACL.

Papineni, K., Roukos, S., Ward, T., & Zhu, W. (2002). BLEU: A method for automatic evaluation of machine translation. In *Proceedings of the 20th Annual Meeting of the Association for Computational Linguistics*. ACL.

Sarkar, A., Haffari, G., & Ueffing, N. (2007). Transductive learning for statistical machine translation. In *Proceedings of the Annual Meeting of the Association for Computational Linguistics*. Prague, Czech Republic: ACL.

Stolcke, A. (2002). SRILM-An extensible language modeling toolkit. In J. H. L. Hansen & B. Pellom (Eds.), *Proceedings of the ICSLP*, (vol. 2, pp. 901-904). Denver, CO: ICSLP.

Ueffing, N. (2006). Using monolingual source-language data to improve MT performance. In *Proceedings of the IWSLT*. IWSLT.

Ueffing, N., Simard, M., Larkin, S., & Johnson, J. H. (2007). NRC's portage system for WMT 2007. In *Proceedings of the ACL Workshop on SMT*. ACL.

KEY TERMS AND DEFINITIONS

Active Learning: An emerging area in machine learning that explores methods that rely on actively participating in the collection of training examples rather than random sampling.

BLEU: An IBM-developed metric which measures how close a candidate translation is to a reference translation by doing an n-gram comparison between both translations.

Machine Learning: The field of study that gives computers the ability to improve performance using experience.

Machine Translation: Computerized systems that utilize software to translate text from one natural language into another with or without human assistance.

***n*-Gram:** A contiguous sequence of *n* items from a given sequence of text.

Semi-Supervised Learning: The use of both labeled and unlabeled data for training.

Statistical Machine Translation (SMT): Statistical machine translation uses a probabilistic framework to automatically translate text from one language to another.

Chapter 5
Selection of an Optimal Set of Features for Bengali Character Recognition

Hasan Sarwar
United International University, Bangladesh

Saima Hossain
LEADS Corporation Limited, Bangladesh

Mizanur Rahman
Institute of Science and Technology (IST), Bangladesh

Sabrina Ahmed
Local Government Engineering Department (LGED), Bangladesh

Nasreen Akter
St. Francis Xavier University, Canada

Chowdhury Mofizur Rahman
United International University, Bangladesh

ABSTRACT

Feature extraction is an essential step of Optical Character Recognition. Accurate and distinguishable feature plays a significant role to leverage the performance of a classifier. The complexity level of feature identification algorithm differs for alphabet sets of different languages. Apart from generic algorithms to find features of different alphabet sets, these algorithms take care of individual characteristic common for a particular alphabet set. Dominant features of one alphabet set might completely differ from that of another set. Since there always remains the chance that inaccurate features may cause inefficient recognition, special attention should be given to identify the set of optimal features of a character set. Bengali characters also have some specific issues apart from the existing issues of other character sets. For example, there are about 300 basic, modified, and compound character shapes in the script, the characters in a word are topologically connected, and Bengali is an inflectional language. Literature survey shows that several authors have used different features and classification algorithms. The authors have extensively reviewed all these feature sets. In order to identify an optimal feature set, variability analysis has been proposed here. They focus on the specific peculiarities of Bengali alphabet sets, its different usage as vowel and consonant signs, compound, complex, and touching characters. The authors also took care to generate easily computable features that take less time for generation. However, more attention needs to be given in order to choose an efficient classifier.

DOI: 10.4018/978-1-4666-3970-6.ch005

1. INTRODUCTION

1.1. Background

The necessity to have a workable Bangla Optical Character Recognizer (OCR) is felt by all Bengali speaking people. Bangla (or Bengali), one of the more important Indo-Iranian languages, is the sixth-most popular in the world and spoken by a population that now exceeds 250 million. Geographical Bangla-speaking population percentages are as follows: Bangladesh (over 95%), and the Indian States of Andaman & Nicobar Islands (26%), Assam (28%), Tripura (67%), and West Bengal (85%). The global total includes those who are now in diaspora in Canada, Malawi, Nepal, Pakistan, Saudi Arabia, Singapore, United Arab Emirates, United Kingdom, and United States. The history of developing a complete Bangla Optical Character Recognizer (OCR) dates back to 1990s(Alam & Kashem, 2010; Chaudhuri & Pal, 1998; Mahmud et al., 2003; Omee et al., 2011). Recent trend of digitizing knowledge repositories, implementation of E-Governance requires easy entry of already printed data into computer. A lot of research effort has already been committed to solve many individual intricate issues. A detailed summary is found here (Hossain, Akter, Sarwar & Rahman, 2010). Research toward a commercially viable Basic OCR still deserves considerable amount of effort. A survey of the existing literature exhibits that most of the authors have tried to develop an OCR considering all the steps of a pattern recognition system. For example, all published literature have considered the tasks of preprocessing, noise elimination, skew detection, segmentation, feature selection and extraction, classification and post processing. A complete in-depth focus on any particular aspect, involving the inherent nature of Bangla Language, is still missing in the whole spectrum of research works in this particular area. Here, we have tried to focus on the feature identification part of the whole issue. In our view, this process deserves special attention and care to be paid in order to build a successful OCR. In our knowledge, this is the first attempt so far taken in the domain of Bangla OCR development.

1.2. A Brief on Bangla Alphabet

The basic Bengali character set comprises of 11 vowels, 39 consonants, and 10 numerals. There are also compound characters being combination of consonant with consonant as well as consonant with vowel. A vowel following a consonant sometimes takes a modified shape and is called a vowel modifier. Similarly there are consonants take the shape of a modifier when comes with another consonant. In general, there are 300 basic, modified and compound character shapes. These characters in a word are topologically connected. Bangla is known as an inflectional language. Some of the characters are shown in Box 1.

Box 1.

Vowels অ আ ই ঈ উ ঊ ঋ এ ঐ ও ঔ

Vowel Modifiers ◌া ◌ি ◌ী ◌ু ◌ূ ◌ৃ ◌ে ◌ৈ ◌ো ◌ৌ

Consonants ক খ গ ঘ ঙ চ ছ জ ঝ ঞ ট ঠ ড ঢ ণ ত থ দ ধ ন প ফ ব ভ ম য র ল শ ষ স ড় ঢ় য় ৎ ◌ং ঃ ◌ঁ

Numerals ০ ১ ২ ৩ ৪ ৫ ৬ ৭ ৮ ৯

Some Compound Characters ষ্ফ ক্ক ঙ্গ ত্ত ঞ্জ ষ্ক ঙ্ক স্তু ন্ধ ষ্ঠ

Basic and modified characters which are about 75 in number occupy about 96% of the text corpus (Chaudhuri, & Pal, 1998). In another way, majority character identification with no or minimal error will ensure more than 90% of efficiency alone. Many characters of Bengali script have a horizontal line at the upper part called '*matra*' or headline. A Bengali text may be partitioned into three zones shown in Figure 1. The upper zone denotes the portion above the headline, the middle zone covers the portion of basic characters or compound characters below the headline and lower zone is the portion where some of the modifiers can reside.

Some common properties in Bengali language are given below (Chaudhuri & Pal, 1998; Das et al., 2010):

- Bengali script flows from left to right.
- Characters are not classified as uppercase or lowercase.
- A vowel with a consonant takes a modified shape known as vowel modifier.
- A consonant with a consonant takes a modified shape known as consonant modifier.
- The vowel (অ) always occurs at the beginning of the word.
- There are about 250 compound characters.
- Many characters have a "*matra*" or headline with them. Some characters have a signature extended above the headline (e.g. ই, ঈ, উ).
- In a standard text piece, 95.63% percent of the characters are basic characters and the rest 4.27 percent are compound characters.

Figure 1. Partitioning line into zones

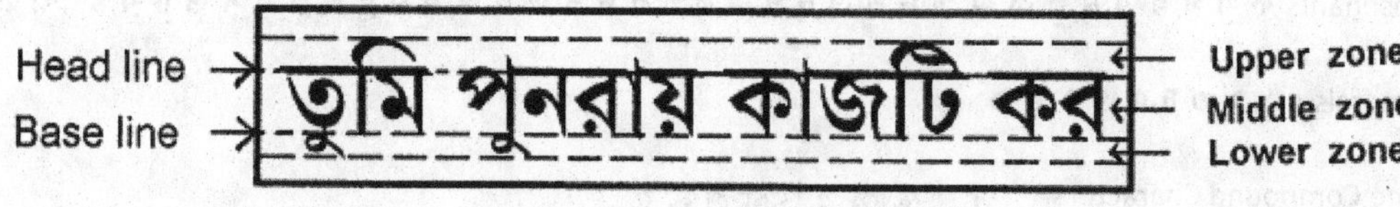

1.3. The Importance of Feature Selection

Generally, a pattern recognition system involves image acquisition phase, followed by image conversion to suitable format, noise elimination, segmentation, feature extraction, classification, and post processing (see Figure 2).

As stated in the first part of introduction that most of the authors, when faced with solving the OCR problem, developed a complete OCR. A part of the literature sets devoted on classification problem of handwritten scripts while another group worked to find solution for printed documents. In most of the cases, isolated characters

Figure 2. Steps in a pattern recognition system

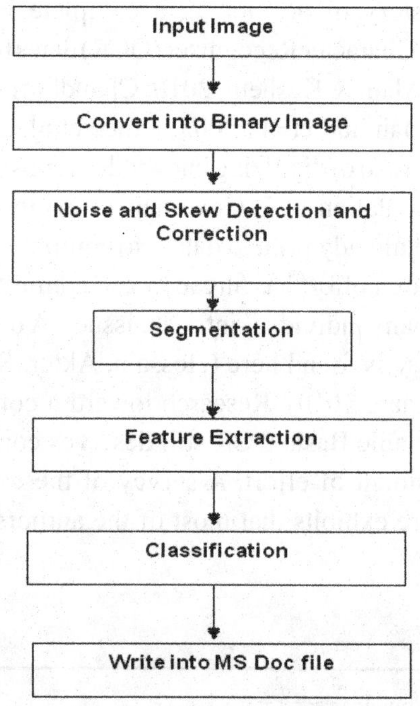

were extracted from segmentation. During feature selection phase, different authors have selected features from different perspectives. These features were later fed to the classifier of choice. A brief summary of all the phases of a complete Bangla OCR is given below.

Initially, a scanned document is converted into binary form. Many existing algorithms are able to solve the image binarization issue and the noise elimination issues. Usually digitized images in gray tone (256 level) is converted into two-tone images. A histogram-based thresholding approach is used (Pal & Chaudhuri, 2000). A specific Noise elimination algorithm using features of Bangla script have been proposed in (Chaudhuri & Pal, 1998). Use of Kapur, Sahoo and Won, Otsu algorithms has also been found in literature. So far, any special implementation of de-noising algorithm for Bangla Language has not been found. For skew detection and correction, a good number of effective algorithms are available based on projection profile, Hough transform, Docstrum, and line correlation. Matra or Head Line is a characteristic element that makes the writing of skew detection algorithm easier than that used for any other language (Chaudhuri & Pal, 1997, 1998).

A literature review suggests that segmentation process has been approached in various ways. The goal of segmentation is very clear. Best segmentation should be described the way which gives the shape of each character undistorted and in an isolated fashion. The task of separating each vowel or consonant would not have been so difficult if there were no vowel or consonant modifiers, no compound or touching characters. Modifiers take special shapes with the attaching character and many of them share the same vertical region with the main character. Some characters have upper parts, a part which exists above the headline/*matra* of a word, Figure 3. To make things complicated these might overlap with the modifiers, Figure 3b.

Figure 3. (a) The character has an upper part over the matra line, (b) overlapping of characters and modifiers on same vertical space, (c) disconnected component – a point below the character

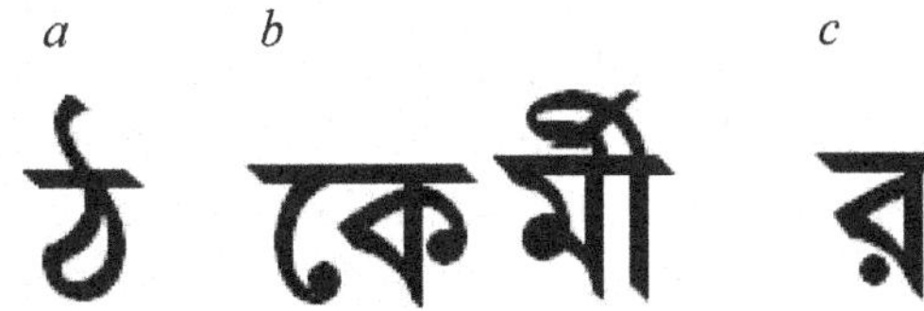

Many of the character have some disconnected components, Figure 3c. This chapter does not deal with the segmentation process. The reader is suggested to go through Abdullah & Rahman, 2003; Akter et al., 2008; Bhowmik et al., 2005; Hasnat & Khan, 2009; Roy et al., 2005; Shukla et al., 2011. In general, most of the authors have considered isolated character recognition system.

In order to perform the recognition process, feature identification is an eventual process after segmentation. This part is the only component of an OCR which has to deal with the specific peculiarities of the shape of each character. So naturally, authors have suggested many different features in their corresponding works. Among all the papers on both printed and handwritten characters, the major features identified are curvature based stroke features (Dutta & Chaudhury, 1993), linear stroke features (Chaudhuri, & Pal, 1998), shadow, longest run (Das N., Das B., Sarkar, Basu, Kundu & Nasipuri, 2010), quad tree based center of gravity (Das N. et al., 2010), chain code (Alam & Kashem, 2010), curvelet coefficient (Dutta & Chaudhury, 1993), structural or topological feature (Dutta & Chaudhury, 1993), fuzzy feature (Hoque & Rahman, 2007), the binary image itself, etc.

The last stage of recognition system is the classifier itself. Many different classifiers are available on the net now. It is the designer's choice which classifier he is really interested to work with. Still now, no such write-up is available which shows a comparative analysis of different classification scheme in the context of Bengali script classification. Different authors have chosen classifiers with feature of their choice. No attempts so far have been noted where a new classifier or a modified classifier has been used. In all the cases, existing and established classifier algorithms have been used. To date, used classifiers are MLP classifier used for both handwritten and printed character (Basu et al., 2005; Bhattacharya et al., 2002; Bhowmik et al., 2004), Kohonen network (Chowdhury & Saha, 2005b; Shatil & Khan, 2006), ANN (Alam & Kashem, 2010; Barman et al., 2010; Bhowmik et al., 2005; Chowdhury & Saha, 2005a; Sarowar et al., 2009), decision tree (Chaudhuri & Pal, 1998; Pal & Chaudhuri, 2000), NN for handwritten numeral only (Bhattacharya et al., 2002b; Islam et al., 2005;Mahmud et al., 2003), Genetic Algorithm for handwritten digit (Alam & Anwer, 2005), Hamming Network (Hasan et al., 2005), Nearest Subspace Classifier (Majumdar & Ward, 2009), Hidden Markov Model for Handwritten character (Parui et al., 2008), SVM for handwritten character (Das N. et al., 2010).

2. TYPES OF FEATURES

There are many types of features authors have proposed. Some of the features have been used for handwritten scripts, while some others have been used for printed characters. Here a compilation of most of the features is given.

2.1. Stroke Feature: Curvature-Based

A stroke is a set of dark pixels such that for all except two of its members there are two dark neighbors from among the members of the set itself (see Figure 4).

A stroke consists of one or more segments. A segment is also a set of dark pixels. Except two pixels, all the other pixels have two dark neighbors from the same set. Of those two pixels, at least one has a junction. There will be no other junction pixel. A junction is a dark pixel, which has at least three dark 8-neighbors. A character may be represented in terms of the structural constraints imposed by junction points and the primitives/segments meeting at junctions. A stroke generates eight feature vectors. Detailed calculation will be found in Pal & Chaudhuri (2000). Values are:

Figure 4. DE, AC, BC are segments; ACB, DE are strokes; DEG is a loop; C and D are junctions (Das et al., 2010)

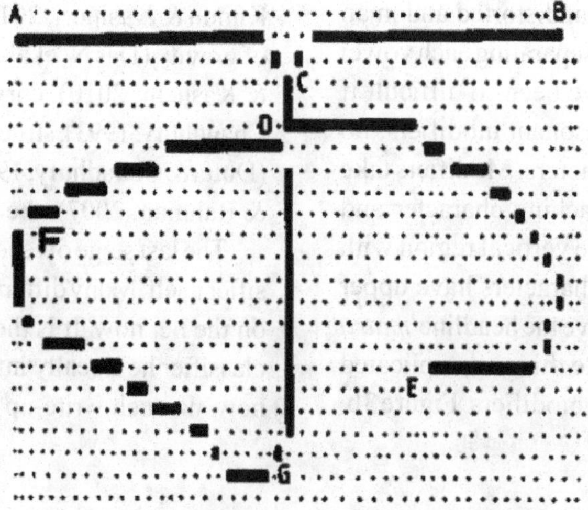

1. Number of points of curvature maxima: If the curvature of a point along a stroke is greater (in magnitude) than that of its two immediate neighbors on both sides, the count of curvature maxima is increased by one.
2. Number of points of curvature minima: If the curvature of a point along a stroke is less (in magnitude) than that of its two immediate neighbors on both sides, the count of curvature minima is increased by one.
3. Number of points of inflexion from –ve to +ve curvature: For each pixel of a stroke, a count is incremented if its two predecessor points' curvature is non-negative and non-zero and two successor points' curvature is non-positive and non-zero.
4. Number of points of inflexion from +ve to –ve curvature: For each pixel of a stroke, a count is incremented if its two predecessor points' curvature is non-positive and non-zero and two successor points' curvature is non-negative and non-zero.
5. Normalized positions with respect to the stroke-length for the points considered in 1 (Number of components=4).
6. Normalized positions with respect to the stroke-length for the points considered in 2 (Number of components=4).
7. Normalized positions with respect to the stroke-length for the points considered in 3 (Number of components=4).
8. Normalized positions with respect to the stroke-length for the points considered in 4 (Number of components=4).

2.2. Stroke Feature: Mostly Linear

Chaudhuri and Pal (1998) have elaborated another way of identifying strokes from a character. These stroke features are mostly linear in structure. A total of 8 stroke features have been used here shown in the ninth figure. The information of existence or non-existence of these strokes are used in classification. These strokes are described below:

1. A horizontal continuous line over the character, known as a *matra*, and assumed to occupy 75% of character width.
2. A vertical continuous line assumed to occupy approximately 75% of the character middle zone.
3. A diagonal line along +45° with horizontal, occupies 40% of the height of middle zone.
4. A diagonal line in the lower half part of middle zone along 45° direction.
5. Existence of both stroke 3 and stroke 4.
6. Length of the arms is assumed to be 30% of the width of the middle zone of the character, and the angle between them is 315°.
7. Stroke 7 is a cup-shaped feature where the bottom of the cup touches the base line.
8. A combination of stroke 1 and stroke 2, whose length is 40% of the height of the middle zone.
9. It is in the lower part of the middle zone.

Here, the stroke lengths are standardized with respect to the character middle zone height because this height is constant for characters of single font and size.

Figure 5. Strokes as proposed in Bhowmik et al. (2005)

2.3. Shadow Features

Nibaran et al used shadow features in recognizing handwritten bangle basic and compound character (Das N. et al., 2010). Here, an image box is divided into 8 octants as shown in Figure 5. On each side of an octant, length of projection of the image is calculated. Thus 24 shadow features are extracted from each digit image. These values are normalized by dividing the maximum possible length of projection on a particular side (see Figure 6).

2.4. Longest Run Features

Along with shadow features, Nibaran et al. also used longest run features (Das N. et al., 2010). Within a rectangular image region of a character, longest run features are computed row wise, column wise and two major diagonal wise. Row-wise longest run feature corresponds to the sum of the lengths of the longest bars of consecutive dark pixels along each of all the rows of the region. The three other longest-run features within the rectangle are computed in the same way. Each of the longest run feature values is to be normalized by dividing it with the product of the height (h) and the width (w) of the entire image (see Figure 7).

2.5. Quad-Tree-Based Feature

A quad-tree is a tree data structure in which each node except the leaf nodes has up to four children. A character pattern is subdivided into 4 regions. Horizontal and vertical lines are drawn through the Center of Gravity (CG) of black pixels in that region. The coordinates of the CG of any image frame, (Cx, Cy), is calculated as follows:

$$C_x = \frac{1}{mn}\sum_{mn} x.f(x,y);\; C_y = \frac{1}{mn}\sum_{mn} y.f(x,y)$$

Figure 6. An illustration for shadow features

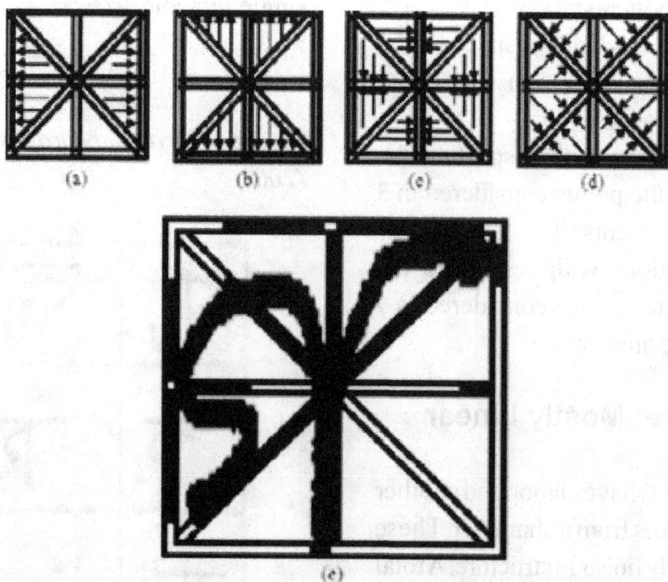

Figure 7. An illustration for computation of the longest–run feature

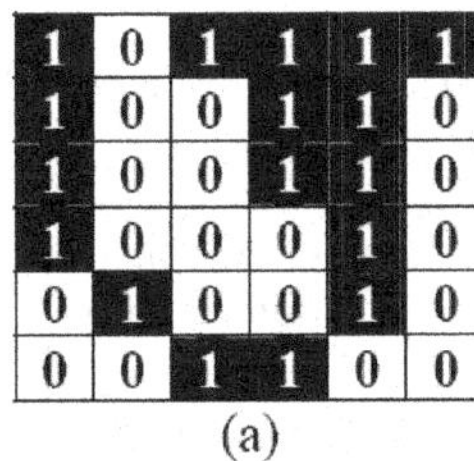

1	0	1	1	1	1
1	0	0	1	1	0
1	0	0	1	1	0
1	0	0	0	1	0
0	1	0	0	1	0
0	0	1	1	0	0

(a)

						Length of the Longest Bar
1	0	4	4	4	4	4
1	0	0	2	2	0	2
1	0	0	2	2	0	2
1	0	0	0	1	0	1
0	1	0	0	1	0	1
0	0	2	2	0	0	2
					Sum =	12

(b)

where x and y are the pixel coordinates of an image of size m x n pixels. Both equal partitioning and CG based partitioning may be used to generate quad-tree. Graphical illustration is shown in Figure 8.

2.6. Structural and Topological Features

In recognizing Bangla numerals, Bhattacharya *et al.* (2002a, 2002b) have used the topological feature set for handwritten Bengali numerals. Numerals are represented as graphs. Different parts or units of the graphs, such as, junction, terminal vertex, lowest vertex, lowest terminal vertex, open arm, right open arm, cycle volume, character height, cycle centroid and some more have been used in order to calculate the feature

Figure 8. Quad tree features

(a) Sample images	(b) Equal Partitioning	(c) CG based partitioning of depth 2

Figure 9. Structural features

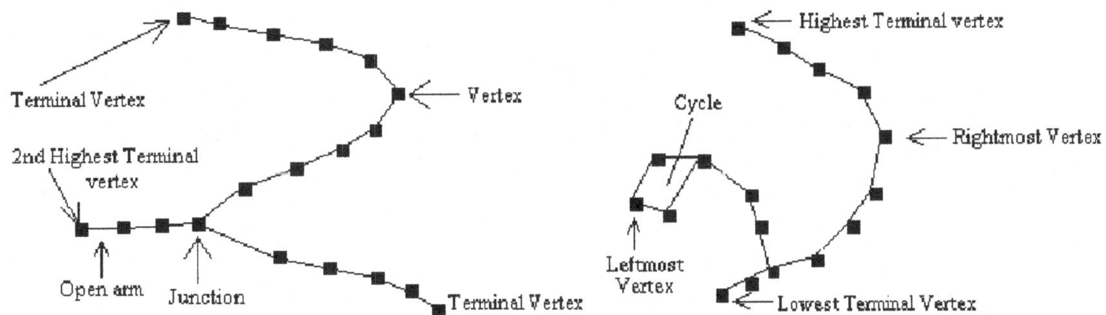

Figure 10. Structural feature vectors

Notation	Description
$HD1$	The horizontal distance between the junction and lowest terminal vertex normalized with respect to character width; (If there exists more than one junction, we consider the lowest such junction).
$HD2$	Horizontal distance between the highest terminal vertex and the lowest terminal vertex normalized with respect to character width; (If there exists only one terminal vertex, this distance is assumed to be zero).
$HD3$	Horizontal distance between the highest terminal vertex and the second highest terminal vertex normalized w.r.t. character width; (If there exists only one terminal vertex, this distance is assumed to be zero).
Vol	Cycle volume
$SgnM$	This variable takes the value -1 if the cycle centroid is situated to the left of the junction; else, it takes the value +1. If any one of the cycle or junction is not unique, then we consider the lowest such objects.
$DistR$	Dist. between the rightmost vertex and the rightmost terminal vertex.
$GradR$	Slope of right open arm.
$GradL$	Slope of left open arm.

vectors shown in Figure 9. A list of important feature vectors with definition are found in Figure 10.

2.7. Watershed

Pal and Chaudhuri (2000) have used water-flow model from the concept of water overflow. They have used it to find features of hand-written numerals. The principle is, if we pour water from the above of numeral, the position where water is stored as reservoir, the shape of the reservoir as hole, etc are noticed (Figure 11). Feature vectors found from this model are:

1. Existence of holes and its number.
2. Position of holes with respect to its bounding box.
3. Ration of hole length to height of the numerals.
4. Center of gravity of the holes.

Figure 11. Features using water flow model

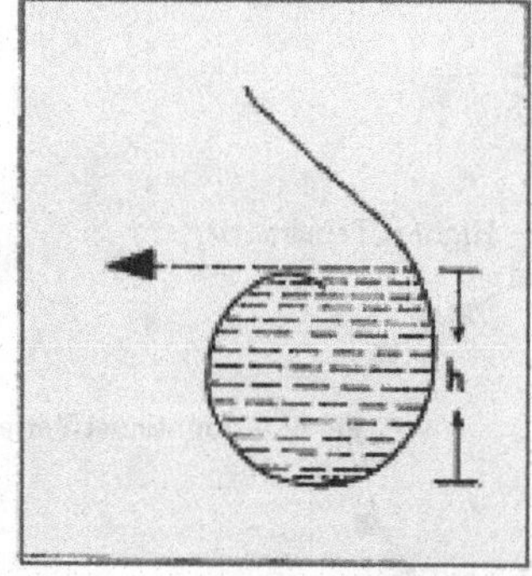

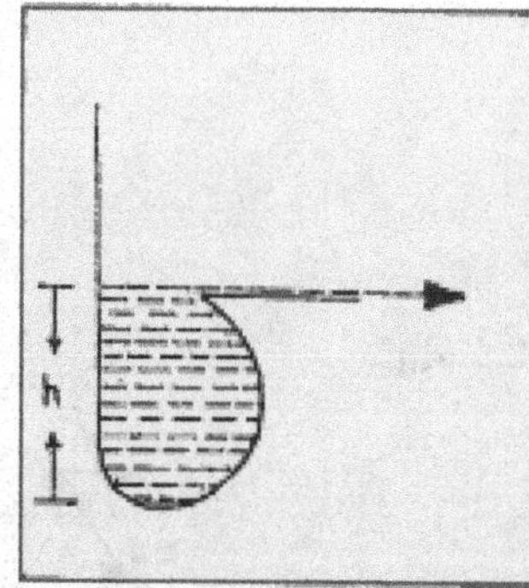

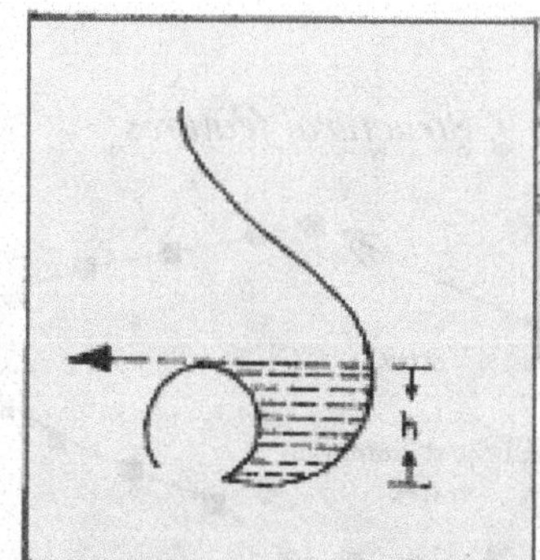

5. Number of crossings in a particular region of the numeral.
6. Convexity of holes, etc.

2.8. Chain Code

Mahmud et al. (2003) and also Alam and Kashem (2010) used chain code to extract feature for connected components of Bengali characters. Each connected component has been divided into four regions indicating four quadrants in 2D geometric system. There are several chain code convention used for image representation, but the most popular one is Freeman chain code. Freeman chain code is based on the observation that each pixel has eight neighborhood pixels (see Figure 12).

A connected component is divided into 4 regions by a horizontal and a vertical line that go through the center of mass. In each zone, contour of the connected component is traversed. The frequency of each directional slope is counted. There are 8 directional slopes in a region, shown in Figure 11. As a result, in total, 32 directional slopes are found. These 32 values are the feature vectors, which are normalized by dividing them with square root of the sum of squares of all feature values.

Figure 12. Slope convention for Freeman chain code

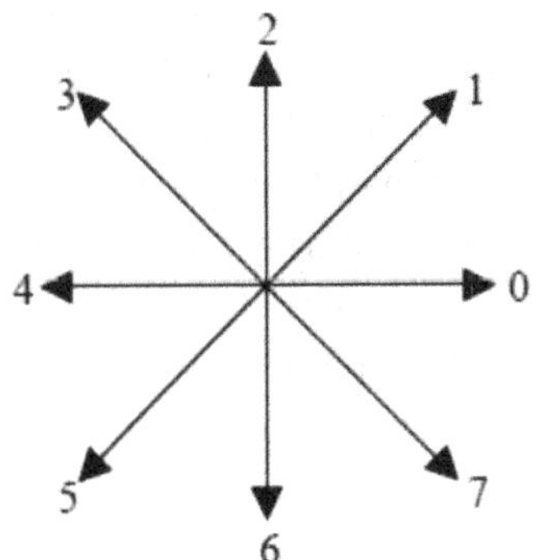

2.9. Concatenated Strokes

Bhowmik, Bhattacharya, and Parui (2004) have proposed a stroke-based feature set for recognizing Bengali handwritten character images. Vertical and horizontal strokes are identified and characterized with 10 features. If there are 6 points in a stroke including the terminal points, that is P_0, P_1, P_2, P_3, P_4, P_5, P_6, then the feature values for each curve/stroke C are:

1. Θ_i (i =1..6), 6 angles created by the lines $P_{i-1}P_i$.
2. Degree of linearity L_1 - A ratio between Euclidean distance between P_0 and P_6 and curve length of C.
3. C_X, C_Y – Center of gravity of the positions of the pixels in C.

2.10. Curvelet Coefficient

Majumdar (2007) has introduced a new feature extraction method based on the curvelet transform of morphologically altered versions of an original character image. Curvelets are known to provide a very good representation of edges in an image. By thinning or thickening an image morphologically, the position of the edges can be changed. Five versions of an image is used during recognition, where one image is the original one, two are thickened images and rest two are thinned images. The variation in position of edges are encoded in the transformed domain. Curvelet coefficients for the five versions are classified using k-NN classifiers. The main idea behind using this scheme is that if a character is failed to be recognized in its original form from its edge information, it may be recognized if the edge positions are slightly varied. Detailed discussion on curvelet transformation can be found in (Majumdar, 2007). Transformation scheme of an image into frequency domain is shown in Figure 13.

Figure 13. Scheme for pictorial ridgelet transform

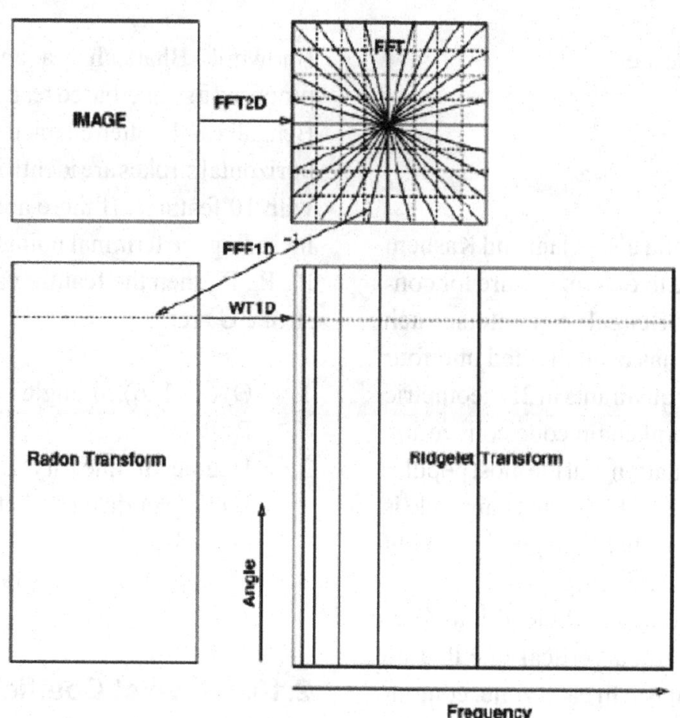

2.11. Some Other Features

Some authors have chosen other types of features which are very easy to compute. Here, each character has been reduced to an image of 16x16 matrix. Then each pixel value is converted into a 0 or a 1, i.e., A pixel is replaced with 0 if it's value is less than a certain threshold value.

Another group has segmented a word or character image into frames. Discrete Cosine Transformation has been done on these frames and the transformed values have been used as feature values. A transformation scheme is shown in Figure 13.

2.12. Proposed Structural Feature: Existential

Here we are proposing some existential features. Existential features are basically different types of stroke features, which are described below:

1. **Existence of Matra:** A horizontal line of dark pixel at the upper zone of the character image and covering 80% of the width of character (e.g ক, ছ, ফ, ষ, ছ, ষ, ন, ছ, চ). It can be detected through Horizontal Projection Count (HPC) at upper part of the character.
2. **First Right Side Bar:** A vertical continuous line assumed to occupy approximately 80% of the character middle zone and exists within the rightmost 20% columns (e.g. ণ, য, ম, ন). It can be detected through Vertical Projection Count (VPC) of first 20% columns, starting from left most position and

compare the VPC values with a predefined threshold value (80% of middle zone height).

3. **Left Side Bar:** A vertical continuous line assumed to occupy approximately 80% of the character middle zone and exists within the leftmost 20% columns (e.g. চ, ট, ঢ, ঢ়, ন,). Detecting technique same as first right side bar, but starting from left most character position.
4. **Middle Bar:** A vertical continuous line assumed to occupy approximately 80% of the character middle zone and exists within the central 40% columns. It can also be detected through Vertical Projection Count (VPC) and compare the VPC values with a predefined threshold value (80% of middle zone height) and search should be limited within 40% of central columns (e.g. ঐ, ক, ঞ, ফ).
5. **Loop with Matra:** A closed loop that has two junctions with matra. Distance between the two junctions is assumed to 80% of the character width. It is easy to detect loop with matra by searching two connection points with matra with a minimum threshold distance (80% of character width) between two junction points (e.g., য, ম, স).
6. **Left Side Bottom to Top Curve:** Existence of a curve that starts from top left corner and gradually shifted to right up to bottom point of a character. This property is detected by left projection profiles. From near left top positions, left profile gradually decrease up to bottom of the character (i.e., অ, আ, উ, ঊ, ও, ঔ, ঙ, জ, ড, ত, ভ, ড়).
7. **Left Side Triangle Shape:** Applicable for characters, which have no left side bar. Using left projection Profile, it should be checked whether the character has a mount at middle of left side and gradually deeper to ward above and below (i.e., ক, ঝ, ব, র).
8. **Having Upper Part:** Whether any part is above the matra line (i.e., ই, ঈ, উ, ঊ, ঐ, ট, ঠ). Most of character upper part starts from right portion of the character.

2.13. Proposed Structural Feature: Calculated

Some more features have been proposed here. This feature values need are calculated by observing the morphology of a character. Some are described below:

1. **Left Projection Profile (LPP):** Projection from left side of the character. Feature is measured by counting the number of non-black pixel until reaching starting left side portion of the character for all rows.
2. **Right Projection Profile (RPP):** Projection from right side of the character. Feature is measured by counting the number of non-black pixel until reaching starting right side portion of the character for all rows.
3. **Horizontal Projection Count (HPC):** Number of black pixels in each row (list of number is generated).
4. **Vertical Projection Count (VPC):** Number of black pixels in each column (list of number is generated).
5. **Quadratic Center of Mass (QCOM):** Determining the centre of mass for the whole character and centre of mass for four equal parts of the character.
6. **Vertical Aspect Ratio (VAR):** Measure the ratio of character height with middle zone height.

3. OPTIMAL FEATURE IDENTIFICATION

Many different segmentation schemes have been proposed. The main objective of a good segmentation scheme is to separate each unit of character or modifier intact. There are 50 basic characters, 10+ vowel and consonant modifiers, and 270 compound characters. Compared to English language, total number of each character is 340 in number while English may contain maximum 61 characters. So at the outset, the problem of classifying Bangla characters becomes a large problem. The idea of classification has been proposed by various authors in several ways. However, a little observation suggests that a two phased classification scheme reduces the problem size within a manageable level. Eventually a better performance may be assumed. In the first phase of this scheme, isolated characters are grouped in clusters. Where each cluster contains several characters having similar morphology. As a result one may conclude that an effective classifier will be composed of two phases. The first phase will break up a bigger part into smaller ones. Existential type of features may be used to create the clusters. Usually, features, which show little or no change with the variation of font type, size and shapes, are taken as existential feature. In the second stage more rigorous classification is required. Here one can use Artificial Neural Network, SVM, HMM or even simple Nearest Neighbor Classifier. Whatever the tools used for classification, a better result may be anticipated only when the features collected from a character image varies less with the variation in font size, type, or shapes. Selection of features may be based on some of the points mentioned below.

- **Thinning Independence:** Thinning is a process which have been used by some author. The purpose of thinning is to create a character that contains a broader width for each stroke. Some feature values may become dependent on thinned or thickened character. It should be noted that a thinning independent feature may avoid the process of thinning, thereby, reducing the time required in the process of thinning.
- **Computational Complexity:** This is another parameter which might be a matter of concern. For example, an algorithm that produces features at a cost of more time compared to another algorithm that produces a less qualified feature at an equivalent time period should be taken for consideration. Of course, the differential ability of those features also should be taken care of.
- **Usage During Classification:** Features should be chosen depending on their use in the classification scheme. For example, in the first phase of classification where only clusters are identified and where a decision tree can be the choice of tool, a feature capable enough to distinguish two clusters of similar characters, known as Existential Feature, can be used easily. But, in the second phase, features having numerical values are more preferred.

It is an exhaustive task to find out the optimal set of features. Here, we have shown a principle for selection, which may be used in order to find the best set of features for a Bangla OCR. Both the existential features and value center features have been considered.

3.1. Choice of Existential Features

In Figure 14, some existential features have been evaluated for a set of basic characters. The features are

- Existence of *matra* over a character (used as Stroke 1 in Chaudhuri, & Pal, 1998).
- Existence of a middle bar (used as Stroke -2 in Chaudhuri, & Pal, 1998)
- Left facing triangular shape (used as Stroke 5 in Chaudhuri, & Pal, 1998).
- First right side bar.
- Bottom to top curve.
- Left side bar.
- Existence of an upper part.

The character অ has a *matra*. A detection algorithm has correctly found the existence of matra on this character. It is seen that different font sizes, namely 18, 19, 20, 21, 22, 23, 24, produce

Figure 14. A set of existential features

	Font Size	Matra Detect? (Stroke-1)	Middle Bar(Stroke-2)	Left Side Triangle Shape(Stroke-5)	First Right Side Bar	Bottom to top Curve	Left Side Bar	Having Upper Pat
অ	24	Y(R)	N(R)	N(R)	Y(R)	Y(R)	N(R)	N(R)
	23	Y(R)	N(R)	N(R)	Y(R)	Y(R)	N(R)	N(R)
	22	Y(R)	N(R)	N(R)	Y(R)	Y(R)	N(R)	N(R)
	21	Y(R)	N(R)	N(R)	Y(R)	Y(R)	N(R)	N(R)
	20	Y(R)	N(R)	N(R)	Y(R)	Y(R)	N(R)	N(R)
	19	Y(R)	N(R)	N(R)	Y(R)	Y(R)	N(R)	N(R)
	18	Y(R)	N(R)	N(R)	Y(R)	Y(R)	N(R)	N(R)
ঋ	24	Y(W)	Y(R)	N(W)	Y(R)	N(R)	N(R)	N(R)
	23	Y(W)	Y(R)	N(W)	Y(R)	N(R)	N(R)	N(R)
	22	Y(W)	Y(R)	N(W)	Y(R)	N(R)	N(R)	N(R)
	21	Y(W)	Y(R)	N(W)	Y(R)	N(R)	N(R)	N(R)
	20	Y(W)	Y(R)	N(W)	Y(R)	N(R)	N(R)	N(R)
	19	Y(W)	Y(R)	N(W)	Y(R)	N(R)	N(R)	N(R)
	18	Y(W)	Y(R)	N(W)	Y(R)	N(R)	N(R)	N(R)
ক	24	Y(R)	Y(R)	Y(R)	N(R)	N(R)	N(R)	N(R)
	23	Y(R)	Y(R)	Y(R)	N(R)	N(R)	N(R)	N(R)
	22	Y(R)	Y(R)	Y(R)	N(R)	N(R)	N(R)	N(R)
	21	Y(R)	Y(R)	Y(R)	N(R)	N(R)	N(R)	N(R)
	20	Y(R)	Y(R)	Y(R)	N(R)	N(R)	N(R)	N(R)
	19	Y(R)	Y(R)	Y(R)	N(R)	N(R)	N(R)	N(R)
	18	Y(R)	Y(R)	Y(R)	N(R)	N(R)	N(R)	N(R)
ট	24	Y(R)	N(R)	N(R)	N(R)	N(R)	Y(R)	Y(R)
	23	Y(R)	N(R)	N(R)	N(R)	N(R)	Y(R)	Y(R)
	22	Y(R)	N(R)	N(R)	N(R)	N(R)	Y(R)	Y(R)
	21	Y(R)	N(R)	N(R)	N(R)	N(R)	Y(R)	Y(R)
	20	Y(R)	N(R)	N(R)	N(R)	N(R)	Y(R)	Y(R)
	19	Y(R)	N(R)	N(R)	N(R)	N(R)	Y(R)	Y(R)
	18	Y(R)	N(R)	N(R)	N(R)	N(R)	Y(R)	Y(R)
ঝ	24	Y(R)	Y(R)	Y(R)	Y(R)	N(R)	N(R)	N(R)
	23	Y(R)	Y(R)	Y(R)	Y(R)	N(R)	N(R)	N(R)
	22	Y(R)	Y(R)	Y(R)	Y(R)	N(R)	N(R)	N(R)
	21	Y(R)	Y(R)	Y(R)	Y(R)	N(R)	N(R)	N(R)
	20	Y(R)	Y(R)	Y(R)	Y(R)	N(R)	N(R)	N(R)
	19	Y(R)	Y(R)	N(W)	Y(R)	N(R)	N(R)	N(R)
	18	Y(R)	Y(R)	N(W)	Y(R)	N(R)	N(R)	N(R)

correct result, shown in Figure 14 as Y(R), where Y(yes) indicates that matra exists and R indicates that the finding is right. Again when we see the character ঋ, a *matra* has been detected for all size of fonts, which is a wrong finding, mentioned as W(Wrong). We may decide that existence of matra might not always be of full proof feature.

In case of another character ঝ, left side triangular shaped stroke could not rightly be detected for 18 and 19 fonts. As a result, right (R) detection of this stroke has been done for font sizes of 20-24. From these examples it can be inferred that certain existential features have the potential to discriminate clusters of characters.

3.2. Choice of Features Having Values

Features that have numeric values can be used as input parameter for different types of classifier. However, no standard way of measuring the distinguishable capacity of these features have been proposed so far. Here we have performed some analysis on some of the features and showed their effectiveness in terms of their differentiation capacity. The features we have considered here are chain code values, quadrature center of mass values, shadow feature, and left projection profile.

3.2.1. Chain Code

In order to verify the distinguishability of chain code feature, we did some statistical analysis on some of the characters. Figure 15 shows generated chain code values for the character K, for five different font sizes. 32 chain code values for each character have been generated. Standard deviation among corresponding chain code values have been calculated, and finally the average of all the standard deviations is found, which stands at 4.18

approximately. Similar calculation is performed for characters ক, ঋ, ঝ, ট. Final average 7.65 of average of standard deviations for each character is shown in table d of Figure 15.

Later, following similar approach, another total average has been found out. This average is the standard deviation of corresponding values of chain code for each of the five characters (ক, অ, ঋ, ঝ, ট). Average deviations among the five characters have been found to be 12.19. Now, if we observe the value of average deviation of chain code values for each of the character, it is 7.65. The difference is significant.

Figure 15. (a, b) Shows the 32 chain code values for character ক; (c) average standard deviation for all 32 values of ক; (d) average of five characters within themselves and average of same five character among themselves

ক	Bold-16	0.45	0.39	0.74	0.74	0	0.04	0.1	0	0	0.54	0.63	0	0	0.07	0.02	0
ক	Bold-18	0.44	0.39	0.57	0.8	0	0.04	0.09	0	0	0.44	0.77	0	0	0.05	0	0
ক	Bold-20	0.47	0.4	0.62	0.83	0	0.03	0.09	0	0	0.37	0.74	0	0	0.13	0	0
ক	Bold-22	0.55	0.24	0.64	0.81	0	0.02	0.05	0	0	0.54	0.69	0	0	0.1	0	0
ক	Bold-24	0.49	0.49	0.37	0.75	0	0.08	0.03	0	0	0.44	0.88	0	0	0.13	0	0
Average of s.d. for each value		0.044	0.09	0.137	0.039	0	0.023	0.03	0	0	0.073	0.094	0	0	0.036	0.009	0

(a)

ক	Bold-16	0.84	0.73	0.21	0	0.11	0	0.02	0	0.29	0.12	0.02	0.63	0.03	0.05	0	0.23
ক	Bold-18	0.82	0.81	0	0	0.11	0.01	0	0	0.34	0.02	0.26	0.54	0.05	0	0.09	0.26
ক	Bold-20	0.84	0.83	0	0	0.1	0.03	0	0	0.24	0.04	0.24	0.5	0	0.03	0.09	0.23
ক	Bold-22	0.72	0.8	0	0	0.16	0	0	0	0.39	0	0.33	0.52	0.03	0	0.1	0.29
ক	Bold-24	0.83	0.73	0	0	0.19	0.03	0	0	0.21	0.09	0.29	0.46	0.02	0.1	0.03	0.47
Average of s.d. for each value		0.051	0.047	0.094	0	0.039	0.015	0.009	0	0.073	0.05	0.121	0.063	0.018	0.042	0.044	0.1

(b)

Average standard deviation of all 32 sds of ক	4.189931248

(c)

ক	4.189931248
অ	15.8115552
ঋ	4.383953295
ঝ	6.752735745
ট	7.149010438
Average deviation within chain code values of five characters, sample set 1 (ক,অ,ঋ,ঝ,ট)	7.65743719
Average deviation among chain code values of five characters, sample set 1 (ক,অ,ঋ,ঝ,ট)	12.19145029
Average deviation within chain code values of five characters, sample set 2 (অ,ক,ঠ,স,হ)	7.711969549
Average deviation among each other's corresponding chain code values of five characters, sample set 2 (অ,ক,ঠ,স,হ)	13.07021741

(d)

3.2.2. Quadratic Center of Mass (QCOM)

The effectiveness of quadratic center of mass has been analyzed here. We have calculated mass values for five samples of A shown in Figure 16. Standard deviation of the all the masses on one column have been averaged. A final average of these averages are calculated and found as 3.262. Similar calculations are performed for F, S, K, U and values found are 4.72, 3.2, 2.7, 4.19, respectively. Average value has been taken again and found to be 3.624 of these five characters.

Figure 16. (a) Shows 10 values of quadrature center of mass values for character A; (b) average standard deviation for all 10 values of A

অ	Bold-16	70	42	67	47	63	57	83	33	70	41
অ	Bold-18	68	41	64	38	61	57	77	43	69	42
অ	Bold-20	67	41	62	51	61	58	80	31	72	40
অ	Bold-22	64	42	59	47	60	59	78	27	68	38
অ	Bold-24	63	45	57	55	63	57	74	28	62	37
S.D. of Center of Mass		2.881	1.643	3.962	6.309	1.342	0.894	3.362	6.387	3.768	2.074
Average of S.D. of Center of Mass of character অ 3.262											

(a)

অ	3.262
ঋ	4.722
ঝ	3.205
ক	2.733
ট	4.198
Average deviation within quadrature center of mass values of five characters, sample set 1 **(ক,অ,ঋ,ঝ,ট)**	3.624
Average deviation among quadrature center of mass values of` five characters, sample set 1 **(ক,অ,ঋ,ঝ,ট)**	7.651
Average deviation within quadrature center of mass values of five characters, sample set 2 **(অ,ক,ঠ,স,হ)**	3.045
Average deviation among each other's corresponding quadrature center of mass values of` five characters, sample set 2 **(অ,ক,ঠ,স,হ)**	10.627

(b)

We see that the average of standard deviation, 3.624 within different font sizes of five characters is less than the average of standard deviation, 7.651 among each of the corresponding center of masses of each character. This same trend is observed for another sample set where the values are respectively 3.045 and 10.627.

3.2.3. Left Projection Profile (LPP)

Left Projection Profile feature has been calculated for two sets of samples, (K,A,F,S) and (A,K,V,m,n). Five different font sizes, 16, 18, 20, 22, 24 have been used for each of the characters.

Feature values of the character A are shown in Figure 17. The average values of standard deviation among the fifteen values of LPP for each five characters are shown in Figure 17b. The average of standard deviation of LPP values within four characters (K,A,F,S) is 8.479 and within the five characters (A,K,V,m,n) is 8.472. While the average of standard deviation among different characters are 11.172 and 18.959, respectively.

3.2.4. Shadow Features

Shadow features are generated following definition given in Das N. et al. (2010). We took two

Figure 17. (a) Shows 15 values of left projection profile values for character A; (b) average standard deviations for sample set 1 and sample set 2

অ	Bold-16	5.55	5.55	5.55	27.8	19.5	11.1	16.7	19.4	22.2	27.8	44.5	61.1	61.1	63.9	66.7
অ	Bold-18	6.66	6.66	6.66	21	25.6	24.1	56.9	20	56.9	34.4	30.8	54.9	80	81	86.7
অ	Bold-20	5.78	5.78	9.78	11.6	13.8	17.3	17.8	23.1	28.4	33.3	59.6	77.8	80.9	81.8	86.7
অ	Bold-22	5.83	5.83	10.8	11.7	11.7	15.4	20.8	23.3	25.8	33.3	52.5	82.9	87.5	87.9	93.3
অ	Bold-24	8.63	6.27	6.27	6.27	8.23	12.5	15.3	18.8	22.4	29	40	81.6	99.2	100	106
Average		0.929	1.847	7.242	7.343	5.7	13.23	12.11	11.23	9.957	10.61	17.84	13.66	12.78	13.24	14.32

(a)

অ	10.136
ঋ	7.824
ঝ	9.382
ক	6.574
Average deviation within Left Projection Profile values of five characters, sample set 1 (ক,অ,ঋ,ঝ)	8.479
Average deviation among Left Projection Profile values of` five characters, sample set 1 (ক,অ,ঋ,ঝ)	11.172
Average deviation within Left Projection Profile values of five characters, sample set 2 (অ,ক,ঠ,স,হ)	8.472
Average deviation among each other's corresponding Left Projection Profile values of` five characters, sample set 2 (অ,ক,ঠ,স,হ)	18.959

(b)

sample sets as above and generated twenty-four features for each character of 5 font sizes each. The first set generated an average standard deviation of 1.665 within feature values of same character. The second set generated 1.822. Average standard deviation among feature values of different characters for sample set 1 is found to be 4.007. This value has been found to be 5.459 for sample set 2. Values are shown in Figure 18.

Figure 18. Average standard deviation calculated for two different sets of samples

অ	1.289
ঋ	2.026
ঝ	1.581
ক	1.513
ট	1.916
Average deviation within Shadow Feature values of five characters, sample set 1 (ক,অ,ঋ,ঝ,ট)	1.665
Average deviation among Shadow Feature values of five characters, sample set 1 (ক,অ,ঋ,ঝ,ট)	4.007
Average deviation within Shadow Feature Profile values of five characters, sample set 2 (অ,ক,ঠ,স,হ)	1.822
Average deviation among each other's corresponding Left Projection Profile values of five characters, sample set 2 (অ,ক,ঠ,স,হ)	5.459

Figure 19. Summary results for sample set 1 and sample set 2

	Sample Characters	Feature averages of individual Characters	For Different Characters	Difference Bet two S.D.	
Chain Code:	অ ঋ ক ঝ ট	7.657437	12.19145	4.534013	(1st Highest Difference)
Quadrate Centre of Mass:	অ ঋ ক ঝ ট	3.624591	7.651633	4.027042	(2nd Highest Difference)
Left Projection Profile :	অ ঋ ক ঝ	8.479407	11.17337	2.693964	(3rd Highest Difference)
Shadow Features	অ ঋ ক ঝ ট	1.665653	4.007753	2.34	(4th Highest Difference)
	Sample Characters	Feature averages of individual Characters	For Different Characters	Difference Bet two S.D.	
chain Code	অ ক ঠ স হ	7.71197	13.07022	5.358248	(3rd Highest Difference)
Quadrate Centre of Mass:	অ ক ঠ স হ	3.045183	10.62761	7.582426	(2nd Highest Difference)
Left Projection Profile:	অ ক ঠ স হ	8.47247	18.95996	10.48749	(1st Highest Difference)
Shadow Features::	অ ক ঠ স হ	1.822356	5.459128	3.636772	(4th Highest Difference)

3.2.5. Results Analysis

Existential features are easily computable. Moreover, these features can be generated during the segmentation procedure, so no extra effort is required to produce these values. Later, we have tried to understand the variability of features. In order to get that proper understanding, we first found the standard deviation of corresponding feature values of one character having different font sizes. These standard deviations of all the features have been averaged. It is expected that a good feature set should produce a small average deviation. A low value indicates that the variability of corresponding feature values for different font sizes is less, that is, feature values does not vary too much with varying font sizes. On the contrary, our expectation is that the same measurement taking two different characters should produce a higher value of standard deviation among the feature values. A larger value indicates that corresponding feature values for two different characters have a greater difference compared to the difference between the feature values of different font sizes. A larger difference among feature values of different characters will make it easier to use them in any classifier. The summary results are shown in Figure 19. It is found that for sample set 1 (A F K S U), chain code produces the best feature values, confirmed by observing the first highest difference between two standard deviations. In case of sample set 2 (A K V m n), we find that the best set of distinguishable feature is produced by LPP, which is confirmed by observing the highest difference between the averaged standard deviation.

4. CONCLUSION

We have extensively reviewed most of the feature sets so far found in the literature involved to develop a complete OCR for Bangla script. A test of variability among feature values have been performed on some chosen features. Existential features show effective way of clustering similar shaped characters into one group. Other features, produced by different algorithms, exhibits efficiency for certain set of character. From this observation, it can be concluded that, before going into developing an OCR employing a certain classification scheme, one should first choose a set of distinguishable features.

REFERENCES

Abdullah, A. B. M., & Rahman, A. (2003). A survey on script segmentation for Bangla OCR: An implementation perspective. In *Proceedings of 6th International Conference on Computer and Information Technology (ICCIT),* (pp. 856-860). ICCIT.

Akter, N., Hossain, S., Islam, M. T., & Sarwar, H. (2008). An algorithm for segmenting modifiers from Bangla text. In *Proceedings of 11th International Conference on Computer and Information Technology (ICCIT),* (pp. 177 - 182). Khulna, Bangladesh: ICCIT.

Alam, M. M., & Anwer, M. (2005). Feature subset selection using genetic algorithm for Bengali handwritten digit recognition. In *Proceedings of the National Conference on Computer Processing of Bangla,* (pp. 258-263). Independent University.

Alam, M. M., & Kashem, D. M. A. (2010). A complete Bangla OCR system for printed characters. *Journal of Computer and Information Technology, 1*(1), 30–35.

Barman, S., Samanta, A. K., Kim, T., & Bhattacharya, D. (2010). Design of a view based approach for Bengali character recognition. *International Journal of Advanced Science and Technology, 15*(2), 49–62.

Basu, S., Das, N., Sarker, R., Kundu, M., Nasipuri, M., & Kumar, B. D. (2005). Handwritten Bangla alphabet recognition using an MLP based classifier. In *Proceedings of the 2nd National Conference on Computer Processing of Bangla (NCCPB),* (pp. 285-291). Independent University.

Bhattacharya, U., Das, T. K., Datta, A., Parui, S. K., & Chaudhuri, B. B. (2002). A hybrid scheme for handprinted numeral recognition based on a self-organizing network and MLP classifiers. *International Journal of Pattern Recognition and Artificial Intelligence, 16*(7), 845–864. doi:10.1142/S0218001402002027.

Bhattacharya, U., Das, T. K., Datta, A., Parui, S. K., & Chaudhuri, B. B. (2002). Recognition of handprinted Bangla numerals using neural network models. In N.R. Pal & M. Sugeno (Eds.), *Proceedings of the 2002 AFSS International Conference on Fuzzy Systems,* (vol. 2275, pp. 228-235). Calcutta: Springer.

Bhowmik, T. K., Bhattacharya, U., & Parui, S. K. (2004). Recognition of Bangla handwritten characters using an MLP classifier based on stroke features. In *Proceedings of the International Conference on Neural Information Processing,* (pp. 814-819). Kolkata, India: Springer.

Bhowmik, T. K., Roy, A., & Roy, U. (2005). Character segmentation for handwritten Bangla words using artificial neural network. In *Proceedings of International Workshop on Neural Networks and Learning in Document Analysis and Recognition,* (pp. 28-32). IEEE.

Chaudhuri, B. B., & Pal, U. (1997). Skew angle detection of digitized Indian script documents. *IEEE Transactions on Pattern Analysis and Machine Intelligence, 19*(2), 182–186. doi:10.1109/34.574803.

Chaudhuri, B. B., & Pal, U. (1998). A complete printed Bangla OCR system. *Pattern Recognition, 31*(5), 531–549. doi:10.1016/S0031-3203(97)00078-2.

Chowdhury, N., & Saha, D. (2005a). A neural network based text classification method: A possible application for bengali text classification. In *Proceedings of the National Conference on Computer Processing of Bangla,* (pp. 183-188). Independent University.

Chowdhury, N., & Saha, D. (2005b). Bengali text classification using Kohonen's self organizing network. In *Proceedings of the National Conference on Computer Processing of Bangla* (pp. 196-200). Independent University.

Das, N., Das, B., Sarkar, R., Basu, S., Kundu, M., & Nasipuri, M. (2010). Handwritten Bangla basic and compound character recognition using MLP and SVM classifier. *Journal of Computing, 2*(2), 109–115.

Dutta, A., & Chaudhury, S. (1993). Bengali alpha-numeric character recognition using curvature features. *Pattern Recognition, 26*(12), 1757–1770. doi:10.1016/0031-3203(93)90174-U.

Hasan, M. A. M., Alim, M. A., & Islam, M. W. (2005). A new approach to Bangla text extraction and recognition from textual image. In *Proceedings of the 8th International Conference on Computer and Information Technology* (pp. 1 – 5). IEEE.

Hasnat, M. A., & Khan, M. (2009). Rule based segmentation of lower modifiers in complex Bangla scripts. In *Proceedings on the Conference on Language and Technology* (pp. 94-101). National University of Computer and Emerging Sciences.

Hoque, M. M., & Rahman, S. M. F. (2007). Fuzzy features extraction from Bangla handwriten character. In *Proceedings of the International Conference on Information and Communication Technology (ICICT)* (pp. 72-75). Dhaka, Bangladesh: ICICT.

Hossain, S., Akter, N., Sarwar, H., & Rahman, C. M. (2010). Development of a recognizer for Bangla text: Present status and future challenges. In Mori, M. (Ed.), *Character Recognition* (pp. 83–112). InTech.

Islam, M. W., Hasan, M. A. M., & Debanath, R. C. (2005). Handwritten Bangla numerical recognition using back-propagation algorithm with and without momentum factor. In *Proceedings of the National Conference on Computer Processing of Bangla* (pp. 177-182). Independent University.

Mahmud, J. U., Raihan, M. F., & Rahman, C. M. (2003). A complete OCR for continuous Bengali characters. In *Proceedings of the IEEE Tencon, Conference on Convergent Technologies for the Asia-Pacific* (pp. 1372-1376). Bangalore, India: IEEE.

Majumdar, A. (2007). Bangla basic character recognition using digital curvelet transform. *Journal of Pattern Recognition Research, 2*(1), 17–26.

Majumdar, A., & Ward, R. K. (2009). Nearest subspace classifier: Application to character recognition. In *Proceedings of the International Conference on Image Processing*. IEEE.

Omee, F. Y., Himel, S. S., & Bikas, M. A. N. (2011). A complete workflow for development of Bangla OCR. *International Journal of Computers and Applications, 21*(9), 1–6. doi:10.5120/2543-3483.

Pal, U., & Chaudhuri, B. B. (2000). Automatic recognition of unconstrained off-line Bangla handwritten numerals. In T. Tan, Y. Shi, & W. Gao (Eds.), *International Conference on Multimodal Interfaces* (LNCS), (vol. 1948, pp. 371-378). Springer-Verlag.

Parui, S. K., Guin, K., Bhattacharya, U., & Chaudhuri, B. B. (2008). Online handwritten Bangla character recognition using HMM. In *Proceedings of the 19th International Conference on Pattern Recognition* (pp. 1-4). Tampa, FL: IEEE.

Roy, A., Bhowmik, T. K., Parui, S. K., & Roy, U. (2005). A novel approach to skew detection and character segmentation for handwritten Bangla words. In *Proceedings of the Digital Imaging Computing: Techniques and Applications*. IEEE.

Sarowar, G., Naser, M. A., Nizamuddin, S. M., Hamid, N. I. B., & Mahmud, A. (2009). Enhancing Bengali character recognition process applying heuristics on neural network. *International Journal of Computer Science and Network Security, 9*(6), 154–158.

Shatil, A. M. S., & Khan, M. (2006). Minimally segmenting high performance Bangla OCR using Kohonen network. In *Proceedings of 9th International Conference on Computer and Information Technology* (pp. 160-164). Dhaka, Bangladesh: IEEE.

Shukla, M. K., Patnaik, T., Tiwari, S., & Singh, D. S. K. (2011). Script segmentation of printed Devnagari and Bangla languages document images OCR. *International Journal of Computer Science and Technology, 2*(2), 367–370.

Chapter 6
Bangla Character Recognition Using Optical Joint Transform Correlation

Mohammed Nazrul Islam
SUNY Farmingdale, USA

Mohammad Ataul Karim
Old Dominion University, USA

ABSTRACT

Automatic Bangla character recognition has been a great challenge for research and development because of the huge number of characters, change of shape in a word and in conjunctive characters, and other similar reasons. An optical joint transform correlation-based technique is developed for Bangla character recognition which involves a simple architecture, but can operate at a very high speed because of optics, and offer a very high level of accuracy with negligible false alarms. The proposed correlation technique can successfully identify a target character in a given input scene by producing a single correlation peak per target at the target location. The discrimination between target and non-target correlation peaks is found to be very high even in noisy conditions. The recognition performance of the proposed technique is observed to be insensitive to the type and number of targets. Further improvement of the technique is made by incorporating a synthetic discriminant function, which is created from distorted images of the target character and hence can make the system efficiently recognize Bangla characters in different practical scenarios.

INTRODUCTION

Optical Character Recognition (OCR) represents the technique of automatically detecting the alphanumeric characters from a given document and translating them into computer encoded character data (Mori, Nishida & Yamada, 1999). Research interests in Bangla character recognition is relatively new and its associated challenges are both many and complex (Chaudhuri Pal, 1998). First, the number of characters in Bangla language is significantly larger than that in most

DOI: 10.4018/978-1-4666-3970-6.ch006

other languages. In addition, there are several sets of characters that have nearly similar shapes, some characters extend beyond the average span, and the language also includes many conjunctive characters. Then, within the context of a word, characters are often interconnected. Recognition of handwritten Bangla characters is a rather challenging task also in part because the written form varies rather widely from person to person.

Digital character recognition techniques have inherent limitations arising from more processing steps and slow speed because of serial processing. Real time character recognition requires a very high processing speed so that instantaneous detection of characters and translation to computer characters can be achieved (Dong, Wejinya, Zhou, Shan & Li, 2009). Additional requirements are efficient recognition of characters in a given input document/scene where characters might also have variations in scale, rotation, and font style.

Optical image processing-based techniques can be applied to real-time character recognition applications, which would recognize a character based on shape and size. Optoelectronics-based image processing techniques employ optical light source, Fourier lenses and other optical components to process the given images in parallel, which implies a very fast operation and provides with almost instantaneous output (Weaver & Goodman, 1966). Optical pattern recognition systems are mainly based on either VanderLugt filter (VanderLugt, 1964) or Joint Transform Correlation (JTC) (Perez & Karim, 1989; Alam, Awwal & Karim, 1991; Alam & Karim, 1993). A VanderLugt correlator as well as its variations such as that involving either phase-only filter (Horner & Gianino, 1984) or amplitude-modulated phase-only filter (Awwal, Karim & Jahan, 1990) necessitate generation of a pre-fabricated complex filter that needs to be accurately aligned with the optical axis in the Fourier plane. When VanderLugt correlator is designed properly, phase of the input and phase of the complex matched filter cancels each other out at the Fourier plane. Presence of a strong correlation peak at the output indicates the location of a match. In comparison, in the case of JTC technique, the reference image and the given image are introduced simultaneously before the optical lens thus eliminating the requirements of complex filter and optical alignment sensitivity issues.

Optical JTC-based technique can also be employed for character recognition in real time (Perez & Karim, 1989; Alam, Awwal & Karim, 1991). However, the classical JTC technique has been observed to suffer from a number of problems, including strong but unwanted auto-correlation signals, duplicate cross-correlation signals, and poor discrimination between a target object and any non-target object present in the input scene (Nomani, Bari, Islam, Haider & Islam, 2007). A number of important modifications of the optical JTC technique have been studied in the literature, including binary JTC (Haider, Islam & Alam, 2006), phase-encoded JTC (Javidi & Kuo, 1988), Fourier plane power spectrum subtraction, fringe-adjusted filter (Alam & Karim, 1993), and synthetic discriminant function (Cherri & Alam, 2001; Riasati, Banerjee, Abushagur & Howell, 2000). An efficient phase-shifted and phase-encoded fringe-adjusted JTC technique has been developed, which can successfully detect multiple objects in one processing step and ensures better utilization of the space-bandwidth resource by generating one correlation peak per target object (Haider, Islam, Alam & Khan, 2005; Islam, Purohit, Asari & Karim, 2008).

Optical JTC technique incorporating synthetic discriminant function has been developed to efficiently recognize Bangla characters. The technique has been observed to be capable to detecting characters with scale and rotation variations present in the input. Further research work is being carried out to enhance the technique so that character recognition performance is invariant to handwriting and font-style variations. Optical JTC-based character recognition technique is investigated through mathematical analyses and computer simulation. Performance of the optical technique is evaluated under various practical scenarios. This chapter provides the researchers and industries with a detail analysis, performance evaluations and future directions for Bangla character recognition systems.

CHALLENGES IN BANGLA CHARACTER RECOGNITION

Bangla is one of the oldest and well-developed languages in the world, spoken by a population exceeding 250 million. However, there has been rather insignificant development in digital processing of the language. Outside of the political issues, the language itself offers a number of challenges for the digital technology some of which are discussed below (Majumdar, 2007; Chaudhuri & Pal, 1998; Barman, Samanta, Kim & Bhattacharyya, 1998):

1. The number of Bangla alphabets is significantly higher than most of the other languages. There are 49 – 51 Bangla alphabets. Some characters are rarely used while some others are being slowly de-emphasized by modern language authorities. There has always been a debate on standardization of the alphabet set for Bangla language. A list of Bangla characters is shown in Figure 1.
2. There are many alphabets with similar shapes. Figure 2 shows a few examples of alphabet sets which make an automatic recognition difficult.

Figure 1. List of Bangla characters

Bangla Digits	০ ১ ২ ৩ ৪ ৫ ৬ ৭ ৮ ৯
Bangla Vowels	অ আ ই ঈ উ ঊ ঋ এ ঐ ও ঔ
Bangla Consonants	ক খ গ ঘ ঙ চ ছ জ ঝ ঞ ট ঠ ড ঢ ণ ত থ দ ধ ন প ফ ব ভ ম য র ল হ শ ষ স ড় ঢ় য়

Figure 2. Examples of groups of alphabets having similar shape

অ আ	ই ঈ	উ ঊ ড ড়		এ ঐ
ও ঔ	ঢ ঢ়	ণ ন	চ ছ	ত ভ
ক খ ঘ ঝ থ ধ ফ ব ম য র ষ য়				

3. Some alphabets extend beyond the average span as shown in Figure 3.
4. Alphabets join together to form conjunctive characters, which is not a common feature in other languages. As can be obvious from Figure 4 that the conjunctive characters may often take shapes totally different from the original characters.
5. Within the context of a word, the characters get connected to each other usually through the top bars, named as matra, as shown in Figure 5. The connected characters in a word offer another difficulty in identifying alphabets from one another.
6. Handwritten characters vary significantly from person to person. As depicted in the example of Figure 6, the characters might differ from the standard form so much that an automated recognition system may easily fail.

DIGITAL TECHNIQUES FOR BANGLA CHARACTER RECOGNITION

Several digital techniques have so far been developed for automatic recognition of Bangla characters, which are mainly based on the principle of Optical Character Recognition (OCR). A Bangla OCR algorithm is proposed utilizing feature extraction process (Chaudhury & Pal, 1998); however, it was limited to printed characters and only a specific font. Neural network-based techniques have also received interests in recognition of Bangla characters (Sarowar, Naser, Nizamuddin, Hamid, & Mahmud, 2009; Hasnat, Habib & Khan, 2008). Majumdar (2007) employed digital curvelet transform to extract the features for recognition purpose. Several other attempts have been made to recognize handwritten Bangla character, including local chain code histogram features (Bhattacharya, Shridhar & Parui, 2006), multistage

Figure 3. Alphabets extending beyond the average span

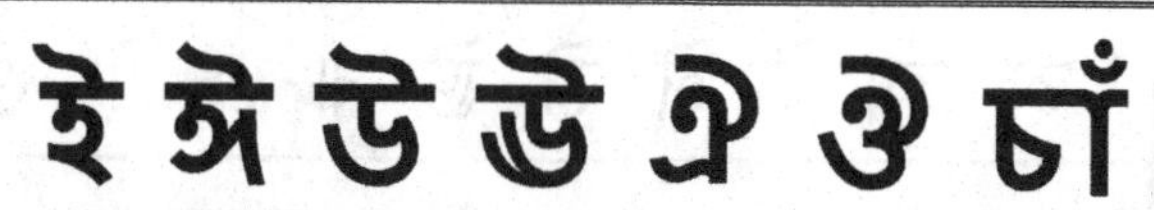

Figure 4. Examples of formation of conjunctive characters

ক+ত=ক্ত	ব+ধ=ব্ধ	ন+ত=ন্ত
ন+হ=হ্ন	ক+ষ=ক্ষ	ঞ+চ=ঞ্চ

Figure 5. Alphabets connecting together while forming words

আমার সোনার বাংলা

Figure 6. Handwritten characters varying significantly

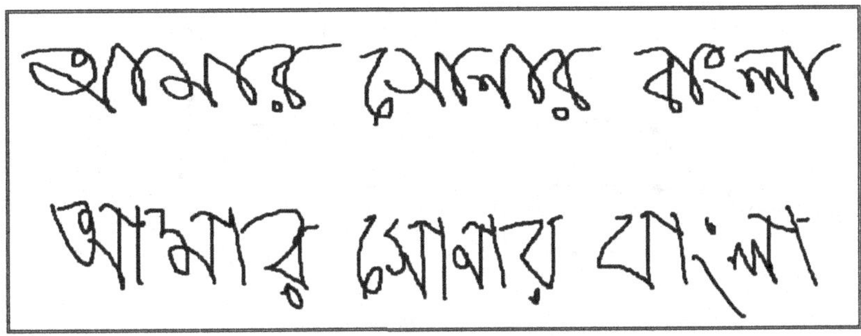

scheme for formation of sub-groups within character set (Fairhurst, Rahman & Rahman, 2002), curvature features (Dutta, & Chaudhury, 1993) and syntactic method (Rahman & Saddik, 2007). However, majority of the digital techniques suffer from low processing speed, requirement of large database for training, ineffectiveness with variations of font and handwriting style, and failure to function successfully under variable and noisy environmental conditions.

OPTICAL JOINT TRANSFORM CORRELATION

Optical correlation techniques were initially based upon the VanderLugt scheme which involves matched filter as shown in Figure 7. The filter needs be pre-fabricated from the reference image and then be placed with perfect alignment in the optical axis in order to recognize a target in the input scene. However, as can be obvious that the VanderLugt correlator was not popular because of several limitations, including the fabrication of a complex filter and the optical alignment issues. On the other hand, the Joint Transform Correlation (JTC)-based technique recognizes an object of interest in a given unknown scene by performing correlation operation between the spatial features of two images as shown in Figure 7(b). For this purpose, it places the two images side-by-side in front of an optical lens and hence eliminates any requirement of a complex filter to perform cross-correlation operation or of alignment of the optical devices (Islam & Karim, 2010).

Basic Principle of Optical JTC Technique

As shown in the block diagram of Figure 7(b), the reference image, $r(x, y)$, which contains the information about the object of interest, and the input image containing unknown objects, $t_i(x, y)$, are placed side-by-side in a joint image plane. The joint input image can be expressed as

$$f\left(x,y\right)=r\left(x,y\right)+\sum_{i=1}^{n}t_{i}\left(x-x_{i},y-y_{i}\right) \qquad (1)$$

where x and y are the spatial domain variables, x_i and y_i's are the displacements of the input scene objects from the origin of the joint image plane, and n is the number of objects in the input image. The joint input image is then Fourier transformed using an optical lens which results in a signal given by

$$F\left(u,v\right)=\left|R\left(u,v\right)\right|\exp\left[j\varphi_{r}\left(u,v\right)\right] +\sum_{i=1}^{n}\left|T_{i}\left(u,v\right)\right|\exp\left[j\varphi_{ti}\left(u,v\right)-jux_{i}-jvy_{i}\right] \qquad (2)$$

where u and v are mutually independent Fourier domain variables scaled by a factor of $2\pi/\lambda f$, λ is

Figure 7. Optical correlation techniques: (a) VanderLugt correlator, (b) joint transform correlator

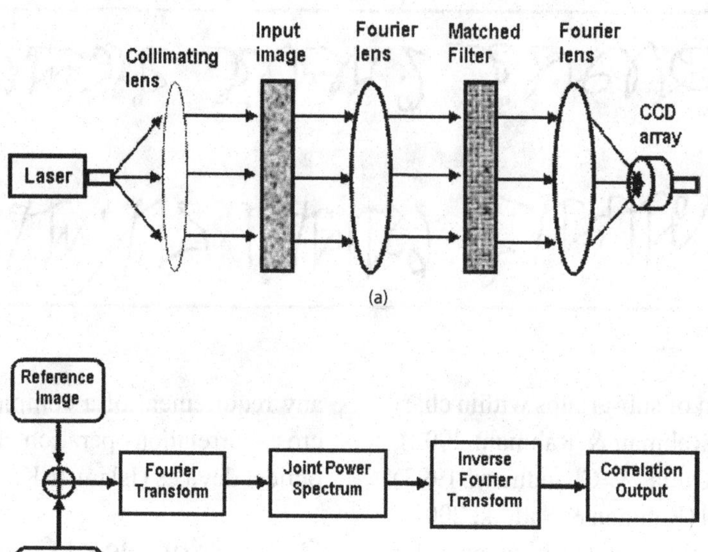

(a)

Reference Image
Input Image
Fourier Transform
Joint Power Spectrum
Inverse Fourier Transform
Correlation Output

(b)

the wavelength of collimating light, f is the focal length of Fourier optical lens, $F(u,v)$ denote the Fourier transform of $f(x,y)$. Also $|R(u,v)|$ and $|T_i(u,v)|$ are the corresponding magnitudes, and $\varphi_r(u, v)$ and $\varphi_i(u, v)$ are the corresponding phases of the Fourier transforms of $r(x,y)$ and $t_i(x,y)$, respectively.

The JTC technique then records the magnitude spectrum of the Fourier transform of the joint image. The Joint Power Spectrum (JPS) signal can be written as in Box 1.

In Equation 3, the superscript * represents a complex conjugate of the original signal. Now an inverse Fourier transform of the JPS signal can yield the correlation output as given by Equation 4 in Box 2.

In Equation 4, $\otimes$ denotes the convolution operation. The correlation signal in the above equation includes the auto-correlation of the reference image and input scene images, respectively, in the first two terms, which are called the zero-order correlation terms because they appear

Box 1.

$$\begin{aligned}E(u,v) &= \left|F(u,v)\right|^2 = F(u,v)F^*(u,v) = \left|R(u,v)\right|^2 + \sum_{i=1}^{n}\left|T_i(u,v)\right|^2 \\ &+ \sum_{i=1}^{n}\left|R(u,v)\right|\left|T_i^*(u,v)\right|\exp\left[j\varphi_r(u,v) - j\varphi_i(u,v) + jux_i + jvy_i\right] \\ &+ \sum_{i=1}^{n}\left|R^*(u,v)\right|\left|T_i(u,v)\right|\exp\left[-j\varphi_r(u,v) + j\varphi_i(u,v) - jux_i - jvy_i\right] \\ &+ \sum_{i=1}^{n}\sum_{k=1,k\neq i}^{n}\left|T_i(u,v)\right|\left|T_k^*(u,v)\right|\exp\left[j\varphi_i(u,v) - j\varphi_k(u,v) - ju(x_i - x_k) - jv(y_i - y_k)\right]\end{aligned} \quad (3)$$

Box 2.

$$e(x,y) = r(x,y) \otimes r(x,y) + \sum_{i=1}^{n} t_i(x,y) \otimes t_i(x,y) + \sum_{i=1}^{n} r(x - x_i, y - y_i) \otimes t_i(x - x_i, y - y_i)$$
$$+ \sum_{i=1}^{n} r(x + x_i, y + y_i) \otimes t_i(x + x_i, y + y_i) \quad (4)$$
$$+ \sum_{i=1}^{n} \sum_{k=1,k\neq i}^{n} t_i(x - x_i + x_k, y - y_i + y_k) \otimes t_i(x - x_i + x_k, y - y_i + y_k)$$

at the origin of the correlation output plane. The third and fourth terms yield the desired cross-correlation between the reference image and the input scene images. The cross-correlation terms are displaced at (x_i, y_i) and $(-x_i, -y_i)$, respectively, which also indicate that they are basically the mirrors of each other. The last term in the above equation represents the cross-correlation among the input scene objects themselves.

Simulation Results

Optical JTC technique was investigated through computer simulation program using MATLAB software. Several Bangla alphabets were employed as binary objects each of which has a size of 32×32 pixels.

Figure 8 shows a joint input image where the left half of the plane contains the reference image which is the alphabet "Ba" (ব) and the right half contains the input scene image which is the same as the reference image. The resultant correlation output is depicted in Figure 8(b), where the peak at the center of the plane corresponds to the auto-correlation terms of the reference and input images. The desired cross-correlation terms between the reference and input images are displaced from the origin as can be seen in the figure.

Figure 9 shows another joint input image where a non-target object, where the input-scene object

Figure 8. Simulation result for JTC technique with single Bangla character: (a) joint input image containing reference image and a target image, (b) correlation output for joint image in (a)

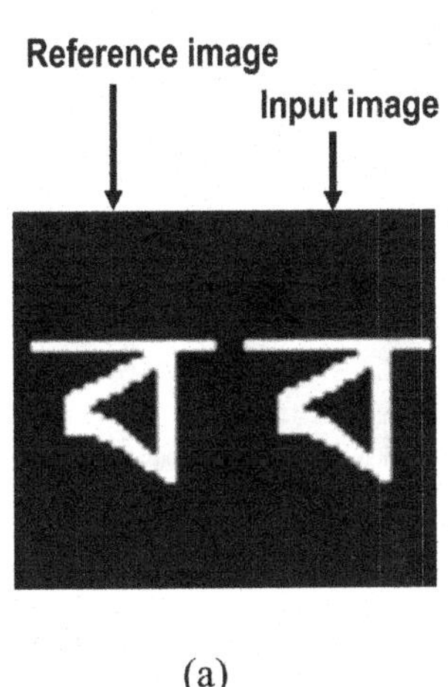

(a)

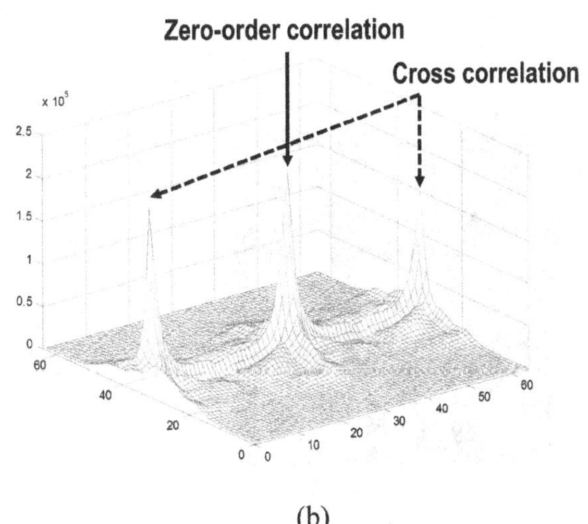

(b)

Figure 9. Simulation result for JTC technique with single Bangla character: (a) joint input image containing reference image and a non-target image, (b) correlation output for joint image in (a)

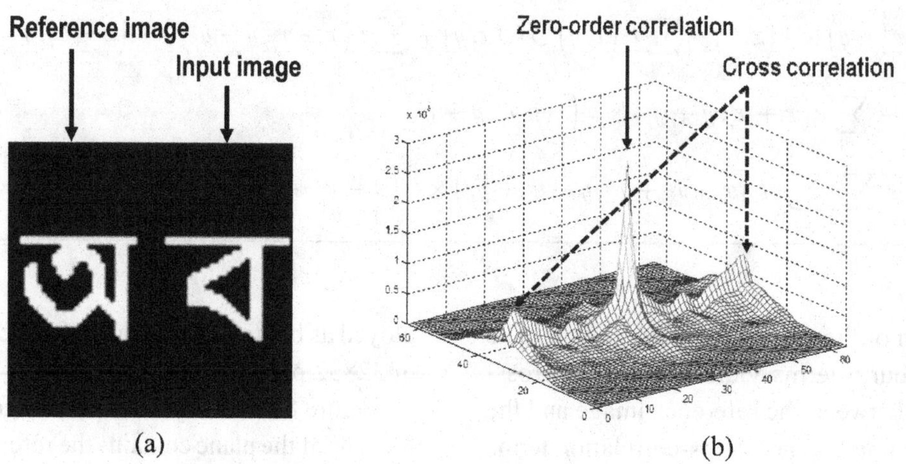

"Ba" (ব) does not match with the reference object "A" (অ). It can be observed from the correlation output shown in Figure 9(b) that the cross-correlation terms are significantly lower in magnitude as compared to those of Figure 8(b) because of mismatching between the input image and the reference image. However, the auto-correlation signal is still very strong as in Figure 8(b), which imposes a big challenge for automatic detection of the cross-correlation terms in the correlation plane.

Next, a simulation experiment was carried out with more than one object in the input scene. Figure 10 shows the joint input image where the alphabet "Ba" (ব) on the left represents the reference image. The objects to the right of the reference object plane represent the input scene which contains two targets and four non-target objects.

Figure 10. Simulation result for JTC technique with single Bangla character: (a) joint input image containing reference image and multiple-object input image, (b) correlation output for joint image in (a)

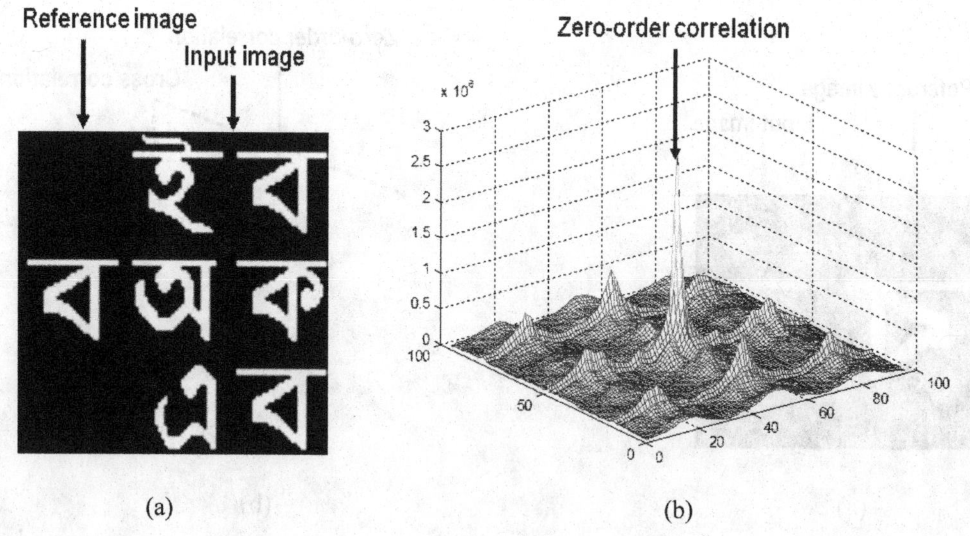

It can be observed from the correlation output shown in Figure 10(b) that the auto-correlation term is much stronger than any cross-correlation terms because all the objects in the joint input image contribute to this zero-order correlation signal. The correlation output contains all the cross-correlation terms between any pair of objects in the joint image, which are scattered in the plane. But the very low strength of these cross-correlation signals makes it almost impossible to identify any target objects and distinguish them from non-target objects in the input scene.

Limitations and Challenges

The optical JTC-based character recognition technique offers a number of salient features over other matched-filter based correlation techniques, some of which are listed below:

- No prior fabrication of a complex-matched filter is required.
- Free from meticulous alignment along the optical axis.
- The reference image can be updated in real time.
- The character recognition tool can be operated at video frame rates.

However, as is obvious from the simulation results in the previous section, the basic JTC technique suffers from a number of problems which impose limitations on practical application of the technique in a real-time, real-life field:

- Very strong zero-order correlation signal overshadows the cross-correlation signals.
- Duplicate cross-correlation signals are generated for every pair of objects resulting in spatial inefficiency.
- The cross-correlation terms are not produced at the target locations, rather are displaced at larger distance from the center, which does not allow an automatic technique to detect the position/location of the targets. Moreover, it requires a larger size of the correlation plane and results in additional limitation on the optical setup of the technique.
- The cross-correlation terms are not very distinctive, rather contain wide side lobes, and hence they may overlap in case of multiple objects in the input scene.
- The joint input image requires that the reference and input images cannot overlap which offers less flexibility in developing the joint image.
- Failure of recognizing targets efficiently in a noisy input scene.

BANGLA CHARACTER RECOGNITION USING PHASE-SHIFTED AND PHASE-ENCODED JTC TECHNIQUE

An efficient character recognition technique is developed based on the optical JTC scheme. The proposed technique employs phase shifting and phase encoding on the reference image and hence enhances the performance by eliminating majority of the above-mentioned limitations.

Performance Analysis

The proposed Phase-Shifted and Phase-Encoded JTC (PSEJTC) technique is depicted in the block diagram of Figure 11. The reference image containing the target Bangla alphabet is first phase-encoded using a random phase mask, $\varphi(x, y)$. The phase encoding process is accomplished through multiplication of the Fourier-transformed signals in the frequency domain. The phase-encoded reference image can be expressed as:

Figure 11. Block diagram of phase-shifted and phase-encoded JTC technique

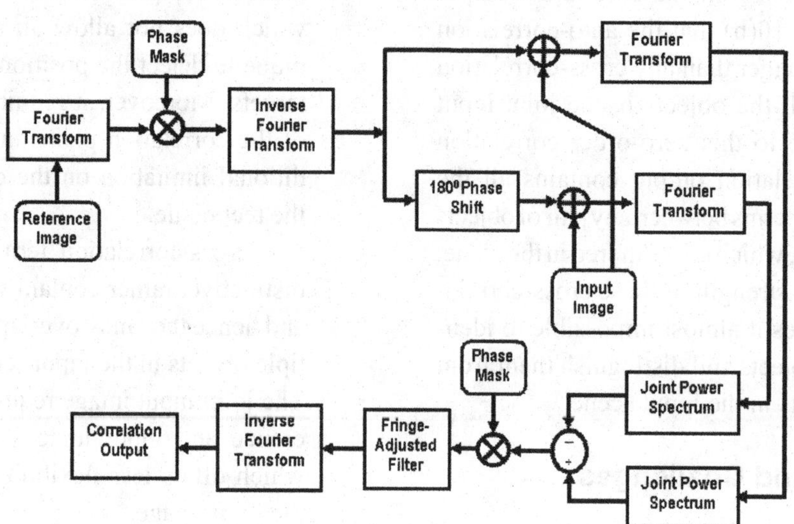

$$r_p(x,y) = \Im^{-1}\left\{\left|R(u,v)\right|\exp\left[j\Phi_r(u,v)\right]\times\Phi(u,v)\right\} = r(x,y)\otimes\varphi(x,y) \quad (5)$$

The phase-encoded reference image is then fed to two channels where the second channel introduces a phase shifting of 180°. The phase-encoded reference images are then combined with the unknown input scene images to form the input joint images as given by:

$$f_1(x,y) = r(x,y)\otimes\varphi(x,y)+\sum_{i=1}^{n} t_i(x-x_i,y-y_i) \quad (6)$$

$$f_2(x,y) = -r(x,y)\otimes\varphi(x,y)+\sum_{i=1}^{n} t_i(x-x_i,y-y_i) \quad (7)$$

The joint input images are then Fourier transformed to yield two Joint Power Spectra (JPS) as given by:

$$\begin{aligned}\left|F_1(u,v)\right|^2 &= \left|R(u,v)\right|^2+\sum_{i=1}^{n}\left|T_i(u,v)\right|^2 \\ &+\sum_{i=1}^{n} R(u,v)T_i^*(u,v)\exp\left[jux_i+jvy_i\right]\Phi(u,v) \\ &+\sum_{i=1}^{n} R^*(u,v)T_i(u,v)\exp\left[-jux_i-jvy_i\right]\Phi^*(u,v)\end{aligned} \quad (8)$$

$$\begin{aligned}\left|F_2(u,v)\right|^2 &= \left|R(u,v)\right|^2+\sum_{i=1}^{n}\left|T_i(u,v)\right|^2 \\ &-\sum_{i=1}^{n} R(u,v)T_i^*(u,v)\exp\left[jux_i+jvy_i\right]\Phi(u,v) \\ &-\sum_{i=1}^{n} R^*(u,v)T_i(u,v)\exp\left[-jux_i-jvy_i\right]\Phi^*(u,v)\end{aligned} \quad (9)$$

Next a modified JPS is generated by subtracting the JPS of Equation 9 from that of Equation 8 and then multiplying the output by the same phase mask used earlier, $\Phi(u, v)$. The modified JPS signal is given by Equation 10 in Box 3.

To further enhance the correlation performance, a fringe-adjusted filter (FAF) is developed whose transfer function in the Fourier domain is given by:

Box 3.

$$E(u,v)=\left[\left|F_1(u,v)\right|^2-\left|F_2(u,v)\right|^2\right]\times\Phi(u,v)$$
$$=2\times\begin{bmatrix}\sum_{i=1}^{n}R(u,v)T_i^*(u,v)\exp\left[jux_i+jvy_i\right]\Phi(u,v)\Phi(u,v)\\+\sum_{i=1}^{n}R^*(u,v)T_i(u,v)\exp\left[-jux_i-jvy_i\right]\end{bmatrix} \quad (10)$$

$$H_f(u,v)=\frac{\alpha(u,v)}{\left[\beta(u,v)+\left|R(u,v)\right|^2\right]} \quad (11)$$

where $\alpha(u,v)$ and $\beta(u,v)$ are either constants or functions of u and v. The parameter $\alpha(u,v)$ is used to avoid having an optical gain greater than unity, while $\beta(u,v)$ is used to overcome the pole problem otherwise associated with a normal inverse filter. Since the power spectra of the reference image can be pre-calculated, implementation of this filter does not deteriorate the system processing speed.

The modified JPS signal of Equation 10 is multiplied by the FAF transfer function of Equation 11 to obtain the fringe-adjusted power spectrum. An inverse Fourier transform of fringe-adjusted JPS yields the desired correlation output for each target object in the class. See Box 4.

It can be observed from the above equation that the unwanted zero-order correlation terms and noisy cross-correlation terms in the correlation plane are automatically cancelled out from the correlation output. Though the final correlation output includes two cross-correlation terms, but the first term is scattered in various directions due to the random nature of the phase mask and so do not produce any peak in the correlation plane of interest. Therefore, the cross-correlation between a reference image and a target contributes to a single correlation peak per target in the output plane. It can also be noted in the above equation that the correlation peak can be produced exactly at the target location.

Simulation Results

The proposed PSEJTC technique was investigated through computer simulation by employing the filter parameters as, $\alpha(u, v) = 1$ and $\beta(u, v) = 10^{-4}$. Figure 12 shows the reference image which is the Bangla character "Ba" (ব). The input scene with four different characters is depicted in Figure 12(b) where there is one target character and three non-target characters. Now the reference image of Figure 12(a) phase encoded, which results in scattering of the image all over the plane, and then added to the input scene as shown in Figure 12(c), which includes the input scene objects

Box 4.

$$e(x,y)=2\sum_{i=1}^{n}r(x+x_i,y+y_i)\otimes t_i(x+x_i,y+y_i)\otimes\varphi(x,y)\otimes\varphi(x,y)\otimes h_f(x,y)$$
$$+2\sum_{i=1}^{n}r(x-x_i,y-y_i)\otimes t_i(x-x_i,y-y_i)\otimes h_f(x,y) \quad (12)$$

along with the phase-masked reference image in the background. It is obvious from the resultant correlation output shown in Figure 12(d) that the proposed technique produces a single correlation peak for the target character in the input scene and very insignificant peaks for all other non-target objects. Thus, the technique produces a high discrimination between the target and the non-target objects in present the input scene. Also, the target peak is very sharp, almost like a delta function and it occurs exactly at the target location.

Figure 13 shows another set of simulation results with the same reference image. This time the input scene contains two target characters as shown in Figure 13(a). The correlation output of Figure 13(c) confirms that the technique can efficiently and successfully identify the target characters in a given unknown input scene by producing sharp peaks at the target locations.

Next, the simulation investigation included a Bangla character "Ka" (ক), which is similar in shape with the target character that is being considered as the reference object, as shown in the input scene of Figure 14. Another similar character "Ja" (য) is included in the input scene of Figure 14(c). The corresponding correlation outputs shown in Figures 14(b) and 14(d), respectively, make it obvious that the technique can efficiently reject any non-target character even if it is similar in shape because it produces single sharp peak only at the target locations.

Now a bigger input scene was included in the simulation experiment containing larger number of characters. In a classical JTC technique, the larger the number of objects in the input scene, the stronger the zero-order correlation term is and the worse the space-bandwidth efficiency is. But the proposed technique performs independent of

Figure 12. Simulation result for the PSEJTC technique: (a) reference image, (b) input image, (c) joint input image, and (d) correlation output

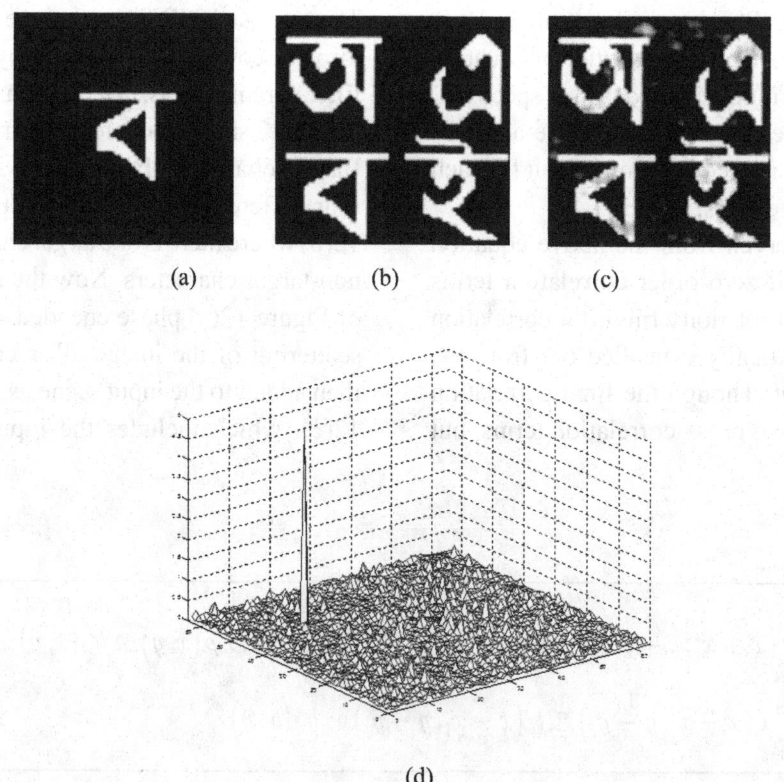

Figure 13. Simulation result for the PSEJTC technique: (a) input image, (b) correlation output

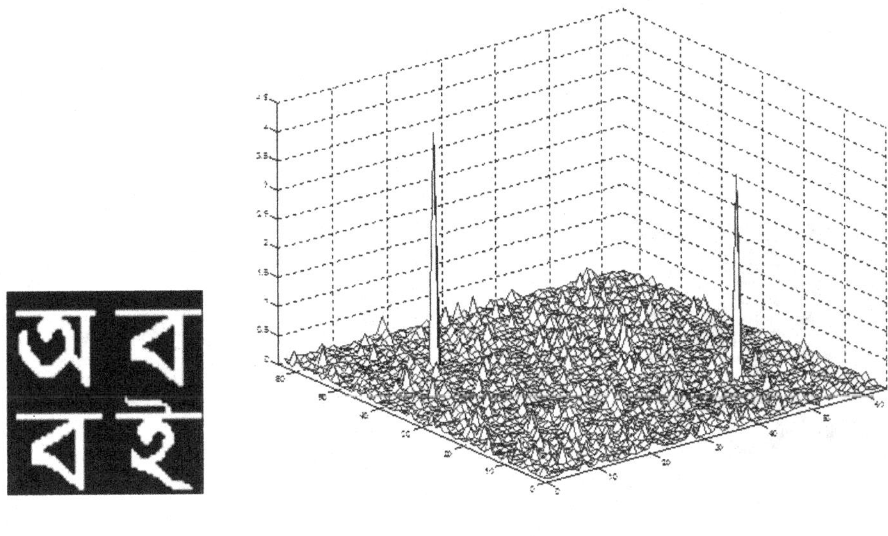

(a) (b)

the number of input-scene objects as can obvious from the results of Figure 15. The input scene of Figure 15(a) contains three target characters, three non-target but similar characters and three other characters. The correlation output shown in Figure 15(b) includes three sharp peaks corresponding to the targets and negligible peaks for other characters.

Simulation experiment was extended to noisy environment. The input scene of Figure 16 was intentionally corrupted by random noise to simulate a practical scenario where the recorded photo or video might not be as clear as the target image available in the database. It can be easily understood by comparing Figures 15(a) and 16(a) that any traditional character recognition technique might fail to identify the target character from such noisy scene. However, the correlation output of Figure 16(b) proves that the proposed technique is as successful in recognizing the target characters in a noisy scene by producing sharp and discriminant peaks.

Next a class-associative character recognition performance was investigated with the proposed technique. In this case, the technique would be looking for more than one class of target characters in a given input scene simultaneously. For this purpose, two different characters, "Ba" (ব) and "I" (ই), were considered as two reference classes of characters as shown in Figure 17. The input scene of Figure 17(b) includes both the target characters as well as other characters similar to those in the reference class. However, Figure 17(c) verifies the efficiency of the proposed technique by producing sharp peaks only for the target characters while rejecting any non-target characters.

BANGLA CHARACTER RECOGNITION USING SYNTHETIC DISCRIMINANT FUNCTION-BASED JTC

A major problem in character recognition applications is that the target character may vary in shape and size as well as may have distortion as compared to the clean image available in the database, which might easily deteriorate the recognition performance. To make the character

Figure 14. Simulation result for the PSEJTC technique: (a) input image, (b) correlation output for input image of (a), (c) another input image, (d) correlation output for input image of (c)

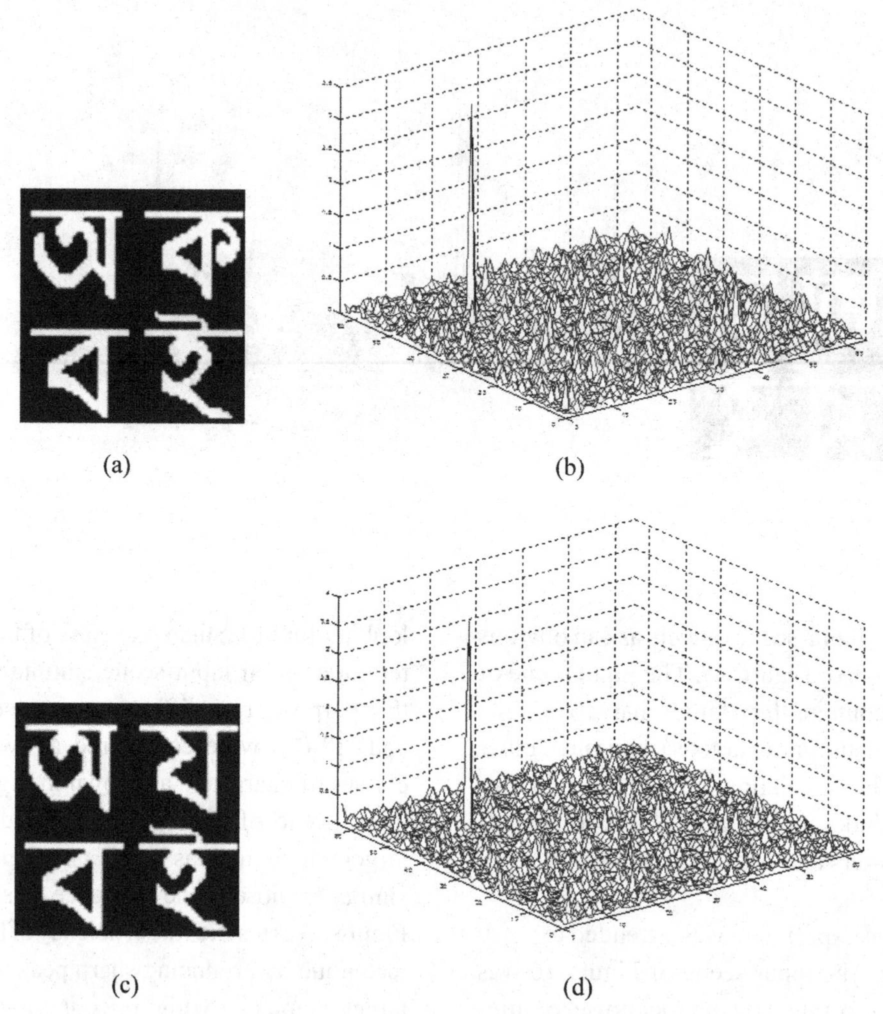

Figure 15. Simulation result for the PSEJTC technique: (a) input image, (b) correlation output

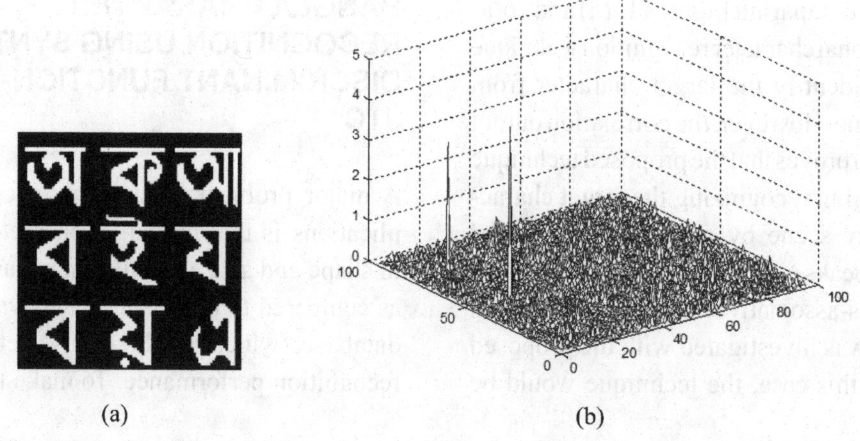

Figure 16. Simulation result for the PSEJTC technique: (a) noisy input image, (b) correlation output

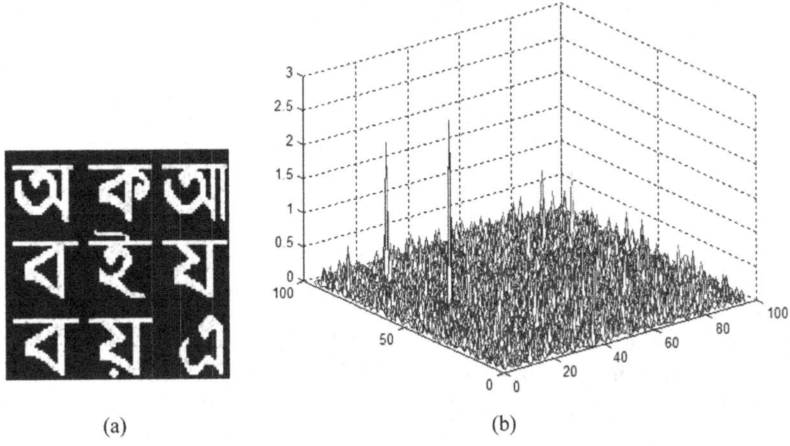

Figure 17. Simulation result for the PSEJTC technique: (a) reference image with target characters, (b) input image, (c) correlation output

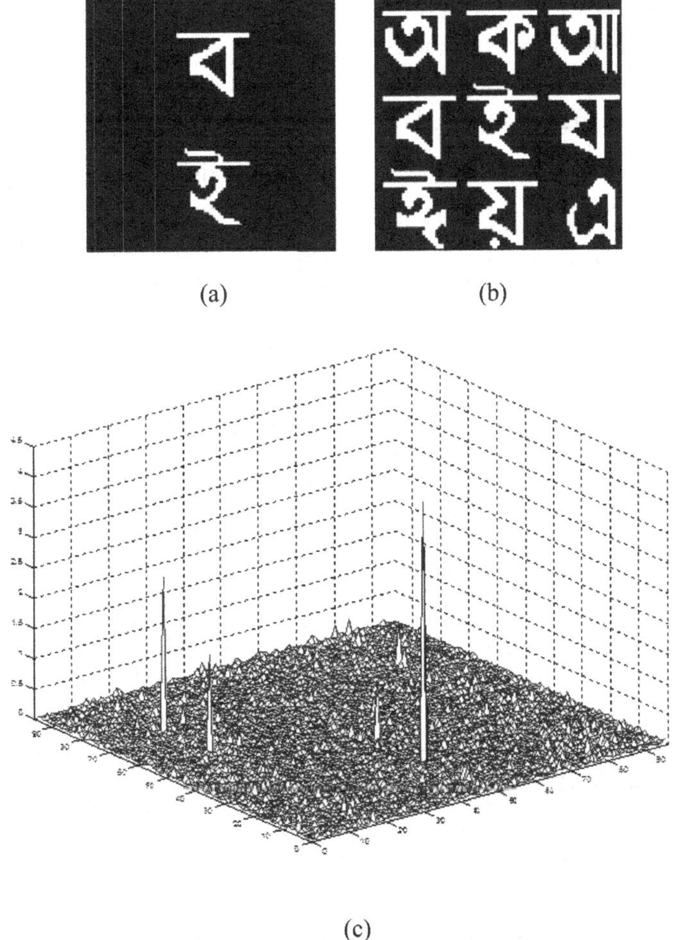

identification invariant to variations and distortions, a synthetic discriminant function is incorporated in the phase-encoded and phase-shifted JTC technique (Riasati, Banerjee, Abushagur, & Howell, 2000).

Performance Analysis

A set of synthetic images of the reference character was used with probable distortions to train the system prior to real-time operation. Multiple SDF reference images can then be fused together to form a composite SDF reference image, which is then fed to the class-associative character recognition technique.

Figure 18 shows the block diagram for the generation of the SDF from a set of training images of the target character. Let there be a total of N number of training images, $r_1(x, y), r_2(x, y)$... $r_N(x, y)$, containing the possible distorted features of the to-be-detected character, which were used to construct the spatial SDF image, $r_{SDF}(x, y)$. The SDF can be synthesized as a weighted average function of the training images as given by:

$$r_{\mathrm{SDF}}\left(x,y\right) = \frac{\sum_{i=1}^{N} a_i r_i\left(x,y\right)}{\sum_{i=1}^{N} a_i} \tag{13}$$

where a_i are the associated coefficients for the respective training images, which can be selected such that the SDF produces a uniform correlation peak with each of the training images. A simplified iterative process is developed, where the iteration begins by initializing all the coefficients equal to unity.

The resultant SDF image thus obtained is then correlated with each of the training images and a correlation matrix is developed.

$$\mathrm{corr}_i^k = r_{\mathrm{SDF}}^k\left(x,y\right) \otimes r_i\left(x,y\right) \tag{14}$$

where k is the iteration number. Then the correlation peak intensities corresponding to each training image are evaluated:

$$C_i^k \in \max\left(\mathrm{corr}_i^k\right) \tag{15}$$

Finally, the maximum peak intensity among the training image components is estimated as:

$$C_{\max}^k \in \max\left(C_i^k\right) \tag{16}$$

Now to ensure an equal correlation peak intensity for all images in the training set, the coefficients a_i of Equation 13 are updated using the empirical relation given by:

$$a_i^{k+1} = a_i^k + \left(C_{\max}^k - C_i^k\right)\delta \tag{17}$$

Figure 18. Formation of the SDF reference image for distortion-invariant pattern recognition (Islam & Karim, 2010)

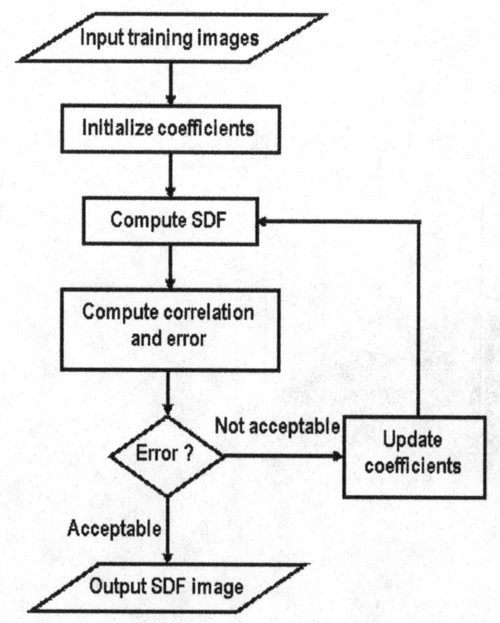

where δ is the relaxation factor that determines the rate of changing the coefficients from one iteration to the next. The iterative process is continued until the difference between the maximum and the minimum correlation peak intensities reduces to an error limit, expressed as:

$$\zeta^{k} = \frac{\left(C_{\max}^{k} - C_{\min}^{k}\right)}{C_{\max}^{k}} \tag{18}$$

Simulation Results

An example of the generation of an SDF image is shown in Figure 19, where a set of eight distorted images of the reference characters "Ba" (ব) were employed for training purpose as shown in Figure 19(a). The SDF image thus obtained is shown in Figure 19(b).

Now the SDF image of Figure 19(b) was employed as the reference image for the proposed PSEJTC technique along with an input scene, as shown in Figure 20(a), which contains one regular and two distorted target characters. It can be observed from the correlation output shown in Figure 20(b) that the technique is very successful and efficient in detecting all three target characters though they were distorted and, at the same time, in rejecting all non-target characters in the input scene.

Figure 19. Simulation result for formation of the SDF reference image: (a) training images, and (b) SDF image

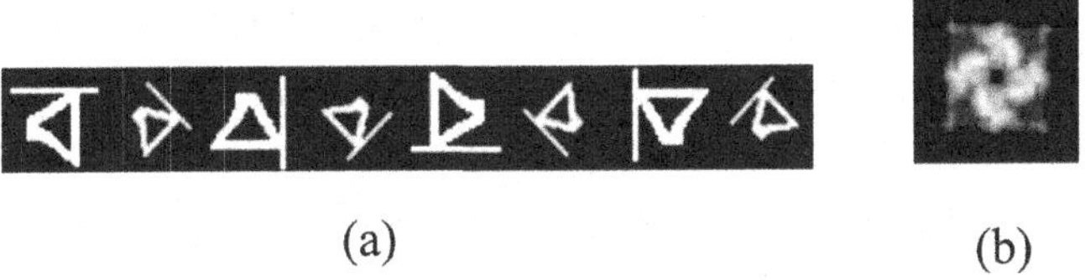

(a) (b)

Figure 20. Simulation result for distortion-invariant character recognition using the PSEJTC technique: (a) input image, and (b) corresponding correlation output

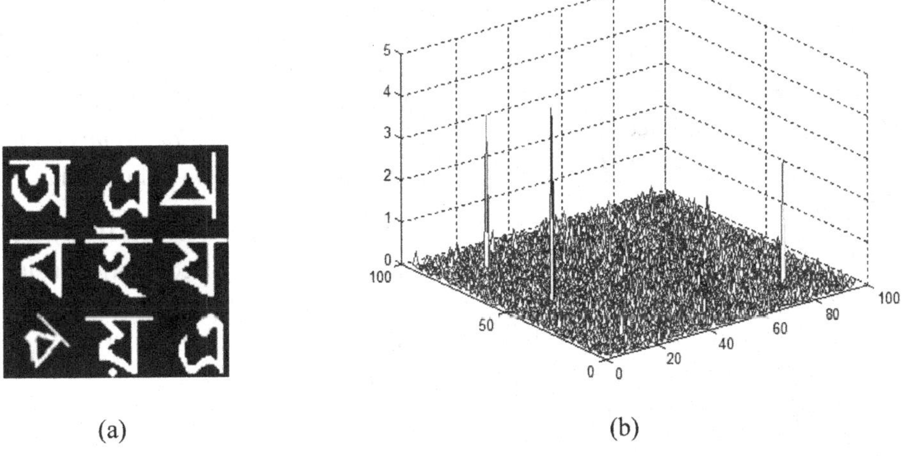

(a) (b)

CONCLUSION

Real-time character recognition is a challenging task which requires simple architecture, fast speed and a very high level of accuracy with negligible false alarms. The proposed optics-based phase-encoded and phase-shifted joint transform correlation technique yields single correlation peak per target and thus ensures the best utilization of the input and output plane space-bandwidth resource. The discrimination between target and non-target correlation peaks is found to be very high which yields an efficient and automatic detection of targets in an input scene. This technique is also observed to be insensitive to the number of targets and the presence of noise in the input scene. Incorporation of a synthetic discriminant function can make the system efficiently recognize Bangla characters in different practical scenario. Though the chapter presents recognition results with "Ba" (ব) as the target characters, simulation experiments were carried out with other Bangla characters as reference images and in every case the proposed technique was observed to perform successfully and efficiently. The salient feature of the proposed technique is that the character recognition is based on the spatial features of the target character and hence the recognition performance is not subject to which character we are looking for.

REFERENCES

Alam, M. M., & Kashem, M. A. (2010). A complete Bangla OCR system for printed characters. *International Journal of Computer and Information Technology*, *1*(1), 30–35.

Alam, M. S., Awwal, A. A. S., & Karim, M. A. (1991). Improved correlation discrimination using joint Fourier-transform optical correlator. *Microwave and Optical Technology Letters*, *4*, 103–106. doi:10.1002/mop.4650040305.

Alam, M. S., & Karim, M. A. (1993). Fringe-adjusted joint transform correlation. *Applied Optics*, *32*, 4344–4350. doi:10.1364/AO.32.004344 PMID:20830091.

Awwal, A. A. S., Karim, M. A., & Jahan, S. R. (1990). Improved correlation discrimination using an amplitude-modulated phase-only filter. *Applied Optics*, *29*, 233–236. doi:10.1364/AO.29.000233 PMID:20556091.

Barman, S., Samanta, A. K., Kim, T., & Bhattacharyya, D. (2010). Design of a view based approached for Bengali character recognition. *International Journal of Advanced Science and Technology*, *15*, 49–62.

Bhattacharya, U., Shridhar, M., & Parui, S. K. (2006). On recognition of handwritten Bangla characters. In *Proceedings of Indian Conference on Computer Vision, Graphics and Image Processing*, (pp. 817–828). IEEE.

Chaudhuri, B. B., & Pal, U. (1998). A complete printed Bangla OCR system. *Pattern Recognition*, *31*(5), 631–649. doi:10.1016/S0031-3203(97)00078-2.

Cherri, A. K., & Alam, M. S. (2001). Reference phase-encoded fringe-adjusted joint transform correlation. *Applied Optics*, *40*, 1216–1225. doi:10.1364/AO.40.001216 PMID:18357108.

Dong, Z., Wejinya, U. C., Zhou, S., Shan, Q., & Li, W. J. (2009). Real-time written-character recognition using MEMS motion sensors: Calibration and experimental results. In *Proceedings of IEEE International Conference on Robotics and Biometrics*, (pp. 687–691). IEEE.

Dutta, A., & Chaudhury, S. (1993). Bengali alpha-numeric character recognition using curvature features. *Pattern Recognition*, *26*(12), 1757–1770. doi:10.1016/0031-3203(93)90174-U.

Fairhurst, M. C., Rahman, A. F. R., & Rahman, R. (2002). Recognition of handwritten Bengali characters: A novel multistage approach. *Pattern Recognition*, *35*(5), 997–1006. doi:10.1016/S0031-3203(01)00089-9.

Haider, M. R., Islam, M. N., & Alam, M. S. (2006). Enhanced class associative generalized fringe-adjusted joint transform correlation for multiple target detection. *Optical Engineering (Redondo Beach, Calif.)*, *45*(4). doi:10.1117/1.2192471 PMID:20052302.

Haider, M. R., Islam, M. N., Alam, M. S., & Khan, J. F. (2005). Shifted phase-encoded fringe-adjusted joint transform correlation for multiple target detection. *Optics Communications*, *248*, 69–88. doi:10.1016/j.optcom.2004.11.102.

Hasnat, M. A., Habib, S. M. M., & Khan, M. (2008). A high performance domain specific OCR for Bangla script. In Proceedings of Novel Algorithms and Techniques in Telecommunications, Automation and Industrial Electronics, (pp. 174–178). Springer.

Horner, J. L., & Gianino, P. D. (1984). Phase-only matched filtering. *Applied Optics*, *23*, 812–816. doi:10.1364/AO.23.000812 PMID:18204645.

Islam, M. N., & Karim, M. A. (2010). Optical pattern recognition systems and techniques. In Ramakrishnan, S., & El-Omary, I. M. M. (Eds.), *Computational Intelligence Techniques in Handling Image Processing and Pattern Recognition*. Lambert Academic Publishing.

Islam, M. N., Purohit, I. K., Asari, K. V., & Karim, M. A. (2008). Distortion-invariant pattern recognition using synthetic discriminant function-based shifted phase-encoded joint transform correlator. *Optical Engineering (Redondo Beach, Calif.)*, *47*(10), 108201-1–108201-9. doi:10.1117/1.3000589.

Javidi, B., & Kuo, C. (1988). Joint transform image correlation using a binary spatial light modulator at the Fourier plane. *Applied Optics*, *27*, 663–665. doi:10.1364/AO.27.000663 PMID:20523656.

Majumdar, A. (2007). Bangla basic character recognition using digital curvelet transform. *Journal of Pattern Recognition Research*, *1*, 17–26.

Mori, S., Nishida, H., & Yamada, H. (1999). *Optical character recognition*. New York: John Wiley & Sons.

Nomani, M. W. K., Bari, S. M. K., Islam, T. Z., Haider, M. R., & Islam, M. N. (2007). Invariant Bangla character recognition using projection-slice synthetic-discriminant-function based algorithm. *Journal of Electronic and Electrical Engineering*, 7(2), 403–409.

Perez, O., & Karim, M. A. (1989). An efficient implementation of a joint Fourier transform correlator using a modified LCTV. *Microwave and Optical Technology Letters*, *2*, 193–196. doi:10.1002/mop.4650020602.

Rahman, M. A., & Saddik, A. E. (2007). Modified syntactic method to recognize Bengali handwritten characters. *IEEE Transactions on Instrumentation and Measurement*, *56*(6), 2623–2632. doi:10.1109/TIM.2007.907955.

Riasati, V. R., Banerjee, P. P., Abushagur, M., & Howell, K. B. (2000). Rotation-invariant synthetic discriminant function for optical pattern recognition. *Optical Engineering (Redondo Beach, Calif.)*, *39*, 1156–1161. doi:10.1117/1.602479.

Sarowar, G., Naser, M. A., Nizamuddin, S. M., Hamid, N. I. B., & Mahmud, A. (2009). Enhancing Bengali character recognition process applying heuristics on neural network. *International Journal of Computer Science and Network Security*, *9*(6), 154–158.

VanderLugt, A. (1964). Signal detection by complex spatial filtering. *IEEE Transactions on Information Theory*, *10*, 139–146. doi:10.1109/TIT.1964.1053650.

Weaver, C. S., & Goodman, J. W. (1966). A technique for optically convolving two functions. *Applied Optics*, *5*, 1248–1249. doi:10.1364/AO.5.001248 PMID:20049063.

Chapter 7
Parsing Bangla Grammar Using Context Free Grammar

Al-Mahmud
Khulna University of Engineering and Technology (KUET), Bangladesh

Bishnu Sarker
Khulna University of Engineering and Technology (KUET), Bangladesh

K. M. Azharul Hasan
Khulna University of Engineering and Technology (KUET), Bangladesh

ABSTRACT

Parsing plays a very prominent role in computational linguistics. Parsing a Bangla sentence is a primary need in Bangla language processing. This chapter describes the Context Free Grammar (CFG) for parsing Bangla language, and hence, a Bangla parser is proposed based on the Bangla grammar. This approach is very simple to apply in Bangla sentences, and the method is well accepted for parsing grammar. This chapter introduces a parser for Bangla language, which is, by nature, a predictive parser, and the parse table is constructed for recognizing Bangla grammar. Parse table is an important tool to recognize syntactical mistakes of Bangla sentences when there is no entry for a terminal in the parse table. If a natural language can be successfully parsed then grammar checking of this language becomes possible. The parsing scheme in this chapter works based on a top-down parsing method. CFG suffers from a major problem called left recursion. The technique of left factoring is applied to avoid the problem.

INTRODUCTION

Language plays the most important role in human communication. Human communication is based on exchange of feelings, sharing of knowledge, etc. Feelings can be exchanged through voice, symbols and signs. Language provides the most convenient way of expressing the expressions of feelings through providing those necessary phonetics that could be spoken and the symbols that could be written to be preserved. Language is the driving force to human communication. Language is the most important medium to represent and express human knowledge and human communication.

DOI: 10.4018/978-1-4666-3970-6.ch007

Bangla (or Bengali) is one of the more important Indo-Iranian languages, is the sixth most popular in the world and spoken by a population that now exceeds 250 million. Geographically, Bangla-speaking population percentages are as follows: Bangladesh (over 95%), and the Indian States of Andaman & Nicobar Islands (26%), Assam (28%), Tripura (67%), and West Bengal (85%). The global total includes those who are now in diaspora in Canada, Malawi, Nepal, Pakistan, Saudi Arabia, Singapore, United Arab Emirates, United Kingdom, and United States.

Bangla is still in degraded stage at least as far as work in the area of computational linguistics is concerned. Natural languages like English and even Hindi is rapidly progressing as far as work done in processing by computers is concerned. Unfortunately, Bangla lags more or less behind in some crucial areas of research like parts of speech tagging, text summarization and categorization, information retrieval and most importantly in the area of grammar checking. The grammar checking for a language has a wide variety of applications.

The activity of breaking down a sentence into its constituent parts is known as parsing. Parsing is an earlier term for the diagramming of sentences of natural languages, and is still used for the diagramming. Parsing a sentence involves the use of linguistic knowledge of a language to discover the way in which a sentence is structured. Exactly how this linguistic knowledge is represented and can be used to understand sentences is one of the questions that has engaged the interest of psycholinguists, linguists, computational linguists, and computer scientists. Bangla parsing is a challenging task. This chapter has a detail discussion over Bangla parsing using Context Free Grammar.

BACKGROUND

In computing, a parser is one of the components in an interpreter or compiler that checks for correct syntax and builds a data structure (often some kind of parse tree, abstract syntax tree or other hierarchical structure) implicitly in the input tokens. Parsing can be defined as a method where a parser algorithm is used to determine whether a given input string is grammatically correct or not for a given grammar. Parsing is a fundamental problem in language processing for both machines and humans. In general, the parsing problem includes the definition of an algorithm to map any input sentence to its associated syntactic tree structure (Saha, 2006). The parser often uses a separate lexical analyzer to create tokens from the sequence of input characters. Parsers may be programmed by hand or may be automatically or semi-automatically generated (in some programming languages) by a tool.

A parse tree for a grammar is a tree where the root of the tree is the start symbol for the grammar, the interior nodes are the non-terminals of the grammar, the leaf nodes are the terminals of the grammar and the children of a node starting from the left to the right correspond to the symbols on the right hand side of some production for the node in the grammar. Every valid parse tree represents a string generated by the grammar (Yarowsky, 1995).

A parser analyzes the sequence of symbols presented to it based on the grammar (Yarowsky, 1995). Natural language applications namely Information Extraction, Machine Translation, and Speech Recognition, need to have an accurate parser (Haque & Khan, 2005). Parsing natural language text is more difficult than the computer languages such as compiler and word processor because the grammars for natural languages are complex, ambiguous, and infinite in number of vocabulary. It is difficult to prepare formal rules to describe informal behavior even though it is clear that some rules are being followed. For a syntax based grammar checking the sentence is completely parsed to check the correctness of it. If the syntactic parsing fails, the text is considered incorrect. On the other hand, for statistics based approach, Parts of Speech (POS) tag sequences are prepared from an annotated corpus, and hence the frequency and the probability (Sengupta & Chaudhuri, 1997). The text is considered correct if the POS-tagged text contains POS sequences with frequencies higher than some threshold (Anwar, Anwar & Bhuiyan, 2009)

In this chapter, we implemented Bangla dictionary in XML format using the corresponding word as tag name and it's POS as value. It is a very useful technique because it needs less time to store data as well as data retrieval from this data storage is very easy and fast compared to other popular forms of data storage. It helps to search the dictionary very fast. Bangla grammar has a large number of forms and rules. The aim of this chapter is to describe a parser that parses a Bangla sentence, rather than generating sentences. A parse tree is displayed if the Bangla parser decides that sentence is correct otherwise parse tree are not generated. This technique of parsing system with XML checks whether every sentence of given Bangla passage is grammatically correct or not correct. It also indicates the location of problems. If any sentence of the passage is found accepted or correct then it generates a parse tree.

There has been a structural difference between the Bangla and English grammar. It is challenging to parse Bangla and English sentence with the same grammatical structure. If we match word to word with Bangla and English grammar structure then the parser will not give the correct answer.

For example, considering the grammatical structure:

Subject + verb + object (I + eat+ rice)

In Bangla it appears as:

আমি + খাই + ভাত.

But it is a non-traditional form. The traditional form is:

আমি + ভাত + খাই.

If we transfer it as word to word then the English form will become:

I + rice + eat.

Here, in English object is appeared after the verb whereas in Bangla the object is appeared before the verb. It's clearly states that how difficult to parse Bangla sentences rather than English sentences.

Roughly speaking, phrases and idioms are expressions whose meaning cannot be completely understood from the meanings of the component parts. For example, whereas it is possible to work out the meaning of (1a) on the basis of knowledge of English grammar and the meaning of words, this would not be sufficient to work out that (1b) can mean something like 'If Sam dies, her children will be rich'. This is because *kick the bucket* is an idiom.

1a: *If Sam mends the bucket, her children will be rich.*

1b: *If Sam kicks the bucket, her children will be rich.*

The problem with phrases and idioms, in a parsing context, is that it is not usually possible to parse them using the normal rules.

Throughout the chapter there will be a detailed discussion over Context Free Grammar for parsing Bangla Text and predictive Bangla parser for constructing parse table. Here a top down parsing scheme is adopted and the problem of left recursion is avoided applying left factoring over the proposed CFG.

RELATED WORKS

Modern Bangla morphology is very productive, especially for verbs, with the root verbs takes around 168 different forms. Bangla lexicon also has a very large number of compound words

(words that have more than one root), which can be created from at most any combination of nouns, pronouns and adjectives. An effort is made at building a complex morphological parser for Bangla, where it can only handle simple words with a single root. Though the addition of inflectional suffixes in Bangla compound word is fairly complex, the compound word's individual root words may retain their inflectional suffixes. Such a compound word morphological parser is developed which can efficiently parse compound words having inflectional suffix and also resolves ambiguities. Some rules are used to develop the morphological analysis of simple and compound Bangla words that can be used to make Universal Natural Language (UNL)-Bangla dictionary for converting the natural Bangla sentences to UNL documents and vice versa.

There has been no organized formal initiative for generating a context-free grammar for Bangla Language. There are some books available on context-free grammars for Bangla but most of them have been limited to the writers' way of generating the grammar rather than producing a generic grammar to cover the whole language (Anwar, Anwar & Bhuiyan, 2009; Aho, Sethi & Ullman, 2002).

Shift-reduce parsing is the simplest kind of bottom-up parsing. Here the parser takes an input string (sentence) and repeatedly pushes the next input word onto a stack which is the shift operation. If the top n items on the stack match the n items on the right-hand side of some production, then they are popped off the stack and the item on the left-hand side of the production is pushed on the stack. This replacement operation is the reduce part of the parsing. The parser ends its work when all the input is consumed and there is only one item remaining on the stack which is a parse tree with the start symbol of the grammar as its root. The parser fails to parse a sentence when there are no remaining input words to shift or when there is no way to reduce the remaining items on the stack. The second problem occurs because the parser blindly reaches the root of terminal using the productions (Sengupta & Chaudhuri, 1997).

Recursive descent Parsing is another way to produce parse trees for an input sentence. This parser interprets the grammar as a specification of how to break a high-level goal into several lower-level sub-goals. The top-level goal is to find the start symbol of the grammar and sub-goals are the production that breaks down the start symbols of the grammar. Such sub-goals are matched with an input sentence and succeed to its next state if the next word is matched. If there is no match the parser backtracks to a previous node and tries a different alternative. One problem with this recursive decent method is that when a production is recursive, the parser keeps on generating a never-ending parse tree when it selects the recursive production (Sengupta & Chaudhuri, 1997). An advantage for recursive decent over the shift-reduce method is that the parser can be forced to choose a specific production to continue parsing. Thus, this makes it easier to produce correct parse tree of a sentence in a given grammar which may not be possible with a shift-reduce parser for the same grammar.

A rule-based Bangla parser has been proposed in (Saha, 2006), that handles semantics as well as POS identification from Bangla sentences and ease the task of handling semantic issues in machine translation.

An open source morphological analyzer for Bangla using finite state technology is described in (Faridee & Tyers, 2009). They developed the monolingual dictionary called Monodix, stored in XML file.

Anwar, Anwar & Bhuiyan (2009) address a method to analyze syntactically Bangla sentence using context-sensitive grammar and interpret the input Bangla sentence to English using the NLP conversion unit. The system is based on analyzing an input sentence and converting into a structural representation.

There have been several parsing technique proposed for Bangla Language. A parsing methodology for Bangla natural language sentences is proposed by Hoque and Ali (2003) and shows how phrase structure rules can be implemented by top-down and bottom-up parsing approach to parse simple sentences of Bangla. An approach named Predicate Preserving Parser (PPP) is described in (Ali, Ripon and Allayear 2012) which maps Bangla text in UNL which then can be translated to any other natural languages. A technique of unsupervised morphological learning for Bengali language is introduced in (Dasgupta & Ng, 2006). A Bengali Dependency Parser based on statistical data driven parsing system followed by a rule based post processing is presented in (Ghosh et. al., 2010). A comprehensive approach for Bangla syntax analysis was developed (Mehedy, Arifin & Kaykobad, 2003) where a formal language is defined as a set of strings. Each string is a concatenation of terminal symbols.

Some other approaches such as Lexical Functional Grammar (LFG) (Sengupta & Chaudhuri, 1997), and Context Sensitive Grammar (CSG) (Hoque & Ali, 2004; Murshed, 1998; Selim & Iqbal, 1999) have also been developed for parsing Bangla sentences. LFG is a monotonic theory of syntax. Instead of postulating different derivational levels represented in the same formal language, it incorporates different parallel levels of information, which can all potentially access each other, each with its own formal language. The assumption about parallel levels of information extends even to non-syntactic aspects of grammar. Thus, for example, semantic information is assumed to be available to various levels of syntax, and syntactic levels can input into phonology (Joshi, 1993).

Some developed Bangla parser using SQL to check the correctness of sentence; but its space complexity is inefficient. Besides, it takes more time for executing SQL command. As a result those parsers becomes slower. A technique is implemented to perform structural analysis of Bangla sentences of different tenses using Context-Free Grammar (CFG) rule (Anwar, Shume & Bhuiyan, 2010). A methodology for analyzing the Bangla sentences in semantic manner is presented in (Hoque, Rahman & Dhar, 2007) and (Hasan, Mondal & Saha, 2010) presents a technique for detecting the named entity based on classifier for Bangla documents. But these papers (Anwar, Shume & Bhuiyan, 2010; Hoque, Rahman & KumarDhar, 2007; Hasan, Mondal & Saha, 2010) do not deal with the detail grammar recognition for Bangla sentences.

PARSING BANGLA SENTENCES WITH CONTEXT FREE GRAMMAR

Context Free Grammar

The most commonly used and mathematical system for modeling constituent structure in natural languages is the Context-Free Grammar, or CFG. Context-free grammars are also called Phrase Structure Grammars. A Context-Free Grammar (CFG) is a set of recursive rewriting rules called productions used to generate string patterns. A CFG consists of the following components (Aho, Sethi & Ullman, 2002):

1. A start symbol for the grammar.
2. A set of terminal symbols that are characters that appear in the strings generated by the grammar.
3. A set of non-terminal symbols that are placeholders for patterns of terminal symbols that can be generated by the non-terminal symbols.
4. A set of productions that are used to replace the non-terminals with other non-terminals or terminals.

A formal language is context-free if there is a context-free grammar that generates it.

This chapter describes a way of producing CFG for Bangla Language and designing a Bangla parser. The grammar discussed throughout the chapter can successfully parse a number of sentences. We have defined a tag set and according to the tag set, we tagged the word. In the next step of producing CFG, we defined the constituents and finally the rules were generated. We used top-down parsing techniques for designing Bangla parser by using XML. Our parser decides which sentence is correct and which is to be rejected. And finally generate a parse tree for this sentence by using Bangla Parser.

There are a number of important subclasses of the context-free grammars:

- LR(*k*) grammars (also known as deterministic context-free grammars) allow parsing (string recognition) with deterministic pushdown automata, but they can only describe deterministic context-free languages.
- Simple LR, Look-Ahead LR grammars are subclasses that allow further simplification of parsing.
- LL(*k*) and LL(*) grammars allow parsing by direct construction of a leftmost derivation as described above, and describe even fewer languages.
- Simple grammars are a subclass of the LL(1) grammars mostly interesting for its theoretical property that language equality of simple grammars is decidable, while language inclusion is not.
- Bracketed grammars have the property that the terminal symbols are divided into left and right bracket pairs that always match up in rules.
- Linear grammars have no rules with more than one non terminal in the right hand side.
- Regular grammars are a subclass of the linear grammars and describe the regular languages, i.e., they correspond to finite automata and regular expressions.

Context-free grammars play a central role in the description and design of programming languages and compilers. They are also used for analyzing the syntax of natural languages. Noam Chomsky (1956) has posited that all human languages are based on context-free grammars at their core, with additional processes that can manipulate the output of the context-free component (the transformations of early Chomskyan theory).

It is found that most parsing methods fall into one of these two classes, named as top-down parsing method and bottom-up parsing method. These terms refer to the order in which nodes in the parse tree are constructed.

In top-down parsing method, construction starts at the root and proceeds towards the leaves i.e., this method works from sentence symbol to the sentence. Parsers designed using top-down parsing method are known as top-down parsers.

On the contrary, in case of bottom-up parsing method, construction starts at the leaves and proceeds towards the root, i.e., this method works from the sentence to sentence symbol. And parsers which are designed using bottom-up parsing method are known as bottom-up parser.

There are some well-recognized problems when concerning with bottom up parsing. Bottom up parsing suffers from termination problem. It is inefficient when dealing with empty categories. Bottom up parsing is data directed as it attempts to parse the words that are there and inefficient when there is great lexical ambiguity (grammar-driven control might help here).

Parsing of Bangla sentences by using grammar rules is still in a rudimentary stage. Very little research has been conducted regarding parsing of Bangla sentences but a significant number of research activities have been conducted on the recognition of Bangla characters. Some developers developed Bangla parser using SQL to check the correctness of sentence. But it takes more space on our computers, meaning its space complexity is inefficient. Besides, it takes more time for executing SQL command. As a result those parsers becomes slower. To decrease time and space, XML files re used for storing data which is more speedy and takes up less space.

The extensions and refinements presented in this chapter over previous works especially in Hasan et al. (2011) are as follows:

- A set of CFG rules.
- Store data into XML file.
- Design a Bangla Parser by using table-driven method with top-down approach.
- Remove grammar ambiguity by using left factoring.
- Construct a parse tree.

Bangla words are stored as tag and its corresponding constituents or POS are used as value. More over the idea of left factoring have been applied to remove the left recursion and ambiguity of the grammar and hence according to the designed grammar, the parser can detect the errors in a Bangla sentence.

SOLUTION AND RECOMMENDATIONS

A Parsing Scheme for Bangla Grammar Recognition

A predictive parser is an efficient way of implementing recursive decent parsing by handling the stack of activation record.

The predictive parser is composed of four elements namely:

1. **Input:** Contains the string to be parsed or checked, followed by a $, the right end marker.
2. **Stack:** Contains a sequence of grammar symbols.
3. **Parse Table:** A two dimensional array M[A,*n*] where A is nonterminal and n is a terminal or $ sign.
4. **Output.**

Building the Word Repository/ Dictionary Using XML

XML (eXtensible Markup Language) has been designed as a markup language and a textual format. It provides for a description of a document's contents, with non-predefined tags, and does not provide for any presentational characteristics. The eXtensible Markup Language (XML) is now used almost everywhere for its simplicity and ease of use. It is a good format to store any kind of data. The tasks behind using XML are always the same: reading data from XML and writing data into it. XML have several advantages. Some of them are:

1. Ease of access.
2. Efficient in response to access time.
3. Easy to format the grammar structure.
4. No need to use any space consuming DBMS.
5. Ease of defining the category of words.
6. Easy to implement and integrate.

The general format of XML tag is

<tag_name>value</tag_name>

A dictionary is a very basic Natural Language Processing (NLP) tool used to get the meaning, parts of speech, and usage of a word and can also be used as a spell-checker to detect errors in a sentence and correct them by providing a set of correct alternatives which includes the intended word. To design the dictionary in XML, we consider *Bangla word* as tag_name and *value* as its corresponding POS. An example of XML file is shown in Figure 1.

Figure 1. XML word repository

```
<?xml version="1.0" encoding="ISO-8859-1"?>
<!-- Edited by XMLSpyΠ-->

<WORD>
        <আমি>pronoun</ আমি >
        <খাই> verb</খাই>
        <একটি>modifier</একটি>
        <এবং>conjunction</এবং>
        <আমরা>pronoun</আমরা>
        <না>neg</না>
</WORD>
```

Categorization of Words

Each sentence is composed of one or more phrases. So if the syntactic constituents of sentences are identified, it will be easier to obtain the structural representation of the sentence (Hoque & Ali, 2003; Mehedy, Arifin & Kaykobad, 2003). Bangla words are tagged with their respective Parts-Of-Speech (POS), modifier, pattern, number (Haque & Khan, 2005), and stored in XML file.

Table 1 shows the tag sets used in XML file for storing Bangla words. Every word is tagged with the appropriate member of the tag set and stored in the XML file in a definite format.

Table 1. Tag set description for Bangla grammar

Tag Name (Symbol)	Examples
Noun (noun)	রহিম, বিদ্যালয়ে, ছেলে, বই, ভাত,টাকা।
Pronoun (pronoun)	আমি, আমরা, তুমি, সে, তারা।
Adjective (adjective)	ভাল, দশ, অনেক, শখ।
Verb (verb)	খাই, খেলে, পড়ছে,পড়া।
Conjunction (conjunction)	এবং, ও, চেয়ে।
Negative Description (neg)	না , নয়।
Modifier (modifier)	এ, একটি, একদিন।

Defining Constituents and Phrases

Each sentence is to be partitioned into its constituents. A constituent expresses the complete meaning for a specific context. After tagging the words, each sentence is to be broken down into their constituent parts. The constituents of the sentences found out are shown in the Table 2.

Grammar Design with CFG

Once constituents have been identified, the productions for Context-Free Grammar (CFG) are developed for Bangla sentence structures. Table 3 shows the productions along with their respective constituents. As Bangla grammar has different forms, the same production term can be used only by reorganizing the in the grammar. For example, following three forms can be applied by reorganizing the production terms.

1. আমি ভাত খাই |
2. আমি খাই ভাত |
3. ভাত আমি খাই |

CFG Productions for Bangla Grammar

The CFG productions for the Bangla grammar G is defined as follows:

S –> NP VP

NP –> noun conjunction noun | noun ip| noun pronoun conjunction pronoun| noun pronoun ip| noun pronoun noun| noun pronoun adjective| noun pronoun pronoun| noun pronoun tp| noun adjective| noun noun conjunction pronoun| noun noun aw| noun noun| noun| noun pronoun| pronoun conjunction pronoun| pronoun ip| pronoun noun conjunction noun| pronoun noun ip| pronoun noun adjective| pronoun noun conjunction pronoun| pronoun noun aw| pronoun noun| pronoun adjective| pronoun pronoun conjunction pronoun|

Table 2. Defining constituents

No.	Constituents	Symbol	Definitions	Examples
1	Noun Phrase	NP	Noun phrase may be consists of only noun or pronoun. It may be modified by quantifier, post position, specifier, plural marker etc.	রহিম, আমি, এ পথে।
2	Verb Phrase	VP	A group of words including a verb and its complements, objects, or other modifiers that functions syntactically as a verb. In English a verb phrase combines with a noun or noun phrase acting as subject to form a simple sentence.	বই পড়ছে, পথ্য সেবন করে, খাওয়া হল না।
3	Adjective Phrase	AP	A group of words including an adjective and its complements or modifiers that functions as an adjective, as too openly critical of the administration.	দশ, ভাল ছেলে।

Table 3. Constituents for developing the grammar

Constituents (Symbol)	Productions	Examples
Noun Phrase (NP)	NP –> noun NP → pronoun NP → modifier noun etc.	রহিম, আমি, এ পথে।
Verb Phrase (VP)	VP –> noun verb VP –> noun verb verb VP –> noun verb ptrn etc.	বই পড়ছে, পথ্য সেবন করে, খাওয়া হল না।
Adjective Phrase (AP)	AP –> adjective AP –> adjective noun etc .	দশ, ভাল ছেলে।

pronoun pronoun aw| pronoun pronoun| pronoun tp| pronoun| modifier noun| modifier adjective ptrn| modifier adjective| modifier pronoun| modifier conjunction adjective| modifier| adjective noun| adjective pronoun| adjective conjunction adjective| adjective ptrn| adjective| ip| tp| xp ip| xp pronoun conjunction pronoun| xp pronoun ip| xp pronoun noun| xp pronoun adjective| xp pronoun tp| xp adjective| xp noun conjunction pronoun| xp noun aw| xp noun| xp tp| xp aw| tp pronoun| tp adjective| tp ip| tp pronoun conjunction pronoun| tp pronoun noun| tp pronoun adjective| tp pronoun tp| tp noun conjunction pronoun| tp noun aw| tp aw.

AP –> adjective noun| adjective pronoun| adjective ptrn

VP –> noun verb| noun verb verb ptrn| noun verb verb adjective verb| noun verb verb adjective noun| noun verb verb adjective pronoun| noun verb verb adjective| noun verb verb noun adjective verb| noun verb verb noun ptrn| noun verb verb noun aw| noun verb verb noun adjective verb| noun verb verb noun verb ptrn| noun verb verb noun verb aw| noun verb verb noun verb adjective| noun verb verb noun ptrn| nounverb verb noun pronoun| noun verb verb| pronoun adjective verb| pronoun verb verb ptrn| pronoun verb verb adjective verb| pronoun verb verb adjective noun| pronoun verb verb adjective pronoun| pronoun verb ptrn| pronoun verb aw| pronoun verb adjective| pronoun verb pronoun| pronoun verb noun| pronoun ptrn | verb verb verb adjective| verb verb verb adjective verb| verb verb verb ptrn| verb verb verb pronoun| verb verb ptrn| verb verb adjective verb| verb verb adjective noun| verb verb adjective pronoun| verb verb noun adjective verb| verb verb noun verb ptrn| verb verb noun verb aw| verb verb noun verb adjective| verb verb noun ptrn| verb verb noun verb pronoun| verb adjective| verb adjective verb ptrn| verb adjective noun| verb adjective verb noun| verb adjective verb noun verb | adjective noun verb adjective verb| adjective noun verb ptrn| adjective noun verb pronoun| adjective noun adjective ptrn| adjective noun adjective aw| adjective noun adjective | adjective pronoun| adjective ptrn | conjunction

Left Factoring

The above grammar G is ambiguous. The parser generated from this kind of grammar is not efficient as it requires backtracking. To remove the ambiguity from the grammar the grammar productions are reconstructed by left factoring.

Left factoring is a grammar transformation useful for producing a grammar suitable for predictive parsing. The basic idea is that when it is not clear which of the productions are to use to expand a non terminal then it can defer to take decision until we get an input to expand it. In general, if we have productions of form:

$$A \rightarrow \alpha\beta_1 \,\middle|\, \alpha\beta_2$$

We left factored productions by getting the input α and break it as follows:

$$A \rightarrow \alpha A'$$
$$A' \rightarrow \beta_1 \,\middle|\, \beta_2$$

The above grammar is correct and is free from conflicts. After left factoring the grammar G, the reconstructed left factored grammar productions are as below:

S -> NP VP

NP -> noun NP1|pronoun NP2|modifier AP1|conjunction NP1| AP | NP2 |xp NP1 |tp NP1

NP1 -> conjunction noun |ip | pronoun NP2 | adjective | noun NP3 | tp | aw |ε

NP2 -> conjunction pronoun | ip | noun NP1 | adjective | pronoun NP3 | tp | ε

NP3 -> conjunction pronoun| aw | ε

AP -> adjective AP1

AP1 -> noun | adjective AP2 | pronoun | conjunction AP | ε

AP2 -> ptrn | ε

VP -> noun VP1| pronoun VP4 | verb VP2 | AP VP3 | conjunction

VP1 -> verb VP2 | adjective VP3 | pronoun noun |noun pronoun

VP2 -> verb VP3 | ptrn | aw | AP VP3 | ε

VP3 -> verb VP4 | ptrn | adjective VP5 | noun VP4 | ε

VP4 -> AP verb | verb VP2| ptrn | pronoun

VP5 -> verb| noun VP4| pronoun AP1

There have been lexical productions which are as follows:

noun -> রহিম । বিদ্যালয়ে। ছেলে। বই। ভাত। টাকা । কণে । সিংহ । ঘাস

pronoun -> আমি । আমরা । তুমি । সে । তারা

verb -> খাই । খেলে । করবে । পড়া । চলে । যাই

adjective -> ভাল । বলবান । গুণবান । একটু । দশ । অনেক । শখ । দ্রুত

conjunction -> এবং । ও । চেয়ে

modifier -> এ । একটি । একদিন । এই

ptrn -> না । নয়

Designing Bangla Parser

A parser for a grammar G is a program that takes a string as input and produces a parse tree as output if the string is a sentence of G or produces an error message indicating that the sentence is not according to the grammar G. The idea of predictive parser design is well understood in compiler design (Murshed, 1998). A predictive parser is proposed in (Hasan et al., 2011) that can recognize mistakes of Bengali sentences when there is no entry for terminal in parse table.

To construct a predictive parser for grammar G two functions namely FIRST() and FOLLOW() are important. These functions allow the entries of a predictive parse table for G. Once the parse table has been constructed any string could be verified whether it satisfy the grammar G or not. The FIRST() and FOLLOW() determines the entries in the parse table. Any other entries in the parse table are considered invalid.

Computation of FIRST and FOLLOW

FIRST(α) be the set of terminals that begin the strings derived from α. If α → ε then ε is also included in FIRST(α). The rules of computing FIRST (Aho, Sethi & Ullman, 2002) are as follows:

- If X is a terminal symbol ⇒ first(X) ={X}
- If X is a non-terminal symbol and X → ε is a production rule ⇒ ε is in first(X).
- If X is a non-terminal symbol and X → $Y^1Y^2.Y^n$ is a production rule ⇒ first(X) = first(Y1).

According to the rules of computing FIRST(α) (Aho, Sethi & Ullman, 2002) the values for FIRST() are computed for the grammar G and are shown here:

FIRST(S) = {noun, pronoun, modifier, adjective, conjunction, xp, tp}

FIRST(NP) = {noun, pronoun, modifier, adjective, conjunction, xp, tp}

FIRST(NP1) = {conjunction, ip, pronoun, adjective, noun, tp, aw, ε }

FIRST(NP2) = {conjunction, ip, pronoun, adjective, noun, tp, ε }

FIRST(NP3) = {conjunction, aw, ε}

FIRST(AP) = {adjective}

FIRST(AP1) = {noun, adjective, pronoun, conjunction, ε}

FIRST(AP2) = {ptrn, ε }

FIRST(VP) = {noun, pronoun, verb, adjective, conjunction}

FIRST(VP1) = {verb, adjective, pronoun, noun}

FIRST(VP2) = {verb, ptrn, aw, adjective, ε}

FIRST(VP3) = {noun, verb, adjective, ptrn, ε}

FIRST(VP4) = {verb, ptrn, pronoun, adjective, ε}

FIRST(VP5) = {verb, noun, pronoun}

FOLLOW(A) of a non terminal *A* is the set of terminals *a* that can appear immediately to the right of A. If A is the right most symbol in the sentential form then $ is added to FOLLW(A). The rules for computing FOLLOW (Aho, Sethi & Ullman, 2002) of a non terminal *A* is as follows:

- If S is the start symbol ⇒ $ is in follow(S).
- If A → αBβ is a production rule ⇒ everything in first(β) is follow(B) except ε.
- If (A→ αB is a production rule) or (A→ αBβ is a production rule and ε is in

first(β))⇒ everything in follow(A) is in follow(B).

According to the rules of computing FOLLOW(S) the values for FOLLOWS() are computed for the grammar G and are shown as follows:

FOLLOW(S) = {noun, adjective, pronoun, modifier, ip, xp, tp, conjunction}

FOLLOW(NP) ={noun, verb, adjective, pronoun}

FOLLOW(NP1) = {noun, verb, adjective, pronoun}

FOLLOW(NP2) = {noun, verb, adjective, pronoun}

FOLLOW(NP3) = {noun, verb, adjective, pronoun}

FOLLOW(AP) = {noun, verb, adjective, pronoun, ptrn, modifier, ip, xp, tp, conjunction}

FOLLOW(AP1) = {noun, verb, adjective, pronoun, ptrn, modifier, ip, xp, tp, conjunction}

FOLLOW(AP2) = {noun, verb, adjective, pronoun, ptrn, modifier, ip, xp, tp, conjunction}

FOLLOW(VP) = {noun, adjective, pronoun, modifier, ip, xp, tp, conjunction, $}

FOLLOW(VP1) ={noun, adjective, pronoun, modifier, ip, xp, tp, conjunction, $}

FOLLOW(VP2) = {noun, adjective, pronoun, modifier, ip, xp, tp, conjunction, $}

FOLLOW(VP3) = {noun, adjective, pronoun, modifier, ip, xp, tp, conjunction, $}

FOLLOW(VP4) = {noun, adjective, pronoun, modifier, ip, xp, tp, conjunction, $}

FOLLOW(VP5) = {noun, adjective, pronoun, modifier, ip, xp, tp, conjunction, $}

Parse Table Construction

Parse table is a two-dimensional array where each row is leveled with non terminal symbol and each column is marked with terminal or special symbol $. Each cell holds a production rule.

Let M[m, n] be a matrix where m is the number of non terminals in grammar G and n is the number of distinct input symbols that may occur in a sentence of grammar G. Table 4 shows the resulting parse table for the grammar G constructed by applying the following rules:

1. For each production of the form A → α of the grammar G for each terminal *a* in first(α), add A → α to M[A, a].
2. If ε is in first(α) then for each terminal in FOLLOW(A) add A → α to M[A, a].

The table shows all the valid entries for the parse table. Entries not in this table are error entries. All other undefined entries of the parsing table are error entries.

Parse Tree Generation

A parse tree for a grammar G is a tree where the root is the start symbol for G, the interior nodes are the non terminals of G and the leaf nodes are the terminal symbols of G. The children of a node T (from left to right) correspond to the symbols on the right hand side of some production for T in G. Every terminal string generated by a grammar has a corresponding parse tree and every valid parse tree represents a string generated by the grammar. We store the parse table M using a

Table 4. Predictive parse table for the grammar G

	Noun	Pronoun	Modifier	Adjective	Verb	Conjunction	ptrn	ip	aw	xp	tp	$
S	NP VP	NP VP	NP VP	NP VP		NP VP		NP VP		NP VP	NP VP	
NP	noun NP1	pronoun NP2	modifier noun	AP		conjunction NP1		NP2	aw	xp NP1	tp NP1	
NP1	noun NP3	pronoun NP2	NP	Adjective	ε	conjunction VP2		ip			tp	
NP2	noun NP1	pronoun NP3		Adjective	ε	conjunction pronoun		ip			tp	
NP3	ε	ε		ε	ε	conjunction AP			aw			
AP				adjective AP1								
AP1	noun	pronoun	ε	adjective AP2	ε	conjunction AP	ε	ε		ε	ε	ε
AP2	ε	ε	ε	ε	ε	ε	ptrn		ε	ε	ε	ε
VP	noun VP1	pronoun VP4		AP VP3	verb VP2	conjunction						
VP1	noun pronoun	pronoun noun		adjective noun	verb VP2							
VP2	noun VP3	ε	ε	AP VP3	verb VP3	ε	ptrn	ε	aw	ε	ε	ε
VP3	noun VP4	ε	ε	adjective VP5	verb VP4	ε	ptrn	ε		ε	ε	ε
VP4		pronoun		AP verb	verb VP2	ε	ptrn	ε		ε	ε	ε
VP5	noun VP4	pronoun	AP1		Verb							

two-dimensional array. To read an element from a two-dimensional array, we must identify the subscript of the corresponding *row* and then identify the subscript of the corresponding *column*. For example, the production "*NP→ modifier noun*" is in row 2, column 3, (see Table 4) so it is identified as M[2][3].

Let us explain the grammar for the sentence একটি ছেলে বই পড়ছে. Using the XML data file we get the tags "*modifier noun noun verb*". Using the production *S→ NPVP* of the grammar G the sentence matches to *NP noun verb*; in the second iteration the *noun verb* part matches to *noun VP1*. The *VP1* in turn matches to *verb VP4* and *VP4* produces ε. Table 5 shows the moves of our implementation using a stack.

Initially, the parser is in a configuration with s$ in the input buffer and the start symbol S on top of the stack and then $.

Managing Non-Traditional Forms

The structure of Bangla language may change in a sentence although the meaning does not change. For example, the sentence আমি ভাত খাই can also be written as আমি খাই ভাত or ভাত আমি খাই. The latter two forms are also correct and have the same meaning. Hence it is sometimes difficult to detect such reorganized non traditional forms in a single grammar. The proposed grammar can detect the the non traditional forms. For example, the grammar G detects the forms "আমি খাই ভাত" and "ভাত আমি খাই" are shown in Table 6 and

Table 5. Moves made by a Bangla parser on input "modifier noun noun verb" for correct sentence

Stack	Input	Action
$ S	modifier noun noun verb $	
$ VP NP	modifier noun noun verb $	S->NP VP
$ VP noun modifier	modifier noun noun verb $	NP-> modifier noun
$ VP noun	noun noun verb $	Poped
$ VP	noun verb $	Poped
$ VP1 noun	noun verb $	VP-> noun VP1
$ VP1	verb $	Poped
$ VP2 verb	verb $	VP1-> verb VP2
$ VP2	$	Poped
$	$	VP2-> ε
$	$	Sentence is accepted

Table 6. Moves made by a Bangla parser on input "pronoun verb noun" for correct sentence "আমি খাই ভাত"

Stack	Input	Action
$ S	pronoun verb noun $	
$ VP NP	pronoun verb noun $	S->NP VP
$ VP NP2 pronoun	pronoun verb noun $	NP->pronoun NP2
$ VP NP2	verb noun $	poped
$ VP	verb noun $	NP2->zero
$ VP3 verb	verb noun $	VP->verb VP3
$ VP3	noun $	poped
$ noun	noun $	VP3->noun
$	$	poped
$	$	Sentence is accepted

Table 7. Moves made by a Bangla parser on input "noun pronoun verb" for correct sentence "ভাত আমি খাই"

Stack	Input	Action
$ S	noun pronoun verb $	
$ VP NP	noun pronoun verb $	S->NP VP
$ VP NP1 noun	noun pronoun verb $	NP->noun NP1
$ VP NP1	pronoun verb $	Poped
$ VP	pronoun verb $	NP1->zero
$ verb AP pronoun	pronoun verb $	VP->pronoun AP verb
$ verb AP	verb $	Poped
$ verb	verb $	AP->zero
$	$	Poped
$	$	Sentence is accepted

Figure 2. Parse tree for Bangla parser on input "modifier noun noun verb"

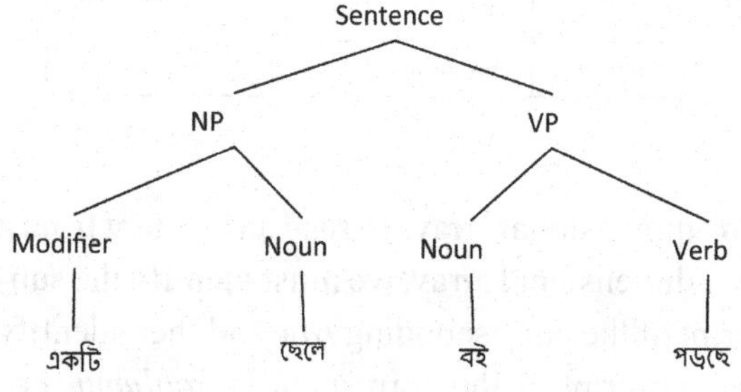

Figure 3. Parse tree for Bangla parser on input "pronoun verb noun"

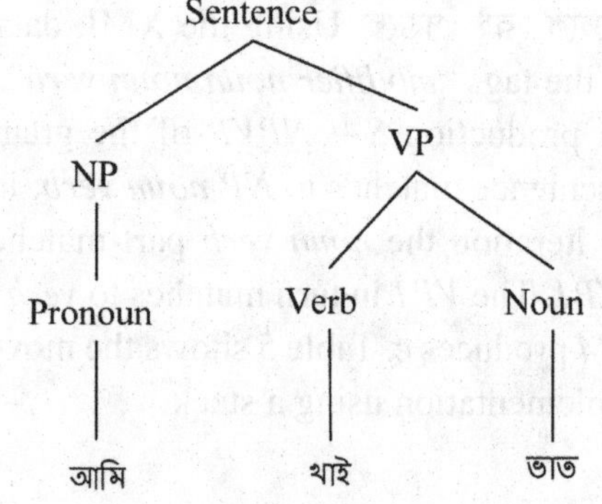

Figure 4. Parse tree for Bangla parser on input "noun pronoun verb"

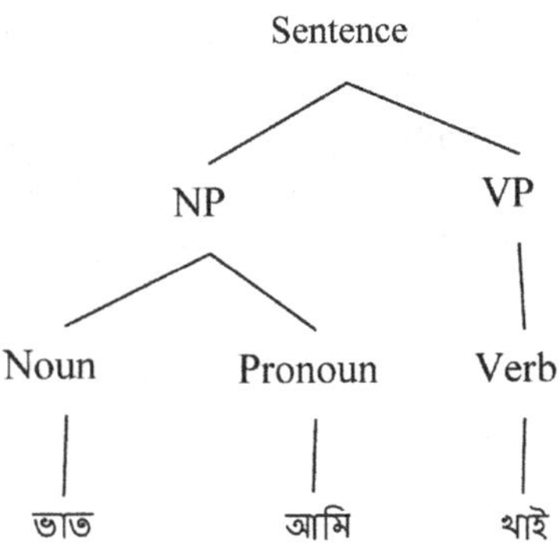

Table 8. Moves made by a Bangla parser on input "noun noun" for incorrect sentence

Stack	Input	Action
$ S	noun noun $	
$ VP NP	noun noun $	S->NP VP
$ VP NP1 noun	noun noun $	NP->noun NP1
$ VP NP1	noun $	Popped
$ VP NP3 noun	noun $	NP1->noun NP3
$ VP NP3	$	Popped
		Sentence is rejected

Table 7 respectively. Figure 3 and Figure 4 show the corresponding parse tree. Table 8 shows the moves for an incorrect sentence "রহিম বিদ্যালয়ে" of the form *"noun noun"*. The sentence is rejected because there is no verb in the sentence and such types of productions are not presented in the grammar G (see Algorithm 1).

Algorithm 1 is for parsing which uses the parse table *M* (Table 4) to produce a Bangla parser for the input of a Bangla sentence. Figure 2 shows the parse tree generated by the grammar G for the input একটি ছেলে বই পড়ছে of the form modifier *noun noun verb*.

PERFORMANCE ANALYSIS OF DESIGNED BANGLA PARSER

Some input sentences are considered to be used for performance analysis of the designed parser. There are three types of sentences used for this purpose:

1. Simple and traditional form
2. Some non-traditional form
3. Paragraphs

Algorithm 1. Parsing with table M

```
1.  Set Input Pointer(IP) to point to the first word of w;
2.  Set X to the top stack word;
3.  While (X! = $)
     Begin   /* stack is not empty */
       a.  If  X is a terminal,  pop the stack and advance IP;
       b.  If X is a Non terminal and  M[X,IP] has  the production  X → Y1Y2…Yk
             Output the production X -> Y1Y2 -Yk;
               Pop the stack;
               Push Yk, Yk-1,. . ., Y1 onto the stack, with Y1 on top;
       c.  If X=$, Sentence is Accepted.
     End
```

The paragraphs are collected from newspaper. By non-traditional form we mean the same meaning of another sentence having structural similarity. For example, "আমি ভাত খাই" and "খাই আমি ভাত" sentences are approximately similar but later on is rarely used. Table 4 shows the success rate of our proposed grammar.

- **Input Sentences:**

তিনি কি ভাল না?, আমি ভাত খাই । আমি কি ভাত খাই?, আমি কি ভাত খাই না? "বাহ! পাখিটি তো খুব সুন্দর"। শিতে আমরা খুব কষ্ট পাই । তোমরা আগামীকাল এসো । আমি, তুমি ও সে বাড়ি যাই । আগামীকাল কি তুমি আসবে?

- **Input Paragraphs:**

মাঝরাতে হঠাৎ করেই আপনার অসুখ করল। চিকিৎসক বা হাসপাতাল আশপাশে নেই।ভয় পাওয়ার কোন কারণ নেই । যদি আপনার হাতের কাছেই মোবাইল পান,তবে ডায়াল করুন হেল্প লাইনে । শীঘ্রই আপনি পেয়ে যাবেন দরকারি পরামর্শ।

আমরাই একমাত্র জাতি যারা ভাষার জন্য যুদ্ধ করেছি । মায়ের ভাষা বাংলাকে ছিনিয়ে এনেছি । ভাষার এই যুদ্ধ এখানেই বন্ধ হয়নি । বাংলাকে আলাদা করে প্রতিষ্ঠিত করার জন্য শুরু হয়েছে প্রযুক্তির ব্যাবহার । সেই যুদ্ধে ঝাঁপিয়ে পড়েছে মেধাবী জনতা।

একসময় বাংলা ভাষা যে হুমকির মুখে ছিল, তার মূলে ছিল উপনিবেশিক শাসন।যা ছিল সংখ্যাগুরুর ওপর চাপিয়ে দেওয়া সংখ্যালঘুর শাসন । তার বিরুদ্ধে লড়াই করেছিল বাংলা ভাষাভাষী বেশির ভাগ মানুষ । কিন্তু একটি ভাষার শক্তি এর ব্যাবহারকারীদের মোট শক্তির সমান । ফলে বাংলা ভাষার বিরুদ্ধকারীরা পরাজিত হয়েছে । যেহেতু তারা সংখ্যায় বেশি ছিল না।

From Table 9, it is clearly viewed that the parser is about 70-80% correct.

Table 9. Success rate for different Bangla sentences

Types of Sentences	Total No. of Sentences per Paragraph (I)	Correctly Detected (D)	Acceptance Rate A=(D/I)*100%
Traditional	120	100	83.33%
Nontraditional	80	58	72.5%
Paragraph	25	18	72%

FUTURE RESEARCH DIRECTIONS

In this chapter, a context free grammar for Bangla language is described and hence a Bangla parser based on the grammar is developed. The approach is very much general to apply in Bangla Sentences and the method is well accepted for parsing a language of a grammar. The structural representation that has been built can cover the maximum simple, complex, and compound sentences. But the sentences composed of idioms and phrases are beyond the scope of this chapter.

There are lots of research scopes on the fields of Bangla Natural Language Parser. The future development may include the following.

1. More extensive CFGs with the addition of more constituents for parsing complex and compound sentences of Bangla NL more efficiently.
2. Efficient algorithm for Bangla NL Parser to solve the problem of ambiguity.
3. Parser for semantic analysis of Bangla natural sentences.

Fusion of top-down and bottom-up parsing technique could result in a more robust and powerful parsing technique.

CONCLUSION

It is well established that parsing natural language text is much more difficult than strictly defined computer languages. One reason is that grammars for natural languages are often complex, ambiguous, and specified by collections of examples rather than complete formal rules. The aim of this Chapter was to Design and Develop algorithms for Bangla Parser, which can parse Bangla language. Parsing is a process of transforming natural language into an internal system representation, which can be trees, dependency graphs, frames or some other SR (Structural Representation). If a natural language is successfully parse then grammar checking from this language becomes easy. Parsing a sentence that involves finding a possible legal structure for sentence and finally gets an SR. An SR generally graphic object and this representation cannot be deals with computer. The standard representation of an SR is a list that are one of the data structure that can be implemented and manipulated very easily within a computer. Our proposed CFG rules can be assigned all types of Bangla sentences into an SR. To represents a complex and a compound sentence into an SR, we used the decomposition technique. Further modify and extending the CFG rules (with the addition of sentences consisting of idioms and phrases, double word, change of voice, and narration), we can able to represents the all kinds of Bangla sentences which are used as an input of an MT engine to produced other equivalent sentences.

REFERENCES

Aho, A. V., Sethi, R., & Ullman, J. D. (2002). *Compilers principles, techniques and tools*. New York: Pearson Education.

Ali, M. N. Y., Ripon, S., & Allayear, S. M. (2012). UNL based Bangla natural text conversion: Predicate preserving parser approach. *International Journal of Computer Science Issues*, *9*(3), 259–265.

Anwar, M. M., Anwar, M. Z., & Bhuiyan, M. A. A. (2009). Syntax analysis and machine translation of Bangla sentences. *International Journal of Computer Science and Network Security*, *9*(8), 317–326.

Anwar, M. M., Shume, N. S., & Bhuiyan, M. A. A. (2010). Structural analysis of Bangla sentences of different tenses for automatic Bangla machine translator. *International Journal of Computer Science and Information Security*, *8*(9).

Dasgupta, S., & Ng, V. (2006). Unsupervised morphological parsing of Bengali. *Language Resources and Evaluation*, *40*, 311–330. doi:10.1007/s10579-007-9031-y.

Faridee, A. Z. M., & Tyers, F. M. (2009). Development of a morphological analyzer for Bengali. In *Proceedings of the First International Workshop on Free/Open-Source Rule-Based Machine Translation,* (pp. 43-50). IEEE.

Ghosh, A., Das, A., Bhaskar, P., & Bandyopadhyay, S. (2010). *Bengali parsing system*. Paper presented at ICON NLP Tool Contest 2010.

Haque, M. N., & Khan, M. (2005). Parsing Bangla using LFG: An introduction. *BRAC University Journal*, *2*(1), 105–110.

Hasan, K. M. A., Mahmud, A., Mondal, A., & Saha, A. (2011). Recognizing Bangla grammar using predictive parser. *International Journal of Computer Science & Information Technology*, *3*(6). doi: doi:10.5121/ijcsit.2011.3605.

Hasan, K. M. A., Mondal, A., & Saha, A. (2010). A context free grammar and its predictive parser for Bangla grammar recognition. In *Proceedings of International Conference on Computer and Information Technology,* (pp. 87 – 91). IEEE.

Hoque, M. M., & Ali, M. M. (2003). A parsing methodology for Bangla natural language sentences. In *Proceedings of International Conference on Computer and Information Technology*, (277-282). IEEE.

Hoque, M. M., & Ali, M. M. (2004). Context-sensitive phrase structure rule for structural representation of Bangla natural language sentences. In *Proceedings of International Conference on Computer and Information Technology*, (pp. 615-620). IEEE.

Hoque, M. M., Rahman, M. J., & Dhar, P. K. (2007). Lexical semantics: A New approach to analyze the Bangla sentence with semantic features. In *Proceedings of the International Conference on Information and Communication Technology*, (pp. 87 – 91). IEEE.

Joshi, S. (n.d.). *Selection of grammatical and logical functions in Marathi*. (PhD Thesis). Stanford University. Palo Alto, CA.

Mehedy, L., Arifin, N., & Kaykobad, M. (2003). Bangla syntax analysis: A comprehensive approach. In *Proceedings of International Conference on Computer and Information Technology (ICCIT)*, (pp. 287-293). ICCIT.

Murshed, M. M. (1998). Parsing of Bengali natural language sentences. In *Proceedings of International Conference on Computer and Information Technology (ICCIT)*, (pp. 185-189). ICCIT.

Saha, G. K. (2006). Parsing Bengali text: An intelligent approach. *ACM Ubiquity*, 7(13), 1–5. doi:10.1145/1132512.1127026.

Selim, M. R., & Iqbal, M. Z. (1999). Syntax analysis of phrases and different types of sentences in Bangla. In *Proceedings of International Conference on Computer and Information Technology (ICCIT)*, (pp. 175-186). ICCIT.

Sengupta, P., & Chaudhuri, B. B. (1997). A delayed syntactic-encoding-based LFG parsing strategy for an Indian language – Bangla. *Computational Linguistics*, *23*(2), 345–351.

Yarowsky, D. (1995). Unsupervised word sense disambiguation rivaling supervised methods. In *Proceedings of 33rd Annual Meeting of the ACL*, (pp. 189-196). ACL.

KEY TERMS AND DEFINITIONS

Bottom-Up Parsing: Construction starts at the leaves and proceeds towards the root, i.e. this method works from the sentence to sentence symbol.

Context-Free Grammar (CFG): A set of recursive rewriting rules called productions used to generate string patterns.

FIRST(): FIRST(α) be the set of terminals that begin the strings derived from α. If $\alpha \rightarrow \varepsilon$ then ε is also included in FIRST(α).

FOLLOW(): FOLLOW(A) of a non terminal A is the set of terminals a that can appear immediately to the right of A. If A is the right most symbol in the sentential form then $ is added to FOLLOW(A).

Parse Tree: A tree where the root of the tree is the start symbol for the grammar, the interior nodes are the non-terminals of the grammar, the leaf nodes are the terminals of the grammar and the children of a node starting from the left to the right correspond to the symbols on the right hand side of some production for the node in the grammar.

Parser: A parser analyzes the sequence of symbols presented to it based on the grammar.

Parsing: A method where a parser algorithm is used to determine whether a given input string is grammatically acceptable or not for a particular language.

Top-Down Parsing: In top-down parsing method, construction starts at the root and proceeds towards the leaves i.e., this method works from sentence symbol to the sentence. Parsers, which are designed using Top-down parsing method, are known as top-down parser.

Chapter 8
Dependency Parsing in Bangla

Utpal Garain
Indian Statistical Institute, India

Sankar De
Gupta College of Technological Sciences, India

ABSTRACT

A grammar-driven dependency parsing has been attempted for Bangla (Bengali). The free-word order nature of the language makes the development of an accurate parser very difficult. The Paninian grammatical model has been used to tackle the free-word order problem. The approach is to simplify complex and compound sentences and then to parse simple sentences by satisfying the Karaka demands of the Demand Groups (Verb Groups). Finally, parsed structures are rejoined with appropriate links and Karaka labels. The parser has been trained with a Treebank of 1000 annotated sentences and then evaluated with un-annotated test data of 150 sentences. The evaluation shows that the proposed approach achieves 90.32% and 79.81% accuracies for unlabeled and labeled attachments, respectively.

1. INTRODUCTION

Dependency parsing is a method of analyzing natural language sentences and outputs a tree of word-on-word dependencies (as opposed to constituent trees of context-free derivations) in a sentence. Dependency is defined as a binary asymmetric relation between two words. Dependency relations are close to semantic relations, which facilitate semantic interpretation of the sentence. This is why dependency parsing gained a lot of attention and popularity for natural language analysis and understanding in recent years.

DOI: 10.4018/978-1-4666-3970-6.ch008

Dependency parsing can be broadly divided into grammar-driven and data-driven parsing. Most of the modern grammar-driven dependency parsers parse by eliminating the parses which do not satisfy the given set of constraints. They view parsing as a constraint-satisfaction problem. Some of the constraint based parsers known in the literature can be found in (Karlsson, 1995; Maruyama, 1990; Bharati, 1993; Bharati, 2002; Tapanainen, 1998; Schröder, 2002; Debusmann, 2004). Multi-dimensional paradigm proposed in these studies attempted to capture various aspect of a language. Data-driven parsers, on the other hand, use a corpus to induce a probabilistic model for disambiguation (Nivre, 2005).

Constraint based parsing has been successfully tried for Indian languages (Bharati, 1993; Bharati, 2002). Under this scheme the parser exploits the syntactic cues present in a sentence and forms Constraint Graphs (CG). It then translates the CG into an Integer Programming problem. The solutions to the problem provide the possible parses for the sentence. Recent works of Bharati (2008b, 2009a, 2009b) show a substantial improvement in grammar driven IL parsing. But most of the works are confined to Hindi only.

Bangla, like other ILs, is a morphologically rich free-word order language. Parsing such types of languages is very challenging (Saha, 2006; Sarkar, 2006; & Hasan, 2011). In this paper we have used dependency based framework and Paninian model (Bharati, 1993; Bharati, 1995) for parsing Bangla sentences. Complex and compound sentences have been simplified to derive two or more simple sentences. A constraint-based approach has then been applied to parse the simple sentential structures. The method also includes the demand-source concept of Paninian grammar described later in this paper.

The very next section of the paper describes the demand-source approach of Paninian grammar. After that, the overall parsing approach is presented. The approach makes use of demand frames and therefore, the important concepts of demand frames are presented in the next section and it is shown that how frames are changed depending on the TAM of the verbs. The subsequent sections describe the constraints applied and it is discussed that how such constraints can be applied to reduce the problem to a bipartite graph matching problem. The algorithm for parsing a simple sentence is then explained. Evaluation results and error analysis has been discussed in the sections thereafter.

2. PANINIAN GRAMMAR

The Paninian framework was originally designed more than two millennia ago for writing a grammar for Sanskrit. This framework is now being adapted for analyzing modern Indian Languages (ILs) which are actually the derivatives of Sanskrit. Paninian grammar is particularly suited for morphologically rich free word ordered languages like most ILs including Bangla.

As conceived by the syntactico-semantic model of Paninian Grammar, every verbal root (*dhaatu*) denotes an action consisting of: (1) an activity and (2) a result. Result is the state which when reached the action is complete. Activity consists of actions carried out by different *participants* or *Karakas* (mostly noun groups) involved in the action. The Karakas have direct relation to the verb. The Paninian model used only six such Karakas such as K1, K2, K3, K4, K5, K7. Some additional relations have been described in (Bharti, 2009c) and the complete tag set has been given in Appendix A. In this approach the verb demands some karakas carryout the activity. Thus verb groups are known as Demand Groups and Karakas as the Source Groups or arguments. So for a very simple sentence (single Demand Group) like S1, the verb group is the root of the dependency tree connecting some noun groups with appropriate Karaka labels (Bharati, 1993). Consider the sentence in Box 1. The parsed output will be shown in Figure 1.

In sentence S1, Ram is performing the act of eating. So Ram is marked as K1 (karta/doer/subject). The activity eating directly affects *bhat* (rice). It is thus marked as K2 (karma/object).

Box 1.

<table>
<tr><td rowspan="4">S1:</td><td>রাম</td><td>ভাত</td><td>খায়</td></tr>
<tr><td>Ram</td><td>bhat</td><td>khay</td></tr>
<tr><td>Ram</td><td>rice</td><td>eats</td></tr>
<tr><td colspan="3">Ram eats rice.</td></tr>
</table>

Figure 1. Parsed output of S1

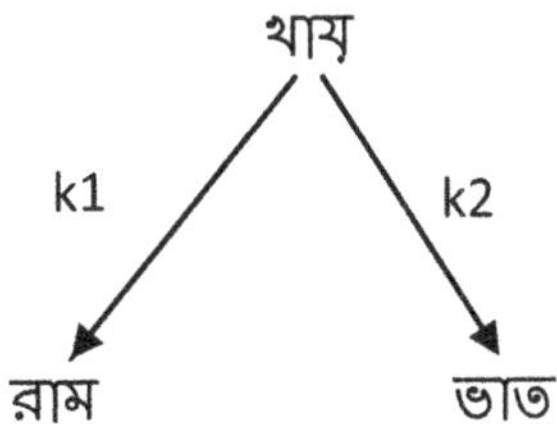

Simple sentences are parsed using the demand frames and transformation rules (Cormen, 2009) to handle the situation better. About 500 demand frames or Karaka frames including mixed verbs, main verbs and their causative forms have been considered in the present study.

3. THE PARSING APPROACH

This section describes the broad algorithmic approach of the parser. It also describes how compound and complex structures have been handled with the help of grammatical rules.

3.1. The Parsing Algorithm

Input: A sentence with all morphological and chunking information.

Output: A dependency tree having the chunked phrases as nodes.

Step 1: If the sentence is compound then divide the sentence to get two or more simple or complex sentences. Pass each of them to Step 2 one by one.
Otherwise pass the sentence to Step 2.

Step 2: If the sentence is complex then divide the sentence to get two or more simple sentences. Pass each of them to Step 3 one by one.
Otherwise pass the sentence to Step 3.

Step 3: Parse the simple sentence.

Step 4: Rejoin the parsed sentences divided in Step 2 with proper links and labels.

Step 5: Rejoin the parsed sentences divided in Step 1 with proper link and label.

Step 6: Return the parsed sentence.

3.2. Parsing of Compound Sentences

The sentences which have sentence level coordinate conjuncts have been treated as compound sentences and handled in Step 1 of the Algorithm. Consider the sentence in Box 2.

In the above sentence, two simple sentences shown within braces are joined with sentence label conjunct *ebam* (and) to form a compound sentence. Our approach is to identify these sentence label conjuncts and divide the sentence to make the parsing task easier. After parsing the two simple sentences the roots of the two sentences are linked with the conjunct with 'ccof' relation as is shown in Figure 2.

3.3. Parsing of Complex Sentences

The sentences having relative clauses are considered as complex sentences and handled in Step 2 of the Algorithm. Consider the sentence in Box 3.

The first part of the sentence is a relative clause which modifies '*se*' (he). '*je*' and '*se*' are grammatical markers of relative clause and main clause, respectively. Thus '*jekhane-sekhane*' (where-there), '*jar-tar*' (whose-his), etc., are such clause markers. With the help of those clause markers, a complex sentence is divided into multiple simple sentences which are then parsed in Step 3 and rejoined in Step 4 as shown in Figure 3.

Box 2.

S2:	(রাম ভাত খায়) এবং (শ্যাম রুটি খায়)
	(*Ram bhat khay*) ***ebam*** (*shyam rutl khay*)
	(Ram rice eats) **and** (Shyam bread eats)
	Ram eats rice **and** Shyam eats bread.

Figure 2. Rejoining simple structures to form original compound structure

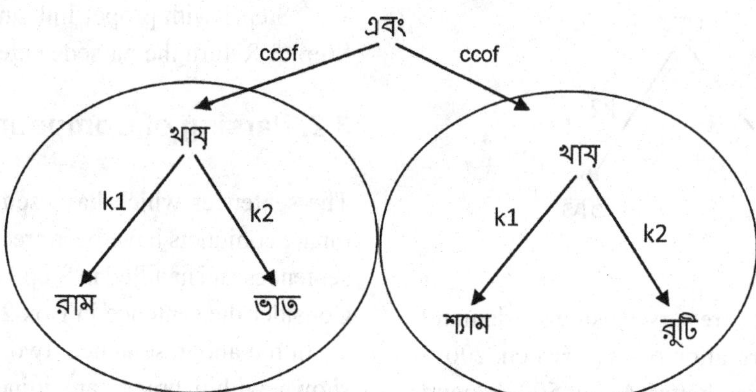

3.4. Demand Frames and their Transformations

Simple sentences have been parsed with demand satisfaction approach. Here comes the role of Demand Frames or Karaka Frames. A Demand Frame or Karaka Frame of a verb is a tabular listing of the demands it makes i.e. the list of all possible Karakas it can take to form a meaningful sentence (Begum, 2008b; De, 2009). A mapping is also specified in the list between Karaka relations and Vibhaktis (post-positions, suffix). The mapping depends on the verbal semantics and the Tense, Aspect, and Modality (TAM) label. The basic frame or default frame of a verb is prepared for present indefinite form of the verb (Bhattacharya, 1993). Other TAMs may have their own transformation rules depending on which the basic frame is changed. The Demand Frame of a verb also specifies what Karakas are mandatory or optional for the verb and what Vibhaktis (post-positions) they take. Thus, for a given verb with some TAM label, the appropriate Karaka frame can be obtained using the basic frame and the corresponding transformation rules.

Box 3.

S3:	(যে ছেলেটি সেখানে বসে আছে) (সে আমার ভাই হয়)
	(je chheleti sekhane base achhe) *(se amar bhai hay)*
	(The boy who there sitting is) (he my brother is)
	The boy who is sitting there is my brother.

Figure 3. Joining two clauses

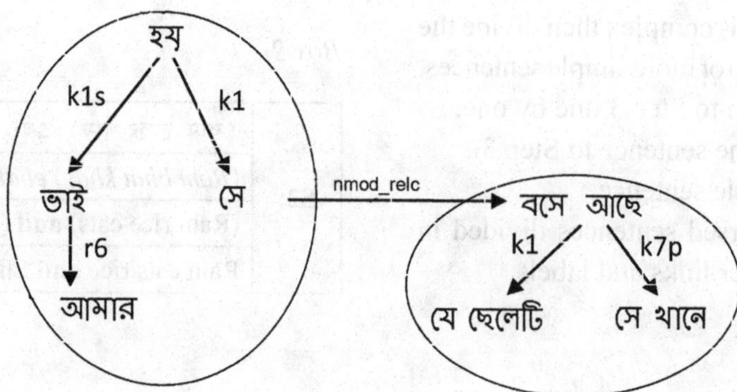

3.4.1. Implementation Issues

Development of Karaka frames is discussed below.

- **Verb:** গোনে (*gon*)
- **Verb Type:** Transitive
- **English Gloss:** To count

Table 1 can be derived from the real life examples encountered in day to day life with the verb '*gon*.' In Box 4 and Box 5, k1 and k2 in both the sentences are mandatory (m), without them the sentences seem to be incomplete. Other Karakas are desirable (d).

Table 1. Karaka frame for verb 'gon' (to count)

Arc_label	Necessity	Vibhakti	Lexical Type
k1	m	Φ	Noun
k2	m	Φ	Noun
k3	d	দিয়ে/এ	Noun
k7t	d	Φ/কে/এ/তে/এতে/য়	Noun
k7p	d	তে/এতে/য়	Noun

3.4.2. Transformations

The above frame is the default frame as it has been prepared for the present indefinite form of the verb. This frame may change with the change of the form of the verb, i.e., TAM labels. If the present indefinite form '*gon*' is changed to '***gunte hay***', we have to apply 'te_ha' (TAM) transformation rule to obtain the frame corresponding to this form. Consider the example with the '***gunte hay***' form of the verb '*gon*.' The example S5 becomes S6 (Box 6).

This example clearly shows that the Vibhakti corresponding to the karaka K1 changes from 'ф' to '*ke*.' So the transformation rule for the 'te_ha' TAM becomes Table 2.

We have prepared an exhaustive TAM list in Bangla and transformation rules, if exists, have been framed for each of them.

3.5. Constraint Graph

For a given sentence after the word groups have been formed, the verb groups are identified. Then each of the source groups are tested against the Karaka restrictions in each Karaka frame (transformed according to TAM rules). When testing

Box 4.

S4:	রাম **ф** (k1)	সন্ধ্যায় (k7t)	আকাশে (k7p)	তারা **ф** (k2)	গোনে (verb)
	Ram **ф** (k1)	*sandhyay* (k7t)	*akase* (k7p)	*tara* **ф** (k2)	*gon* (verb)
	Ram	evening - Loc	sky - Loc	star	count (3rd person)
	Ram counts stars in the sky in the evening.				

Box 5.

S5:	রাম **ф** (k1)	হাতে (/হাত **দিয়ে**) (k3)	টাকা **ф** (k2)	গোনে (verb)
	Ram **ф** (k1)	*hate* (/*hat* ***diye***)(k3)	*taka* **ф** (k2)	*gon* (verb)
	Ram	hand – Loc (/hand with)	money (k2)	count (3rd person)
	Ram counts money with his hand.			

Box 6.

S6:	রামকে (k1)	সন্ধ্যায় (k7t)	আকাশে (k7p)	তারা ϕ (k2)	গুনতে হয় (verb)
	Ramke (k1)	*sandhyay* (k7t)	*akase* (k7p)	*tara* ϕ (k2)	*gunte hay*
	Ram - dat	evening - Loc	sky - Loc	star	count (to have)
	Ram has to count stars in the sky in the evening.				

Table 2. Transformation rule for te_ha TAM for 'gon' verb

Arc_label	Necessity	Vibhakti	Lexical Type
k1	m	Φ	noun

a source group against the Karaka restrictions of a demand group, vibhaki information is checked and if found satisfactory the source group becomes a candidate for the Karaka of the demand group. This can be shown in the form of a Constraint Graph (CG) (Bharati, 2008b, 2009a). Nodes of the graph are the word groups and there is an arc from a verb group to a source group labeled by a Karaka, if the source group satisfies the Karaka restrictions in the Karaka chart.

A restricted CG can be obtained by following certain rules as mentioned below:

1. **Leftness Rule:** In most of the Indian languages, source groups occur before the demand groups. Although some exceptions are seen. This can be well handled by including an extra column in the demand frame as src_pos (source position) which may be '*l*' (can occur at the left of a demand group) or 'r' (can occur at the right of a demand group).
2. **Gender, Number, Person (GNP) Agreement:** The 'Karta Karaka' (k1) always agrees in GNP (gender, number, person) for non-passive sentences and k2 for passive.
3. Lexical type of the source must match that in the Karaka frame.

For example, consider the sentence S7 (Box 7) and see how its CG is constructed. The demand frame for খা (*kha*) can be seen in Table 3. No transformation is needed for present indefinite form of the verb '*kha*' has been directly used. The CG (restricted) corresponding to the above sentence becomes Figure 4.

3.5.1. Constraints

A parse is a sub-graph of the constraint graph containing all the elements of the CG and satisfying the following constraints:

C1: For each of the mandatory Karakas in a Karaka frame for each demand group, there should be exactly one outgoing edge labeled by the Karaka from the demand group.

C2: For each of the desirable or optional Karakas in a Karaka frame for each demand group, there should be at most one outgoing edge labeled by the Karaka from the demand group.

C3: There should be exactly one incoming edge into each source group.

If several sub-graph of the CG satisfies the above conditions, the sentence is probably ambiguous. We have tried to resolve ambiguities by applying more grammatical constraints as discussed later.

Box 7.

S7:	আমি	দুপুরে	ভাত	খাই
	ami **ф**	*dupure*	*bhat* **ф**	*khai*
	I	noon - Loc	rice	eat (1st person)
	I eat rice at noon.			

3.5.2. Parsing as Bipartite Graph Matching Problem

The parsing problem now can be reduced to a bipartite graph matching problem (Bharati, 1995, Cormen, 2009). The bipartite graph (BG) G is defined as a three-tuple (D,S,E) where D={(d_i, k_j), for each demand group d_i and its Karaka demands k_j's in its demand frame}, S is the set of all source groups {s}, E is the set of edges from D to S, i.e. E={(d_i,k_j,s_t), if an attachment is possible from (d_i, k_j) to a source group s_t and D∩S=ф. For a weighted BG, E is redefined as E={(d_i,k_j,s_t,w), where w is called the weight of the edge. We have set a weight of 2 for mandatory Karakas and 1 for desirables, so that a mandatory Karaka surely gets an arc. Now we define a matching M on the bipartite graph as M⊆E such that for all vertices v∈D or v∈S, at most one edge of M is incident on v. A vertex v will be matched by M if some edge of M is incident on v; otherwise v is unmatched. The matching problem is to find a maximum matching of G, i.e., matching M with maximum cardinality. A maximal matching is called complete if every node in D and S has an edge (one-to-one and onto).

Table 3. Karaka Frame for verb 'kha' (to eat)

Arc_label	Necessity	Vibhakti	Lexical Type	Src_pos
k1	m	Φ	noun	l
k2	d	Φ	noun	l
k3	d	দিয়ে/এ	noun	l
k7t	d	Φ/এ/তে/এতে/য়	noun	l
k7p	d	এ /তে/এতে/য়	noun	l

Figure 4. Restricted CG for S7

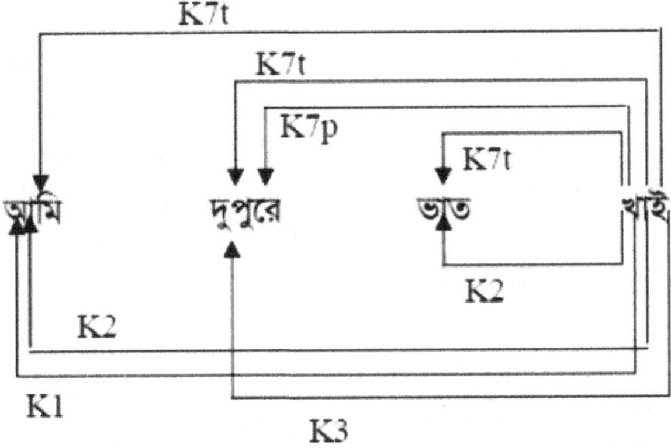

3.5.3. Constructing Initial Bipartite Graph

The initial bipartite graph is constructed in three stages:

1. For every source node s in the constraint graph form a node s in S.
2. For every demand node d in the constraint graph and for every Karaka k in the Karaka frame for d, form a node (d, k) in D.
3. For every edge (d, s) in the constraint graph labeled by Karaka k, create an edge 'e' (d, k, s, w) in E where w=2 if k is mandatory, w=1 if k is desirable, w is called the weight of the edge 'e.'

3.6. Parsing of Simple Sentences

Pre-assumptions: (1) Chunking has been done with full accuracy, (2) Demand Frames are complete in the sense that the set of arc-labels (Karaka labels) is exhaustive, Karaka-Vibhakti mapping is accurate and the transformation rules are exhaustive for a particular verb, (3) Demand Frames are exhaustive in the sense that every verb that is used in the language has a Demand Frame.

Algorithm 2. Parse_simple_sentence

Input: Chunked simple sentence with all morphological information.
Output: A maximal matching M.
Step 1: Identify demand groups in the sentence.
Step 2: Load demand frame for each one.
Step 3: Transform demand frames according to TAM rules if there is any.
Step 4: Form initial weighted bipartite graph G_w={D,S,E}.
Step 5: Set matching M←ϕ // initially M contains no edge.
Step 6: Search a node (d_i, k_j) in D such that it has a unique outgoing edge (d_i,k_j,s_t,2) /* for mandatory demands only*/.
Step 7: Set M←M + (d_i, k_j, s_t, 2).

E←E-(d_i, k_j, s_t, 2)

Step 8: Remove all other edges incident on s_t.
Step 9: Search a node s_p in S such that it has a unique incoming edge (d_m, k_n, s_p, w).
Step 10: Set M←M + (d_m, k_n, s_p, w).

E←E-(d_m, k_n, s_p, w)

Step 11: Remove all other edges originating at (d_m, k_n).
Step 12: Repeat Step 6 to Step 11 until E= ϕ or no nodes are found in Step 6 and 9.
Step 13: If E≠ ϕ then apply a grammatical constraint discussed in 7.1, to resolve for an edge 'e.' Add the edge 'e' to M, subtract 'e' and other related edges from E. Go to Step 6.
Step 14: Return M.

3.6.1. Ambiguity Resolution

For resolving ambiguities, we had to use some constraints. Relative Karaka position played an important role in this case. For this purpose, there is a thumb rule in Bangla. The Karakas in a sentence occur in a sequence like k1 k7 k3 k5 k2 k4 v. We have used this with a little modification: k1 k7t k7p k3 k5 k2/k2p k1s k2g/ k4 v.

Here we discuss an example which is solved by ambiguity resolution (Box 8).

The restricted CG corresponding to the above sentence becomes Figure 5.

Before ambiguity resolution, the sentence gives two parses as shown in Figures 6 and 7.

In the ambiguity resolution stage, we apply the constraint that k7t occurs before k7p. Thus the final parse becomes parse-1.

Box 8.

S8:	আমি	বিকালে	সেখানে বসে	ছিলাম
	ami φ	*bikale*	*sekhane*	*base chhilam*
	I	afternoon – Loc	there – Loc	sitting was
	I was sitting there in the afternoon.			

Figure 5. CG for S8

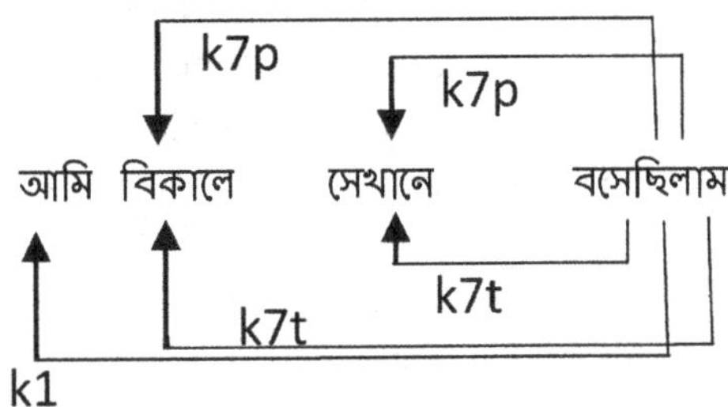

Figure 6. Parse-1 for S8

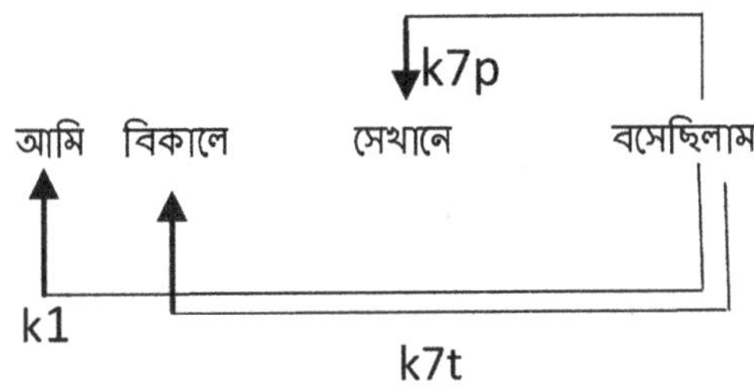

Figure 7. Parse-2 for S8

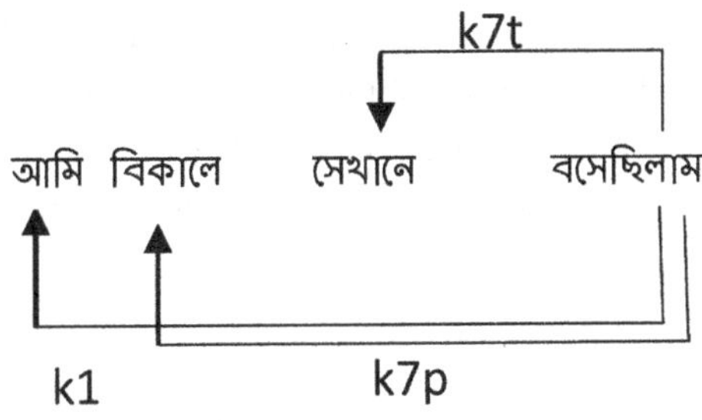

4. EVALUATION

As mentioned before the parser has been trained with a Treebank of 1000 annotated sentences and then evaluated with un-annotated test data of 150 sentences. Then the output has been verified with the gold standard data and per token evaluation has been done. The evaluation metric is as follows:

- **Labeled Attachment Score (LAS):** Percentage of tokens with correct head and label.
- **Unlabeled Attachment Score (UAS):** Percentage of tokens with correct head.
- **Label Accuracy Score (LS):** Percentage of tokens with correct label.

The evaluation shows the accuracies of the proposed approach as follows: UAS = 90.32%; LAS = 79.81%; and LA=81.27%. This evaluation was done by ICON 2009 NLP Tool Contest Committee (ICON, 2009) and showed the best accuracy among all the participating teams. A comparative result is being given in Table 4.

From the table it is also clear that when a little course dependency tag set is chosen, the result is improved significantly. The course LAS, UAS and LS as shown in the table are 84.29, 90.32 and 85.95 respectively.

Table 4. Comparative study of ICON 2009 tools contest results for Bangla

Groups	Teams	Score Type	Dependency Tag Set	
			Fine	Coarse
1	Ghosh (JU, India)	LAS	53.90	19.04
		UAS	74.09	32.88
		LS	61.71	29.14
2	Nivre (UU, Sweden)	LAS	70.45	76.07
		UAS	88.66	88.97
		LS	72.94	79.60
3	Zeman (CU, Czech)	LAS	66.60	71.49
		UAS	86.68	86.89
		LS	71.28	76.59
4	Our system (ISI Kolkata)	LAS	79.81	**84.29**
		UAS	90.32	**90.32**
		LS	81.27	**85.95**
5	Ambati (IIIT-H, India)	LAS	72.63	78.25
		UAS	88.45	90.22
		LS	75.34	81.69
6	Chatterji (IIT-Kgp, India)	LAS	60.46	
		UAS	82.21	
		LS	65.97	
7	Mannem (IIIT-H, India)	LAS	67.74	70.34
		UAS	85.33	83.56
		LS	69.93	73.05

4.1. Analysis of Errors and Possible Solutions

A rigorous error analysis has been done for 150 sentences of gold test data. The following points were identified from the analysis.

Box 9.

S9:	সে	ঘাড়	ঘুরিয়ে	ওকে	দেখল
	se **Φ**	*ghar* **Φ**	*ghuriye*	*oke*	*dekhlo*
	He	neck	turning	her – dat	saw
	Turning his neck he saw her.				

1. About 30% of the errors are associated with the Karaka Label 'k7t' i.e. either 'k7t' has been wrongly assigned or another Karaka Label has been wrongly associated in place of 'k7t'. This is possibly because of the fact that almost all Vibhaktis can be associated with k7t. This can be better understood if we take a look on the Karaka frames.
   This problem can be solved with a little change in the POS tag set. The nouns which are used for expressing time, e.g. today, tomorrow, afternoon, etc, have to be given a POS different from other nouns (may be NNT). Having done that, it is obvious that k7t will always be associated with NNT with proper Vibhakti and vice versa.
2. A significant number of errors have occurred for shared arguments. A shared argument is a Karaka which fulfils the demands of two verbs at a time. Consider a sentence in Box 9 from the test data.
   In S9 two verbs, Guriyze (turning-participle) and ZeKlo (saw-main) share the same Karta (k1) '*se*' (he). The symbol 'Φ' represents NULL (or *sunyo*) Vibhakti. Here '*se*' (he) is a shared argument which occurs only once in the sentence but is semantically related to both the verbs. Analysis shows that the shared arguments have been attached to the verb close to it.
   A solution for this has been proposed in (Bharti, 2009c). A null phrase may be introduced in the sentence and may be associated with the participle form (turning) with a co-

reference to the original argument (he). The original argument is then associated with main verb. Introduction of the null phrase must be done in the stage of chunking.

3. Some errors are observed for missing arguments. Bengali frequently omits an argument which is mandatory to the verb in action. Consider a sentence in Box 10.
   In S10 *balla* (said) is a verb with mandatory demand od Karta Karaka (k1). But here k1 is omitted. In this case the parser gets confused and word occurring before the verb (said) with zero Vibhakti (necessary for k1) is assigned the Karaka label k1 (here tArapara). This problem can also be solved as in 2.
4. Some errors are observed due to the mixed verbs used in the test data but were not included in the mixed verb list. Bengali uses a lot of mixed verbs, to find and include all of them in the list and also prepare a demand frame for that is very difficult. The solution for this can be achieved with more rich linguistic resources, e.g., verb list, demand frames, etc.
5. Some errors have been propagated due to the errors in demand frames. Cross checking of the demand frames and preparing an exhaustive set of demand frames may significantly decrease the errors.

5. CONCLUSION

This paper presents grammar-driven dependency parser for Bengali. The linguistics rules are mostly collected from the language grammar and ICON 2009 data. A brief review of the parsing techniques for Indic language including Bengali is also presented. The experimental shows that the proposed parser works well for the ICON data. However, it has to be tested with other datasets which is not used to extract linguistics rules. The errors show that the verb net developed under this research is not complete and in future, it has to be upgraded to include more verbs and their corresponding demand frames.

The overall approach, though presently proposed for Bangla, would work well for other morphologically rich free-word-order languages (like many of the Indian languages). One major requirement is to use the lexical resources (demand frames) for the corresponding language. We plan to try it for other ILs in near future. As this approach is fully grammar driven, more grammatical rules should have been applied for better accuracy.

Another important use of this parser is in developing a statistical parser for Bengali. A data-driven parser like MaltParser (Nivre, 2006) requires large amount of annotated data and preparation of such a big dataset manually is a difficult task. Instead, we use our parser to parse more data to generate tree-banks which are later manually checked and corrected by linguists. This way (semi-automatically), we would be able to generate a large annotated dataset to be used for developing a data-driven dependency parser for Bengali.

Box 10.

S10:	তারপর	বলল	“খুব	খিদে	পেয়ে	গেছে”
	tarpar	*balla*	*“Kub*	*KiZe*	*peyze*	*geCe”*
	Then	said	very	hunger	got	has
	Then said “I am very hungry.”					

ACKNOWLEDGMENT

The research embodied in this paper is partially funded by the Society for Natural Language Technology Research (SNLTR), Kolkata, India.

REFERENCES

Begum, R., Husain, S., Sharma, D. M., & Bai, L. (2008b). Developing verb frames for Hindi. In *Proceedings of LREC-2008*. LREC.

Begum, R., Husain, S., Sharma, D. M., Bai, L., & Sangal, R. (2008a). Dependency annotation scheme for Indian languages. In *Proceedings of IJCNLP-2008*. IJCNLP.

Bharati, A., Chaitanya, V., & Sangal, R. (1995). *Natural language processing: A paninian perspective*. New Delhi: Prentice-Hall of India.

Bharati, A., Husain, S., Ambati, B., Jain, S., Sharma, D. M., & Sangal, R. (2008a). Two semantic features make all the difference in parsing accuracy. In *Proceedings of the 6th International Conference on Natural Language Processing (ICON-08)*. CDAC.

Bharati, A., Husain, S., Sharma, D. M., & Sangal, R. (2008b). A two-stage constraint based dependency parser for free word order languages. In *Proceedings of the International Conference on Asian Language Processing (IALP)*. Chiang Mai, Thailand: IALP.

Bharati, A., Husain, S., Sharma, D. M., & Sangal, R. (2009a). Two stage constraint based hybrid approach to free-word order language dependency parsing. In *Proceedings of the 11th International Conference on Parsing Technologies (IWPT09)*. Paris, France: IWPT.

Bharati, A., Husain, S., Vijay, M., Deepak, K., Sharma, D. M., & Sangal, R. (2009b). Constraint based hybrid approach to parsing indian languages. In *Proceedings of the 23rd Pacific Asia Conference on Language, Information and Computation (PACLIC 23)*. Hong Kong: PACLIC.

Bharati, A., & Sangal, R. (1993). Parsing free word order languages in the paninian framework. In *Proceedings of ACL-1993*. ACL.

Bharati, A., Sharma, D. M., Husain, S., Bai, L., Begum, R., & Sangal, R. (2009c). *AnnCorra: TreeBanks for Indian languages, guideline for annotating Hindi TreeBank v2.0*. Hydearabad, India: IIIT.

Bhattacharya, K. (1993). *Bengali-oriya verb morphology: A contrastive study*. Kolkata, India: Das Gupta & Co. Private Limited.

Cormen, T. H., Leiserson, C. E., Rivest, R. L., & Stein, C. (2009). *PHI learning private limited*. New Delhi: Academic Press.

De, S., Dhar, A., & Garain, U. (2009). Karaka frames and their transformations for Bangla verbs. In *Proceedings of the 31st All-India Conference of Linguists*. Hyderabad, India: AICL.

Hasan, K. M. A., Mahmud, A., Mondal, A., & Saha, A. (2011). Recognizing Bangla grammar using predictive parser. *International Journal of Computer Science & Information Technology, 3*(6), 61–73. doi:10.5121/ijcsit.2011.3605.

Husain, S., Gadde, P., Bharat, A., Sharma, D. M., & Rajeev, R. (2009). A modular cascaded approach to complete parsing. In *Proceedings of the International Conference on Asian Language Processing (IALP)*. Singapore: IALP.

ICON. (2009). *ICON2009 NLP tools contest: Indian language dependency parsing*. Retrieved from http://ltrc.iiit.ac.in/nlptools2009/CR/all-papers-toolscontest.pdf

Maruyama, H. (1990). Structural disambiguation with constraint propagation. In *Proceedings of ACL*. Pittsburgh, PA: ACL.

Nivre, J., Hall, J., & Nilssion, J. (2006). Malt-Parser: A data-driven parser-generator for dependency parsing. In *Proceedings of LREC*, (pp. 2216-2219). LREC.

Saha, G.K. (2006, April). Parsing Bengali text: An intelligent approach. *Magazine Ubiquity*.

Sarkar, M. Z. H., Rahman, S., & Mottalib, M. A. (2006). Parsing algorithms for Bengali parser to handle affirmative sentences. *Asian Journal of Information Technology*, *5*(5), 504–511.

APPENDIX

Table 5. Dependency tag-set

k1	karta (doer/agent/subject)
k2	karma (object/patient)
k3	karana (instrument)
k4	sampradaana (recipient)
k5	apaadaana (source)
k7t	kaalaadhikarana (location in time)
k7p	deshadhikarana (location in space)
k7	vishayaadhikarana (location elsewhere)
ras	upapada__ sahakaarakatwa (associative)
rd	prati upapada (direction)
rh	hetu (cause-effect)
k*u	saadrishya (similarity)
rt	taadarthya (purpose)
k1s	vidheya karta (karta samanadhikarana)
k2s	vidheya karma (karma samanadhikarana)
r6	shashthi (possessive)
pk1	prayojaka karta (causer)
mk1	madhyastha karta (causer2)
jk1	prayojya karta (causee)
nmod	Noun modifiers
jjmod	Adjectival modifiers
adv	kriyaavisheshana ('manner adverbs' only)
rad	Address words
ccof	Conjunct of relation
pof	Part of relation
nmod_relc	Noun modifier of the type relative clause
jjmod_relc	Adjectival modifier of the type relative clause.
rbmod_relc	Adverbial modifier of the type relative clause

Chapter 9
Speech Feature Evaluation for Bangla Automatic Speech Recognition

Mohammed Rokibul Alam Kotwal
United International University, Bangladesh

Foyzul Hassan
United International University, Bangladesh

Mohammad Nurul Huda
United International University, Bangladesh

ABSTRACT

This chapter presents Bangla (widely known as Bengali) Automatic Speech Recognition (ASR) techniques by evaluating the different speech features, such as Mel Frequency Cepstral Coefficients (MFCCs), Local Features (LFs), phoneme probabilities extracted by time delay artificial neural networks of different architectures. Moreover, canonicalization of speech features is also performed for Gender-Independent (GI) ASR. In the canonicalization process, the authors have designed three classifiers by male, female, and GI speakers, and extracted the output probabilities from these classifiers for measuring the maximum. The maximization of output probabilities for each speech file provides higher correctness and accuracies for GI speech recognition. Besides, dynamic parameters (velocity and acceleration coefficients) are also used in the experiments for obtaining higher accuracy in phoneme recognition. From the experiments, it is also shown that dynamic parameters with hybrid features also increase the phoneme recognition performance in a certain extent. These parameters not only increase the accuracy of the ASR system, but also reduce the computation complexity of Hidden Markov Model (HMM)-based classifiers with fewer mixture components.

DOI: 10.4018/978-1-4666-3970-6.ch009

INTRODUCTION

Conventional Automatic Speech Recognition (ASR) systems use stochastic pattern matching techniques, where a word candidate is matched against word templates represented by Hidden Markov Models (HMMs) (Young, 2005). Although these techniques have a fair performance in limited applications, they suffer from huge computational cost at classifier stages, and also they always reject a new vocabulary or so-called Out-Of-Vocabulary (OOV) word. On the other hand, a traditional segmentation-based phone decoding technique can be used to solve these problems, but, until now, its recognition accuracy is far from sufficient performance.

These ASR systems could not be able to provide enough performance at anytime and everywhere. One of the reasons is that the Acoustic Models (AMs) of a Hidden Markov Model (HMM)-based classifier include many hidden factors such as speaker-specific characteristics that include gender types and speaking styles. It is difficult to recognize speech affected by these factors, especially when an ASR system contains only a single acoustic model. One solution is to employ multiple acoustic models, one model for each type of gender. Though the robustness of each acoustic model prevails to some extent, the whole ASR system can handle gender effects appropriately.

Most of these ASR systems use Mel Frequency Cepstral Coefficients (MFCCs) of 39 dimensions (12-MFCC, 12-ΔMFCC, 12-ΔΔMFCC, P, ΔP and ΔΔP, where P stands for raw energy of the input speech signal). Here, Hamming window of 25 ms is used for extracting the feature. The value of pre-emphasis factor is 0.97. Although these standard MFCCs are prevalent to current ASR system, but these features do not provide better performance because frequency domain information are not incorporated within the feature vector during the extraction process.

Recently, dynamic parameters such as velocity and acceleration coefficients of speech showed its necessity for embedding them as features to resolve the coarticulation effect due to widening the context window size. Though the coarticulation effects can be solved by incorporating the triphone models (Young, 2005), but a large-scale speech corpus is required to negotiate all the triphones. Besides, the training of triphone models incurs many complexities in HMM based classifiers. To eliminate these complexities at cost we need some parameters like dynamic parameters for solving the problem of left and right context.

Contemporary Bangla automatic speech recognition suffers from some difficulties: (1) lack of large scale speech corpus, (2) unavailability of labeled speech data, and (3) insufficient research opportunities though more than 220 million people speak in Bangla as their native language, which is ranked sixth based on the number of native speakers. These problems should be reduced immediately for constructing an ASR system for recognizing the voice.

The objective of this chapter is to design some ASR systems based on the above mentioned ground and to incorporate the some other speech features inside the ASR for improving the performance by eliminating the gender effects. The followings explicate the objectives of the chapter in details.

1. To construct a phoneme recognizer based on standard MFCC features to solve OOV problem.
2. To innovate a canonicalization method that resolves gender factor by incorporating both types of genders (male and female) in the process after selecting the maximum hypothesis.
3. To incorporate time and frequency domain information, new feature called local feature instead of standard MFCC is extracted from an input speech for an ASR system.
4. To extract phoneme probabilities based on time delay neural network by using MFCCs as input feature.

5. To embed dynamic parameters such as velocity (Δ) and acceleration ($\Delta\Delta$) coefficients as features for resolving coarticulation effects.
6. To design a labeled medium scale speech corpus for evaluating the recognition performance.
7. To extract hybrid features based on phoneme probabilities extracted by a neural network and acoustic features derived from the input speech.

BACKGROUND

There have been many literatures in Automatic Speech Recognition (ASR) systems for almost all the major languages in the world. Unfortunately, only a very few works have been done in ASR for Bangla (can also be termed as Bengali), which is one of the largely spoken languages in the world. A major difficulty to research in Bangla ASR is the lack of proper speech corpus. Some efforts are made to develop Bangla speech corpus to build a Bangla text to speech system (Kishore, 2003). However, this effort is a part of developing speech databases for Indian Languages, where Bangla is one of the parts and it is spoken in the eastern area of India (West Bengal and Kolkata as its capital). But most of the natives of Bangla (more than two thirds) reside in Bangladesh, where it is the official language. Although the written characters of Standard Bangla in both the countries are same, there are some sounds that are produced variably in different pronunciations of Standard Bangla, in addition to the myriad of phonological variations in non-standard dialects (Wikipedia, 2012). Therefore, there is a need to do research on the main stream of Bangla, which is spoken in Bangladesh, ASR.

Some developments on Bangla speech processing or Bangla ASR can be found in (Hossain, 2007; Hasnat, 2000; Karim, 2002; Houque, 2006; Roy, 2002; Hassan, 2003; Rahman, 2003; Hossain, 2004). For example, Bangla vowel characterization is done in (Hossain, 2007); isolated and continuous Bangla speech recognition on a small dataset using Hidden Markov Models (HMMs) is described in (Hasnat, 2007); recognition of Bangla phonemes by Artificial Neural Network (ANN) is reported in (Roy, 2002; Hassan, 2003). Continuous Bangla speech recognition system is developed in (Rahman, 2003), while (Hossain, 2004) presents a brief overview of Bangla speech synthesis and recognition. However, most of these works are mainly concentrated on simple recognition task on a very small database, or simply on the frequency distributions of different vowels and consonants.

MAIN FOCUS OF THE CHAPTER

Bangla Phonetic Schema

Eight short vowels, (অ, আ, ই, উ, এ, ঐ, ও, ঔ), excluding long vowels (ঈ, ঊ) and 29 consonants are in the Bangla phonetic inventory. Table 1 shows Bangla vowel phonemes with their corresponding International Phonetic Alphabet (IPA) and our proposed symbols. On the other hand, the consonants, which are used in Bangla language, are presented in Table 2. Here, the Table exhibits the same items for consonants like as Table 1. In the Table 2, the pronunciation of /শ/, /ঘ/ and /স/ are same by considering the words বিশ (/biʃ/), বিঘ (/biʃ/) and ড়িস (/ḍiʃ/), respectively, which is shown in Figure 1. Here the meanings of বিশ, বিষ and ড়িস are English language "twenty (20)", "poison" and "bowl", respectively. On the other hand, in the words জাম (/dʒam/) and ঘাক (/dʒak/), there is no difference between the pronunciation of /জ/ and /ঘ/, respectively that depicted in Figure 2. Here the meanings of জাম and ঘাক are English language "black berry" and "go", respectively. Again, Figure 3 shows that there is no difference between /ণ/ and /ন/ in the words হরিণ (/hɾin/) and নাতিন (/natin/), respectively. Here the meanings

Table 1. Bangla vowels

Letter	IPA	Our Symbol
অ	/ɔ/ and /o/	a
আ	/a/	aa
ই	/i/	i
ঈ	/i/	i
উ	/u/	u
ঊ	/u/	u
এ	/e/ and /æ/	e
ঐ	/oj/	oi
ও	/o/	o
ঔ	/ow/	ou

of হরিণ and নাতিন are English language "deer" and "granddaughter," respectively. Moreover, phonemes /ড়/ and /ঢ়/ carry same pronunciation in the words পাহাড় (/pahaɽ/) and আষাড় (/aʃaɽ/), respectively, which is shown in the Figure 4. Here the meanings of পাহাড় and আষাড় are English language "hill" and "rainy season," respectively.

Initial consonant cluster is not allowed in the native Bangla: the maximum syllable structure is CVC (i.e., one vowel flanked by a consonant on each side) (Masica, 1993). Sanskrit words borrowed into Bangla possess a wide range of clusters, expanding the maximum syllable structure to CCCVC. English or other foreign borrowings add even more cluster types into the Bangla inventory.

This phonetic scheme did not consider context effect which yields less recognition performance for the utterance that is not more frequent. Therefore, a phonetic scheme with context dependency is needed to get better performance.

Triphone Design

Figure 5 depicts a triphone model for the Bangla word চাঁদ (pronounced as '*chaad*' and English meaning is 'Moon'). Here, five states three loops left-to-right HMM model is used.

Figure 6 shows the partial part of tree.hed, which contains the instructions regarding which contexts to examine for possible clustering, can be rather long and complex (Young, 2005). It is noted that this script is only capable of creating the TB commands (decision tree clustering of

Table 2. Bangla consonants

Letter	IPA	Our Symbol	Letter	IPA	Our Symbol
ক	/k/	k	ধ	/d̪ʱ/	dh
খ	/kʰ/	kh	ন	/n/	n
গ	/g/	g	প	/p/	p
ঘ	/gʱ/	gh	ফ	/pʰ/	ph
ঙ	/ŋ/	ng	ব	/b/	b
চ	/tʃ/	ch	ভ	/bʱ/	bh
ছ	/tʃʰ/	chh	ম	/m/	m
জ	/dʒ/	j	য	/dʒ/	j
ঝ	/dʒʱ/	jh	র	/ɾ/	r
ট	/ʈ/	ta	ল	/l/	l
ঠ	/ʈʰ/	tha	শ	/ʃ/ / /s/	s
ড	/ɖ/	da	ষ	/ʃ/	s
ঢ	/ɖʱ/	dha	স	/ʃ/ / /s/	s
ণ	/n/	n	হ	/h/	h
ত	/t̪/	t	ড়	/ɽ/	rh
থ	/t̪ʰ/	th	ঢ়	/ɽ/	rh
দ	/d̪/	d	য়	/e̯/ /-	y

Figure 1. Spectrogram of Bangla phonemes /k/, /l/ and /m/ in the words বিশ (/biʃ/), বিষ (/biʃ/) *and* ড়িস (/ɖiʃ/) *respectively*

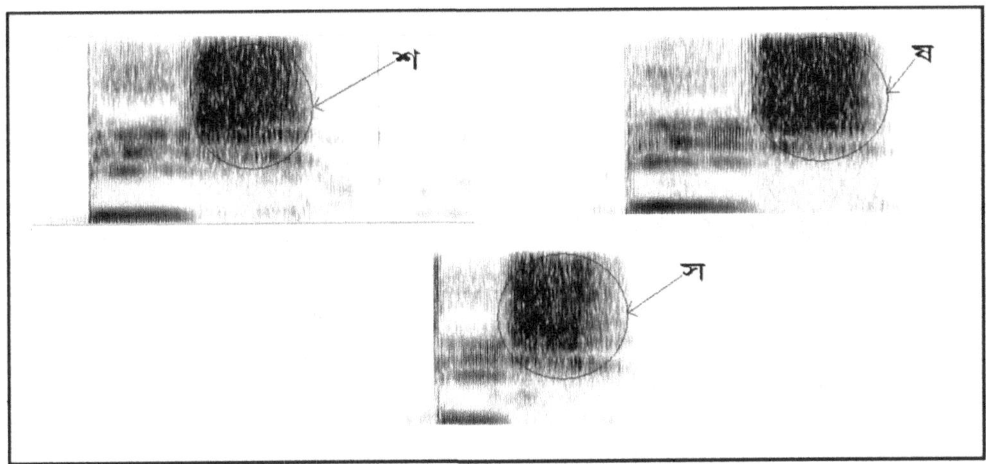

Figure 2. Spectrogram of Bangla phonemes /R/ and /h/ in the words জাম *(/dʒam/) and* যাক *(/dʒak/) respectively*

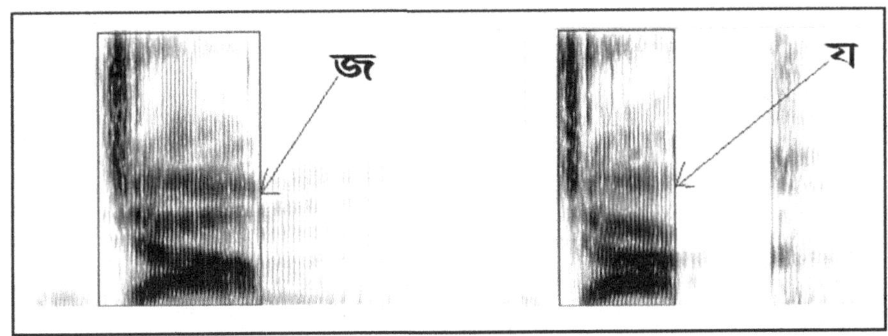

Figure 3. Spectrogram of Bangla phonemes /Y/ and /b/ in the words হরিণ (/hɾin/) *and* নাতিন *(/natin/) respectively*

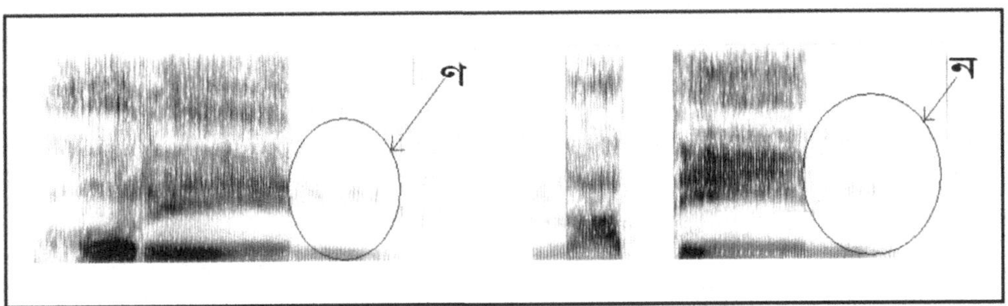

Figure 4. Spectrogram of Bangla phonemes /o/ and /p/ in the words পাহাড় *(/pahaɽ/) and* আষাড় *(/aʃaɽ/) respectively*

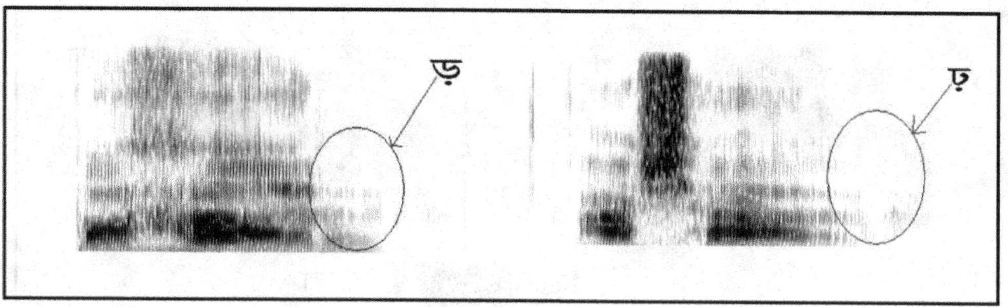

Figure 5. Triphone model for the Bangla word চাঁদ

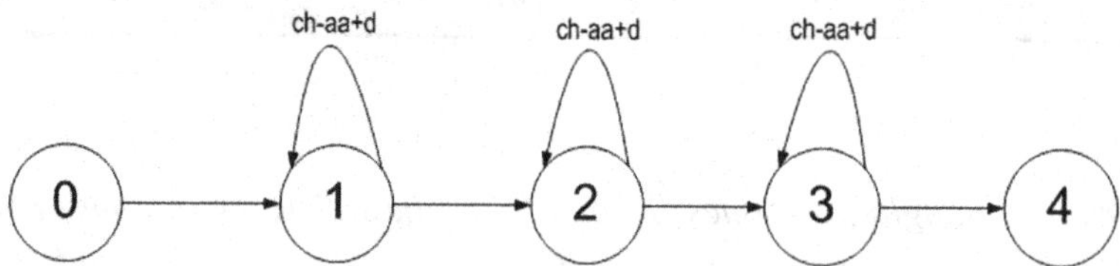

Figure 6. Fragments of tree.hed for Bangla phonemes

```
RO 100 stats

TR 0

QS  "R_NonBoundary"     { *+* }
QS  "L_NonBoundary"     { *-* }
QS  "R_Silence"         { *+sil }
QS  "L_Silence"         { sil-* }
QS  "R_Stop"            { *+p,*+pd,*+b,*+t,*+td,*+d,*+dd,*+k,*+kh,*+kd,*+g }
QS  "L_Stop"            { p-*,pd-*,b-*,t-*,td-*,d-*,dd-*,k-*,kh-*,kd-*,g-* }
QS  "R_Nasal"           { *+m,*+n,*+en,*+ng }
QS  "L_Nasal"           { m-*,n-*,en-*,ng-* }
....
QS  "R_w"               { *+w }
QS  "L_w"               { w-* }
QS  "R_y"               { *+y }
QS  "L_y"               { y-* }
QS  "R_z"               { *+z }
QS  "L_z"               { z-* }

TR 2

TB 350 "ST_aa_2_"  {("aa","*-aa+*","aa+*","*-aa").state[2]}
TB 350 "ST_ch_2_"  {("ch","*-ch+*","ch+*","*-ch").state[2]}
TB 350 "ST_ey_2_"  {("ey","*-ey+*","ey+*","*-ey").state[2]}
....
TB 350 "ST_sil_4_"{("sil","*-sil+*","sil+*","*-sil").state[4]}
TB 350 "ST_bh_4_"  {("bh","*-bh+*","bh+*","*-bh").state[4]}
TB 350 "ST_u_4_"   {("u","*-u+*","u+*","*-u").state[4]}

TR 1

AU "fulllist"
CO "tiedlist"

ST "trees"
```

states). The questions (Qs) still need defining by the user. The entire script appropriate for clustering Bangla phone models is too long to show here in the text, however, its main components are given by the following fragments.

However, triphone model solves coarticulation effects by considering left and right contexts, the design of these models need huge speech corpus to negotiate all the necessary triphones. Besides, it is very difficult to obtain all the triphones in almost same frequency in speech corpus. Moreover, complexities in triphone-based modeling are inherent in HMM-based classifier.

Bangla Speech Corpus

At present, a real problem to do experiment on Bangla phoneme ASR is the lack of proper Bangla speech corpus. In fact, such a corpus is not available or at least not referenced in any of the existing literature. On the other hand, Muhammad (2009) designed a medium size speech corpus for bangle digits where '0' [Zero ()] to '9' [Nine ()] are recorded. They selected 50 male (m01-m50) and 50 female (f01 – f50), so a total of 100 speakers. All of the speakers are Bangladeshi nationals and native speakers of Bangla. The age of the speakers ranges from 16 to 60 years. They recorded 10 trials of each digit from each speaker: 5 trials in quiet condition and 5 trials in typical Bangladeshi office environment, where ceiling fans were switched on and windows were open, and some low level street or corridor noise could be heard. These two types of trails were recorded in two sessions. A total of 50 utterances were recorded from each speaker in quiet condition (5 trials and 10 digits) and 50 utterances in office environment. The experiment of this paper involves only quiet condition utterances. This digit corpus is medium in size, but it is designed only for digit recognition. Besides, the large scale Bangla speech database designed by the BRAC University, Dhaka, Bangladesh (Alam, 2010) is not segmented or labeled to use in supervised learning.

Acoustic Features

This is an introduction to front-end processing and acoustic features for ASR. The front-end of an ASR system is the part that transforms speech to a vector of features that is suitable for further processing (Rosell, 2006).

The aims behind the front-end processing are:

- The parameters/features should capture the salient aspects of the speech signal. These should also be perceptually meaningful if it is possible. To capture the salient aspects it is necessary to capture the spectral dynamics, the change of the spectra over time.
- The features should be robust in the sense that the particular task should not be affected by the distortions that can appear, due to among other things environmental aspects and/or transmission medium. For instance should a general ASR-application be able to recognize speech from different persons.

Figure 7, from (Picone, 1993), divides the digital signal processing (DSP) of the front-end into three parts: spectral shaping, spectral analysis, and parametric transform. Statistical modeling is sometimes thought of as a part of the speech recognizer. The features or parameters that are a result of the front-end are analyzed statistically to define similarity between feature vectors and sometimes also to reduce the size of the representation (eg quantization).

Spectral shaping is the process of converting the analogue sound signal into a digital signal, A/D conversion. It also often involves some filtering, emphasizing important frequency components.

Spectral analysis is what the name suggests – the analysis of the spectrum in order to capture the salient aspects of the signal.

Parameter transform is the name for the molding of the measurements achieved through spectral analysis. Here the different features are

Figure 7. Digital speech signal processing

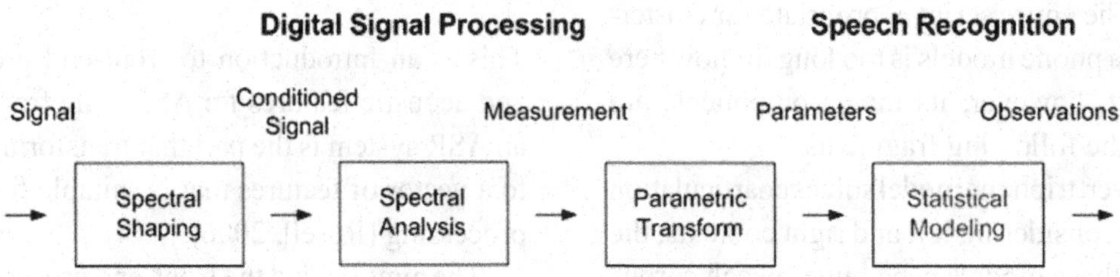

put together in one vector. At this stage the differences between consecutive frames (small time intervals) can be used to capture the dynamics of the signal.

Channel normalization is not accounted for in the picture. It is a process in which the properties of the medium are taken into consideration. By the medium we mean the environment in which the speech was uttered and the channel through which it reached the spectral analyzer. Channel normalization is applied after the spectral analysis and is often accomplished by analyzing a short time interval, so we consider it a part of the parameter transforms.

Mel Frequency Cepstral Coefficients (MFCCs)

Spectral Shaping

To convert an analogue sound wave to digital form one first filters the signal (reduces frequency information) and then samples it. Theoretically, to represent a frequency of *x*Hz a sampling frequency of 2*x*Hz is needed. The ear can perceive a dynamic range (amplitude ratio) of 20 bits (1 to 106). Normally each sample is stored in 16 bits, for telephone speech 8-12 bits are used.

The intensity of the speech sound is not evenly distributed over the frequency range. It falls with approximately 6 dB per octave. Often the signal is pre-emphasized to compensate for this.

Spectral Analysis

To analyze the spectrum the sampled signal is divided into frames, short time intervals. If these frames are short enough the signal appears static and can be represented by a feature vector. On the other hand, they have to be long enough to contain at least one cycle of the lowest frequency one is interested in. A normal length is 20-25 ms, which includes a few periods of the glottis. Usually the frames are set to overlap so that their centers lie only 10 ms apart. Each frame is multiplied by a tapered window, so that the values near the edges become zero. This prevents the discontinuities at the edges to affect the result of the further processing.

The sound signal is represented by a feature vector for each frame. The methods for extracting features for a single frame, described in the following sections, could be combined in several ways. Figure 8 shows some of the possibilities.

Filter Banks

The information needed in each frame is a description of the frequency distribution, i.e. how the power of the signal is distributed over different frequencies. A filter bank, in its simplest form, is a set of band pass filters with different frequencies covering the interesting part of the spectrum (the fundamental frequency and the formants). The output of the filters during a frame can be used as features.

Figure 8. Spectral analysis

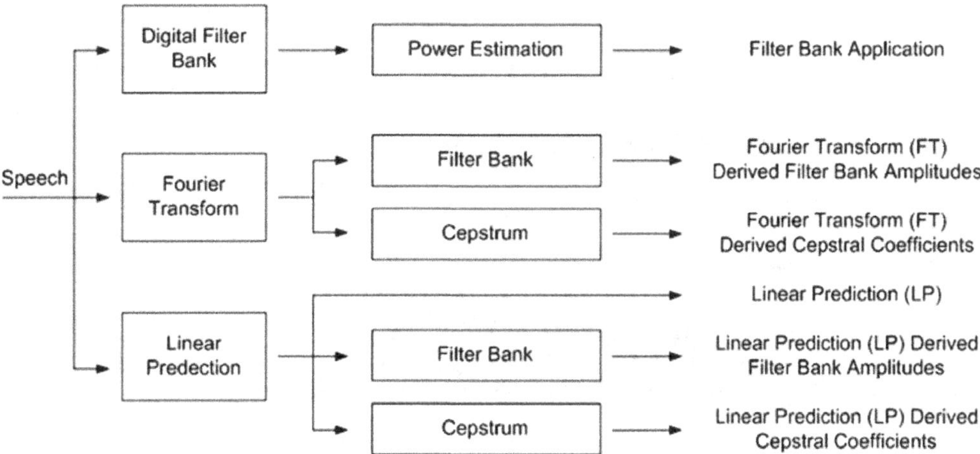

The center frequencies of the filters can be chosen in several ways. Usually they are set according to some perceptually motivated scale. The perceived pitch of a sound is not equal to the actual frequency. A popular approximation of the real mapping is the mel scale, the mel frequency (fmel) given in Equation 1.

$$f_{mel} = 2595 \log10(1 + f/700.0) \quad (1)$$

Here f is the actual frequency. An increase in frequency is easier to recognize in the lower register than in the higher.

The human auditory system cannot distinguish between frequencies that are close to each other. The higher the frequency the bigger are these critical bands (the intervals within which the frequencies cannot be separated from the center frequency). Using for instance the mel frequency the size of the critical band is approximated by Equation 2:

$$BW_{critical} = 25 + 75[1 + 1.4(fmel/1000)2]0.69 \quad (2)$$

In a critical band filter bank the bandpass filters are linearly spaced on a perceptually motivated scale (for instance the mel scale). The bandwidth of the filters is set to the critical bandwidth for the center frequency. An important approximation to a critical band filter bank is based on the mel scale. Between 100Hz and 1kHz ten filters are spaced linearly. Above 1kHz five filters are assigned for each doubling of the frequency. That is, they are logarithmically spaced. The bandwidths are set so that the 3dB point (half the power) is half-way between the centers of consecutive filters. Normally samples from the 20 first filters are used.

Figure 9 shows the critical band filter bank and mel-filter bank, including the pre-emphasis usually connected to them.

Another way to accomplish a corresponding feature vector is to use the Fourier transform to sample the signal at the desired frequencies (like for instance the centers of the filters in the mel-filter bank). This gives a Fourier filter bank and is accomplished using the Discrete Fourier Transform (DFT) performed by Equation 3.

$$S(f) = \sum_{n=0}^{N_S-1} s(n) e^{-i\frac{2\pi f}{fs}n} \quad (3)$$

where f is the frequency, S(f) is the Fourier coefficient for the particular frequency, s(n) is the sampled speech signal, f_s is the sampling frequency and N_s is the number of samples in the window under consideration. Often the signal is sampled

Figure 9. Two perceptually motivated filter banks

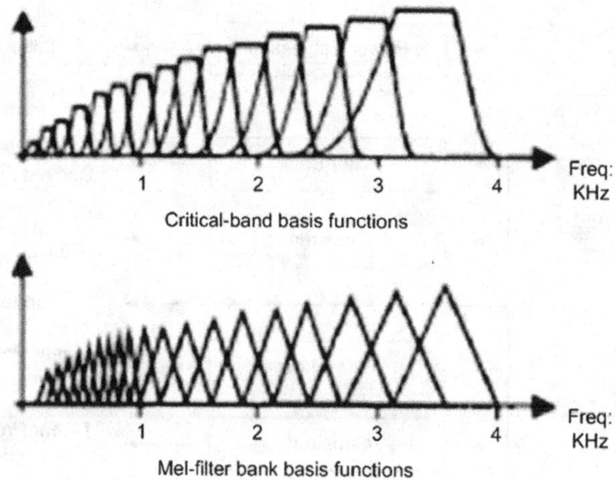

at a higher resolution in frequency and then the values for each "filter" is calculated as an average over several frequencies.

Cepstral Analysis

The spectrum of a speech signal is the result of the sound source (in voiced speech the oscillating vocal folds) and the vocal tract acting like a filter. The fundamental frequency of the glottis is resonated resulting in harmonics and partials, some of which are strengthened and others weakened by the vocal tract. In the time domain (the ordinary sampled speech signal) the signal s(n) is modeled by a convolution given in Equation 4.

$$s(n) = g(n) \otimes v(n) \quad (4)$$

where g(n) is the excitation signal, the signal coming from the glottis, and v(n) is the vocal tract filter. In the frequency domain (after for instance a Fourier transform) this is a product shown by Equation 5.

$$S(f) = G(f)V(f) \quad (5)$$

By instead considering the logarithm of the intensity the filtering process becomes a simple addition expressed in Equation 6:

$$\log(S(f)) = \log(G(f)) + \log(V(f)) \quad (6)$$

Hence, the logarithm of the spectrum can be viewed as a superposition of the source or excitation signal and the vocal tract resonance.

Figure 10 shows the steps of cepstral analysis. The spectrum of a sound signal may also be viewed as a superposition of several waves in the frequency domain. The waves with high frequency correspond to the harmonics of the excitation signal, while the more slowly varying represent the vocal tract shape. The cepstrum is the series of coefficients when doing the Fourier transform of the spectrum. In this new domain the lower order coefficients represents the slowly varying parts of the spectrum. Usually there is a spike in this series that corresponds to the harmonic series of the vocal folds. Considering only the coefficients lower than this spike gives a representation of the vocal tract shape.

By truncating the cepstral coefficient series and using the inverse transforms a smoothed spectrum is achieved. This is called a cepstral smoothing and ideally shows the slow trends in the spectrum, i.e. the formants, Figure 10.

The perhaps most common use of cepstral analysis is when constructing the mel-frequency cepstral coefficients (MFCCs). The right side of Figure 11 shows the steps involved.

Figure 10. Cepstral analysis

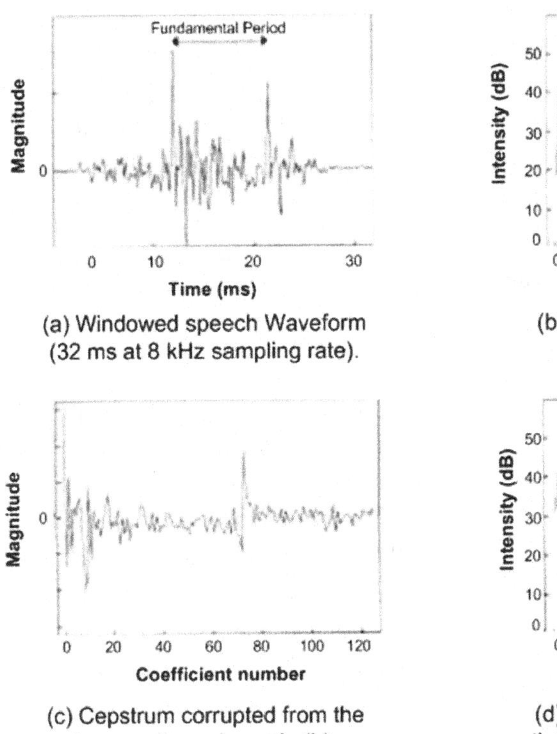

(a) Windowed speech Waveform (32 ms at 8 kHz sampling rate).

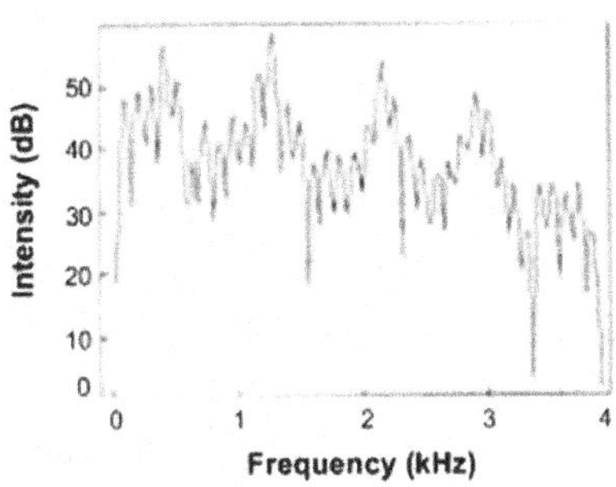

(b) Log spectrum (from a Fourier Transformation).

(c) Cepstrum corrupted from the log spectrum shown in (b).

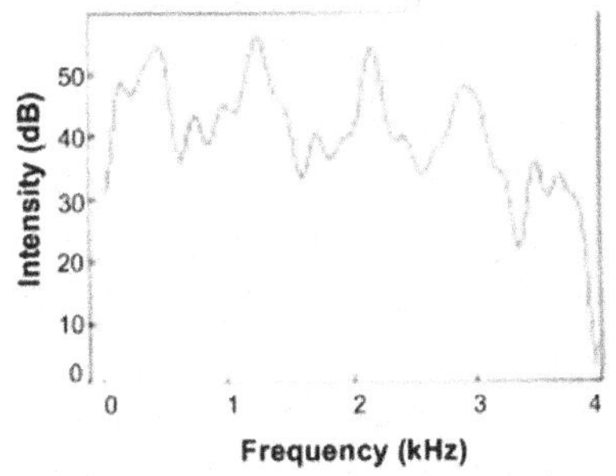

(d) Log spectrum reconstructed from the first 40 cepstral coefficients in (c).

Figure 11. MFCC extraction procedure

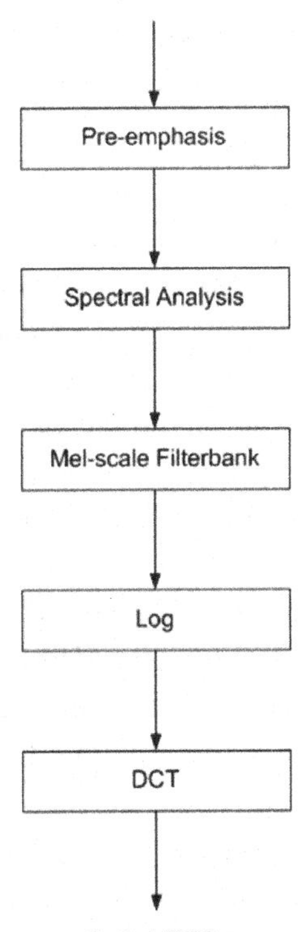

These extracted features called MFCCs embed only the time domain information, while frequency domain information is not incorporated. Due to the lacking of information in frequency domain these features shows lower recognition performance during the time of classification.

Solutions and Recommendations

Speech Corpus Construction

At present, a real problem to do experiment on Bangla phoneme ASR is the lack of proper Bangla speech corpus. In fact, such a corpus is not available or at least not referenced in any of the existing literature. Therefore, we develop a medium size Bangla speech corpus, which is described below.

Hundred sentences from the Bengali newspaper *Prothom Alo* (*Daily Prothom Alo*) are uttered by 30 male speakers of different regions of Bangladesh. These sentences (30x100) are used as male training corpus (D1). On the other hand, 3000 same sentences uttered by 30 female speakers are used as female training corpus (D2).

Besides, different 100 sentences from the same newspaper uttered by 10 different male speakers and by 10 different female speakers are used as male test corpus (D3) and female test corpus (D4), respectively. All of the speakers are Bangladeshi nationals and native speakers of Bangla. The age of the speakers ranges from 20 to 40 years. We have chosen the speakers from a wide area of Bangladesh: Dhaka (central region), Comilla – Noakhali (East region), Rajshahi (West region), Dinajpur – Rangpur (North-West region), Khulna (South-West region), Mymensingh and Sylhet (North-East region). Though all of them speak in standard Bangla, they are not free from their regional accent.

Recording was done in a quiet room located at United International University (UIU), Dhaka, Bangladesh. A desktop was used to record the voices using a head mounted close-talking microphone. We record the voice in a place, where ceiling fan and air conditioner were switched on and some low level street or corridor noise could be heard.

Jet Audio 7.1.1.3101 software was used to record the voices. The speech was sampled at 16 kHz and quantized to 16 bit stereo coding without any compression and no filter is used on the recorded voice.

Phoneme Recognizer Based on Standard MFCCs

Although all ASR techniques based on HMM perform adequately in certain limited applications, they always reject a new vocabulary or a so-called Out-Of-Vocabulary (OOV) word (See Figure 12). Therefore, an accurate phonetic typewriter or a phoneme recognizer is expected to assist next-generation ASR systems in resolving this OOV-word problem via a short interaction (talk-back) by automatically adding the word into a word lexicon from the phoneme string of an input utterance (Bazzi, 2000; Seneff, 2005; Kirchhoff, 2007) (See Figure 13).

Figure 12. Problem related to OOV

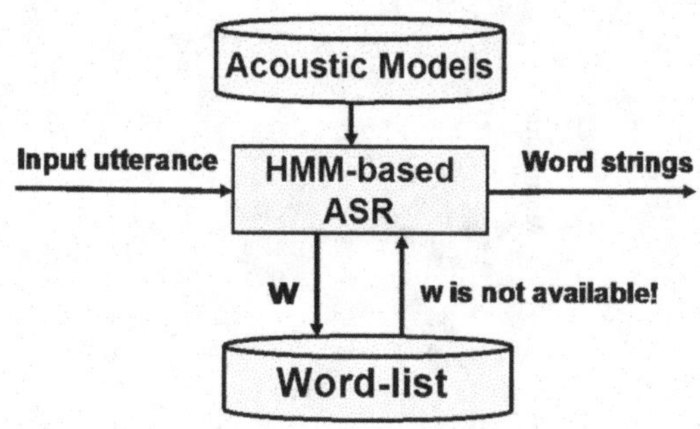

Traditional approach of ASR systems uses MFCC as feature vector to be fed into a HMM-based classifier for constructing a phoneme recognizer and the system diagram is shown in Figure 14. Parameters (mean and diagonal covariance of hidden Markov model of each phoneme) are estimated, from MFCC training data, using Baum-Welch algorithm. For different mixture components, training data are clustered using the K-mean algorithm. During recognition phase, a most likely phoneme sequence for an input utterance is obtained using the Forward algorithm.

Experimental Setup

The frame length and frame shift (frame shift between two consecutive frames) are set to 25 ms and 10 ms, respectively, to obtain acoustic features (MFCCs) from an input speech. MFCCs comprised of 39 dimensional (12-MFCC, 12-ΔMFCC, 12-ΔΔMFCC, P, ΔP and ΔΔP, where P stands for raw log energy of the input speech signal) features vector.

For designing the phoneme recognizer, Phoneme Correct Rates (PCRs) and Phoneme Accuracies (PAs) for D3 data set are evaluated using an HMM-based classifier. The D1 data set is used to design 39 Bangla monophones (8 vowels, 29 consonants, sp, sil) HMMs with five states, three loops, and left-to-right models. Input features for

Figure 13. An ASR system with OOV detection

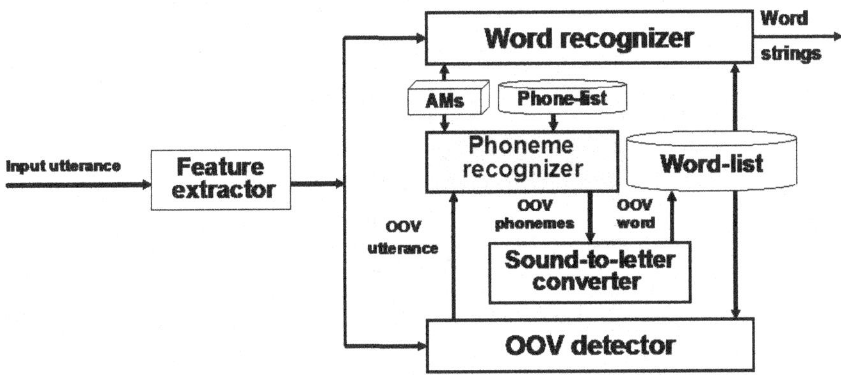

Figure 14. MFCC-based phoneme recognition method

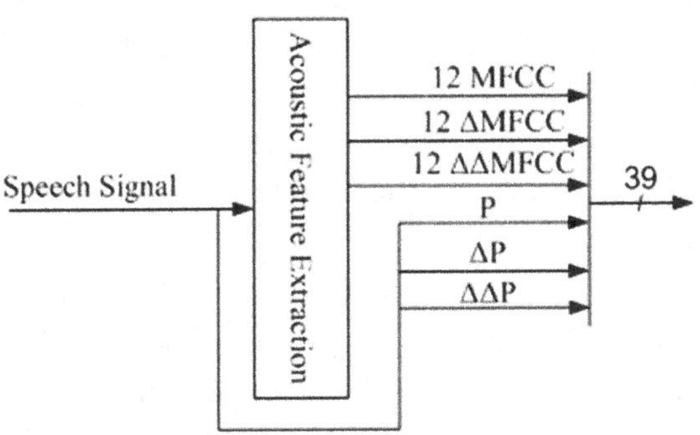

the classifier are 39 dimensional MFCCs. In the HMMs, the output probabilities are represented in the form of Gaussian mixtures, and diagonal matrices are used. The mixture components are set to 1, 2, 4, 8, 16 and 32.

Experimental Results and Analysis

The PCRs and PAs for test data are shown in the Table 3 for the method based on standard MF-CCs. From the table, it is noted that the mixture component 32 provides the highest recognition performance (both PCRs and PAs) among all the mixture components investigated. Moreover, it is exhibited from the table that the increment of mixture components improves the PRCs and PAs within a certain limit. The reason for these trends is that better training of HMM-based classifier provides better performances.

Effect of Dynamic Parameters on Phoneme Recognizer

Multilayer Neural Network-Based Method

Figure 15 shows the phoneme recognition method using MLN. At the acoustic feature extraction stage, input speech is converted into MFCCs of 39 dimensions (12-MFCC, 12-ΔMFCC, 12-ΔΔMFCC, P, ΔP and ΔΔP, where P stands for raw log energy of the input speech signal). MFCCs are input to an MLN with three layers, including 2 hidden layers, after combining preceding (t-3)-th and succeeding (t+3)-th frames with the current t-th frame. The MLN has 39 output units (total

Table 3. Phoneme recognition performance for D3 data set

	Mix	Mix2	Mix4	Mix8	Mix16	Mix32
PCRs	57.61	62.24	65.37	69.09	71.34	73.15
PAs	41.77	49.50	52.86	56.67	59.12	60.88

Figure 15. Phoneme recognition performance for D3 data set

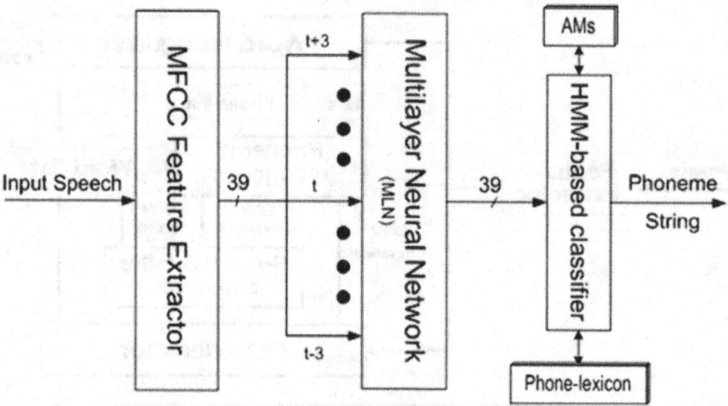

39 monophones) of phoneme probabilities for the current frame t. The two hidden layers consist of 300 and 100 units, respectively. The MLN is trained by using the standard back-propagation algorithm. This method yields comparable recognition performance. However, the single MLN suffers from an inability to model dynamic information precisely.

Multilayer Neural Network-Based Method with Dynamic Parameters (Kotwal, 2010)

Figure 16 shows the proposed phoneme recognition method, which comprises two stages: 1) a Multilayer Neural Network (MLN), which converts acoustic features, MFCCs, into phoneme probabilities of 39 dimensions, 2) the phoneme probabilities obtained from the first stage and corresponding Δ and ΔΔ parameters calculated by LR are inserted into a Hidden Markov Model (HMM) based classifier to obtain more accurate phoneme strings.

The architecture of MLN and its learning algorithm is similar to the procedure described in multilayer neural network based phoneme recognition method. The 39 dimensional output probabilities obtained by the MLN and corresponding Δ and ΔΔ calculated by using three point LR (39x3) are inserted into a HMM-based classifier. Input

Figure 16. Phoneme recognition method using dynamic parameters

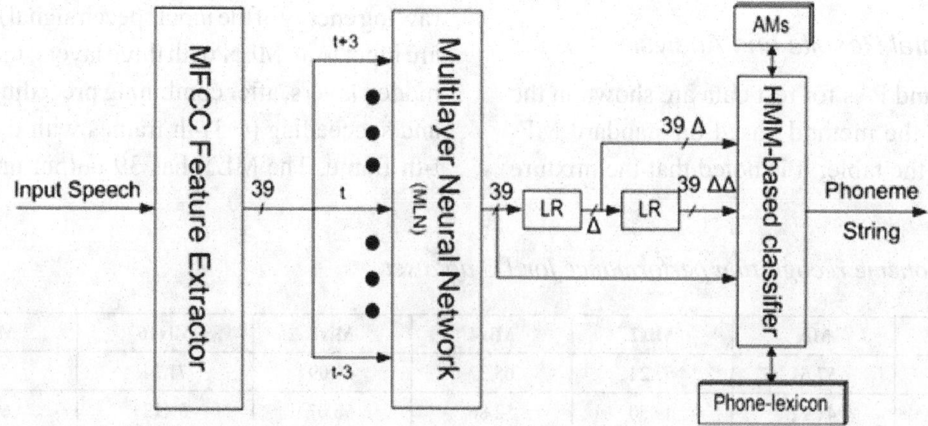

features of 117 dimensions (39x3) for the HMM-based classifier are derived by combining output probabilities obtaining by the MLN, and corresponding Δ and ΔΔ.

Experimental Setup

MFCCs, which comprised of 39 dimensional features vector, are extracted by setting up the same frame length and frame shift sizes already described.

For designing the phoneme recognizers in this section, PCRs and PAs for D3 data set are evaluated using an HMM-based classifier. The D1 data set is used to design 39 Bangla monophone (8 vowels, 29 consonant, sp, sil) HMMs with five states, three loops, and left-to-right models. Input features using the methods MFCC+MLN, MFCC+MLN+Δ and MFCC+MLN+Δ.ΔΔ 39, 78, and 117 dimensions, respectively. In the HMMs, the output probabilities are represented in the form of Gaussian mixtures, and diagonal matrices are used. The mixture components are set to 1, 2, 4, 8, 16, and 32.

In our experiments of the MLN, the non-linear function is a sigmoid from 0 to 1 (1/(1+exp(-x))) for the hidden and output layers.

To obtain the PCRs and PAs we have designed the following experiments:

1. MFCC+MLN
2. MFCC+MLN+Δ
3. MFCC+MLN+Δ.ΔΔ.

Experimental Results and Analysis

Figures 17 and 18 show the PCRs and PAs respectively for the investigated methods using training data set D1. It is shown from the figures that the method, (3) provides a higher phoneme recognition performance than the other methods investigated. For an example, at 32 mixture component, the method, (3) shows 70.78% PCR, while the methods, (1) and (2) exhibit 67.75% and 70.37% PCRs, respectively. On the other hand, at the same mixture component, the accuracies of the methods (1), (2), and (3) are 52.98%, 59.95%, and 61.31%, respectively.

On the other hand, the PCRs and PAs for test data, D3 are shown in the Figures 19 and 20, respectively for the investigated methods. The method, (3) outperformed the other methods for both the evaluations (PCRs and PAs) in the mixture components 2, 4, 8, 16 and 32. It is noted

Figure 17. Phoneme correct rate for training data (D1) using investigated methods

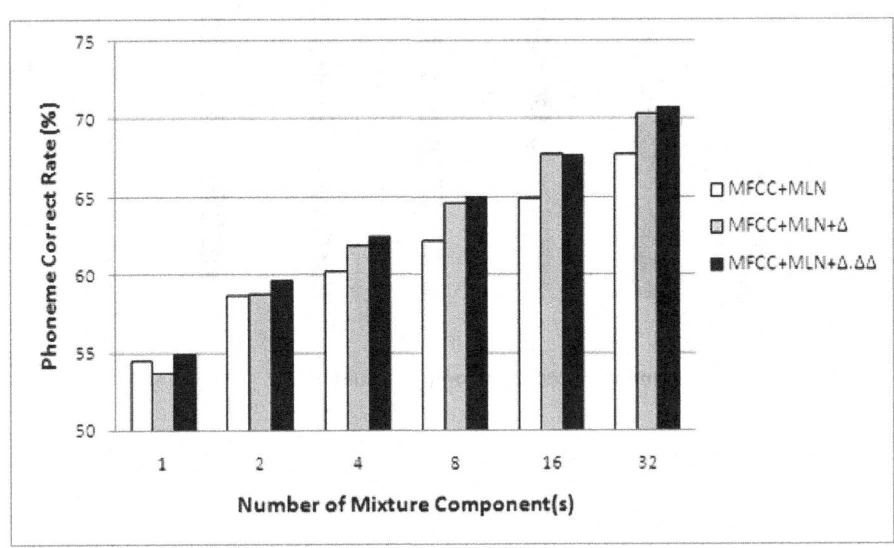

Figure 18. Phoneme accuracy for training data (D1) using investigated methods

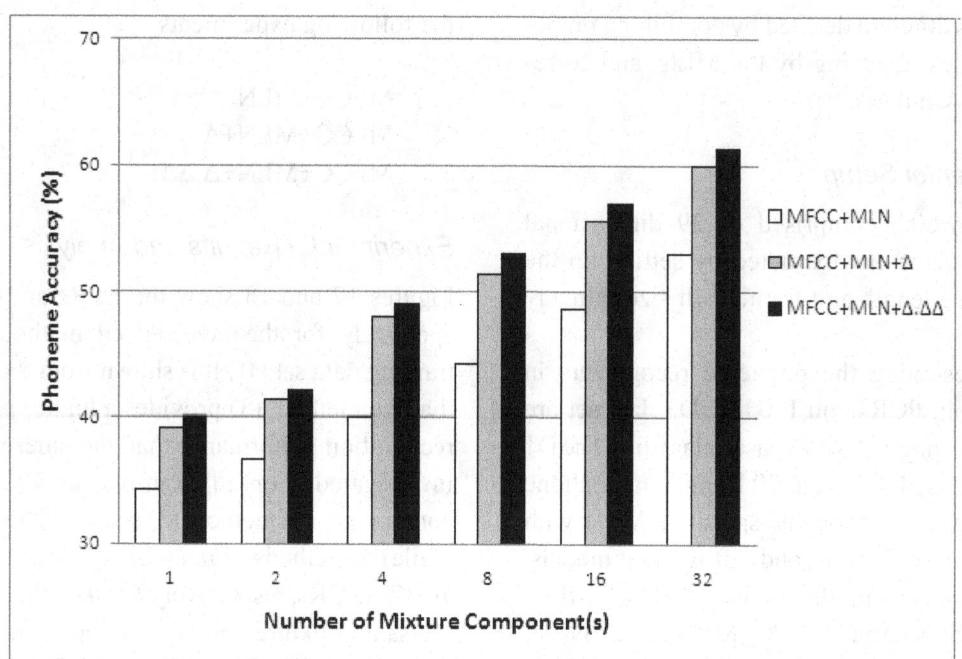

Figure 19. Phoneme correct rate for test data (D3) using investigated methods

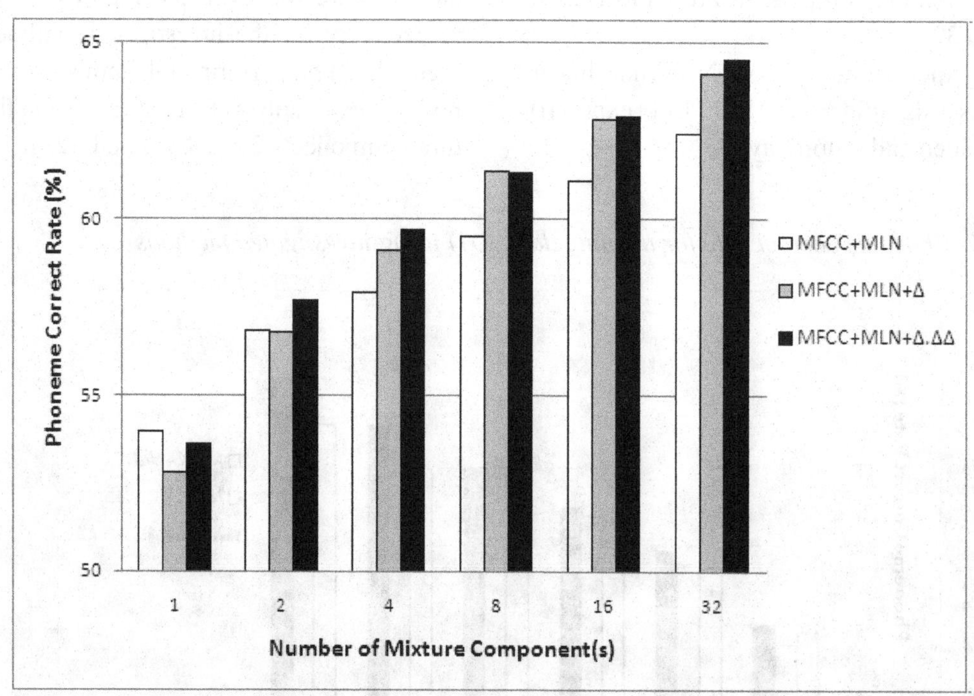

Figure 20. Phoneme accuracy for test data (D3) using investigated methods

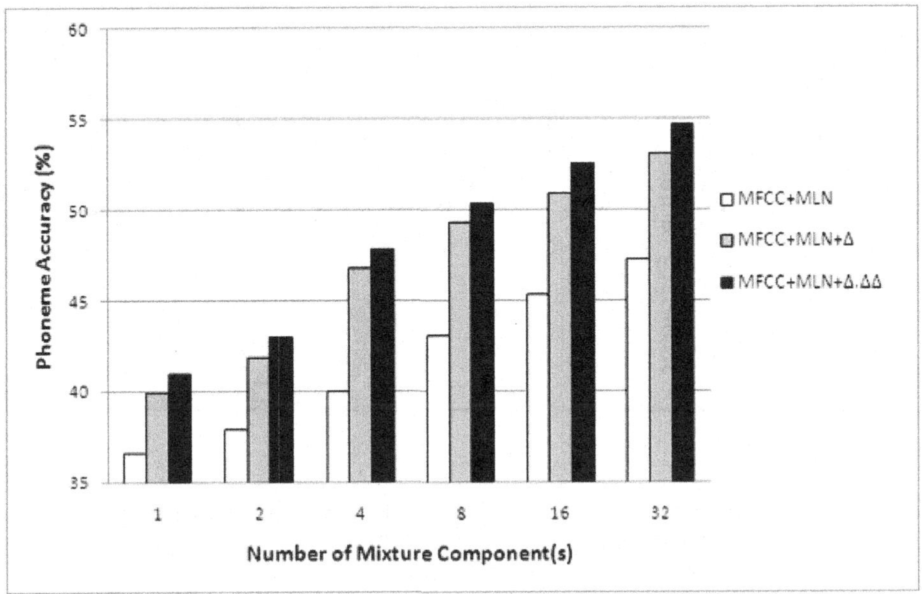

from the mixture component 32 from the Figure 20 that the method (3) having 54.66% accuracy shows its better recognition performance over the other methods accuracies.

The reason for providing better result by the method (3) is Δ and ΔΔ (dynamic parameters), while the method, (1) contains no dynamic parameters. On the other hand, the second investigated method, (2) embeds only velocity coefficient (Δ) which covers a context window of limited size and consequently, provides a higher recognition performance than the method, (1). Since the method, (3) incorporates both velocity (Δ) and acceleration coefficients (ΔΔ), it shows better performance than the method, (2).

It is claimed that the method, (3) reduces mixture components in HMMs and hence computation time. For an example from the Figure 20, approximately 47.50% phoneme recognition accuracy is obtained by the methods (1) and (3) at mixture components 32 and four, respectively.

Effect of Hybrid Features on Phoneme Recognizer

MLN-Based Method

Features (39-dimensional phoneme probabilities) extracted by the method described in multilayer neural network based phoneme recognizer are embedded with the input MFCC features of 39 dimensions to construct hybrid features for this method. Then these 78 dimensional hybrid features are inserted into HMM-based classifier for achieving more accurate phoneme recognizer. Figure 21 shows the system diagram for this method.

MLN-Based Method with Dynamic Parameters (Kotwal, 2011)

Figure 22 shows a phoneme recognition method using hybrid features and dynamic parameters. The method comprises three stages: at first stage, a Multilayer Neural Network (MLN) converts acoustic features, Mel Frequency Cepstral Coefficients (MFCCs), into phoneme probabilities, where the second stage computes Δ and ΔΔ parameters from the phoneme probabilities by using

Figure 21. MLN-based phoneme recognition method using hybrid features

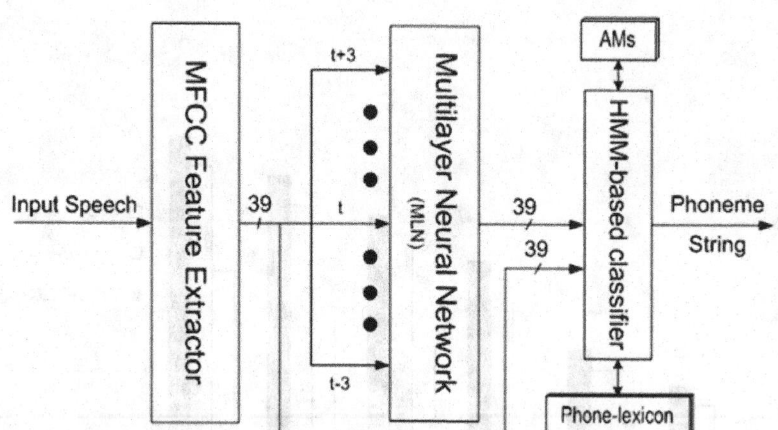

Figure 22. Proposed phoneme recognition method using dynamic parameters and hybrid features

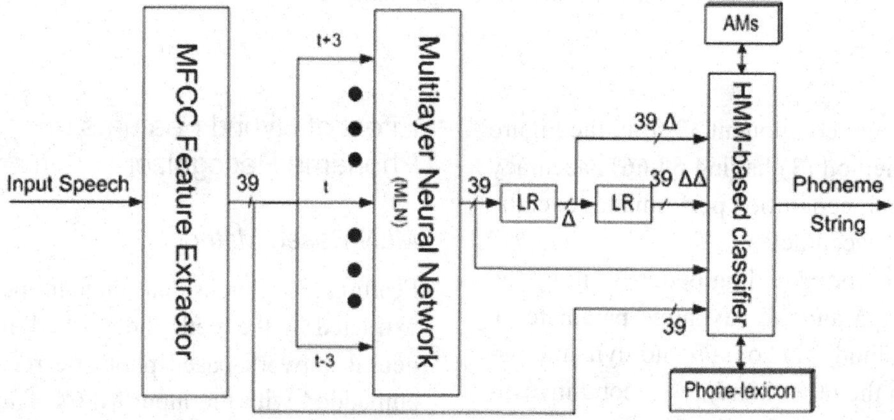

three point Linear Regression (LR). Finally, the phoneme probabilities, Δ and ΔΔ coefficients and the input MFCCs, combined as hybrid features, are fed into a Hidden Markov Model (HMM) based classifier to obtain more accurate phoneme strings. The architecture of MLN and its learning method is similar to the method described in MLN-based phoneme recognizer.

Experimental Setup

The dimensionality of MFCCs, and frame size and frame shift during extraction procedure are already illustrated. For designing phoneme recognizer in this section, PCRs and PAs for D3 data set are evaluated using an HMM-based classifier. The D1 data set is used to design 39 Bangla monophones (8 vowels, 29 consonant, sp, sil) HMMs with five states, three loops, and left-to-right models. Input features using the methods (1) and (3), and (2) and (4) are 39 and 78 dimensions, respectively. In the HMMs, the output probabilities are represented in the form of Gaussian mixtures, and diagonal matrices are used. The mixture components are set to 1, 2, 4, 8, 16, and 32. In our experiments of the single MLN and two-MLN the non-linear function is a sigmoid from 0 to 1 (1/(1+exp(-x))) for the hidden and output layers.

To obtain the PCRs and PAs we have designed the following experiments:

1. MFCC + MLN
2. MFCC + MLN + MFCC
3. MFCC + MLN + Δ
4. MFCC + MLN + Δ + MFCC
5. MFCC + MLN + Δ.ΔΔ
6. MFCC + MLN + Δ.ΔΔ + MFCC

Experimental Results and Analysis

Figures 23 and 24 show the PCRs and PAs respectively for the investigated methods. It is shown from the figures that the method, (6) provides a higher phoneme recognition performance than the other methods investigated. For an example, at 32 mixture component, the method, (6) shows 69.57% PCR, while the methods, (1), (3), and (5) without hybrid features, and (2) and (4) with hybrid features exhibit 62.40%, 64.13% and 64.54%, and 68.72% and 69.34% PCRs, respectively. On the other hand, at the same mixture component, the accuracies of the methods (1), (2), (3), (4), (5), and (6) are 47.26%, 55.87%, 53.07%, 59.23%, 54.66%, and 59.77%, respectively.

The effect of hybrid features over the methods (1), (3), and (5) are shown in the Figures 25, 26, 27, 28, 29, and 30. It is observed from all the figures that the method, which comprise hybrid features, provide better phoneme recognition performance than the counter one. From the Figures 27 and 28, at mixture component 32, the methods (3) and (4) show 64.13% and 69.34% PCR (from Figure 25), respectively, while PA values for the corresponding methods are 53.07% and 59.23% (from Figure 26), respectively.

An improvement by the method, (6) over the method (5) that does not incorporate hybrid features is shown in Figure 31. From the figure, it is observed that the method, (6) shows its highest level improvements of PCR and PA at mixture components 32 and two, respectively, where the improvement of PCR and PA are 5.03% and 5.64%, respectively

Local Feature Extraction

At the acoustic feature extraction stage, the input speech is first converted into LFs that represent a variation in spectrum along the time and frequency axes. Two LFs are then extracted by applying three-point Linear Regression (LR) along the time (t) and frequency (f) axes on a Time Spectrum pattern (TS), respectively. Figure 32 exhibits an

Figure 23. Phoneme correct rate for investigated methods

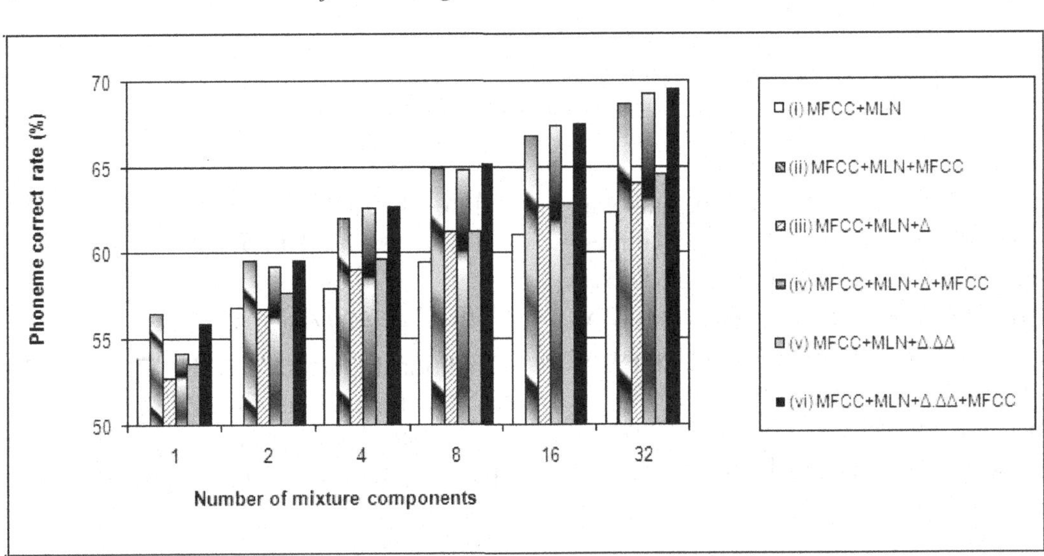

Figure 24. Phoneme accuracy for investigated methods

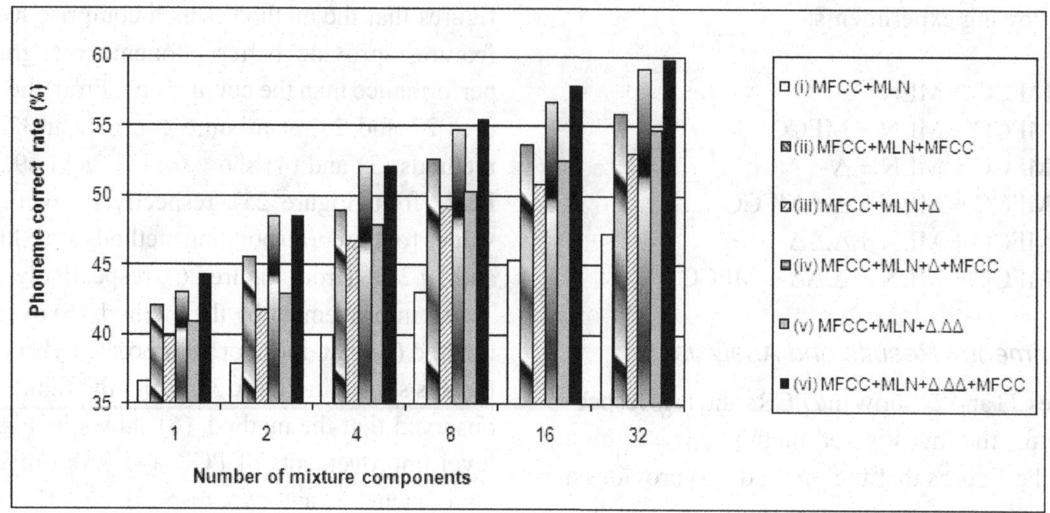

Figure 25. Effects of hybrid features for phoneme correct rate using method (1) and (2) without incorporating dynamic parameters

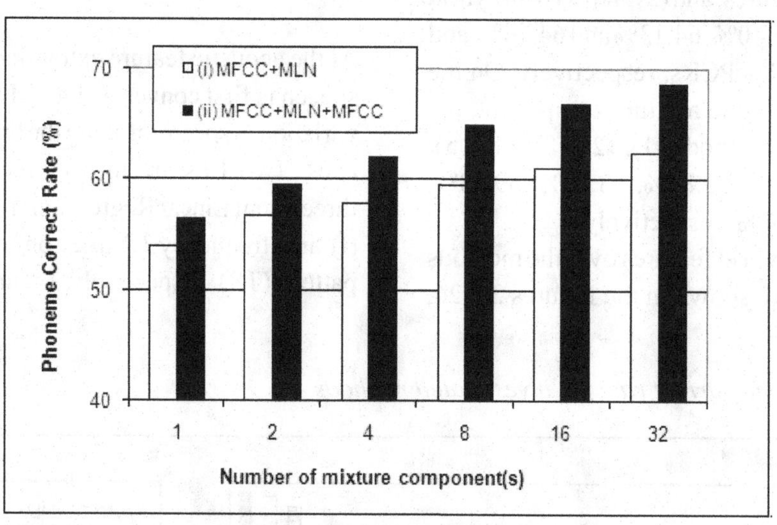

example of LFs for an input utterance, /gaikoku/. After compressing these two LFs with 24 dimensions into LFs with 12 dimensions using discrete cosine transform (DCT), a 25-dimensional (12 Δt, 12 Δf, and ΔP, where P stands for the log power of a raw speech signal) feature vector called LF is extracted (Kotwal, 2011). Figure 33 shows the local feature extraction procedure.

Male-Dependent ASR Using Triphone-Based HMM

MFCC-Based ASR

Traditional approach of ASR systems uses MFCC of 39 dimensions (12-MFCC, 12-ΔMFCC, 12-ΔΔMFCC, P, ΔP and ΔΔP, where P stands for raw log energy of the input speech signal) as

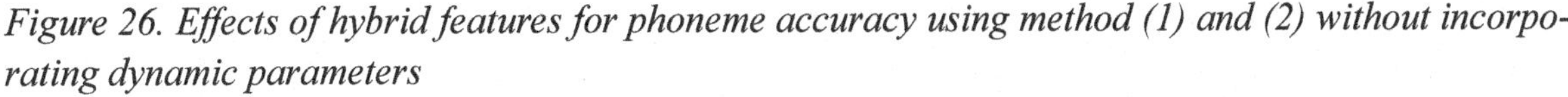

Figure 26. Effects of hybrid features for phoneme accuracy using method (1) and (2) without incorporating dynamic parameters

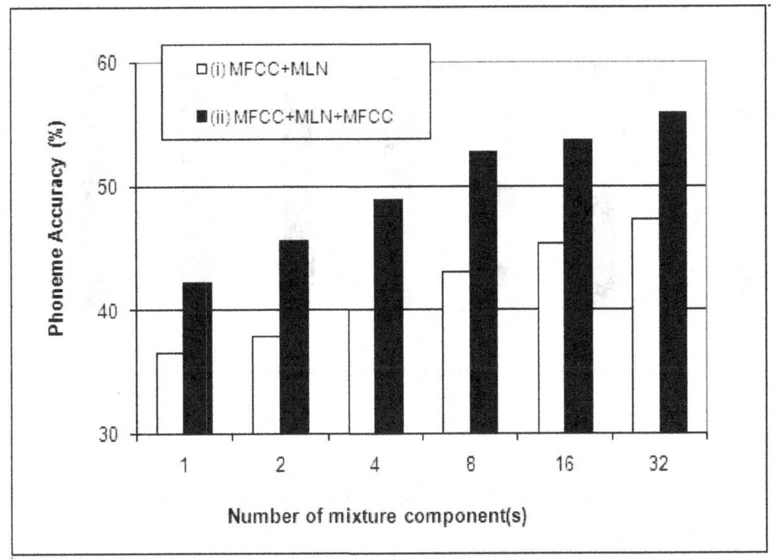

Figure 27. Effects of hybrid features for phoneme correct rate using method (3) and (4) incorporating only velocity (Δ) coefficient

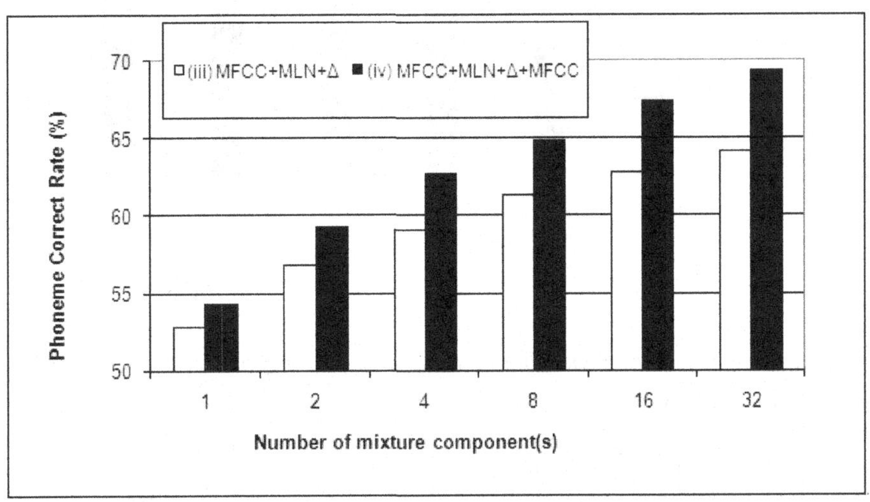

feature vector to be fed into a HMM-based classifier and the system diagram is shown in Figure 34. Parameters (mean and diagonal covariance of hidden Markov model of each phoneme) are estimated, from MFCC training data, using Baum-Welch algorithm. For different mixture components, training data are clustered using the K-mean algorithm. Triphone models are configured using training data instead of monophone. During recognition phase, a most likely word for an input utterance is obtained using the Viterbi algorithm.

Figure 28. Effects of hybrid features for phoneme accuracy using method (3) and (4) incorporating only velocity (Δ) coefficient

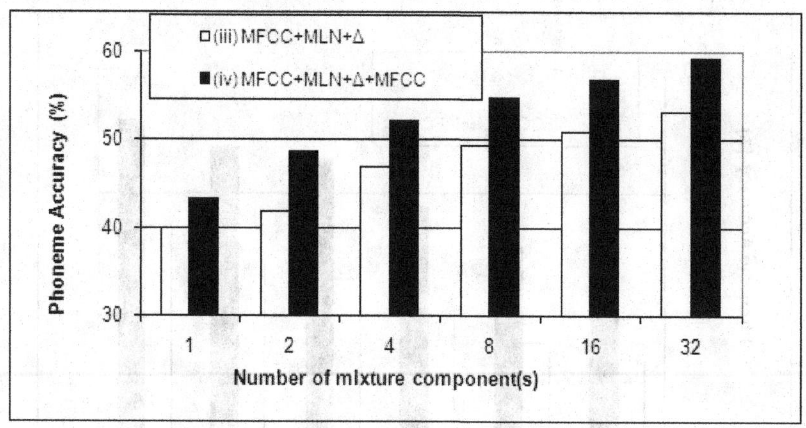

Figure 29. Effects of hybrid features for phoneme correct rate using method (5) and (6) incorporating dynamic (Δ and ΔΔ) parameters

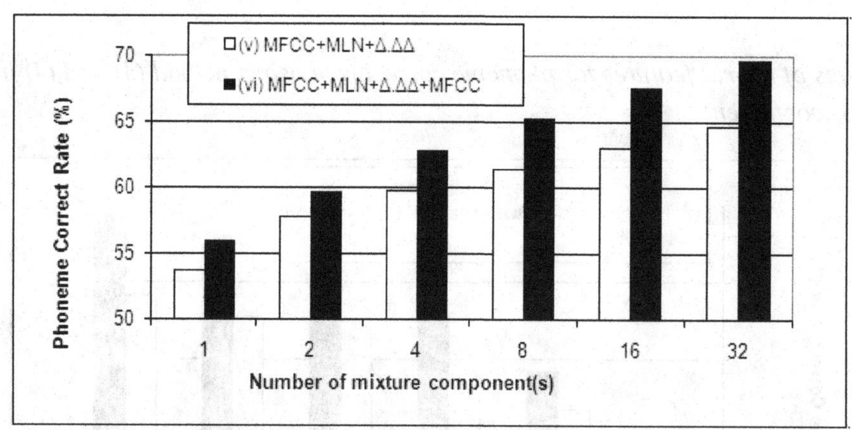

Figure 30. Effects of hybrid features for phoneme accuracy using method (5) and (6) incorporating dynamic (Δ and ΔΔ) parameters

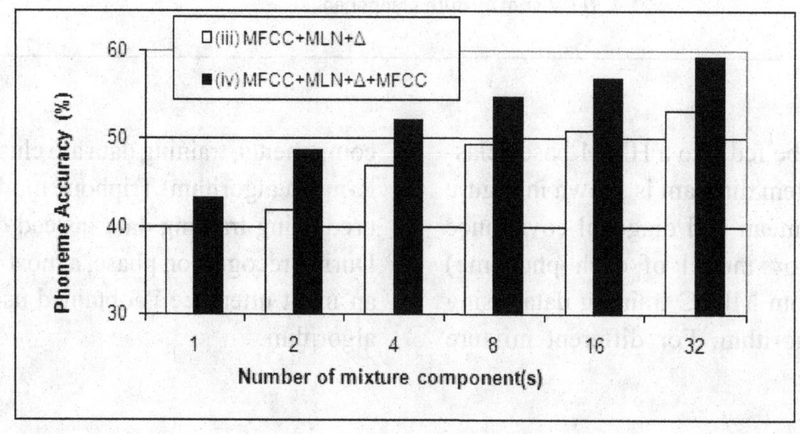

Figure 31. Effect of hybrid features in the method, (6) over the method (5)

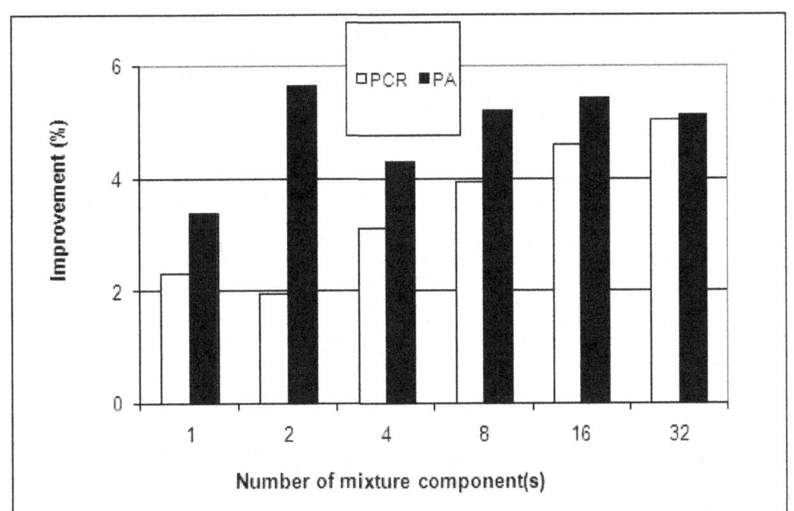

Figure 32. Example of local features

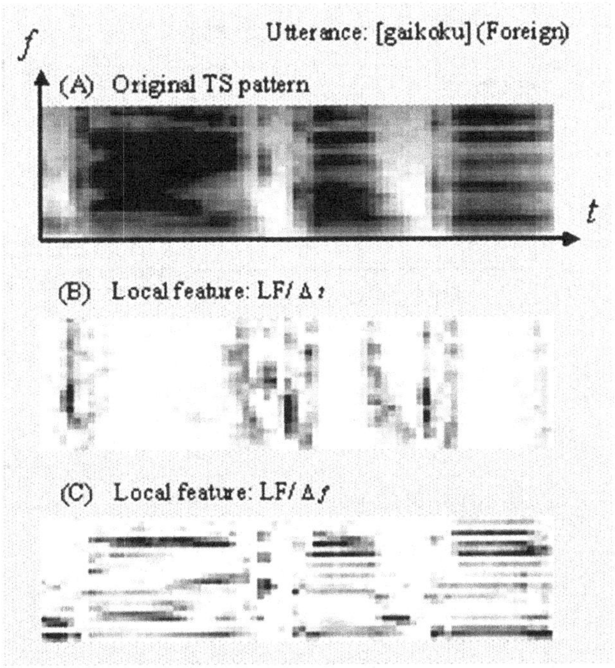

LF-Based ASR

At an acoustic feature extraction stage, firstly, input speech is converted into Local Features (LFs) of 25 dimensions that is already described in local feature extraction section (Nitta, 1999). Recognition results using triphone model are found after inserting these 25-dimnsional data vectors into HMM-based classifier, which is similar to the conventional approach. Figure 35 shows the system diagram of LF-based ASR.

Figure 33. Local feature extraction procedure

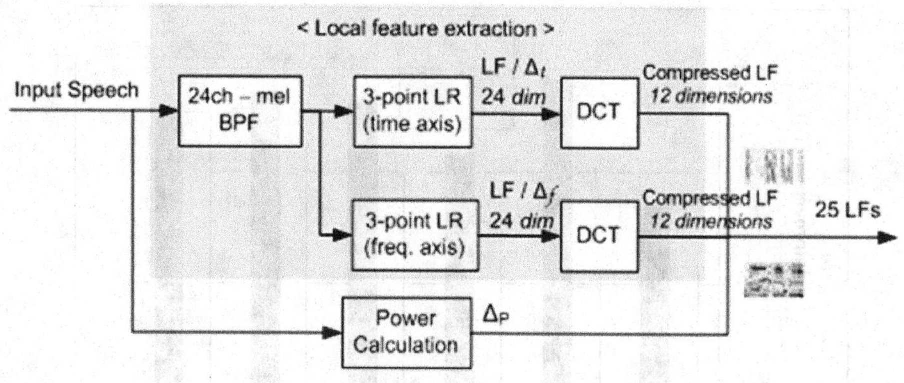

Figure 34. Conventional approach of MFCC-based word recognizer

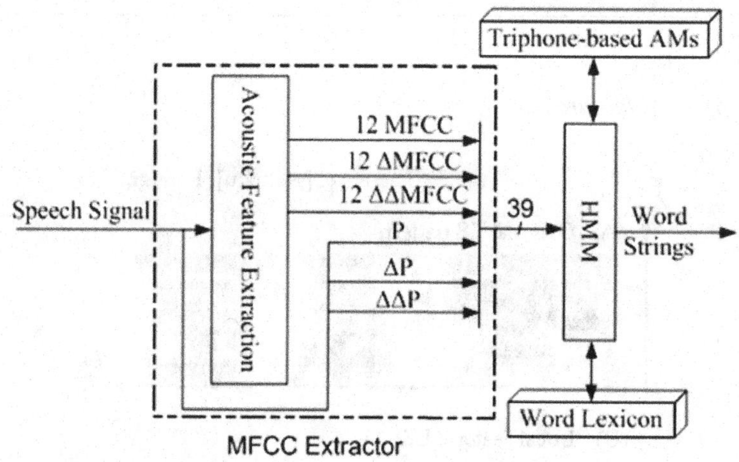

Figure 35. LF-based word recognizer

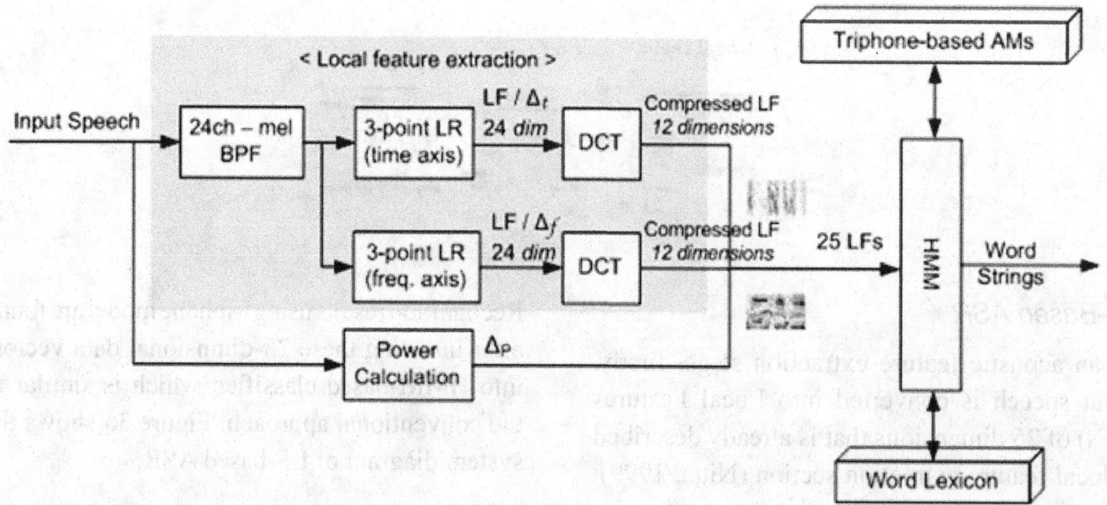

Phoneme Probability-Based ASR (Hassan, 2011)

Figure 36 shows the word recognition method using MLN. At the acoustic feature extraction stage, input speech is converted into MFCCs of 39 dimensions that are input to an MLN with four layers, including three hidden layers, after combining preceding (t-3)-th and succeeding (t+3)-th frames with the current t-th frame. The MLN has 53 output units (all phonemes including sp and sil) of phoneme probabilities for the current frame t. The three hidden layers consist of 400, 200 and 100 units, respectively. The MLN is trained by using the standard back-propagation algorithm. These phoneme probabilities are inserted into the triphone based HMM to obtain more accurate word strings. This method embeds short and long vowels, and some instances of allophones for designing triphone HMMs.

Experimental Setup

The frame length and frame rate are set to 25 ms and 10 ms (frame shift between two consecutive frames), respectively, to obtain acoustic features (MFCCs and LFs) from an input speech. MFCC comprised of 39 dimensional features. LFs are a 25-dimensional vector consisting of 12 delta coefficients along time axis, 12 delta coefficients along frequency axis, and delta coefficient of log power of a raw speech signal (Nitta, 1999).

For designing an accurate continuous word recognizer, Word Correct Rates (WCRs), Word Accuracy (WAs), and Sentence Correct Rates (SCRs) for D3 data set are evaluated using an HMM-based classifier. The D1 data set is used to design Bangla triphones HMMs with five states, three loops, and left-to-right models. Input features for the classifier are 39 dimensional MFCC. In the HMMs, the output probabilities are represented in the form of Gaussian mixtures, and diagonal matrices are used. The mixture components are set to one, two, four, and eight.

To obtain the WCRs, WAs and SCRs we have designed the following experiments for D1 (close test) and D3 (open test) data sets:

a. MFCC39+Triphone-HMM[Conventional].
b. LF25 + Triphone-HMM.
c. MFCC39 + MLN + Triphone-HMM.

Experimental Results and Discussion

Figure 37 shows the comparison of WCR using D1 data set among the systems, MFCC39+ Triphone-HMM, LF25+Triphone-HMM and MFCC39+MLN+Triphone-HMM. It is observed from the figure that the system, (c) always provides

Figure 36. Phoneme probability-based word recognizer

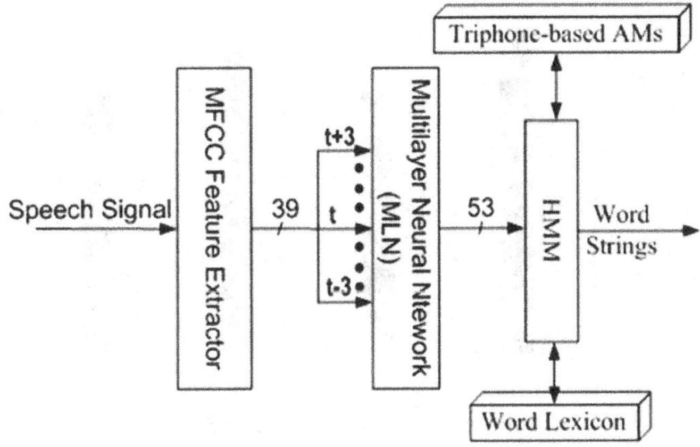

Figure 37. Word correct rate for D1 data set

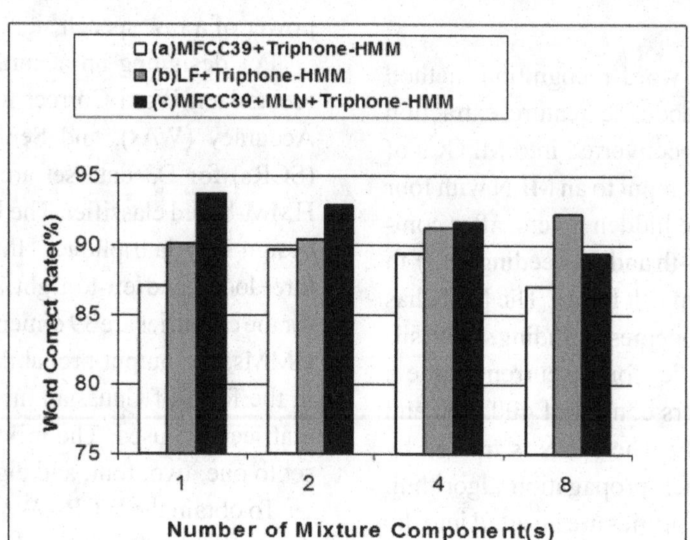

higher WCR than the other method investigated at lower mixture components (One, Two and Four). For an example, at mixture component one, the system, (c) exhibits 93.71% correct rate, while 87.13% and 90.08% WCRs are obtained by the methods, MFCC39+Triphone-HMM and LF25+Triphone-HMM, respectively. On the other hand, Figure 38 gives corresponding WA for the methods investigated. It is also shown from this figure that similar types of results are obtained. These results exhibit the excellence of the system, (c) over the other methods investigated. It is observed from the figure that the method, (c) shows the highest word recognition performance

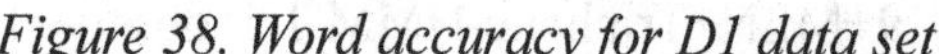

Figure 38. Word accuracy for D1 data set

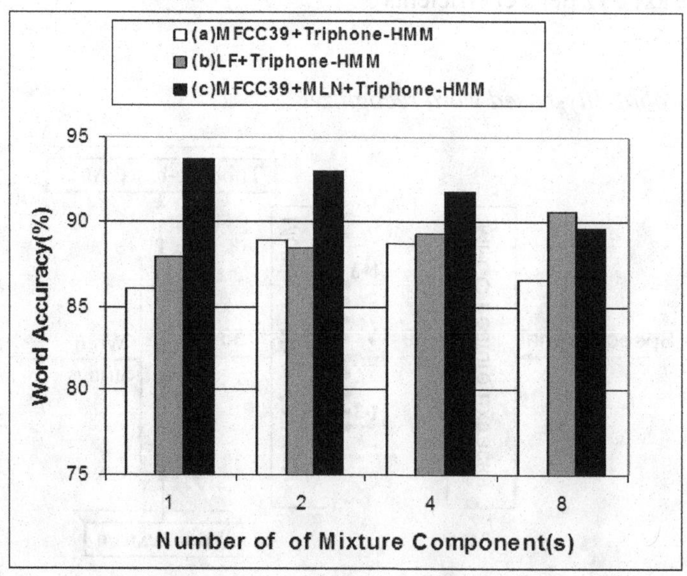

over the methods, MFCC39+Triphone-HMM and LF25+Triphone-HMM at mixture component one. Figure 39 shows sentence correct rate (SCR) for the investigated methods using D1 data set. From the figure, it is shown that the method, (c) always provides highest level correctness for the mixture components one, two and four. If we observe the Figures 37, 38 and 39 for comparing the methods, (a) and (c), it provides strong evidence that the incorporation of MLN with longer context input (Seven Frames: from "t-3" th frame to "t+3" th frame) has significant role for improving the performances. Moreover, the method, (c) requires fewer mixture components to obtain better result than the other methods investigated.

Tables 4, 5, and 6 show the word recognition performance for the methods, MFCC39+ Triphone-HMM, LF25+Triphone-HMM and MFCC39+ MLN+Triphone-HMM, respectively using the D1 data set. It is observed from the tables that highest number of recognized words, H by the methods (c), (b) and (a) are 10824, 10658 and 10353 at mixture components one, eight and two respectively for the total number of training words, 11550. Again, the lowest number of total deletions for the methods (c), (b) and (a) are 217, 51 and 180 in mixture component one, four and one respectively, which indicates that the method (b) exhibits the lowest deletions among the all methods investigated. Moreover, the methods, (c), (b) and (a) substitute 509, 839 and 989 words that represent lowest substitution at mixture component one, eight and four respectively. Finally, the least number of insertions for the corresponding methods, which measures the word accuracy, are found 13, 188 and 54 for the mixture component eight.

The sentence recognition performance for the methods (c), (b) and (a) are shown in Tables 7, 8, and 9 respectively using the D1 data set. The total numbers of correctly recognized sentences for the corresponding methods are 2813, 2729 and 2678 at mixture component one, eight and two out of 3000 training sentences, respectively. These recognized values indicate highest number of sentence correction rate among all the investigated mixture components. The method, (c) recognizes highest number of sentences because of having more context information over the other methods investigated.

Figure 39. Sentence correct rate for D1 data set

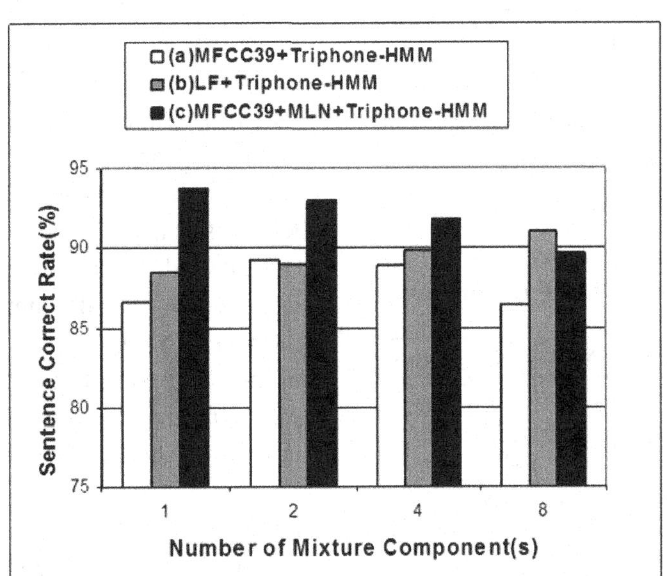

Table 4. Word recognition performance for MFCC39+triphone-HMM using D1 data set

	Mix1	Mix2	Mix4	Mix8
Correctly Recognized, H	10063	10353	10320	10056
Deletion, D	180	183	241	391
Substitution, S	1307	1014	989	1103
Insertion, I	131	86	71	54
Total, N	11550	11550	11550	11550

Table 5. Word recognition performance for LF25+triphone-HMM using D1 data set

	Mix1	Mix2	Mix4	Mix8
Correctly Recognized, H	10404	10446	10537	10658
Deletion, D	60	68	51	53
Substitution, S	1086	1036	962	839
Insertion, I	246	233	225	188
Total, N	11550	11550	11550	11550

Table 6. Word recognition performance for MFCC 39 +MLN +triphone-HMM using D1 data set

	Mix1	Mix2	Mix4	Mix8
Correctly Recognized, H	10824	10726	10586	10327
Deletion, D	217	249	329	447
Substitution, S	509	575	635	776
Insertion, I	16	20	21	13
Total, N	11550	11550	11550	11550

Table 7. Sentence recognition performance for MFCC 39 +triphone-HMM using D1 data set

	Mix1	Mix2	Mix4	Mix8
Correctly Recognized, H	2598	2678	2667	2591
Substitution, S	402	322	333	409
Total, N	3000	3000	3000	3000

Table 8. Sentence recognition performance for LF 25 +triphone-HMM using D1 data set

	Mix1	Mix2	Mix4	Mix8
Correctly Recognized, H	2655	2669	2694	2729
Substitution, S	345	331	306	271
Total, N	3000	3000	3000	3000

Table 9. Sentence recognition performance for MFCC 39 +MLN +triphone-HMM using D1 data set

	Mix1	Mix2	Mix4	Mix8
Correctly Recognized, H	2813	2790	2753	2689
Substitution, S	187	210	247	311
Total, N	3000	3000	3000	3000

WCRs using the D2 data set for the methods, MFCC39+Triphone-HMM, LF25+Triphone-HMM and MFCC39+MLN+Triphone-HMM systems are depicted in Figure 40. From the figure, it is observed that the system, (c) provides higher WCR than the other methods investigated at the lowest mixture components (One). The system, (c) proclaims 91.91% correct rates at mixture component one, while 88.57% and 88.18% WCRs are obtained by the methods, MFCC39+Triphone-HMM and LF25+Triphone-HMM, accordingly. Besides, Figure 41 illustrates WA for the corresponding methods investigated. These results exhibit that the system, (c) provides better result than the other methods investigated. The method, (c) produces highest recognition performance over the methods, MFCC39+ Triphone-HMM and LF25+Triphone-HMM at mixture component one. Sentence correct rates (SCRs) for the investigated methods using the D3 data set are shown in Figure 42. From the figure, it is clearly visible that the method, (c) provides highest level correctness at mixture component one. Longer context window for the neural network

Figure 40. Word correct rate for D3 data set

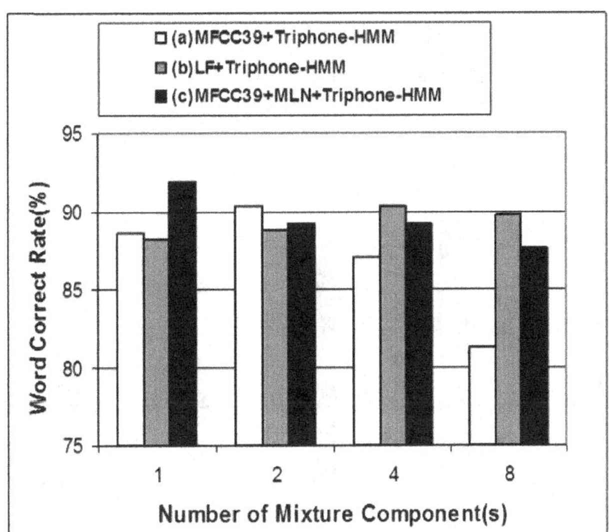

Figure 41. Word accuracy for D3 data set

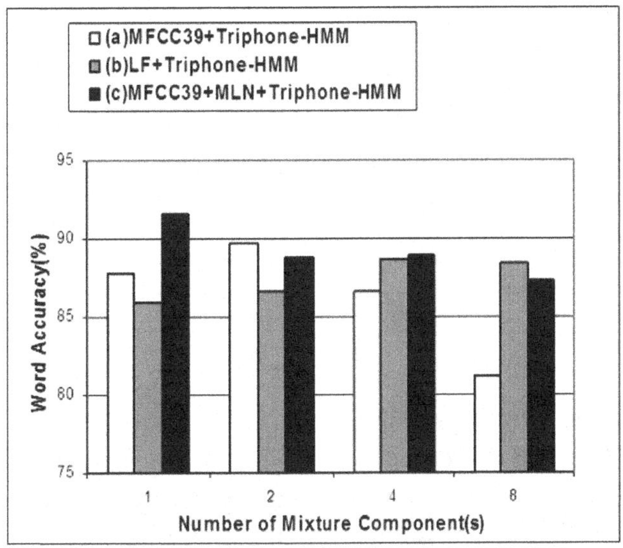

input contain more information to resolve co-articulation effect and consequently, the system, (c) provides better result than the other methods investigated in fewer mixture component.

Word recognition performance for the methods, MFCC39+Triphone-HMM, LF25+Triphone-HMM and MFCC39+MLN+Triphone-HMM using the D3 data set are shown in Tables 10, 11 and 12. The method, (c) outperformed the other methods for the correctly recognized word, H at mixture components one using D3 data set. The methods, (c), (b) and (a) provide the lowest number of deletions, 88, 33 and 74 at mixture components one, two and two, respectively. On the other hand, the lowest substitutions, 178, 284 and 244 at mixture components one, four and two are

Figure 42. Sentence correct rate for D3 data set

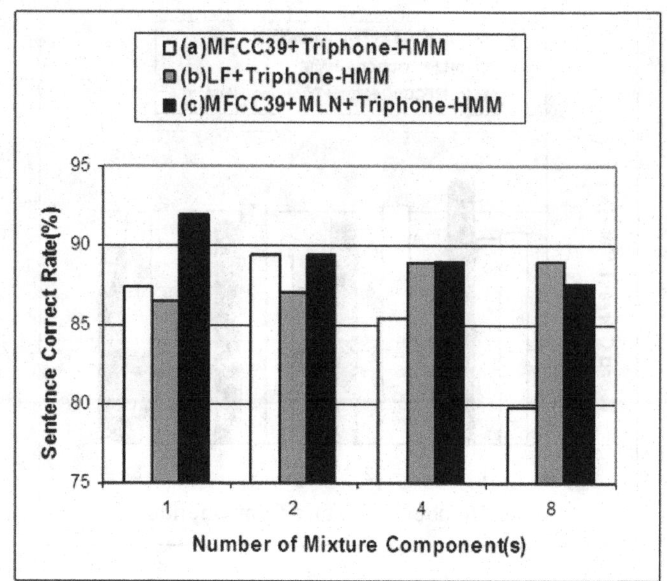

Table 10. Word recognition performance for MFCC39+triphone-HMM using D3 data set

	Mix1	Mix2	Mix4	Mix8
Correctly Recognized, H	2914	2972	2865	2676
Deletion, D	88	74	104	181
Substitution, S	288	244	321	433
Insertion, I	24	21	17	5
Total, N	3290	3290	3290	3290

Table 11. Word recognition performance for MFCC 39 +triphone-HMM using D3 data set

	Mix1	Mix2	Mix4	Mix8
Correctly Recognized, H	2901	2922	2973	2954
Deletion, D	43	38	33	45
Substitution, S	346	330	284	291
Insertion, I	74	73	56	47
Total, N	3290	3290	3290	3290

Table 12. Word recognition performance for MFCC 39 +MLN +triphone-HMM using D3 data set

	Mix1	Mix2	Mix4	Mix8
Correctly Recognized, H	3024	2935	2935	2882
Deletion, D	88	109	129	151
Substitution, S	178	246	325	257
Insertion, I	9	12	11	10
Total, N	3290	3290	3290	3290

produced by the methods (c), (b), and (a), respectively. Finally, the methods, (c), (b) and (a) provide the lowest number of insertions, 9, 47 and 5 at mixture components one, eight and eight respectively.

Tables 13, 14 and 15 depict Sentence Correct Rates (SCRs) comparison among the methods, (a), (b), and (c) using the D3 data set. The highest number of correctly recognized sentences by the methods, (c), (b) and (a) are 920, 890 and 894 at mixture components one, eight and two out of

Table 13. Sentence recognition performance for MFCC 39 +triphone-HMM using D3 data set

	Mix1	Mix2	Mix4	Mix8
Correctly Recognized, H	874	894	855	798
Substitution, S	126	106	145	202
Total, N	1000	1000	1000	1000

Table 14. Sentence recognition performance for LF 25 +triphone-HMM using D3 data set

	Mix1	Mix2	Mix4	Mix8
Correctly Recognized, H	865	871	889	890
Substitution, S	135	129	111	110
Total, N	1000	1000	1000	1000

Table 15. Sentence recognition performance for MFCC 39 +MLN +triphone-HMM using D3 data set

	Mix1	Mix2	Mix4	Mix8
Correctly Recognized, H	920	894	890	876
Substitution, S	80	106	110	124
Total, N	1000	1000	1000	1000

1000 test sentences, respectively. The method, (c) recognizes the highest number of sentences at lowest mixture component. The reason for these results is that the phoneme probabilities obtained by using the longer context window in MLN are used to design triphone HMM instead of acoustic features. This behavior is independent of any speech language, but related to neural network based model.

Male-Dependent ASR Using Triphone-Based HMM

MFCC-Based Method

Method-I without Incorporating GI Classifier (Kotwal, 2011)

Figure 43 shows the system diagram of MFCC-based gender factor canonicalization method without incorporating GI classifier, where MFCC features are extracted from the speech signal using the MFCC extractor already described and then male and female HMM classifiers are trained using the D1 and D2 data sets, respectively. Here, triphone acoustic HMMs are designed and trained using D1 and D2 data sets. Output hypothesis is

Figure 43. MFCC-based suppression method without GI classifier

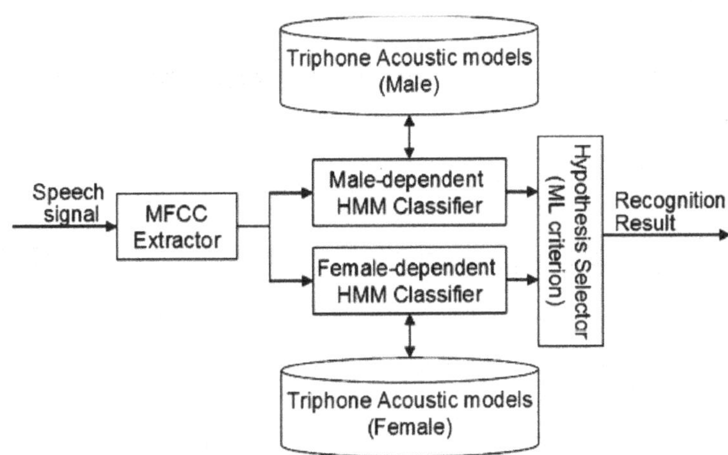

selected based on maximum output probabilities after comparing male and female hypotheses, and passed the best matches hypothesis to the output.

Method-II Incorporating GI Classifier (Hassan, 2011)

The diagram of the MFCC-based gender factor suppression method incorporating GI classifier is depicted in Figure 44. Here, the extracted MFCC features from the input speech signal are inserted into the male, female, and GI HMM-based classifiers. The male, female, and GI HMM-based classifiers are trained using the D1, D2 and (D1+D2) data sets. Here, output hypothesis is selected based on maximum output probabilities after comparing male, female and gender independent hypotheses, and passed the best matches hypothesis to the output.

Experimental Setup

The frame length and frame rate are set to 25 ms and 10 ms (frame shift between two consecutive frames), respectively, to obtain acoustic features (MFCCs of 39 dimensions) from an input speech.

For designing an accurate continuous word recognizer, Word Correct Rates (WCRs), Word Accuracy (WAs) and Sentence Correct Rate (SCRs) for (D3+D4) data set are evaluated using an HMM-based classifier. The D1 and D2 data sets are used to design Bangla triphones HMMs with five states, three loops, and left-to-right models. Input features for the classifier are 39 dimensional MFCC. In the HMMs, the output probabilities are represented in the form of Gaussian mixtures, and diagonal matrices are used. The mixture components are set to 1, 2, 4, and 8.

For evaluating the performance of different methods including the MFCC-based suppression method incorporating the GI classifier, we have designed the following experiments:

a. MFCC (Train: 3000 male, Test: 1000 male + 1000 female).
b. MFCC (Train: 3000 female, Test: 1000 male + 1000 female).
c. MFCC (Train: 3000 male + 3000 female, Test: 1000 male + 1000 female).
d. MFCC (Train: 3000 male, Train: 3000 female, Test: 1000 male + 1000 female).
e. MFCC (Train: 3000 male, Train: 3000 female, Train: 3000 male + 3000 female, Test: 1000 male + 1000 female).

Experimental Results and Analysis

Figure 45 shows the comparison of word correct rates among all the investigated methods, (a), (b), (c), (d), and (e). Among all the mixture components investigated, the method, (e) shows higher performance in comparison with the other

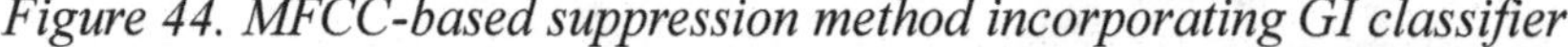

Figure 44. MFCC-based suppression method incorporating GI classifier

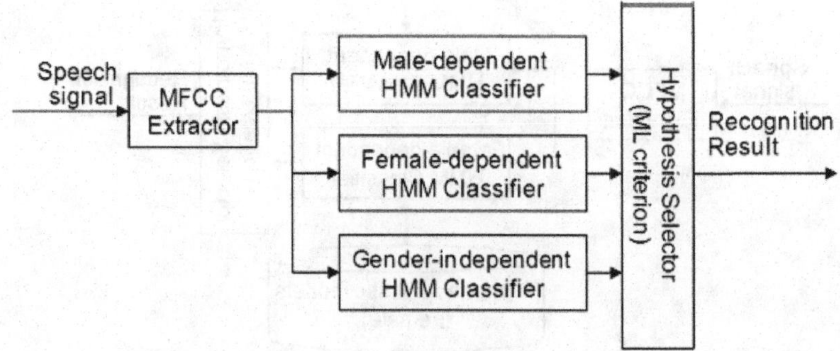

Figure 45. Word correct rate comparison among all the investigated methods

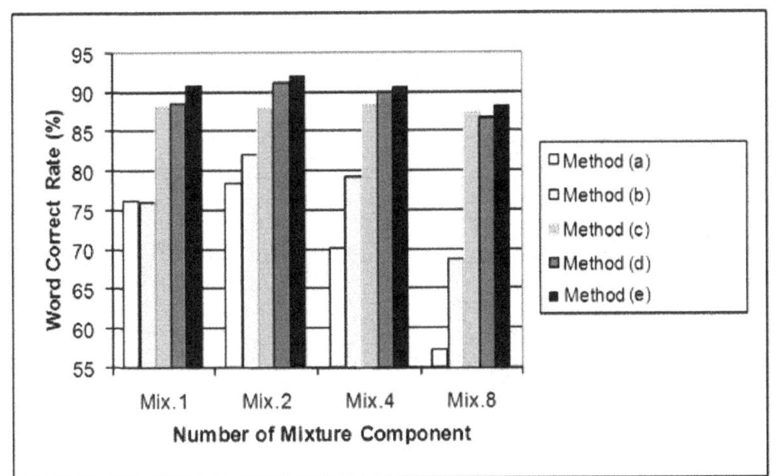

method evaluated. It is noted that the method, (e) exhibits its best performance (92.17%) at mixture component two.

Word accuracies for different investigated methods are depicted in Figure 46. From the figure, it is observed that the highest level performance (91.64%) at mixture component two is found by the method, (e) compared to the other methods investigated. Here, the performance of the methods, (a), (b), (c), (d), and (e) at mixture component two are 77.58%, 81.47%, 87.39%, 90.78%, and 91.64%, respectively.

It is shown from the Figure 47 that sentence correct rates for the investigated methods, (a), (b), (c), (d), and (e) are 77.20%, 81.45%, 86.60%, 90.45%, and 91.30%, respectively, where the proposed method, (e) provides its best performance. The methods, (a), (b), and (c) give less performance in comparison with the method (d) because (d) incorporates both HMM-based classifiers for male and female. Again, the method, (e) incorporates GI HMM-based classifier over the method (d), which increases sentence correct rate significantly. Since the maximum output

Figure 46. Word accuracy comparison among all the investigated methods

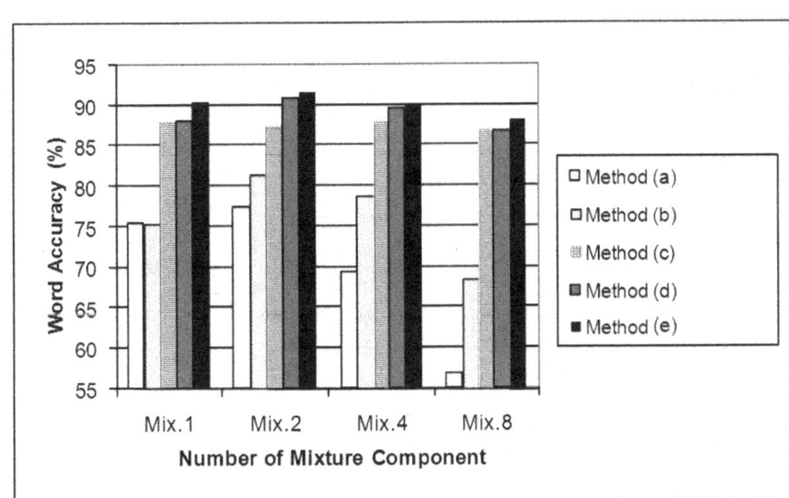

Figure 47. Sentence correct rate comparison among all the investigated methods

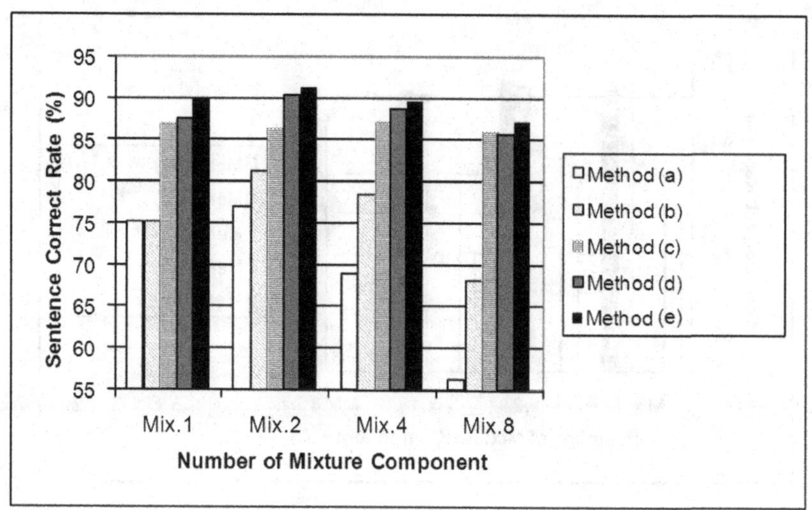

probability is generated by the method, (e) after comparing the probabilities among male, female and GI classifiers, the suppression method, (e) shows its superiority.

Improvements by the GI classifier in the proposed method (e) over the method (d) that does not incorporate GI classifier is shown in Figure 48. From the figure, it is observed that the method, (e) shows its highest level improvement at mixture components one, where the improvement of sentence correct rate, word accuracy and word correct rate are 2.4%, 2.36% and 2.32%, respectively.

LF-Based Method

The diagram of the LF-based method is depicted in Figure 49. Here, the extracted LFs (Nitta, 1999) from the input speech signal are inserted into the male, female and GI HMM-based classifiers. The

Figure 48. Effect of gender-independent classifier in the proposed method (e) over the method (d)

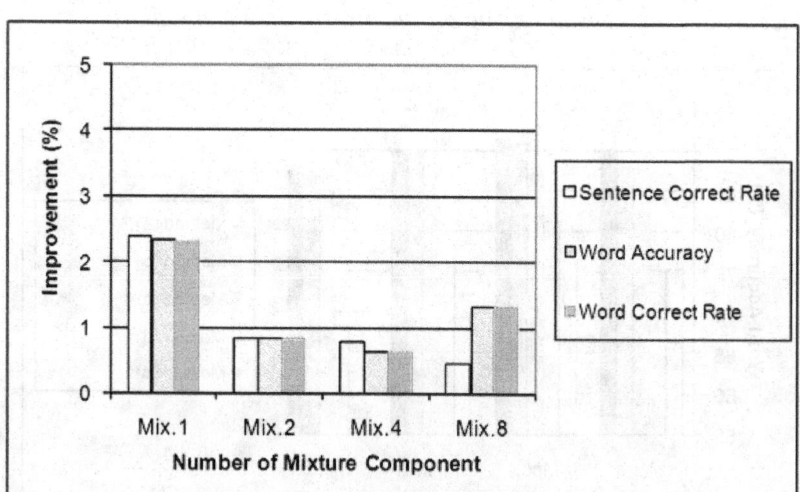

Figure 49. LF-based suppression method incorporating GI classifier

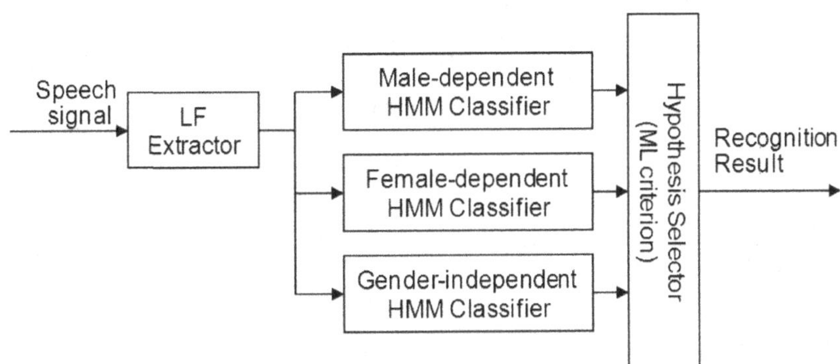

male, female and GI HMM-based classifiers are trained using the D1, D2 and (D1+D2) data sets. Here, output hypothesis is selected based on maximum output probabilities after comparing male, female and gender independent hypotheses, and passed the best matches hypothesis to the output.

Experimental Setup

The frame length and frame rate are set to 25 ms and 10 ms (frame shift between two consecutive frames), respectively, to obtain acoustic features (LFs) from an input speech. LFs comprised of 25 dimensional features vector (Nitta, 1999).

For designing an accurate continuous word recognizer, Word Correct Rate (WCR), Word Accuracy (WA) and Sentence Correct Rate (SCR) for (D3+D4) data set are evaluated using an HMM-based classifier. The D1 and D2 data sets are used to design Bangla triphones HMMs with five states, three loops, and left-to-right models. Input features for the classifier are 39 dimensional MFCC. In the HMMs, the output probabilities are represented in the form of Gaussian mixtures, and diagonal matrices are used. The mixture components are set to 1, 2, 4, and 8.

For evaluating the performance of different methods including the LF-based suppression method incorporating GI classifier, we have designed the following experiments:

a. LF (Train: 3000 male, Test: 1000 male + 1000 female).
b. LF (Train: 3000 female, Test: 1000 male + 1000 female).
c. LF (Train: 3000 male + 3000 female, Test: 1000 male + 1000 female).
d. LF (Train: 3000 male, Train: 3000 female, Train: 3000 male + 3000 female, Test: 1000 male + 1000 female).

Experimental Results and Analysis

Word Correct Rates (WCRs), Word Accuracies (WAs), and Sentence Correct Rates (SCRs) for LF and MFCC based methods, (a), (b), (c), and (d)/(e) using (D3+D4) data set are shown in Table 16. Here, methods (d) and (e) represent LF-based and MFCC-based suppression methods with gender independent (GI) classifiers, respectively. From the experiment #1, where the HMM-based classifier is trained with D1 data set and evaluated with (D3+D4) data set, a tremendous improvement of WCRs, WAs and SCRs are exhibited by the LF-based ASR that incorporates gender effect canonicalization module in the ASR process. Similarly, the same pattern of performance is also achieved in the experiment #2, where the HMM-based classifier is trained with D2 data set and evaluated with (D3+D4) data set. This trend explicates the LFs, which embeds time and frequency domain information in its extraction procedure, as

Table 16. Word correct rates (WCRs), word accuracies (WA), and sentence correct rates (SCRs) for LF and MFCC based methods, (a), (b), (c), and (d)/(e) using (D3+D4) data set. Here, methods (d) and (e) are LF-based and MFCC-based suppression methods with gender independent (GI) classifiers, respectively.

Experiments	Methods	WCR (%)	WA (%)	SCR (%)
1	LF-based (a)	88.63	85.53	86.60
	MFCC-based (a)	76.38	75.41	75.30
2	LF-based (b)	86.29	93.65	84.50
	MFCC-based (b)	76.16	75.50	75.45
3	LF-based (c)	92.22	90.43	90.85
	MFCC-based (c)	88.39	87.83	87.15
4	LF-based (d)	94.94	93.86	93.95
	MFCC-based (e)	91.00	90.43	90.05

excellent feature for the Bangla automatic speech recognition system. Again, the experiment #3, which shows the GI ASR for Bangla language based on LF and MFCC features, is trained with (D1+D2) and evaluated with (D3+D4) data sets and provides 3.83%, 2.60% and 3.70% improvements by the LF-based method in comparison with the MFCC-based counterpart. Finally, the methods in the experiment #4 imply two ASR systems for GI Bangla ASR by integrating gender factor canonicalization process in its architecture and shows the highest level performance for WCRs, WAs and SCRs compare to the corresponding the methods in the experiments #1, #2 and #3. Since these methods of the experiment #4 always maximizes the output probabilities obtained from the three classifiers: male, female and GI, it shows its maximum level of performance. Besides, the LF-based methods improves the WCRs, WAs and SCRs by 3.94%, 3.43% and 3.90%, respectively than the method that inputs MFCC features in the HMM-based classifier in the gender effect suppression process.

On the other hand, Table 17 exhibits sentence recognition performance for LF and MFCC based methods, (a), (b), (c), and (d)/(e) using (D3+D4)

Table 17. Sentence recognition performance for LF and MFCC based methods, (a), (b), (c), and (d)/(e) using (D3+D4) data set. Here, methods (d) and (e) are LF-based and MFCC-based suppression methods with gender independent (GI) classifiers, respectively.

Experiments	Methods	Word Recognition Performance (Total 6580 Words)			
		Correctly Recognized, H	Deletion, D	Substitution, S	Insertion, I
1	LF-based (a)	5832	58	690	204
	MFCC-based (a)	5026	438	1116	64
2	LF-based (b)	5678	89	813	174
	MFCC-based (b)	5011	448	1121	43
3	LF-based (c)	6068	55	457	118
	MFCC-based (c)	5816	152	612	37
4	LF-based (d)	6247	33	300	71
	MFCC-based (e)	5988	140	452	38

data set, where the methods (d) and (e) represent LF-based and MFCC-based suppression methods with Gender Independent (GI) classifiers, respectively. Here, experiments #1, #2, #3 and #4 use same corpora for training and evaluation that we explained earlier. From all the experiments, it is evident that the LF-based method reduces the number of incorrectly recognized sentences with respect to its counterpart. The experiment #4 shows the highest number of correctly recognized sentences than the corresponding methods in the other experiments, #1, #2 and #3 investigated. For an example, in the LF-based and MFCC-based methods of experiment #4, the numbers of correctly recognized sentences are 1879 and 1801, respectively that are the highest numerical figures among the corresponding methods of all the experiments. It is noted that two significant phenomenon contributed more for obtaining the best experimental results by the LF-based method of experiment #4: 1) both time and frequency domain information and 2) selection of maximum probability among the three output probabilities calculated by the male, female and GI HMM-based classifiers.

Moreover, word recognition performance for LF and MFCC based methods, (a), (b), (c), and (d)/(e) using (D3+D4) data set are summarized in the Table 18. In the table, methods (d) and (e) represent LF-based and MFCC-based suppression methods with Gender Independent (GI) classifiers, respectively. The same speech corpora for training and evaluation are used for the experiments #1, #2, #3 and #4 which is already described in the earlier. It is observed from all the experiments that the LF-based method increases the number of correctly recognized words in comparison with its counterpart. The highest number of correctly recognized words shown by the experiment #4 with respect to their corresponding methods in the other experiments, #1, #2 and #3 are evident from the table. It can be mentioned as an example that the LF-based and MFCC-based methods of experiment #4 provide the highest numbers of correctly recognized words, which are 6247 and 5988, respectively, dictates the respective numerical figures obtained for the corresponding methods of all the other experiments. The reason for obtaining the best experimental results by the LF-based method of experiment #4 is also illustrated earlier.

Table 18. Word recognition performance for LF and MFCC based methods, (a), (b), (c), and (d)/(e) using (D3+D4) data set. Here, methods (d) and (e) represent LF-based and MFCC-based suppression methods with gender independent (GI) classifiers, respectively.

Experiments	Methods	Sentence Recognition Performance (Total 2000 Sentences)	
		Correctly Recognized, H	Incorrectly Recognized, S
1	LF-based (a)	1732	268
	MFCC-based (a)	1506	494
2	LF-based (b)	1690	310
	MFCC-based (b)	1509	491
3	LF-based (c)	1817	183
	MFCC-based (c)	1743	257
4	LF-based (d)	1879	121
	MFCC-based (e)	1801	199

FUTURE RESEARCH DIRECTIONS

Some issues are not considered and resolved during the whole study. For example, speech is collected in a noise corrupted environment that integrated corridor noise, street noise and air condition noise, etc, but noise suppression procedure is not included in this study. Besides, the gender effect suppression procedure was embedded for suppressing gender-factor in this research, but consideration of suppression of speaking style was not done. Consequently, a canonicalization process is needed that suppress both noise of different SNRs (Signal to Noise Ratios) in the different acoustic environments and gender factor with low cost (memory and computation). Again, current HMM-based classifier cannot resolve OOV problem and hence, a phonetic typewriter functionality design is needed for inserting the OOV word automatically in the word lexicon by call back procedure instead of generating errors. Moreover, incorporation of language model will reduce grammatical errors, which is not dealt in this study. On the other hand, an interface design is also needed for hearing impaired people of Bangladesh for recognizing the continuous speech. Another major concern is that, people of different areas of Bangladesh make conversation with different dialects and therefore, further research is also recommended for resolving the dialects. In addition, an interface design for constructing email by uttering the speech avoids the necessity of typing in the email editor that will be done in near future.

CONCLUSION

This chapter has discussed some ASR techniques for Bangla language by evaluating the different speech features. In this study, phoneme recognizer based on standard MFCC features generates phoneme strings for resolving the OOV word problem of current HMM-based classifier. In addition, a canonicalization method also resolves gender factor by incorporating both types of genders (male and female) in the process after selecting the maximum hypothesis. Here, incorporation of local features, which comprised of time and frequency domain information, show significant improvement of word correct rates, word accuracies and sentence correct rates compared to the method that uses standard MFCCs. Moreover, phoneme probabilities based on MFCCs are extracted by using a multilayer neural network, where these output probabilities increase the word and sentence recognition performance of male-dependent ASR. In the experiments of phoneme recognition, dynamic parameters, such as velocity (Δ) and acceleration ($\Delta\Delta$) coefficients for resolving coarticulation effects increase recognition performance and reduce computation cost by taking fewer mixture components in the HMM-based classifier. A labeled medium scale Bangla speech corpus for evaluating the recognition performance is designed in this research which can be used in any supervised learning algorithm. Finally, phoneme recognition performance can be improved by incorporating hybrid features in the classifier.

REFERENCES

Bazzi, I., & Glass, J. R. (2000). Modeling OOV words for ASR. In *Proceedings of the International Conference on Spoken Language Processing (ICSLP)*. Beijing, China: ICSLP.

Daily Prothom Alo. (n.d.). Retrieved from www.prothom-alo.com

Firoj, A., Murtoza, H. S. M., Afroza, S. D., & Mumit, K. (2010). BRAC university institutional repository. *Development of Annotated Bangla Speech Corpora.* Retrieved June 28, 2012, from http://dspace.bracu.ac.bd/handle//10361//633

Hasnat, M. A., Mowla, J., & Khan, M. (2007). Isolated and continuous Bangla speech recognition: Implementation performance and application perspective. In *Proceedings of International Symposium on Natural Language Processing (SNLP)*. Hanoi, Vietnam: SNLP.

Hassan, F., Kotwal, M. R. A., & Huda, M. N. (2011). Bangla ASR design by suppressing gender factor with gender-independent and gender-based HMM classifiers. In *Proceedings of WICT 2011*. Mumbai, India: WICT.

Hassan, M. R., Nath, B., & Bhuiyan, M. A. (2003). Bengali phoneme recognition: A new approach. In *Proceedings of the 6th International Conference on Computer and Information Technology (ICCIT03)*. Dhaka, Bangladesh: ICCIT.

Hossain, S. A., Rahman, M. L., & Ahmed, F. (2007). World academy of science, engineering and technology. *Bangla Vowel Characterization Based on Analysis by Synthesis*, *20*, 327–330.

Hossain, S. A., Rahman, M. L., Ahmed, F., & Dewan, M. (2004). Bangla speech synthesis, analysis, and recognition: An overview. In *Proceedings of the National Conference on Computer Processing of Bangla (NCCPB04)*. NCCPB.

Houque, A. K. M. M. (2006). *Bengali segmented speech recognition system*. (Unpublished Undergraduate Thesis). BRAC University. Bangladesh.

Karim, R., Rahman, M. S., & Iqbal, M. Z. (2002). Recognition of spoken letters in Bangla. In *Proceedings of the 5th International Conference on Computer and Information Technology (ICCIT02)*. Dhaka, Bangladesh: ICCIT.

Kirchhoff, K. (2007). OOV detection by joint word/phone lattice alignment. In *Proceedings of ASRU*. Kyoto, Japan: ASRU.

Kishore, S., Black, A., Kumar, R., & Sangal, R. (2003). *Experiments with unit selection speech databases for Indian languages*. Paper presented at National Seminar on Language Technology Tools: Implementation of Telugu. Hyderabad, India.

Kotwal, M. R. A., Bonik, M., Eity, Q. N., Huda, M. N., Muhammad, G., & Alotaibi, Y. A. (2010). Bangla phoneme recognition for ASR using multilayer neural network. In *Proceedings of the International Conference on Computer and Information Technology (ICCIT10)*. Dhaka, Bangladesh: ICCIT.

Kotwal, M. R. A., Hasan, F., Ahmed, F., Alam, M. S., Daud, S. I., & Huda, M. N. (2011). Incorporation of dynamic parameters in hybrid feature-based Bangla phoneme recognition using multilayer neural networks. In *Proceedings of the International Conference on Computer and Information Technology (ICCIT11)*. Dhaka, Bangladesh: ICCIT.

Kotwal, M. R. A., Hassan, F., Daud, S. I., Alam, M. S., Ahmed, F., & Huda, M. N. (2011). Gender effects suppression in Bangla ASR by designing multiple HMM-based classifiers. In *Proceedings of CICN 2011*. Gwalior, India: CICN.

Magnus, R. (2006). *An introduction to front-end processing and acoustic features for automatic speech recognition*. Swedish National Graduate School of Language Technology.

Masica, C. P. (1993). *The Indo-Aryan languages*. Cambridge, UK: Cambridge University Press.

Muhammad, G., Alotaibi, Y. A., & Huda, M. N. (2009). Automatic speech recognition for Bangla digits. In *Proceedings of the International Conference on Computer and Information Technology (ICCIT09)*. Dhaka, Bangladesh: ICCIT.

Nitta, T. (1999). Feature extraction for speech recognition based on orthogonal acoustic-feature planes and LDA. *Proceedings of ICASSP*, *99*, 421–424.

Picone, J. Staples, Kondo, & Arai. (1993). *Processing system of Japanese language.* Japanese Patent No. TIJ-18107. Tokyo: Japanese Patent Office.

Rahman, K. J. Hossain, Das, Islam, & Ali. (2003). Continuous Bangla speech recognition system. In *Proceedings of the 6th International Conference on Computer and Information Technology (ICCIT03).* Dhaka, Bangladesh: ICCIT.

Roy, K. Das, & Ali. (2002). Development of the speech recognition system using artificial neural network. In *Proceedings of the 5th International Conference on Computer and Information Technology (ICCIT02).* Dhaka, Bangladesh: ICCIT.

Seneff, S. (2005). A two-pass for strategy handling OOVs in a large vocabulary recognition task. In *Proceedings of Interspeech.* Lisbon, Portugal: Interspeech.

Wikipedia. (2012). *Bengali phonology.* Retrieved June 28, 2012, from http://en.wikipedia.org/wiki/Bengali_phonology

Young, S. (2005). *The HTK book.* Cambridge, UK: Cambridge University Engineering Department.

KEY TERMS AND DEFINITIONS

Automatic Speech Recognition (ASR): An automated computer based system that recognizes an input speech as a text.

Canonization: A neutralization/normalization process for gender effects.

Dynamic Parameters: The velocity (Δ) and acceleration (ΔΔ) coefficients of an input speech.

Hidden Markov Model (HMM): A statistical Markov model in which the system being modeled is assumed to be a Markov process with unobserved (hidden) states. An HMM can be considered as the simplest dynamic Bayesian network.

Hybrid Feature: A feature that is derived by the amalgamation of acoustic features and phoneme probabilities extracted by neural networks with/without dynamic parameters.

Local Feature: A new acoustic feature of 25 dimensions (12 delta coefficients along time axis, 12 delta coefficients along frequency axis, and delta coefficient of log power of a raw speech signal).

Mel Frequency Cepstral Coefficient (MFCC): An acoustic feature of 39 dimensions (12-MFCC, 12-ΔMFCC, 12-ΔΔMFCC, P, ΔP and ΔΔP, where P stands for raw energy of the input speech signal).

Multilayer Neural Network: A Neural Network (NN) of multiple layers is a mathematical model or computational model that is inspired by the structure and/or functional aspects of biological neural networks. A neural network consists of an interconnected group of artificial neurons, and it processes information using a connectionist approach to computation. In most cases an Artificial Neural Network (ANN) is an adaptive system that changes its structure based on external or internal information that flows through the network during the learning phase.

Phoneme Recognizer: An Automatic Speech Recognition (ASR) system for recognizing an input speech as a text of phoneme strings.

Word Recognizer: An ASR system for recognizing an input speech as a text of word strings.

Chapter 10
Bangla Speech Analysis, Synthesis, and Vowel Nasality

Shahina Haque
Daffodil International University, Bangladesh

ABSTRACT

The chapter provides an overview of the theory of speech production, analysis, and synthesis, and status of Bangla speech processing. As nasality is a distinctive feature of Bangla and all the vowels have their nasal counterpart, both Bangla vowels and nasality are also considered. The chapter reviews the state-of-the-art of nasal vowel research, cross language perception of vowel nasality, and vowel nasality transformation to be used in a speech synthesizer.

1. INTRODUCTION

In this section a brief overview of Bangla language is given. Then the importance of Bangla speech processing is discussed. The aim of this chapter is pointed out in Section 1.4.

1.1. Brief Description of Bangla

Bangla, one of the more prominent Indo-Iranian languages, is the sixth-most popular in the world and spoken by a population that now exceeds 250 million. Geographical distribution of Bangla-speaking population percentages are as follows: Bangladesh (over 95%), and the Indian States of Andaman & Nicobar Islands (26%), Assam (28%), Tripura (67%), and West Bengal (85%). The global total includes those who are now in diaspora in Canada, Malawi, Nepal, Pakistan, Saudi Arabia, Singapore, United Arab Emirates, United Kingdom, and United States. Bangla has two literary styles: one is called *Sadhubhasa* (elegant form) and the other *Chaltibhasa* (commonly used form). The differences between the two styles are not huge and involve mainly forms of pronouns and verb conjugations.

The origin of modern Bangla derives from Vedic Sanskrit (1500 BC – 1000 BC). Bangla writing system evolved from the Brahmi script, which is closely related to the *Devanagari* alphabet, from which it started to diverge in the 11th century AD. The current printed form of Bangla

DOI: 10.4018/978-1-4666-3970-6.ch010

alphabet first appeared in 1778 when Charles Wilkins developed printing in Bangla. Its script includes two types of symbols, the letters (Varnas) and signs (Cinhas). The letters are vowels, consonants and conjunct consonants. The signs used are vowel signs and prosodic signs. When the vowel is used with the consonant except in the first position, it is written in sign symbols. Among prosodic signs Chandrabindu [(] and Hasant [$] are noticeable. Chandrabindu or moon dot is a graphic sign for nasalization and is written on top of a letter when the vowel following immediately is to be expressly nasalized. The writing system is more syllabic than phonemic as there is an inherent vowel [ɔ] with all the consonant phonemes except three consonants. It has the ambiguity of being phonetic, syllabic or alphabetic in nature (Hai, 1985; Chaudhury, 1984). When Hasant is appended to a consonant, the pronunciation is consonantal alone, so the inherent vowel [ɔ] is not functioning anymore. Bangla is an intonation language having no tone, accent or stress (Shaw, 1996). Normal Bangla speech is heard more or less on a monotone with slight rise and fall of pitch and loudness within the sentence. Just as the written form of a language is a sequence of elementary alphabet, speech is also a sequence of elementary acoustic sounds or symbols known as phonemes that convey the spoken form of a language (Hai, 1985). Bangla is heard more or less in monotone. But the interesting point in Bangla is nasality. All the 7 vowels in Bangla have their corresponding nasal counterparts. Nasalization of vowel changes meaning of some words in Bangla. The contrast lies in the spectrum of nasal and oral vowels as shown in Figure 1. Besides, there are 29 simple consonants, 19 diphthongs and two semivowel phonemes as shown in Table 1. There are monosyllabic to seven syllabic words in Bangla. Vowel is the nucleus of a syllable. Some vowel itself has meaning and is treated as a word. The general syllable structure of Bangla is:

(C)(C)(C)V(V)(C)

where **C** and **V** stand for consonants and vowels. When two or more consonants occur consecutively without any vowel in between they are written in cluster form. The second consonant is written below the first consonant, and the third consonant below the second. These consonant clusters are called double and triple consonant, respectively.

1.2. Nasality in Bangla

The nasality feature is found in many of the world's languages. 96.5% of the 451languages from UPSID database (UCLA Phonological Segment Inventory Database use this feature in their consonantal system. It is also the most frequent secondary dimension used in vocalic systems (22.4% of UPSID languages), on a par with the dimension of length.

Vowel nasality has differing prosodic properties across languages. In many languages vowel nasalization is strictly local, i.e. it does not spread to an adjacent segment, even if vocalic, as in French /oseã/ which surfaces as [oseã] 'ocean.' In other languages, vowel nasality, inherent or from an adjacent nasal consonant, may spread onto and across adjacent segments. In Apurinã, all vowels adjacent to a nasal vowel are obligatorily nasalized. Directionality of nasal spread

Figure 1. Spectrum of oral Bangla vowel /i/ and its nasal counterpart /i)/

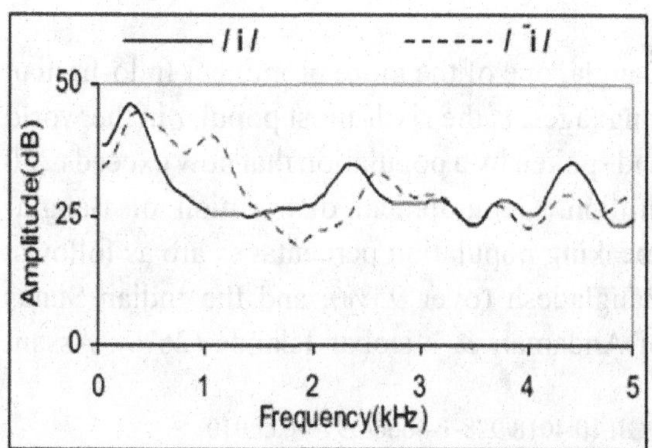

Table 1. Number of phonemes and characters in Bangla

Vowel		Consonants				Semi vowels	Prosodic signs
Letter	Sign						
অ[ɔ]		ক[k]	ট[ʈ]	প[p]	য়	য[j]	্
আ[a]	া	খ[kh]	ঠ[ʈh]	ফ[ph]	য	ওয়[w]	ʃ
ই[i]	ি	গ[g]	ড[ɖ]	ব[b]	স		ঁ
ঈ	ী	ঘ[gh]	ঢ[ɖh]	ভ[bh]	ৎ		‹
উ[u]	ু	ঙ	ত[t]	ম[m]	ঃ		ʹ
ঊ	ূ	চ[tʃ]	থ[th]	র[r]	ং		ˋ
ঋ	ৃ	ছ[tʃh]	দ[d]	ল[l]	ঁ		
এ[e]	ে	জ[dz]	ধ[dh]	ড়[ɽ]			
ঐ	ৈ	ঝ[dzh]	ন[n]	ঢ়[ɽh]			
ও[o]	ো	হ[h]	ষ	ঞ			
ঔ	ৌ	শ[ʃ]		ণ			
অ্যা[æ]	্যা						

across segments also varies. It may be mostly mono directional as in Warao (Venezuela), where it is left to right, or bidirectional as in Barasano (Tucanoan, Colombia).

In Bangla, all the 7 major vowels have nasal counterparts and the nasality of vowels is phonemic. The nasal-oral distinction of vowels, therefore, acquires an additional importance compared to those languages where nasality of vowels is non-phonemic. It is likely that for this group of languages, i.e., where nasality is phonemic, both the production and perception mechanisms would be more meaningfully organized. A study of the acoustic properties of nasality and their role in perception has, therefore, been a subject of great cognitive interest. Most of these studies relate to the languages where nasality of vowels is non-phonemic and the perception studies have been done on synthetic speech. It should be noted that all the acoustic properties that bear signatures of nasality may not be perceptually significant. The vowels are nasalized by a direct coupling of the nasal cavity with the oral one affected by the opening of soft velum. Again different vowels have different sizes of the back and front oral cavities as well as different degrees of coupling between them according to the positions of the tongue hump both in horizontal and vertical directions. Spectral changes in the signal due to nasal coupling, therefore, may be different from vowel to vowel. The degree of prominence of different nasal cues may have variances with respect to the vowels as well as the gender of the speakers. Such variances, if any, are likely to be reflected in our perception of oral-nasal characteristics.

Bangla and Brazilian Portuguese and are the only languages with substantial phonetic data in oral and nasal vowels. In Bangla, all the 7 major vowels have nasal counterparts and the nasality of vowels is phonemic. The nasal-oral distinction of vowels, therefore, acquires an additional importance compared to those languages where nasality of vowels is non-phonemic. Most of the studies relate to the languages where nasality of vowels is non-phonemic and the perception studies are typically carried out on synthetic speech as all the acoustic properties that bear signatures of nasality may not be perceptually significant.

Now, let us consider some examples of pure and nasalized vowels of Bangla. A comparative set of such cases are listed in the following illustration of pure and nasalized vowels in Bangla:

1. i – ĩ ihar (of this) – ĩhar (of him/her-polite)
2. u – ũ uki (a hiccup) – ũki (a peep)
3. e – e eke (to him/ her- informal) – eke (to him/her-formal)
4. o – õ ora (they-informal) – õra (they-formal)
5. æ – a) æk (one) – ha) (yes)
6. ɔ – ɔ) ɔkejo (useless) – ɔ))k (a nasal sound)
7. a – ã baʃi (stale) – bãʃi (flute)

Here, most of the pairs are minimal pairs (except æ – a_ and ɔ – ɔ). Among all the vowels in Bangla [a] (and [ã] from nasal ones) is the most frequent vowel. This set of pure and nasalized vowels provide the maximum number of minimal pairs in Bangla. (Bykova, 1981) has pointed out two important characteristics of the nasalization of Bangla vowels, namely, the frequency of occurrences of the nasalized vowels and the dependency of nasality. Although the grapheme to phoneme mapping is not so strong in this corpus, we get a fairly strong support of the data provided by (Ferguson & Chowdhury, 1960). We see the most frequent nasal vowel in Bangla is [ã] and the least frequent one is [ɔ)]. These observations are almost identical to those found in the data presented by (Bykova, 1981) where [ã] and [õ] are reported as the most frequent ones. The other aspect of Bangla nasal vowels is the dependency factor. It is essential to distinguish between dependent or positional and independent or phonological vowels in Bangla (Hai, 1985). Dependent or positional nasality of a vowel is caused by the influence of the preceding or (partly) following nasal consonant (of neighboring syllable). This is just an echo of the other nasal sound and not a phonological element of real vowel nasality. On the other hand, we have pure nasal vowels which occur irrespective of their environment. (Hai, 1985) termed this type of events as phonological nasality.

1.3. Necessity for Bangla Speech Processing

Computers are becoming an integral part of our life. People with access to computers have access to a wide variety of useful information through use of ICT. The uneducated masses and those who live in the rural areas outside of the reach of available bandwidth, as well as handicapped people are missing out on these advantages. People have to be reasonably computer skilled and educated to use or to access the computer based resources. Most of the information resources are in English. Therefore, people have to know English in addition to being educated. This is more so true since most of these resources of information, journals, books, etc. are not readily available in Bangla.

With advances in the fields of signal processing, microelectronics, and communication technologies, the users have increased flexibilities in part because of the presence of mobile devices, robots and other interactive systems. Interaction between man and machine are based often on the same concepts as those between humans. Speech is one of the most natural means of human interactions. Speech processing techniques are therefore developed for communication with machines and any class of people whether literate or illiterate can understand it. Therefore, many of the technologically advanced societies are trying to produce and use voice enabled devices. To make the life of the entire community easier to use and access computer based work and related items must be easier and voice enabled. Therefore humans would rather have machines that can understand speech easily. The branch of science that deals with the making of machines that understand speech or make the machines speak like humans, is referred to as speech processing. The idea of giving computers the ability to process human language is as old as the idea of computers themselves. It includes topical areas of speech recognition, machine translation, speaker recognition, speech synthesis, speech coding etc.

The goal of speech processing is to get computers to perform useful tasks involving human language, tasks such as enabling human-machine communication, improving human-human communication, or simply doing useful processing of text or speech. Interfacing between speech processing and its real world application is the technology to implement the ideas. Language Technology (LT) includes computational methods, computer programs, and electronic devices that are specialized for analyzing, producing, or modifying texts and speech. These systems must be based on an understanding of human language. Therefore, language technology defines the engineering branch of computational linguistics. Although the existing language technology systems are far from achieving human ability but they have numerous possible applications.

Works in languages such as English, Japanese, and Chinese are now rather advanced and has expanded to include speech processing and LT. This is not the case with Bangla for a whole host of technological, financial, and political reasons.

1.4. Aim of This Chapter

The aim of this chapter is to provide:

- A background of speech and how it is produced.
- A brief overview of speech analysis methods, synthesis methods and vowel nasalization.
- A brief overview on Bangla speech analysis, Bangla speech synthesis and vowel nasality research.
- Challenges of Bangla Speech Analysis, Synthesis and Vowel Nasality.
- Conclusion.

2. BACKGROUND

In this section, the background of the present research work is presented. Speech production and phoneme is discussed along with the phoneme perception in computation. Speech processing techniques are also discussed for Analysis, Synthesis. This chapter provides a comprehensive background on the speech signal generation, representation, synthesis and vowel nasality perception in computational perspectives.

2.1. An Overview of Speech Production

Thoughts originating in the neurons of the brain are converted to speech through a complex mechanical motion by using lungs, vocal folds and vocal tract to create a linguistic utterance that convey information. The acoustic signal of speech is the product of the operations of language expression and the input to the processes of language comprehension. The speech signal consists of variation in pressure, measured directly in front of the mouth, as a function of time. The amplitude variations of such a signal correspond to deviations from atmospheric pressure caused by traveling waves. The signals are nonstationary and constantly changing as the muscles of the vocal tract contract and relax. Speech is generated by compression of the lung volume causing airflow which is modulated in the vocal tract and nasal tract and is radiated through mouth and nose into the air to produce the audible sound of speech. If the sound is radiated through both oral and nasal cavity the speech is said to be nasalized. Nasality is a distinctive feature of a language.

The process of speech production involves the following:

- **Respiration:** Lungs providing the energy source.
- **Phonation:** Vocal folds converting the energy into audible sound.

- **Articulation:** Articulators transforming the sound into intelligible speech.

An overview of the vocal tract showing structures that are important in speech sound production and speech articulation is shown in Figure 2. As shown in the Figure 2, the human speech production mechanism consists of the lungs, trachea (windpipe), larynx, pharyngeal cavity (throat), buccal cavity (mouth), nasal cavity, velum (soft palate), tongue, jaw, teeth, and lips as shown in a simplified tube model in Figure 3. The lungs and trachea make up the respiratory subsystem of the mechanism. These elements provide the source of energy for speech when air is expelled from the lungs into the trachea. Speech production can be viewed as a filtering operation in which a sound source excites a vocal tract filter (Furui, 2001).

The production of each phonemic sound is affected by the context of the neighboring phonemes. This is called coarticulation. Speech signals convey much more than spoken words. The information conveyed by speech is multi-layered and includes time frequency modulation of such carriers of information as formants and pitch intonation. Formants are the resonances of vocal tract and pitch is the sensation of the fundamental frequency of the opening and closings of the glottal folds. The information conveyed in speech includes the following:

Figure 2. Human vocal and nasal tract. The dot shows the location where the nasal cavity couples with the rest of the vocal tract; it also divides the vocal tract into pharyngeal and oral cavities.

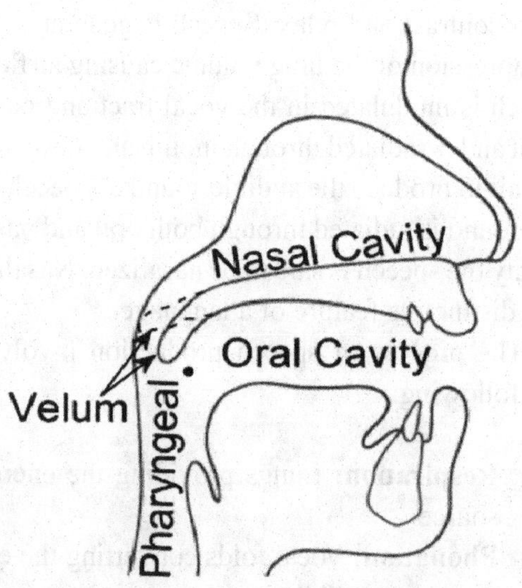

Figure 3. A simplified tube model of the human speech production system

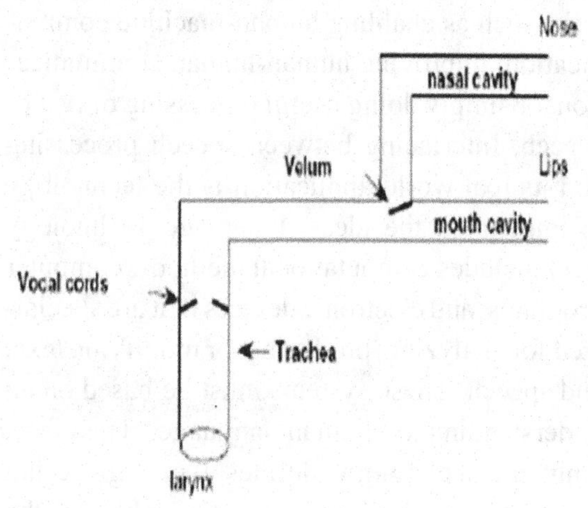

- **Acoustic Phonetic Symbols:** These are the most elementary speech units from which larger speech units such as syllables and words are formed.
- **Prosody:** These are rhythms of speech mostly intonation signals carried by changes in the pitch trajectory and stress. Prosody help to signal such information as the boundaries between segments of speech, link sub-phrases and clarify intention and remove ambiguities such as whether a spoken sentence is a statement or a question.
- **Gender Information:** Gender is conveyed by the pitch (related to the fundamental frequency of voiced sounds) and the size and physical characteristics of the vocal tract. Due to differences in vocal anatomy, female voice has higher resonance fre-

quencies and formants), pitch intonation, duration, emphasis and stress.

- **Speaker's Identity:** Conveyed by the physical characteristics of a person's vocal folds, vocal tract, pitch intonations and stylistics.
- **Emotion and Health, Conveyed by Changes in:** Vibrations of vocal fold, vocal tract resonance, duration, and stress and by the dynamics of pitch and vocal tract spectrum.

In the remainder of this chapter, we will perform a brief review of how various acoustic correlates of speech and speaker can be modelled and used for speech processing applications.

Vowels are produced by exciting a fixed vocal tract with quasi-periodic pulses of air caused by vibration of the vocal chords. The resonant frequency of the tract (formants) varies with the cross sectional area and the dependence of cross-sectional area upon distance long the tract, which is known as area function is determined primarily by the position of the tongue, but the positions of the jaw, lips, and, to a small extent, the velum also influences the resulting sound (Rabiner, 1978). The chief characteristic of the vowels is the freedom with which the air stream, once out of the glottis, passes through the speech organs. The supra-glottal resonators do not cut off or constrict the air; they cause only resonance, that is to say, the reinforcement of certain frequency ranges (Deller & Hansen, 2000).

2.2. An Overview of Speech Analysis, Synthesis, and Vowel Nasalization

Speech processing is the process by which speech signals are interpreted, understood, and acted upon. It specifically refers to the processing of human speech by computerized systems, as in voice recognition software or voice-to-text programs. Speech processing is important to many fields for both theoretical and practical uses, ranging from voice activation and control in phones to the development of functional artificial intelligence in computer science. Interpretation and production of coherent speech are both important in the processing of speech; some concerns do favor one over the other, however, as the application needs of speech processing are very diverse. Research in speech processing by computer has traditionally been focused on a number of somewhat separable, but overlapping, problem areas. One of these is speech analysis, speech synthesis, speech perception, speech recognition, etc.

2.2.1. Speech Analysis

Speech analysis is the branch of science which deals with the analysis of speech sounds taking into consideration their method of production, modeling the method of production by a suitable model and estimating the parameters of the model. These parameters should procure all the required information underlying the speech and will form the acoustic feature vector of that speech sound. There are several speech analysis methods. Proper selection and use of speech analysis technique greatly affects the extracted speech feature. Therefore, the first task of a specific language processing should be the proper selection of a speech analysis method that will procure enough information required to reproduce the speech or to recognize the speech from the parameters. Therefore, depending on the language, proper speech analysis technique has to be used. Otherwise analysis fails to procure all the required speech parameters which may give rise to errors in speech synthesis or recognition. The primary objective of speech analysis is to parameterize speech signal to reduce the bandwidth and to characterize the speech signal with only a few features. Speech analysis assumes that speech is short time stationary and formulate a feature vector that captures the important information in the speech signal for future.

Formants and pitch period are the important parameters of speech (Furui, 2001). Pitch is periodic rate at which the vocal cord vibrates and formant frequencies are the resonance frequencies of the vocal tract. The first three formants F1, F2, and F3 among several formant have the significant perceptual effect of speech.

There are several methods of speech analysis. Now, we discuss three type of speech analysis methods. Mostly popular is the methods which are based on Fourier transform e.g. Cepstral and Linear Predictive Coding (LPC). Then we discuss in brief recently used Wavelet Transform (WT) technique. Most of the works those are reported on Bangla speech analysis and synthesis are based on Fourier transform method.

2.2.1.1. Cepstral Analysis Technique

Cepstral method represents the vocal tract by pole-zero digital filters characterized by the cepstral coefficients which is suitable for characterizing all kinds (oral, nasal, fricatives, etc.) of speech signals. The observed speech signal x[n] is the result of convolution of excitation source signal *v*[*n*] and the linear system impulse response v[n] in the time domain or a product of the excitation source and the system spectra in frequency domain. x[n]=v[n]*u[n]. In frequency domain, the above equation can be expressed as X[ω]= V[ω]U[ω]. Taking log of the above equation splits the product of two spectra into a summation. The cepstrum of the speech sequence is actually the sum of the vocal tract cepstrum and the glottal excitation cepstrum. Cepstrum c[n] is the inverse Fourier transform of the short time logarithmic amplitude spectrum *X*(w) of the speech waveform (Furui, 2001) as given by Equation 1.

$$c_x[n] = \frac{1}{2\pi} \int_{-\pi}^{\pi} \log\left|X\left(e^{j\omega}\right)\right| e^{j\omega n} d\omega \quad (1)$$

From the high frequency part the pitch period is obtained. The first few cepstral coefficients of the low-frequency part of the speech cepstrum contain the characteristics of the vocal tract.

2.2.1.2. LPC Analysis Technique

LPC analysis decomposes digitized speech signal into its fundamental frequency (F0 and its amplitude i.e. loudness of the source) and the vocal tract is represented as all pole filters, which can be modeled by a number of coefficients known as LPC order. This system is excited by an impulse train for voiced speech or a random noise sequence for unvoiced speech. Thus, the parameters of this model are: voiced/unvoiced classification, pitch period for voiced speech, gain parameter *G*, and the coefficients $\{a_k\}$ of the digital filter. Equation 2 expresses the transfer function of the filter model in z-domain, where *V*(*z*) is the vocal tract transfer function. *G* is the gain of the filter and $\{a_k\}$ is a set of autoregression coefficients called Linear Prediction Coefficients. The upper limit of summation, *p*, is the order of the all-pole filter.

$$V(z) = \frac{G}{1 - \Sigma_{k=1}^{p} z^{-k} a_k} \quad (2)$$

Figure 4 shows the spectrum of Bangla oral and nasal vowel /i/ obtained using cepstral and LPC method of analysis. Figure 5 shows the vowel space constructed using the extracted formants for all the oral nasal vowel pairs of Bangla.

Figure 4. Spectrum of oral-nasal pairs of Bangla vowel / i / obtained using cepstral and LPC analysis techniques

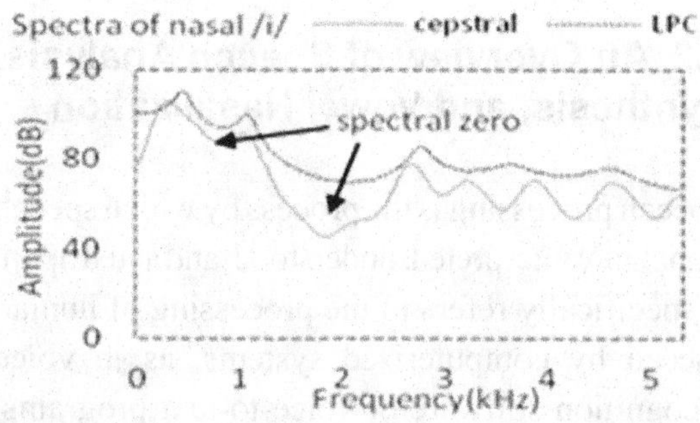

Figure 5. Vowel space of oral-nasal vowel pairs of Bangla

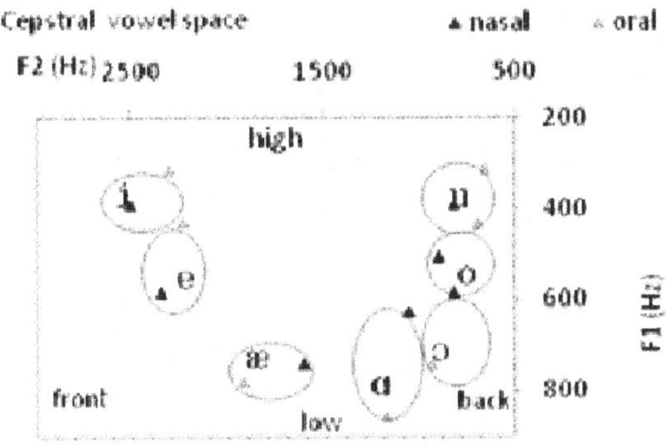

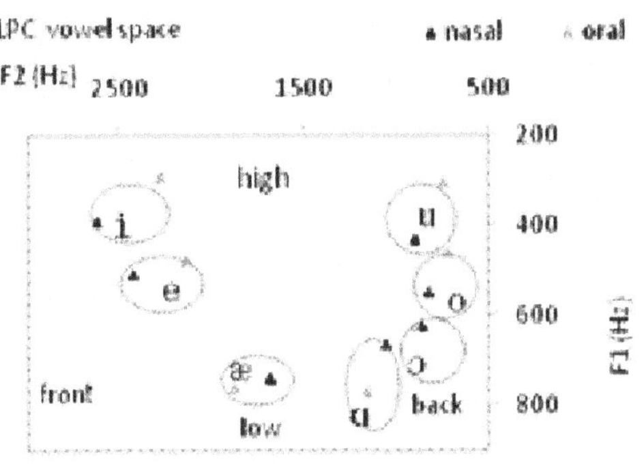

2.2.1.3. Wavelet Analysis Technique

The fundamental idea behind wavelets is to analyze according to scale. The wavelet analysis procedure is to adopt a wavelet prototype function called an analyzing wavelet or mother wavelet. Any signal can then be represented by translated and scaled versions of the mother wavelet. Wavelet analysis is capable of revealing aspects of data that other signal analysis techniques such as Fourier analysis miss aspects like trends, breakdown points, discontinuities in higher derivatives, and self-similarity. Furthermore, because it affords a different view of data than those presented by traditional techniques, it can compress or de-noise a signal without appreciable degradation (Agbinya, 1992). A major drawback of Fourier analysis is that in transforming to the frequency domain, the time domain information is lost (Graps, 2001). A low-scale compressed wavelet with rapidly changing details corresponds to a high frequency. A high-scale stretched wavelet that is slowly changing has a low frequency. Figure 6 shows the speech waveforms for Decomposing and reconstructing Bangla vowel /i/ using WT.

2.2.2. Synthesis Method

Speech synthesis is a process which artificially produces speech for various applications, diminishing the dependence on using a person's recorded voice (Furui, 2001). The speech synthesis methods enable the machine to pass on instructions or information to the user through speaking. The applications include information supply services over telephone, such as banking services, directory services, announcement services, reading email, reading Web pages, voice output in machine translation, word processor with voice output for handicapped people and speaking aid for vocally handicapped people, etc.

There are many techniques available for speech synthesis like formant synthesis or rule-based synthesis, concatenative synthesis or synthesis based on analysis synthesis, articulatory synthesis, etc. Figure 7 shows the block diagram of a speech synthesizer where demisyllable is used as the speech unit. Now, a brief overview of these methods is presented.

2.2.2.1. Formant Synthesis

Formant synthesis, also known as rule-based synthesis, creates the acoustic speech data entirely through rules on the acoustic correlates of the various speech sounds. In this method feature parameters for fundamental small units of speech such as syllable, phonemes or one-pitch-period speech are stored and connected by rules. Prosodic features pitch and amplitude The quality of fundamental units for synthesis and control rules for acoustic parameters plays important roles, and they must be connected based on phonetic and linguistic characteristics of natural speech.

Figure 6. Decomposing and reconstructing Bangla vowel /i / using WT

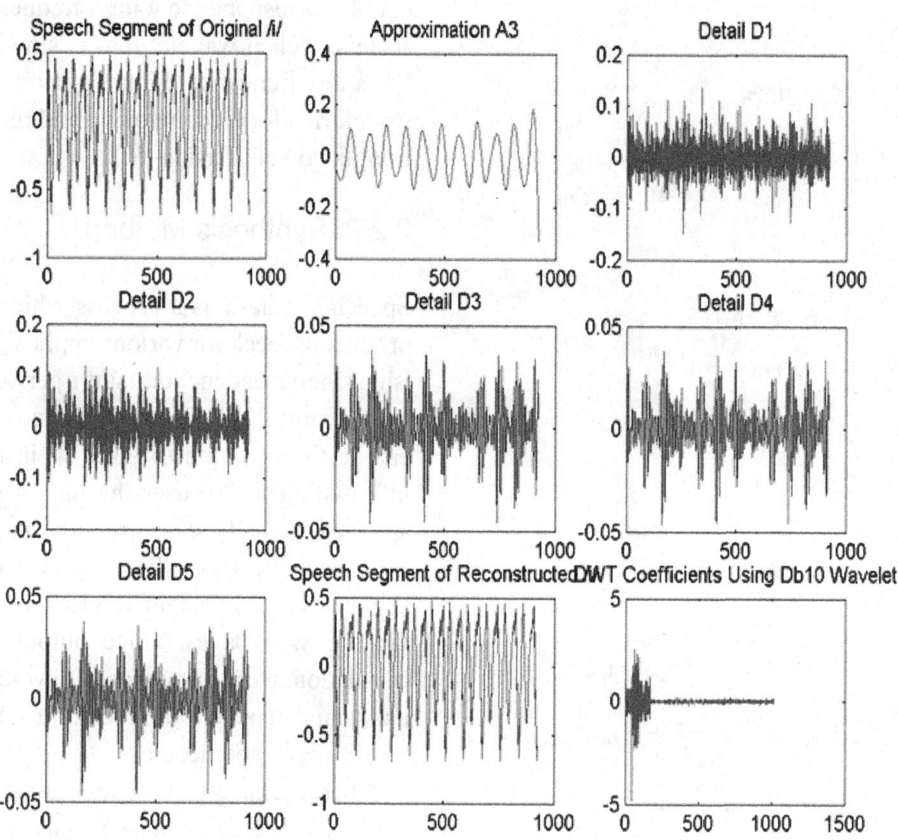

Figure 7. Block diagram of a speech synthesizer

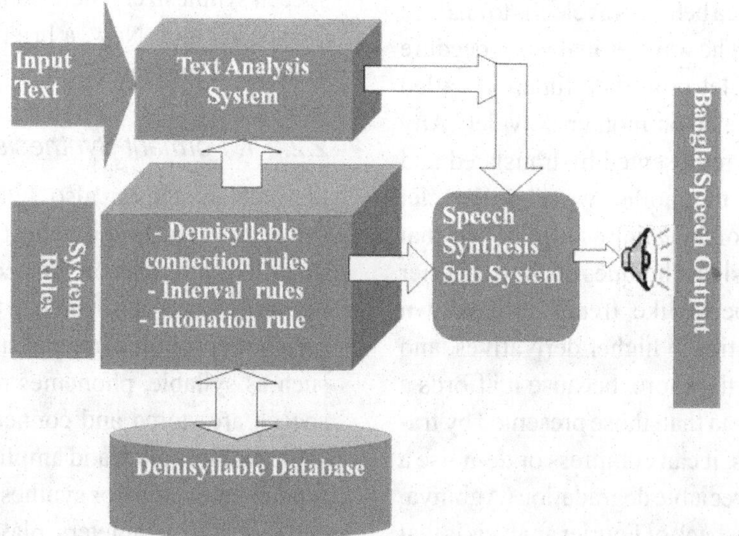

To produce natural and distinct speech temporal transition of pitch, stress and spectrum must be smooth and pause, location must be appropriate. No human speech recordings are involved at run time and if the rules are not appropriate the resulting speech sounds relatively unnatural and "robot-like" compared to state-of-the-art concatenative systems, but a large number of parameters related to both voice source and vocal tract can be varied quite freely. This is interesting for modeling emotional speech. In this method high degree of control is provided. Despite of the reduced naturalness, because of the high degree of flexibility and control over acoustic parameters that this technique provides has advantages. With high degree of control it is helpful to find good acoustic correlates of naturalness.

2.2.2.2. Concatenative Synthesis

In concatenative synthesis, recordings of a human speaker are concatenated in order to generate the synthetic speech. Concatenative model uses different length of prerecorded samples derived from natural speech, is probably the easiest way to produce intelligible and natural sounding synthetic speech. One of the most important aspects in concatenative synthesis is to find correct unit length of speech components. The selection is usually trade-off between longer and shorter units. With longer units high naturalness, less concatenation points and good control of co-articulation are achieved, but the amount of required units and memory is increased. With shorter units, less memory is needed, but the sample collecting and labeling procedures becomes more difficult and complex. In concatenative synthesis the speech units are usually words, syllables, demisyllable, phonemes, and sometimes-even tri-phones. The use of diphones, i.e., stretches of the speech signal from the middle of one speech sound ("phone") to the middle of the next, is common. Diphone recordings are usually carried out with a monotonous pitch. At synthesis time, the required F0 contour is generated through signal processing techniques which introduce a certain amount of distortion, but with a resulting speech quality usually considered more natural than formant synthesis. In most diphone synthesis systems, only F0 and duration (and possibly intensity) can be controlled. In particular, it is usually impossible to control voice quality.

2.2.2.3. Unit Selection Method of Synthesis

The synthesis technique often perceived as being most natural is unit selection or waveform coding, or large database synthesis, or speech re-sequencing synthesis. Short segments of human voice like words, phrases are stored and desired sentence is synthesized by selecting and connecting the appropriate units. Acoustic feature include spectral envelop, amplitude, fundamental frequency and speaking rate. If large units are stored the sound intelligibility and naturalness of the speech is better. If small units are used the speech quality is highly degraded. Instead of a minimum speech data inventory as in diphone synthesis, a large inventory (e.g., one hour of speech) is used. Out of this large database, units of variable size are selected which best approximate a desired target utterance defined by a number of parameters. These parameters can be the same as used in diphone synthesis, i.e. phoneme string, duration and F0, or they could be different. The weights assigned to the selection parameters influence which units are selected. If well-matching units are found in the database, no signal processing is necessary. While this synthesis method often gives very natural results, the results can be very bad when no appropriate units are found.

Synthesis systems based on waveform coding method are simple and provide high quality speech but are low versatile. Synthesis by rule systems feature great versatility but are highly complex and yet of limited quality. In practical cases it is desirable to select the method most appropriate for objectives fully taking the performance and properties of each method into consideration.

2.3. An Overview of Vowel Nasalization

Speech perception is the process by which the sounds of language are heard, interpreted and understood. The study of speech perception is closely linked to the fields of phonetics and linguistics and cognitive psychology and perception in psychology. Research in speech perception seeks to understand how human listeners recognize speech sounds and use this information to understand spoken language. Speech perception research has applications in building computer systems that can recognize speech, in improving speech recognition for hearing- and language-impaired listeners, as well as in foreign-language teaching. Categorical perception is involved in processes of perceptual differentiation. People perceive speech sounds categorically, that is to say, they are more likely to notice the differences between categories (phonemes) than within categories. The perceptual space between categories is therefore warped, the centers of categories working like a sieve or like magnets for incoming speech sounds.

The perceptual effect of nasality is produced by the nasalization process by lowering the velum to couple between the oral and nasal cavities so that part of the sound wave is free to pass through the nasal cavity. The nasal and oral cavities resonate together and lower the energy of the whole spectrum, as well as they broaden $F1$ bandwidths and introduce nasal poles and zeros in the spectrum (Deller & Hansen, 2000). The sounds which can be nasalized are usually vowels, but it can also include semivowels (Ladefoged, 1982), thus encompassing the complete set of sonorant sounds. Vowel nasalization can occur in three ways. Vowel nasality has differing prosodic properties across languages. In almost all the languages nasalization occurs when nasals are adjacent to vowels called coarticulatory nasalization (Krakow, 1993; Beddor, 1993). Phonemic nasalization occurs when the vowel itself is nasalized and it occurs in almost 22% of the world's languages (Maddieson, 1984; Ruhlen, 1978). In functional nasalization nasality is introduced because of defects in the functionality of the velopharyngeal mechanism (Cairns, 1996).

2.3.1. Importance of Nasalization Modeling

Nasalization research has implications for speech processing, the biomedical diagnosis and treatment of velopharyngeal dysfunction, phonetics, and phonology. For Text-To-Speech (TTS) system we need to model more accurately the spontaneous speech features. Modeling spontaneous speech, improving the language models, we need to detect vowel nasalization accurately. Nasalization of vowels is an essential feature for languages with phonemic nasalization. Thus, detection of vowel nasalization is essential for rule-based TTS synthesis system.

Nasalization of vowels also makes it difficult to recognize vowels themselves because of a contraction of the perceptual vowel space due to the effects of nasalization. Experiments conducted by Bond (1975) confirmed this by showing that vowels excised from nasal contexts are more often misidentified than are vowels from oral contexts. Mohr and Wang (1968) and Wright (1986) also showed that the perceptual distance between members of nasal vowel pairs was consistently less than that between oral vowels. The ability to detect vowel nasalization in a non-intrusive fashion can be used for detecting certain physical/motor-based speech disorders like hypernasality. Detection of hypernasality is indicative of anatomical, neurological, or peripheral nervous system problems, and is therefore important for clinical reasons. Accurate detection of vowel nasalization can also be used for speech intelligibility enhancement of hypernasal speech by enabling selective restoration of stops that are weakened by inappropriate velar port opening (Niu, 2005).

Vowel nasalization is not an easy feature to study because the exact acoustic characteristics of nasalization vary not only with the speaker (that is, with changes in the exact anatomical structure of the nasal cavity), but also with the particular sound upon which nasalization is superimposed (that is, vowel identity in this case) and with the degree of nasal coupling (Fant, 1960). One of the main acoustic characteristics of nasalization is the introduction of zeros in the acoustic spectrum. These zeros do not always manifest as clear dips in the spectrum, and are extremely hard to detect given the harmonic spectrum, and the possibility of pole-zero cancellations. Further, even though the articulatory maneuver required to introduce nasalization (that is, a falling velum) is very simple, the acoustic consequences of this coupling are very complex because of the complicated structure of the nasal cavity. Spectral changes in the signal due to nasal coupling, therefore, may be different from vowel to vowel. It is expected that degree of prominence of different nasal cues may have some variances with respect to the vowels as well as the sex of the speaker. Such variances, if any, are likely to be reflected in the perception of oral-nasal distinction also.

3. LITERATURE SURVEY OF ANALYSIS, SYNTHESIS, AND VOWEL NASALITY

Speech is the most natural means of communication among humans. In future, spoken language processing will play an important role in bridging the gap between humans and machines. As we have the speaking and speech understanding machines within ourselves, if we can make the devices around us which speaks and understands speech and work like humans then life will become very comfortable. This fact is reflected in modern technology as machines are used to transmit, store, manipulate, recognize and create speech. For all these tasks, the speech signal is usually represented digitally. Today, speech and dialog based software applications and hardware systems are available in the developed world. This speech based application interface is creating a new paradigm of human-computer interaction for the blind. Based on the above observations, BLP has gained tremendous importance to enable Bangla as the means of communication with the computer applications through voice as well as phonetic classification and parameterization for computer speech recognition. Analysis of speech in general is complicated as speech is highly a stochastic process and different factors influence the production of the same set of speech corpus. Applications for such activities of speech research are not limited to communication research areas; rather, they are applicable to a wide range of areas, including weather analysis, earthquake analysis, stock market analysis, consumer trends, automatic speech recognition, computer vision, radar, and many others. Currently, computers can only understand human speech in a very limited capacity. A person has to learn certain skills before they can use a computer. Therefore, it would be much easier for anyone to use a computer if the computer could understand the person's natural communication method. Speech recognition could also be used to provide access for anybody who is handicapped that prevents him from the use of a keyboard. There is an entire class of people that cannot use a computer at all because they are disabled.

A review of research papers, literatures, and related survey works is performed to become familiar with the problem area and related developments and their processes. This section will explore what is done and are being done on Bangla language processing in the area of Bangla speech analysis, synthesis, and vowel nasalization.

3.1. Literature Survey of Bangla Speech Analysis

Speech analysis is the branch of science which deals with the analysis of speech sounds taking into consideration their method of production, modeling the method of production by a suitable model and estimating the parameters of the model. These parameters should procure all the required information underlying the speech and will form the acoustic feature vector of that speech sound. Proper selection and use of speech analysis technique greatly affects the extracted speech feature. Therefore, the first task of a specific language processing should be the proper selection of a speech analysis method that will procure enough information required to reproduce the speech or to recognize the speech from the parameters. Therefore, depending on the language, proper speech analysis technique has to be used. Otherwise analysis fails to procure all the required speech parameters which may give rise to errors in speech synthesis or recognition.

In the history of more than three decades of Bangla speech processing, very few unified work have been reported. Researchers are still working scatteredly on many unexplored areas of Bangla speech processing. Bangla speech analysis has been an interesting area of investigation for the researchers for more than three decades and researchers are still working scatterdly and exploring ways to parameterize Bangla speech for machine understanding, recognition, synthesis, machine translation etc. Bangla computational speech analysis first started its journey in the year 1975 by Pramanik and Kido (1975, 1976, 1977) during his doctoral research in Japan. He analyzed the Bangla vowels spoken in isolation and at word initial position, extracted formant frequencies and synthesized them. They also performed auditory experiment of natural and synthetic vowels. In acoustical study of Bangla vowels for limited set of Bangla phonemes, he extracted formants of isolated Bangla vowels only and compared them with those of Japanese vowels and vowel like sounds. Unlike Japanese and American English vowels, he found that the formants of non-initial vowels of Bangla words do not change much with respect to vowels uttered in isolation. He investigated Bangla vowels in isolation without coarticulatory effect on the formant transition of vowels and vowel normalization. The computer available in the laboratory is a NEC 3200/50. The programs were written using the combination of Fortran and Assembly languages. Paramanik recorded Bangla speech signal with a frequency limit of 4.8 kHz and were digitized with 12 kHz sampling frequency by an A/D conversion unit DATAC-1500.

Ali (1990, 1993) during research work with short duration signals investigated spectral properties of Bangla phonemes. They were able to capture some Bangla vowel phoneme for the experimental observation through digital storage oscilloscope and measured FFT spectrum of three Bangla vowels and compared their real and imaginary parts of the spectrum. In another work on Bangla speech, Hossain (1991) analyzed duration of Bangla phonemes and investigated Bangla voiced speech to track the fundamental frequency contour using cepstral smoothing technique. He measured short time cepstral parameters of few Bangla vowels and consonant phonemes. Talukder (1992) also investigated the spectral and formant properties of Bangla speech and applied time and frequency domain processing techniques on a limited set of Bangla speech corpora containing isolated utterances of Bangla vowels, 39 consonants and 36 consonant clusters. They also measured power spectrum, amplitude spectrum, and relative phase between the real and imaginary parts of the FFT coefficients and discussed formant analysis from the representation of spectra.

In another research work, Rahman (1992) investigated power spectrum and related properties of Bangla speech. They measured the first three formants and bandwidths of all Bangla vowels using C programming and approximated formants and other measurements from the spectral measurements rather than using an efficient peak picking method or other mathematical transformations. Beside analyzing Bangla speech, researchers also developed software tool for efficient Bangla speech processing. Hamid et al (1995) developed software for the basic processing of Bangla speech. They used Hamming windowed speech segment of isolated utterance of Bangla vowels and consonants from three age groups of male speakers and investigated short-time spectrum, pitch period, fundamental frequency, power spectrum and the first three formant frequencies investigated the spectral properties of Bangla phonemes and measured short time spectrum and power spectrum of Bangla vowels and consonants. In the area of speaker identification in Bangla, Hossain (1997) investigated efficient tracking of fundamental frequency of Bangla voiced speech for the identification of speakers. Haque (1997) extracted speech parameters pitch and the first formant frequency of all the vowel and consonant phonemes for different age and sex groups and showed how pitch and first formant varies with age and sex groups. She also synthesized Bangla voiced phonemes using extracted parameters.

Over the years, several contributions are already made in Bangla speech analysis, synthesis. A detailed study on speech production mechanism of Bangla phoneme and classification criteria for computer analysis and synthesis of Bangla speech is carried out (Hossain, et al., 2005, 2007, 2008). They also differentiated between vowel and consonant both from the context of linguistics as well as computer processing point of view. Later on Centre of Research for Bangla Language Processing (CRBLP) BRAC University a group working on different aspects of Bangla. The acoustics of Bangla vowels and diphthongs of male and female voices were done by Alam et al. (2007a, 2007b) and vowel and consonant inventory was designed and presented.

Acoustic categorization of Bangla oral-nasal vowel pairs were done by Haque and Takara (2011a) and they showed how nasal vowel space shrinks and moves towards front with respect to its oral vowel space. She also extracted the oral-nasal vowel parameters by cepstral (pole-zero) and LPC (all pole) method and made a comparative study of the extracted parameters obtained using the two methods. She discussed that for a language like Bangla having phonemic nasality, cepstral method which is a pole-zero method is suitable for feature extraction Most of these works of analysis and synthesis of Bangla speech are based on Fourier transform based methods like Linear Predictive Coding (LPC), Cepstral method. As Fourier transform has resolution problem, so in order to produce better accuracy, (Haque, 2011b) used Wavelet Transform (WT) with several wavelet families for analyzing and synthesizing the seven Bangla vowels. The performance of several wavelets on Bangla vowel analysis, synthesis and compression was measured by several parameters and the optimal wavelet for Bangla vowel synthesis and compression was identified.The parameters for performance evaluation for selecting optimal wavelet for Bangla phoneme synthesis were Normalized Root Mean Square Error (NRMSE), Signal to Noise Ratio (SNR), Peak Signal to Noise Ratio (PSNR), and Retained Energy (RE) of the first few coefficients of the first approximation decomposition at the decomposition level 5. The works were centered on the following wavelet families: Haar, Daubechies, Coiflet, Symmlet, Biorthogonal and Reverse Biorthogonal. It is observed from the study that symmlet8(sym8) wavelet at decomposition level 5, stores more than 98% of the energy in the first few approximation coefficient with moderate SNR, PSNR, and reproduces the signal with lowest NRMSE.

3.2. Literature Survey of Bangla Speech Synthesis

In this age of information technology, information exchange methodologies, which overcome the barrier of human limitations, have gained importance. Since speech is a primary mode of communication among human beings, it is natural for people to expect to be able to carry out spoken dialogue with computers. This involves the integration of speech input/output technologies and language technologies. Speech synthesis is the automatic generation of artificial speech signal by the computer. The function of TTS system is to convert an arbitrary text to a spoken waveform. This generally involves two steps, i.e., text processing and speech generation. Text processing is used to convert the given text to a sequence of synthesis units while speech generation of an acoustic wave form corresponding to each of these units in the sequence. This technology is a great help to people with physical impairments like visually handicapped and vocally disabled. The ability to convert text to voice reduces the dependency, frustration, and sense of helplessness of these people. In the last few years, this technology has been widely available for several languages for different platform ranging from personal computer to stand alone systems. If the vocabulary is very limited, very natural speech is possible by merely concatenating stored speech units. Most of "voice response systems", such as paying bill through telephone, apply this method, which is much simpler than a real speech synthesizer. A true TTS system should be able to accept any input text in the chosen language including new words and typographical errors.

The modeling of emotion in speech relies on a number of parameters like fundamental frequency (F0) level, voice quality, or articulation precision. Different synthesis techniques provide control over these parameters to vary different degrees. Bangla speech synthesis and automatic generation of Bangla speech waveforms, have been under research and development for last few years. Recent progress in speech synthesis has produced synthesizers with very high intelligibility but the sound quality and naturalness still remain a major problem. The researchers are still investigating different techniques for improving quality of Bangla speech synthesis. The area of Bangla speech synthesis has been found to be emerging and new research works are in progress. At present, the Bangla speech synthesis research and development works are based on concatenative approach of speech synthesis. Besides, the research on articulatory based speech synthesis in Bangla is still at the early stage.

Bangla script is mostly phonological in nature, the utterance of some graphemes of a word is not always identical with their utterance in isolation. Various scholars tried to find utterance rules that are limited mainly to word-initial position. To find new rules Dash et al. (1988) used a sample corpus of 5,000,000 words and a dictionary of about 60,000 words These rules were applied to a TTS system. In another work on TTS synthesis for Bangla, Choudhury et al. (2001) employed concatenative synthesis technique. The authors investigated the prosodic modification issues to generate natural speech through synthesis. This prosodic modification used part of the phoneme at the concatenation point during synthesis.

One of the earliest works on Bangla voice synthesis was conducted by Alam, et al. (1995), The author used concatenative approach of speech synthesis and investigated voice synthesis through spectral measurements. In another work (Examination Roll:841, 1997) on TTS system for Bangla, the author captured Bangla text from the keyboard and the extracted words were segmented into appropriate synthesis segments according to the category of vowels, consonants, consonants with vowel allographs etc. These synthesis segments were prerecorded speech segments, which were concatenated to form the speech. Tanbeer et al (2000) investigated Bangla voice synthesis by considering sequential flow of phonemes. The author used sequential flow of phoneme sets defined by the rule of linguistics and proposed a synthesis scheme using the synthesis chip Vortex SC.

Some important issues of Bangla TTS System which is based on a partneme were done by Bandyopadhyay (2002). The system is based on concatenative method. Concatenation of signal segments was done using ESOLA (Epoch Synchronization and Overlap Add) method and broad windows were used to help in Spectral smoothing of the transition between the segments. The concatenation module consists of joining two partnemes (part of a phoneme) using certain rules. Signal elements of the dictionary are terminated at both ends at positive going zero crossing to avoid phase mismatch. The constant pitch allows a large overlap of the signals. The signal dictionary has been extracted from a corpus recorded by Bangla speaker by keeping a constant pitch during the pronunciation to facilitate the initial pitch modification. The synthesized sentence is fairly clear with good degree of phonetic naturalness. Another speech synthesizer was developed which produced improved quality of speech using LPC smoothing and HMM techniques by Sen (2001). Chowdhury et al. (2001) worked on intonation modeling for Bangla.

Seddiqui et al. (2002) also used algorithmic approach to synthesize voice from Bangla text. DasMandal et al. (2002) reports successful development of TTS system of Bengali. They used concatenative system with partneme as the basic unit of speech. Using the above technology, developed TTS system deliver a good quality speech output which can be deployed in many kind of application like online news paper reading from Internet, overcome literacy barrier, empowering visual impaired population, enhancing other information system. The various steps involved and problems encountered in development of such solutions are highlighted. They conclude with the description and demonstration of reading newspaper on line from Website, which is one of the typical application of this technology. This system can help to overcome the literacy barrier of common mass, can also empower the visually impaired population and increase the possibilities of improved man-machine interaction through on-line newspaper reading from Internet.

Bandyopadhyay et al. (2003) discussed some important issues of Bangla TTS. He discussed the basic building blocks of a synthesizer using partneme (part of a phoneme) as the basic speech unit and their implementation strategies. The approach for Bangla text analysis has also been included. Author(s) tried to make clear the importance of interpretation of phonological information in Bangla. The concatenation of partneme signal segments is done by concatenation rules using ESOLA (Epoch Synchronization and Overlap Add) method are applied to broad windows to help in Spectral smoothing of the transition between the segments. Signal elements of the dictionary are terminated at both ends at positive going zero crossing to avoid phase mismatch. The constant pitch allows a large overlap of the signals. The signal dictionary has been extracted from a corpus recorded by Bangla speaker with a constant pitch to facilitate the initial pitch modification. The synthesized sentence is fairly clear with good degree of phonetic naturalness.

As discussed earlier, Bangla is an intonation language, having no tone, stress or accent. Adding naturalness or prosody to the speech synthesizer is another aspect of speech processing research. It is well known that the F0 contour plays an important role in conveying prosodic information but the process of synthesizing the F0 contour from the underlying linguistic information has not been elucidated. Bandyopadhyay et al., (2003) discussed generation of intonated speech for natural speech synthesis using prosody generation model. He observed the effect of pitch modification through pitch contour stylization for parameter extraction and time scale modification for its implementation. He described an approach for close-copy syllabic stylization. In the latter part, he mentioned algorithm for implementation of time scale modification with necessary approximation for sinusoidal signal and showed the experimental results of applying the technique for pitch modification on Bangla sentence. The output shows satisfactory performance of sound quality after necessary pitch modification to make synthetic speech natural.

Haque and Takara (2004) performed rule based Bangla speech synthesis system using cepstral method and Log Magnitude Approximation (LMA) filter. Intonation used was a simple declining (falling) line in log frequency domain.

The system used demisyllable as the basic speech unit. The intelligibility of the system for oral vowel, nasal vowel, initial C, final C, monosyllabic, CCV, CCCV was checked and was found to have acceptable value. She also discussed that Bangla oral vowels can be transformed to their nasal counter by two methods, one is using a simple sine curve model and another is using neural network. She also discussed if demisyllable or syllable is used as the basic speech unit in a speech synthesizer then the database size can be reduces to half by using the vowel nasality transformation technique, e.g. for Bangla if demisyllable is used as the basic speech unit then we need around 1400 units for Bangla. But if vowel nasality transformation technique is used to transform oral vowel part to nasal vowel then the speech database size can be reduced to around 700. Chowdhury et al. (2005), presented a partneme based TTS system. Mandal et al. (2007) detected word boundary based on suprasegmental features. He used Epoch Synchronous Non-Over Lapping Add (ESNOLA) Method for Concatenative Synthesis System for Bangla. Mandal et al. (2010) modeled sentence medial pauses for Bangla readout speech. The system proposed by Alam et al. (2007) presents a TTS synthesis system for Bangla language using the open-source Festival TTS engine. Festival is a complete concatenative TTS system using diphone or other unit selection speech unit, with components supporting front-end processing of the input text, language modeling, and speech synthesis using its signal processing module. This system uses Unicode to ASCII conversion rules with its own ASCII conversion Chart. It separates each character of word of text and tokenizes them based on whitespace and punctuation. Pronunciation of words is detected according to LTS (Letter to Sound) rule based on Bangla syllable rule and stress on lexicon. This method keeps the sound file of each character in the database, searches them, and concatenates them for producing speech. On 19 February 2009, CRBLP of BRAC University announced the first official release of its Bangla language processing software package *'Katha'* which converts Bangla text into speech (Mahboob, 2009). The TTS run on Linux, Windows, and Mac OSX. There is also a Web-enabled front-end for the TTS.

The other method proposed by Islam *et al.* (2009b) uses syllable rules. It splits words into syllables. The method uses normalization rules for Bangla language and supports Unicode directly. It keeps the specific sound files of syllables and characters in the database. When the system reads the text, it searches the corresponding sound files of syllable and character from the database and concatenates them for producing speech. In their system, they keep the sound files of syllables and characters in the sound database and that makes their database size huge. Searching any element from the larger database takes more time than from a small database.

LTS indicate how the written text has to be spoken. Most of the American and European languages have their own specific letter to sound rules. In case of Bengali language, LTS rules are not as simple as other Indian languages. In Basu et al. (2009), Ghosh et al. (2010), derived simple LTS rules for Bengali and incorporated in speech synthesis systems. They used Letter-To-Sound (LTS) rules for generating speech from text. Narendra et al. (2011) presents the design and development of unrestricted TTS system in Bengali language. He used syllables as basic units for synthesis with added feature in Festival framework. He evaluated the system output in four stages by conducting objective and subjective listening tests on synthesized speech. Talukder et al. (2011) proposed a method for Bangla speech generation from Bangla PDF document using three major tasks. One is PDF to text conversion, then text to ASCII conversion, and then follows the character and modifier rules while reading text and finally speech generation from the concatenate sound files of text. Authors analyzed the proposed method and the existing methods with respect to error rate of reading all the Bangla words and also the time complexity.

Project TTS systems for Indian Languages (TTS-IL) (2009) develops TTS systems for Indian languages (in the first phase for Hindi, Bangla, Marathi, Telugu, Tamil and Malayalam) using open source Festival Speech Synthesis engine. Syllable based unit selection technique adopted by the consortium, gives more natural speech compared to the existing TTSs in Indian languages to date. TTS systems in these 6 Indian languages have been developed and integrated with NVDA and ORCA screen readers. Training programs for the Visually Challenged persons in the vernacular using NVDA and ORCA at different sites across India are now being conducted. Testing and evaluation of the system is being carried out by C-DAC and STQC jointly. GIST QA has evolved the initial draft of testing strategy, benchmarking and evaluation strategy for TTS synthesis system. Test data was collected from the Web and text books for all six languages supported by TTS. A syllable based TTS system was developed by Narendra et al. in 2011. Mukherjee et al. (2012) proposed an android based Bengali TTS systems for a resource limited device such as a mobile phone. They used ESNOLA based concatenative speech synthesis technique which uses the partnemes as the smallest signal units for concatenations.

Basu et al. (2012) used Fujisaki model for modeling intonation for Bangla. They found the Fujisaki's command response model parameters by analyzing 200 declarative Bangla sentences. Based on the analysis, rules are constructed for predicting both phrase and accent command parameters of the model for generating the F0 contours. A perceptual evaluation test for the naturalness of prosody shows that there is no significant difference between synthetic speech with model generated F 0 contours and the original natural speech.

3.3. Literature Survey of Vowel Nasality

Nasality is a distinctive feature of Bangla. Nasality of vowels at word-initial syllable (except in some very rare cases) which is not a standard feature of many languages) changes meaning of some words in Bangla. As Bangla has a very weak history in nasality processing so we discuss the overview of nasality in general. Research on Bangla are going on scatteredly on several areas of speech processing. But there are few researches on acoustic details of Bangla nasal vowel. Works are done by the phoneticians on Bangla nasality, but this field is almost untouched by the computational researchers for Bangla.

Nasalization occurs when the velum drops to allow coupling between the oral and nasal cavities. When this happens, the oral cavity is still the major source of output but the sound gets a distinctly nasal characteristic. The sounds which can be nasalized are usually vowels, but it can also include semivowels (Ladefoged, 1982, p. 208), thus encompassing the complete set of sonorant sounds. Non-sonorant nasalized sounds are much less frequent because leakage through the nasal cavity would cause a reduction in pressure in the oral cavity, thus stripping the obstruent sounds of their turbulent/bursty characteristics and making them very hard to articulate. Further, contrasts between nasalized and non-nasalized consonants (including semivowels) do not occur in any language (Ladefoged, 1982, p. 208). Thus, the scope of this chapter will be limited only to nasalized vowels.

Panini in 5th century BC first described the linguistics of nasal sound. The history of nasal sound began when the comparative grammarian in indo European language (e.g. Grimm, 1822) were searching for the nasal sound pattern. The nasal process have been the focus of a large amount of scientific articles and monographs that are briefly reviewed below. Early studies in experimental phonetics involved the investigation of nasal sounds using inventive instrumentation. (e.g. Rousselot). Phonetic studies in the 60's and the 70's mainly concentrated on the production of nasal sounds using a variety of data and techniques such as (cine)radiography, electromyography, fiberoscopy, aerodynamic data (e.g. Björk, 1961; Bell-Berti, 1976; Benguerel et al., 1974, 1977), and specific devices like the nasograph (Ohala, 1971). Nasal studies much contributed to the elaboration of coarticulation theories and models (Farnetani & Recasens, 1999). Our understanding of the perception of nasalization has made much progress in the 80s and the 90s with the development of synthesized speech and modelisation (e.g. Krakow et al., 1988; Beddor, 1990; Kingston & MacMillan, 1995).

Many issues need further exploration and the interest for nasalization remains considerable, as evidenced by the number of dissertations that have been defended in the last years, whether on languages that were poorly described regarding nasalization (e.g. Diakoumakou, 2004; Onsuwan, 2005) or on more documented ones (e.g. on French: Rossato, 2000; Delvaux, 2003; Amelot, 2004). The scientific literature on nasal disorders developed somewhat apart from phonetic and phonological studies. Physicists started to investigate the specific (nasal) disabilities of cleft palate speakers in the mid-50's (e.g. Warren, 1964). Weinber and colleagues (1968) showed that hypernasality in speech is the primary cue to diagnose velopharyngeal incompetence. Although there has been a growing body of literature on nasal disorders in the last decades, the cooperation between phoneticians and pathologists still needs to be reinforced.

Now, summary of acoustic correlates and the acoustic parameters corresponding to the articulatory opening of the velopharyngeal port, proposed in past literature is presented. This section also summarizes the perceptual experiments that have been performed in past to confirm these acoustical correlates.

3.3.1. Acoustic Correlates of Vowel Nasalization

House and Stevens (1956) found that as coupling to the nasal cavity is introduced, the first formant amplitude reduces and its bandwidth and frequency increase. A spectral prominence around 1000 Hz and a zero in the range of 700-1800 Hz were also observed along with an overall reduction in the amplitude of the vowel. Reduction in the amplitude of the third formant and changes in the amplitude of the second formant were also observed, although the changes in second formant amplitude were less systematic than those of the third formant. Hattori et al. (1958) identified the following characteristic features for nasalization for the five Japanese vowels: a dull resonance around 250 Hz, a zero at about 500 Hz, and comparatively weak and diffuse components filling valleys between the oral formants. It was also mentioned in this study that when the nostrils are closed, the zero shifts from 500 Hz to 350Hz. Fant (1960) reviewed the acoustic characteristics of nasalization pointed out in the literature until then, and from his own observations confirmed the reduction in the amplitude of the first formant due to an increase in its bandwidth, and the rise in the first formant frequency. An extra formant at around 2000 Hz (seen in the form of a split third formant), and a pole-zero pair below that frequency (with the exact locations varying with the vowel) were also observed. It was also pointed out that the exact acoustic consequences of nasality vary with vowels, speakers (the physical properties of the nasal tract), and the degree of coupling between the nasal cavity and the oral cavity.

Dickson (1962) studied several measures and found the following measures to occur in the spectrograms of some nasal speakers (although no measure consistently correlated with the degree of judged nasality): an increase in F1 and F2 bandwidths, an increase or decrease in the intensity of harmonics, and an increase or decrease in F1, F2 and F3 frequency. Fujimura and Lindqvist

(1971) studied the effects of nasalization on the acoustic characteristics of the back vowels /aa/, /ow/ and /uw/ using sweep-tone measurements. They observed a movement in the frequency of the first formant toward higher frequencies, and the introduction of pole-zero pairs in the first (often below the first formant) and third formant regions on the introduction of nasal coupling. Lindqvist-Gauffin and Sundberg (1976), and later Maeda (1982b) suggested that the low frequency prominence observed by Fujimura and Lindqvist (1971) and several others was produced by the sinus cavities. In more recent work, Dang et al. (1994) and Dang and Honda (1996) suggested that the lowest pole-zero pair was due to the maxillary sinuses. Maeda (1982c) suggested that a flattening of the spectra in the range of 300 to 2500 Hz was the principal cue for nasalization.

Hawkins and Stevens (1985) suggested that a measure of the degree of prominence of the extra pole in the vicinity of the first formant was the basic acoustic property of nasality. They also proposed that there were additional secondary properties like shifts in the low-frequency center of gravity. It was also suggested that at higher frequencies, nasalization may introduce shifts in formants, modification of formant amplitudes, and additional poles. However, they noted that these effects were not as consistent across speakers as those in the vicinity of the first formant. Bognar and Fujisaki (1986) in a study on the four French nasal vowels found that all nasal vowels showed an upward frequency shift of F3, and a downward shift of F2 resulting in widening of the F2-F3 region. From an analysis-synthesis procedure, two pole-zero pairs were found to have been introduced between 220 Hz and 2150 Hz. The main effect of the lower pole-zero pair was an increase in the amplitude of the second harmonic. Stevens et al. (1987b) also proposed that the main effect of nasalization was the replacement of the single non-nasal pole, F1, by a pole-zero-pole pair. They also said that the main reason behind the reduction in the amplitude of F1 was the presence of the nasal zero, not the increase in the bandwidth of poles. A splitting of the F1 peak was observed in cases where the non-nasal F1 frequency was close to the frequency of the nasal zero. Further, they suggested that nasal poles at high frequencies occur with a very high density and manifest themselves as small notches in the spectrum.

3.3.2. Perception of Vowel Nasalization

Several studies have shown the correspondence between the properties suggested above and perception of nasalization. House and Stevens (1956) found that the amplitude of F1 needed to be reduced by 8 dB for the nasality response to reach the 50% level. Hattori et al. (1958) also performed a perceptual experiment to confirm the correlation between the acoustic correlates suggested by them, and the perception of nasalization. They concluded that adding the pole around 250 Hz gave some perception of nasality, but adding the zero at 500 Hz did not. However, the combination of the two gave a much improved perception of nasality. Further, for high vowels like /iy/ and /uw/, it was necessary to modify the higher frequency spectrum by adding additional poles between regular formants to produce the percept of nasality. Maeda (1982c) confirmed the importance of spectral flattening at low frequencies in producing the perception of nasality by listening tests.

Hawkins and Stevens (1985) used the Klatt synthesizer (Klatt, 1980) to simulate a continuum of CV syllables (/t/ followed by one of the five vowels /iy, ey, aa, ow, uw/) from non-nasal to nasal. Nasalization was introduced by inserting a pole- zero pair in the vicinity of the first formant. The degree of nasalization was varied by changing the spacing between the pole and zero. Wider spacing of the pole-zero pair was found to be necessary for the perception of nasality. Bognar and Fujisaki (1986), in their perceptual study of nasalization of French vowels, evaluated the role of the formant shifts and of pole-zero pairs on phonemic and phonetic judgements of nasality of synthetic stimuli generated by using parameter values (i.e. F1, F2, F3 frequencies and the frequency separation between the extra pole-zero pair) which varied between those for an oral /eh/ and its nasalized version /~eh/. Their results suggested that whatever one's phonemic framework, a certain degree of pole-zero separation is perceived as nasalization. However, they found that the phonemic sys- tem of the French speaker strongly influenced his phonetic perception of an acoustic feature like formant shift. In other words, the contribution of the formant shifts and pole-zero separation was almost equal for the phonemic task of distinguishing between /eh/ and /~eh/, whereas the contribution of formant shifts was negligible for the phonetic task of discriminating nasalized vowels from non-nasalized vowels (that is, the listener only had to say whether the sound was nasalized or not, and did not have to worry about specifying the exact phonemic identity of the sound). Beddor (1993) presented a review of past literature on the perception of vowel nasalization.

3.3.3. Independence from Category of Nasality

Although, there are no studies which directly address the question of similarities/differences between the acoustic manifestations of the three different categories of nasality, a lot of studies suggest that they are similar. Dickson (1962) performed an acoustic study of nasality for the vowels /iy/ and /uw/ in the words 'beet' and 'boot' for 20 normal speakers, 20 speakers classified as having functional nasality, and 20 speakers with cleft-palate and nasality. In this study, no means was found to differentiate nasality in cleft-palate and non-cleft-palate individuals either in terms of their acoustic spectra or the variability of the nasality judgements (listeners were consistently able to judge nasality irrespective of what had caused it). Further, the acoustic correlates found to occur in the spectrograms of the nasal speakers were exactly the same as correlates that are usually cited for coarticulatory nasalization. Other studies have cited similar acoustic correlates for languages with phonemic nasalization.

3.3.3.1. Vowel Independence

All of the acoustic studies cited above (House and Stevens, 1956; Hattori et al., 1958; Fant, 1960; Dickson, 1962; Fujimura and Lindqvist, 1971; Maeda, 1982b, 1982c; Hawkins and Stevens, 1985; Bognar and Fujisaki, 1986; Stevens et al., 1987b) have shown that irrespective of the vowel identity, the most important and stable effects of nasalization are in the low frequency regions. These effects are in the form of prominence of the extra poles, modification of F1 amplitude and bandwidth, and spectral flattening. Perceptual studies across different vowels have confirmed that reduction in the amplitude of F1 (House and Stevens, 1956), spectral flattening (Maeda, 1982c), or increasing separation between the extra pole-zero pair inserted at low frequencies (Hawkins and Stevens, 1985) are sufficient to produce the perception of nasality. It seems, then, that there is a vowel independent cue for nasality. Hawkins and Stevens (1985) went one step further and suggested that this vowel independent property was a measure of the degree of spectral prominence in the F1 region.

Results shown by Hawkins and Stevens (1985) do show a small variation in thresholds that listeners use for oral-nasal distinction across vowels. Bognar and Fujisaki (1986) have shown that a native speaker of Japanese, when asked to judge the phonetic quality (nasalized vs non-nasalized) of synthetic stimuli of a vowel which does not belong to the phonetic system of his mother tongue, was able to correctly perceive nasalization in the stimuli with increasing separation between the nasal pole and zero. However, more experiments are required to confirm this for natural speech stimuli.

3.3.4. Language Independence: Cross-Language Perception

Perceptual experiments using speakers of different languages with and without phonemic nasalization have shown that different language groups give similar responses for the presence or absence of nasalization. In a cross-language study to investigate the effect of linguistic experience on the perception of oral-nasal distinction in vowels, Beddor and Strange (1982) presented articulatory synthesized continua of [baa-b˜aa] to Hindi and American English speaking subjects (nasalization being phonemic for Hindi). They found no consistent differences across continua in the identification responses of Hindi and American English speakers. In another cross-language study on speakers of American English, Gujarati, Hindi and Bengali (Gujarati, Hindi, and Bengali have phonemic nasalization), Hawkins and Stevens (1985) found no significant differences in the 50% crossover points of the identification functions. They suggested the existence of a vowel and language independent acoustic property of nasality and proposed that this measure was a measure of the degree of spectral prominence in the vicinity of the first formant. They also postulated that there are one or more additional acoustic properties that may be used to various degrees in different languages to enhance the contrast between a nasal vowel and its non-nasal congener. Shifts in the center of gravity of the low-frequency prominence and changes in overall spectral balance were cited as examples of such additional secondary properties. In another cross-language study of the perception of vowel nasalization in VC contexts using native speakers of Portugese, English and French, which differ with respect to the occurrence of nasal vowels in their phonological systems, Stevens et al. (1987a) found that different language groups gave similar responses with regard to the presence or absence of nasalization.

Even though it seems that speakers of different languages use the same acoustic cues to make oral-nasal distinction among vowels, behavioral differences have been found. Beddor and Strange (1982) found that the perception of oral-nasal vowel distinction was categorical for Hindi speakers, and more continuous for speakers of American English. Stevens et al. (1987a) found that the judgments of naturalness of the stimuli depended on the temporal characteristics of nasalization in the stimuli. English listeners preferred some murmur along with brief nasalization in the vowel, whereas French listeners preferred a longer duration of nasalization in the vowel and gave little importance to the presence of a murmur. Responses of Portugese listeners were intermediate.

Results presented by Beddor and Strange (1982) and Hawkins and Stevens (1985) suggest that the nasality detection used by the listeners across language might be the same. However, it has also been shown that even though the 50% crossover points might be similar, the identification functions do get tuned for categorical perception when the speakers native language has phonemic nasalization. Thus, speakers of these languages find it harder to correctly perceive the degree of nasalization. In summary, language background will strongly bias test responses.

3.3.5. Effects of Vowel Properties on Perceived Nasalization

Studies using natural stimuli have shown that low vowels are perceived as nasal more often than non-low vowels (Ali et al., 1971; Lintz and Sherman, 1961). Studies using synthetic stimuli, however, have shown that low vowels need more velar coupling to be perceived as nasal as compared to non-low vowels (Abramson et al., 1981; House and Stevens, 1956; Maeda, 1982c). One plausible explanation is as follows: high vowels are more closed in the oral cavity than low vowels, and hence offer a higher resistance path (looking into the oral cavity from the coupling point). Therefore, even a small coupling with the nasal cavity is sufficient to lower the impedance enough to let a sufficient amount of air to pass through the nasal cavity, thus making it nasalized. In the case of low vowels, however, the velum needs to drop a lot more to reduce the impedance to a value equal to or lower than the impedance offered by the oral cavity. Further, the apparent contradiction between the results of studies using natural and synthetic stimuli can be explained by the fact that low vowels are produced with a lower velum even in oral contexts (Ohala, 1971).

In a study with synthetic stimuli, Delattre and Monnot (1968) presented stimuli differing only in vowel duration to French and American English listeners and found that shorter vowels were identified as oral and longer vowels as nasal. In this study, vowel nasalization was held constant and was intermediate between that of an oral and that of a nasal vowel in terms of the F1 amplitude. In another study, Whalen and Beddor (1989) synthesized vowels /aa/, /iy/ and /uw/ with five vowel durations and varying degree of velopharyngeal opening, and found that American English listeners judged vowels with greater velopharyngeal opening, and the vowels with longer duration as more nasal.

Perceived vowel nasality is also influenced by the phonetic context in which the vowels occur. Lintz and Sherman (1961) showed that the perceived nasality was less severe for syllables with a plosive environment than for syllables with a fricative environment. Kawasaki (1986) found that perceived vowel nasality was enhanced as adjacent nasal consonants were attenuated. Krakow and Beddor (1991) found that nasal vowels presented in isolation or in oral context were more often correctly judged as nasal, than when present in the original nasal context. These studies show that listener' knowledge of coarticulatory overlap leads them to attribute vowel nasalization to the adjacent nasal contexts, thereby hearing nasal vowels in nasal context as nonnasal. Further, in a study with listeners of a language with phonemic nasalization, Lahiri and Marslen-Wilson (1991) found that vowel nasality was not interpreted as a cue to the presence of a nasal consonant by such listeners.

3.3.6. Effects of Nasalization on Perceived Vowel Properties

It has been suggested by Beddor and Hawkins (1990) that the height of vowels is influenced by the location of the low-frequency center of gravity instead of just F1. Introduction of extra poles in the low frequency region in nasalized vowels (either above or below F1) leads to a change in the center of gravity of these vowels. Thus, high and mid nasal vowels tend to sound like vowels of lower height, and low vowels become higher. This was confirmed by Wright (1986) in a study of oral and nasal counterparts of American English vowels /iy, ey, eh, ae, aa, ow, uh, uw/. This shift was also confirmed by Arai (2004) in more recent experiments. Further, it has been shown by Krakow et al. (1988) that, in the case of contextual nasalization, American English listeners adjust for the low frequency spectral effects of nasalization to correctly perceive vowel height. However, in the case of non-contextual nasalization, the perceptual effect of this spectral shift was to lower the perceived vowel height. Arai (2004) has also shown that a nasalized vowel is recognized with higher accuracy than a non-nasal vowel with the same formant frequencies as the nasal vowel, thus, confirming the existence of a compensation effect. Arai (2005) has also tried to study the compensation effect for formant shifts on the production side. In a study with American English vowels /iy, ih, eh, ah, ae, aa/ he found that the positions of the articulators showed no compensation effect except for vowel /aa/. It was concluded that there might be no compensation effect on the production side because American English does not distinguish between oral and nasal vowels phonemically. It could, however, be true for languages with phonemic nasalization. No such consistent effects of nasalization have been found on perceived vowel backness until now.

In effect, then, the low frequency spectral effects of nasalization lead to a con- traction of the perceptual space of nasalized vowels. Bond (1975) confirmed this by showing that vowels excised from nasal contexts are more often misidentified than are vowels from oral contexts. Mohr and Wang (1968) and Wright (1986) also showed that the perceptual distance between members of nasal vowel pairs was consistently less than that between oral vowels.

3.3.7. Acoustic Parameters

This section describes the Acoustic Parameters (APs) that have been suggested by various researchers in the past to capture the acoustic correlates described earlier in this chapter. The algorithms suggested may or may not be automatic. Glass (1984) and Glass and Zue (1985) developed a set of APs which were automatically extracted and tested on a database of 200 words, each spoken by 3 male and 3 female speakers. To capture nasality they used the following parameters: (1) the center of mass in 0-1000 Hz, (2) the standard deviation around the center of mass, (3) the maximum and minimum percentage of time there is an extra pole in the low frequency region, (4) the maximum value of the average dip between the first pole and the extra pole, and (5) the minimum value of the average difference between the first pole and the extra pole. Parameters 1 and 2 tried to capture the smearing in the first formant region. Parameter 3 tried to capture the presence of the extra nasal pole in the first formant region, and Parameters 4 and 5 tried to capture the distinctiveness of the extra nasal pole due to a higher amplitude and a deeper valley. They were able to obtain an overall accuracy of 74% correct nonnasal-nasal distinction using a circular evaluation procedure.

Huffman (1990) identified the average difference between the amplitude of the first formant (A1) and the first harmonic (H1), and change in A1 − H1 over time as good parameters to capture the decrease in A1 with the introduction of nasality. In this study, listeners were presented with oral and coarticulatorily nasalized vowels, and the results were correlated with the proposed APs. The nasalized vowels con- fused as oral vowels were those with higher overall values of A1 − H1. However, the oral vowels which were sometimes confused to be nasal vowels were the ones which showed a marked decrease in A1 − H1 over the course of the vowel rather than a lower value of A1 − H1. These results highlighted the role of dynamic information in the perception of nasality.

Maeda (1993, p. 160) proposed the use of the difference in frequency between two poles in the low-frequency region to capture the spectral "spreading" or "flattening" in the low frequency regions. Each of these poles could either be a nasal pole, or an oral formant. The choice of the two poles to use depended heavily on the vowel and the coupling area and the poles were identified by visual inspection (i.e. not automatically). This spectral measure was only tested on three vowels /aa/, /iy/ and /uw/ synthesized by using the digital simulation method proposed in Maeda (1982a) with the velar coupling area varying between 0 to 2.5 cm^2 in six steps. While a good match was found between the spectral measure and perceptual judgments of nasality for /aa/ and /iy/, it was not so for /uw/, where a high degree of nasalization was predicted for the non-nasalized /uw/ vowel. It was suggested that the reason for this discrepancy was that the spectrum of oral /uw/ at low fre- quencies looked quite similar to that for nasalized /iy/ with coupling area of 0.2-0.4 cm^2.

Chen (1995, 1996, 1997) proposed two parameters for extraction of vowel nasalization. These parameters were the difference between the amplitude of the first formant (A1) and the extra nasal pole above the first formant (P 1) and the difference between the amplitude of the first formant (A1) and the extra nasal pole below the first formant (P 0). The first parameter captures the reduction in the amplitude of the first formant and increase in its bandwidth because of higher losses due to the large shape factor of the nasal cavity, and the increasing prominence of the extra nasal pole above the first formant because of an increase in the velopharyngeal opening. The second parameter captures the nasal prominence at very low frequencies introduced because of coupling to the paranasal sinuses. P 1 was estimated by using the amplitude of the highest peak harmonic around 950 Hz, and P 0 was chosen as the amplitude of the harmonic with the greatest amplitude at low frequencies. Chen (1995, 1997) also modified these parameters to make them independent of the vowel context. However, these parameters were not automatically extracted from the speech signal. In later work, Chen (2000a, 2000b) also used these parameters in detecting the presence of nasal consonants for cases where the nasal murmur was missing.

Cairns et al. (1994, 1996b, 1996a) proposed the use of a nonlinear operator to detect hypernasality in speech in a noninvasive manner. The basic idea behind the approach was that normal speech is composed of just oral formants, whereas nasalized speech is composed of oral formants, nasal poles and zeros. Therefore, lowpass filtering with a properly selected cutoff frequency would filter just the first formant for normal speech, and a combination of first oral formant, nasal poles and zeros for hypernasal speech. However, bandpass filtering around the first formant would only return first formant in both cases. This multicomponent nature of hypernasal speech was exploited using a nonlinear operator called the Teager Energy operator. They used the correlation coefficient between the Teager energy profiles of lowpass filtered and bandpass filtered speech as a measure of hypernasality, where a low value of the correlation coefficient suggested hypernasality. The final decision making was done with a likelihood ratio detector. Even though the correlation parameter was extracted automatically, this approach had several problems: First, back vowels were not studied because of the difficulty in filtering out the second formant. This raises a question about its application across all vowels. Second, the parameters of the probability densities used for the likelihood ratio detector varied over different speaker groups and over different vowels. Finally, there were different thresholds for different vowels and different speaker groups. These limitations make it too restrictive for a generalized application across all speakers and vowels.

Hasegawa-Johnson et al. (2004, 2005) also worked on vowel nasalization detectors using a large set of APs which included Mel-Frequency Cepstral Coefficients (MFCCs), Knowledge-Based APs (Bitar, 1997a), rate-scale parameters (Mesgarani et al., 2004), and formant parameters (Zheng and Hasegawa-Johnson, 2004). All the acoustic observations were generated automatically once every 5 ms. MFCCs generated once every 10ms were also included. A frame-based vowel-independent common classifier to distinguish nasal frames from non-nasal frames using these parameters in a linear SVM framework was able to achieve 62.96% accuracy on a test set extracted from a combination of WS96 and WS97 databases. Vijayalakshmi and Reddy (2005a) used the modified group delay function proposed by Murthy and Gadde (2003) and Hegde et al. (2004, 2005) to extract APs for detecting hypernasality. The idea behind using the modified group delay function was that conventional formant extraction techniques like Linear Prediction and Cepstral smoothing are unable to resolve the extra pole around 250 Hz introduced due to hypernasality, because of a poor frequency resolution capability and the influence of adjacent poles. Group delay, on the other hand, has been shown to have a much better ability to identify closely spaced poles because of the additive property of phase (Yegnanarayana, 1978; Vijayalakshmi and Reddy, 2005b). However, the group delay function is very spiky in nature due to pitch peaks, noise and window effects. The modified group delay function reduces the spiky nature of the group delay function. Stevens et al. (1987b) also proposed that the main effect of nasalization was the replacement of the single non-nasal pole, F1, by a pole-zero-pole pair. They also said that the main reason behind the reduction in the amplitude of F1 was the presence of the nasal zero, not the increase in the bandwidth of poles. A splitting of the F1 peak was observed in cases where the non-nasal F1 frequency was close to the frequency of the nasal zero. Further, they suggested that nasal poles at high frequencies occur with a very high density and manifest themselves as small notches in the spectrum.

In summary, early research results do not support a general model.

Today's most well accepted acoustic parameters for vowel nasality in speech are:

1. The standard deviation around center of mass in the band below 1kHz, and the percentage of time of observed extra poles at low frequencies (Glass, 1985).
2. df_P0 and df_P1, that is the frequency of the nasal extra poles P0 and P1 with respect to the frequency of F1 (Maeda, 1993).
3. dA_P0 and dA_P1, the amplitudes of the extra poles with respect to the amplitude of F1 (Chen,1995).
4. F1 bandwidth and other F1 profile criteria, and the number of peaks above a threshold 40dB below signal peak, and two criteria relating the amplitude of the first formant to the first harmonic (Pruthi, 2007).

Different sets of some 10 to 20 of these and other APs are usually taken as a knowledge-based parameter set to solve binary nasality classification tasks. Most of these studies deliver an accuracy between 60% and 90%. Some of the APs introduced by Glass in 1985 are now expressed by the nasal poles P0 and P1 around F1, and their relation to F1 in terms of frequency and amplitude (Glass, 1985) P0 and P1 are usually dominated by F1 and F2 and are difficult to separate.

The speech community seems to have settled with the search for appropriate APs, most of which are located around F1 and well below 1 kHz. There is full awareness that there are many more APs at higher frequencies, however, with little chance for modeling. Pruthi has shown in his simulations, that velum motion causes extra poles and zeros across the full range between 1 kHz and 3 kHz, depending on the size of the coupling area between the vocal and the nasal tract, and depending on the vowel context (Pruthi, 2007). This confirms the complexity issue and explains the problem of generalization for APs at the higher frequencies. Today the speech community investigates additional cues to improve speech-to-text categorical tasks: phonetic context and murmur thresholds and energy over time fluctuations (Berger, 2007; Hajro, 2004).

The special session on New Trends in Vowel Nasalization: The Articulation of Nasal Vowels in 13th Annual Conference of the International Speech Communication Association September 9-13, 2012, Portland, Oregon, USA concentrated on the unique problems of studying vowel nasalization through a novel perspective: oropharyngeal articulation. A significant challenge in the study of nasal vowels is separating the relative contribution of the oral and nasopharyngeal tracts to the acoustic output. A growing body of research shows that it is possible to measure differences in the physical configuration of the oro-pharyngeal tract during nasal and oral vowel congeners. These articulatory differences have acoustic consequences relating to the oral/nasal contrast. This research has implications for speech processing, the biomedical diagnosis and treatment of velopharyngeal dysfunction, phonetics, and phonology.

Now a summary of the very few works reported on Bangla vowel nasality computation is presented.

Datta (1998a, 1998b) et al studied the perception of nasality in Bangla vowels with the role of fundamental and the first formant frequency. Datta (1998b) et al also studied the spectral cues of nasality of inherently nasal Bangla vowels. Haque and Takara (2004) showed that oral vowels can be transformed into nasal vowel inserting a simple pole-zero pattern in the vicinity of the first formant region of the oral vowel and its application to Bangla speech synthesizer.

In another work, Haque and Takara (2006) observed an interesting result from cross-language vowel nasality perception study that Japanese listeners perceive most Bangla nasal /˜i/ as Japanese non-nasal /u/. As the amount of nasalization of /˜i/ was increased synthetically, perception of this vowel change was found to be more categorical for Japanese listeners than that of Bangla listeners' vowel perception. But interesting case arises among the two language groups in case of perceiving /˜i/. All Bangla listeners perceive /˜i/ as /˜i/, whereas Japanese listeners perceive most (more than 50%) of the natural /˜i/ as /u/. This result of perceiving /˜i/ as /u/ (across vowel category) by Japanese listeners has similarity with the result obtained with natural stimuli. They also observed that for Japanese listeners, the change of perception of vowels is more categorical: The graph of the listening tests of is fitted with a normal cumulative density function and threshold of phoneme change (50% crossover point of nasal vowel recognition) and slope of the curve at threshold were measured and took these two quantities as a measure of comparing the difference in perception of the listeners of the two language groups. Average value of 3 speakers' threshold of phoneme change is observed to be higher (10.6dB) for Japanese than Bangla listeners (9.3dB). At threshold, Japanese listener's perception from /i/ to /u/ has steeper slope (19%/dB, more categorical) than change of slope of /i/ to /˜i/ (11.8%/dB, continuous) of Bangla listeners. Therefore, as vowel nasality increases, Japanese listeners perceive from /˜i/ to /u/ which is more categorical than the change of perception from /i/ to /˜i/ of Bangla listeners. They concluded that, due to Japanese listeners' categorical perception of vowels, similar spectral location of nasal formant of /˜i/ and F2 of /u/ results in perceptual illusion of perceiving /u/ which is the nearest vowel quality for them.

4. CHALLENGES OF BANGLA SPEECH ANALYSIS, SYNTHESIS, AND VOWEL NASALITY

Despite presence of over 250 million Bangla speakers, organized efforts in developing Bangla software and ICT systems have been rather insignificant. To develop a robust ICT infrastructure, we need to have established standards for encoding the language. The first attempt to use Bangla in computing was made in the early 1980swithBangla font developed mostly in the Windows environment. These efforts were led by commercial vendors. Introduction of 'ShahidLipi' and 'Bijoy,' while they provided for new possibilities, weren't able to overcome the compatibility issue of Bangla language in different platforms. Bangla was not usable as a general language on every system as there was still no unique way to represent Bangla. In the late 1990s with introduction and use of Unicode, the process of Bangla computing began to take a new shape in Bangladesh, in particular.

The open source movement has some impact on Bangla in computing. In 1998, J. Ahmed (wiki.mozilla.org/L1on:Teams:bn-BD), a software developer in Bangladesh, first solved the Bangla issue in computing and started a process of Bangla version of Linux. In the late 1990s, a voluntary group named Ankur (www.ankurbangla.org) started Bangla open source software like Linux, OpenOffice.org, Gaim, etc (Islam, 2009a). Another voluntary organization, Ekushey (ekushey.org), started developing open source unicode fonts and a Bangla input system (i.e. determining how Bangla fonts can be arranged using the existing keyboard). In 2004, the Bangladesh Computer Council came up with a national Bangla keyboard mapping and a collation sequence. The Bangladesh

Open Source Network (BdOSN: bdosn.org) was formed in 2005 with local open source volunteers. BdOSN took Bangla in computing as one of its main issues. As a result, open source in Bangla has started to thrive. Though there is a positive movement on BLP research to use Bangla for the benefit of common masses to use and learn ICT, but it faces the various following challenges that limit the most comprehensive use of Bangla in ICT:

There is no standard corpus in Bangla with a superior quality of the speech recordings. This will need to be developed to aid in spelling and grammar checking, and speech reconstruction. Enlarging the corpus, since it increases the probability that acceptable units will be found in the database (e.g., the 16-h corpus ATRECCS provided for the Blizzard Challenge 2006 (Bennett, 2006)).

No standard has yet been developed for recording speech, dialect selection, recording environment, phonetically trained speaker selection, pronunciation selection, unit selection. Individual data are being used for research purpose.

Lack of large volume and high resolution of speech data continue to be a limitation. Improvements to optimize the quality of the output speech such as: paying extreme attention to a superior quality of the speech recordings to make them consistent, having accurate phonetic labels and pitch marks, highest possible SNR, etc. Also, the more speech data is available and the higher its resolution is, the better the achieved quality can be. This, however, requires huge memory capacities to be able to provide random access to the speech data involved..

There is a lack of detailed acoustic and morphological analysis of Bangla language which is essential to develop software framework for application level support. It is still not clear which speech unit should be selected for it to be efficient in Bangla and whether the existing DSP processor can handle real-time processing.

Lack of a large and representative lexicon of Bangla language and the various lexicons currently in use do not provide for a large number of ever expanding colloquial terms and proper nouns.

Most of the current Bangla language computing tools are primarily based on Microsoft Windows operating system. As the open source operating system greatly improves and supports Unicode fonts, and Linux operating system, focus needs to be shifted to cover these free platforms fully.

For proper TTS synthesis, we need to model more accurately the spontaneous speech features, coarticulation effect, emotions, and nasalization.

There continues to be only very limited work on Bangla prosody; more research is needed on this intonation modeling of Bangla. Improvements to optimize the quality of the output speech such as reducing involved signal processing as much as possible by producing a speech corpus that as best as possible reflects the textual and prosodic characteristics of the target speech. There are many methods to produce speech sounds after text and prosodic analysis. All these methods have some benefits and problems of their own. Therefore a suitable method will need to be adopted.

Till now there exists no standard synthetic speech evaluation technique. This might be achieved by moving away from forced-choice tests using abstract emotion words towards tests measuring the perceived naturalness of an utterance given an emotion defining context.

For TTS synthesis, we need to model more accurately the spontaneous speech features. Modeling spontaneous speech improving the language models, we need to detect vowel nasalization accurately. Therefore a speech analysis technique should be selected which should capture all the essential features of Bangla.

Synthesis techniques currently seem to show a trade-off between flexibility of acoustic modeling and perceived naturalness. In order to express a large number of emotional states with a natural sounding voice, either the rule-based techniques need to become more natural sounding or the selection-based techniques must become more flexible.

A significant challenge lies in the study of nasal vowels to separate the relative contribution of the oral and nasopharyngeal tracts to the acoustic output.

A standard colloquial dialect database and customized dialog system should be built for easy access for all people to the necessary information according to their need.

5. CONCLUSION

This chapter provides a brief survey of the research work on Bangla speech analysis, synthesis, and vowel nasality. In comparison with the language processing efforts in Europe, America and Japan, it seems that we have progressed rather little on BLP and has a long way to go to reap the full benefit of it. Technologies for handheld devices with open platforms have made rapid progresses. Recently open-platforms Android is being used for building Bangla speech synthesis system that can produce an acceptable quality of synthesized output in almost real-time on mobile devices.

Further research work can be carried out incorporating the results of the present survey in the area of automatic speech feature extraction, text to speech and speech to speech and speech to text synthesis, automatic vowel nasality extraction, nasality modeling for a speech synthesizer and other related areas of speech technology.

REFERENCES

Abramson, A. S., Nye, P. W., Henderson, J., & Marshall, C. W. (1981). Vowel height and the perception of consonantal nasality. *The Journal of the Acoustical Society of America, 70*(2), 329–339. doi:10.1121/1.386781 PMID:7288023.

Agbinya, I. (1996). Discrete wavelet transform techniques in speech processing. In *Proceedings of the IEEE Tencon Digital Signal Processing Applications*. IEEE.

Alam, F., Habib, S. M., & Khan, M. (2008a). *Acoustic analysis of Bangla vowel inventory*. Dhaka, Bangladesh: BRAC University.

Alam, F., Habib, S. M., & Khan, M. (2008b). Acoustic analysis of Bangla consonants. In *Proceedings of Spoken Language Technologies for Under Resourced Language (SLTU'08)*, (Vol 1, pp. 108-113). SLTU.

Alam, F., Nath, P. K., & Khan, M. (2007). Text to speech for Bangla language using festival. In *Proceeding of First International Conference on Digital Communication and Computer Applications (DCCA 2007)*. Irbid, Jordan: DCCA.

Alam, S. E. (1995). *Bengali voice synthesis*. (MSs Thesis). University of Dhaka. Bangladesh.

Ali, A. M. A. (1999). *Auditory-based acoustic-phonetic signal processing for robust continuous speaker independent speech recognition*. (Ph.D. Thesis). University of Pennsylvania. Philadelphia, PA.

Ali, L., Gallagher, T., Goldstein, J., & Daniloff, R. (1971). Perception of coarticulated nasality. *The Journal of the Acoustical Society of America, 49*(2), 538–540. doi:10.1121/1.1912384 PMID:5100276.

Ali, M. G. (1990). *Digital processing of short duration signals and design of digital filters*. (MSc Thesis). Rajshahi University. Rajshahi, Bangladesh.

Amelot, A. (2004). *Etude aérodynamique, fibroscopique, acoustique et perceptive des voyelles nasales du français*. (Ph.D. Dissertation). Université Paris III. Paris.

Arai, T. (2004). Formant shifts in nasalization of vowels. *The Journal of the Acoustical Society of America, 115*(5), 2541.

Arai, T. (2005). Comparing tongue positions of vowels in oral and nasal contexts. In *Proceedings of Interspeech*. Lisbon, Portugal: Interspeech.

Bandopadhay, A., Mandal, S. D., & Pal, B. (2003). *Effects of pitch contours stylization and time scale modification on natural speech synthesis*. Paper presented at the Workshop on Spoken Language Processing, TIFR. Mumbai.

Bandyopadhyay, A. (2002). *Some important aspects of bengali speech synthesis system*. Paper presented at IEMCT. Pune.

Basu, J. B., Mitra, T., Mandal, M., & Das, S. K. (2009). Grapheme to phoneme (g2p) conversion for Bangla. In *Proceedings of Oriental COCOSDA*. COCOSDA. doi:10.1109/ICSDA.2009.5278373.

Basu, T., & Warsi, A. H. (2012). *Analysis and synthesis of F0 contours for Bangla readout speech*. Paper presented at the Workshop on Tone and Intonation: Theory, Typology and Computation, WTI, IIT. Guwahati, India.

Beddor, P. S. (1993). The perception of nasal vowels. In Phonetics and Phonology: Nasals, Nasalization and the Velum (pp. 171–196). Academic Press.

Beddor, P. S., & Hawkins, S. (1990). The influence of spectral prominence on perceived vowel quality. *The Journal of the Acoustical Society of America*, *87*(6), 2684–2704. doi:10.1121/1.399060 PMID:2373803.

Beddor, P. S., & Strange, W. (1982). Cross language study of perception of the oral- nasal distinction. *The Journal of the Acoustical Society of America*, *71*(6), 1551–1561. doi:10.1121/1.387809 PMID:7108030.

Bell-Berti, F. (1976). An electromyographic study of velopharyngeal function in speech. *Journal of Speech and Hearing Research*, *19*, 225–240. PMID:979198.

Benguerel, A. P. (1974). Nasal airflow patterns and velar coarticulation in French. *Speech Communication Seminar Proceedings*, *2*, 105-112.

Benguerel, A.P., & Hirose, H., S, M., & Ushijima, T. (1977). Velar coarticulation in French: A fiberscopic study. *Journal of Phonetics*, *5*(2), 149–158.

Bennett, C., & Black, A. (2006). *The blizzard challenge 2006*. Paper presented at the Blizzard Challenge Workshop. Pittsburgh, PA.

Berger, M. A. (2007). *Measurement of vowel nasalization by multidimensional acoustic analysis*. (M.Sc. Thesis). University of Rochester. Rochester, NY.

Bitar, N. N. (1997a). *Acoustic analysis and modeling of speech based on phonetic features*. (Ph.D. Thesis). Boston University. Boston, MA.

Björk, L. (1961). Velopharyngeal function in connected speech. *Acta Radiologica*, *202*, 1–94.

Bognar, E., & Fujisaki, H. (1986). Analysis, synthesis and perception of French nasal vowels. In *Proceedings of ICASSP*, (pp. 1601–1604). ICASSP.

Bond, Z. S. (1975). Identification of vowels excerpted from neutral and nasal contexts. *The Journal of the Acoustical Society of America*, *59*(5), 1229–1232. doi:10.1121/1.380988 PMID:956518.

Bykova, E. M. (1981). *The Bengali language, translation of Bengalskii jazyk, languages of Asia and Africa*. Nauka Publisher.

Cairns, D. A., Hansen, J. H. L., & Kaiser, J. F. (1996a). Recent advances in hypernasal speech detection using the nonlinear Teager energy operator. In *Proceedings of ICSLP*, (pp. 780–783). ICSLP.

Cairns, D. A., Hansen, J. H. L., & Riski, J. E. (1994). Detection of hypernasal speech using a nonlinear operator. In *Proceedings of IEEE Conference on Engineering in Medicine and Biology Society*, (pp. 253–254). IEEE.

Cairns, D. A., Hansen, J. H. L., & Riski, J. E. (1996b). A noninvasive technique for detecting hypernasal speech using a nonlinear operator. *IEEE Transactions on Bio-Medical Engineering, 43*(1), 35–45. doi:10.1109/10.477699 PMID:8567004.

Chaudhury, F. (1984). *Collected works of Mufazzal Haider Chaudhury* (*Vol. 3*). Bangla Academy.

Chen, M. Y. (1995). Acoustic parameters of nasalized vowels in hearing-impaired and normal-hearing speakers. *The Journal of the Acoustical Society of America, 98*(5), 2443–2453. doi:10.1121/1.414399 PMID:7593928.

Chen, M. Y. (1996). *Acoustic correlates of nasality in speech.* (Ph.D. Thesis). MIT. Cambridge, MA.

Chen, M. Y. (1997). Acoustic correlates of English and French nasalized vowels. *The Journal of the Acoustical Society of America, 102*(4), 2360–2370. doi:10.1121/1.419620 PMID:9348695.

Chen, M. Y. (2000a). Acoustic analysis of simple vowels preceding a nasal in standard Chinese. *Journal of Phonetics, 28*(1), 43–67. doi:10.1006/jpho.2000.0106.

Chen, M. Y. (2000b). Nasal detection module for a knowledge-based speech recognition system. *Proceedings of ICSLP, 4*, 636–639. Beijing, China: ICSLP..

Choudhury, S. Datta, A. K., & Chaudhuri, B. B. (2001b). *Concatenative synthesis for a group of languages*. Paper presented at the 17th International Congress on Acoustics. Rome, Italy.

Chowdhury, S., Datta, A. K., & Chaudhuri, B. B. (2001). Study of intonation patterns for text reading in standard colloquial Bengali. In *Proceedings of the Sixth International Workshop on Recent Trends in Speech, Music and Allied Signal Processing (IWSMSP)*. New Delhi, India: IWSMSP.

Chowdhury, S., Moushumi, G., & Anupam, B. (2005). Partneme as the speech inventory for Bangla text to speech synthesis. In *Proceedings of International Conferences on Computer Processing of Bangla.* Dhaka, Bangladesh: IEEE.

Dang, J., & Honda, K. (1996). Acoustic characteristics of the human paranasal sinuses derived from transmission characteristic measurement and morphological observation. *The Journal of the Acoustical Society of America, 100*(5), 3374–3383. doi:10.1121/1.416978 PMID:8914318.

Dang, J., Honda, K., & Suzuki, H. (1994). Morphological and acoustical analysis of the nasal and the paranasal cavities. *The Journal of the Acoustical Society of America, 96*(4), 2088–2100. doi:10.1121/1.410150 PMID:7963023.

Dash, N.S., & Chaudhuri. (1988). Utterance rules for Bangla words and their computer implementation. In *Proceedings of the International Conference of Computational Linguistics, Speech and Document Processing (ICCLSDP '98)*, (pp. 51-58). ICCLSDP.

DasMandal, S. K., & Pal, B. (2002). *Bengali text-to-speech synthesis system, a novel approach for crossing literacy barrier*. Regional Winner paper in CSI-YITPA(E).

DasMandal, S. K., Saha, A., & Basu, T. (2010). Modeling of sentence medial pauses in bangla readout speech: Occurrence and duration. *Proceedings of Interspeech, 2010*, 1764–1767.

Datta, A. K., Sengupta, D., Banerjee, R. N., & Nag, D. (1998a). *Perception of Nasality in Bangali Vowels: Role of Harmonics between F0, F1.* Proceedings of International Conferences on Computational Linguistics, Speech and Document Processing, India.

Datta, A. K., Sengupta, D., Banerjee, R. N., & Nag, D. (1998b). *Spectral cues of nasality in inherently nasal bangla vowels.* Paper presented at the International Conferences on Computational Linguistics, Speech and Document Processing. India.

Delattre, P., & Monnot, M. (1968). The role of duration in the identification of french nasal vowels. *International Review of Applied Linguistics, 6*, 267–288. doi:10.1515/iral.1968.6.1-4.267.

Deller, J. R., & Hansen, J. H. L. (2000). *Discrete-time processing of speech signals*. IEEE Press.

Delvaux, V. (2003). *Contrôle et connaissance phonétique: Le cas des voyelles nasales du français*. (Ph.D. Dissertation). Université Libre de Bruxelles. Brussels, Belgium.

Diakoumakou, E. (2004). *Coarticulatory vowel nasalization in modern Greek*. (PhD Dissertation). University of Michigan. Ann Arbor, MI.

Dickson, D. R. (1962). Acoustic study of nasality. *Journal of Speech and Hearing Research, 5*(2), 103–111. PMID:13886213.

Examination Roll. 841. (1997). *A text-to-speech synthesis system for bangla language using concatenative technique*. (MS Thesis). Rajshahi University. Rajshahi, Bangladesh.

Fant, G. (1960). *Acoustic theory of speech production*. The Hague, Netherlands: Mouton.

Farnetani, E., & Recasens, D. (1999). *Coarticulation models in recent speech production theories*. Hardcastle.

Ferguson, C. A., & Choudhury, M. (1960). Phonemes of Bengali: Part I. *Language, 36*(1). doi:10.2307/410622.

Fujimura, O., & Lindqvist, J. (1971). Sweep tone measurements of vocal tract characteristics. *The Journal of the Acoustical Society of America, 49*, 541–558. doi:10.1121/1.1912385 PMID:5541748.

Furui, S. (2001). *Digital speech processing, synthesis, and recognition* (2nd ed.). Marcel Dekker, Inc..

Ghosh, K., Reddy, R. V., Narendra, N. P., Maity, S., Koolagudi, S. G., & Rao, K. S. (2010). *Grapheme to phoneme conversion in bengali for festival based TTS framework.* Paper presented at the 8th International Conference on Natural Language Processing (ICON). New Delhi.

Glass, J. R. (1984). *Nasal consonants and nasalised vowels: An acoustical study and recognition experiment*. (Master's Thesis). MIT. Cambridge, MA.

Glass, J. R., & Zue, V. W. (1985). Detection of nasalized vowels in American English. In *Proceedings of ICASSP*, (pp. 1569–1572). ICASSP.

Graps, A. (2001). An introduction to wavelets. *IEEE Computational Sciences and Engineering*. Retrieved from http://www.amara.com/IEEEwave/IEEEwavelet.html

Grimm, J. (1822). *Deutsche grammatik* (2nd ed.). Göttingen.

Hai, A. (1985). *Dhvani-vignan o bangla dhvani tattwa*. Mullick Brothers.

Hajro, N. (2004). *Automated nasal feature detection for the lexical access from features project*. (Master's Thesis). MIT. Cambridge, MA.

Hamid, M. E., Siddique, S. A., Chisty, K. J. A., & Sobhan, M. A. (1995). *Power spectrum analysis of bangla vowels and consonants by windowed short time fourier transforms*. Rajshahi University Studies.

Haque, S. (1997). *Comparative study of extractive features of bangla phonemes with different age and sex groups and synthesis of voiced phonemes with developed software.* (M.Sc. Dissertation). Rajshahi University. Bangladesh.

Haque, S., & Takara, T. (2004). Rule based speech synthesis by cepstral method for standard bangle. In *Proceedings of 18th International Congress on Acoustics, ICA 2004*. Kyoto, Japan: ICA.

Haque, S., & Takara, T. (2006). Nasality perception of vowels in different language background. In *Proceedings of INTERSPEECH 2006 – ICSLP*. Pittsburgh, PA: ICSLP.

Haque, S., & Takara, T. (2011a). Bangla oral-nasal vowel pairs: Acoustic categorization and comparative study of feature extraction methods. *Journal of Computing*, *3*(7).

Haque, S., & Takara, T. (2011b). Optimal wavelet for bangla vowel synthesis. *International Journal of Scientific and Engineering Research*, *2*(1).

Hasegawa-Johnson, M., Baker, J., Borys, S., Chen, K., Coogan, E., & Greenberg, S. ... Wang, T. (2004). Landmark-based speech recognition. Baltimore, MD: Johns Hopkins.

Hasegawa-Johnson, M., Baker, J., Borys, S., Chen, K., Coogan, E., & Greenberg, S. ... Wang, T. (2005). Landmark-based speech recognition. In *Proceedings of ICASSP*, (pp. 213–216). ICASSP.

Hattori, S., Yamamoto, K., & Fujimura, O. (1958). Nasalization of vowels in relation to nasals. *The Journal of the Acoustical Society of America*, *30*(4), 267–274. doi:10.1121/1.1909563.

Hawkins, S., & Stevens, K. N. (1985). Acoustic and perceptual correlates of the non- nasal-nasal distinction for vowels. *The Journal of the Acoustical Society of America*, *77*(4), 1560–1575. doi:10.1121/1.391999 PMID:3989111.

Hegde, R. M., Murthy, H. A., & Ramana Rao, G. V. (2004). Application of the modified group delay function to speaker identification and discrimination. In *Proceedings of ICASSP*, (pp. 517–520). ICASSP.

Hegde, R. M., Murthy, H. A., & Ramana Rao, G. V. (2005). Speech processing using joint features derived from the modified group delay function. In *Proceedings of ICASSP* (pp. 541–544). ICASSP.

Hossain, S. A. (1991). *Experimental and computer aided analysis of active filters and analog and digital processing of music and bangla speech signals*. (MSc Thesis). Rajshahi University. Bangladesh.

Hossain, S. A. (2008). *Analysis and synthesis of bangla phonemes for computer speech recognition*. (Ph.D. Dissertation). University of Dhaka. Dhaka, Bangladesh.

Hossain, S. A., Rahman, M. L., & Ahmed, F. (2005). Acoustic space of bangla vowels. In *Proceedings of WSEAS 5th International Conference on Speech and Image Processing*, (pp. 138-142). Corfu, Greece: WSEAS.

Hossain, S. A., Rahman, M. L., & Ahmed, F. (2007). Acoustic classification of bangla vowels. World Academy of Science, Engineering and Technology, 26.

Hossain, S. A., & Sobhan, M. A. (1997). Fundamental frequency tracking of bangle voiced speech. In *Proceedings of National Conference on Computer and Information Systems*. IEEE.

House, A. S., & Stevens, K. N. (1956). Analog studies of the nasalization of vowels. *The Journal of Speech and Hearing Disorders*, *21*(2), 218–232. PMID:13320522.

Huffman, M. K. (1990). The role of f1 amplitude in producing nasal percepts. *The Journal of the Acoustical Society of America*, *88*(S1), S54. doi:10.1121/1.2029054.

Islam, M. R., Saha, R. S., & Hossain, A. R. (2009b). Automatic reading from Bangla PDF document using rule based concatenative synthesis. In *Proceeding of ICCDA*. Singapore: ICCDA.

Islam, M. S. (2009a). *Research on bangla language processing in Bangladesh: Progress and challenges*. Paper presented at the 8th International Language & Development Conference. Dhaka, Bangladesh.

Kawasaki, H. (1986). Phonetic explanation for phonological universals: The case of distinctive vowel nasalization. In *Experimental Phonology*. Academic Press.

Kingston, J., & Macmillan, N. A. (1995). Integrality of nasalization and f1 in vowels in isolation and before oral and nasal consonants: A detection-theoretic application of the garner paradigm. *Journal of the American Society of Acoustics*, *97*, 1261–1285. doi:10.1121/1.412169 PMID:7876447.

Klatt, D. H. (1980). Software for cascade/parallel formant synthesizer. *The Journal of the Acoustical Society of America*, *67*, 971–995. doi:10.1121/1.383940.

Krakow, R. A. (1993). Nonsegmental influences on velum movement patterns: Syllables, sentences, stress and speaking rate. In *Phonetics and Phonology: Nasals, Nasalization and The Velum*. Academic Press.

Krakow, R. A., & Beddor, P. S. (1991). Coarticulation and the perception of nasality. In *Proceedings of The 12th International Congress of Phonetic Sciences*. IEEE.

Krakow, R. A., Beddor, P. S., Goldstein, L. M., & Fowler, C. (1988). Coarticulatory influences on the perceived height of nasal vowels. *The Journal of the Acoustical Society of America*, *83*, 1146–1158. doi:10.1121/1.396059 PMID:3356819.

Ladefoged, P. (1982). *A course in phonetics*. New York: Harcourt Brace Jovanovich.

Lahiri, A., & Marslen-Wilson, W. (1991). The mental representation of lexical form: A phonological approach to the recognition lexicon. *Cognition*, *38*, 245–294. doi:10.1016/0010-0277(91)90008-R PMID:2060271.

Lindqvist-Gauffin, J., & Sundberg, J. (1976). Acoustic properties of the nasal tract. *Phonetica*, *33*, 161–168. doi:10.1159/000259720 PMID:996111.

Lintz, L. B., & Sherman, D. (1961). Phonetic elements and perception of nasality. *Journal of Speech and Hearing Research*, *4*, 381–396. PMID:14465667.

Maddieson, I. (1984). *Patterns of sounds*. Cambridge University Press. doi:10.1017/CBO9780511753459.

Maeda, S. (1982a). A digital simulation method of the vocal-tract system. *Speech Communication*, *1*, 199–229. doi:10.1016/0167-6393(82)90017-6.

Maeda, S. (1982b). The role of the sinus cavities in the production of nasal vowels. *Proceedings of ICASSP*, *2*, 911–914.

Maeda, S. (1982c). Acoustic cues for vowel nasalization: A simulation study. *The Journal of the Acoustical Society of America*, *72*, S102. doi:10.1121/1.2019690.

Maeda, S. (1993). Acoustics of vowel nasalization and articulatory shifts in french nasal vowels. In *Phonetics and Phonology: Nasals, Nasalization and The Velum*. Academic Press.

Mahboob, M. (2009). *TechSpotlight: The power of Bangla*. The Daily Star.

Mesgarani, N., Slaney, M., & Shamma, S. (2004). Speech discrimination based on multiscale spectrotemporal features. In *Proceedings of ICASSP*. ICASSP.

Mohr, B., Wang & W. S.-Y. (1968). Perceptual distance and the specification of phonological features. *Phonetica, 18*, 31–45. doi:10.1159/000258597.

Mukherjee, S., & Das Mandal, S. K. (2012, July). A Bengali speech synthesizer on android. In *Proceedings of The 1st Workshop on Speech and Multimodal Interaction in Assistive Environments, Association for Computational Linguistics*. Jeju, Republic of Korea: ACL.

Murthy, H. A., & Gadde, V. (2003). The modified group delay function and its application to phoneme recognition. In *Proceedings of ICASSP*. ICASSP.

Narendra, N. P. K., Rao, K., Ghosh, K., Vempada, R. R., & Maity, S. (2011). Development of syllable-based text to speech synthesis system in bengali. *International Journal of Speech Technology, 14*, 167–181. doi:10.1007/s10772-011-9094-4.

Niu, X., Kain, A., & Santen, J. P. H. (2005). *Estimation of the acoustic properties of the nasal tract during the production of nasalized vowels*. Paper presented at Interspeech. Lisbon, Portugal.

Ohala, J. J. (1971). Monitoring soft palate movements in speech. *The Journal of the Acoustical Society of America, 50*, 140. doi:10.1121/1.1977664.

Onsuwan, C. (2005). *Temporal relations between consonants and vowels in Thai syllables*. (PhD Dissertation). University of Michigan. Ann Arbor, MI.

Pramanik, K., & Kido, K. (1975). On the formant frequencies of bengali vowels uttered in isolation. *ASJ Trans. of The Com. on Speech Res., S75-02*, 1--8.

Pramanik, K., & Kido, K. (1976a). On the formant structure of bengali (bangla)vowels uttered in isolation. *ASJ Trans. of The Com. on Speech Res., S75-16*, 57--64,

Pramanik, K., & Kido, K. (1976b). Extraction of, formant frequencies of initial vowels of bengali words. *ASJ Trans. of The Com. on Speech Res., S75-61*, 1—8.

Pramanik, K., & Kido, K. (1977). Auditory experiments of natural and synthesized bengali vowels. *ASJ Trans. of the Com. on Speech Res., S77-22*, 1-7.

Pruthi, T. (2007). *Analysis, vocal-tract modeling and automatic detection of vowel nasalization*. (Ph.D. Dissertation). University of Maryland. College Park, MD.

Rabiner, L. R., & Schafer, R. W. (1978). *Digital processing of speech signal*. New York: Prentice Hall.

Rahman, M. (1992). *Power spectrum and formants extraction of bangla speech*. (MSc Thesis). Rajshahi University. Rajshahi, Bangladesh.

Rossato, S. (2000). *Du son au geste, inversion de la parole: le cas des voyelles nasales*. (PhD Dissertation). INPGrenoble. Grenoble, France.

Ruhlen, M. (1978). Nasal vowels. In *Universals of Human Language* (pp. 203–242). Stanford University Press.

Seddiqui, M. H., Azim, M. A., Rahman, M. S., & Iqbal, M. J. (2002). Algorithmic approach to synthesize voice from bangla text. In *Proceeding of 5th ICCIT Conference*. ICCIT.

Sen, A. (2001). *Speech synthesis in indian language*. Paper presented at the Pre-Workshop Tutorial on Speech and Music Signal Processing.

Stevens, K. N., & Andrade, A., Viana & M. C. (1987a). Perception of vowel nasalization in VC contexts: A cross-language study. *The Journal of the Acoustical Society of America, 82*, S119. doi:10.1121/1.2024621.

Stevens, K. N., Fant, G., & Hawkins, S. (1987b). *Some acoustical and perceptual correlates of nasal vowels*. Foris Publications. doi:10.1515/9783110886078.241.

Talukder, K. H., Rahman, M. M., & Ahmed, T. (2011). An efficient speech generation method based on character and modifier of bangla pdf document. In *Proceedings of 2nd ICCPB Conference*. Dhaka, Bangladesh: ICCPB.

Talukder, M. M. R. (1992). *Spectral and formant analysis of bangla speech (alphabets)*. (MSc Thesis). Rajshahi University. Rajshahi, Bangladesh.

Tanbeer, S. K., Alam, M. S. E., & Mottalib, M. A. (2000). *Study of phonemes for bangla voice synthesis*. Paper presented at the International Conferences on Computer and Information Technology. Dhaka, Bangladesh.

Vijayalakshmi, P., & Reddy, M. R. (2005a). *Detection of hypernasality using statistical pattern classifiers*. Paper presented at Interspeech. Lisbon, Portugal.

Vijayalakshmi, P., & Reddy, M. R. (2005b). *The analysis of band-limited hypernasal speech using group delay based formant extraction technique*. Paper presented at Interspeech. Lisbon, Portugal.

Warren, D. W., & Dubois, A. B. (1964). A pressure flow technique for measuring velopharyngeal orifice area during continuous speech. *The Cleft Palate Journal, 1*, 52–71. PMID:14116541.

Weinberg, B., Bosma, J. F., Shanks, J. C., & DeMyer, W. (1968). Myotonic dystrophy initially manifested by speech disability. *Journal of Sport and Health Research, 33*, 51–59. PMID:5643961.

Whalen, D. H., & Beddor, P. S. (1989). Connections between nasality and vowel duration and height: Elucidation of the eastern algonquian intrusive nasal. *Language, 65*, 457–486. doi:10.2307/415219.

Wright, J. T. (1986). The bahavior of nasalized vowels in the perceptual vowel space. In *Experimental Phonology* (pp. 45–67). Academic Press.

Yegnanarayana, B. (1978). Formant extraction from linear-prediction phase spectra. *The Journal of the Acoustical Society of America, 63*, 1638–1640. doi:10.1121/1.381864.

Zheng, Y., & Hasegawa-Johnson, M. (2004). Formant tracking by mixture state particle filter. In *Proceedings of ICASSP*. ICASSP.

KEY TERMS AND DEFINITIONS

Demisyllable: Speech units obtained by dividing syllables in half, with the cut during the vowel where the effects of co-articulation are minimal.

Formants: The frequencies at which the vocal tract and nasal tract resonates while producing the speech sound.

Nasalization: The production of the sound while the velum—that fleshy part of the palate near the back—is lowered, so that some air escapes through the nose during the production of the sound by the mouth.

Pitch Period: The frequency at which the vocal cord vibrates while producing voiced sound.

Speech Analysis: The branch of science which deals with the analysis of speech sounds taking into consideration their method of production, modeling the method of production by a suitable model and estimating the parameters of the model.

Speech Perception: The process by which the sounds of language are heard, interpreted and understood.

Speech Synthesis: A process which artificially produces speech for various applications, diminishing the dependence on using a person's recorded voice.

Chapter 11
Perception of Vowels and Dental Consonants in Bangla Speech Processing

Syed Akhter Hossain
Daffodil International University, Bangladesh

M. Lutfar Rahman
Daffodil International University, Bangladesh

Faruk Ahmed
Independent University Bangladesh, Bangladesh

M. Abdus Sobhan
Independent University Bangladesh, Bangladesh

ABSTRACT

The aim of this chapter is to clearly understand the salient features of Bangla vowels and the sources of acoustic variability in Bangla vowels, and to suggest classification of vowels based on normalized acoustic parameters. Possible applications in automatic speech recognition and speech enhancement have made the classification of vowels an important problem to study. However, Bangla vowels spoken by different native speakers show great variations in their respective formant values. This brings further complications in the acoustic comparison of vowels due to different dialect and language backgrounds of the speakers. This variation necessitates the use of normalization procedures to remove the effect of non-linguistic factors. Although several researchers found a number of acoustical and perceptual correlates of vowels, acoustic parameters that work well in a speaker-independent manner are yet to be found. Besides, study of acoustic features of Bangla dental consonants to identify the spectral differences between different consonants and to parameterize them for the synthesis of the segments is another problem area for study. The extracted features for both Bangla vowels and dental consonants are tested and found with good synthetic representations that demonstrate the quality of acoustic features.

DOI: 10.4018/978-1-4666-3970-6.ch011

INTRODUCTION

A fundamental distinctive unit of sound of a language is called phoneme. It is distinctive in the sense that differentiates words of a language (Pickett, 1980). In English the words "cat," "bat," and "hat" consists of three speech sounds having distinctive meaning due to different phoneme classes. Different languages contain different phoneme sets. Syllable contains one or more phonemes, while words are formed with one or more syllables, concatenated to form phrases and sentences. Phonemes can differ across languages despite similar grammatical rules.

A phoneme arises from a combination of vocal fold and vocal tract articulatory features. Articulatory features include the vocal fold state i.e. whether vocal folds are vibrating or open; the tongue position and height, i.e. whether it is in the front, central or back along the plate and whether its constriction is partial or complete; and the velum state i.e. whether a sound is nasal or not. In English, the combination of features are such as to give 40-44 phonemes, while in other languages the features can yield a smaller or a larger phoneme set (Quatieri, 2002).

Bangla (or Bengali), one of the more important Indo-Iranian languages, is the sixth-most popular in the world and spoken by a population that now exceeds 250 million. Geographical Bangla-speaking population percentages are as follows: Bangladesh (over 95%), and the Indian States of Andaman & Nicobar Islands (26%), Assam (28%), Tripura (67%), and West Bengal (85%). The global total includes those who are now in diaspora in Canada, Malawi, Nepal, Pakistan, Saudi Arabia, Singapore, United Arab Emirates, United Kingdom, and United States.

In linguistic relationship, Bangla is closer to Assamese then to Oriya and Hindi. The general structural patterns show numerous resemblances to the Dravidian languages of south India. About sixty percent of the word types in formal Bangla are classical Sanskrit; the rest contains British English, Persian, Portuguese and other South Asian languages (Islam, 1970). The Bangla script is historically derived from ancient Indian Brahmi, itself a modification of ancient southern Arabic (Hai, 1966).

Bangla is read and written from left to right and has no capitals. It uses diacritics in all four directions to indicate non-initial vowels and some consonants. There are ten vowels (among which two are diphthongs), three semivowels and thirty-five (phonetically twenty-nine) consonants in present day Bangla, but in early days two more vowels namely *hri* (ঋ) and *hli* (ঌ) were used. Any kind of combination of vowels, semivowels and consonants can form a syllable in Bangla but a consonant is always uttered with the first vowel /আ/ or [a] which is called an inherent vowel unless it is followed by a sign called hash sign called diacritics (Islam, 1970).

According to Bangla Linguistics, based on the IPA (International Phonetic Alphabet) representation, there are eight classified cardinal vowels grouped into categories of frontal and back vowels and one central or neutral vowel /আ/ [aa]. The frontal vowels are /ই/ [e], /এ/ [a], /ঐ/ [ae] and back vowels are /অ/ [ao], /ও/ [o], /ঔ/ [ou] and /উ/ [u] respectively (Hai, 2000).

The goals of this study are: to develop linguistic classification of Bangla vowels based on relevant normalized acoustic features applicable to Bangla vowels; to propose a Bangla vowel system for the normalized acoustic parameters based on formant frequency extracted from males and females; and to make a comparative study of Bangla dental consonants. In the review of the literature, various non-linguistic speaker-dependent sources of variation and previous normalization procedures are examined. Then, this particular study evaluates two specific methods: one using formant values in Hz, the other using the values in Bark units, and compares the two versions with other procedures in terms of minimization of male and scaled female differences in database.

LITERATURE SURVEY

Bangla speech analysis has been an exciting area of investigation for the researchers for more than three decades and researchers explored and are still exploring avenues to parameterize Bangla speech for the machine understanding and recognition of Bangla phonemes.

One of the earliest acoustic studies on Bangla speech was conducted by Paramanik (1976) during his doctoral research in Japan. In acoustical study of Bangla vowels for limited set of Bangla phonemes, he extracted formants of isolated Bangla vowels only and compared them with those of Japanese vowels and vowel like sounds. Unlike Japanese and American English vowels, he found that the formants of non-initial vowels of Bangla words do not change much with respect to vowels uttered in isolation.

In one of the earlier research (Ali, 1990; Ali & Sobhan, 1993) work with short duration signals, the researchers investigated spectral properties of Bangla phonemes. They were able to capture some Bangla vowel phoneme for the experimental observation through digital storage oscilloscope and measured FFT spectrum of three Bangla vowels and compared their real and imaginary parts of the spectrum. In another work on Bangla speech (Hossain, 1991; Hossain & Sobhan, 1997) the researchers analyzed duration of Bangla phonemes and investigated Bangla voiced speech to track the fundamental frequency contour using cepstral smoothing technique. The investigation measured short time cepstral parameters of few Bangla vowels and consonant phonemes. Talukder (1992) also investigated the spectral and formant properties of Bangla speech and applied time and frequency domain processing techniques on a limited set of Bangla speech corpora containing isolated utterances of 11 Bangla vowels, 39 consonants and 36 consonant clusters. They also measured power spectrum, amplitude spectrum and relative phase between the real and imaginary parts of the FFT coefficients and discussed formant analysis from the representation of spectra.

In another research work, Rahman (1992) investigated power spectrum and related properties of Bangla speech. They measured the first three formants and bandwidths of all Bangla vowels using C programming and approximated formants and other measurements from the spectral measurements rather than using an efficient peak picking method or other mathematical transformations.

Alongside the analysis of Bangla speech, researchers also attempted at the tool development for efficient Bangla speech processing. Hamid (1993) developed software solution for the basic processing of Bangla speech. They used Hamming windowed speech segment of isolated utterance of Bangla vowels and consonants from three age groups of male speakers and investigated short-time spectrum, pitch period, fundamental frequency, power spectrum and the first three formant frequencies using C program.

In another work on Bangla speech processing, Uddin (1993) and Hamid and Sobhan (1995) investigated the spectral properties of Bangla phonemes and measured short time spectrum and power spectrum of Bangla vowels and consonants. In the area of speaker identification in Bangla, Hossain & Sobhan (1997) investigated efficient tracking of fundamental frequency of Bangla voiced speech for the identification of speakers.

Datta and Nag (1998) studied the perception of nasality in Bangla vowels with the role of fundamental and the first formant frequency. They also studied the spectral cues (Datta & Nag, 1998) of nasality of inherently nasal Bengali vowels. Datta and Nag (1998) in another work presented fundamental frequency for speaker identification in Bengali. In this experiment they used a distance classifier based on euclidean distance weighted with the inverse of class variance at word level.

The spectral properties of different analysis window namely Hamming, Hanning, etc., was investigated by Uddin and Chisty (2001) et al. on the extraction of formant frequencies of Bangla phonemes. Hossin and Ahmed (2005) et al also reviewed the general features of Bangla phoneme production and perception from the perspective of research for Bangla speech recognition. In this work, the author illustrated spectral features of different classes of Bangla vowels and consonants. In another perceptional work on Bangla vowels, Hossain and Ahmed (2007) et al. worked on various classes of Bangla vowels and investigated in detail the acoustic features responsible for classification of Bangla vowels. Based on the investigation, the authors proposed a classification scheme on vowel triangular map using normalized acoustic feature vectors. Beside these accomplished research works on Bangla speech analysis, a significant research work is required in the area of Bangla speech perception, classification, and acoustic-linguistic relationship to create semantic representation of Bangla phonemes and speech for the purpose of machine recognition.

In another research on developing Bangla speech corpus for Phone recognizer using optimum text, Mandal and Basu (2011) et al proposed a technique for phonetic representation of text selected for phone recognition. The proposed work used linguistically defined vowel and consonant maps. In a work on effect of aging on speech features and phoneme recognition for Bangla voicing vowels, Das and Basu (2012) studied on different voice source features including fundamental frequency, formants, etc and applied spectral processing techniques including cepstral domain analysis, MFCC, etc. for the determination of phoneme dissimilarity features among the age groups.

Acquisition of Bangla speech corpus as it has been observed from the review of the research works is not linguistically defined with complete coverage for all the Bangla vowels and consonants including clusters as well as the isolated and co-articulated utterances. Multiple speakers are used in many cases during research works as described in previous paragraphs for speaker specific feature identification but appropriate normalization has not been applied for the generalization of the feature vectors as well as the experimental results. Bangla vowel study has not been accomplished for linguistic perception and classification along with the Bangla vowel normalization throughout the past decades of the Bangla speech research. Bangla consonants also require independent research study for classification and parameterization for the computer recognition of Bangla consonants. The better the classification and parameterization of Bangla phonemes, the better the machine understanding of Bangla phonemes.

In the present study, the Bangla speech corpus used for the research study is developed from the Bangla linguistics point of view with the help of linguist. This compilation comprises of a total of 1800 isolated Bangla words containing all the vowels and consonants both in CVC (Consonant-Vowel-Consonant) and VCV (Vowel-Consonant-Vowel) forms with co-articulatory effects from thirty-five native Bangla speakers both male and female of different age group.

ANALYSIS OF BANGLA VOWELS

Phonemes are the linguistically contrastive or significant sounds of a language. Such a contrast is usually demonstrated by the existence of minimal pairs or Contrast in Identical Environment (CIE). Minimal pairs are pairs of words which vary only by the identity of the segment at a single location in the word (e.g. [mæt] and [kæt]) or /দাও/ [dao] and /খাও/ [khao] for Bangla. If two segments contrast in identical environment then they must belong to different phonemes.

Speech Materials and Pre-Processing

Vowel material consists of the Bangla vowels from the utterance of words with different Consonant Vowel Consonant (CVC) and Vowel Consonant Vowel (VCV) segmental combination such as

"কাধ [kaf], কাব [kab], কাভ [kabh], কাধ [kadh], কাঠ [kath], কাচ [koch], কোঘ [kogh], কোধ [kof], কিট [kit], কীট [kiit], কুপ/কূপ [kup], কেন [kaen], কোন [kon], কান [kan], কৌস [koum], কর [kaor], কার [kar], কাল [kaol], কোল [kol], কিল [kil], কুল/কূল [kul], কস [kash], কেশ [kaesh], কোস [kosh], কুহ [kuh], কস [kam]. These token stimuli were drawn from multi-talker in this study.

A total of 60 vowel tokens were used for acoustic analysis: 30 vowel tokens produced by male speakers, and 30 vowel tokens produced by female speakers. There were 6 tokens of each of 8 vowels, 3 produced by male speakers and 3 produced by female speakers. A total of 15 different male speakers and 20 female speakers produced 60 vowel tokens. Each speaker produced only a subset of 8 vowels.

Based on the linguistic classification of Bangla and the CVC and VCV combination requirement of this study, a detail word list was prepared. These words were selected with different combination of Bangla consonants, vowels and diacritics.

Consonant material consists of Bangla retroflex and dental consonants. The consonants were in the form of vowel consonant vowel syllables. Some of the speech corpora used in this study were from Bangla words "আতা [ata], উতি [utee], আদা [ada], উদি [udee], আধা [adha], উধি [udhee], আপা [apaa], উপি [upee], আঘা [afaa], উঘি [ufee], আবা [abaa], উবি [ubee], আচা [ataa], উটি [utee], আঠা [atha], উঠি [uthee], আভা [abha], উভি [ubhe], আসা [amaa], উসি [umee], আকা [akaa], উকি [ukee], আখা [akha], উখি [ukhee], আগা [agaa], উগি [ugee], আঘা [agha], উঘি [ughee]." The stimuli were drawn from the word list prepared for the purpose of the study. A total of 88 consonant tokens were used for acoustic analysis: 44 consonants produced by male speakers and 44 consonants produced by female speakers.

Prior to the analysis, the Bangla vowel data set was manually and visually segmented to consonant vowel consonant segments. The starting and ending times of each vocalic nuclei was measured by hand from high-resolution digital spectrograms. In order to avoid the effect of formant transitions due to the role of consonants, acoustic measurements were made starting from 20% of the vowel duration to 80% of the vowel duration. The vocalic segments were segmented into frames of 10-20ms and acoustic analyses were done on these frames.

For Bangla stop consonants, the release burst were analyzed over a 10ms interval or the total burst duration, whichever was found smaller, starting from the burst. This was done in order to be consistent with the methodology followed in the studies by Steven and Blumenstein (Blumstein & Steven, 1979), Lahiri et al. (Gerwirth & Blumstein, 1984) and Loizou and Dorman (Dorman & Loizou, 1996).

Acoustic Measurements for Perception

Vowel Duration: The vowels in each target word were manually segmented on the waveform based on the corresponding wide-band spectrogram. Markers were placed at the acoustic onset and offset of the first and second vowels.

Vowel onset and offset were determined by observing both the spectrogram and the amplitude tracing. On the spectrogram, each vowel tended to begin with a glottal pulse and clear formant bars following the weak noise of preceding consonant. Vowel onset was identified as the point where the 40dB threshold was crossed. Vowel offset was assigned to the point where the amplitude fell and the formant bars terminated on the spectrogram. Vowel onset and offset were used to determine total vowel duration. The duration was measured at the word initial, word medial and word end position for multi speaker and multiple vowel tokens.

Fundamental Frequency: In this experiment, for each vowel token, the fundamental frequency F0 was extracted automatically with the programs developed using Matlab 7.0, based on the autocorrelation method. The fundamental frequency measurement was further evaluated and verified using the phonetic tool Praat. The range to estimate F0 for male speaker was set between 50Hz and 300Hz and between 100Hz and 500Hz for female speakers.

Formant Frequency: Formant frequency measures were taken one-third into the vowel (i.e., at the point determined by adding one-third of the total duration to vowel onset). Formant values were both automatically computed by spectral analysis using Matlab and visually verified using the spectrographic display; these methods almost always converged. The fundamental frequency F0 was gathered from computer estimates by an auto-correlation method while checking its validity against the duration of a vocal fold pulse on the waveform. When formant values of the same vowel and subject show wide variation, they are double-checked by listening to and comparing the spectrograms of three tokens.

The frequencies of F0, F1, F2, F3, and F4 were automatically measured every 10ms with an overlap of 5ms over the entire utterance using the analysis module developed in Matlab and verified using visualization tools. The settings of the formant tracker are the following: low-pass filtering at 10 kHz; pre-emphasis constant: 0.94; LPC order: 12. F0, F1 and F2 frequencies at the acoustic midpoint of the vowel segment were automatically extracted. Formant frequency values were then verified manually.

For each speaker and each vowel segment, extreme frequency values were checked using both an FFT spectrum and an LPC spectrum computed over a 20ms window centered at the midpoint of the vowel, together with a wide-band spectrogram, and they were corrected when it was found that the formant had not been correctly located by the automatic formant tracker.

Logarithmic Distance: Once the formant frequencies were obtained, the logarithmic distance was calculated between two formants, for example, between F2 and F1 *log10*(F2_transition/F1_transition), from now on *log10(F2/F1)*. The logarithmic distance were measured as *log10(F2/F1)*, *log10(F3/F2)*, and *log10(F4/F3)* for the relative measurements of differences between the formant frequencies in the identification of the respective vowels.

Normalization of Vowels: In this step, the linear formant frequency scale was converted to a Bark scale using the formula (Traunmuller, 1988) shown in Equation 1:

$$D_M^B = 26.81 \times \left(\frac{F_i}{1960 + F_i} \right) - 0.53 \qquad (1)$$

where F_i represents the frequency in Hz of the i-th formant and the corresponding value in Bark.

In agreement with Ladefoged and Maddieson (Ladefoge & Maddieson, 1996), among others, $D(F1)$ and $[D(F2) - D(F1)]$ were taken as acoustic/auditory correlates of the vowel-height and front-back dimensions, respectively, as these dimensions are traditionally defined. Syrdal and Gopal (Syrdal & Gopal, 1986) pointed out that the relationship between $[D(F2) - D(F1)]$ and the front-back dimension may not be universal, and found that the latter is more closely related to $[D(F3) - D(F2)]$ than to $[D(F2) - D(F1)]$ in American English. In the current research the acoustic characteristics of vowels in Bangla has been found to have a tighter relationship between the front-back distinction and $[D(F2) - D(F1)]$ compared to $[D(F3) - D(F2)]$.

In another work on the perception of vowel height, Hoemeke and Diehl (Hoemeke & Diehl, 1994) has suggested that $[D(F1) - D(F0)]$ is a more reliable cue to this contrast than $D(F1)$ alone both across and within speakers. More specifically, $[D(F1) - D(F0)]$ may contribute to factor out speaker-dependent variations in the frequency of $F1$, insofar as these are correlated with variations in the fundamental frequency.

It has also been assumed that $[D(F1) - D(F0)]$ varies to a greater extent than $D(F1)$ depending on vowel height because of the well-known correlation shown by $F0$ itself with vowel height for a given speaker. However, differences in intrinsic fundamental frequency are expected to be minimal among the mid vowels on which this study is focused. Statistical analyses were performed on the Bark-transformed formant frequencies. Bangla vowel classification in the present work was carried out on the Bark transformed F0, F1, F2, F3 and F4 along with F1 complement.

Experimental Results

The mean duration of Bangla vowel tokens for both male and female speakers were investigated at the word-initial position and the measured duration of each vowel token is shown in the Figure 1 and Figure 2 in graphical forms.

Averaged across all speakers and vowel contexts, in word-initially, the mean duration for the vowels /আ/ [aa], and /ও/ [o] are about 85ms and 88ms respectively and follows identical variations for both male and female speakers. The vowels /অ/ [a] and /ই/ [e] for the female speaker shows 130ms and 132ms in duration compared to 93ms for average male speakers producing the same vowel segments at the word-initial positions. This hypothesize that low vowel like /অ/ [a] and high vowel like /ই/ [e] for female speakers takes longer duration at the word initial position compared to male speakers producing the same vowel segments.

In case of word-medially position shown in Figure 3, the mean duration for the vowels /আ/ [aa], and /উ/ [u] are about 95ms and 100ms respectively and indistinguishable for both male and female speakers. The vowels /অ/ [a] for the

Figure 1. Comparison of mean duration of Bangla vowels in word-initial position for female speakers

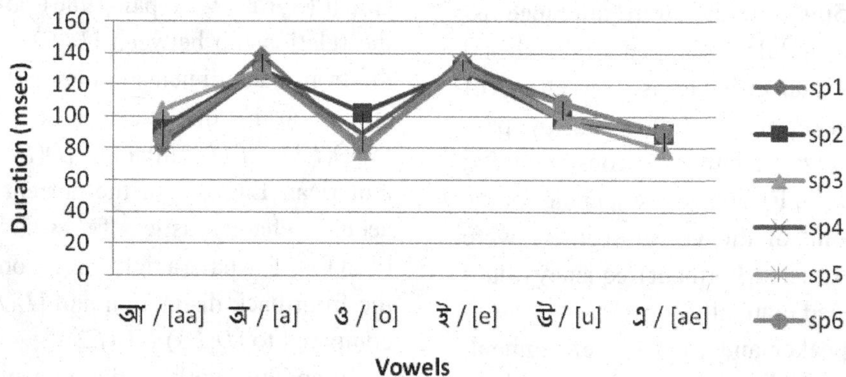

Figure 2. Comparison of mean duration of Bangla vowels in word-initial position for male speakers

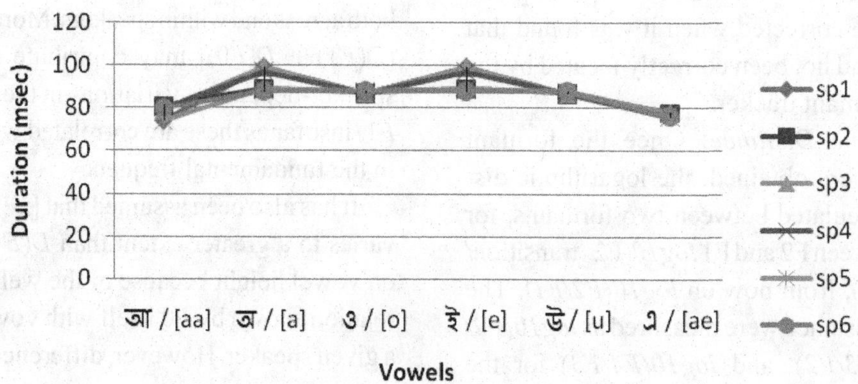

Figure 3. Comparison of mean duration of Bangla vowels in word-medially position for female speakers

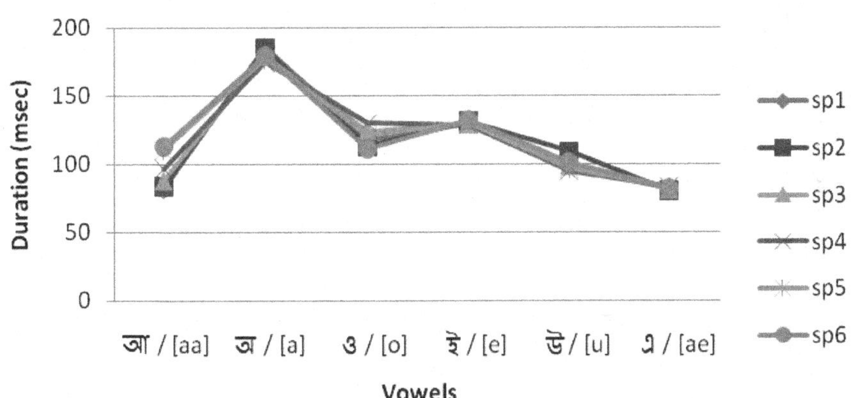

female speakers stays at about 180ms compared to 100ms for male speakers producing the same vowel segments at the word-medially positions.

This again hypothesizes that low vowels like /অ/ [a] for female speakers take longer duration at the word medially position compared to male speakers producing the same vowel segments. See Figure 4.

The mean duration of Bangla vowel tokens for both male and female speakers were also investigated at the word-end position and the measurements are shown in the Figure 5 and Figure 6.

The mean durational statistics is shown in the Table 1. The duration of vowel /ই/ [e] at the word initial position is higher than the other Bangla vowels while the duration of vowel /অ/ [a] at the word medial position is higher and the duration of vowel /ই/ [e] at the word end position is also higher compared to the other Bangla vowels.

The fundamental frequency of Bangla vowel tokens for both male and female speakers are measured and five different speakers from speaker data sets in the category of male and female is shown in the following Table 2 and Table 3 (Hossain, 2003).

As seen from the tables, the fundamental frequency of each Bangla vowel is characterized through speaker specific variations, stress properties, emotions and changes across the vowels based on position and manner of articulation. These differences in the fundamental frequency

Figure 4. Comparison of mean duration of Bangla vowels in word-medially position for male speakers

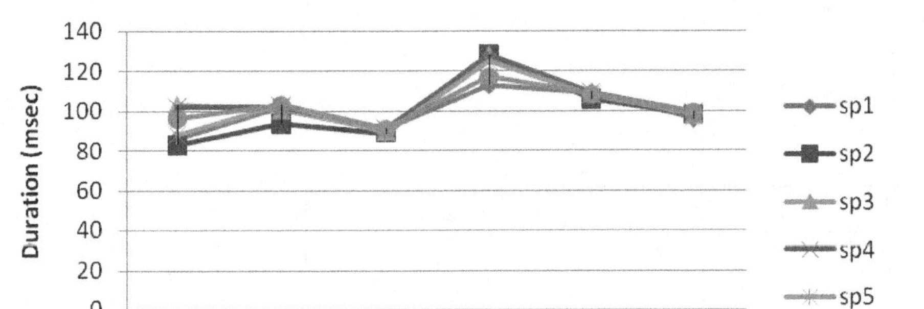

Figure 5. Comparison of mean duration of Bangla vowels in word-end position for female speakers

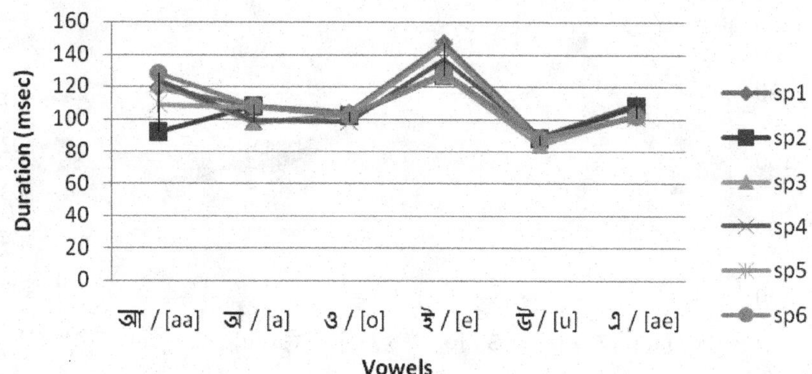

Figure 6. Comparison of mean duration of Bangla vowels in word-end position for male speakers

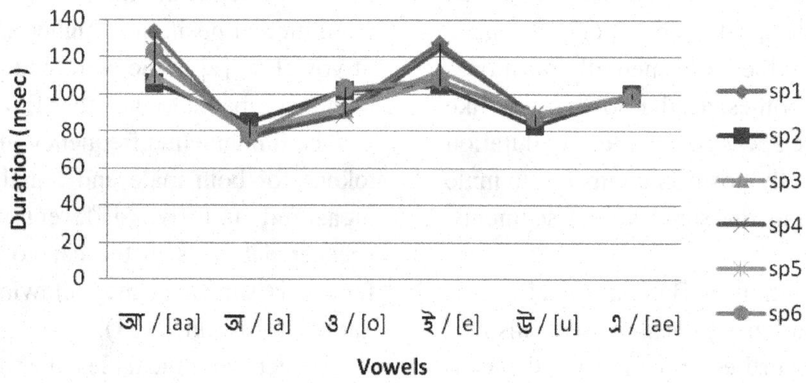

Table 1. Mean segment and phoneme duration (ms) in word-initial, -medial, and -end position. The figures in the parenthesis indicate standard deviation.

Position	/অ/ [a]	/আ/ [aa]	/ও/ [o]	/ই/ [e]	/উ/ [u]	/এ/ [ae]
Initial	106 (26)	92 (8)	82 (8)	113 (21)	95 (8)	82 (6)
Medial	141 (42)	94 (11)	105 (16)	127 (6)	104 (5)	90 (9)
End	92 (14)	117 (11)	99 (6)	124 (14)	87 (2)	101 (4)

Table 2. Mean and standard deviation of fundamental frequency of Bangla vowels produced by adult male speakers (values in Hz)

No.	/অ/ [a]	/আ/ [aa]	/ও/ [o]	/ই/ [e]	/উ/ [u]	/এ/ [ae]
1	149 (1.34)	132 (1.56)	135 (2.11)	151 (1.45)	169 (1.37)	154 (2.13)
2	130 (2.61)	139 (2.12)	155 (1.34)	147 (1.46)	177 (1.39)	136 (1.18)
3	125 (1.35)	126 (2.14)	150 (1.67)	122 (1.23)	165 (1.36)	123 (2.12)
4	145 (1.39)	119 (2.18)	147 (1.46)	148 (1.38)	158 (1.33)	142 (2.11)
5	140 (1.76)	143 (2.11)	121 (1.44)	155 (1.39)	175 (1.38)	138 (2.17)

Table 3. Mean and standard deviation of fundamental frequency of Bangla vowels produced by adult female speakers (values in Hz)

No.	/অ/ [a]	/আ/ [aa]	/ও/ [o]	/ই/ [e]	/উ/ [u]	/এ/ [ae]
1	238 (2.34)	221 (2.46)	235 (1.56)	242 (1.45)	244 (1.67)	244 (2.56)
2	234 (2.56)	243 (3.11)	244 (1.67)	242 (1.55)	237 (1.46)	226 (2.11)
3	222 (2.38)	217 (3.13)	224 (1.58)	243 (1.49)	239 (1.58)	241 (2.15)
4	236 (2.55)	226 (3.12)	199 (1.48)	230 (1.39)	242 (1.66)	240 (2.19)
5	237 (2.24)	214 (2.57)	229 (1.57)	240 (1.38)	241 (1.44)	244 (2.27)

may not play significant role in Bangla vowel recognition but the fundamental frequency is used in this study with the first formant frequency to characterize Bangla vowels. From the measurements of mean fundamental frequency shown in the Table 2 and Table 3, a male to female duration ratio of approximately 0.6 is observed.

The average formant frequency variation of first four formants of all Bangla vowels produced by male and female speakers are shown in the Figure 7 and Figure 8. The means and standard deviations calculated for F1, F2, F3 and F4 frequencies give an average set of values for each vowel (Hossain, 2004; 2005).

Figure 7. Variation of formants for each Bangla vowel for female speakers

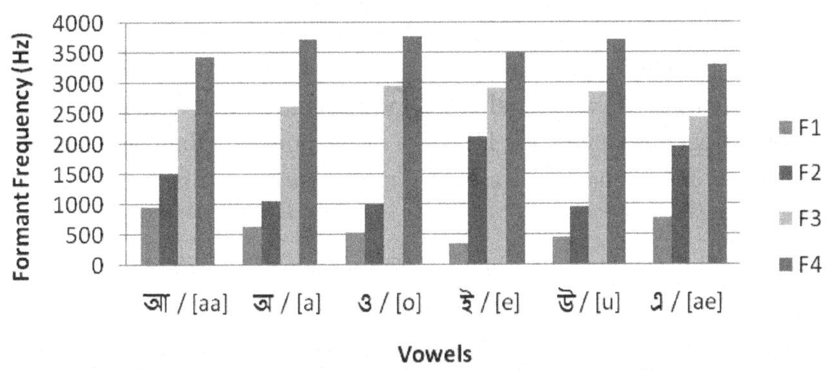

Figure 8. Variation of formants for each Bangla vowel for male speakers

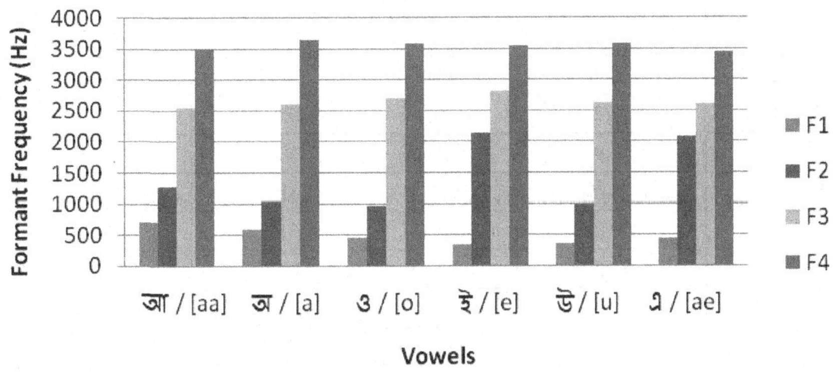

The mean value of the first formant frequency F1 for each Bangla vowel produced by different speakers is shown below in Table 4 and the summary measurement is given in the Table 5.

As can be seen from the Table 4, the mean value of the first formant frequency F1 of all Bangla vowels produced by different male and female speakers are having standard deviation less than about 70Hz. In case of Bangla vowel /অ/ [a], F1 varies within 511Hz to 618Hz for male speakers and from 685Hz to 726Hz for female speakers with standard deviation less than 50Hz.

In Table 5, the mean value of formant frequencies along with the bandwidth and the standard deviation of Bangla vowels produced by different male and female speakers are tabulated and this represents overall formant frequency representation for Bangla vowels. For males, the standard deviations for F1 across different Bangla vowels are generally less than about 80Hz. But for F2, F3 and F4, the standard deviations are larger than F1. The values for F2 generally are less than 1500Hz, with the exception of /ই/ [e] and /এ/ [ae]. Generally, the standard deviations for F2 are smaller than those for F3 but larger than those for F4. For females, the standard deviations for F1 are, with exceptions, less than 100Hz. The standard deviation for F2, F3 and F4 still seems to be larger than those for F1.

The formant log distance for each Bangla vowels for both male and female speakers are shown in the Figure 9 and Figure 10.

As seen from the formant log distance between different formant frequencies of male speakers in the Figure 9, Bangla vowel /অ/ [a] and /আ/ [aa] demonstrate close ratio measurement of 0.253 and 0.244 for F2/F1 respectively whereas the ratio F3/F2 demonstrate significant difference of more than 0.1 for all the vowel samples. The vowel /ও/ [o] as shown has 0.318 for the ratio F2/F1 and 0.453 for F3/F2 which seems moderate and distinguishable and the vowel /ই/ [ee] as shown has 0.799 for the ratio of F2/F1 and 0.119 for F3/F2 being prominent in the ratio measurements. The log ratio for the vowel /উ/ [u] has 0.451 in F2/F1 and 0.435 in F3/F2 and for the vowel /এ/ [ae] has 0.674 in F2/F1 and 0.0980 in F3/F2 respectively.

As seen from the formant log distance between different formant frequencies of female speakers in the Figure 10, Bangla vowel /অ/ [a] and /আ/ [aa] demonstrate similar variation as male speakers.

Table 4. Mean value of the first formant F1 of each Bangla vowel for different speakers (values in Hz; M=male, F=female, SD = standard deviation)

Speaker	/অ/ [a] (SD)	/আ/ [aa] (SD)	/ও/ [o] (SD)	/ই/ [e] (SD)	/উ/ [u] (SD)	/এ/ [ae] (SD)
M1	511 (40)	959 (10)	393 (27)	365 (8)	360 (16)	466 (15)
M2	579 (8)	828 (11)	449 (10)	318 (5)	373 (8)	382 (27)
M3	587 (11)	812 (68)	450 (10)	306 (38)	324 (29)	435 (11)
M4	603 (13)	819 (26)	415 (18)	294 (22)	354 (12)	472 (12)
M5	618 (25)	814 (26)	463 (21)	349 (7)	410 (12)	448 (15)
M6	589 (15)	879 (23)	435 (15)	320 (12)	346 (7)	441 (12)
F1	695 (28)	972 (97)	548 (11)	309 (3)	321 (14)	801 (14)
F2	743 (28)	1038 (51)	543 (4)	319 (6)	315 (7)	624 (66)
F3	685 (20)	1070 (56)	585 (8)	311 (2)	318 (7)	536 (36)
F4	796 (18)	1083 (32)	483 (29)	302 (5)	328 (18)	775 (12)
F5	725 (20)	982 (32)	542 (8)	301 (20)	385 (10)	787 (6)
F6	726 (18)	988 (24)	532 (14)	310 (12)	335 (16)	746 (12)

Table 5. Mean value of formant frequency and bandwidth of Bangla vowels for both male and female speakers (values in Hz; M=male, F=female, Fx=formant frequency, Bx=bandwidth, Ax=amplitude, SD=standard deviation)

Phoneme	F1 (SD)	B1/A1	F2 (SD)	B2/A2	F3 (SD)	B3/A3	F4 (SD)	B4/A4
/অ/ (F)	728 (42)	26.51/ 0.17	1142 (81)	53.8/ 0.13	2700 (137)	40/ 0.17	3807 (129)	32.35/ 0.28
[a] (M)	581 (37)	30.31/ 0.13	1075 (44)	53.72/ 0.11	2468 (261)	35.5/ 0.16	3452 (197)	30.43/ 0.23
/আ/ (F)	1038(50)	81.79/ 0.19	1511 (222)	53.56/ 0.15	2904 (72)	85.97/ 0.05	4271 (146)	145.41/ 0.04
[aa] (M)	819 (80)	65.9/ 0.25	1316 (76)	58.08/ 0.29	2540 (95)	36.04/ 0.22	3885 (147)	46.51/ 0.26
/ই/ (F)	310 (7)	28.78/ 0.09	2717 (92)	52.57 0.01	3297 (88)	47.0/ 0.09	4418 (62)	233/ 0.06
[e] (M)	327 (27)	21.0/ 0.22	2090 (189)	46.45/ 0.12	2714 (170)	65.0/ 0.09	3326 (155)	143.5/ 0.08
/এ/ (F)	718 (99)	23/ 0.063	2049 (321)	54.76/ 0.07	2604 (250)	48.0/ 0.013	3606 (511)	217.22/ 0.07
[ae] (M)	445 (35)	13.0/ 0.40	2082 (181)	52.24/ 0.21	2580 (237)	50.0/ 0.10	3399 (282)	233.5/ 0.29
/ও/ (F)	535 (35)	53.0/ 0.15	985 (88)	86.4/ 0.07	2822 (102)	33.0/ 0.02	3981 (181)	49.47/ 0.05
[o] (M)	428 (30)	30.23/ 0.07	938 (89)	45.0/ 0.10	2653 (157)	33.0/ 0.06	3471 (123)	37.10/ 0.11
/উ/ (F)	333 (26)	46.64/ 0.03	886 (94)	71.67/ 0.03	2554 (286)	50.39/ 0.04	3374 (169)	75.76/ 0.03
[u] (M)	361 (29)	30.5/ 0.04	909 (85)	51.0/ 0.02	2495 (256)	61.25/ 0.03	3380 (179)	81.88/ 0.06

Figure 9. Formant log distance of Bangla vowels for male speakers

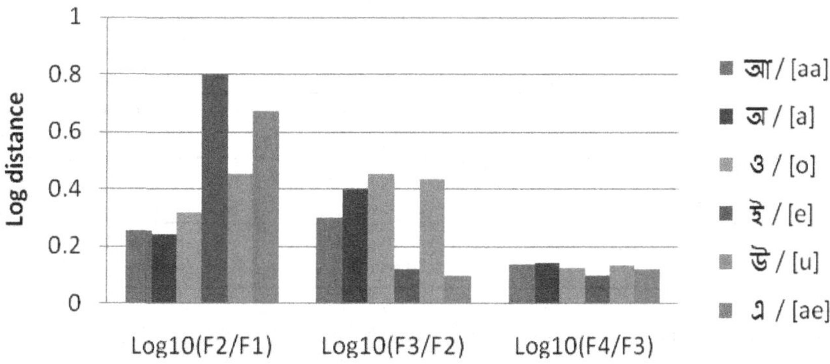

The vowel /ও/ [o] as shown has 0.272 for the ratio F2/F1 and 0.459 for F3/F2 which seems moderate and distinguishable and the vowel /ই/ [ee] as shown has 0.762 for the ratio of F2/F1 and 0.151 for F3/F2 being same prominent the male speakers. The log ratio for the vowel /উ/ [u] has 0.328 in F2/F1 and 0.474 in F3/F2 and for the vowel /এ/ [ae] has 0.397 in F2/F1 and 0.0960 in F3/F2 respectively.

Figure 10. Formant log distance of Bangla vowels for female speakers

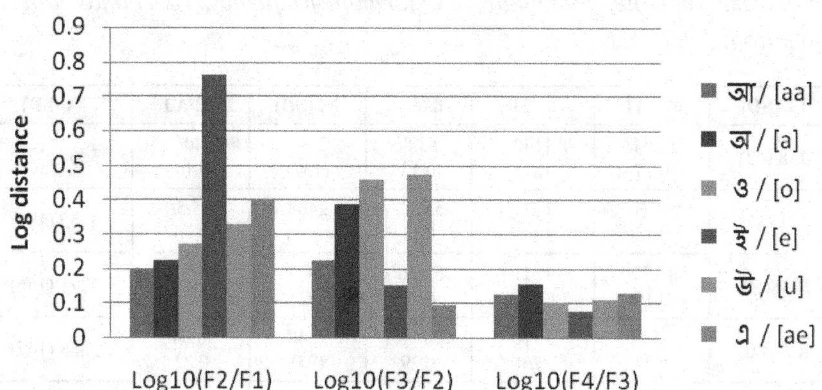

All the prediction measurements related to Bangla vowel openness, backness, and roundness are given in Tables 6, 7, and 8. The vowel openness or tongue height correlates to the F1 and the vowel backness correlates to tongue advancement and F2 measurements.

As seen from the Table 6 on the effectiveness of F1 in categorizing High-Low vowels, Bangla vowel /অ/ [a] and /আ/ [aa] both shows F1>4.5 Bark for all sixty vowel tokens. The vowel /ই/ [ee] shows F1<=4.5 Bark for all the vowel tokens. The vowel /ও/ [o] also shows the same count as the vowels /অ/, and /আ/. But the vowel /এ/ [ae] shows 42% in the area of High and 58% in the area of Low vowels and the vowel /উ/ [u] shows 58% in the area of High and 42% in the area of Low vowel category.

As seen from the Table 7 on the effectiveness of F1-F0 in categorizing High-Low vowels, Bangla vowel /অ/ [a] and /আ/ [aa] shows F1-Fo > 3.0 Bark for all sixty vowel tokens. The vowel /ই/ [ee] shows F1-F0 <= 3.0 Bark for all sixty vowel tokens. The vowel /ও/ [o] shows 20% in the area of High and 80% in the area of Low vowel category. The vowel /এ/ [ae] shows 50% in the area of High and 50% in the area of Low vowels and

Table 6. Effectiveness of F1 in categorizing high-low vowels (openness predictor)

Phoneme		F1 (Bark Scale)		Total
		F1 <= 4.5 Bark High	F1 > 4.5 Bark Low	
/অ/ [a]	Count % of Phoneme	0 0.0%	60 100.0%	60 100.0%
/আ/ [aa]	Count % of Phoneme	0 0.0%	60 100.0%	60 100.0%
/ই/ [e]	Count % of Phoneme	60 100.0%	0 0.0%	60 100%
/এ/ [ae]	Count % of Phoneme	25 42.0%	35 58.0%	60 100.0%
/ও/ [o]	Count % of Phoneme	0 0.0%	60 100.0%	60 100.0%
/উ/ [u]	Count % of Phoneme	35 58.0%	25 42.0%	60 100.0%

Table 7. Effectiveness of F1-F0 in categorizing high-low vowels (openness predictor)

Phoneme		F1-F0 (Bark Scale)		Total
		F1-F0 <= 3.0 Bark High	F1-F0 > 3.0 Bark Low	
/অ/ [a]	Count % of Phoneme	0 0.0%	60 100.0%	60 100.0%
/আ/ [aa]	Count % of Phoneme	0 0.0%	60 100.0%	60 100.0%
/ই/ [e]	Count % of Phoneme	60 100.0%	0 0.0%	60 100.0%
/এ/ [ae]	Count % of Phoneme	30 50.0%	30 50.0%	60 100.0%
/ও/ [ʊ]	Count % of Phoneme	12 20.0%	48 80.0%	60 100.0%
/উ/ [u]	Count % of Phoneme	55 91.0%	5 9.0%	60 100.0%

Table 8. Effectiveness of F2 in categorizing front-back vowels (backness predictor)

Phoneme		F2 (Bark Scale)			Total
		F2 <= 9.5 Bark Back	9.5 < F2 <=13 Central	F2 > 13 Front	
/অ/ [a]	Count % of Phoneme	22 37.0%	38 63.0%	0 0.0%	60 100.0%
/আ/ [aa]	Count % of Phoneme	0 0.0%	60 100.0%	0 0.0%	60 100.0%
/ই/ [e]	Count % of Phoneme	0 0.0%	0 0.0%	60 100.0%	60 100.0%
/এ/ [ae]	Count % of Phoneme	0 0.0%	13 33.0%	47 67.0%	60 100.0%
/ও/ [o]	Count % of Phoneme	55 91.0%	5 9.0%	0 0.0%	60 100.0%
/উ/ [u]	Count % of Phoneme	55 91.0%	5 9.0%	0 0.0%	60 100.0%

the vowel /উ/ [u] shows 91% in the area of High and 9% in the area of Low vowels.

As seen from the Table 8 on the effectiveness of F2 in categorizing Front-Back vowels, Bangla vowel /অ/ [a] has F2<=9.5 Bark in case of 37% and within the range 9.5 to 13 Bark in case of 63%. The vowel /আ/ [aa] shows F2 in the range 9.5 to 12 Bark for all sixty vowel tokens. The vowel /ই/ [ee] shows F2 > 13 Bark for all sixty vowel tokens. But the vowel /এ/ [ae] shows 33% in the area of Central and 67% in the area of Front vowels. The vowel /ও/ [o] and /উ/ [u] both shows 91% in the area of Back and 9% in the area of Central vowel category.

As seen in the Table 9 on the effectiveness of F2-F0 in categorizing Front-Back vowels, Bangla vowel /অ/ [a] has F2-F0<=7 Bark in case of 6% and within the range 7 to 11 Bark in case of 94%. The vowel /আ/ [aa] shows F2-F0 in the range 7 to 11 Bark for all sixty vowel tokens. The vowel /ই/ [ee] shows F2-F0 > 11 Bark for all sixty vowel tokens. But the vowel /এ/ [ae] shows 16%

in the area of Central and 84% in the area of Front vowels. The vowel /ও/ [o] shows 58% in the area of Back and 42% in the area of Central vowels and /উ/ [u] shows 84% in the area of Back and 16% in the area of Central vowel category.

As seen in the Table 10 on the effectiveness of F2-F1 in categorizing Front-Back vowels, Bangla vowel /অ/ [a] has F2-F1<=4 Bark for all sixty vowel tokens. The vowel /আ/ [aa] shows F2-F1<=4 for 50% tokens and F2-F1 in the range 4 to 6 Bark for the rest 50% vowel tokens. The vowel /ই/ [e] shows F2-F1 <= 4 Bark for all sixty vowel tokens. The vowel /এ/ [ae] shows F2-F1>6 for sixty vowel tokens. The vowel /ও/ [o] shows 75% in the area of Back, 34% in the area of Central and 9% in the area of Front vowels and /উ/ [u] shows 50% in the area of Back, 34% in the area of Central and 16% in the area of Front vowel category.

As seen in the Table 11 on the effectiveness of F3-F2 in categorizing Front-Back vowels, Bangla vowel /অ/ [a] has F2-F1<=3 Bark for 6%, F3-F2 in the range of 3 to 6 Bark for 81% and F3-F2>6 for the rest 13% of vowel tokens. The vowel /আ/ [aa] shows F3-F2<=3 for 12% tokens and F3-F2 in the range 3 to 6 Bark for the rest 88% vowel tokens. The vowel /ই/ [ee] shows F3-F2 <= 3 Bark for all sixty vowel tokens. The vowel /এ/ [ae] shows F3-F2<=3 for sixty vowel tokens. The vowel /ও/ [o] shows 8% in the area of Back, 16% in the area of Central and 76% in the area of Front vowels and /উ/ [u] shows 16% in the area Central and 84% in the area of Front vowel category.

As seen in the Table 12 on the effectiveness of F2′ in categorizing roundness of vowels, Bangla vowel /অ/ [a] has F2'<=9 Bark for 18% and F2' >9 Bark for the rest 82% of vowel tokens. The vowel /আ/ [aa] shows F2'>9 Bark for all the vowel tokens. The vowel /ই/ [ee] shows F2' > 9 Bark for all sixty vowel tokens. The vowel /এ/ [ae] shows F2' > 9 Bark for sixty vowel tokens. The vowel /ও/ [o] shows 84% in the area of Rounded and 16% in the area of unrounded vowels and /উ/ [u] shows 84% in the area of Rounded and 16% in the area of unrounded vowel category.

As seen in the Table 13 on the effectiveness of F2'-F0 in categorizing roundness of vowels, Bangla vowel /অ/ [a] has F2'-F0 <=7 Bark for 6% and F2'-F0 >7 Bark for the rest 94% of vowel tokens. The vowel /আ/ [aa] shows F2'-F0> 7 Bark for all the vowel tokens. The vowel /ই/ [ee] shows F2'-F0 > 7 Bark for all sixty vowel

Table 9. Effectiveness of F2-F0 in categorizing front-back vowels (backness predictor)

Phoneme		F2-F0 (Bark Scale)			Total
		F2 - F0 <= 7 Back	7 < F2 - F0 <= 11 Central	F2 - F0 > 11 Front	
/অ/ [a]	Count % of Phoneme	4 6.0%	56 94.0%	0 0.0%	60 100.0%
/আ/ [aa]	Count % of Phoneme	0 0.0%	60 100.0%	0 0.0%	60 100.0%
/ই/ [e]	Count % of Phoneme	0 0.0%	0 0.0%	60 100.0%	60 100.0%
/এ/ [ae]	Count % of Phoneme	0 0.0%	10 16.0%	50 84.0%	60 100.0%
/ও/ [o]	Count % of Phoneme	39 58.0%	21 42.0%	0 0.0%	60 100.0%
/উ/ [u]	Count % of Phoneme	50 84.0%	10 16.0%	0 0.0%	60 100.0%

Table 10. Effectiveness of F2-F1 in categorizing front-back vowels (backness predictor)

Phoneme		F2-F1 (Bark Scale)			Total
		F2 - F1 <= 4 Back	4 < F2 - F1 <= 6 Central	F2 - F1 > 6 Front	
/অ/ [a]	Count % of Phoneme	60 100.0%	0 0.0%	0 0.0%	60 100.0%
/আ/ [aa]	Count % of Phoneme	30 50.0%	30 50.0%	0 0.0%	60 100.0%
/ই/ [e]	Count % of Phoneme	60 100.0%	0 0.0%	0 0.0%	60 100.0%
/এ/ [ae]	Count % of Phoneme	0 0.0%	0 0.0%	60 100.0%	60 100.0%
/ও/ [o]	Count % of Phoneme	45 75.0%	10 16.0%	5 9.0%	60 100.0%
/উ/ [u]	Count % of Phoneme	30 50.0%	20 34.0%	10 16.0%	60 100.0%

Table 11. Effectiveness of F3-F2 in categorizing front-back vowels (backness predictor)

Phoneme		F3-F2 (Bark Scale)			Total
		F3 - F2 <= 3 Back	3 < F3 - F2 <= 6 Central	F3 - F2 > 6 Front	
/অ/ [a]	Count % of Phoneme	4 6.0%	49 81.0%	7 13.0%	60 100.0%
/আ/ [aa]	Count % of Phoneme	7 12.0%	53 88.0%	0 0.0%	60 100.0%
/ই/ [e]	Count % of Phoneme	60 100.0%	0 0.0%	0 0.0%	60 100.0%
/এ/ [ae]	Count % of Phoneme	60 100.0%	0 0.0%	0 0.0%	60 100.0%
/ও/ [o]	Count % of Phoneme	5 8.0%	10 16.0%	45 76.0%	60 100.0%
/উ/ [u]	Count % of Phoneme	0 0.0%	10 16.0%	50 84.0%	60 100.0%

tokens. The vowel /এ/ [ae] shows F2'-F0 > 7 Bark for sixty vowel tokens. The vowel /ও/ [o] shows 66% in the area of rounded and 34% in the area of unrounded vowels and /উ/ [u] shows 84% in the area of rounded and 16% in the area of unrounded vowel category.

Based on the analysis of all the formants and formant contours and the transition of formant frequencies in the generation of Bangla vowels are identified as shown in the Table 14.

As shown in the Table 14, in the production of vowel /অ/ [a], the first formant frequency F1 tends to increase while F2, F3 and F4 do not show noticeable transition. In case of vowel /আ/ [aa], both F1 and F2 tend to increase without changes in F3 and F4. Interestingly, in the production of the vowel /ই/ [e] the first formant frequency F1 tends to decrease while F2, F3 and F4 tend to increase. In the production of the vowel /এ/ [ae] the first formant frequency F1 tends to decrease

Table 12. Effectiveness of F2' in categorizing roundness of bangla vowels (roundness prediction)

Phoneme		F2' (Bark Scale)		Total
		F2' <= 9 Rounded	F2' > 9 Unrounded	
/অ/ [a]	Count % of Phoneme	11 18.0%	49 82.0%	60 100.0%
/আ/ [aa]	Count % of Phoneme	0 0.0%	60 100.0%	60 100.0%
/ই/ [e]	Count % of Phoneme	0 0.0%	60 100.0%	60 100.0%
/এ/ [ae]	Count % of Phoneme	0 0.0%	60 100.0%	60 100.0%
/ও/ [o]	Count % of Phoneme	50 84.0%	10 16.0%	60 100.0%
/উ/ [u]	Count % of Phoneme	50 84.0%	10 16.0%	60 100.0%

Table 13. Effectiveness of F2'-F0 in categorizing roundness of Bangla vowels

Phoneme		F2'-F0 (Bark scale)		Total
		F2'-Fo <= 7 Rounded	F2'-Fo > 7 Unrounded	
/অ/ [a]	Count % of Phoneme	4 6.0%	56 94.0%	60 100.0%
/আ/ [aa]	Count % of Phoneme	0 0.0%	60 100.0%	60 100.0%
/ই/ [e]	Count % of Phoneme	0 0.0%	60 100.0%	60 100.0%
/এ/ [ae]	Count % of Phoneme	0 0.0%	60 100.0%	60 100.0%
/ও/ [o]	Count % of Phoneme	40 66.0%	20 34.0%	60 100.0%
/উ/ [u]	Count % of Phoneme	50 84.0%	10 16.0%	60 100.0%

while F2 tends to increase and there is no change in the F3 and F4. For the vowel /ও/ [o] the first formant frequency F1 tends to decrease without noticeable change in F2, F3 and F4. In the vowel /উ/ [u] the first and second formant frequencies F1 and F2 both tend to decrease while F3 tends to increase without any change in F4. The effect of transition of higher formant F4 in the production of vowels is less significant.

Based on the acoustic and perceptional research with Bangla vowels and experimental observations and study as furnished in Table 6 through Table 13, the articulatory description of Bangla vowels could be summarized as shown in the Table 15.

As shown in the Table 15, the vowel /অ/ [a] is identified as low and central vowel from the articulatory point of view and is also unrounded. It is neither tense nor lax. The vowel /আ/ [aa] is identified in the same category as /অ/ [a] but with lax in the measure of tenseness. The vowel /ই/ [e] is identified as high and front vowel with being unrounded and tense. The vowel /এ/ [ae] is in the

Table 14. Vowel formant transitions (F1: first formant; F2: second formant; F3: third formant; F4: fourth formant)

Formant Frequency	Bangla Vowel Phonemes					
	/অ/ [a]	/আ/ [aa]	/ই/ [e]	/এ/ [ae]	/ও/ [o]	/উ/ [u]
F1	Increase	Increase	Decrease	Decrease	Decrease	Decrease
F2	-	Increase	Increase	Increase	-	Decrease
F3	-	-	Increase	-	-	Increase
F4	-	-	Increase	-	-	-

Table 15. Articulatory descriptions of Bangla vowels

Phoneme	Height	Frontness	Tenseness	Roundness	Manner
/অ/ [a]	Low	Central	-	Unrounded	Vowel
/আ/ [aa]	Low	Central	Lax	Unrounded	Vowel
/ই/ [e]	High	Front	Tense	Unrounded	Vowel
/এ/ [ae]	Low-Mid	Front	-	Unrounded	Vowel
/ও/ [o]	Low	Back	Tense	Rounded	Vowel
/উ/ [u]	High	Back	Tense	Rounded	Vowel

category of low-mid and front vowel. It is unrounded and neither tense nor lax. The vowel /ও/ [o] is in the category of low and back vowel being tense and also rounded. The vowel /উ/ [u] is identified as high and back vowel with being both tense and rounded.

From the articulatory description of vowels shown in the Table 15, the proposed six-vowel system for Bangla vowels is plotted as shown the Figure 11 and Figure 12.

As shown in the Bangla vowel chart of the Figure 11 and Figure 12, the Bangla vowels are represented in a two dimensional plane defined by the first and the second formant frequency F1 and F2 respectively. This vowel chart signifies the place and manner of articulation for each Bangla vowel phonation.

ANALYSIS OF BANGLA DENTAL CONSONANTS

The section describes in detail the result of the analysis of the Bangla dental consonants /ট/ [t], /ঠ/ [th], /ড/ [d] and /ঢ/ [dh] in different context of Bangla vowels.

Speech Materials and Pre-Processing

The speech material consist of minimal pairs from the corpus originated from the Bangla word আতা [ata], আত [at], উতি [uti], অদা [ada], অদ [ad], উদি [udi], আধা [adha], আধ [adh], উধি [udhi], আপা [apa], আপ [ap], উপি [upi], আফা [afa], আফ [af], উফি [ufi], আবা [aba], আব [aab], উবি [ubi], আটা [ata], আট [at], উটি [uthi], আঠা [atha], আঠ [ath], উঠি [uthi], আভা [abha], আভ [abh], উভি [ubhi], আমা [ama], আম [aam], উমি [umi], আকা [aka], আক [akh], উকি [uki], আখা [akha], আখ [akh], উখি

Figure 11. Bangla vowels plot of six-vowel system

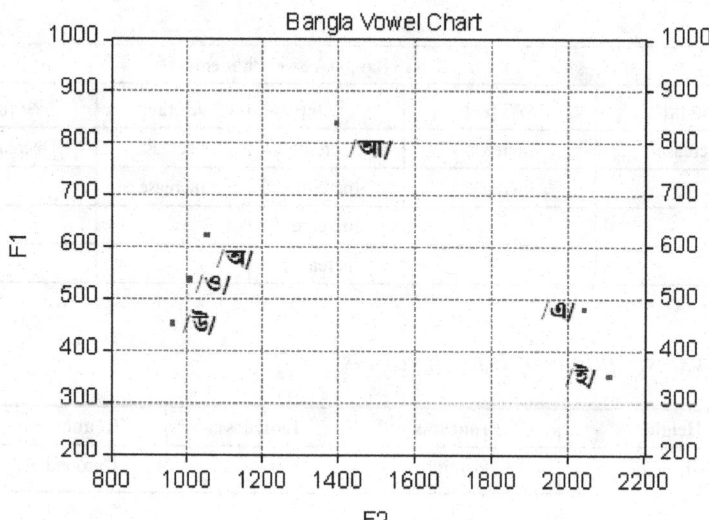

Figure 12. Bangla vowels plot (inverted and reversed)

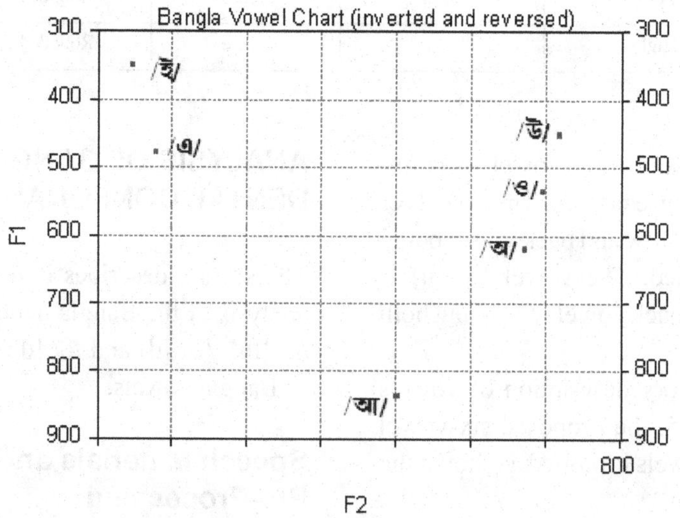

[ukhi], আগা [aga], আগ [agh], আগি [ugi], আঘা [agha], আঘ [agh], উঘি [ughi]. These sounds were analyzed in six long vowel contexts /আ/ [a], /ই/ [i], /ও/ [o], and /উ/ [u] for an accurate description of their acoustic characteristics/features and the differences between the corresponding cognate sounds in the two classes. Various parameters like duration of closure/voice bar, duration of burst, voice onset time, duration of aspiration, rate of second formant transition and burst frequencies and amplitudes have been studied in details.

Prior to any analysis, the complete consonant data set was manually segmented to [Vowel Consonant Vowel]. The starting and ending times of the vocalic nuclei was measured by hand from high-resolution digital spectrograms. Only the first 10ms of the release burst or the whole burst was considered.

The spectral analysis of these syllables was carried out using digital spectrograms and other techniques like short time FFT and LPC spectra, pitch, formants, waveforms and envelope displayed together. Using the spectrogram most of the important acoustical events were studied in time as well as frequency domain. Duration and sequences of events in each sound/syllable was noted down using time scale of the spectrogram. Unlike other sounds, which can be described largely in terms of steady-state spectra, stops are transient phonemes and thus are acoustically complex. Bangla consonant-vowel (CV) syllables of the type stop plus vowel consist of at least four phonetic segments, viz. the closure or voicebar, burst, voice onset time (VOT), aspiration and a voiced interval for vowel.

Acoustic Measurements for Perception

Burst Frequency: The burst frequency is the frequency at which the maximum amplitude in the frequency spectrum occurred. The burst frequency was estimated from the frequency spectrum of the release burst. Burst frequency measurements were made using a 20-pole LPC spectrum. A half-Hamming window of 20ms was used that is (only the latter half of the Hamming window was multiplied with the 10ms of the release burst samples). The LPC spectrum was obtained using a 512-point FFT. The frequency of the maximum amplitude of spectral peak was extracted from LPC spectrum using a global peak picking algorithm. Once this acoustic analysis was done for the clean consonants, the frequencies at which the peaks for the consonants occurred were computed and plotted.

Burst frequencies depend on the place of articulation of the stop as well as the vowel context. The spectral difference among the stop consonants across the places of articulation are primarily reflected in the spectra of the burst and formant transitions of the target vowel. The burst frequencies of the same consonants do show slight variation in different vowel contexts.

Experimental Results

The FFT and LPC smoothed spectra along with the formant contour and log Mel power spectrum of the same speech segments are captured in another two frames. The formant contour clearly demonstrates the transition of formant frequencies due to vowel-consonant-vowel phonation. The first formant F1 tends to increase due to the closure of the oral tract and decreases again due to the opening.

In English, in the production of /t/ and /d/ sounds, the tip of the tongue comes in contact with the alveolar ridge while in Bangla, there is no alveolar sound, rather it has either dental consonants or retroflex. These sounds are produced by the tip of the tongue in interaction with the back part of the alveolar ridge.

As can be seen from the Table 16, the place of articulation and the vowel context determine the burst frequencies of dental and retroflex sounds. The burst and formant transition of the target vowel varies across the stop consonants. The same stop consonant shows variation in the formant frequency transition in different vowel context. The vowel context /ই/ [i] shows significant difference in formant transition between firsṭ formant F1 and second formant F2 for all the retroflex sounds of Bangla except for the phonation /ট/ [t]. The formant transition between the second and third formant frequency F2 and F3 is consistent throughout different retroflex and dental sounds. Besides, the context /উ/ [u] and /ও/ [o] shows persistent formant transitions for different retroflex sounds as can be seen from the Table 16.

The relative burst amplitudes of various retroflex and dental sounds of Bangla in different

Table 16. Comparison of burst frequencies of dental and retroflex sounds

Formant	/ত/ [t]	/ট/ [t]	/থ/[th]	/ঠ/ [th]	/দ/ [d]	/ড/ [d]	/ধ/ [dh]	/ঢ/[dh]
a. /আ/ [a] context								
F1 (Hz)	600	950	950	600	380	350	750	550
F2 (Hz)	1450	1900	2000	1800	1700	1850	1900	1750
F3 (Hz)	2700	3100	2900	2750	2700	2850	3000	2650
F4 (Hz)	3400	3450	3900	3500	3350	3600	3850	3650
b. /ই/ [i] context								
F1 (Hz)	400	1050	450	350	350	300	450	350
F2 (Hz)	2150	1750	1850	2050	2150	2100	2150	2100
F3 (Hz)	2550	3150	2950	2850	2900	2950	2800	2950
F4 (Hz)	3800	3350	4150	3850	3250	3900	3750	3950
c. /উ/ [u] context								
F1 (Hz)	550	400	450	400	375	250	350	300
F2 (Hz)	1600	1650	1750	1950	1650	1500	1600	1625
F3 (Hz)	2750	2850	3150	3050	2750	2650	3000	3250
F4 (Hz)	3850	3450	3550	3500	3450	3700	3950	4150
d. /ও/ [o] context								
F1 (Hz)	550	500	500	550	250	450	450	300
F2 (Hz)	1500	1850	1900	2050	1725	1550	1450	1600
F3 (Hz)	2850	2650	2550	2770	2550	2550	2850	2850
F4 (Hz)	3550	3500	3950	3350	3950	3450	3900	3800

vowel contexts were measured using the same settings and all the measurements were recorded in the Table 17 and Table 18 as shown.

Table 17 and Table 18 postulate the relative burst amplitude of retroflex and dental sounds in different vowel contexts. As can be seen from the Table 17, the consonant /ত/ [t] in the vowel context /আ/ [aa] shows relatively higher burst amplitude for second formant frequency compared to higher formant frequencies. While the consonant /ত/ [t] in the vowel context /ই/ [i], /উ/ [u] and /ও/ [o] shows relatively higher amplitude for the burst for higher formant frequency compared to lower formant frequencies. The consonants /থ/ [th], /দ/ [d], and /ধ/ [dh] shows higher relative burst amplitude in the vowel context /আ/ [aa] and /ই/ [i].

The consonant /ট/ [t] shows higher relative burst amplitude in higher formant frequencies in all vowel contexts. In case of consonant /ঠ/ [th] the relative burst amplitude is high in higher formant frequencies except for the vowel context /আ/ [aa]. The consonant /ড/ [d] also shows higher relative burst amplitude in higher formant frequencies except for the vowel contexts /আ/ [aa] and /উ/ [u]. In case of consonant /ঢ/ [dh] the relative burst amplitude is higher in higher formant frequencies for all vowel contexts under the present study.

The formant frequency transition of various retroflex and dental sounds of Bangla in different vowel contexts were measured through the formant contour observation and all the measurements were recorded in Table 19 and Table 20 as shown.

Table 17. Relative burst amplitudes of retroflex sounds in vowel contexts (with relative level difference; A2F: F2 amplitude; A3F: F3 amplitude; A4F: F4 amplitude)

Consonant	/আ/ [aa]	/ই/ [i]	/উ/ [u]	/ও/ [o]
/ত/ [t]	A2F> A3F> A4F	A4F> A3F> A2F	A4F> A2F> A3F	A4F> A2F> A3F
/থ/ [th]	A4F> A2F> A3F	A4F> A2F> A3F	A2F> A3F> A4F	A3F> A4F> A2F
/দ/ [d]	A4F> A2F> A3F	A3F> A4F> A2F	A2F> A3F> A4F	A4F> A3F = A2F
/ধ/ [dh]	A4F> A2F> A3F	A3F> A4F> A2F	A2F> A3F> A4F	A2F> A3F> A4F

Table 18. Relative burst amplitudes of dental sounds in vowel contexts (with relative level difference; A2F: F2 amplitude; A3F: F3 amplitude; A4F: F4 amplitude)

Consonant	/আ/ [aa]	/ই/ [i]	/উ/ [u]	/ও/ [o]
/ত/ [t]	A3F> A4F> A2F	A4F> A3F> A2F	A4F> A3F> A2F	A4F> A2F> A3F
/থ/ [th]	A2F> A4F> A3F	A3F> A2F> A4F	A4F> A3F> A2F	A4F> A3F> A2F
/দ/ [d]	A2F> A4F> A3F	A3F> A4F> A2F	A2F> A4F> A3F	A4F> A3F> A2F
/ধ/ [dh]	A4F> A3F> A2F	A4F> A2F> A3F	A4F> A3F = A2F	A4F> A3F> A2F

Table 19. Formant transition of retroflex sounds to and from the vowel segment

Consonant	F1	F2	F3	F4
/ত/ [t]	high – low – high	Steady	low-high	high-low
/থ/ [th]	high – low – high	Steady	low-high	high-low
/দ/ [d]	high – low – high	Steady	low-high	high-low
/ধ/ [dh]	high – low – high	Steady	low-high	high-low

Table 20. Formant transition of dental sounds to and from the vowel segment

Consonant	F1	F2	F3	F4
/ত/ [t]	high – low – high	low-high	high-low-high	Steady
/থ/ [th]	high – low – high	low-high	high-low-high	Steady
/দ/ [d]	high – low – high	low-high	high-low-high	Steady
/ধ/ [dh]	high – low – high	low-high	high-low-high	Steady

As can be seen from the Table 19 and Table 20, for all the retroflex and dental sounds of Bangla, the first formant frequency F1 transits from high to low during the movement towards the vowel segment and to high during the retraction from the vowel segment. In case of retroflex sounds, the second formant frequency is steady during the transition but the third formant frequency transits from low to high and the fourth formant frequency from high to low while the segment moves to and from the vowel. In case of dental sounds as can be seen from the Table 20, the fourth formant frequency is steady during the transition but the second formant frequency transits from low to high and the third formant frequency from high to low during movement towards the vowel and to high while the segment moves away from the vowel.

FUTURE RESEARCH DIRECTIONS

Further research work can be carried out incorporating the results of the present investigations in the area of automatic speech recognition, text to speech, speech to speech and speech to text synthesis and other related areas of speech production and perception by the machine. There are many directions in which this research can be further extended. Some of the possible ideas are discussed in this section.

Bangla Vowel Duration and Logarithmic Distance

Even though the Bangla vowel durational study presented in this work has given an understanding of the durational characteristics of vowels in word intial-, medial-, and end- positions and has shown variations that exists in different context. The phonological processes like aspiration, word final devoicing, and the long vowels are not considered in the present study. Thus a more detailed study considering the phonological aspects of Bangla is required to map the vowel duration with articulatory variation for the speech recognizer. Specifically, durational description of Bangla vowels in other environments and in different syllable settings needs to be made.

Bangla Vowel Classification and Vowel Space

The classification of Bangla cardinal vowels /আ/ [aa], /অ/ [a], /ই/ [e], /এ/ [ae], /ও/ [o], and /উ/ [u] based on the articulatory perception from spectral measurements presented in this work which has shown vowels location in F2-F1 vowel plane. The gender specific as well as age group classification within the vowel space is not considered in the present study. Thus another study covering both the gender and age group is required to define the general classification scheme more effectively in case of automatic labeling and recognition of phonemes. Besides, cross linguistic study of vowel space is required to identify features of both common and uncommon for language identification.

Bangla Retroflex Consonants

In this research work, Bangla dental consonants have been studied to identify the spectral characteristics in different vowel contexts. The burst frequency and the formant transition to and from the consonant segment along with the relative amplitude measurements have been considered in this work. The durational characteristics and acoustic moment measurements are not covered along with the gender specific analysis in this work. This study is required to address durational characteristics, acoustic moments and gender specific analysis to provide a framework for synthesis and recognition of Bangla retroflex sounds.

DISCUSSION AND CONCLUSION

The mean duration of Bangla vowels are recorded at different word initial, medial and end position of the word as shown in the Figure 1 through Figure 6 and summary observations are recorded in Table 1 through Table 3. The comparison of duration of vowels revealed that manner of articulation can be robustly distinguished by evaluating the phoneme length of the vowels in word-initial, -medial, and -end positions.

The fundamental frequency, along with the formant frequencies for different vowel tokens, are recorded as shown in Table 2 through the Table 5 and in Figure 7 and Figure 8. The fundamental frequency variation in different vowel contexts showed the speaker dependence property. Table 5 showed the mean value of formant frequencies along with the bandwidth and the standard deviation of Bangla vowels produced by different male and female speakers and summarizes the formant characteristics of Bangla vowels.

The logarithmic distance between the formant frequencies were recorded as shown in the Figure 9 and Figure 10. This measurement revealed that distance between F3 and F2 signifies the difference between Bangla vowel /অ/ [a] and /আ/ [aa]. The distance between formant F2 and F1 signifies the vowel /ও/ [o] and the vowel /ই/ [e] is also distinguished through the distance between F2 and F1.

The analysis of Bangla vowel and consonant phonemes are accomplished and results are postulated in Table 6 through Table 15 and some of the results analysis is displayed in Figure 7 and Figure 8 both for male and female speakers.

Furthermore we have investigated different vowel normalization techniques and validated the procedure used for the vowel normalization. We have successfully classified Bangla vowels through acoustic characterization and proposed a vowel system for computer analysis, synthesis and recognition of Bangla. Vowel normalization is applied on the formant vectors derived across speakers to identify the classification of vowels in the form of open, close or round category and all the respective measurements are recorded in Table 6 through Table 13. The classification is summarized in Table 14.

The relationship between the first and second formants is mainly summarized in a vowel space plot. Here this was done by matching grid references of first and second formants of each vowel. Thus, as shown in Figure 11, based on the formant frequency values, a vowel space plot of Bangla vowels was developed. The resultant plot shown in Figure 11 is not what we normally encounter in phonetics. So it was inverted to achieve the common way of the presentation which is called inverted and reversed model. In this graph the X axis, which is based on second formant values, starts with the lowest frequency and ends with the highest, and the Y axis starts with the lowest and goes up in terms of frequency values as shown in Figure 12.

As indicated in the Figure 11 and Figure 12, distribution of the three vowels /অ/ [a], /ই/ [e] and /উ/ [u] in the vowel space supports the idea of sufficiency of these three vowels as the major means of communication in the majority of the languages of the world in general and in Bangla in particular. That is, in majority of the languages, including Bangla, these vowels are present and they are the basic vowels. The graphic investigation of the place of occurrence of these vowels in the plot shows that, in Bangla, they happen to occur at the corners of this plot. The relative and symmetrical distance of these vowels from one another, which creates a triangular shape in the vowel space, is an indication of a kind of pressure to form a systematic pattern in the vowel system of Bangla language. In addition to these cornering vowels, Bangla language has developed three other intermediate vowels /ই/ [e], /আ/ [aa], and /ও/ [o] to create a symmetrically distributed vowel system to cater the communicative needs of the language users.

As regards to Bangla language this chart is believed to be the first authentic chart which has ever been developed on acoustic grounds. The findings indicate the presence of six vowels distributed symmetrically in the vowel space plot. The findings further lend support to the idea of efficiency of the three vowels /অ/ [a], /ই/ [e], and /উ/ [u] as the major means of communication in the majority of languages of the world. In Bangla these vowels appear to occur at the corners of this vowel space. Furthermore, the results suggest that the pressure to form pattern has made Bangla language to develop a vowel system which could be described in a triangular auditory space. In addition to these cornering vowels, Bangla language has developed three other intermediate vowels /ই/ [e], /আ/ [aa], and /ও/ [o] to create a symmetrically distributed vowel system to cater the communicative needs of the language.

The findings and results of the present study could be utilized in linguistic studies such as dialectology, or practical studies like developing a computer based devise aiming at helping the foreign language learners to improve their pronunciation.

Bangla dental consonants are analyzed for spectral representations and the results are postulated in Table 17 through Table 19. It has been observed at the burst position that formants three and four contained most of the energy in case of retroflex sounds while formants four contained most of the energy in case of dentals. Retroflex sounds have a very strong burst release as compared to the corresponding dental sounds. Also there is general lowering of the third and fourth formants in case of retroflex as compared to dentals. Voice bar frequency is about 10 to 15% lower in case of retroflex as compared to dentals.

In case of voiced stops, it has been observed that the center frequency of the voice bar varies between 200-300 Hz, and the amplitude of the first resonance is high while all higher resonance are strongly damped. This type of spectral shape is obtained by using a spectral tilt factor. In case of voiced aspirated stops /থ/ [th] and /ধ/ [dh], a break in the voice bar prior to the aspiration is observed. Duration of voice bar is around 70-75ms in retroflex and 60 to 65ms in dental sounds depending on the vowel context under this study.

It has also been observed that the bandwidths of the formants are narrower (i.e. the formant peaks are better defined) in the case of voiced aspirated sounds /দ/ [d], /ধ/ [dh], /ড/ [d], and /ঢ/ [dh] as compared to unvoiced aspirated sounds /ত/ [t], /থ/ [th], /ট/ [t], and /ঠ/ [th]. The formant transitions from burst frequency to the target vowel frequency are part of the aspiration segment. Aspiration duration is about 90-110ms in case of retroflex sounds, while the duration is 80-100ms for dental sounds.

REFERENCES

Ali, M. G. (1990). *Digital processing of short duration signals and design of digital filters*. (M.Sc. Thesis). Rajshahi University. Rajshahi, Bangladesh.

Ali, M. G., Aziz, M. A., & Sobhan, M. A. (1993). Short-duration voice signal analysis of selected Bangla vowels. *The Rajshahi University Studies, 21*.

Blumstein, S., & Stevens, K. (1979). Acoustic invariance in speech production. *The Journal of the Acoustical Society of America, 66*, 1001–1017. doi:10.1121/1.383319 PMID:512211.

Das, B., Mandal, S., Mitra, P., & Basu, A. (2012). Effect of aging on speech features and phoneme recognition: A study on Bengali voicing vowels. In *International Journal of Speech Technology*. Springer. doi:10.1007/s10772-012-9147-3.

Datta, A. K., Sengupta, R., Dey, N., Banerjee, B. M., & Nag, D. (1998a). Perception of nasality in bangali vowels: Role of harmonics between F0, F1. In *Proceedings of International Conferences on Computational Linguistics, Speech and Document Processing*. IEEE.

Datta, A. K., Sengupta, R., Dey, N., Banerjee, B. M., & Nag, D. (1998b). Spectral cues of nasality in inherently nasal bengali vowels. In *Proceedings of International Conferences on Computational Linguistics, Speech and Document Processing*. IEEE.

Datta, A. K., Sengupta, R., Dey, N., Banerjee, B. M., & Nag, D. (1998c). Speaker Identification using pitch in Bengali. In *Proceedings of International Conferences on Computational Linguistics, Speech and Document Processing*. IEEE.

Dorman, M., & Loizou, P. (1996). Relative spectral change and formant transitions as cues to labial an alveolar place of articulation. *The Journal of the Acoustical Society of America, 100*, 3825–3830. doi:10.1121/1.417238 PMID:8969483.

Gerwirth, L. L., & Blumstein, S. (1984). A reconsideration of acoustic invariance for place of articulation in diffuse stop consonants: Evidence from a cross-language study. *The Journal of the Acoustical Society of America, 76*, 391–404. doi:10.1121/1.391580 PMID:6480990.

Hai, M. A. (1966). *Bengali language handbook*. Washington, DC: Center for Applied Linguistics.

Hai, M. A. (2000). *Dhani vignan 0 bangla dhvanitattwa*. Mullick Brothers.

Hamid, M. E. (1993). *Software development for computer processing of bangla speech*. (M.Sc. Thesis). Rajshahi University. Rajshahi, Bangladesh.

Hamid, M. E., Siddique, S. A., Chisty, K. J. A., & Sobhan, M. A. (1995). *Power spectrum analysis of bangla vowels and consonants by windowed short time fourier transforms. Rajshahi University Studies*. Rajshahi.

Hoemeke, K. A., & Diehl, L. R. (1994). Perception of vowel height: The role of F1-F2 distance. *The Journal of the Acoustical Society of America, 96*, 661–674. doi:10.1121/1.410305 PMID:7930066.

Hossain, S. A. (1991). *Experimental and computer aided analysis of active filters and analog and digital processing of music and bangla speech signals*. (M.Sc. Thesis). Rajshahi University. Rajshahi, Bangladesh.

Hossain, S. A., Rahman, M. L., & Ahmed, F. (2005). A review on bangla phoneme production and perception for computational approaches. In *Proceedings of 7th WSEAS International Conference on Mathematical Methods and Computational Techniques in Electrical Engineering*. Sofia, Bulgaria: IEEE.

Hossain, S. A., Rahman, M. L., & Ahmed, F. (2007). Acoustic classification on bangla vowels. In *Proceedings of XX International Conference on Computer, Information, and Systems Science, and Engineering*, (Vol. 20, p. 321). Barcelona, Spain: IEEE.

Hossain, S. A., & Sobhan, M. A. (1997). Fundamental frequency tracking of bangla voiced speech. In *Proceedings of National Conference on Computer and Information Systems (NCCIS)*. Dhaka, Bangladesh: NCCIS.

Islam, R. (1970). *An introduction to colloquial Bangali*. Dhaka, Bangladesh: Central Board for Development of Bangla.

Ladefoged, P., & Maddieson, I. (1996). *The sounds of the world's languages*. Oxford, UK: Blackwell Publishers.

Mandal, S., Das, B., Mitra, P., & Basu, A. (2011). Developing Bengali speech corpus for phone recognizer using optimum text selection technique. In *Proceedings of the International Conference on Asian Language Processing*. Penang, Malaysia: IEEE.

Paramanik, A. K. (1977). *Acoustical study on the vowel structure of Bengali language*. (Doctoral Dissertation). Tohoku University. Japan.

Paramanik, M., & Kido, K. (1976). Bengali speech: Formant structure of single vowels and initial vowels of words. In *Proceedings of the IEEE International Conference on ICASSP*. ICASSP.

Pickett, J. M. (1980). *The sounds of speech communication*. Austin, TX: Pro-Ed, Inc..

Quatieri, T. F. (2002). *Discrete-time speech signal processing*. New York: Prentice Hall.

Rahman, M. L. (1992). *Power spectrum and formants extraction of bangla speech*. (M.Sc. Thesis). Rajshahi University. Rajshahi, Bangladesh.

Syrdal, A. K., & Gopal, H. S. (1986). A perceptual model of vowel recognition based on the auditory representation of American English vowels. *The Journal of the Acoustical Society of America*, *79*, 1086–1100. doi:10.1121/1.393381 PMID:3700864.

Talukder, M. M. R. (1992). *Spectral and formant analysis of bangla speech (alphabets)*. (M.Sc. Thesis). Rajshahi University. Rajshahi, Bangladesh.

Traunmuller, H. (1988). Paralinguistic variation and invariance in the characteristic frequencies of vowels. *Phonetica*, *45*, 1–29. doi:10.1159/000261809 PMID:3237776.

Uddin, M. J. (1993). *Computer aided spectral analysis of bangla phonemes*. (M.Sc. Thesis). Rajshahi University. Rajshahi, Bangladesh.

Uddin, M. J., Sobhan, M. A., & Chisty, K. J. A. (2001). Effect of window length on the formant frequency extraction of bangla phoneme. In *Proceedings of International Conferences on Computer and Information Technology*. Dhaka, Bangladesh: IEEE.

Chapter 12
Bengali (Bangla) Information Retrieval

Debasis Ganguly
Dublin City University, Ireland

Johannes Leveling
Dublin City University, Ireland

Gareth J. F. Jones
Dublin City University, Ireland

ABSTRACT

This chapter introduces Bengali Information Retrieval (IR) to students by explaining the fundamental concepts of IR such as indexing, retrieval, and evaluation metrics. This chapter also provides a survey of and comparisons between various Bengali language-specific methodologies, and hence can serve researchers particularly interested in the state-of-the-art developments in Bengali IR. It can also act as a guideline for application developers on how to set up an information retrieval system for the Bengali language. All steps for creating and evaluating an information retrieval system are introduced, including content processing, indexing, retrieval models, and evaluation. Special attention is given to language-specific aspects of Bengali information retrieval. In addition, the chapter discusses cross-lingual information retrieval, where queries are entered in English with an objective to retrieving Bengali documents.

INTRODUCTION

The World Wide Web is growing at an astounding rate, both in terms of the volume of content available and the number of individuals with access to the Web. The majority of professionally authored content is typically still produced in English. However, potentially valuable content is being created in a multitude of other languages. Machine-Translated (MT) versions of this content may be generated for some languages, but the limited availability of high quality MT means that this is not always possible for all language pairs. At the same time, access to digital information is becoming more important and, due to the increase in amount and diversity of data, more difficult.

DOI: 10.4018/978-1-4666-3970-6.ch012

Bangla (or Bengali), one of the more important Indo-Iranian languages, is the sixth-most popular in the world and spoken by a population that now exceeds 250 million, of which more than 193 million are native speakers[1]. Geographical Bangla-speaking population percentages are as follows: Bangladesh (over 95%), and the Indian states of Andaman and Nicobar Islands (26%), Assam (28%), Tripura (67%), and West Bengal (85%). The global total includes those who are now in diaspora in Canada, Malawi, Nepal, Pakistan, Saudi Arabia, Singapore, United Arab Emirates, United Kingdom, and the United States. However, compared to languages such as English, Bengali is a low-resource language, i.e. the range of natural language processing tools and linguistic resources is still small. For example, the English Wikipedia comprises almost 4 million articles while the Bengali Wikipedia has little more than 20,000 articles. Research on language-specific aspects of Bengali information retrieval is still in its infancy.

The process of Information Retrieval (IR) can be broadly defined as satisfying a user's information need by retrieving relevant documents from a collection of documents, where relevant means that a document contains the information necessary to satisfy the user's need. IR encompasses search on collections of text documents, either structured or unstructured, but also search over collections of spoken recordings, music and other audio data, images and video. Most IR approaches still focus on text retrieval or on text annotations of multimedia data. In designing an IR System (IRS), the key issues are to determine methodologies for: (1) document representation; (2) query representation; and (3) a similarity measure for comparing a query with documents. Language-specific adaptations are particularly required for the first two components, namely finding suitable representations for the documents and queries.

Early IR research focused on development of techniques for English (e.g. at TREC, http://trec.nist.gov). More recent work has explored development of effective techniques for European (e.g. at CLEF, http://clef2012.org/) and Asian languages (e.g. at NTCIR, http://research.nii.ac.jp/ntcir/index-en.html). The inception and success of FIRE, the Forum for Information Retrieval and Evaluation (http://www.isical.ac.in/~clia/) has shown the interest in the development and automatic evaluation of IRS for Indian languages and has resulted in the creation of additional language resources for Bengali to aid Natural Language Processing (NLP) and IR.

The rest of this chapter is organized as follows: Section 1 (The Search Process) introduces the search process in general. Section 2 (Content Preprocessing) presents different normalization and conversion methods for transforming a set of files into a document collection. Section 3 (Indexing) introduces content processing and the most widely used index structure, the inverted file. Section 4 (Retrieval Models) presents alternative retrieval models. Section 5 (Enhancing IR effectiveness by Relevance Feedback) describes methods to improve IR effectiveness. Section 6 (Cross-Language IR) presents approaches to cross-language IR. Section 7 (Evaluation) presents evaluation metrics and the most important research results from evaluation initiatives and Section 8 (Bengali IR Benchmarking) reviews the various Bengali IR tasks undertaken till date in open evaluation forums. This is followed by Section 9 (Towards Best Practises), which provides a comparison between various approaches undertaken for Bengali IR. Section 10 (Tools and Resources) provides a list of tools and resources useful for starting Bengali IR experiments. Finally, Section 11 (Conclusion) concludes this chapter.

1. THE SEARCH PROCESS

From a user's point of view, the search process starts with an information need and comprises submitting a search query which attempts to express this need to an IRS. The IRS responds with a list of potentially relevant documents, typically ordered by likelihood of relevance to the query. The user then browses through the results, views selected documents, and may repeat the search with a reformulated query until the information need is satisfied. From a researcher's point of view, the task is to optimize the quality of the retrieval process based on search effectiveness measurements on standard evaluation data sets. Typically, evaluation metrics such as precision and recall are employed to measure the quality of an IRS, evaluating its ability to retrieve all and only relevant documents. The practical objective is to minimize user efforts required to satisfy their information needs.

Figure 1 shows a generic IRS. The user formulates his information need as a query and submits it to the IRS. The IRS comprises a document index which contains representations of a collection of documents. The query is compared to the document representations in the index and their similarity is computed. The user then examines the retrieved set of documents until the information need is satisfied or he decides to reformulate the query. The query reformulation process can also be automated as part of the IRS (e.g. automatic query expansion, discussed in Section 5). The output of the IRS is typically a ranked list of documents ordered by decreasing similarity to the query.

Figure 1. Generic information retrieval system

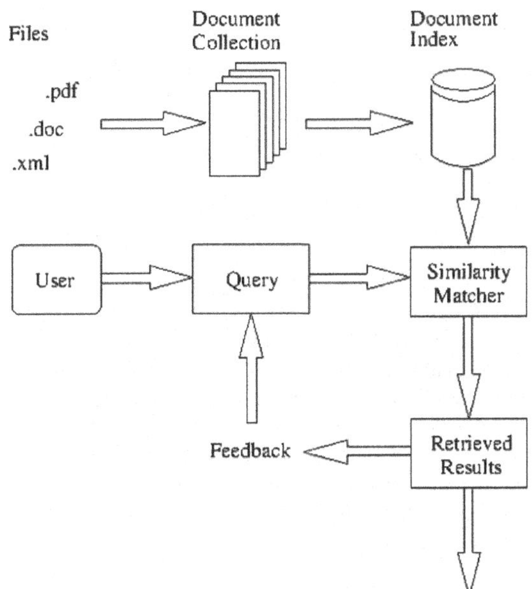

The quality of the retrieved set of documents can be improved by explicit user feedback, i.e. by asking the user which documents are relevant and which are not. The system then attempts to improve on the search results with the help of this explicit user feedback. This process is known as relevance feedback (RF). However, in practice users of a search system are reluctant to make the effort to provide explicit feedback. When the user does not provide feedback, an IRS then can assume that a number of top ranked documents are relevant, and use this information for a second retrieval step to improve on the initial retrieval results. Since the process is automatic and does not rely on actual relevance information or manual user intervention, it is known as Pseudo-Relevance Feedback (PRF) or blind relevance feedback. Since often not all documents presumed to be relevant actually are, PRF can have an adverse effect on IR effectiveness on some queries.

One major challenge in developing an IRS is to adapt the similarity matching process to reflect the importance of terms with respect to the information need. Consider, for example, the query "Find documents on Bengali information retrieval." Normally, there will be very few documents containing all query terms. and documents containing the terms "Bengali" and "retrieval" should be scored higher than documents containing "find" and "on", because the latter two do not characterize the information need well and occur frequently in non-relevant documents. Thus, query terms are associated with different term weights for document scoring.

Two additional problems typically make the task of finding relevant document more difficult: polysemy and synonymy. Polysemy occurs when one word has different meanings. For instance, the English word "bank" could refer to the financial institution or to a river bank. This implies that a search for "bank" would return documents about both senses. Synonymy means that the same concept can be expressed with different words. For example "bank" and "financial institution" can be used interchangeably in most contexts. This means that a search for "bank" would not find documents with the term "financial institution". An example of polysemy in Bengali can be seen by the use of the word "জাল" which could mean "net" or "forged." Note that the ambiguous word "জাল", with an intended meaning of "forged," in fact occurs in the description text of the sample query shown in Box 1. Polysemy and synonymy are among the main causes for low IR effectiveness.

Throughout the chapter, we will use a Bengali query example to explain the working principles of each method that we will be discussing later on. This example Bengali query is a sample from the FIRE-2010 ad-hoc test set, and is shown in Box 1, along with the equivalent query in English. The structure of the queries and the significance of each XML tag is discussed in more detail in Section 7.1. For now, let us assume that the text enclosed within the <title> tag is the ad-hoc query used.

2. CONTENT PREPROCESSING

Before document content can be entered into an IRS, various stages of preprocessing are required. The exact preprocessing methods applied are language-specific and vary depending on the retrieval algorithms to be used and on the functionality of the IRS. In broad terms, the preprocessing stages extract features from the documents which can be used for search by applying selected linguistic processing. The basic search feature extracted is typically the word, but phrases or other multi-word units may be supported, possibly in conjunction with other information such as proximity of words in a document. Typically, the same preprocessing techniques are applied to both the queries and documents. The extraction process includes transforming data to a format that the IRS can process, e.g. converting a PDF document into raw text or text with minimal markup. The conversion is supported by tools such as the Apache Tika toolkit (http://tika.apache.org/), which detects and extracts structured text from various document formats using existing parser libraries. File formats supported by Tika include DOC, RTF, PDF, MP3, MP4, and HTML.

Structured documents in HTML, XML, or SGML are usually easy to parse for feature extraction with suitable parsers, but pose problems when their markup is invalid or broken, when

Box 1. A sample query (taken from the FIRE-2010 test topics for ad-hoc IR)

<top lang="bn"> <num>100</num> <title>অবৈধ পাসপোর্ট মামলায় মণিকা বেদী</title> <desc>মণিকা বেদীর বিরুদ্ধে হায়দরাবাদ থেকে জাল পাসপোর্ট করানোর অভিযোগ</desc> <narr>প্রাসঙ্গিক নথিতে মণিকার বিরুদ্ধে নাম ভাঁড়িয়ে হায়দরাবাদে পাসপোর্ট জালিয়াতির অভিযোগ বা সে বিষয়ে সিবিআই তদন্ত সংক্রান্ত তথ্য থাকা চাই । অন্য কোথাও করানো জাল পাসপোর্ট সংক্রান্ত তথ্য এখানে প্রাসঙ্গিক নয় । </narr> </top>	<top lang="en"> <num>100</num> <title>Monica Bedi and the passport forgery case</title> <desc>Monica Bedi charged with obtaining forged passports at Hyderabad.</desc> <narr>A relevant document should contain information about charges against Monica Bedi of acquiring a forged passport under a false name at Hyderabad, and the investigations conducted by the CBI in this regard. Information about forged passports obtained elsewhere is not relevant.</narr> </top>

named characters or character encodings are used incorrectly, or when the content is not just text, but binary data (e.g. an image). This requires robust processing of the documents, which is supported by error-correcting parsers such as TagSoup (http://ccil.org/~cowan/XML/tagsoup/) or Beautiful Soup (http://lxml.de/elementsoup.html).

The heterogeneous nature of text documents means that text normalization is often an important preprocessing stage. This text normalization can include multiple steps, and is especially important for languages such as Bengali. For example, the Bengali script uses visually similar glyphs (writing symbols), which can result from incorrect conversion (OCR errors) or input by non-native speakers. Inconsistent character encodings can also pose a significant problem and require normalizations.

Character normalization is an essential preprocessing step, because unnormalized texts encoded with UTF-8 may use different multi-byte character encodings for the same character. For example, the typographical ligature character "ff" (UTF-8 character code U+FB00) is semantically equivalent to two consecutive characters "f". As an example in Bengali, the vowel "ো" can be represented with two possible encodings either as a single character U+09C8, or as two consecutive characters "ে" (U+09C7) and "া" (U+09BE).

An IR application should aim to normalize queries and documents in the same manner. For example, it is convenient to substitute every occurrence of U+09C7 followed by U+09BE in the document collection to a single character U+09C8, this step being called character normalization. Returning to our example query, if the word "পাসপোর্ট" (EN: passport) is encoded with the single vowel "ো" in the query, whereas in the document index it is encoded with "ে" followed by "া", these two will essentially be treated as different words and we will miss out on results for this particular query term.

A minimum normalization for an UTF-8 encoded text can be obtained by following the guidelines for canonical decomposition from the International Components for Unicode (ICU), implementing the standard normalization forms described in the Unicode Standard Annex #15 - Unicode Normalization Forms (http://www.unicode.org/unicode/reports/tr15/). These normalization steps guarantee a fixed order of characters where multiple variants are allowed.

In addition to standard character normalization as per Unicode Standard, character normalization rules specific to Bengali have successfully been applied in Bengali IR (Leveling & Jones, 2010), using the following normalization rules in sequence:

1. Internal word space is removed (e.g. characters U+200C and U+200D).
2. "ঁ" (*Chandra Bindu*) and "ং" (*Anusvara*) are mapped to "ং" (*Chandra Bindu*).
3. "ঁ" followed by a vowel is mapped to the corresponding vowel.
4. The punctuation character "।" (*Dari*) is removed.
5. Combinations of "্" (*Hrasanta*) and a consonant are replaced by the corresponding consonant character.
6. Long vowels are mapped to the corresponding short form.
7. Accents (which are typically part of transcribed foreign names) are removed.
8. Digit symbols in Bengali, i.e. "০" - "৯" are mapped to corresponding numeric literals in Roman script, i.e. "0" - "9", because documents may contain both forms.

These rules serve as a means to normalize orthographic variants, similar to work described by (Pal, Majumder, Mitra, Mitra, & Sen, 2006) on newspaper article retrieval and (Pingali, Jagarlamudi, & Varma, 2006) for Web pages. The result of the preprocessing stage is a cleaned up document or query, consisting of a sequence of tokens, which is used in the subsequent IR stages, for example in the indexing stage.

3. INDEXING

The objective of the indexing process is to organize the information in documents into efficient data structures for easy comparison to an ad-hoc search query. During search, the IRS determines a set of potentially relevant documents by matching the query with the available documents. Indexing in IR encompasses the first component as mentioned in the introduction viz. document and query representation. The most widely used data structure for effectively matching documents against a given query is the inverted file data structure (Witten, Moffat, & Bell, 1999). The principle of the inverted file structure is language-independent. Prior to being inserted into the inverted file, the document content must be processed to form the selected indexing units (e.g. words, phrases, character n-grams), broadly referred to as terms. The following sections focus on Bengali language-specific issues of choosing effective indexing units, leading to a basic overview of the construction of the inverted file. This will be illustrated with two sample Bengali documents and a query.

3.1. Tokenization

The first stage of term construction is tokenization, which is the process of converting text into a sequence of tokens for indexing. It aims at finding word boundaries and can be extended to include additional pre-processing operations such as removing punctuation characters, and case folding. For Bengali, words are usually delimited by whitespace or punctuation (a working definition of token could be a sequence of alphanumeric characters). Case folding (i.e. conversion to lower or upper case) is not necessary for Bengali script, but may prove useful as a token normalization step if foreign proper nouns or acronyms in different capitalization forms are present in a document. For example, the tokens obtained from the Bengali query shown in Box 1, are “অবৈধ” (EN: illegal), “পাসপোর্‌ট” (EN: passport), “মামলায়” (EN: case), “মণিকা” (EN: Monica), and “বেদী” (EN: Bedi).

Alternatives to tokenizing text into words are truncation, i.e. using word prefixes of fixed length as indexing units, and using character n-grams, where an n-gram is a sequence of characters from a word (McNamee, 2008). For example, the prefix of length 3 for the word “পাসপোর্ট” is “পাস”, while the other character 3-grams are: “◌াসপ”, “সপো”, “পোর্”, “◌োর্ট”. N-gram tokenization has also been shown to be effective for other applications in Bengali, such as Bengali text classification (Mansur, 2006). For an inflectional language such as Bengali, the use of fixed length character n-grams as indexing units can be an effective substitute for stemming in practise. In fact, it has been shown in FIRE ad-hoc tasks that character n-gram indexing units produce better retrieval results than whole words for Bengali retrieval (Leveling & Jones, 2010). Compared to stemming, these approaches do not rely on language-specific stemming rules and do not require additional linguistic analysis of document collections.

3.2. Stopword Removal

Some words such as articles, prepositions, pronouns, etc., commonly occur in the majority of documents in the collection. These terms do not play an important role in distinguishing relevant from non-relevant documents. They are referred to as stopwords in IR and are filtered from the extracted token sequence.

Stopwords are contained in a predetermined fixed list. Creating a stopword list involves three steps. In the first step, the most frequent or least meaningful terms in a document collection are identified, e.g. by the term frequency in the document collection. Returning to our example query of Box 1, Bengali words such as “থেকে” (EN: from) and “করানোর” (EN: done) in the description (enclosed within the “<desc>” tags) can be considered as stopwords. Additional stopwords, specific to a collection, can be obtained from collection-level statistics such as normalized *document frequency* which is the ratio of the number of documents in which a term occurs to the total number of documents in the collection, or *collection frequency* which is the number of times a term occurs in the collection divided by the collection size. Words having a normalized document frequency or collection frequency above a predefined threshold *t* (e.g. $t=0.8$) are considered as stopwords (Fox, 1992). In the next step, the list of terms is manually examined and high-frequency terms which are not considered as stopwords are removed from the list (e.g. frequent proper nouns). This step also includes completing the stopword list by adding missing word forms (e.g. morphological variants).

An alternative way to create a stopword list is to translate an existing one for another language, either manually or automatically (Chen & Gey, 2002). There are several stopword lists for Bengali available on the Internet[2]. As for other languages, stopword removal seems to benefit IR effectiveness for Bengali IR (Dolamic & Savoy, 2008; Leveling, Ganguly, & Jones, 2010a). The approach of eliminating terms based on collection-level statistics has been successfully applied for Bengali as well as other languages (Dolamic & Savoy, 2008).

3.3. Term Conflation

The goal of term conflation is to reduce different derivational or inflectional variants of the same word to a single indexing form to increase IR effectiveness and efficiency. To see how this is important for IR, let us take an example from our sample query, as shown in Box 1. The root form of the word "মামলায়" (EN: in a case) is "মামলা" (EN: case). Now let us assume that both these forms exist in the collection. There might exist relevant documents in the collection which contain the form "মামলা" but not the form "মামলায়". If an IR system treats these words differently, such relevant documents containing only the word "মামলা" may not be retrieved at high rank because of the dissimilarity with the query term "মামলায়", which means that the query and the document terms do not match. The process of term conflation in IR attempts to reduce word forms to a common form so as to treat these equivalently. This amounts to mapping both "মামলা" and "মামলায়" to the same term. For simplicity, we presume that a word consists of a root form *"r"*, to which morphological suffixes *"s"* are concatenated to obtain word forms. For example, the word form "cats" has the root form "cat" and the derivational suffix "s".

The linguistic-based approach to reduce word forms to their base form is called lemmatization (Manning & Schütze, 1999). Lemmatization removes word affixes and reduces word forms to well-formed words with the same word category (part of speech). In contrast, stemming usually focuses on removing word suffixes, the result does not have to be an existing word in the language, and stemming conflates word forms across word categories. For example, the words "মামলায়", "মামলাতে", "মামলার", "মামলারই" can all be reduced to "মামল" even though it is not a valid word of the Bengali vocabulary. In contrast, lemmatization would produce the correct Bengali word "মামলা" (EN: case).

The most important approach to term conflation is stemming, where full word forms are mapped to a common form. This can be achieved by either stripping the longest matching suffix in a list of derivational suffixes from the word, or iteratively removing suffixes from the word to account for compositionality of morphological suffixes. For example, the Porter stemmer for English (Porter, 1980) applies suffix removal rules in 5 phases to incrementally remove suffixes. Stemming approaches can be classified into different categories, e.g. by the results produced by the stemmer, e.g. light stemming (Harman, 1991) vs. aggressive stemming (Krovetz, 1993) or by the resources used, e.g. corpus-based (Xu & Croft, 1998) vs. dictionary-based (Majumder et al., 2007).

Light stemming focuses on removing only the most frequent suffixes from word forms. It has been researched as a less complex and less aggressive means to reduce words to their root form. For English, the s-stemmer, which removes only the "s", "es", and "ies" suffixes from words and other light stemming approaches have been proposed (see, for example, (Harman, 1991; Savoy, 2006)). Light stemming decreases the risk of *overstemming* (i.e. reducing two distinct words to the same common form, such as stemming "experiment" and "experience" to the same form), while it bears a risk of *understemming* (i.e. reducing words corresponding to the same root form to different forms, such as stemming "industry" and "industrial" to two different forms). In contrast, aggressive stemming as in the Krovetz stemmer tries to remove more or longer suffixes from words to map more word forms to the same common form. This has a lower risk of understemming, but a higher risk of overstemming compared to light stemming. The problems of over- and understemming indicate that stemming is not perfect. For example, the word "news" in English will usually be incorrectly stemmed to "new," unless a list of stemming exception is employed.

Stemmers can be classified as either light or aggressive depending on the number of suffix characters they remove. A too light stemming approach may not reduce word forms completely as a result of which the stemmed version of a word may still not match with the original root form of it. For example, a light stemmer may reduce the Bengali word "বেদীর" (EN: Bedi's) to "বেদী" (EN: Bedi) whereas an aggressive stemmer may reduce it to "বেদ" (EN: Bed, the name of a religious book). As can be seen from the example, a light stemmer suits this particular word, since the aggressive one reduces the given word to a word of different semantic category. For some cases on the other hand, an aggressive stemmer can yield better results, e.g. it requires an aggressive stemmer to reduce the word "জালিয়াতির" (EN: pertaining to forgery) to "জাল" (EN: forged), whereas a light stemmer may reduce it only to "জালিয়াতি" (EN: forgery) or "জালিয়াত" (EN: forger), as a result of which "জাল" (EN: forged) and "জালিয়াত" (EN: forger) might be treated as different words in the index. In contrast, too aggressive stemming might result in mapping unrelated words to the same index form, a process known as overstemming. Over- and understemming both have a detrimental effect on IR effectiveness: overstemming means that additional matches between query and document terms are found, which introduces noise into the results; understemming means that not all query terms match document terms, which will prevent finding all relevant documents.

Morphology can be compositional, i.e. multiple suffixes can be added to a word to form a new word (e.g. "hope-less-ness"). To gain control over the stemming process, each suffix corresponds to one stemming rule. The Porter stemmer for English applies about 50 rules roughly corresponding to a single simple suffix in 5 phases. It is typically considered as moderately aggressive (Porter, 1980). Removing the same number of suffixes from words in a different language may result in very light stemming. For example, Russian and Scandinavian languages have a very complex morphology (Kornilov S.A., Rakhlin N.V., & Grigorenko E.L., 2012). Compared to English, Bengali has a much richer morphology and has more complex word formation rules, which is indicated by the higher number of possible morphological suffixes.

Corpus-based stemming approaches derive their knowledge from a global analysis of a large document collection. They are typically language-independent and rely on likely co-occurrences between different forms of the same word. For instance, given the occurrence of the word "জাল" (EN: forged), it is very likely to find an occurrence of the word "জালিয়াতি" (EN: forgery) in the same document. There is nonetheless an implicit risk of deducing false correlations between words of different semantic categories. Moreover, corpus-based methods are prone to training errors and may lead to erroneous stemming for highly frequent proper nouns. A rule-based stemmer on the other hand is much faster because it can directly be applied during the dictionary construction phase of indexing and does not require pre-processing the whole corpus. However, manually creating a stemmer requires linguistic knowledge about the morphology of a language.

YASS is a clustering-based suffix stripper which has been applied to English, French, and Bengali (Majumder et al., 2007). YASS identifies clusters of equivalence classes for words by computing distance measure between strings. This stemmer relies on several dictionaries which have to be extracted from documents, i.e. all words starting with the same character have to be collected in the same word list in a scan over all documents. Similar word forms are then organized into sets, and all grouped elements are reduced to the same form.

Another approach to stemming is to automatically learn stemming rules through repeated trials of splitting up a word into different positions and determine the position which results in maximum frequency of the root in the stem dictionary and the maximum frequency of the suffix in the stem dictionary. This process is known as morpheme induction (Dasgupta & Ng, 2007). As an example of this, consider splitting up the word "জালিয়াতির" (EN: in a forgery) into a root and a suffix. This can be done as "জালিয়াতি" + "র", "জালিয়াত" + "ির", "জালিয়া" + "তির", "জালিয়" + "াতির", "জালি" + "য়াতির", "জাল" + "িয়াতির" etc. Let us assume that out of these candidate splits, "জাল" is the word which occurs with the highest frequency in the collection. The method thus learns to reduce "জালিয়াতির" to "জাল". In a second step, suffix combinations (composite suffixes) are determined via the frequency of potential root forms, allowing for a recursive morphological word structure (e.g. reducing "জালিয়াতগুলোর" (EN: pertaining to forgers) in turn to "জালিয়াতগুলো", "জালিয়াত" and "জাল"). A word is stemmed by removing the longest suffix found in the generated suffix lists or by not removing a suffix, otherwise. This approach is described in (Dasgupta and Ng, 2007) and has been tested on FIRE-2010 English and Bengali ad-hoc IR task (Leveling and Jones, 2010). The following section illustrates Bengali examples of rule-based stemming and morpheme induction methods.

3.3.1. A Rule-Based Stemmer for Bengali

Of all the approaches for stemming introduced in the previous section, it is the rule-based approach which requires language-specific adaptations in particular. We now describe the detailed steps towards developing a rule-based stemmer for Bengali. We review some morphological suffixation rules in Bengali before describing a rule-based stemmer in details.

Morphological affixing in Bengali can be categorized into: (a) inflectional, where the part-of-speech of the inflected word remains unchanged; and (b) derivational, where the part-of-speech of the inflected word changes. It is typically the nouns in Bengali that are affected by inflectional morphology. Bhattacharya, Choudhury et al. (2005) show that noun inflections can group into:

- **Title Markers:** These are titles such as "দেবী" (EN: Mrs.), "বাবু" (EN: Sir) etc. which are added as suffixes to proper nouns.
- **Classifier:** Used to denote plurality and specificity of a noun, e.g. the root word "ছবি" (EN: picture) may be inflected as "ছবিগুলো" (EN: pictures) or "ছবিটা" (EN: the picture). A classifier can also indicate the gender of a noun, e.g. "ছাত্র" (EN: student) may be inflected to "ছাত্রী" to particularly denote a female student.

- **Case Marker:** Used to denote possessive or accusative relations with other words. The possessive case marker for English is the apostrophe character. English does not use accusative markers. An example of a possessive marker is “পরিবারের” where the suffix “ে র” is added to the root form “পরিবার” (EN: family) to mean “of family.”
- **Emphasizer:** These markers are used to emphasize the current word, e.g. “ছবি” (EN: picture) may be inflected to “ছবিই” to denote an equivalent of “only a picture” in English.

All the above suffix types can appear in a word but only in the specified order, e.g. “ছবিগুলোকেও” (EN: also those pictures), where “গুলো” (those: a plurality classifier), “কে” (a case marker) and “ও” (also: an emphasizer) have been concatenated from left to right to compose the inflected form. In English language IR, “also” and “those” can be easily removed since they are stopwords. The trailing s apostrophe (“s’”), which is a plural genitive marker, can also be removed by a simple rule. However, as the example points out, in Bengali it is difficult to do so, since a sequence of words in English, including stopwords, can be equivalent to a single word in Bengali. Not normalizing this word to the base form would cause mismatches between query terms and document terms and lead to a poor retrieval effectiveness.

A rule-based stemming algorithm for Bengali can remove word suffixes in several steps:

- Delete emphasizers.
- Delete classifiers and case markers (e.g. “তা”, “টা”, “টি”, “টুকু”, “কে”, “র”, “◌ের”, “দের”, “ভাবে”).
- Delete title markers (e.g. “কারী”, “শীল”, “দেবী”, “বাবু”, “ভাই”).
- Delete plural suffixes (e.g. “রা”, “গুলো”, “গুলি”, “গুলোতে”, “গুলিতে”).
- Delete derivational suffixes.
- Remove trailing Bengali vowels, Matras, and “য়”.

Table 1 shows examples of particular cases. To handle compound suffixes, multiple rules are applied in a series of steps, as shown in the second row of the table, until no further rules are applicable.

3.3.2. Stemming by Morpheme Induction

In this section, we overview the morpheme induction method used for Bengali indexing in (Leveling & Jones, 2010). This was shown to significantly improve IR effectiveness over indexing surface word forms without stemming. The list of candidate suffixes is produced using a method suggested by (Keshava & Pitler, 2006). After extracting the surface word forms in a document collection, their frequency is computed for morpheme induction. All words *w* are analyzed by successively selecting all possible segmentation points, splitting them into a potential root form *r* and a suffix *s*. Thus, *w* is the concatenation of *r* and *s*. It is usually the case that the vocabulary will not only contain forms corresponding to inflected or derived words, but also the uninflected root forms. If the potential root form *r* is contained in the set of terms (e.g. it is part of the collection vocabulary and the root frequency is higher than 0), *s* is added to the list of suffix candidates and *r* is added to the list of root candidates. Candidate suffixes are filtered as follows:

- Suffixes with a frequency lower than a given threshold t_f are removed.
- A score is assigned to each suffix by multiplying the suffix frequency and the suffix length in characters. Using suffix length as a scoring factor is motivated by the observation that short, low-frequency suffixes are likely to be erroneous (Goldsmith, 2001).

Table 1. Rules for suffix removal with Bengali examples

Suffix Type	Bengali Example	English Translation
Emphasizer	আধিক্যই → আধিক্য	this excessiveness → excessiveness
Emphasizer and plural classifier	মন্ত্রীরাও → মন্ত্রী	ministers themselves → minister
Specific classifier	মুখোশটা → মুখোশ	that mask → mask
Possessive case marker	ভারতের → ভারত	India's → India
Plural accusative case marker	শিল্পীদের → শিল্পী	artists' → artist
Specific classifier and Possessive case marker	দুনিয়াটার → দুনিয়া	this world's → world
Derivational	স্থিতীশীল → স্থিতী	in a state of calm → calm
Title marker	করুণাদেবীর → করুণা	Mrs. Karuna's → Karuna
Plural accusative case marker and derivational	ভারতীয়দের → ভারতীয়	Indians' → Indian

The suffix candidates are then ranked by their score to obtain the top K suffixes. This parameter K depends on the vocabulary size and thus requires language-specific tuning. Composite suffixes are detected by combining all suffixes in the induced candidate list, e.g. "গুলো"+"র" in "গুলোর", where + denote the concatenation of strings. For morphologically rich languages like Bengali, composite suffix detection plays an important role in base form reduction. The detection of composite suffixes s_1+s_2 builds on the assumption that a root form r will also combine with part of the suffix (s_i). This property typically does not hold for non-composite suffixes. The morpheme induction method presumes that s_1+s_2 is a composite suffix if s_1+s_2 and s_1 are similar in terms of the words they can combine with. Specifically, s_1+s_2 and s_1 are considered to be similar if their similarity value, which is calculated as shown in Equation 1, is greater than a threshold t_s (e.g. $t_s > 0.6$).

$$similarity(s_i + s_j, s_i) = P(s_i \mid s_i + s_j) = \frac{|W^{iji}|}{|W^{ij}|} \quad (1)$$

where $|W^{iji}|$ is the number of distinct words that combine with both s_i+s_j and s_i, and $|W^{ij}|$ is the number of distinct words that combine with the compound suffix s_i+s_j. These values correspond to the morphological family size of s_i+s_j and its intersection with s_i, respectively. For example, in analyzing the word "hopelessness", we would find that both "lessness" and "less" are valid suffixes, and that the suffix "less" also combines frequently with other words. Thus, "lessness" is considered a compound suffix.

The analysis of suffixes is performed after indexing words forms. All terms are processed as described and the top ranked suffix candidates and composite suffix candidates are extracted. The extracted suffixes are then collected and the longest match (including composite suffixes) is removed from the word forms to facilitate stemming. The corpus-based stemmer processes words longer than a given threshold t_l ($t_l = 3$). All other words remain unstemmed. The stemmer determines the one longest suffix in the suffix lists (if any) and removes it from the word to produce a root form.

3.4. Phrases and Compounds

While the typical indexing unit for IR is a word, using alternative indexing units may improve IR effectiveness. In general, two cases can be considered: (1) indexing sub-words, to facilitate additional matches between query and documents;

(2) indexing multi-word units, to increase the precision of matches between terms. The first case plays an important role for IR in compounding languages, where a single word (compound) can be a concatenation of several constituent words. The main idea is to index the compound as well as its constituents (i.e. its sub-words), to allow matches even when only the compound is present in a query or documents. The Bengali language is rich in word compounding (known as *Sandhi* in Bengali). An instance of such compounding is the formation of the compound word "কৃষিজমি" (EN: farmland) from the constituents "কৃষি" (EN: farming) and জমি (EN: land). In an information need about "কৃষিজমি" (EN: farmland), it may be useful to retrieve documents on "কৃষি" (EN: farming) as well, i.e. splitting compounds into their constituent terms and indexing the constituents (and the original compound term) will usually benefit IR effectiveness.

The second case would treat a sequence of words as a single indexing unit, which allows differentiating words by context words. For example, "New York" could serve as a single index term, to differentiate it from other occurrences of "new" and "York." For most languages, it is common to find word sequences with a non-compositional meaning, and Bengali is no exception. For example, "পানীয় জল" as a whole translates to "drinkable water," whereas the first constituent "পানীয়" means "a drink." Another example is "তাজ মহল" (EN: Taj Mahal). These "phrases" can be considered as single indexing units, as indexing more than one term might decrease precision.

In compounding languages such as Dutch or German, complex concepts can be expressed in a single word, which comprises of two or more constituent words. Most research on decompounding has focused on European languages. For example, Hedlund (2002) investigates compound splitting for cross-language IR using a dictionary-based approach. For experiments on German, Swedish, and Finnish based on CLEF data, it was found that compound processing, i.e. decompounding a word into its constituents, has in general a positive effect on retrieval performance (Braschler & Ripplinger, 2004). At this point there has been no work directed towards the investigation of automated decompounding techniques and its effectiveness for Bengali IR, but techniques for other morphologically rich languages, such as German, are well established (Braschler & Ripplinger, 2004). For Bengali, the decompounding problem is non-trivial, because a compound word may be formed purely as a result of a phonological process resulting in a fusion of sounds across word boundaries. Decompounding in such cases is thus ambiguous. For example a word ending with a consonant (without the Hrasanta symbol) can be compounded with a word beginning with "অ" by replacing the "অ" character at the start of the second word with the Matra symbol "◌া". A similar result is achieved if either of the constituent words starts with "আ" or ends with "◌া". This effect is illustrated in Table 2.

The decompounding method has to resolve the ambiguity arising at each candidate splitting position, e.g. the method has to choose one of

Table 2. A compounding (Sandhi) rule in Bengali

Compounding Rule	Example
অ + অ = ◌া	মহিষ (buffalo) + অসুর (demon) = মহিষাসুর (buffalo-demon)
◌া+ অ = ◌া	মশা (mosquito) + অরি (enemy) = মশারি (mosquito net)
অ + ◌া= ◌া	মাদক (drug) + আসক্ত (addicted) = মাদকাসক্ত (drug-addict)

“মহিষ + অসুর”, “মহিষা + সুর” or “মহিষ + আসুর” in an attempt to decompound the word “মহিষাসুর” (EN: buffalo-demon). An automatic method can select the decomposition with the smallest number of words (there may be more than two constituent words) and the highest decomposition probability. This approach has proven effective for languages such as German (Chen & Gey, 2004), (Leveling, Magdy, & Jones, 2011). For example, the words “মহিষ” and “অসুর” are valid Bengali words which are more likely to occur in the collection than the other two cases. Thus, these are the most likely constituents of the word “মহিষাসুর.”

Sometimes, word compounds can also be formed of phrasal constituents, e.g. “প্রধানমন্ত্রী” (EN: prime minister). Decompounding such words is not desirable since the decompounded constituent words would lose the compositional meaning of the compounded variant, e.g. decompounding “প্রধানমন্ত্রী” into two separate words “প্রধান” (EN: prime) and “মন্ত্রী” (EN: minister) is likely to degrade retrieval performance. It is thus difficult to decide – and an open research question - when to decompound and when not to.

3.5. Inverted Files

Users generally insist that the response time of an IRS, i.e. the time taken to provide the output set of potentially relevant documents as result of a query input, be as short as possible. A naïve computation of similarity scores by iterating over each document in the collection is therefore infeasible. Documents thus need to be represented in a suitable way so as to enable fast similarity computation. The most widely used data structure in search engines is the inverted file.

It is obvious that a document which does not contain either of the words “পাসপোর্ট” (EN: passport) or “মণিকা” (EN: Monica), is likely to be irrelevant to the query. The challenge in developing an efficient data structure for the search is thus to restrict the similarity computation to a subset of documents, namely the ones which have at least one query term common with the query. This is achieved by maintaining an associated list of documents (called the postings list or simply postings) for every term. The documents in the list are precisely those ones which contain that particular term. Figure 2 shows the schematic diagram of the inverted file data structure for the terms of the sample query. Items in the lists are unique document identifiers. Notice that the

Figure 2. Schematic diagram of an inverted file associating terms (left) with a list of documents containing the terms (right)

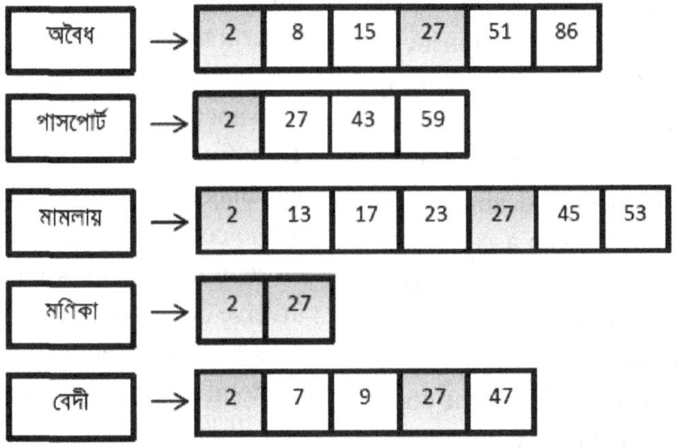

term "অবৈধ" (EN: illegal), being a fairly common word, occurs in 6 documents whereas the word "মণিকা" (EN: Monica) which is a proper noun, occurs in fewer documents. Documents in each list are kept in sorted order so that intersection of the lists can be computed in linear time. In this particular example, the intersection of the lists comprising of the documents 2 and 27, is shown with shaded background. The terms themselves are typically stored in hash-tables or tries, so that the list heads for each query term can be accessed efficiently. The technical detail of the construction of inverted lists is beyond the scope of this book chapter. For brevity, the inverted index shown only contains document IDs. In practice, it may also contain information about term positions in a document and/or term weights. For a more technical introduction to inverted files, the reader is referred to (Manning, Raghavan, & Schütze, 2009; Witten et al., 1999).

4. RETRIEVAL MODELS

The performance of an IRS relies largely on the retrieval model which is used to compute the similarity between query and documents. There are many IR models in use (see, for example Zobel & Moffat, 1998). The next sections will present some retrieval models in detail.

4.1. Vector Space Model

The oldest of the established ranked retrieval models is the Vector Space Model (VSM) (Salton, Wong, & Yang, 1975). In the VSM, the query *q* and each document *d* are represented as vectors over the term space of the entire vocabulary of the document collection. The basic assumption for the operation of the VSM is that the potential relevance of a document to a query is related to the similarity of their vector representation. The advantage of such a representation is that the concept of distance is well defined in a vector space. A query and a document are similar if their vector representation is close, i.e. if the angle between their vectors is small. The Euclidean distance is not particularly interesting for IR, because it heavily depends on the length of vectors, and in IR documents are typically much longer than the queries. As a result, the angle between two vectors is used as a measure of distance, which is in fact proportional to the Euclidean distance between length normalized unit vectors. The cosine of the angle (say φ) between two vectors, which is simply the dot product of two normalized vectors as shown in Equation 2, is easier to calculate than the true angle. The cosine of the angle between a document and the given query vector is thus used directly as a measure of inverse distance or *similarity* (i.e. closeness).

$$sim_{VSM}(d,q) = \sum_{i=1}^{n} d_i q_i = \mid d \mid\mid q \mid \cos\phi \qquad (2)$$

An important issue with regard to the vector space similarity function is how to define the components of the document and query vectors. One obvious way of choosing the components is to assign term frequency of the ith term to the ith component of a vector. The raw term frequency alone may not be a very good indicator of the *importance* of a term in a document. It is thus common practice to assign normalized term frequencies as vector components. Raw term frequency alone however, cannot distinguish between relative importance of term matches, e.g. a match between relatively rare words in the collection is a better indicator of relevance, than matches between frequent words. Term frequencies are therefore scaled by a factor which has a high value if a term is relatively rare in the collection, and a low value if it relatively more common. This factor is referred to as the inverse document frequency (*idf*) and in its standard form is calculated as $\log(N/df_i)$, where N is the total number of documents in the collection and df_i is the number of documents in which the

i^{th} term occurs. The components of a document vector are therefore weighted as d_i=*tf(i). idf(i)*. The simple VSM was shown not to scale well to large document collections in early TREC evaluations, but its effectiveness was improved by the introduction of log-based term frequency functions and the so-called pivoted-length normalization method (Singhal, Buckley, & Mitra, 1996). While established for more than twenty years, the VSM remains a competitive choice for retrieval over collections up to on the order of 100,000 documents.

4.2. BM25

An alternative to the VSM is the theoretically motivated probabilistic model. This was first developed in the 1970s (Robertson & Jones, 1976), but became popular with its extensions to what became known as the BM25 in the mid-1990s (Robertson et al., 1995). The BM25 matching score for a document *d* and a query *q* is defined as:

$$sim_{BM25}(d,q) = \sum_{t \in q} w^{(1)} \frac{(k_1+1)tf}{K+tf} \frac{(k_3+1)qtf}{k_3+qtf} \quad (3)$$

where *q* is the query, containing terms *t* and $w^{(1)}$ is the RSJ (Robertson/Sparck Jones) weight of *t* in *q* (Robertson & Jones, 1976), where

- $w^{(1)} = \log \frac{(r+.5)(N-R-n+r+.5)}{(n-r+.5)(R-r+.5)}$
- k_1, k_3, and *b* are empirically set scalar parameters. The default parameters for the BM25 model used are $b = 0.75$, $k_1 = 1.2$, and $k_3 = 7$.
- *N* is the number of documents in the collection.
- *n* is the document frequency for the term.
- *R* is the number of documents known or presumed to be relevant for a topic.
- *r* is the number of (pseudo) relevant documents containing the term.
- *tf* is the frequency of the term t within a document.
- *qtf* is the frequency of the term in the topic.
- $K = k_1((1-b) + b * \frac{doclen}{avg\_doclen})$
- *doclen* and *avg_doclen* are the document length and average document length in index terms, respectively.

BM25 has been shown to be effective in IR evaluations in different languages and for different IR tasks over the years. It remains a reliable choice for an IR model.

4.3. Language Modeling

Language Modeling (LM) in IR models the query formulation action of a user, i.e. a user's query is likely to comprise of the *key* terms from documents that he wants to retrieve. A document in LM gets a high similarity score to a query if the document is likely to generate the query by a sampling process, which in turn happens if the document contains the query words often. The main difference of LM with BM25 is that, while BM25 ranks documents by decreasing *probability of relevance* to a given query, LM ranks documents by the estimated probabilities of query generation. Relevance is thus modeled implicitly in LM in contrast to BM25.

The LM similarity score between a document *d* and a query *q* is shown in Equation 4.

$$sim_{LM}(q \mid d) = \prod_{t \in q} \lambda \frac{tf(t,d)}{doclen} + (1-\lambda)\frac{cf(t)}{cs} \quad (4)$$

The parameter λ in Equation 4 controls the likelihood of generating the query term from the document, or in other words the emphasis put on the occurrence of a query term in a document. This is estimated simply by the ratio of the total number of times a term occurs in a document to the length of the document, i.e. *tf(t,d)/doclen*. The factor (1- λ) accounts for the probability of generating a term from the collection, which is estimated by the ratio of the total number of times a term occurs in the collection, i.e. the collection frequency, to the total number of tokens in the collection, i.e. the collection size. The parameter λ is also called a smoothing parameter since it avoids the zero probabilities, and effectively smoothes out a probability function by assigning non-zero probability of generating a query term from a document, even if the query term does not exist in the document itself. A higher value of λ tends to rank documents with more number of matching query terms higher than the ones with lesser number of them, a characteristic known as co-ordination level ranking (Hiemstra, 2000). LM has been successfully used in IR experiments on Bengali documents as a state-of-the-art IR model.

5. ENHANCING IR EFFECTIVENESS BY RELEVANCE FEEDBACK

A major problem in IR is the mismatch between query terms and the terms in relevant documents which satisfy a user's information need. This problem of vocabulary mismatch can arise when the query and the documents use alternative descriptions of the same concepts, or may occur simply due to the lack of terms included in the query. The initial retrieval results obtained using one of the models introduced in the preceding section can generally be improved by a process called Relevance Feedback (RF), in which the user provides relevance information on some of the documents retrieved in the initial search which is then used to modify the search with a subsequent rerunning of the retrieval system. Relevance feedback can involve one or both of the two processes: (1) term re-weighting and (2) query expansion. In the absence of manual user feedback, the process of relevance feedback can be automated by the assumption that top k documents are relevant, where k typically is a small number in the range of 5 to 20. The top ranked documents are often referred to as pseudo-relevant documents and the automatic relevance feedback method is known as pseudo or blind relevance feedback (PRF/BRF).

Term reweighting can involve boosting the scores of terms which occur frequently in the relevant documents, and down-weighting the scores of the ones which are frequent in the non-relevant one (Rocchio, 1971). In the context of VSM, this has a simple interpretation of shifting the query vector towards the centroid of the relevant document vectors and away from the centroid of the non-relevant ones. The query modification algorithm as proposed by Rocchio is shown in Equation 5. The parameters α, β, and γ are the weights attached to the original query vector q, the set of judged relevant documents in the feedback step (R), and the complementary set of non-relevant documents (NR) respectively. It has been found that positive feedback is more beneficial than negative feedback, and hence it is a common practise to set $\gamma < \beta$.

$$q' = \alpha q + \frac{\beta}{|R|}\sum_{d \in R} d - \frac{\gamma}{|NR|}\sum_{d \in NR} d \qquad (5)$$

Query Expansion (QE) is a popular technique used to bridge the vocabulary gap between the terms in the query and the documents. QE techniques work by adding terms to the user's original query so as to enrich it to better describe the information need by including additional terms which might have been used in the relevant documents or which augment the terms in the original query, e.g. synonyms (see, for example Rocchio, 1971). If good expansion terms are selected then the retrieval system can retrieve additional relevant documents or improve the rank of documents already retrieved. Query expansion techniques aim to predict the most suitable candidate words to be added to the query so as to increase retrieval effectiveness. The various different methods for IR have corresponding different approaches to QE.

A standard QE approach is typically term-based, i.e. a subset of terms occurring in relevant documents are chosen based on some *term scoring function* aiming to select the good expansion terms. The simplest scoring function which works well in practice in combination with Rocchio's term reweighting, uses term occurrence statistics alone as advocated by (Buckley, Salton, Allan, & Singhal, 1994), where terms occurring in a larger number of (pseudo-)relevant documents are added to the query. The score assigned to a term *t* is in this approach is shown in Equation 6, where *r* is the number of (pseudo)relevant documents that the term occurs in.

$$Occ(t) = r \tag{6}$$

Such a simple scoring function does not distinguish terms by their collection statistics and might end up adding too many common terms (because these terms are also abundant in the relevant documents), thus not increasing IR effectiveness significantly. Scoring functions thus are often augmented by incorporating the *idf* factor.

For the probabilistic model, the most commonly used method to rank potential expansion terms is based on the Robertson Selection Value (RSV) (Robertson, 1995), which is defined as follows:

$$\begin{aligned} &RSV(t) \\ &= r * \log\frac{(r+.5)(N-R-n+r+.5)}{(n-r+.5)(R-r+.5)} \\ &- r * w^{(1)} \end{aligned} \tag{7}$$

In Equation 7, *r* is the number of (pseudo)relevant documents in which the term *t* occurs in, *N* is the total number of documents in the collection, *n* is the document frequency of the term, and *R* is the number of (pseudo-)relevant documents.

Expansion terms in LM feedback are chosen by the odds of generating a term from the set of top ranked pseudo-relevant documents to that of generating it from the collection (Ponte & Croft, 1998).

$$LM(t) = \sum_{j=1}^{R} \frac{P(t \mid d_j)}{P(t)} \tag{8}$$

A limitation of each of these methods is that: (1) these do not restrict the choice of expansion terms over regions of documents which are most similar to the query and in turn thus more likely to be relevant; and (2) deducing importance of feedback terms by occurrence statistics only fails to capture any context information.

Expanding queries by adding the most similar sentences (e.g. based on cosine similarity) from top ranked document proves beneficial for Bengali IR (Ganguly, Leveling, & Jones, 2010). The idea behind sentence-based QE is that expansion based on the constituent terms of a sentence can be useful to enrich the query with sufficient context information which is typically missed in term based expansion, because the constituent words of a sentence do not have to be among the most frequent words occurring in the pseudo-relevant set of documents. Also, such a sentence-based QE approach is able to restrict the choice of candidate expansion terms to regions of documents most similar to the query.

Context information can particularly be helpful for languages rich in word compounding. As an example the word "কৃষিজমি" (farmland) constitutes two component words "কৃষি" (farming) and "জমি" (land). Often in a document, the word "কৃষিজমি"(farmland) can be abbreviated to "জমি"(land) in a pre-defined context of "কৃষি" (farming). In a set of pseudo-relevant documents, the word "জমি" might be among the top most frequent words and thus have a high term score but this might not be true for the word "কৃষি". However in such a scenario, if a query contains the term "কৃষিজমি", it would be beneficial to add both the terms "কৃষি" and "জমি" to the original query. Sentence level expansion is a way to achieve this, because sentences offer an implicit way of capturing the context associated with a term. Recent research has also focused on adapting parameter settings per query instead of using a fixed setting for all queries. For example, the number of feedback terms or feedback documents can be selected per query and feedback terms can be classified into "good" (i.e. terms which increase IR effectiveness) and "bad" expansion terms (Leveling and Jones, 2010).

6. CROSS-LANGUAGE IR

Native Bengali language speakers often prefer to type their queries in English due to the ease of use of the English keyboard, although the final objective is to locate and read relevant Bengali articles. This is precisely the objective of cross-language IR, where it is required to retrieve documents in a language different from that of the query language. In some cases, the English datasets are richer than Bengali resources. For example, the English Wikipedia contains more and longer articles than the Bengali Wikipedia: almost 4 million English articles vs. 22,000 Bengali articles. In these conditions, it helps to translate a less resourced language query to English and retrieve from the English collection. Thus, there is a practical necessity for cross language IR from English to Bengali and vice-versa.

Cross-Language Information Retrieval (CLIR) can be achieved by translating queries, documents, or both. As translation resources for Bengali are still rare and comparatively small, attempts at document translation for IR have, to the best of our knowledge, not yet been made. For European languages, it has been shown that CLIR can achieve up to 90-95% of monolingual IR performance (Di Nunzio et al., 2008). For Bengali, manual query translation by native speakers achieved 81.7%-94.3% of the MAP[3] for the corresponding monolingual experiments (Leveling et al., 2010a). For comparison, manual query translation for English to Hindi was shown to yield 87.0%-92.9% of the MAP for the corresponding monolingual experiments. In comparison, query translation by the Google translate Web service shows a slightly (but not significantly) lower MAP and achieves 85.6%-89.8% of the MAP for the best monolingual Hindi run (Leveling et al., 2010a).

A dictionary-based approach towards translation is particularly useful for short queries. However, translation at word level granularity may not always produce good quality overall translations for larger queries, which offer more context with the presence of natural language sentences. Dictionary-based query translation for Bengali still suffers from a limited coverage. For example, Anubadok (http://anubadok.sourceforge.net/) is based on Ankur's English to Bengali dictionary (http://www.bengalinux.org/english-to-bengali-dictionary/), which contains little more than 17000 edited entries. A Machine Translation (MT) system trained on parallel corpora can be utilized in such cases.

Online machine translation services such as Google translate (http://translate.google.com/) offer content translation for a large number of languages, including Bengali. However, Google translate processes only a limited amount of content in a given time interval. Google also offers a transliteration service (http://www.google.com/transliterate/). Udupa et al. used transliteration for experiments on Hindi to English CLIR to improve the coverage of query translation for proper nouns, which would otherwise remain untranslated (Udupa, Jagarlamudi, & Saravanan,

2008). The same principle can be applied to Bengali to improve CLIR effectiveness.

7. EVALUATION

The preceding sections have introduced the stages and techniques for processing content and constructing indexes such as with or without stemming, with or without stopword removal; different retrieval models ranging from simple *tf-idf* weighting algorithm to more involved techniques such as the BM25 and LM term weightings. The alternative choices in IR make it a highly empirical discipline requiring careful and thorough evaluation of associated methodologies on representative test collections. In this section, we introduce the notion of test collection and evaluation metrics, followed by an empirical evaluation of the Bengali-specific IR adaptations presented in the earlier sections. Formal evaluation of an IR System (IRS) traditionally follows the Cranfield paradigm (Cleverdon, 1991). Typically, publically available and reusable IR benchmarking datasets are created to evaluate the research activities under a common evaluation framework and settings to enable direct comparison of experimental work. We first introduce the components of a standard IR test collection, and then follow it up with a discussion on automatically measuring the effectiveness of an IRS.

7.1. Test Collection Components

A standard IR benchmarking dataset typically comprises of:

- A document collection.
- A test suite of information needs expressed as semi-structured queries.
- A set of manual relevance assessments for each query.

The document collection comprises of a set of structured files with a predefined mark-up specification. Each file may contain more than one document enclosed within. An ad-hoc query is structured into title, description and narrative fields. The title field of a keyword comprises a few keywords and resembles a Web search query found in practise. The description field is an extended version of the title expressed in one or two natural language sentences. The narrative field of a query describes the relevance criteria that a document should possess in order to be relevant to the query. A sample query is shown in Box 1. Retrieval experiments can be conducted by using one or a combination of the text in each query field. The most commonly used queries for IR experiments are T (query constituted of the text within the title field only), TD (text enclosed within the title and description fields), and TDN (title, description and narrative fields).

Relevance is assessed with respect to the underlying information need of a query (as enclosed within the *narrative* tags), and not solely on the query text. For large test collections, it is not possible to collect relevance assessments for each query-document pair. An incomplete set of relevance judgements can be obtained by a process called *pooling*, where the main idea is as follows. A pool of documents is constructed by taking the union of retrieval runs which are to be evaluated. Assuming that each retrieval run returns a finite number of documents in response to the query (typically 1000), and that there is sufficient amount of overlap between the documents retrieved, the number of documents that need to be judged is kept manageable. The relevance judgement for each query document pair is typically a binary decision of whether the document is relevant or not to the underlying information need of the query.

7.2. Evaluation Metrics

The evaluation of an IRS measures its ability to retrieve *all* and *only* relevant information. These two aspects of IR quality correspond to: (1) precision (P), which measures how much relevant content is there in the retrieved set, and (2) recall (R), which measures how much relevant content have been retrieved from the collection. These notions can be made clear by examining the contingency table (Table 3).

The definition of precision and recall are thus:

$$P = \frac{tp}{tp + fp} \tag{9}$$

$$R = \frac{tp}{tp + fn} \tag{10}$$

The set-based definition of recall, as shown in Equation 10 can directly be applied to ranked document lists as well. The set-based definition of precision, as shown in Equation 9 can be applied to ranked lists by limiting the ranked list to sets of top *k* documents. Hence the quality of a ranked list of documents is often measured by the simple metric P@*k* denoting precision at top *k* documents, or the number of relevant documents found in the top k documents. However, this metric fails to distinguish the quality of retrieval runs by the ranks of relevant documents, e.g. a ranked list of documents with relevant documents at ranks 2, 3, 4 should be rated better than a one with relevant documents at 7, 8, 9, although P@10 for both is 3/10. Furthermore, P@*k* does not take into account the recall factor, which in fact can be ignored for cases such as the web search.

A common metric of IR quality measurement which combines the two aspects of precision on ranked lists and recall, is the mean average precision (MAP). For a single information need, average precision (AP) is the average of the precision values obtained for the top set of k documents, after each relevant document is retrieved. This value, when averaged over a query set, is called the mean average precision (MAP). The fact that a non-zero component, i.e. the precision at k^{th} rank,

Table 3. Contingency table for precision-recall

	Relevant	Non-Relevant
Retrieved	True positives (tp)	False positives (fp)
Non-Retrieved	False negatives (fn)	True negatives (tn)

is added for every relevant document retrieved at rank *k*, tends to favour retrieval results with higher recall and relevant documents retrieved at lower (better) ranks. The mathematical expression for AP for a single query is shown in Equation 11, and its average over the set of queries i.e. MAP is shown in Equation 12. It is assumed that the relevant set of documents for a query $q \in Q$, is $\{d_1, ..., d_m\}$, *m* being the number of total number of relevant documents (not necessarily retrieved) for the query *q*, and R_k denoting the ranked list of documents from d_k to d_1.

$$AP(q) = \frac{1}{m}\sum_{k=1}^{m} Precision(R_k) \tag{11}$$

$$MAP(Q) = \frac{1}{|Q|}\sum_{j=1}^{Q} AP(q) \tag{12}$$

Coming back to our earlier example, AP of the ranked list {2, 3, 4} is 1/3(1/2 + 2/3 + 3/4) = 0.638, whereas AP of the ranked list {7, 8, 9} is 1/3(1/7 + 2/8 + 3/9) = 0.242. This clearly shows that MAP prefers ranked lists with more relevant documents at early ranks. Although MAP was designed to address both aspects of retrieval quality viz. precision and recall, yet it can be argued that MAP is more biased towards precision than recall, as can be realized by the progressively decreasing amounts of contribution added to the AP value for increasing ranks. A recall oriented metric, recently devised for patent retrieval, is the Patent Retrieval Evaluation Score (PRES), which overcomes the excessive precision biasness of MAP (Magdy & Jones, 2010).

The standard tool for IR evaluation given retrieval results for a set of topics and the corresponding relevance assessments is *trec_eval*. The tool is made available from the TREC Web site (http://trec.nist.gov/trec_eval/). It generates output on performance metrics such as mean average precision and recall at different cut-off points. So far, no Bengali-specific IR evaluation metrics have emerged, as evaluation metrics are presumed to be language-independent. For more information on evaluation metrics, the reader is referred to (Manning, Raghavan, & Schütze, 2009).

8. BENGALI IR BENCHMARKING

In this section, we present a timeline for the developments in Bengali IR, starting from the early days in CLEF 2007, when the experiments in Bengali IR were only of the cross-language type (Bengali-English) because of the unavailability of a Bengali document collection. The first reported monolingual Bengali IR experiments became possible with the inception of FIRE in 2008. Since then, the Bengali document collection has been growing bigger in each subsequent year of FIRE.

8.1. Early Days (CLEF 2007)

The first IR evaluation task involving Bengali was organized at CLEF 2007, as part of a cross-language retrieval exercise for Indian languages. Resources for Bengali natural language processing and information retrieval were even scarcer at that time. Mandal et al. (2007) state that "neither we had any effective Bengali-English bilingual lexicon nor any parallel corpora to build a statistical lexicon" (p. 1). They used phoneme-based transliterations to generate equivalent English queries from Bengali topics and achieved a MAP of 0.07 in their best experiment for Bengali to English CLIR on newspaper articles. In contrast, monolingual English experiments yielded a MAP of 0.36.

8.2. FIRE 2008-2012

Similar to other IR evaluation initiatives such as the Text Retrieval Conference (TREC, http://trec.nist.gov/), the NII Test Collection for Information Retrieval (NTCIR, http://research.nii.ac.jp/ntcir/), or the Cross-Language Evaluation Forum (CLEF, http://www.clef-campaign.org), the Forum for Information Retrieval Evaluation (FIRE, http://www.isical.ac.in/~clia/) aims at comparing the retrieval performance of different systems and approaches and at investigating evaluation methods for IR. FIRE started in 2008 with document collections for English, Bengali, Hindi, and Marathi and has since added IR topics and documents in other Indian languages. While standard document collections for ad-hoc IR on English and other major European languages have been in existence from early to mid-90s, the test collections for Indian languages such as Hindi and Bengali are still in their infancy. The Forum for Information Retrieval and Evaluation (FIRE) is playing a major role in building up freely downloadable reusable document collections in Bengali and other Indian languages.

The Bengali document collection of FIRE-2010 comprises of over 120,000 news articles crawled from the Bengali daily "*Anandabazar Patrika*" (http://www.anandabazar.com/index.html). The crawled Web pages are cleaned up by removing advertisements and other unnecessary accessories, and semi-structurally formatted with SGML mark-up. Box 2 shows a sample document from the FIRE-2010 Bengali ad-hoc IR collection. Each SGML formatted document comprises a document name (or identifier) enclosed within the DOCNO tags. The textual content is enclosed within the TEXT tags. The first line is the title of the document, which is followed by the news source location in the second line. A total of 150 test queries, 50 for each year's evaluation, along with 25 training queries have been released since the inception of FIRE in 2008.

Box 2. A sample document from the FIRE Bengali collection (left) and a similar (not exact translation) document from the FIRE English collection (right)

<table>
<tr>
<td><DOC>
<DOCNO>1070404_4desh7.pc.utf8</DOCNO>
<TEXT>
20 চৈত্র 1413 বুধবার 4 এপ্রিল 2007
বার্ড ফ্লু নিয়ে বিশেষ সতর্কতা উত্তর পূর্বে
নিজস্ব সংবাদদাতা গুয়াহাটি ও শিলচর
মায়ানমার ও বাংলাদেশের বার্ড ফ্লুর আতঙ্ক এ বার ছড়াল উত্তর পূর্ব ভারতেও । কেন্দ্রীয় সরকার এ নিয়ে যে প্রতীরোধমূলক ব্যবস্থার কথা ভাবছে, তাতে সামিল করা হচ্ছে পশ্চিমবঙ্গকেও । আগামী বৃহস্পতিবার বার্ড ফ্লু নিয়ে কলকাতায় বৈঠক ডেকেছে কেন্দ্র । সেখানে পশ্চিমবঙ্গের সঙ্গে নাগাল্যাণ্ড, মণিপুর, ত্রিপুরা ও মিজোরামের পশুপালন দফতরের কর্তারাও উপস্থিত থাকবেন । পরের দিন একই ধরনের বৈঠক হবে গুয়াহাটিতে । মণিপুর ও মিজোরামের পরে এ বার অসম, ত্রিপুরা ও অরুণাচল প্রদেশেও বাংলাদেশ বা মায়ানমার থেকে পোলট্রিজাত পণ্য আমদানির উপরে বিধিনিষেধ জারি হয়েছে । সমস্ত শুল্ক দফতরকে রাজ্য সরকার এ বিষয়ে সতর্ক করে দিয়েছে ।...
</TEXT>
</DOC></td>
<td><DOC>
<DOCNO>en.3.382.302.2007.7.30</DOCNO>
<TITLE> India steps up bird flu vigil after Myanmar cases
</TITLE>
<TEXT>
NEW DELHI, July 30 (bdnews24.com/Reuters) - India has stepped up vigil on the Myanmar border after receiving "credible" reports of an outbreak of bird flu in its neighbour, which has witnessed several outbreaks this year. The OIE, the global organisation for animal health, reported an outbreak among chickens in Mon state in southern Myanmar on July 24. Upma Chawdhry, joint secretary in India's Animal Husbandry Department, told Reuters that authorities in the remote state of Mizoram had been told to ensure no poultry was smuggled in from Myanmar…
</TEXT>
</DOC></td>
</tr>
</table>

The FIRE-2012 edition will provide a larger document collection in Bengali, English, Gujarati, Hindi, Marathi, and Tamil and topics in the same languages as well as in Telugu. The Bengali topics are also made available in transliterated form in Roman script.

The FIRE evaluation campaign 2012 is moving a step ahead of the traditional IR evaluation paradigm by organizing the following advanced tasks. RISOT (Retrieval from Indian Script OCR'd Text) is a task concerned with the investigating optical character recognition (e.g. scanning text documents) and improving recognition errors. Typical approaches include automatic correction or error modelling. The Morpheme Extraction Task (MET) involves identifying morphemes, the smallest meaningful units of language, in Indian Languages. The output of morpheme extraction can help in machine translation or IR to build morphological analyzers lemmatizers or stemmers for Bengali.

9. TOWARDS BEST PRACTICES

In this section, we present a brief overview of the reported works on Bengali IR, referring back to the IR techniques introduced earlier.

Dolamic & Savoy (2008) use the BM25 IR model, divergence from randomness (DFR) and language modeling (LM) for FIRE-2008 and 2010 experiments on Bengali, Marathi, and Hindi documents. Their approach includes light stemming (Savoy, 2006) and stopword removal based on small stopword lists (less than 200 words). They also apply Rocchio feedback (with $\alpha = \beta = 0.75$) using 3-10 feedback documents and 20-100 feedback terms and find that blind relevance feedback seems to be a useful techniques for enhancing retrieval effectiveness. The best performance is based on data fusion of results from different IR models. For Bengali, the best result was 0.4134 MAP using the title and description fields from the FIRE-2008 topics. They showed that applying a stemmer outperforms no stemming and using an aggressive stemmer outperforms light stemming.

On the FIRE-2010 topics, they achieve 0.4862 MAP for TD queries.

Dolamic and Savoy (2010) show that the choice of a suitable stemming technique also depends on the retrieval model being chosen. Some retrieval models work better with light stemming, while some work well with aggressive stemming. Table 4, reproduced from (Dolamic & Savoy, 2010), shows the Mean Average Precision (MAP) values with different stemming techniques. It can be seen that BM25 works best with an aggressive stemming approach whereas the Divergence From Randomness (DFR) model works best with a light stemming policy. To predict which stemming approach for Bengali would be most suitable for a particular retrieval method is an interesting open research question.

Experiments with the rule-based stemmer as shown in Table 5, following the rules described in Section 3.3.1, show that it achieves a MAP close to the one obtained by Dolamic & Savoy (2010), who use an aggressive stemmer on DFR. The experiments make use of the topic title (T), description (D), and narrative (N). Note that the baselines in Table 4 and Table 5 are different due to different implementations of LM under different frameworks.

Table 4. MAP values of various stemming techniques with different retrieval models on TD queries

Retrieval Model	No Stemming	Light Stemming	Aggressive Stemming
BM25	0.3640	0.4256	0.4446
DFR	0.3629	0.4405	0.4366
LM	0.3481	0.3310	0.3523

Table 5. MAP obtained by applying rule-based stemmer with LM on FIRE-2010 Bengali queries

Rule-Based Stemming	T	TD	TDN
No	0.2627	0.3718	0.4311
Yes	0.3422	0.4333	0.4904

These results illustrate that different stemming techniques work best for different IR models and careful tuning or adaptation to different tasks and domains can benefit IR effectiveness.

N-grams are frequently used for Bengali IR, because of their robust retrieval performance for noisy document collections and because creating language-specific stemmers can be considered as time-consuming. McNamee (2008) employs n-grams and skipgrams (n-grams with wildcards) as indexing units for IR on English, Bengali, Hindi, and Marathi documents using Language Modelling (LM) as a retrieval model (Hiemstra, 2000). He experimented with different but fixed numbers of expansion terms for different indexing methods: 50 feedback terms for words, 150 for 4-grams and 5-grams, and 400 for skip-grams. Additional experiments on the FIRE-2008 data use n-grams on running text, and word truncation (prefixes) (McNamee, 2008). Significant improvements for indexing n-grams compared to the baseline of indexing words are observed. The best effectiveness for Bengali is achieved when using 4-grams (MAP: 0.3582).

McNamee et al. (2009) investigate stemming techniques for 18 languages and 5 different writing systems. For the FIRE-2008 data, they find that overlapping characters 4-grams performs best (MAP: 0.3247). They found that overlapping character n-grams (with n=4 or n=5) and n-prefixes (truncation after n characters) perform best across languages with a relative improvement of 40-80% in some languages.

Paik and Parui (2008) experiment with n-gram based indexing using the Terrier engine for FIRE-2008. They employ different retrieval models on the training data, including BM25, DFR, and *tf-idf*, and observe that 3-grams perform best on the Bengali data. They achieve 0.4232 MAP in their official submission using the IFB2 retrieval model and conflating terms with a common prefix.

Leveling and Jones (2010) perform monolingual Bengali experiments on the FIRE-2010 collection. They experimented with BM25 and different indexing techniques (stems, word prefixes, and character n-grams). They proposed a corpus-based, language-independent stemming approach was implemented following a morpheme induction approach described by Dasgupta and Ng, which has been evaluated for English and Bengali (Dasgupta & Ng, 2006), (Dasgupta & Ng, 2007). The stemmer relies on a list of candidate suffixes which are induced by a frequency analysis of word roots and suffixes. In a second step, suffix combinations (composite suffixes) are determined via the frequency of potential root forms, allowing for a recursive morphological word structure. A word is stemmed by removing the longest suffix found in the generated suffix lists or by not removing a suffix, otherwise. They found that using 5-prefixes outperforms corpus-based stemming and indexing raw word forms. The best performance was achieved using BM25 with 5-prefixes and blind relevance feedback using 10 documents and 20 terms (0.4526 MAP).

Leveling et al. (2010) experimented with corpus and rule-based stemming approaches on the FIRE-2010 data, using BM25 and language modelling. In their monolingual IR experiments, the best performance (MAP: 0.4526) was again achieved using 5-prefixes and blind relevance feedback (10 documents, 20 terms). They also conducted bilingual (Bengali-English) IR experiments, using native speakers to translate topics into English (MAP: 0.37).

Loponen et al. (2010) investigate the use of different language normalizers: one stemmer, YASS, and two lemmatizers, GRALE and StaLe on the FIRE-2011 document collection. The performances of the three normalizers are close to each other, all the TD runs delivered results close to 0.44 MAP. The best results were achieved best with YASS and manually pruning stemmed output (0.4511 MAP).

Kettunnen et al. (2011) apply Frequent Case Generation (FCG) as a means of text normalization. FCG is a method based on the skewed distributions of word forms in natural languages and is suitable for morphologically complex languages. They show that FCG achieves 30% improvement over the plain word baseline on the FIRE-2011 document collection (MAP: 0.3457).

Banerjee and Pal (2011) performed initial experiments with the Terrier retrieval engine on FIRE-2011 data. They apply the YASS stemmer and query expansion. The best results are achieved with Terrier's PL2-Poisson model with Laplace after-effect and normalization 2 model (MAP: 0.2929).

As an example of cross-language IR experiments, Bandyopadhyay et al. (2007) proposed a semi-automatic query term list preparation. Their experiments for CLEF 2007 are based on simple tf-idf ranking and zonal indexing. For Bengali to English bilingual experiments, they employed query translation and transliteration based on an online Bengali dictionary[4]. They achieve about 10% MAP for Bengali to English bilingual ad-hoc IR experiments.

Bhaskar et al. (2010) applied k-means clustering to the documents, partitioning the document collection into different theme clusters, using the Lucene retrieval engine. They achieved 0.4002 MAP for Bengali monolingual retrieval on the FIRE-2010 data.

In summary, the combination of IR different models performs well for Bengali and state-of-the-art IR models which yield good performance in other languages also seem to perform well for Bengali.

10. TOOLS AND RESOURCES

This section surveys the freely available general purpose IR tools and Bengali language-specific linguistic resources on the Web. The objective of the section is thus to introduce the readers to the available resources, and prepare them for building and testing their own IR systems so that they can readily participate in the Bengali IR tasks at evaluation forums.

Most IR search engines come equipped with different stemmers and stopword lists. A stemmer for most European languages is Snowball (http://snowball.tartarus.org/). Adaptation of IR to Indian languages requires a little more effort. Jacques Savoy has compiled an excellent Web page with stopword lists and implementations of stemmers for many other languages, including Bengali, Hindi, and Marathi (http://members.unine.ch/jacques.savoy/clef/index.html).

The SMART (System for the Mechanical Analysis and Retrieval of Text) Information Retrieval System is an information retrieval system developed at Cornell University in the 1960s. Many important concepts in IR were developed as part of research on the SMART system (ftp://ftp.cs.cornell.edu/pub/smart/) including the vector space model, and relevance feedback.

Apache Lucene (http://lucene.apache.org/) is an open source IR library, implemented in Java. It is supported by the Apache Software Foundation. At the core of Lucene's logical architecture is the idea of a document containing fields of text. This flexibility allows Lucene's API to be independent of the file format. Text from PDFs, HTML, Microsoft Word, and OpenDocument documents, as well as many others (except images), can all be indexed as long as their textual information can be extracted. Additionally, the tool also supports spellchecking, hit highlighting, advanced content analysis and tokenization capabilities.

Terrier (http://terrier.org/) is a highly flexible, efficient, and effective open source search engine written in Java. Terrier implements state-of-the-art indexing and retrieval functionalities, and provides an ideal platform for the rapid development and evaluation of large-scale retrieval applications. Terrier is a comprehensive, flexible and transparent platform for research and experimentation in IR and has been used on standard TREC and CLEF test collections.

Managing Gigabytes for Java (MG4J, http://mg4j.di.unimi.it/) is a free full-text search engine for large document collections written in Java (Boldi & Vigna, 2005). MG4J is highly customisable and provides state-of-the-art IR models such as BM25/BM25F. MG4J aims at efficiency and supports distributed processing (indexing) and multi-threading.

Moses (http://www.statmt.org/moses/) is a statistical machine translation system which allows to automatically train translation models based on a parallel corpus. Moses supports two types of translation models: phrase-based and tree-based models (Koehn et al., 2007).

The EMILLE/CIIL (Xiao, McEnery, Baker, & Hardie, 2004) Corpus has been created in the EMILLE project by Lancaster University, UK, and the Central Institute of Indian Languages (CIIL), Mysore, India. EMILLE is distributed by ELRA, the European Language Resources Association (Catalog Reference: ELRA-W0037). The corpus consists of monolingual, parallel and annotated data in more than 14 South Asian languages. The parallel corpus consists of 200,000 words of text in English with translations into Hindi, Bengali, Punjabi, Gujarati, and Urdu. It can be employed to train a statistical machine translation system for English-Bengali.

11. CONCLUSION

Bengali IR is a relatively new research topic. A large community of Bengali speakers could benefit from improved search and better linguistic resources. Most early research has focused on applying generic IR approaches to Bengali IR and only recently research on language-specific aspects for Indian languages in general has gained interest. The interest has been supported largely by initiatives such as FIRE, where the need to build up resources and benchmark collections has been identified. FIRE is also a step towards building a research community in Bengali-speaking countries. This chapter has introduced to information retrieval, showing all steps from creating IR experiments to their evaluation.

ACKNOWLEDGMENT

This research is supported by the Science Foundation Ireland (Grant 07/CE/I1142) as part of the Centre for Next Generation Localisation (CNGL) project.

REFERENCES

Bandyopadhyay, S., Mondal, T., Naskar, S. K., Ekbal, A., Haque, R., & Godhavarthy, S. R. (2007). Bengali, Hindi and Telugu to English ad-hoc bilingual task at CLEF 2007. In C. Peters, V. Jijkoun, T. Mandl, H. Müller, D. W. Oard, A. Peñas, V. Petras, et al. (Eds.), *Advances in Multilingual and Multimodal Information Retrieval, 8th Workshop of the Cross-Language Evaluation Forum, CLEF 2007, Budapest, Hungary, September 19-21, 2007, Revised Selected Papers* (Vol. 5152, pp. 88–94). Springer.

Banerjee, R., & Pal, S. (2011). ISM@FIRE-2011: Monoliongual task. In *Proceedings of FIRE 2011, Third workshop of the Forum for Information Retrieval Evaluation*. FIRE.

Bhaskar, P., Das, A., Pakray, P., & Bandyopadhyay, S. (2010). Theme-based English and Bengali ad-hoc monolingual information retrieval in FIRE 2010. In *Proceedings of Working Notes of the Forum for Information Retrieval Evaluation, 2010*. FIRE.

Bhattacharya, S., Choudhury, M., Sarkar, S., & Basu, A. (2005). Inflectional morphology synthesis for Bengali noun, pronoun and verb systems. In *Proceedings of the National Conference on Computer Processing of Bangla (NCCPB)*, (pp. 34–43). NCCPB.

Boldi, P., & Vigna, S. (2005). MG4J at TREC 2005. In E. M. Voorhees & L. P. Buckland (Eds.), *The Fourteenth Text REtrieval Conference (TREC 2005) Proceedings*. NIST.

Braschler, M., & Ripplinger, B. (2004). How effective is stemming and decompounding for german text retrieval? *Information Retrieval*, *7*(3/4), 291–316. doi:10.1023/B:INRT.0000011208.60754.a1.

Buckley, C., Salton, G., Allan, J., & Singhal, A. (1994). Automatic query expansion using SMART: TREC 3. In *Proceedings of TREC* (pp. 69–80). NIST.

Chen, A., & Gey, F. C. (2002). Building an Arabic stemmer for information retrieval. In *Proceedings of the Eleventh Text REtrieval Conference (TREC 2002)*. NIST.

Chen, A., & Gey, F. C. (2004). Multilingual information retrieval using machine translation, relevance feedback and decompounding. *Information Retrieval*, *7*(1-2), 149–182. doi:10.1023/B:INRT.0000009444.89549.90.

Cleverdon, C. W. (1991). The significance of the Cranfield tests on index languages. In *Proceedings of the 14th Annual International ACM SIGIR Conference on Research and Development in Information Retrieval - SIGIR '91* (pp. 3–12). New York: ACM Press.

Dasgupta, S., & Ng, V. (2006). Unsupervised morphological parsing of {B}engali. *Language Resources and Evaluation*, *40*, 311–330. doi:10.1007/s10579-007-9031-y.

Dasgupta, S., & Ng, V. (2007). High-performance, language-independent morphological segmentation. In C. L. Sidner, T. Schultz, M. Stone, & C. Zhai (Eds.), *Proceedings of the Human Language Technology Conference of the North American Chapter of the Association of Computational Linguistics, (NAACL HLT 2007), April 22--27, 2007* (pp. 155–163). Rochester, NY: ACL.

Di Nunzio, G. M., Ferro, N., Mandl, T., & Peters, C. (2008). Advances in multilingual and multimodal information retrieval. In Peters, C., Jijkoun, V., Mandl, T., Müller, H., Oard, D. W., & Peñas, A. et al. (Eds.), *CLEF* (*Vol. 5152*, pp. 13–32). Berlin: Springer.

Dolamic, L., & Savoy, J. (2008). UniNE at FIRE 2008: Hindi, Bengali, and Marathi IR. In *Proceedings of Working Notes of the Forum for Information Retrieval Evaluation*. Kolkata, India: FIRE.

Dolamic, L., & Savoy, J. (2010). UniNE at FIRE 2010: Hindi, Bengali, and Marathi IR. In *Proceedings of Working Notes of the Forum for Information Retrieval Evaluation, 2010*. FIRE.

Fox, C. (1992). Lexical analysis and stoplists. In *Information Retrieval: Data Structures and Algorithms* (pp. 102–130). New York: Prentice-Hall.

Ganguly, D., Leveling, J., & Jones, G. J. F. (2010). Exploring sentence level query expansion in the language model. In D. M. Sharma, R. Sangal, & S. Sarkav (Eds.), *Proceedings of ICON-2010: 8th International Conference on Natural Language Processing* (pp. 18–27). Macmillan Publishers.

Goldsmith, J. (2001). Unsupervised learning of the morphology of a natural language. *Computational Linguistics*, *27*, 153–198. doi:10.1162/089120101750300490.

Harman, D. (1991). How effective is suffixing? *Journal of the American Society for Information Science American Society for Information Science*, *42*(1), 7–15. doi:10.1002/(SICI)1097-4571(199101)42:1<7::AID-ASI2>3.0.CO;2-P.

Hedlund, T. (2002). Compounds in dictionary-based cross-language information retrieval. *Information Research, 7*(2).

Hiemstra, D. (2000). *Using language models for information retrieval*. Enschede, The Netherlands: Center of Telematics and Information Technology, AE.

Keshava, S., & Pitler, E. (2006). A simpler, intuitive approach to morpheme induction. In *Proceedings of the PASCAL Challenge Workshop on Unsupervised Segmentation of Words Into Morphemes - MorphoChallenge 2005*. Venice, Italy: MorphoChallenge.

Kettunen, K., Paik, J., Pal, D., & Järvelin, K. (2011). Frequent case generation in ad hoc retrieval of the Indian languages. In *Proceedings of FIRE 2011, Third workshop of the Forum for Information Retrieval Evaluation*. FIRE.

Koehn, P., Hoang, H., Birch, A., Callison-Burch, C., Federico, M., & Bertoldi, N. et al. (2007). *Moses: Open source toolkit for statistical machine translation*. ACL. doi:10.3115/1557769.1557821.

Kornilov, S. A., Rakhlin, N. V., & Grigorenko, E. L. (2012). Morphology and Developmental language disorders: New tools for Russian. *Psychology in Russia: State of the Art*, *5*, 371–387.

Krovetz, R. (1993). Viewing morphology as an inference process. In R. Korfhage, E. Rasmussen, & P. Willett (Eds.), *Proceedings of the 16th Annual International ACM SIGIR Conference on Research and Development in Information Retrieval* (pp. 191–202). Pittsburg, PA: ACM.

Leveling, J., Ganguly, D., & Jones, G. J. F. (2010a). Term conflation and blind relevance feedback for information retrieval on indian languages. In *Proceedings of Working Notes of the Forum for Information Retrieval Evaluation, 2010*. Gandhinagar, India: FIRE.

Leveling, J., & Jones, G. J. F. (2010). Sub-word indexing and blind relevance feedback for English, Bengali, Hindi, and Marathi IR. *ACM Transactions on Asian Language Information Processing, 9*(3), 1–30. doi:10.1145/1838745.1838749.

Leveling, J., Magdy, W., & Jones, G. J. F. (2011). An investigation of decompounding for cross-language patent search. In W.-Y. Ma, J.-Y. Nie, R. A. Baeza-Yates, T.-S. Chua, & W. B. Croft (Eds.), *Proceeding of the 34th International ACM SIGIR Conference on Research and Development in Information Retrieval, SIGIR 2011,* (pp. 1169–1170). ACM.

Leveling, J. G. J. F. J. (2010). Classifying and filtering blind feedback terms to improve information retrieval effectiveness. In *Proceedings of RIAO'2010: Adaptivity, Personalisation and Fusion of Heterogeneous Information* (pp. 156–163). RIAO.

Loponen, A., Paik, J., & Jarvelin, K. (2010). UTA stemming and lemmatization experiments in the Bengali ad hoc track at FIRE 2010. In *Proceedings of Working Notes of FIRE 2010.* FIRE.

Magdy, W., & Jones, G. J. F. (2010). PRES: A score metric for evaluating recall-oriented information retrieval applications. ACM. *Proceedings of SIGIR, 2010,* 611–618.

Majumder, P., Mitra, M., Parui, S. K., Kole, G., Mitra, P., & Datta, K. (2007). YASS: Yet another suffix stripper. *ACM Transactions on Information Systems, 25*(4), 18–20. doi:10.1145/1281485.1281489.

Mandal, D., Gupta, M., Dandapat, S., Banerjee, P., & Sarkar, S. (2007). Bengali and Hindi to English CLIR evaluation. In C. Peters, V. Jijkoun, T. Mandl, H. Müller, D. W. Oard, A. Peñas, V. Petras, et al. (Eds.), *Advances in Multilingual and Multimodal Information Retrieval, 8th Workshop of the Cross-Language Evaluation Forum, CLEF 2007,* (Vol. 5152, pp. 95–102). Springer.

Manning, C. D., Raghavan, P., & Schütze, H. (2009). *An introduction to information retrieval.* Cambridge, UK: Cambridge University Press.

Manning, C. D., & Schütze, H. (1999). *Foundations of statistical natural language processing.* Cambridge, MA: MIT Press.

Mansur, M. (2006). *Analysis of n-gram based text categorization for bangla in a newspaper corpus.* BRAC University.

McNamee, P. (2008). N-gram Tokenization for {I}ndian language text retrieval. In *Proceedings of Working Notes of the Forum for Information Retrieval Evaluation.* Kolkata, India: IEEE.

McNamee, P., Nicholas, C., & Mayfield, J. (2009). Addressing morphological variation in alphabetic languages. In J. Allan, J. A. Aslam, M. Sanderson, C. Zhai, & J. Zobel (Eds.), *Proceedings of the 32nd Annual International ACM SIGIR Conference on Research and Development in Information Retrieval, SIGIR 2009,* (pp. 75–82). Boston, MA: ACM.

Paik, J. H., & Parui, S. K. (2008). A simple stemmer for inflectional languages. In *Proceedings of the Working Notes of the Forum for Information Retrieval Evaluation.* Kolkata, India: FIRE.

Pal, D., Majumder, P., Mitra, M., Mitra, S., & Sen, A. (2006). Issues in searching for Indian language web content. In *Proceedings of iNEWS'08* (pp. 93–94). Napa Valley, CA: ACM.

Pingali, P., Jagarlamudi, J., & Varma, V. (2006). Web khoj: Indian language IR from multiple character encodings. In *Proceedings of WWW 2006, May 23--26* (pp. 801–809). Edinburgh, Scotland: ACM.

Ponte, J. M., & Croft, W. B. (1998). A language modeling approach to information retrieval. In *Proceedings of the 21st Annual International ACM SIGIR Conference on Research and Development in Information Retrieval* (pp. 275–281). New York, NY: ACM.

Porter, M. F. (1980). An algorithm for suffix stripping. *Program, 14*(3), 130–137. doi:10.1108/eb046814.

Robertson, S. E., & Jones, K. S. (1976). Relevance weighting of search terms. *Journal of the American Society for Information Science American Society for Information Science, 27*(3), 129–146. doi:10.1002/asi.4630270302.

Robertson, S. E., Walker, S., & Beaulieu, M. (1998). Okapi at TREC-7: Automatic ad hoc, filtering, VLC and interactive track. In D. K. Harman (Ed.), *The Seventh Text REtrieval Conference (TREC-7)* (pp. 253–264). Gaithersburg, MD: National Institute of Standards and Technology (NIST).

Robertson, S. E., Walker, S., Jones, S., Hancock-Beaulieu, M. M., & Gatford, M. (1995). Okapi at TREC-3. In D. K. Harman (Ed.), *Overview of the Third Text Retrieval Conference (TREC-3)* (pp. 109–126). Gaithersburg, MD: National Institute of Standards and Technology (NIST).

Rocchio, J. J. (1971). Relevance feedback in information retrieval. In Salton, G. (Ed.), *The SMART retrieval system -- Experiments in automatic document processing*. Englewood Cliffs, NJ: Prentice Hall.

Salton, G., Wong, A., & Yang, C. S. (1975). A vector space model for automatic indexing. *Communications of the ACM, 18*(11), 613–620. doi:10.1145/361219.361220.

Savoy, J. (2006). Light stemming approaches for the French, Portuguese, German and Hungarian languages. In H. Haddad (Ed.), *Proceedings of the 2006 ACM Symposium on Applied Computing (SAC),* (pp. 1031–1035). ACM.

Singhal, A., Buckley, C., & Mitra, M. (1996). Pivoted document length normalization. In *Proceedings of the 19th Annual International ACM SIGIR Conference on Research and Development in Information Retrieval - SIGIR '96* (pp. 21–29). New York: ACM Press.

Udupa, R., Jagarlamudi, J., & Saravanan, K. (2008). Microsoft research at FIRE 2008: Hindi-English cross-language information retrieval. In *Proceedings of the Working Notes of the Forum for Information Retrieval Evaluation*. Kolkata, India: FIRE.

Witten, I. H., Moffat, A., & Bell, T. C. (1999). *Managing gigabytes: Compressing and indexing documents and images*. San Francisco, CA: Morgan Kaufmann.

Xiao, Z., McEnery, A., Baker, P., & Hardie, A. (2004). Developing Asian language corpora: Standards and practice. In V. Sornlertlamvanich, T. Tokunaga, & C. Huang (Eds.), *Fourth Workshop on Asian Language Resources* (pp. 1–8). Sanya.

Xu, J., & Croft, B. (1998). Corpus-based stemming using co-occurence of word variants. *ACM Transactions on Information Systems, 16*(1), 61–81. doi:10.1145/267954.267957.

Zobel, J., & Moffat, A. (1998). Exploring the similarity space. *ACM SIGIR Forum, 32*(1), 18–34.

ENDNOTES

1. http://en.wikipedia.org/Bengali_language.
2. See http://www.isical.ac.in/~fire/stopwords_list_ben.txt and http://members.unine.ch/jacques.savoy/clef/bengaliST.txt.
3. MAP is a retrieval effectiveness measure which is described in more detail in Section 7.2.
4. http://dsal.uchicago.edu/dictionaries/biswas-bengali.

Chapter 13
The Bengali Literary Collection of Rabindranath Tagore:
Search and Study of Lexical Richness

Suprabhat Das
Indian Institute of Technology Kharagpur, India

Anupam Basu
Indian Institute of Technology Kharagpur, India

Pabitra Mitra
Indian Institute of Technology Kharagpur, India

ABSTRACT

Rabindranath Tagore is one of the most prolific authors of Bengali literature. He has added a vast amount of richness in style and language to the Bengali text. The present study aims at a quantitative study of vocabulary size and lexical richness as well as effective search engine for his works. Several statistical measures of term distribution have been used to measure lexical richness. An initial attempt has been made to build a search engine, Anwesan, for Rabindra Rachanabali collection. The first complete digital Rabindra Rachanabali released by Society for Natural Language Technology Research, Kolkata, in 2010, has been used in the study. It was observed that a high lexical richness value was characteristics of most of Rabindranath Tagore's work.

INTRODUCTION

One of the most prolific writers in Bengali literature is Nobel laureate Rabindranath Tagore (May 7, 1861 - August 7, 1941). He had dominated both the Bengali and Indian philosophical and literary scene for decades. He was a social reformer, patriot and above all, a great humanitarian and philosopher. He had modernized Bengali art by changing its rigid classical forms. He was the ambassador of Indian culture to the rest of the world. For his eternal writing *Gitanjali*, he was awarded the Nobel Prize for Literature in the year of 1913, becoming the first Asian Nobel laureate.

DOI: 10.4018/978-1-4666-3970-6.ch013

He is the only litterateur who penned anthems of two countries, *Jana Gana Mana*, the Indian national anthem and *Amar Shonar Bangla*, the Bangladeshi national anthem.

Different statistical techniques in stylistic analysis of literary texts have been studied for long time. An empirical law to estimate vocabulary size from collection size, which is known as Heaps' law (Heaps, 1978), is now becomes a benchmark in the field of information retrieval, though it is not well-known in linguistics. Besides that, there are multinomial Bayesian approaches (Boender & Rinnooy Kan, 1987) and few essential but rarely followed procedures (Nation, 1993) to estimate the vocabulary size. Many lexical richness measures have also been studied and applied on English and other languages for years. Different measures of lexical richness were applied on the data from the works of three contemporary French singers (Ratkowsky & Hantrais, 1975), the volumes of the *Travaux de Linguistique Quantitative* (TLQ) series (Ratkowsky, 1988), which was initiated by Swiss publishing firm Slatkine in 1978, Biblical texts (Holmes, 1994) and sixteen works from eight English authors (Tweedie & Baayen, 1998) to study different lexical styles. The hidden connections in the medical literature have also been reported using lexical statistics (Lindsay & Gordon, 1999 May). The corpora of three playwrights, Euripides – a great tragedian of classical Athens, Aristophanes – a comic playwright of ancient Athens, and Terence – a playwright of the Roman Republic, was studied to compare the trends in vocabulary richness over time (Smith & Kelly, 2002). The number of different types in the first fifty thousand words in each text from the twelve texts of twelve different authors along with the effects of text-doubling and text-combining on measures of vocabulary richness have been reported (Hoover, 2003). Besides that, the studies of vocabulary richness have been done for child language and second language research to monitor changes in children and adults with vocabulary difficulties. Primarily type/token ratio was used to measure lexical diversity in child language research (Richards, 1987). After that, different advanced measures in child language and second language have been reported by many researchers (Bogaards & Laufer-Dvorkin, 2004; Haznedar & Gavruseva, 2008; Richards & Malvern, 2000 September). There is a large body of research works on information retrieval methods, including several commercial search engines for English speaking users. There are search engines for the literary works of Shakespeare.

There were no major works on statistical analysis as well as search engines for Bengali literary works. We have made an initial attempt on Rabindra Rachanabali collection to study vocabulary size and different lexical richness measures. Various measures of lexical richness have been computed for different genres of Rabindra Rachanabali collection and different chronological intervals. The statistical measures are also compared with the measures from another Bengali author Bankim Chandra Chattopadhyay. We also build a search engine, Anwesan, for Rabindra Rachanabali collection.

The rest of the paper is organized as follows: The details of the Rabindra Rachanabali collection along with available metadata are given in next section. How the vocabulary size is correlated with Heaps' law and the analysis of estimated vocabulary size using Heaps' law are described in the following sections. Next sections describe a brief overview of different measures of lexical richness and the analysis of lexical richness, chronological study and comparative study with another Bengali author. After that, the details of Anwesan, its architecture, components, advanced features and usage statistics have been given. In the last section, we have concluded about our evaluation result and some other features are also discussed that can be included in future works for the betterment of our research work.

THE RABINDRA RACHANABALI COLLECTION

Rabindranath Tagore made his remarkable contributions in every genre, from poetry to novels, stories, plays and songs. He had also written dramas and essays of all kinds, travel diaries etc. There are more than five thousand documents in the complete Rabindra Rachanabali collection. This comprehensive collection of complete Rabindra Rachanabali is mainly used in our study. Society for Natural Language Technology Research (SNLTR)[1] provide us the complete Rabindra Rachanabali collection along with relevant information (metadata), like date and place of writing, date of publications, name of main characters and many others. The distribution of complete Rabindra Rachanabali collection according to genres and list of available metadata for every genre are given in Table 1.

CORRELATION WITH HEAPS' LAW

A vocabulary is commonly defined as the set of distinct tokens from the collection. Heaps proposed the simplest possible relationship between collection size and vocabulary size, which is known as Heaps' law (Heaps, 1978; Manning et al., 2008). It relates the vocabulary size, i.e. the number of unique words in a collection as a function of collection size, i.e. the number of tokens it contains.

$$V = kN^b \quad (1)$$

where V is the estimated vocabulary size and N is the collection size. The values for the parameters b and k depend on collection. These parametric values are quite variable because vocabulary growth depends a lot on the nature of the collection and how it is processed. The relationship between collection size and vocabulary size is linear in log-log space.

$$\log_{10} V = b \log_{10} N + \log_{10} k \quad (2)$$

Though Heaps' law simply predicts the number of different tokens from test corpus, it is perhaps the most intuitive measure of lexical richness (Ordan et al., 2010). Vocabulary size was used for new lexical richness measure in second-language learners' writing also (Laufer & Nation, 1995).

MEASURES OF LEXICAL RICHNESS

The traditional study of stylistics has been done on literary works for many years. Mathematical linguistics introduced the quantitative component resulting from the computation of textual features.

Table 1. The complete Rabindra Rachanabali collection with metadata

Genres	No. of Documents	List of Available Metadata
Story	162	Date/place of writing, date of publication, publisher, name of book, main characters, film (name, director, producer, release date, actors), other implementation
Poetry	2,475	First line, date/place of writing, date of publication, name of book, transformation
Drama	64	Type, date/place of writing, date/place of performance, name of book, main characters, other implementation, old form
Novel	13	Date/place of publication, main characters, film (name, director, producer, release date, actors), other implementation
Song	1,815	First line, stage (*porjay*), order (*krom*), where used, notation, rhythm, collection, domestic and foreign influence, original song
Essay	719	Name of book, date/place of publication, date/place of writing, magazine name, objective of writing
Total	**5,248**	

In statistical linguistics, there are many measurement techniques, models, constants to measure the level of lexical richness.

Type/Token Ratio (TTR)

The best known and basic measure of lexical richness is undoubtedly type/token ratio (TTR) (Hess et al., 1989; Thomas, 2005; Williamson, 2009). In order to study lexical richness, we must count the number of tokens as well as the number of types from the test corpus. The number of tokens, indicated by N, is the total number of words in the text sample and the number of types, indicated by V, is the total number of distinct words in the same sample. The equation of type/token ratio is as follows:

$$\text{Type/Token Ratio (TTR)} = \frac{V}{N} \tag{3}$$

A high TTR indicates a large amount of lexical variation and a low TTR indicates relatively little lexical variation. This measure depends on the length of the text to a great extent. With increasing text length, the value of TTR decreases systematically. Mainly two types of approaches have been taken to obtain measures that are independent of text length.

1. Using simple functions of N, such as square root or logarithm.
2. Using spectrum elements.

Measures Normalized with Text Length

Various mathematical transformations of the type/token ratio have also been proposed. We have studied three of them.

Index of Guiraud: Guiraud had made an attempt to remove the effect of text length. Guiraud Index or the 'Indice de Richness' (Guiraud, 1954, 1960) is calculated by dividing the number of types by the square root of the number of tokens. The expression for Index of Guiraud is as follows:

$$\text{Index of Guiraud} = \frac{V}{\sqrt{N}} \tag{4}$$

Index of Herdan: Herdan proposed logarithmic type/token ratio (Herdan, 1960; 1964), which is calculated by dividing the logarithmic value of the number of types by the logarithmic value of the number of tokens. The logarithmic type/token ratio is much efficient than simple type/token ratio (Weitzman, 1971).

$$\text{Index of Herdan} = \frac{\log V}{\log N} \tag{5}$$

Uber Index: Dugast proposed Uber Index (Dugast, 1979), a more complicated logarithmic transformation. It is calculated by dividing the square of the logarithmic value of the number of tokens by the difference between logarithmic value of the number of tokens and logarithmic value of the number of types.

$$\text{Uber Index} = \frac{\left(\log N\right)^2}{\left(\log N - \log V\right)} \tag{6}$$

Yule's Characteristic *K*

The spectrum elements $V(i, N)$ is the numbers of types occurring i times in a sample of length N. Yule's Characteristic K (Miranda-García & Calle-Martín, 2005; Yule, 1944) is a word frequency measurement for large blocks of text. Although most of the measures for lexical richness actually depend on text length, Yule's characteristic K is considered to be highly reliable for being text length independent. The expression for Yule's Characteristic K is as follows:

$$K = 10^4\left(\frac{\sum i^2 V(i,N)}{N^2} - \frac{1}{N}\right) \quad (7)$$

where i = number of times a word occurs, N = Total number of tokens, and $V(i, N)$ = Number of words occurring i times

A high value of Yule's Characteristic K implies that the vocabulary is highly concentrated on to those words that are used over and over again. If the vocabulary is concentrated on few words, the number of unique words will be smaller and Type/Token Ratio (TTR) or other simple transformed measures will have lower value. Hence, reciprocal of Yule's Characteristic K has been taken to compare with other measures of lexical richness.

ANALYSIS OF VOCABULARY SIZE USING HEAPS' LAW

Heaps' law predicts the vocabulary size from the collection size. Number of tokens and vocabulary size for every genre are plotted in log-log space. For every collection, the best fit trend line has been calculated. We got the parametric values of b and k from these trend lines for every genre. The distributions of vocabulary sizes for every genre are given in Figure 1.

The list of parametric values of Heaps' law is tabulated in Table 2.

The parametric values for all the collections are: $0.72 < b < 0.78$ and $2.55 < k < 3.25$.

ANALYSIS OF LEXICAL RICHNESS

Firstly, the whole Rabindra Rachanabali collection has been partitioned into different groups according to genres. To make an overall analysis, documents of four different genres (Story, Poetry, Drama and Novel) are taken into consideration to

Table 2. Parametric values of Heaps' law for different genres

Genres	b	$\log_{10}k$	k
Story	0.763	0.413	2.588213
Poetry	0.778	0.407	2.552701
Drama	0.744	0.471	2.958012
Novel	0.721	0.511	3.243396

Figure 1. Distribution of vocabulary sizes for every genre: (a) story, (b) poetry, (c) drama, and (d) novel

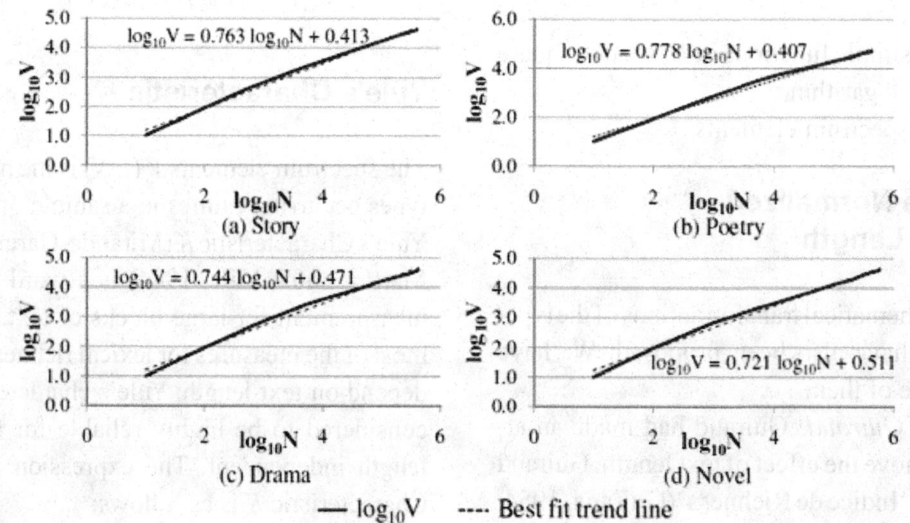

study different measures of lexical richness. The functional dependence of the number of types as well as different lexical richness measures on the number of tokens for Rabindra Rachanabali is given in Figure 2.

From Figure 2, it is seen that all the measures of lexical richness are highest for poetry and lowest for novel. TTR and Index of Herdan have decreasing slopes whereas Index of Guiraud has increasing slope. For smaller token size, Uber Index has decreasing slope; but it becomes almost constant for higher token size. For larger token size, 1/Yule's Characteristic *K* also maintains a text length independent graph. This study will help in genre detection for a test document from Rabindra Rachanabali collection.

Chronological Study

In this section, the whole Rabindra Rachanabali collection has been partitioned into different chronological intervals on the basis of date of writing. Each of the groups has two years duration. There is a problem of incorporating all the documents from Rabindra Rachanabali collection in the study as the dates of writing for every document are not known. Only those documents are included in the study whose dates of writing are known. Almost six hundred documents are taken into consideration whose dates of writing are ranging from 1876 to 1941. Distribution of different lexical richness measures with time are given in Figure 3.

It is seen from Figure 3 that the values of TTR, Index of Guiraud and Index of Herdan have almost

Figure 2. Distribution of number of types and different lexical richness measures with number of tokens for Rabindra Rachanabali collection genre-wise

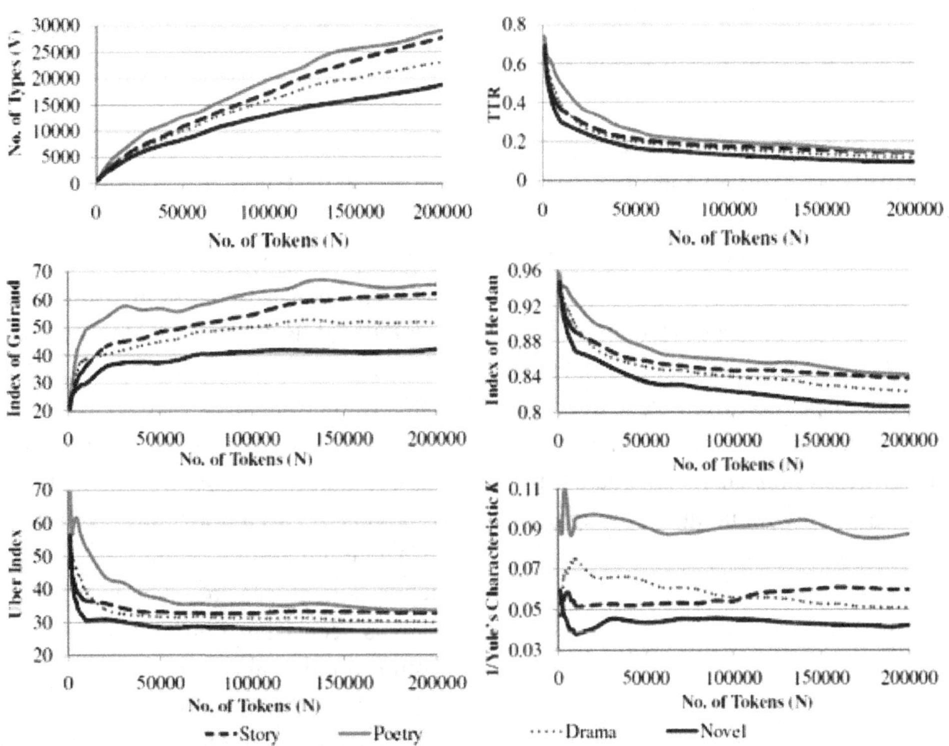

Figure 3. Distribution of different lexical richness measures with time

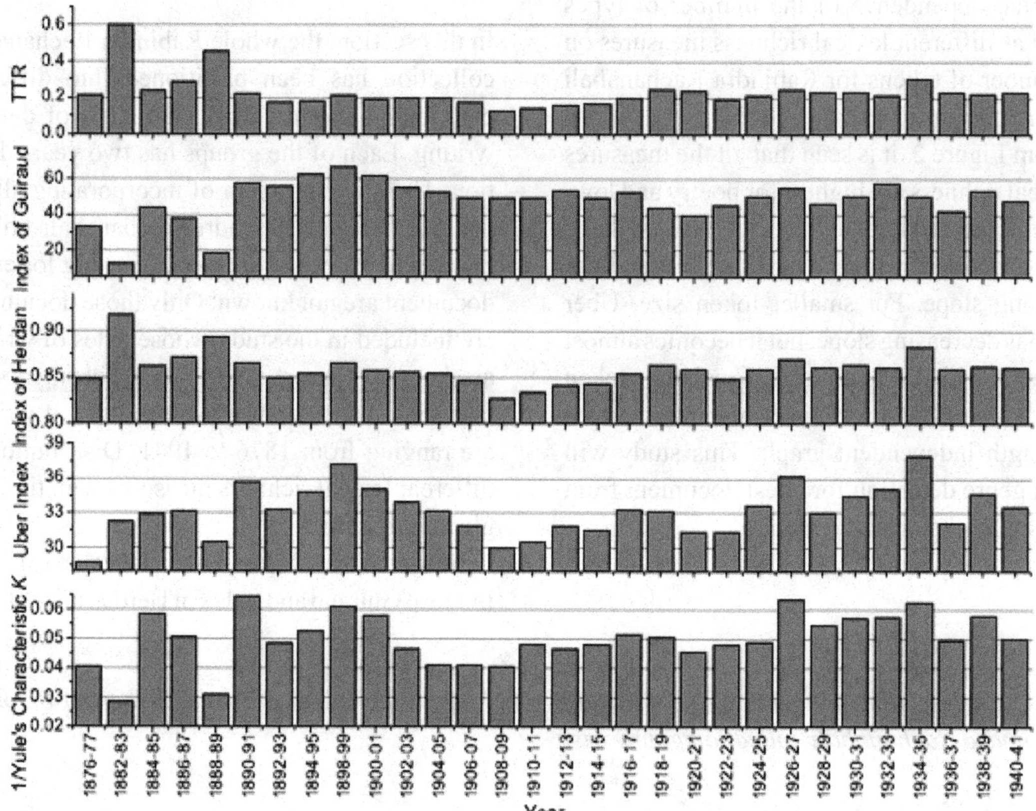

an average value throughout the years except for two values. If the years 1882-83 and 1888-89 are exempted from the calculations, as there are very small number of tokens in these years, average value of TTR,

Index of Guiraud and Index of Herdan will be approximately 0.2, 50, and 0.85 respectively. It is also seen that the dispersion from these average values is very minimal for every other values. In case of Uber Index and Yule's Characteristic *K*, no average values are maintained throughout the years.

Comparative Study with Other Authors

In this part, we present a comparative study of different lexical richness measures between the writings of Rabindranath Tagore and Bankim Chandra Chattopadhyay (1838 - 1894), who predates Rabindranath Tagore by twenty years. All the novels from both of the authors are taken for the comparative study. Details of the collection of novels of two authors are given in Table 3.

The comparative graphs for different lexical richness measures are given in Figure 4.

It is seen from Figure 4 that the documents from Rabindranath Tagore's novel, having token size of below thirty two thousand (<32,000), have higher values than the documents from Bankim

Table 3. Details of the test collection for comparative study

Author Name	No. of Novels	Total No. of Tokens	Total No. of Unique Tokens
Rabindranath Tagore	13	594,757	40,626
Bankim Chandra Chattopadhyay	14	381,119	36,016

Chandra Chattopadhyay's novel of same size for every measures. For token sizes of greater than thirty two thousand (>32,000), the documents from Rabindranath Tagore's novel have lower values than the documents from Bankim Chandra Chattopadhyay's novel. It implies that Bankim Chandra Chattopadhyay had used much unique words than Rabindranath Tagore for longer novels.

ANWESAN: A PLATFORM FOR SEARCHING BENGALI LITERARY WORKS

Anwesan is a digital library as well as search engine for the Rabindra Rachanabali collection. It is developed on the framework of DSpace version 1.5.2. Some major changes have been made on this open-source digital repository DSpace, according to our requirements. Though DSpace supports Unicode encoding, but there were no available tokenizer or stemmer for Bengali language in the existing system of DSpace. A tokenizer and a rule-based stemmer for Bengali have been developed. After integrating these modules with our system, the correctness, i.e. recall value of the search result increases significantly. Besides that, many advanced search features have been incorporated in Anwesan. Perhaps this has been

Figure 4. Comparison of different lexical richness measures between novels of Rabindranath Tagore and Bankim Chandra Chattopadhyay

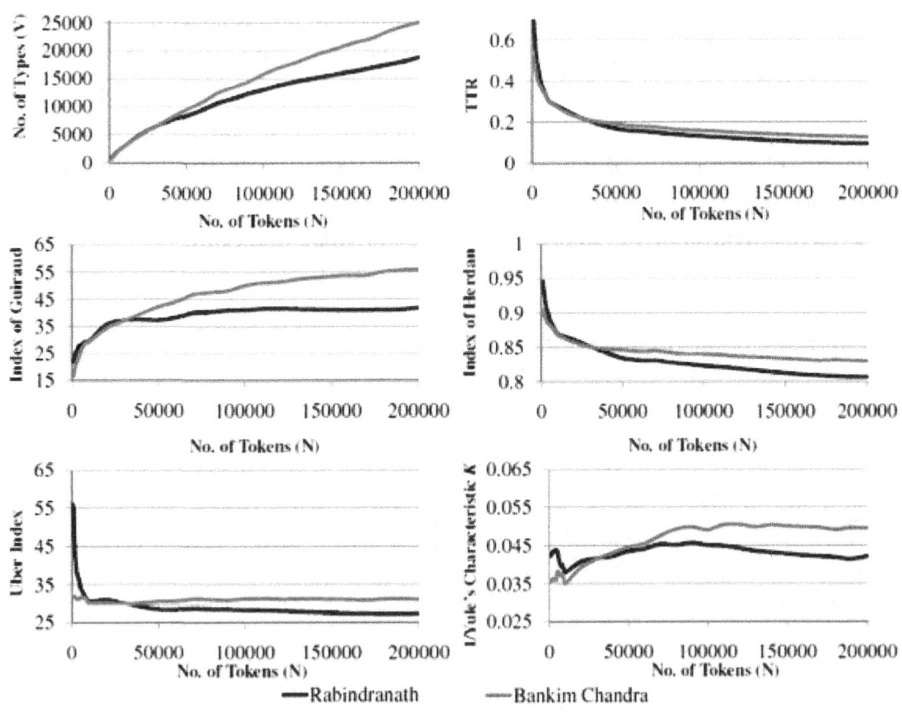

the most extensive exercise in extending DSpace to an Indian language.

Like any other search engines, in Anwesan also, the complete functionality consists of two basic parts. First part is indexing and the second part is retrieval. In the first part, to create an index file from all the documents, we need to extract every token from documents. Tokenizer and the rule-based stemmer are used for this procedure. The whole indexing is done in administrator's side. All the actions in the retrieval part are done in users' side. In the retrieval part, users enter their query and the search engine searches for the user query from that index file and return the correct results, i.e. relevant to the user query. Full-text as well as metadata search are feasible in Anwesan using Lucene, a high-performance, full-featured text search engine library written entirely in Java. This Lucene is used as the search engine in DSpace.

Architecture of Anwesan

In the architecture of Anwesan, there are many supporting modules for indexing and searching procedure. There are tokenizer, stemmer, database and database updating module for indexing procedure. The index file is created for complete Rabindra Rachanabali collection using these modules. In the retrieval part, the users type their query and get search result through user interface. Searching is done using application module and the rank score module is used to return the search result after sorting them by relevancy measure. Each and every module is written in Java, JSP or servlet. The whole architecture of Anwesan is given in Figure 5.

From the architectural view of Anwesan, it is seen that the whole system consists of mainly three modules. The basic three components are as follows.

Display Module: The display module directly interacts with the users. This module maintains the displaying pages, where a user can enter queries or the pages where the search results are displayed. The user queries are sent to the application module for further processing and the search results are received from the application module to display using this module.

Application Module: The application module is most important module in the system. Primarily while indexing, this module reads the documents one by one and redirects the contents of the documents to the database updating module. In time of searching, it takes user query as input, sends it to database updating module to extract root words and finally search for that root word in database. If there are more than one search results for a query, then all the search results are sorted according to the relevancy score and this sorted result is sent to the display module.

Figure 5. Block diagram of the architecture of Anwesan

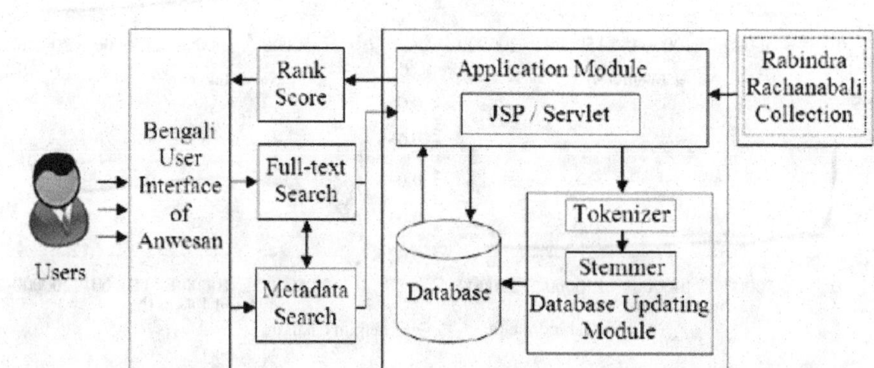

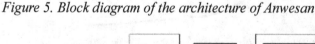

Database Updating Module: The efficiency and correctness of the system depends upon this module. The measures like precision and recall are highly depend upon how efficiently this module can extract root words to store in database and to match with database entries. The contents of the documents and users query are the input to this module. Tokenizer is used to split a string into individual tokens according to a set of delimiters. The resulting tokens are then passed on to stemmer for further processing of the input string. The process can be considered a sub-task of parsing input.

Bengali Stemmer

Stemming (Majumder et al., 2007 October) is the process for reducing inflected or sometimes derived words to their root form. Bengali is morphologically rich language and highly inflectional in nature. Most of the inflectional words in Bengali are generated by adding suffixes to the root word. So, suffix stripping is the best way of getting stems from Bengali words. The stemmer used in Anwesan is a rule-based stemmer (Das & Mitra, 2011 January; Sarkar & Bandyopadhyay, 2008) for inflectional words in Bengali. A set of rules are used to stripe off suffix parts from every tokens and to get the stemmed part. The rule-based stemmer and the tokenizer have been developed in such a way so that it can be integrated with Lucene as Bengali analyzer.

Advanced Search Features

Apart from full-text search, some advanced search features are included in Anwesan. The most promising feature is that user can build query by merging maximum three metadata values by logical operator like AND(^), OR(□), NOT(¬).

Some special search features are included in the system of Anwesan for the benefit of users. Users can search query only from some specialized collection, excluding the remaining part of the whole community. This feature of domain selection makes the whole searching space smaller and makes the search procedure faster.

Figure 6. Number of searches performed per month

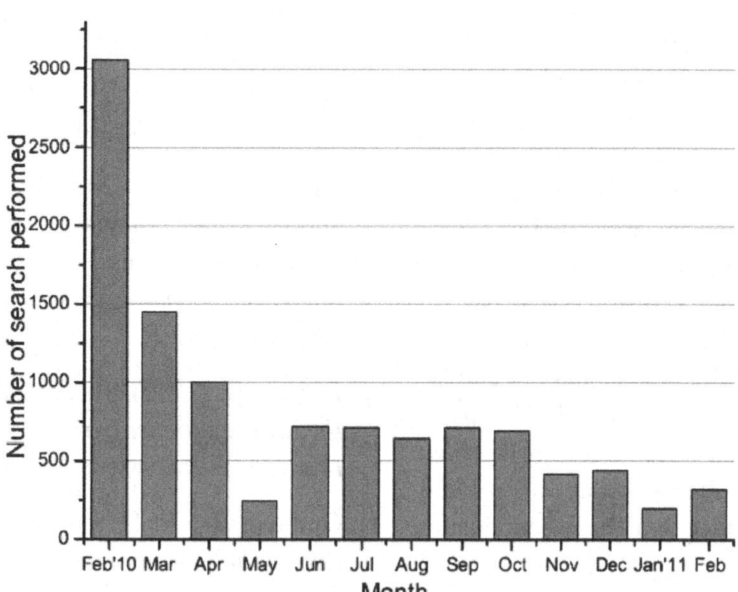

Bengali Virtual Keyboard and Transliteration Engine

As there is no cross-lingual support in Anwesan till now, users must have to type their query in Bengali alphabets only. But typing the queries in Bengali alphabets is a problem for some users, not having any Bengali keyboards, a virtual Bengali keyboard is provided in the Web page of Anwesan. But it is seen from the statistics of previous user queries that some users have been typing query in English alphabets, though a Bengali virtual keyboard is provided. So recently, a transliteration engine is also provided, so that user can type Bengali words in English alphabets phonetically.

Highlighted Query Words

A new feature of highlighted page is invoked in Anwesan, which is not present in DSpace system. In this feature, the content of the document is displayed with query words highlighted. Using this feature, user can be aware about the exact location of query words in the document. This is similar to the cached page of Google search engine.

Usage Statistics

The Website for Anwesan (http://anwesan.iitkgp.ernet.in) was released in Kolkata Book Fair, 2010. After that, many major and minor modifications and addition of some new features to the Website is in the process of continuous up-gradation. The details about the number of search performed, the number of items view, user query and many other features have been tracked in the statistics file of the system. Number of search performed per month for one year from the month of February 2010 to February 2011 is displayed in Figure 6.

From this figure, it is seen that there was huge number of hits just after Anwesan was publicly open, and after that there is a steady continuation of that.

CONCLUSION

This is an initial attempt to quantitatively study the lexical richness of the literary works of Rabindranath Tagore. This is possibly the first such work on a Bengali literature. We have studied the effectiveness of several statistical measures for this purpose. A comprehensive collection of Rabindranath Tagore, released in 2010, was used for this purpose. A cross genre and chronological study may help in genre classification and study of chronological variation. Several other studies are possible, concerning statistics beyond unigrams and bi-grams. Phrases, synonym, affix usage, and deeper structures may be explored.

We have also developed a search engine, Anwesan, for the collection of Rabindra Rachanabali. It is evident that the Website of Anwesan is effective for searching Bengali literary works.

REFERENCES

Boender, C. G. E., & Rinnooy Kan, A. H. G. (1987). A multinomial Bayesian approach to the estimation of population and vocabulary size. *Biometrika, 74*(4), 849–856. doi:10.1093/biomet/74.4.849.

Bogaards, P., & Laufer-Dvorkin, B. (2004). *Vocabulary in a second language: Selection, acquisition, and testing*. Amsterdam, Netherlands: John Benjamins Publishing Company.

Das, S., & Mitra, P. (2011, January). A rule-based approach of stemming for inflectional and derivational words in Bengali. In *Proceedings of IEEE Students' Technology Symposium* (pp. 134-136). Kharagpur: IEEE.

Dugast, D. (1979). *Vocabulaire et stylistique: I théâtre et dialogue: Travaux de linguistique quantitative*. Geneva, Switzerland: Slatkine-Champion.

Guiraud, P. (1954). *Les caractères statistiques du vocabulaire*. Paris: Presses Universitaires de France.

Guiraud, P. (1960). *Problèmes et méthodes de la statistique linguistique*. Paris: Presses Universitaires de France.

Haznedar, B., & Gavruseva, E. (2008). *Current trends in child second language acquisition: A generative perspective*. Amsterdam, Netherlands: John Benjamins Publishing Company.

Heaps, H. S. (1978). *Information retrieval: Computational and theoretical aspects*. Orlando, FL: Academic Press, Inc..

Herdan, G. (1960). *Type-token mathematics: A textbook of mathematical linguistics*. Mouton: Gravenhage.

Herdan, G. (1964). *Quantitative linguistics*. London: Butterworths.

Hess, C. W., Haug, H. T., & Landry, R. G. (1989). The reliability of type-token ratios for the oral language of school age children. *Journal of Speech and Hearing Research*, *32*(3), 536–540. PMID:2779198.

Holmes, D. (1994). Authorship attribution. *Computers and the Humanities*, *28*, 87–106. doi:10.1007/BF01830689.

Hoover, D. L. (2003). Another perspective on vocabulary richness. *Computers and the Humanities*, *37*(2), 151–178. doi:10.1023/A:1022673822140.

Laufer, B., & Nation, P. (1995). Vocabulary size and use: Lexical richness in L2 written production. *Applied Linguistics*, *16*(3), 307–322. doi:10.1093/applin/16.3.307.

Lindsay, R. K., & Gordon, M. D. (1999, May). Literature-based discovery by lexical statistics. *Journal of the American Society for Information Science American Society for Information Science*, *50*, 574–587. doi:10.1002/(SICI)1097-4571(1999)50:7<574::AID-ASI3>3.0.CO;2-Q.

Majumder, P., Mitra, M., Parui, S. K., Kole, G., Mitra, P., & Datta, K. (2007). YASS: Yet another suffix stripper. *ACM Transactions on Information Systems*, *25*(4), 18–20. doi:10.1145/1281485.1281489.

Manning, C. D., Raghavan, P., & Schütze, H. (2008). *Introduction to information retrieval*. New York, NY: Cambridge University Press. doi:10.1017/CBO9780511809071.

Miranda-García, A., & Calle-Martín, J. (2005). Yule's characteristic *K* revisited. *Language Resources and Evaluation*, *39*(4), 287–294. doi:10.1007/s10579-005-8622-8.

Nation, P. (1993). Using dictionaries to estimate vocabulary size: Essential, but rarely followed, procedures. *Language Testing*, *10*(1), 27–40. doi:10.1177/026553229301000102.

Ordan, N., Itskovich, V., Shlesinger, S., & Kanter, I. (2010). Lexical richness revisited: Blueprint for a more economical measure. *Journal of Quantitative Linguistics*, *17*(1), 55–67. doi:10.1080/09296170903395957.

Ratkowsky, D. (1988). Review: The travaux de linguistique quantitative. *Computers and the Humanities*, *22*(1), 77–81. doi:10.1007/BF00056351.

Ratkowsky, D. A., & Hantrais, L. (1975). Tables for comparing the richness and structure of vocabulary in texts of different lengths. *Computers and the Humanities*, *9*(2), 69–75. doi:10.1007/BF02404306.

Richards, B. (1987). Type/token ratios: What do they really tell us? *Journal of Child Language*, *14*(2), 201–209. doi:10.1017/S0305000900012885 PMID:3611238.

Richards, B., & Malvern, D. (2000). *Measuring vocabulary richness in teenage learners of French*. Paper presented at the British Educational Research Association Conference. London.

Sarkar, S., & Bandyopadhyay, S. (2008). Design of a rule-based stemmer for natural language text in Bengali. In *Proceedings of the IJCNLP-08 Workshop on NLP for Less Privileged Languages* (pp. 65-72). Hyderabad, India: IJCNLP.

Smith, J. A., & Kelly, C. (2002). Stylistic constancy and change across literary corpora: Using measures of lexical richness to date works. *Computers and the Humanities*, *36*(4), 411–430. doi:10.1023/A:1020201615753.

Thomas, D. (2005). *Type-token ratios in one teachers classroom talk: An investigation of lexical complexity*. Academic Press.

Tweedie, F. J., & Baayen, R. H. (1998). How variable may a constant be? Measures of lexical richness in perspective. *Computers and the Humanities*, *32*(5), 323–352. doi:10.1023/A:1001749303137.

Weitzman, M. (1971). How useful is the logarithmic type/token ratio? *Journal of Linguistics*, *7*(2), 237–243. doi:10.1017/S0022226700002930.

Williamson, G. (2009). *Type-token ratio*. Retrieved January 10, 2012, from http://www.speech-therapyinformation-and-resources.com/type-token-ratio.html

Yule, G. U. (1944). *The statistical study of literary vocabulary*. Cambridge, UK: Cambridge University Press.

ENDNOTES

1 http://www.nltr.org/SNLTR/

Chapter 14
Sentiment Recognition from Bangla Text

K. M. Azharul Hasan
Khulna University of Engineering and Technology (KUET), Bangladesh

Sajidul Islam
Khulna University of Engineering and Technology (KUET), Bangladesh

G. M. Mashrur-E-Elahi
Khulna University of Engineering and Technology (KUET), Bangladesh

Mohammad Navid Izhar
Khulna University of Engineering and Technology (KUET), Bangladesh

ABSTRACT

Sentiment analysis is a very important area of the natural language processing. In general, sentiment classification means the analysis to determine the expression of a speaker whether he or she holds positive or negative opinion to a specific subject. With the rapid growth of e-commerce, sentiment analysis can greatly influence everyone in their real life. For example, product reviews on the Web have become an important source of information for customers' decision making when they want to buy any product. As the reviews are often too many for customers to go through, how to automatically classify and detect the sentiment from them has become an important research problem. In this chapter, the authors present a Sentiment Analyzer that recognizes the Bangla sentiment or opinion about a subject from Bangla text. They construct some phrase patterns and calculate their sentiment orientation. They add tags to words in the Bangla text to construct the phrase pattern for positive and negative sentiment. Then the authors match the phrase pattern in Bangla text with their predefined phrase pattern and cumulate the sentiment orientation of each sentence.

DOI: 10.4018/978-1-4666-3970-6.ch014

INTRODUCTION

Sentiment analysis or opinion mining is a vast area of Natural Language Processing (NLP). Analyzing sentiment of a language is a challenging task in NLP. In general, the motive of sentiment analysis is to determine the expression of a speaker or a writer with respect to some specific topic or story. The expression may be their opinion, feelings, attitude or comments, which indicate the thinking of the writer or the emotional effect the writer wants to have on reader mind (Picard et al., 2011). The fundamental task in sentiment analysis is classifying the sentimental state of a text in a given document whether the expressed opinion in a document is positive, negative, or neutral (Shaikh et al., 2007).

Bangla (or Bengali), one of the more important Indo-Iranian languages, is the sixth-most popular in the world and spoken by a population that now exceeds 250 million. It is the primary language in Bangladesh and second language in India (Das & Bandyopadhyay, 2010). Lots of research on sentiment analysis has been done on different languages such as English (Picard et al., 2011; Sebastiani, 2002; Lu, Liu, & Zhang, 2006), Chinese (Zhang et al. 2011), Urdu (Sayed et al. 2011) etc. But in contrary, sentiment analysis is still an unsolved research problem in Bangla and such kind of research work is very rare due to lake of resource and the complexity of Bangla language.

The Internet has become a rich platform for people to express their opinion, attitude, feeling, and emotion. From this point of view, Web is an important source of product reviews, news reviews, blog reviews, movie review, stock market reviews, travel advice, social issue discussions, consumer complaints, etc. Nowadays, Bangla has been using widely in the Web. Automatic sentiment classification will become very useful in above applications. Sentiment analysis is now a great interest to the social networking media such as Twitter, Facebook, Google+ as well. Using sentiment analysis, they can track their site for some unexpected posts, comments and share. But they require analyzing many languages.

In this chapter, we present a phrase pattern-based (Fei et al. 2004) method in classifying sentiment orientation of Bangla text. That is to analyze whether the text expresses a favorable or unfavorable sentiment for a specific subject. We construct some phrase patterns and calculate their sentiment orientation by unsupervised learning algorithm. When we classify a document, we first add special tags to some words in the text, and then match the tags within a sentence with some phrase patterns to get the sentiment orientation of the sentence. At last, we add up the sentiment orientation of each sentence. We classify the text according to this summation. The research on Bangla sentiment recognition and classification is in very primary stage. Still more research efforts are needed to reach the user satisfaction level and social demand. We present a sentiment analyzer for Bangla language using machine-learning methodology for paragraph level granularity. Along with the proposal, we determine some technical challenges for Bangla language processing. This analyzing technique basically recognizes the Bangla sentiment or opinion about a subject from Bangla text. We implement the corresponding Bangla dictionary in Extensible Markup Language (XML) format using the word as value and its Parts of Speech (POS) as tag name. The XML is used because it is a very efficient technique for data storing and searching. We believe the proposed method can be applied efficiently for detecting sentiment from Bangla text.

TRENDS AND SOLUTIONS OF SENTIMENT RECOGNITION

What is the opinion of other people has always carried a valuable piece of information in any decision-making process which may help to provide better output. There are two popular procedures for sentiment detection automatically (Esuli & Sebastiani, 2006) one is dictionary-based approach and another is corpus-based approach. The dictionary-based methods mainly determine the sentiment orientation of a particular word based on the sentiment-bearing words in the dictionary. And the corpus-based technique depends on syntactic patterns of words in large texts to determine their sentiment. Modern approaches to Natural Language Processing (NLP) are grounded in machine learning which classifies the reviews with machine learning technology into positive or negative. Some machine learning text labeling algorithms like Conditional Random Field (CRF) (Diederich & Dillon, 2008), Support Vector Machine (SVM) (Das & Bandyopadhyay, 2009) has been used to cluster same type of opinions. Phrase pattern based approach (Fei, Liu, & Wu, 2004) is another popular technique for recognizing sentiment from text. There are also other approaches such as feature level based approach, and subjectivity detection (Pang & Lee, 2004) for recognizing sentiment for popular topics.

There are different levels of studying sentiment of text such as words (Turney, 2002 and Das & Bandyopadhyay, 2009), phrases and sentences (Kim, & Hovy, 2006 and Wilson et al., 2005), and documents (Hu & Liu, 2004). Sentiment has been studied based on keyword spotting, lexical affinity (Valitutti, 2004) statistical methods (Pennebaker, et al. 2003), a dictionary of affective concepts and lexicon, commonsense knowledgebase (Liu et al. 2003), fuzzy logic (Subasic & Huettner, 2001), knowledge-base from facial expression (Fitrianie & Rothkrantz, 2006), machine learning (Wiebe et al. 2005), domain specific classification (Nasukawa & Yi, 2003), proximity-based sentiment analysis (Hasan & Adjeroh, 2011), and valence assignment (Wilson et al., 2005). There are some study that dedicated to domain specific such as text mining with sentiment analysis to invest in stock market (Michael, 2012), Online Health Communities (OHC) to obtain information and seek social support (Baojun et al., 2011).

A semi-supervised approach to sentiment classification is proposed by Dasgupta and Ng (2009) to detect the ambiguous and unambiguous review via a combination of active learning, transductive learning, and ensemble learning. A review is ambiguous when the reviewer discussed both the positive and negative aspects of the subject, which is not uncommon in reviews. Using their model (Dasgupta and Ng, 2009), they automatically identify and label the unambiguous reviews and handle the ambiguous reviews using a discriminative learner to bootstrap from the automatically labeled unambiguous reviews and a small number of manually labeled reviews that are identified by an active learner. Dasgupta and Nga (2009) introduces a sentiment based classification or clustering of documents. The text clustering is usually done by topic, author's mood, sender, age etc. It incorporates the users feedback into the clustering algorithm that helps to detect the dimension on which the clustering to be done using sentiment detection dataset. Consoli (2009) recognized the textual sentiment by classifying the words as Direct Affecting Words (DAW) and Indirect Affecting Words (IAW) where DAW group is formed by words expressing a direct emotional state in the specific domain and other words belong to IAW group. Based on the affectivity of single words they estimate and polarize the opinion in positive or negative with its intensity.

However, to our knowledge, some works addressed automatic sentiment or emotion detection from Bangla text such as Das (2011), Das and Bandyopadhyay (2009), (2010), and Das et al. (2012). Das (2011) proposed the Tracking of emotions based on topic or event by employing sense based affect scoring techniques for Bangla. They analyze the emotions for annotated news stories and blog corpora in Bengali incorporating *SentiWordNet* (Esuli & Sebastiani, 2006) and *WordNet Affect* (Strapparava and Valitutti, 2004). The system identifies the emotions consisting of four inter-connected modules including word, phrase, sentence, and document. Das et al. (2012)

recognizes the emotion of Bangla language Bangla blogs. They developed a pre-processing technique to retrieve and store the bloggers' comments on specific topics. The identified Ekman's (Ekman, 1993) six basic emotions from the bloggers' comments at sentence and paragraph level granularities using the Bengali *WordNetAffect* (Das, & Bandyopadhyay, 2010) which is developed from the affect wordlists already available in English. Das and Bandyopadhyay(2010) detect the opinion from Bangla text based on news corpus using support vector machine (Das & Bandyopadhyay, 2009).

CHALLENGES FOR BANGLA LANGUAGE PROCESSING

Some important challenges for Bangla language processing are pointed out in this Section. The challenges include:

- Bangla is a language that has very flexible structure for constructing a sentence. Suppose the general structure of an English language: Subject + Verb + Object. (Example: I eat rice). Any ordering of the structure is incorrect in English but in Bangla any ordering is correct (Example: আমি ভাত খাই, ভাত আমি খাই, খাই আমি ভাত) and has the same meaning.
- Bangla language has two forms. One is elegant, or chaste (সাধুভাষা), and the other is colloquial (চলিত ভাষা) language. These two forms of Bangla language make it difficult to model.
- **Consonants and Vowels:** Bangla language has vowels and constants as well as symbolic sign of vowels.
- **Compound Letter or Diphthong (যুক্তবর্ণ) Identification:** Diphthong is the special properties of Bangla language but it provides another challenge for modeling Bangla language. For example: বিজ্ঞান (Science), চঞ্চল (Fickle), বন্ধু (Friend), কান্ড (Occurrence), বিহঙ্গ (Bird), কলঙ্ক (Scandal), লাঞ্ছনা (Harassment), ভিক্ষা (Begging).
- **Symbolic Sign:** The vowel letters becomes a symbolic KAR such as ◌া, ◌ি, ◌ী, ◌ু, ◌ূ, ◌ৃ, ◌ে, ◌ৈ, ◌ো, ◌ৌ. Bengali is written from left to right. Space is used to mark word boundaries. Letters are uncased and are grouped together based on place and manner of articulation. When writing, characters merge to form single base line, as shown for the word BAABAA (father) as follows: For example: ব (Letter *Ba*) + ◌া(Vowel *AA*) + ব (Letter *Ba*) + ◌া(Vowel *AA*) = বাবা
- **Miscellaneous Signs:** হসন্ত, ব-ফলা, ম-ফলা, র-ফলা, য-ফলা, রেফ; for example: প্রকাশ (Expose), ব্যস্ত (Busy), জন্ম (Birth), চর্চা (Practice). This is sometimes difficult to detect the word.
- **Standardization of Keyboard:** Still there is no standard key board for Bangla Language typing.
- Besides these, there are some other challenges like huge vocabulary, same word having different meaning for different position in a sentence.

A PHRASE PATTERN SCHEME FOR RECOGNIZING SENTIMENT FROM BANGLA TEXT

In this section, we present a scheme to determine the sentiment of Bangla text. The methodology is based on positive or negative sentiment of words of a Bangla sentence. We are interested in identifying positive or negative sentiment from a Bangla text hence scope of the chapter is limited to sentiment assessment only.

Tagging Bangla Sentimental Words

There are lots of words in a sentence but not all words contain any type of sentiment. According to a linguistic survey, only 4% of the words in a sentence carry sentiment of the author. Hence we analyze the words for selecting the right word containing sentiment and we categorize them according to their sentiment. We write "sentimental word" to indicate the word that contains sentiment. Each word can express two types of sentiment, positive sentiment and negative sentiment. After categorization, we collect those sentimental words and add different tags to the words. By tag we mean the concatenation of sentiment (positive or negative) and parts of speech of the word. Hence every tag name has two parts, first letter of the tag name express sentiment type and second letter express parts-of-speech (POS). For example, the word "খারাপ" has tag *nj*. It means the sentiment orientation is negative(n), and its POS is an adjective(j). Table 1 shows the tagging of Bangla words and their categorization.

Table 1. Bangla word categorization and adding tags

Sl.	Type	Tag	Example
1	Positive noun	pn	সাহায্য, প্রশংসা
2	Negative noun	nn	অপবাদ,বিপক্ষ
3	Positive adjective	pj	ভাল,বড়
4	Negative adjective	nj	খারাপ, দুষ্টু
5	Positive adverb	pa	সবচেয়ে, খুব
6	Negative adverb	na	ধীরেধীরে
7	Positive verb	pv	অর্জন,দেখ
8	Negative verb	nv	পালান, থাম
9	Negative word	nw	না,নয়,নেই
10	Positive word	pw	হ্যাঁ,হাঁ

Storing Words in XML

The Extensible Markup Language (XML) is a very efficient format for storing data. It is now widely used because of its simplicity and efficiency. The tasks behind the XML are always the same, reading data from XML and writing data into it. The basic format of XML tag is *<tag_name>value</tag_name>*. We design a XML file for storing the sentimental words as shown in Table 1. Here we consider Bangla word as *value* and *tag_name* as its corresponding parts-of-speech (POS). Box 1 shows an example of XML data file.

Constructing Phrase Patterns

We construct phrase patterns by using the tags (see Table 1) in a group. Sentiment orientation depends on these constructed phrase patterns. Each phrase pattern consists of noun, adjective, adverb, verb, positive word and negative word. For an example, in the sentence," সে খুব ভাল ক্রিকেট খেলে, the word খুব is a positive adverb *pa*, ভাল is a positive adjective *pj* and খেলে *is* a positive verb *pv.* The phrase pattern of this sentence is pa+aj+pv. There are two types of phrase patterns; positive phrase pattern (represent positive sentiment orientation) and negative phrase pattern (represent negative sentiment orientation). Examples of

Box 1. Data format of XML file

```
<?xml version="1.0" encoding="UTF-8" ?>
- <!-- This document was created with Syntext Serna -->
<word>
<positive_noun> <pn> খেল  </pn>
</positive_noun>
<negative_noun> <nn> বাদ  </nn>
    <nn>দুঃখ</nn>
</negative_noun>
<positive_adjective> <pj> ভালো  </pj>
    <pj> সামর্থ্য  </pj>
</positive_adjective>
</word>
```

some phrase patterns are shown in Table 2. We use another XML file for storing these phrase patterns as in Box 2.

Applying Machine Learning Methodology

Every phrase pattern has its own sentiment orientation either positive or negative. For example, phrase pattern *pn+pj* expresses positive sentiment orientation and phrase pattern *pn+nj* expresses negative sentiment orientation. There are several ways of finding strength of sentiment orientation. Phrase patterns with positive sentiment are evaluated as +1 and the phrase patterns with negative sentiment are evaluated as –1 (Tetsuya & Jeonghee, 2003). In our study, after creating phrase patterns from input text we compare the input text phrase pattern with our predefined phrase patterns. We count the phrase pattern appears in the positive samples and in the negative samples respectively.

Table 2. Phrase patterns

Positive Phase Pattern (Sp)	Negative Phase Pattern (Sn)
pn	nn
pn + pj	pn + nj
pa + pj	pa + nj
pa + pj + pv	pa + nj + pv
pj + pn + pv	pj+ pn + pv + nw

Box 2. Predefined phrase pattern

```
<?xml version="1.0" encoding="utf-8" ?>
<pattern>
<p_pattern>
<sp>pv</sp>
<sp>pj+pj</sp>
<sp>pj+pv</sp>
<sp>pj+pv+pj</sp>
</p_pattern>
<n_pattern>
<sn>pn + nj</sn>
<sn>pj+pv+pv+nw</sn>
</n_pattern>
</pattern>
```

For this purpose we use two different types of counter, *sp* count total number of positive sentiment orientation and *sn* counts total number of negative sentiment orientation. Then we used the following machine learning (Fei, Liu, & Wu, 2004) formula to evaluate the sentiment of a statement.

$$S = \begin{Bmatrix} \log\left(\dfrac{Sp}{Sn}\right); & Sp \neq 0 \middle| Sn \neq 0 \\ \log\left(\dfrac{1+Sp}{1+Sn}\right); & Sp = 0 \text{ or } Sn = 0 \end{Bmatrix}$$

Here, S = sentiment orientation of the text, Sp= total number of positive phrase patterns, and Sn= total number of negative phrase patterns. If $S<0$, it expresses negative sentiment else expresses positive sentiment.

Classification of Sentiment

Every individual person has his/her own individual sentiment for a single text from different point of view. One person's opinion on a particular paragraph may positive; in contrast other may think it as nearly positive. That means there is another state of sentiment which we call weakly positive. To make the result more realistic and acceptable we subdivide the positive and negative sentiment as weakly positive, positive, strongly positive and weakly negative, negative and strongly negative respectively. The classification is shown in Figure 1.

We make this sub-classification based on experimental result and expert's opinion. By doing this we set the range or values for each sub class based on the following inequalities:

$S=0$, neutral
$0 < S \leq +0.3$, weakly positive
$0.3 < S \leq +.8$, positive
$0.8 < S \leq +1.0$, strongly positive

and

Figure 1. Classification of sentiment

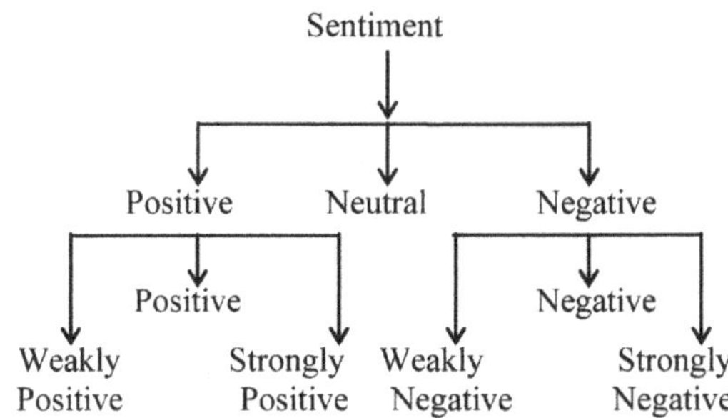

$-0.3 < S \leq 0$, weakly negative
$-0.8 < S \leq -0.3$, negative
$-1.0 < S \leq -0.8$, strongly negative

The threshold values are selected based on empirical study i.e. various threshold values were trialed and these values produced the best classification results.

Sentiment Classification Process

First we match the key words (which contains sentiment) of the input text with our stored XML data storage. Then we make a phrase pattern with these matched words and compare them with our predefined phrase patterns. If one of the constructed phrase patterns matches with predefined phrase patterns, the sentiment orientation of this sentence is equal to the sentiment of the predefined phrase patterns. For example, there is an input text and we tag the key words of the sentence. এখন বায়ুদূষণ (*nn*) ঢাকার প্রধান সমস্যা (*nj*) । So, the constructed pattern is *nn+nj*.

EXPERIMENTAL RESULTS

We have implemented a prototype system using our methodology. To find more realistic results we collect data from various online newspapers as done by Charles et al. (2011). We tested these collected articles using our system. To verify and compare the accuracy of our proposed methodology, we also collected expert opinion for the same article. Some sample data are shown in Table 3 where we worked with 10 sports reviews from www.prothom-alo.com and www.bdnews24.com. 6 of them holds positive sentiment and 4 of them holds negative sentiment. We have also taken opinion from experts (on average 10 people) regarding of our selected reviews. We represent a comparative result of some articles of our experiment in Table 3.

Table 3 shows that for almost all the articles the system result matches with the expert opinion. Among the five articles, we see that most of the articles match with the 70 percent experts' opinion. Article 4 matches with only 60 percent experts' opinion which shows worse result. For article 5, where experts said weakly positive where as our system result shows weakly negative. This is because the expression is positive when Bangladesh team is concerned but the same expression is negative when Australia team is concerned. For example "গুড়িয়ে দেয়ার সামর্থ্য রাখেন" is positive for Bangladesh team and negative for Australia team. There are some other exceptions of Bangla words that contain dual sentiment both negative and positive sentiment. For example, এমন মার দেব মজা টের পাবে. The sentence is a negative sentence but due to the word "মজা" the sentence becomes positive. There are some exceptions also in literal and non-literal meanings of words. Literal word means taking words in their basic sense without metaphor or allegory. For example, "আজ অস্ট্রেলিয়ার বিপক্ষে বাংলাদেশের দ্বিতীয় ম্যাচ।" The literal meaning of this sentence indicates a negative sense (for the word "বিপক্ষে"). But the non-literal meaning of "বিপক্ষে" means a match between Bangladesh vs. Australia. There are lots of sentences in bangle that can be categorized as above. Because of the literal meaning, the system result becomes weakly negative for article 5.

Our proposed methodology is also tested for articles on international women day for performance analysis. In this case we also find good results that reveal the expert peoples opinion. We

Table 3. Experimental articles of sports with opinion

Sl.	Input Text	Expert Opinion (%)	Our System Result
1.	প্রথমে শোনা গিয়েছিল মেসির চোট সারতে ২৫ থেকে ৪৫ দিন লাগবে । পরে জানানো হয়, চোটমুক্ত হতে দুই থেকে তিন সপ্তাহ সময় লাগবে । বাস্তবতা হলো, প্রত্যাশার চেয়েও দ্রুত সেরে উঠছেন লিওনেল মেসি । গত শুক্রবারই যোগ দিয়েছেন অনুশীলনে । সপ্তাহখানেকের মধ্যেই মাঠে ফিরবেন বার্সেলোনা তারকা । চোট-শঙ্কার সঙ্গে কেটে গেছে আরও একটি শঙ্কা । আর্জেন্টিনা জাতীয় দলের হয়ে মেসির জাপান সফরে আর কোনো আপত্তি নেই বার্সেলোনার । একটি প্রীতি ম্যাচ খেলতে আগামী মাসে জাপান সফর করবে আর্জেন্টিনা । জাপান সফরের দলে মেসিকে রেখেছেন আর্জেন্টিনার অন্তর্বর্তী কোচ সার্জিও বাতিস্তা । বার্সেলোনা কোচ পেপ গার্দিওলা এখন বলছেন, আমি আগের অবস্থান থেকে সরে এসেছি । মেসি জাতীয় দলের সঙ্গে থাকবে । আমি মনে করি, ও ভালোই করবে । সূত্র: 26-9-2010, The Daily Prothom-Alo.	70% Positive expression 30% Strongly positive expression	Strongly positive
2.	আর্জেন্টিনার হয়ে লিওনেল মেসি কেন বার্সেলোনার মতো খেলতে পারেন না। কারণ, আর্জেন্টিনায় বার্সেলোনার মতো সমর্থন পান না মেসি—জানা উত্তরটাই আরেকবার জানিয়ে দিলেন বার্সা ডিফেন্ডার দানি আলভেজ। তবে সহজ এই কথাটা বলতে গিয়ে একটা খুব 'কঠিন' কথা বলে দিয়েছেন ব্রাজিলিয়ান ডিফেন্ডার। আলভেজের মতে, আর্জেন্টিনার চেয়ে বার্সেলোনা ভালো দল। আলভেজ কথাটা বলেছেন মেসি প্রসঙ্গেই। বার্সেলোনায় মেসিকে অজস্র বল এগিয়ে দেওয়া আলভেজ বলছেন, 'আমার মনে হয় মেসির আর্জেন্টিনায় কাজটা কঠিন হওয়ার কারণ, বার্সেলোনা ও আর্জেন্টিনা দলের মধ্যে তুলনা চলে না। আর্জেন্টিনা দলের সব খেলোয়াড়ের প্রতি পূর্ণ শ্রদ্ধা রেখেই বলছি, এই দু দলের তুলনা হয় না। বার্সেলোনায় ও আসলে নিজের মান অনুযায়ী খেলতে পারে।' আর্জেন্টিনার চেয়ে বার্সেলোনা ভালো, এই মন্তব্য এবং আলভেজদের জাতীয়তা—এই দুই যোগ করে তাঁকে আর্জেন্টিনা-বিরোধী ধরে নিতে পারেন কেউ কেউ। তবে ব্রাজিলিয়ান এই তারকা সবকিছুর পরও মেসির মঙ্গল কামনা করেন, মেসির প্রশংসা করেন, 'ওর তো বয়স অনেক কম। ওকে এখনই কাঁধে পুরো জাতির দায়িত্ব নিয়ে নিতে হচ্ছে। এটা তো অনেক বড় দায়িত্ব। কিন্তু ও খুবই ভালো ছেলে। কখনোই কোনো কিছু নিয়ে অভিযোগ করে না।' সূত্র: 12-6-2010, The Daily Prothom-Alo.	80% Positive expression 20% Strongly positive expression	Positive
3.	অস্ট্রেলিয়ার বিপক্ষে একদিনের সিরিজ । টিকে থাকতে হলে দ্বিতীয় খেলায় ব্যাটসম্যানদের ঘুরে দাঁড়াতেই হবে । আর অস্ট্রেলিয়া সিরিজ নিশ্চিত করতে চায় এই ম্যাচেই । তিন ম্যাচের সিরিজের প্রথম খেলায় জিতে ১-০ ব্যবধানে এগিয়ে আছে অস্ট্রেলিয়া । এই অবস্থায় বাংলাদেশের ব্যাটসম্যানদের দায়িত্ব নিয়ে খেলতে হবে । অথচ রানের মধ্যে নেই তারা । ব্যাটসম্যানরা বড় রান করতে পারছেন না । ইমরুল কায়েস বিশ্বকাপে রান পেলেও প্রথম খেলায় ব্যর্থ হয়েছেন । শাহরিয়ার নাফীস সেভাবে রানের মধ্যে নেই । হাসি নেই রকিবুল হাসানের ব্যাটেও । ব্যাটিং 'পাওয়ার প্লে'কেও কাজে লাগাতে পারছেন না ব্যাটসম্যানরা । সূত্র: 10-4-2011, bdnews24.com.	70% Weakly negative expression 30% Strongly negative expression	Weakly negative

continued on following page

Table 3. Continued

Sl.	Input Text	Expert Opinion (%)	Our System Result
4.	এই বিশ্বকাপ মাশরাফির কাছে খুব গুরুত্বপূর্ণ । তাই আসন্ন বিশ্বকাপের জাতীয় দল থেকে বাদ পড়ার পর চোখের পানি আটকে রাখতে পারেননি । নিজ দেশে তিনি বিশ্বকাপে খেলতে পারছেন না । এটি তাঁর জীবনের সবচেয়ে দুঃখের দিন । তারপরও একটু যেন আশার আলো রয়েছে । সুস্থ হলে বিশ্বকাপের দ্বার তাঁর জন্য খোলা থাকছে । সেজন্য মাশরাফি জোর চেষ্টা চালিয়ে যাচ্ছেন ফিটনেস ফিরে পেতে । তাই মাশরাফিকে দেখা যাচ্ছে প্রশিক্ষণ শিবিরে । তার সঙ্গে রয়েছেন জাতীয় দলের আরেক বোলার রুবেল হোসেন । শুক্রবার মাশরাফির প্রাকটিসের সময় ছিলেন জাতীয় দলের ফিজিও মাইক হেনরি । তিনি আশা করছেন যে আগামী ৪ ফেব্রুয়ারি থেকেই পুরো রানআপ নিয়ে বোলিং করতে পারবেন মাশরাফি । সূত্র: 22-01-2011, The Daily Prothom-Alo.	60% Positive expression 40% Negative expression	Positive
5.	বাংলাদেশের বোলিং আক্রমণ নিঃসন্দেহে অনেক ভালো । দেশের মাটিতে স্পিনাররা যে কোনো দলকে গুড়িয়ে দেয়ার সামর্থ্য রাখেন । প্রথম খেলায় ২৭০ রানে থামিয়ে দিয়েছেন তারা অস্ট্রেলিয়াকে । আব্দুর রাজ্জাক, সোহরাওয়ার্দী শুভ, মাহমুদুল্লাহ রিয়াদ ও সাকিবকে নিয়ে ভাবতে বাধ্য হচ্ছেন অস্ট্রেলিয়ার অধিনায়ক মাইকেল ক্লার্ক । প্রথম খেলায় ক্যাচ ও রান-আউটের সুযোগ হাতছাড়া করেছেন ফিল্ডাররা । তবে 'গ্রাউন্ড ফিল্ডিং' খুব একটা খারাপ নয় দলের । অন্যদিকে লড়াইয়ের জন্য বাংলাদেশের ব্যাটসম্যানদের রানের মধ্যে ফেরার কোনো বিকল্প নেই । সূত্র: 10-4-2011, bdnews24.com.	90% Weakly positive expression 10% Positive expression	Weakly negative

took 10 articles on international women day from daily newspaper. From the above 10 articles we found 2 articles are strongly positive, 7 articles are positive and 1 article is weakly positive. Also we compare with experts opinion and found matches with higher percentage people's opinion. Table 4 shows 3 example articles and the calculated results.

FUTURE WORKS

We propose the detection of the positive or negative sentiment of a text for paragraph level granularity. The work can be extended to detect the six basic emotions namely anger, disgust, fear, joy, sadness and surprise for Bangla text. Supervised and unsupervised learning methodology can easily be applied on Bangla text for sentiment analysis or opinion mining for specific domain of text. Ambiguous and unambiguous sentiments for Bangla text can be handled using semi supervised methodology. One more direction is, based on Bangla text, the identification of overlapped comments i.e. user's comments on each other about a subject and dual sentiment detection i.e. the same comment is positive for one and negative for another people. To do the above works it will be necessary and useful to develop the standard data sets for Bangla text about review of products or comments on a subject with respect to emotion or sentiment.

CONCLUSION

The aim of this research was to design and develop algorithm for recognizing the overall sentiment of Bangla language from a paragraph level granularity. We found good results from our prototype system. The performance of the system depends

Table 4. Experimental articles of international women day with opinion

Sl.	Input Text	Expert Opinion (%)	Our System Result
1.	আন্তর্জাতিক নারী দিবসে স্ত্রীকে ১০ লাখ লাল গোলাপ পাঠিয়েছেন কাজাখস্তানের এক ব্যক্তি । সোভিয়েত শাসনামলের অত্যন্ত রোমান্টিক একটি গানের কথা অনুসরণ করে প্রিয়তমা স্ত্রীর মান ভাঙাতে এই উপহার হিসেবে তিনি তাঁকে ১০ লাখ গোলাপ পাঠিয়েছেন । এতে অবশ্য স্ত্রীর মান ভেঙেছে কি না, তা আর জানা যায়নি । সংবাদভিত্তিক ওয়েবসাইট এক্সপ্রেস কে.কেজেড জানায়, ওই ব্যক্তি কাজাখস্তানের কাজিলোর্দা শহরের এক ফুল ব্যবসায়ীকে আন্তর্জাতিক নারী দিবসে তাঁর স্ত্রীর কাছে ১০ লাখ গোলাপ পাঠানোর নির্দেশ দেন । তাও যে-সে গোলাপ হলে হবে না, এগুলো হতে হবে হল্যান্ডের বিখ্যাত লাল গোলাপ । ওয়েবসাইট সূত্রে জানা গেছে, ওই দম্পতির মাঝে কিছুদিন ধরে মান - অভিমান চলছিল । কাজাখস্তানে আন্তর্জাতিক নারী দিবস উপলক্ষে আজ বৃহস্পতিবার প্রতিটি গোলাপ বিক্রি হয়েছে তিন থেকে ১৩ ডলারে । সে হিসাবে ১০ লাখ গোলাপের পেছনে ওই ব্যক্তির ব্যয় হয়েছে ৩০ লাখ থেকে এক কোটি ৩০ লাখ ডলার । সূত্র: 08-03-2012, The Daily Prothom-Alo.	80% Positive expression 20% Strongly positive expression	Positive
2.	১৭ বছর আগে ১৯৯৪ সালে মাধ্যমিক স্তরে ছাত্রীদের ভর্তির হার ছিল ৩৩ শতাংশ । এখন ছাত্রদের পেছনে ফেলে ছাত্রীদের ভর্তির হার বেড়ে হয়েছে ৫৪ শতাংশ । শুধু মাধ্যমিকেই নয়; প্রাথমিক, উচ্চমাধ্যমিক ও উচ্চশিক্ষায় নারীর অংশগ্রহণ বেড়েছে । তবে ঝরে পড়া শিক্ষার্থীদের বেশির ভাগ এখনো ছাত্রী । তা ছাড়া ছাত্রীদের শিক্ষার সার্বিক মান এখনো ভালো হয়নি বলে মনে করেন শিক্ষা নিয়ে কাজ করা ব্যক্তিরা । তত্ত্বাবধায়ক সরকারের সাবেক উপদেষ্টা ও গণসাক্ষরতা অভিযানের নির্বাহী পরিচালক রাশেদা কে চৌধুরী প্রথম আলোকে বলেন, শিক্ষায়তনে ছাত্রীদের অভিগম্যতা বেড়েছে, এটা ঠিক । উপবৃত্তি, নতুন নতুন নীতিমালাসহ নানা ধরনের উদ্যোগের কারণে শিক্ষায় নারীদের অংশগ্রহণ বেড়েছে, কিন্তু সার্বিক মান বাড়েনি । দেখা যাচ্ছে, পরীক্ষাগুলোয় প্রথম সারির দিকে মেয়েরা ভালো করছে, যাদের বেশির ভাগই আর্থিকভাবে মোটামুটি সচ্ছল পরিবারের সন্তান । কিন্তু দরিদ্র পরিবারের ছাত্রীরা কিন্তু অতটা ভালো করতে পারছে না । সূত্র: 08-03-2011, The Daily Prothom-Alo.	50% Positive expression 50% Weakly positive expression	Weakly positive
3.	আমার মায়ের নাম ছিল সাঈদা, ডাকনাম ছিল সেবু । তিনি ছিলেন ছয় ছেলে ও ছয় মেয়ের জননী । আমি হচ্ছি তাঁর আট নম্বর সন্তান । তিনি ছিলেন অত্যন্ত ন্যায় ও নীতিবান ব্যক্তি । অনেক কিছুই তাঁর জানা ছিল এবং এ কারণে তাঁর মৃত্যু পর্যন্ত আমাদের জন্য তিনি ছিলেন মূল্যবান জ্ঞানের ভান্ডার । মৃত্যুর সময় তাঁর বয়স হয়েছিল ৯০ বছর । আমার মা অত্যন্ত রূপবতী ছিলেন । কিন্তু রূপবতী হওয়া সত্ত্বেও বহুবার আমার বাবাকে বলতে শুনেছি যে, তিনি আমার মাকে পছন্দ করেছিলেন তাঁর ব্যক্তিত্ব, তাঁর অন্য মানুষের প্রতি সহানুভূতি এবং সবচেয়ে বেশি তাঁর বুদ্ধিমত্তার জন্য। ১৯২০ সালের শেষের দিকে মা তাঁর পছন্দসই একজন ব্যক্তিকে বিয়ে করেছিলেন । আমার বাবা তখন শুধু ইংল্যান্ড থেকে ফিরেছেন একজন ব্যারিস্টার হয়ে । সূত্র: 08-03-2011, The Daily Prothom-Alo.	70% Positive expression 30% Strongly positive expression	Positive

on the developing the negative and positive phrase patterns. If more phrase patterns are included the performance will be better. Again, inclusion of sentimental word in the dictionary increases the performance of the system. We believe that the proposed method is successfully applicable for the Bangla Language for sentiment detection and can be extended to emotion detection.

REFERENCES

Baojun, Q., Kang, Z., Prasenjit, M., Dinghao, W., Cornelia, C., & John, Y. ... Kenneth, P. (2011). Get online support, feel better – Sentiment analysis and dynamics in an online cancer survivor community. In *Proceedings of PASSAT* (pp. 274 – 281). PASSAT.

Charles, B., Choi, Y., Steven, S., & Eduardo, X. (2011). Empath: A framework for evaluating entity-level sentiment analysis. In *Proceedings of CEWIT* (pp. 1 – 6). CEWIT.

Consoli, D. (2009). Textual emotions recognitions with an intelligent software of sentiment analysis. In *Proceedings of the Third International Conference EITM, section Mathematics and Computer Science* (pp. 997-1009). Retrieved November 10, 2012 from http://www.upm.ro/facultati_departamente/stiinte_litere/conferinte/situl_integrare_europeana/Lucrari3/MI/100_consoli_paper.pdf

Das, A., & Bandyopadhyay, S. (2009). Subjectivity detection in English and Bengali: A CRF-based approach. In *Proceeding of ICON*. Macmillan Publishers.

Das, A., & Bandyopadhyay, S. (2010a). Phrase-level polarity identification for bengali. *International Journal of Computational Linguistics and Applications*, *1*(2), 169–181.

Das, D. (2011). Analysis and tracking of emotions in English and Bengali Texts: A computational approach. ACM. *Proceedings of WWW, 2011*, 343–347.

Das, D., & Bandyopadhyay, S. (2010b). Developing Bengali wordnet affect for analyzing emotion. In *Proceedings of 23rd International Conference on the Computer Processing of Oriental Languages (ICCPOL 2010)*, (pp. 35–40). ICCPOL.

Das, D., Roy, S., & Bandyopadhyay, S. (2012). Emotion tracking on blogs - A case study for Bengali. In Jiang, H. et al. (Eds.), *IEA/AIE 2012, (LNAI)* (*Vol. 7345*, pp. 447–456). Springer. doi:10.1007/978-3-642-31087-4_47.

Dasgupta, S., & Ng, V. (2009). Topic-wise, sentiment-wise, or otherwise? Identifying the hidden dimension for unsupervised text classification. In *Proceedings of the 2009 Conference on Empirical Methods in Natural Language Processing (EMNLP)* (pp. 580—589). EMNLP.

Dasgupta, S., & Nga, V. (2009). Mine the easy, classify the hard: A semi-supervised approach to automatic sentiment classification. In *Proceedings of the Joint Conference of the 47th Annual Meeting of the Association for Computational Linguistics and the 4th International Joint Conference on Natural Language Processing of the Asian Federation of Natural Language Processing (ACL-IJCNLP)* (pp. 701—709). ACL.

Diederich, J., & Dillon, D. (2008). Sentiment recognition by rule extraction from support vector machine. In *Proceedings of Computer Games Multimedia & Allied Technology*. IEEE.

Ekman, P. (1993). Facial expression and emotion. *The American Psychologist*, *48*(4), 384–392. doi:10.1037/0003-066X.48.4.384 PMID:8512154.

Esuli, A., & Sebastiani, F. (2005). Determining the semantic orientation of terms through gloss analysis. In *Proceedings of CIKM* (pp. 617–624). CIKM.

Esuli, A., & Sebastiani, F. (2006). A publicly available lexical resource for opinion mining. In *Proceedings of the 5th Conference on Language Resources and Evaluation*. Genova, Italy: ACL.

Esuli, A., & Sebastiani, F. (2006). SENTIWORDNET: A publicly available lexical resource for opinion mining. In *Proceedings of LREC-06*. LREC.

Fei, Z., Liu, J., & Wu, G. (2004). Sentiment classification using phrase patterns. In *Proceedings of the CIT* (pp. 1147 - 1152). CIT.

Fitrianie, S., & Rothkrantz, L. J. M. (2006). Constructing knowledge for automated text-based emotion expressions. In Proceedings of CompSysTech. CompSysTech.

Hasan, S. M. S., & Adjeroh, D. A. (2011). Proximity-based sentiment analysis. In *Proceedings of ICADIWT* (pp. 106 – 111). ICADIWT.

Hu, M., & Liu, B. (2004). Mining and summarizing customer reviews. In *Proceedings of KDD*. ACM.

Kim, S., & Hovy, E. (2006). Identifying and analyzing judgment opinions. In *Proceedings of HLTNAACL*. ACL.

Kim, S.-M., & Hovy, E. (2004). Determining the sentiment of opinions. In *Proceedings of COLING* (pp. 1367-1373). COLING.

Liu, H., Lieberman, H., & Selker, T. (2003). A model of textual affect sensing using real-world knowledge. In *Proceedings of IUI*, (pp. 125–132). ACM.

Lu, L., Liu, D., & Zhang, H. (2006). Automatic mood detection and tracking of music audio signals. *IEEE Transactions on Audio. Speech & Language Processing*, *14*(1), 5–18. doi:10.1109/TSA.2005.860344.

Michael, S. (2012). Boom or ruin--Does it make a difference? Using text mining and sentiment analysis to support intraday investment decisions. In Proceedings of HICSS (pp. 1050 – 1059). ACM.

Mullen, T., & Collier, N. (2004). Sentiment analysis using support vector machines with diverse information sources. In *Proceedings of EMNLP*. EMNLP.

Nasukawa, T., & Yi, J. (2003). Sentiment analysis: Capturing favorability using natural language processing. In *Proceedings of K-CAP* (pp. 70–77). ACM Press.

Pang, B., & Lee, L. (2004). A sentimental education: Sentiment analysis using subjectivity summarization based on minimum cuts. In *Proceedings of the Association for Computational Linguistics (ACL)* (pp. 271-278). ACL.

Pennebaker, J. W., Mehl, M. R., & Niederhoffer, K. (2003). Psychological aspects of natural language use: Our words, our selves. *Annual Review of Psychology*, *54*, 547–577. doi:10.1146/annurev.psych.54.101601.145041 PMID:12185209.

Picard, R. W. (1997). *Affective computing*. Cambridge, MA: MIT Press.

Picard, R. W., Yzas, V., & Healey, J. (2001). Toward machine emotional intelligence: Analysis of affective physiological state. *IEEE Transactions on Pattern Analysis and Machine Intelligence*, *23*(10), 1175–1191. doi:10.1109/34.954607.

Sayed, A. Z., Muhammad, A., & Martinz, A. M. (2011). Adjectival phrases as the sentiment carriers in the urdu text. *Journal of American Science*, *7*(3), 644–652.

Sebastiani, F. (2002). Machine-learning in automated text categorization. *ACM Computing Surveys*, *34*(1), 1–47. doi:10.1145/505282.505283.

Shaikh, M. A. M., Prendinger, H., & Mitsuru, I. (2007). Assessing sentiment of text by semantic dependency and contextual valence analysis. In Paiva, A., Prada, R., & Picard, R. W. (Eds.), *ACII 2007, (LNCS)* (*Vol. 4738*, pp. 191–202). Springer-Verlag. doi:10.1007/978-3-540-74889-2_18.

Strapparava, C., & Valitutti, A. (2004). Wordnet-affect: An affective extension of wordnet. In 4th LREC (pp. 1083-1086). LREC.

Subasic, P., & Huettner, A. (2001). Affect analysis of text using fuzzy semantic typing. *IEEE Transactions on Fuzzy Systems*, *9*(4), 483–496. doi:10.1109/91.940962.

Tetsuya, N., & Jeonghee, Y. (2003). Sentiment analysis: Capturing favourability using natural language processing. In *Proceedings of K-CAP* (pp. 70-77). K-CAP.

Turney, P. (2002). Thumbs up or thumbs down? Semantic orientation applied to unsupervised classification of reviews. In *Proceedings of 40th Annual Meeting of the ACL* (pp. 417–424). ACL.

Valitutti, A., Strapparava, C., & Stock, O. (2004). Developing affective lexical resources. *PsychNology Journal*, *2*(1), 61–83.

Wiebe, J., Wilson, T., & Cardie, C. (2005). Annotating expressions of opinions and emotions in language. *Language Resources and Evaluation*, *39*(2-3), 165–210. doi:10.1007/s10579-005-7880-9.

Wilson, T., Wiebe, J., & Hoffmann, P. (2005). Recognizing contextual polarity in phrase-level sentiment analysis. In *Proceedings of HLT/EMNLP* (pp. 347–354). ACL.

Zhang, H., Yu, Z., Xu, M., & Shi, Y. (2011). Feature-level sentiment analysis for Chinese product reviews. In *Proceedings of 3rd ICCRD* (pp. 135-140). ICCRD.

Chapter 15

যন্ত্র-না (Jantra-Na: Not-Machine) Can Only Feel যন্ত্রনা (Jantrana: Pain)!

Amitava Das
Norwegian University of Science and Technology, Norway

Björn Gambäck
Norwegian University of Science and Technology, Norway

ABSTRACT

Arguably, the most important difference between machines and humans is that humans have feelings. For several decades researchers have been trying to create methods to simulate sentimentality for machines, and currently Sentiment Analysis is the hottest, most demanding, and rapidly growing task in the language processing field. Sentiment analysis or opinion mining refers to the application of Natural Language Processing, Computational Linguistics, and text analytics to identify and extract sentimental (opinionated, emotional) information in a text. The basic task in sentiment analysis is to classify the polarity of a given text at the document, sentence, or feature/aspect level, that is, to decide whether the expressed sentiment in a document, a sentence, or a feature/aspect is positive (happy), negative (sad), neutral (memorable), and so forth. In this chapter, the authors discuss various challenges and solution strategies for Sentiment Analysis with a particular view to texts in Bangla (Bengali).

1. INTRODUCTION: SENTIMENT ANALYSIS (যন্ত্রানুভূতি)

The title of this chapter is inspired by the Bangla science-fiction writer Narayan Sanyal. One of his most popular Sci-Fi novels is *Nakshatraloker Debatatma* [নক্ষত্রলোকেরদেবতাত্মা] (1976), which was inspired by Sir Arthur C. Clarke's novel *2001: A Space Odyssey* (1968). Sanyal's book first describes the evolution of the human race all the way from primitive creatures to intelligent beings building civilisations and ruling the Earth. The book then takes the history further into the space age, with Jupiter exploration and the same

DOI: 10.4018/978-1-4666-3970-6.ch015

super intelligent computer, "HAL" as in Clark's work. Sanyal called HAL "*Jantra-Na*" (যন্ত্রনা), which in Bangla ambiguously means both 'not a machine' (যন্ত্রনা) and 'pain' (যন্ত্রনা), metaphorically portraying the key difference between machines and humans: "The Feelings."

In the late 80s, researchers in Natural Language Processing (NLP) and Artificial Intelligence (AI) started to realize that machines should be able to understand and express sentiment to be intelligent. Since then researchers have attempted textual Sentiment Analysis (SA) for a range of different languages. Sentiment Analysis defines an overall problem, which addresses multiple sub-problems. It is without any doubt a challenging and enigmatic research task. Any scientific research needs to know the proper definitions of its problems in order to solve them. The essential question that is raised at the beginning of the sentiment analysis research is "*What is sentiment or opinion?*" Several researchers have tried to answer this question in the light of a range of research fields, such as Psychology, Philosophy, Psycholinguistics, and Cognitive Science, with many different researchers attempting to give their own definitions, going all the way back to Plato who interpreted opinion as being the medium between Knowledge and Ignorance.

Sentiment analysis research as such started as a content analysis problem in Behavioural Science. The General Inquirer system (Stone et al., 1966) was the first attempt in this direction. The aim was to gain understanding of the psychological forces and perceived demands of the situation that were in effect when a document was written. The system usually counted the occurrences of positive or negative emotion instances in any particular piece of text. The General Inquirer system and work by several researchers from the early 90s onwards (e.g., Wiebe et al., 1990; Hatzivassiloglou and McKeown, 1997; Turney, 2002; Pang and Lee, 2004) are milestones that mark the avenues to the current research trends of today. However, although sentiment analysis research started long ago, the question "*What is sentiment or opinion?*" still remains unanswered. It is very hard to define sentiment or opinion, and to identify the regulating or the controlling factors of sentiment. Moreover, it has not been possible to define a concise set of psychological forces that really affect the writers' sentiments, that is, the human sentiment, broadly speaking. Probably the question cannot be answered by the theories of Computer Science, and maybe the scopes of Medicine, Cognitive Science, Psychology, and other science fields have to be explored. Topically Relevant Opinionated Sentiment detection is better known as Subjectivity Detection (Wiebe et al., 1990). Janyce Wiebe borrowed the definition of opinion from Psycholinguistic research such as Quirk et al. (1985) which states that "an opinion could be defined as a private state that is not open to objective observation or verification."

Sentiment Analysis/Opinion Mining from natural language text is thus both a multifaceted and multidisciplinary AI problem (Liu, 2010). It tries to narrow the communication gap between the highly sentimental human and the sentimentally restricted computers by developing computational systems that can recognize and respond to the sentimental states of the human users. There is a perpetual debate about the best ways of collecting intelligence either by following the functional path of biological human intelligence or by generating new methodologies for completely heterogeneous mechatronic machines and defining a completely new horizon called electronic intelligence. Present research endeavors try to find the optimal solution strategies for machines that either mimic the techniques of self-organized biological human intelligence or can at least simulate the functional similarities of human sentimental intelligence.

Though it might even be impossible to formulate a complete analytical definition of sentiment (Kim and Hovy, 2004), the motivation behind the whole sentiment analysis research field is to develop solution strategies to meet the practical necessities. In today's digital age, text is the primary medium of representing and communicating information, as evidenced by the pervasiveness of e-mails, instant messages, documents, Weblogs, news articles, homepages, and printed materials. Our lives are now saturated with textual information, and there is an increasing urgency to develop technologies to help us manage and make sense of the resulting information overload. While expert systems have enjoyed some success in assisting information retrieval, data mining, and language processing systems, there is a growing need for sentiment analysis systems that can automatically process the plethora of sentimental information available in online electronic text. The increasing social necessity is the driving force for the massive research efforts on Sentiment Analysis/ Opinion Mining. But why does sentiment analysis become so imperative? Because knowing what others think always is a very important factor in our decision making. For example, before buying electronic products like TVs, laptops, iPads or smartphones, or before going to the cinema to watch the latest *Prometheus* or *Skyfall* we google on it to find out, *What do others think?* about the object or subject. With the proliferation of social networking, a plethora of important information is being added to the World Wide Web every day. Only Twitter adds on average over 400 million messages (tweets) per day. This data offers new and exciting opportunities, and there is much useful information that can be learned from meaningful analysis of the data. It has therefore over the last few years been a growing public and enterprise interest in different types of social media and their role in modern society and especially in sentiment analysis (Burwen 2012; Grimes 2012).

As discussed above, sentiment analysis research first started for the English language, but to satisfy the necessities of multilingual users all over the Globe many researchers have made efforts to develop technologies for other languages. Our endeavor was to develop mechanisms to make machines sensitive to Bangla, or Bengali, as it is known as according to the International Standards Organisation (ISO-639 language code: 'ben'). Bangla is the World's 5th most common language in terms of speakers (over 350 million of which about 200 million have it as first language), the second most common in India and the national language of Bangladesh. The main problem of working with Bangla is the scarcity of electronic resources and the morpho-syntactic richness of the language. When we started back in 2006 there were no resources available for Bangla, and we thus had to develop resources like lexica and corpora, and basic processing tools like a stemmer, part-of-speech tagger, etc., to start the actual research. Those resource creation processes are truly inseparable part of language processing research, especially while working with under-resourced languages such as Bangla. In connection to the difficulties of Bangla in particular, we would like to suggest interested readers to read "Why Indian Languages Failed to Make a Mark Online!" (PJ 2010).

This chapter summarizes the research endeavors by the authors on almost every granular aspects of Sentiment Analysis and especially on Bangla. Bangla is a morpho-syntactically and culturally rich language; therefore sentiment analysis from Bangla is undoubtedly tough in itself. Sentiment is not a direct property of languages; therefore an intelligent system needs some prior knowledge to act senti-mentally. Sentiment knowledge is generally wrapped into a computational lexicon, technically called a Sentiment Lexicon. The development process of such a lexicon for Bengali, the *Bengali SentiWordNet* is described in Section 2 (যন্ত্রানুভূতি-সংকলন). Similar to classical pattern recognition problems, Sentiment Analysis can also be divided into the identification and the classification genres, called *sentiment/subjectivity detection* and *polarity classification*, respectively. The proposed techniques for subjectivity detection and polarity classification for Bangla are elaborated in Sections 3 (যন্ত্র-বোধদয়) and 4 (যন্ত্রানুভূতি-মেরুধর্মিতা-নিরূপণ).

The needs of the end users are the driving forces behind sentiment analysis research. The end users are often not looking for just binary (positive/negative) or multi-class sentiment classification, but are more interested in aspectual/structural sentiment analysis. Therefore only sentiment detection and classification is not enough to satisfy the needs of the end users. Proper *structurization* of sentiments is essential before proceeding to any further granular analysis or generation and aggregation. Structurization involves identification of various aspects of a sentiment/opinion, such as sentiment holder, and sentiment topic. The research attempts on structurization are described in Section 5 (যন্ত্রানুভূতি-পর্যেষণা). To meet the satisfaction level of end users, an intelligent sentimental/opinionated information processing system should be capable of presenting an at-a-glance view of aggregated information, scattered over various sources/documents. Textual or visual summarization, visualization or tracking of sentiment are all striking needs from the perspective of the end users. The overall summarization-visualization-tracking research attempts are described in Section 6 (যন্ত্রঃক্রিয়-অনুভূতি-সাংক্ষেপ). Finally, Section 7 discusses the future of sentiment analysis.

2. BANGLA SENTIWORDNET (যন্ত্রানুভূতি-সংকলন)

Sentiment knowledge acquisition in terms of a sentiment lexicon is a vital pre-requisite of any sentiment analysis system. Previous studies have proposed to attach *prior polarity* (Esuli and Sebastiani, 2006) to each sentiment lexicon level. Prior polarities are approximate values and are based on corpus statistics. The techniques for the creation of sentiment lexica can broadly be categorized into two types, one follows the classical manual annotation techniques (Andreevskaia and Bergler, 2006; Wiebe and Riloff, 2005; Mohammad et al., 2008) and the other includes various automatic techniques (Tong, 2001; Mohammad and Turney, 2010). Both types of techniques have some limitations. Automatic techniques demand manual validations and are dependent on the corpus availability in the respective domain. Manual annotation techniques are trustworthy, but in general takes time for development. Manual annotation techniques furthermore require a large number of annotators to balance the sentimentality of individual annotators in order to reach agreement, but qualified human annotators are both costly and difficult to find. There are two issues that should be satisfied by a good quality sentiment lexicon. The first one is coverage and the second is credibility of the associative polarity scores. Automatic processes are good for coverage expansion, but manual methods are trustable for prior polarity assignment. Both the processes have been attempted to develop SentiWordNet(s) (Das and Bandyopadhyay, 2010c; Das and Bandyopadhyay, 2010e) for several languages.

The automatic processes used in the present work are bilingual dictionary based look-up, WordNet-based synonym and antonym expansion, orthographic antonym generation and corpus-based induction. English sentiment lexica were chosen as the source and the synset members were translated into the target language using bilingual dictionaries. WordNet 3.0 was effectively used to expand a given synset via synonym and antonym search. Sixteen hand-crafted suffix/affix rules (like normal – ab-normal, natural – un-natural) were used to orthographically create more antonyms for a given synset, and corpus validation was carried out later to confirm the validity of the orthographically generated forms. The generated sentiment lexicon was used as a seed list. The language specific corpus was automatically tagged with these seed words using the simple tagset of Sentiment Word Positive (SWP) and Sentiment Word Negative (SWN). A Conditional Random Field (CRF) based classifier was trained on the tagged corpus and then applied to the un-annotated corpus to find out new language and culture specific sentimental words. These techniques have been successfully used for three Indian languages: *Bengali*, *Hindi* and *Telugu* (Das and Bandyopadhyay, 2010c; Das and Bandyopadhyay, 2010e). The Bengali SentiWordNet (Das and Bandyopadhyay, 2010f) has already been made publically available.[1]

As there is a high scarcity of human annotators, it was decided to involve the Internet population for creating more credible sentiment lexica (Das and Bandyopadhyay, 2011; Das, 2011). The Internet population is huge and constantly growing (currently ca 2.4 billion; Miniwatts 2012). It consists of people with various languages, cultures, ages, etc., and thus is not biased towards any particular domain, language or society. An interactive online game called *Dr. Sentiment* was developed to collect players' sentiment by asking a set of simple template-based questions to reveal the sentimental status of the player.[2] The lexica tagged by this system are credible as humans tag them. They are not static sentiment lexica, as the prior polarity scores are updated regularly. On average almost 100 players/day currently play *Dr. Sentiment* throughout the world in different languages. *Global SentiWordNet* (Das and Bandyopadhyay, 2010d), SentiWordNets for 57 languages was developed using Google Translate API.

Dr. Sentiment also helps to capture an overall picture of human social psychology regarding sentiment understanding. The age-wise distribution of players' sentimentality is shown in Figure 1. Sentimentality also changes with gender, as reported in Figure 2, and with the players' geospatial location, as exemplified in Figure 3. There it is shown how the word "blue" has been tagged by different players around the world: surprisingly it has been tagged as positive in one part of the world and negative in another part. Most of the negative tags come from the Middle-East and especially from Islamic countries. This might be based on verse 20:102 of the *Qur'an* in which it says that on the day "the Trumpet is blown" (the Day of Resurrection), the sinners shall be gathered, "blue-eyed" – supposedly with their eyes turning blue with fear, hence giving the word "blue" a bad connotation.

Several types of psychological information are currently being incorporated into the existing

Figure 1. Sentimentality age wise

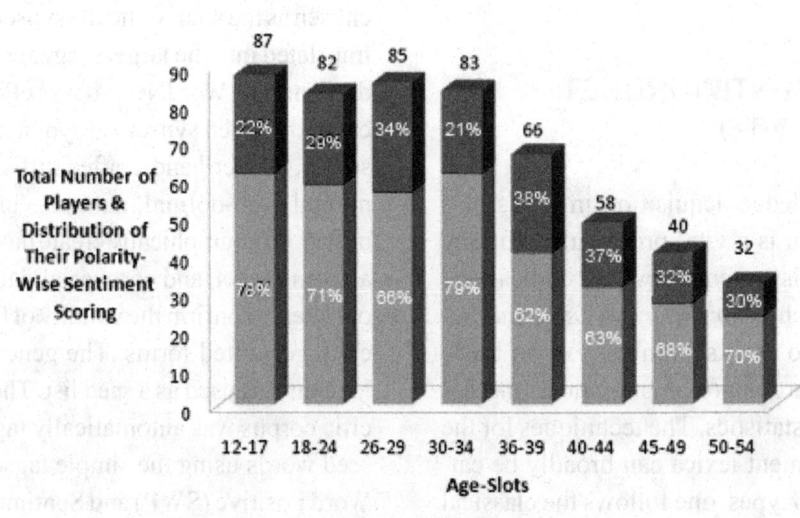

Figure 2. Sentimentality gender wise

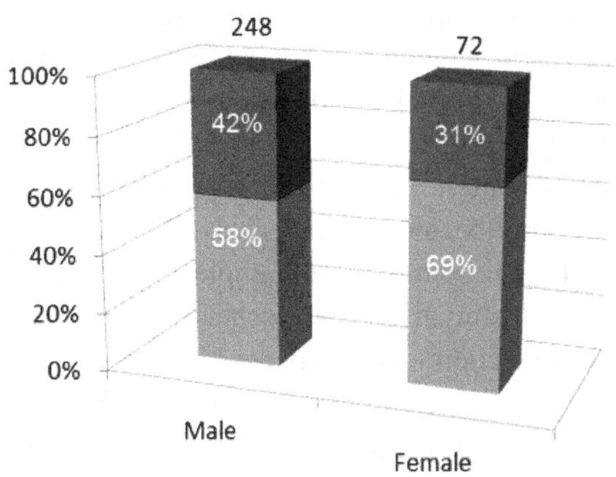

SentiWordNet, with the resultant lexicon being termed the *PsychoSentiWordNet* (Das, 2011). The *PsychoSentiWordNet* holds variable prior polarity scores that may be fetched depending upon the regulating psychological aspects. The example in Table 1 illustrates the definition.

3. SENTIMENT DETECTION AND CLASSIFICATION (যন্ত্র-বোধদয়)

The term subjectivity simply refers to the identification of sentiments in a piece of text. More precisely, the term Subjectivity can be defined as the Topically Relevant Opinionated Sentiment (Wiebe *et al.*, 1990). The subjectivity is concerned with whether the expressed sentiment is related to the relevant topic or fulfills the overall desired goal of a Sentiment Analysis system.

Table 1. Polarity scores dependent on psychological aspect

Aspect Values (Profession)	Input	Polarity
Null	High	Positive
Businessman	High	Negative
Share Broker	High	Positive

Figure 3. Geospatial sentimentality

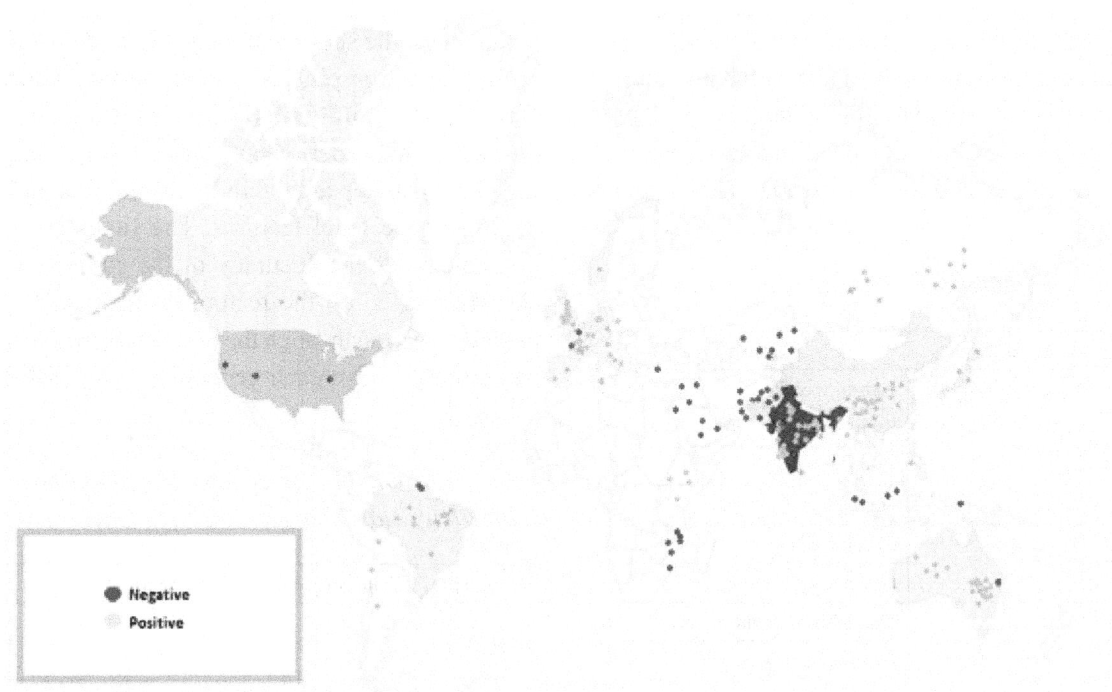

Sentiment or subjectivity detection is a very tough challenge for machines with very limited emotional capabilities and even for human beings. Let us take a look at the following examples.

Example 1: Product Review
"My camera broke in two days."

Example 2: Film Review; Film Name: Deep Blue Sea, Holder: Arbitrary-outside of theatre
"This is blue!"

In the first example, it is very hard to disambiguate whether the author is only talking about an accident or complaining about the quality of the camera. The problem with the second example is that there is no evaluative expression and no indicators at syntactic or semantic levels to identify the sentiment. Previous studied have identified some clues at the lexical and syntactic levels (Aue and Gamon, 2005; Hatzivassiloglou and McKeown, 1997; Nasukawa and Yi, 2003). A series of experiments have been carried out to find the optimal feature set for both the English and Bangla languages. The final feature set used for the experiments has been classified into three types (levels) as reported in Table 2.

On the algorithmic aspect, the experiments started with a*rule-based* (Das and Bandyopadhyay, 2009c) technique and continued with Machine Learning (Das and Bandyopadhyay, 2009b) and hybrid techniques (Das and Bandyopadhyay, 2009a). A Theme Detection technique was developed to detect topical relevant sentiments. The themes relate to the topic of any document, but there may be more unrevealed clues based on human psychology or on complex relationships among the linguistic clues for sentiment / subjectivity detection which may not be extracted with present NLP/simple machine learning techniques.

Thus, experiments have been carried out with Genetic Algorithms (Das and Bandyopadhyay, 2010g) to adopt the biological evolutionary path of the human intelligence for machines. The accuracy of the system with the Genetic-Based Machine Learning (GBML) technique reaches 90.22% (MPQA: news) and 93.00% (IMDB: movie review) for English and 87.65% (news) and 90.6% (blog) for Bangla, respectively, as stated in Table 3. Machine learning algorithms when applied to NLP systems generally utilize various combinations of syntactic and semantic linguistic features to identify the most effective feature set. The sentiment/subjectivity detection problem in the present task was viewed as a Multi-Objective or Multi-Criteria Optimization search problem. The experiments started with a large set of possible extractable syntactic, semantic and discourse level features. The fitness function calculates the accuracy of the subjectivity classifier based on the feature set identified by natural selection through the process of crossover and mutation after each generation. The GBML

Table 2. Features for subjectivity detection

Types	Features
Lexico-Syntactic	Part-of-Speech
	SentiWordNet
	Frequency
	Stemming
Syntactic	Chunk Label
	Dependency Parsing
Discourse Level	Title of the Document
	First Paragraph
	Average Distribution
	Theme Word

Table 3. Results of the genetic algorithm-based subjectivity classifier

Languages	Domain MPQA	Precision	Recall
English	MPQA	90.22%	96.01%
	IMDB	93.00%	98.55%
Bangla	NEWS	87.65%	89.06%
	BLOG	90.6%	92.40%

technique automatically identifies the best feature set based on the principles of natural selection and survival of the fittest. The identified best fitting feature set is then optimized locally, and global optimization is obtained by a multi-objective optimization technique.

4. SENTIMENT POLARITY DETECTION (যন্ত্রানুভূতি-মেরুধর্মিতা-নিরূপণ)

Polarity classification is the classical problem from which Sentiment Analysis started. It involves sentiment/opinion classification into semantic classes such as *positive, negative or neutral* and/or other fine-grained emotional classes like *happy, sad, anger, disgust, surprise,* and maybe others. However, for the present task we stick to standard binary classification, i.e., positive and/or negative. We start by discussing previous research endeavors, in particular elaborating on the birth of prior polarity as a concept, its usage for polarity classification, and the most recent trends in prior polarity research.

Sentiment polarity classification (Is the text positive or negative?) started as a semantic orientation determination problem: by identifying the semantic orientation of adjectives, Hatzivassiloglou *et al.* (1997) proved the effectiveness of empirically building a sentiment lexicon. Turney (2002) suggested positive and negative classification by *Thumbs Up* and *Thumbs Down*, while the concept of a prior polarity lexicon was established with the introduction of *SentiWordNet* (Esuli and Sebastiani, 2006). Higher accuracy for prior polarity identification is very hard to achieve, as prior polarity values are approximations only. Hence, the prior polarity method may not excel alone; additional techniques are required for contextual polarity disambiguation. The use of other NLP or machine learning methods to extend human-produced prior polarity lexica was pioneered by Pang *et al.* (2002). Several researches then tried syntactic-statistical techniques for polarity classification, reporting good accuracy (Seeker *et al.*, 2009; Moilanen *et al.*, 2010). With these research efforts the two-step methodology, i.e., sentiment lexicon followed by further NLP techniques, became the standard method for polarity classification.

The existing reported solutions or available systems are still far from perfect or fail to meet the satisfaction level of the end users. The main issue may be that there are many conceptual rules that govern sentiment and there are even more clues (possibly unlimited) that can convey these concepts from realization to verbalization of a human being (Liu, 2010). A recent trend of prior polarity takes a different way for sentiment knowledge representation, following the mental lexicon model to hold the contextual polarity as in human knowledge representation. To this end, Cambria *et al.* (2011) introduced a new paradigm: *Sentic Computing*, in which they use an emotion representation and a Common Sense-based approach to infer affective states from short texts over the Web. Grassi (2009) conceived the Human Emotion Ontology as a high-level ontology supplying the most significant concepts and properties constituting the centerpiece for the description of human emotions. To overcome the problems of the present proximity-based static sentiment lexicon based techniques, we have introduced a new way to represent sentiment knowledge using Vector Space Models. This representation of the sentiment knowledge in the Conceptual Spaces of distributional Semantics will be referred to as Sentimantics. The new models can store dynamic prior polarity with different contextual information (e.g., "*long*", context: *waiting* polarity: -0.25 or "*long*", context: *live* polarity: +0.50). The concept of Sentimantics is clearly an off-spring of the existing prior polarity concept, but we deviate philosophically in terms of contextual dynamicity, and ideologically follow the path of Minsky (2006), Cambria *et al.* (2011) and Grassi

(2009), but with a different notion. The strategy has been tested on both English and Bangla. The intension behind choosing two distinct language families is to establish the credibility of the proposed methods.

Since the two-step methodology is the most common approach to polarity classification in practice, a syntactic-polarity classifier was developed to compare the impact of the proposed Sentimantics concept to the standard polarity classification technique, in order to produce comparative results. Adhering to the standard two-step methodology (i.e., prior polarity lexicon followed by any NLP technique), a Syntactic-Statistical polarity classifier was quickly developed using Support Vector Machines (SVM) with SVMTool (Giménez and Márquez, 2004). The intension behind the development of the syntactic polarity classifier was to examine the effectiveness and the limitations of the standard two-step methodology. The following feature set was used: *Sentiment Lexicon, Negative Words, Stems, Function Words, Part of Speech and Dependency Relations*, as most previous research indicated that these are the prime features to detect the sentimental polarity from text (Das and Bandyopadhyay, 2010h).

The feature ablation, presented in Table 4 proves the accountability of the two-step polarity classification technique. The prior polarity lexicon (completely dictionary-based) approach gives about 50% accuracy; the further improvements of the system are obtained by other NLP techniques.

Table 4. Performance of the syntactic polarity classifier by feature ablation

Features	Performance	
	English	Bangla
Sentiment Lexicon	50.50%	47.60%
+Negative Words	55.10%	50.40%
+Stemming	59.30%	56.02%
+ Functional Words	63.10%	58.23%
+ Parts Of Speech	66.56%	61.90%
+Chunk	68.66%	66.80%
+Dependency Relations	76.03%	70.04%

The entries in a prior polarity lexicon are attached with two probabilistic values, positivity and negativity, but according to the best of our knowledge no previous research clarifies which value to pick in what context – and there is no information about this in the SentiWordNet. The general trend is to pick the highest one, but which the correct one actually is may depend on the context. An example may illustrate the problem better: Suppose the word "high" (Positivity: 0.25, Negativity: 0.125 for "high" from SentiWordNet) is attached with a positive polarity (since its positivity value is higher than its negativity value) in the sentiment lexicon. However, the polarity of the word may vary by its particular use.

- Sensex reaches high[+].
- Prices go high[-].

Hence further processing is required to disambiguate these types of words. Table 5 shows how many words in the SentiWordNet(s) are ambiguous and need special care. There are 6,619 (English) and 7,654 (Bangla) lexicon entries in SentiWordNet(s) where both the positivity and the negativity values are greater than zero. Similarly, there are 3,187 (English) and 2,677 (Bangla) lexi-

Table 5. Statistics for SentiWordNet (the percentages are based on n/28,430 resp. n/30,000)

Types	English	Bangla
Total number of tokens	115,424	30,000
Positivity>0 OR Negativity>0	28,430	30,000
Positivity>0 AND Negativity>0	**6,619 (23.28%)**	**7,654 (25.51%)**
Positivity>0 AND Negativity=0	10,484 (36.87%)	8,934 (29.78%)
Positivity=0 AND Negativity>0	11,327 (39.84%)	11,780 (39.26%)
Positivity>0 AND Negativity>0 AND |Positivity-Negativity|>=0.2	**3,187 (11.20%)**	**2,677 (8.92%)**

cal entries whose positivity and negativity value difference is less than 0.2. All these lexical entries are ambiguous.

Two different types of models for Sentimantics (Das and Gambäck, 2012) composition have been examined. Both are empirically grounded and can represent the contextual similarity relations among various lexical sentiment and non-sentiment concepts. The experiments started with existing resources such as *ConceptNet* and *SentiWordNet* for English and *SemanticNet* (Das and Bandyopadhyay, 2010n; Das and Bandyopadhyay, 2010p) and *SentiWordNet (Bengali)* for Bangla. The common sense lexica like ConceptNet and SemanticNet were developed for general purposes and the formalization of Sentimantics from these resources faces challenges due to lack of dimensionality. Thus is a second experiment a Vector Space Model (VSM) was developed by a corpus driven semi-supervised method to assign the Sentimantics from scratch. This model performed relatively better than the previous one and was quite satisfactory. Generally, extracting knowledge from this kind of VSM is algorithmically very expensive because the network has a very high dimensionality. An important limitation of this type of model is that it requires very well-defined processed input to extract knowledge such as "Input: (*high*); Context (*sensex, share market, point*)". In the end, a Syntactic Co-Occurrence Based VSM with relatively few dimensions was built. The final model is the best performing lexicon network model and may be described as the acceptable solution to the Sentimantics problem. Each sentiment word in the developed lexical network by the Network overlap technique is assigned a contextual prior polarity. Figure 4 shows the lexical network for the word "long."

5. SENTIMENT STRUCTURIZATION (যন্ত্রানুভূতি-পর্যেষণা)

It is important to keep in mind that the needs of the end users are the driving forces behind the sentiment analysis research: the research endeavors should lead to the development of a real time sentiment analysis system, which successfully satisfies the needs of the end users. Let us have a look at some real life needs of end users. For example, market surveyors from company A may identify the need to find out the changes in public opinion about their product X after release of product Y by another company B. The different aspects of product Y that the public consider better than product X are also points

Figure 4. Sentimantics network developed by the network overlap technique

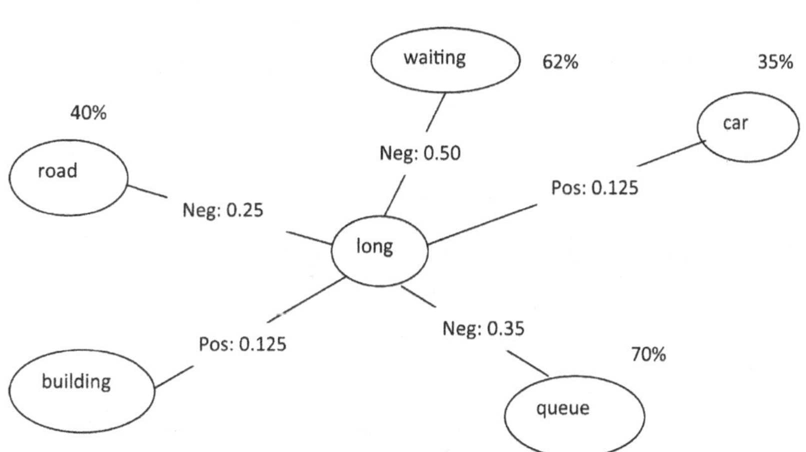

of interest. These aspects could typically be the durability of the product, power options, weight, color and many more other issues that depend on the particular product. In another scenario, a voter may be interested in studying the change of public opinion about a leader or a public event before and after an election. In this case the aspect could be a social event, economic recession and maybe other issues. The end users are not only looking for binary (positive/negative) sentiment classification, but are more interested in aspectual sentiment analysis. Therefore only sentiment detection and classification is not enough to satisfy the needs of the end users: a sentiment analysis system should be capable of understanding and extracting the aspectual sentiments present in a natural language text.

Previous research efforts have proposed several different structures or components for sentiment extraction. Among the proposed sentiment structures the most widely used structures are *Holder* (Kim and Hovy, 2004; Choi et al., 2005; Bethard et al., 2006), *Topic* (Ku et al., 2005; Zhou et al., 2006; Kawai et al., 2007) and other domain-dependent attributes (Kobayashi et al., 2006; Bal and Saint-Dizier, 2009). However, real life users are not always interested in all the aspects at the same time, but rather look for opinion/sentiment changes of any "Who" during "When" and depending upon "What" or "Where" and the reasons behind "Why." With this hypothesis, we have proposed a 5W (Who/কে, What/কি, When/কখন, Where/কোথায় and Why/কেন) constituent extraction technique for sentiment/opinion structurization (Das et al., 2010i). The 5W structure is domain independent and more generic than the existing semantic constituent extraction structures.

Table 6 presents the sentence level co-occurrence patterns of the 5Ws in the Bangla corpus. The 5Ws do not appear together regularly in the corpus. Hence, sequence labeling with 5W tags using any machine learning technique will lead to a label bias problem and may not be an acceptable solution for the present problem of 5W role labeling. Therefore, a system based on a hybrid architecture has been built. It statistically assigns 5W labels to each chunk in a sentence using Maximum Entropy Modeling (MaxEnt). A rule-based post-processor helps to reduce many false hits by the MaxEnt-based system and at the same time identifies new 5W labels. The rules have been developed based on the acquired statistics on the training set and the linguistic analysis of standard Bangla grammar. By analyzing the output of both the MaxEnt and the hybrid systems (MaxEnt followed by the rule-based post-processor system) it can be easily inferred that the hybrid structure is essential to the 5W problem domain.

6. SENTIMENT SUMMARIZATION (যন্ত্রঃক্রিয়-অনুভূতি-সাংক্ষেপ)

Aggregation of information is a necessity from the end users' perspective, but it is nearly impossible to develop consensus on the output format or how the data should be aggregated. Researchers have tried various types of output formats like textual

Table 6. Sentence level co-occurrence patterns of 5Ws in Bangla

Tags	Percentage					
	Who	What	When	Where	Why	Overall
Who	-	58.56%	73.34%	78.01%	28.33%	73.50%
What	58.56%	-	62.89%	70.63%	64.91%	64.23%
When	73.34%	62.89%	-	48.63%	23.66%	57.23%
Where	78.0%	70.63%	48.63%	-	12.02%	68.65%
Why	28.33%	64.91%	23.66%	12.02%	-	32.00%

or visual summary, or overall tracking along the time dimension. Several research attempts can be found in the literature on Topic-wise (Yi *et al.*, 2003; Pang and Lee, 2004; Zhou *et al.*, 2006) and Polarity-wise (Hu, 2004; Yi and Niblack, 2005; Das and Chen, 2007) summarization, and on Visualization (Morinaga *et al.*, 2002; Aue and Gamon, 2005; Carenini *et al.*, 2006) and *Tracking* (Lloyd *et al.*, 2005; Mishne and de Rijke, 2006; Fukuhara *et al.*, 2007). The key issue regarding the sentiment aggregation is how the data shall be aggregated. Dasgupta and Ng (2009) pose an important question: "*Topic-wise, Sentiment-wise, or Otherwise?*" about the opinion summary generation techniques. Actually the output format varies by the end users' requirements and domains. Several output formats have been experimented with in the present work.

The experiments started with multi-document topic-opinion textual summary (Das and Bandyopadhyay, 2010k). A 5W constituent-based textual summarization-visualization-tracking system was devised to meet the need for an at-a-glance presentation. The 5W constituent-based aggregation system is a multi-genre system. The system facilitates users to generate sentiment tracking with a textual summary and a sentiment polarity-wise graph based on any dimension or combination of dimensions they want, for example, "Who" are the actors and "What" their sentiment regarding any topic, changes in sentiment during "When" and "Where" and the reasons for change in sentiment as "Why." The final graph for tracking is generated with a timeline. The 5W constituent-based summarization-visualization-tracking system aims to cover all genres and attempts to answer the philosophical question "*Topic-Wise, Polarity-Wise* or *Other-Wise?*"

- **Topic-Wise:** Users may generate sentiment summaries based on any customized topic like Who, What, When, Where and Why along any dimension or combination of dimensions they want.
- **Polarity-Wise:** The system produces a Gantt chart that can be treated as the overall polarity-wise summary. An interested user can still look into the summary text to find out more details.

Moreover, the end users can structure their information needs by:

- Who was involved?
- What happened?
- When did it take place?
- Where did it take place?
- Why did it happen?

During the development of the multi-document topic-opinion summarization system, a strong semantic lexical network (Das and Bandyopadhyay, 2010j; Das and Bandyopadhyay, 2010k) was proposed following the idea of Mental Lexicon models. The same lexical semantic network was used to develop the 5W system. The present 5W summarization-visualization-tracking system (Das *et al.*, 2012) also provides an overall summary. A snapshot of the 5W Sentiment Summarization-Visualization-Tracking System is presented in Figure 5. Another important aspect of the present system is that a user can leave out the input along a dimension in order to see all the possible information on that dimension.

The working principle of the present 5W summarization-visualization-tracking system is as follows: The system identifies all the desired nodes in the developed semantic constituent network as given by the user in the 5W form. Inter-constituent distances are then calculated from the developed semantic constituent network. For example, suppose the user gave the input shown in Table 7. The calculated inter-constituent distances would then look like those displayed in Table 8.

Next, all the sentences consisting of at least one of the user-defined constituents are extracted from all documents. The extracted sentences are

Figure 5. A snapshot of the 5W summarization-visualization-tracking system

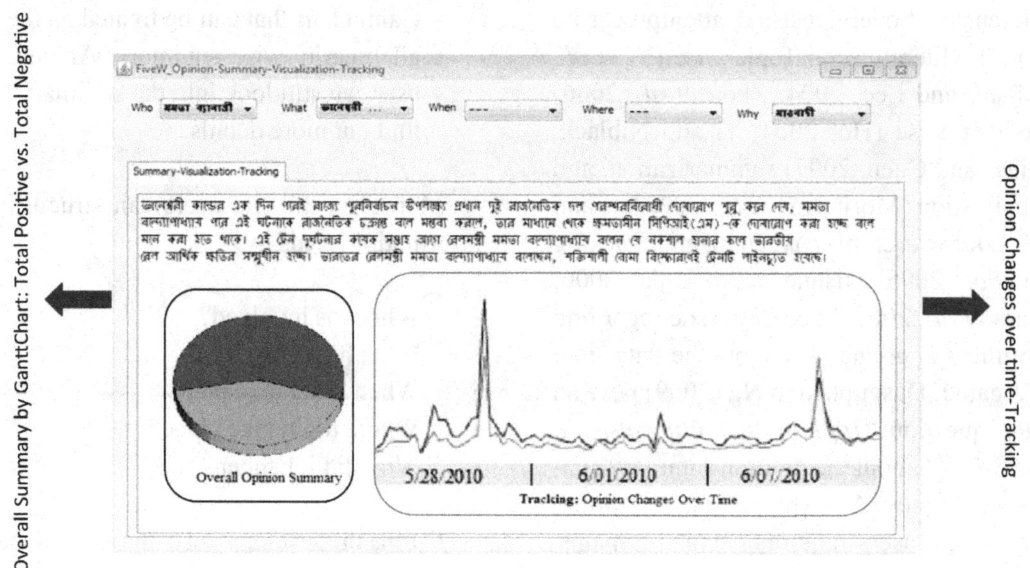

Table 7. Example of 5Ws chosen by end user

	Who	What	When	Where	Why
INPUT	মমতাব্যানার্জী	জ্ঞানেশ্বরীএক্সপ্রেস	মধ্যরাত	ঝাড়গ্রাম	মাওবাদী
	(Mamata Banerjee)	(Gyaneswari Express)	(Midnight)	(Jhargram)	(Maoist)

ranked with the adaptive Information Science Page-Rank algorithm based on the constituents present in the sentence. In the first iteration, the Page-Rank algorithm assigns a score to each sentence based on keyword presence (constituents are treated as keywords at this stage). In the second iteration, the ranks calculated by Page-Rank are multiplied by the inter-constituent distances for those sentences where more than one constituent is present. In the example sentence below two Ws ("Who" and "What") are jointly present. Suppose the assigned rank for the sentence by Page-Rank is *n*. Then in the next iteration the modified score will be *n**0.86, because the inter-constituent distance for "Who" (মমতাবন্দ্যোপাধ্যায়) and "What" (জ্ঞানেশ্বরীএক্সপ্রেস) is 0.86.

Table 8. Calculated inter-constituent distances

Type	Inter-Constituent Distances				
	Who	What	When	Where	Why
Who	-	0.86	0.02	0.34	0.74
What	0.86	-	0.80	0.89	0.67
When	0.02	0.80	-	0.58	0.23
Where	0.34	0.89	0.58	-	0.20
Why	0.74	0.67	0.23	0.20	-

মমতা_বন্দ্যোপাধ্যায়/ **Who** জ্ঞানেশ্বরী_এক্সপ্রেস_ঘটনাকে/ **What** রাজনৈতিকচক্রান্তবলেমন্তব্যকরেন।

English Gloss: Mamta_Bandyopadhyay/ **Who** commented that the Gyaneshwari_Express_incident/ **What** is a political conspiracy.

The ranked sentences are then sorted in descending order and the top-ranked 30% (of all retrieved sentences) are shown as a summary. The ordering of sentences is very important for summarization. We prefer the temporal order of sentences as they occurred in original document, when it was published.

The visual tracking system consists of five drop down boxes. The drop down boxes give options for individual 5W dimension of each unique W that exists in the corpus. An example output from the present 5W summarization-visualization-tracking system is shown in Table 9.

Produced Textual Summary: পরশু মধ্যরাতে ঝাড়গ্রামের অদূরে জ্ঞানেশ্বরী এক্সপ্রেসের লাইনচ্যুত হওয়ার ঘটনাকে বড়সড় রাজনৈতিক ষড়যন্ত্র বলে দাবি করেন মমতা।শ্রীমতী মমতা বন্দ্যোপাধ্যায় পরদিন সকালেই ঝাড়গ্রাম পৌছান ও প্রেসমিটিং-এ জানান, সিবিআইকে দিয়ে ঘটনাটি তদন্ত করা হচ্ছে । তদন্ত শুরু করেছে সিআইডি, তবে রেলমন্ত্রী মমতা বন্দ্যোপাধ্যায় ট্রেন বেলাইন হওয়ার কারণ হিসেবে রেল লাইনে বিস্ফোরণ ঘটার তথ্য দিয়েছেন, যার কোনও প্রমাণ পাওয়া যায়নি । এমনকী এই ঘটনা যে পুরভোটের আগে তাঁকে বেকায়দায় ফেলার চক্রান্ত, এমন ইঙ্গিতও দিয়েছেন মমতা বন্দ্যোপাধ্যায়।

English Gloss: Mamta claimed that the derailment incident of the Jyaneswari Express near Jharagramera, which happened at midnight the day before yesterday is a big political conspiracy. Smt. Mamta Bandyopadhyay reached Jharagrama next morning and said in a press conference that the case will be investigated by CBI. CID has started investigation, but rail minister Mamta Bandyopadhyay has presented a theory of an explosion as a probable reason for the derailment of the train, of which no evidence has stillbeen found. This incident before the municipality election is a conspiracy to ensure her defeat, Mamta Bandyopadhyay has indicated.

7. HOW FAR AWAY IS THE "THE BEST-INFORMED DREAM" OF HAL OR যন্ত্রনা?

Sir Arthur C. Clark's book *2001: A Space Odyssey* was written in 1968 and the ideological replica in Bangla by Narayan Sanyal, *Nakshatraloker Debatatma* [নক্ষত্রলোকেরদেবতাত্মা] in 1976; however, even though approximately four decades have passed after that science fantasy, HAL or "যন্ত্রনা" is still just the "*The Best-Informed Dream*" for researchers in Artificial Intelligence. It is very hard to predict the next probable avenue of this scientific field. Sentiment Analysis is a highly inter-disciplinary research field and it will need to get contributions from research endeavors in disciplines such as Computer Science, AI, Psychology, Philosophy, Psycholinguistics, Cognitive Science, and many more.

How humans understand and express emotions is a complex issue in itself; to make machines understand and express emotions is substantially harder. Textual sentiment analysis is a step in that direction, but it is essential that we manage to identify what particular pieces of text carry what sentiment (at least with some probability). In order to truly start to understand what sentiment and opinion really means, it is also imperative that this is done for many different languages and for people with varying backgrounds and cultures. The research reported in the present chapter is an important contribution in that direction, and

Table 9. Output from the 5W tracking system

	Who	What	When	Where	Why
INPUT	মমতাব্যানার্জী	লাইনচ্যুত	-	ঝাড়গ্রাম	-
	(Mamta Banerjee)	(Derailment)	-	(Jhargram)	-

thus a step towards *understanding* and interpreting sentiment. To be able to do so clearly is a prerequisite for *expressing* emotions. Only when the processes underlying both interpreting and expressing emotions have been fully understood, maybe "the best-informed dream" can be reached and a machine in the future utter, "I am sorry!"

REFERENCES

Andreevskaia, A., & Bergler, S. (2007). Clac and clac-NB: Knowledge-based and corpus-based approaches to sentiment tagging. In *Proceedings of the 4th SemEval-2007*, ACL.

Aue, A., & Gamon, M. (2005). Customizing sentiment classifiers to new domains: A case study. In *Proceedings of RANLP-05*. Borovets, Bulgaria: RANLP.

Bal, K., & Saint-Dizier, P. (2010). Towards building annotated resources for analyzing opinions and argumentation in news editorials. In *Proceedings of LREC 2010*. Valetta, Malta: LREC.

Bethard, S., Yu, H., Thornton, A., Hatzivassiloglou, V., & Jurafsky, D. (2006). Extracting opinion propositions and opinion holders using syntactic and lexical cues. In The Computing Attitude and Affect in Text: Theory and Applications, (pp. 125-141). Academic Press.

Burwen, M. (2012). *Social media: The end of conventional market research?* Technology Futures.

Cambria, E., Hussain, A., & Eckl, C. (2011). Taking refuge in your personal sentic corner. In *Proceedings of the Workshop on Sentiment Analysis: Where AI meets Psychology*. IJCNLP.

Carenini, G., Ng, R., & Pauls, A. (2006). Multi-document summarization of evaluative text. In *Proceedings of the European Chapter of the Association for Computational Linguistics*. EACL.

Choi, Y., Cardie, C., Riloff, E., & Patwardhan, S. (2005). Identifying sources of opinions with conditional random fields and extraction patterns. In *Proceedings of the HLT/EMNLP 2005*. HLT/EMNLP.

Das, A. (2010n). Can we mimic human pragmatics knowledge into computational lexicon? In *Proceedings of the International Conference on Natural Language Processing (ICON 2010)*. ICON.

Das, A., & Bandyopadhyay, S. (2009a). Subjectivity detection in English and Bengali: A CRF-based approach. In *Proceeding of the International Conference on Natural Language Processing (ICON 2009)*. ICON.

Das, A., & Bandyopadhyay, S. (2009b). Theme detection an exploration of opinion subjectivity. In *Proceeding of the Affective Computing & Intelligent Interaction (ACII2009)*. Amsterdam, The Netherlands: ACII.

Das, A., & Bandyopadhyay, S. (2009c). Extracting opinion statements from bengali text documents through theme detection. In *Proceeding of the 17th International Conference on Computing (CIC-09)*. GEOS.

Das, A., & Bandyopadhyay, S. (2010c). Dr sentiment creates SentiWordNet(s) for Indian languages involving internet population. In *Proceeding of IndoWordNet Workshop*. ICON.

Das, A., & Bandyopadhyay, S. (2010d). Towards the global SentiWordNet. In *Proceeding of the Workshop on Model and Measurement of Meaning (M3)*. PACLIC.

Das, A., & Bandyopadhyay, S. (2010e). SentiWordNet for Indian languages. In *Proceeding of the 8th Workshop on Asian Language Resources (ALR 8)*. COLING.

Das, A., & Bandyopadhyay, S. (2010f). SentiWordNet for Bangla. In *Proceedings of the Knowledge Sharing Event-4: Task 2: Building Electronic Dictionary (KSE4)*. Mysore, India: KSE.

Das, A., & Bandyopadhyay, S. (2010g). Subjectivity detection using genetic algorithm. In *Proceeding of the 1st Workshop on Computational Approaches to Subjectivity and Sentiment Analysis (WASSA10)*. ECAI.

Das, A., & Bandyopadhyay, S. (2010h). Opinion-polarity identification in Bengali. In *Proceeding of the 23rd International Conference on the Computer Processing of Oriental Languages (ICCPOL 2010)*. KESE.

Das, A., & Bandyopadhyay, S. (2010j). Opinion summarization in Bengali: A theme network model. In *Proceeding of the 2nd IEEE International Conference on Social Computing (SocialCom-2010)*. SocialCom.

Das, A., & Bandyopadhyay, S. (2010k). Topic-based Bengali opinion summarization. In *Proceeding of the 23rd International Conference on Computational Linguistics (COLING 2010)*. COLING.

Das, A., & Bandyopadhyay, S. (2010p). SemanticNet-Perception of human pragmatics. In *Proceeding of the 2nd Workshop on Cognitive Aspects of the Lexicon: Enhancing the Structure and Lookup Mechanisms of Electronic Dictionaries (COGALEX-II)*. COLING.

Das, A., & Bandyopadhyay, S. (2011). Dr sentiment knows everything! In *Proceeding of the 49th Annual Meeting of the Association for Computational Linguistics: Human Language Technologies (ACL/HLT 2011 Demo Session)*, (pp. 50-55). Portland, OR: ACL.

Das, A., & Gambäck, B. (2012). Sentimantics: The conceptual spaces for lexical sentiment polarity representation with contextuality. In *Proceedings of the 3rd Workshop on Computational Approaches to Subjectivity and Sentiment Analysis (WASSA)*. ACL.

Das, A., Gambäck, B., & Bandyopadhyay, S. (2012). The 5W structure for sentiment summarization-visualization-tracking. In *Proceeding of the 13th International Conference on Intelligent Text Processing and Computational Linguistics (CICLING 2012)*. Delhi, India: CICLING.

Das, A., Ghosh, A., & Bandyopadhyay, S. (2010a). Semantic role labeling for bengali noun using 5Ws: Who, what, when, where and why. In *Proceeding of the International Conference on Natural Language Processing and Knowledge Engineering (IEEE NLPKE2010)*. IEEE.

Das, I. (2011). PsychoSentiWordNet. In *Proceeding of the 49th Annual Meeting of the Association for Computational Linguistics: Human Language Technologies (ACL/HLT 2011 Student Session)*. ACL.

Das, S. R., & Chen, M. Y. (2007). Yahoo! For Amazon: Sentiment extraction from small talk on the web. *Management Science*, *53*(9), 1375–1388. doi:10.1287/mnsc.1070.0704.

Dasgupta, S., & Ng, V. (2009). Topic-wise, sentiment-wise, or otherwise? Identifying the hidden dimension for unsupervised text classification. In *Proceedings of the EMNLP*. Singapore: EMNLP.

Esuli, A., & Sebastiani, F. (2006). SentiWordNet: A publicly available lexical resource for opinion mining. In *Proceedings of the International Conference on Language Resources and Evaluation* (LREC-2006), (pp. 417-422). Genoa, Italy: LREC.

Fukuhara, T., Nakagawa, H., & Nishida, T. (2007). Understanding sentiment of people from news articles: Temporal sentiment analysis of social events. In *Proceedings of the International Conference on Weblogs and Social Media.* ICWSM.

Giménez, J., & Márquez, L. (2004). SVMTool: A general POS tagger generator based on support vector machines. In *Proceedings of the 4th International Conference on Language Resources and Evaluation (LREC'04)*. Lisbon, Portugal: LREC.

Grassi, M. (2009). Developing HEO human emotions ontology. In *Proceedings of the 2009 Joint International Conference on Biometric ID management and Multimodal Communication* (LNCS), (vol. 5707, pp. 244–251). Springer.

Grimes, S. (2012). *DeepMR: Market research mines social sentiment*. GreenBook.

Hatzivassiloglou, V., & McKeown, K. (1997). Predicting the semantic orientation of adjectives. In *Proceedings of the 35th Annual Meeting of the ACL and the 8th Conference of the European Chapter of the ACL*, (pp. 174–181). Madrid, Spain: ACL.

Hu, M., & Liu, B. (2004). Mining and summarizing customer reviews. In *Proceedings of the 10th ACM SIGKDD International Conference on Knowledge Discovery and Data Mining*, (pp. 168–177). Seattle, WA: ACM.

Kawai, Y., Kumamoto, T., & Tanaka, K. (2007). Fair news reader: Recommending news articles with different sentiments based on user preference. In Proceedings of Knowledge-Based Intelligent Information & Engineering Systems (pp. 612-622). KES.

Kobayashi, N., Iida, R., Inui, K., & Matsumoto, Y. (2006). Opinion mining as extraction of attribute-value relations. *Lecture Notes in Artificial Intelligence, 4012*, 470–481.

Ku, L.-W., Lee, L.-Y., Wu, T.-H., & Chen, H.-H. (2005). Major topic detection and its application to opinion summarization. In *Proceedings of the 28th Annual International ACM SIGIR Conference on Research and Development in Information Retrieval*, (pp. 627-628). Salvador, Brazil: ACM.

Liu, B. (2010). Sentiment analysis: A multi-faceted problem. *IEEE Intelligent Systems, 25*(3), 76–80.

Lloyd, L., Kechagias, D., & Skiena, S. (2005). Lydia: A system for large-scale news analysis. LNCS. *Proceedings of String Processing and Information Retrieval, 3772*, 161–166. doi:10.1007/11575832_18.

Minsky, M. (2006). *The emotion machine*. New York: Simon and Schuster.

Mishne, G., & de Rijke, M. (2006). Moodviews: Tools for blog mood analysis. In *Proceedings of the AAAI Symposium on Computational Approaches to Analysing Weblogs* (pp. 153–154). AAAI.

Mohammad, S., Dorr, B., & Hirst, G. (2008). Computing word-pair antonymy. In *Proceedings of the Empirical Methods on Natural Language Processing*. EMNLP.

Mohammad, S., & Turney, P. (2010). Emotions evoked by common words and phrases: Using mechanical turk to create an emotion lexicon. In *Proceedings of the Workshop on Computational Approaches to Analysis and Generation of Emotion in Text*. NAACL.

Moilanen, K., Pulman, S., & Zhang, Y. (2010). Packed feelings and ordered sentiments: Sentiment parsing with quasi-compositional polarity sequencing and compression. In *Proceedings of the 1st Workshop on Computational Approaches to Subjectivity and Sentiment Analysis*. ECAI.

Morinaga, S., Yamanishi, K., Tateishi, K., & Fukushima, T. (2002). Mining product reputations on the web. In *Proceedings of the ACM SIGKDD Conference on Knowledge Discovery and Data Mining*. ACM.

Nasukawa, T., & Yi, J. (2003). Sentiment analysis: Capturing favorability using natural language processing. In *Proceedings of the Conference on Knowledge Capture*. K-CAP.

Pang, B., & Lee, L. (2004). A sentimental education: Sentiment analysis using subjectivity summarization based on minimum cuts. In *Proceedings of the 42nd Annual Meeting on Association for Computational Linguistics*. ACL.

Pang, B., Lee, L., & Vaithyanathan, S. (2002). Thumbs up? Sentiment classification using machine learning techniques. In *Proceedings of the Empirical Methods on Natural Language Processing*. EMNLP.

PJ. (2010). Why Indian languages failed to make a mark online!. *NextBigWhat*.

Quirk, R., Greenbaum, S., Leech, G., & Svartvik, J. (1985). *A comprehensive grammar of the English language*. Academic Press.

Seeker, W., Bermingham, A., Foster, J., & Hogan, D. (2009). *Exploiting syntax in sentiment polarity classification*. Dublin: Dublin City University.

Stone, P. J., Dunphy, D. C., Smith, M. S., & Ogilvie, D. M. (1966). *The general inquirer: A computer approach to content analysis*. Boston: The MIT Press.

Tong, R. M. (2001). An operational system for detecting and tracking opinions in on-line discussions. In *Proceedings of Working Notes from the Workshop on Operational Text Classification*. ACM.

Turney, P. (2002). Thumbs up or thumbs down? Semantic orientation applied to unsupervised classification of reviews. In *Proceedings of the Association for Computational Linguistics*. ACL.

Wiebe, J. (1990). *Recognizing subjective sentences: A computational investigation of narrative text*. (Ph.D. Dissertation). SUNY. Buffalo, NY.

Wiebe, J., & Riloff, E. (2005). Creating subjective and objective sentence classifiers from unannotated texts. In *Proceedings of the 6th CICLing-2005*, (pp. 475-486). CICLing.

Yi, J., Nasukawa, T., Bunescu, R., & Niblack, W. (2003). Sentiment analyzer: Extracting sentiments about a given topic using natural language processing techniques. In *Proceedings of the 3rd ICDM*, (pp. 427-434). Washington, DC: ICDM.

Yi, J., & Niblack, W. (2005). Sentiment mining in WebFountain. In *Proceedings of the International Conference on Data Engineering*. ICDE.

Zhou, L., & Hovy, E. (2006). On the summarization of dynamically introduced information: Online discussions and blogs. In *Proceedings of the AAAI-2006 Spring Symposium on Computational Approaches to Analyzing Weblogs*. Stanford, CA: AAAI.

ENDNOTES

1. http://www.amitavadas.com/sentiwordnet.php
2. http://www.amitavadas.com/Sentiment-Game/

Chapter 16
Building Language Resources for Emotion Analysis in Bengali

Dipankar Das
National Institute of Technology (NIT), India

Sivaji Bandyopadhyay
Jadavpur University, India

ABSTRACT

Rapidly growing Web users from multilingual communities focus the attention to improve the multilingual search engines on the basis of sentiment or emotion and provide the opportunities to build resources for languages other than English. At present, there is no such corpus or lexicon available for emotion analysis in Indian languages, especially for Bengali, the sixth most popular language in the world, second in India, and the national language of Bangladesh. Thus, in the chapter, the authors describe the preparation of an emotion corpus and lexicon in Bengali. The emotion lexicon, termed Bengali WordNet Affect has been developed from its equivalent version in English by traversing the steps of expansion, translation, and sense disambiguation. In addition to emotion lexicon, a Bengali blog corpus for emotion analysis has also been developed by manual annotators with detailed linguistic expressions such as emotional phrases, intensities, emotion holder, emotion topic and target span, and sentential emotion tags.

INTRODUCTION

In recent times, research activities in the areas of Opinion, Sentiment, and/or Emotion in natural language texts and other media are gaining ground under the umbrella of subjectivity analysis and affective computing.

The Subjectivity Analysis is defined as classifying a given text (usually a sentence) into one of two classes: objective or subjective whereas Affective computing is an area of artificial intelligence that focuses on how emotion is expressed, perceived, recognized, processed, and interpreted in text, speech, dialogue, image, video etc.. Text based emotion analysis relies heavily on Natural Language Processing (NLP), which is mostly focused on understanding the semantics of text. By analyzing the texts and obtaining semantic as well as emotional information, the computer can deal with more interpersonal matters such as

DOI: 10.4018/978-1-4666-3970-6.ch016

understanding the relationships between people. Both affective computing and NLP are needed to reach this goal. NLP algorithms are necessary to understand the semantics or explicit message of text, while affective computing is needed to understand the implicit message in text manifested through emotion (Minato *et al.*, 2008).

The identification of emotional state from texts is not an easy task as emotion is not open to any objective observation or verification (Quirk *et al.*, 1985). Genuine opinion, emotion and sentiment are hard to collect, ambiguous to annotate, and tricky to distribute due to privacy reasons. Different forms of modeling exist, and ground truth is never solid due to the often highly different perception of the mostly very few annotators. Thus, the few available corpora suffer from a number of issues due to the peculiarity of these young and emerging fields.

In order to obtain knowledge and information from emotional text it is necessary to have reliable linguistic resources, such as tagged emotion corpora and emotion dictionaries. As the study of emotion recognition combined with natural language processing is rather new, it is still difficult to obtain such linguistic resources.

Among the social media like e-mails, Weblogs, chat rooms, online forums and even twitter, blog is one of the communicative and informative repository of text based emotional contents in the Web 2.0 (Lin *et al.*, 2007). Thus, we have prepared the emotion annotated corpus from Bengali blog documents.

The proposed corpus annotation task was carried out at sentence and document levels. Three annotators have manually annotated the blog sentences, which were retrieved from an open source Bengali Web blog archive (www.amarblog.com). Ekman's (1993) six basic emotion classes (*anger, disgust, fear, happy, sad* and *surprise*) were considered to accomplish our tasks. The emotional sentences are annotated with three types of intensities such as *high*, *medium* and *low* as well as the sentences of non-emotional (*neutral*) and multiple (*mixed*) categories were also identified. The emotional words and phrases were marked by fixing the lexical scope of the emotional expressions. Each of the emoticons is also considered as individual emotional expressions. The emotion holder and relevant topics associated with the emotional expressions were annotated by considering the punctuation marks, conjuncts, rhetorical structures and other discourse information whereas the knowledge of the rhetorical structure helps in removing the subjective discrepancies from the writer's point of view. The annotation scheme is used to annotate 123 blog posts containing 4,740 emotional sentences having single emotion tag and 322 emotional sentences for mixed emotion tags along with 7087 *neutral* sentences in Bengali. Three types of standard agreement measures such as Cohen's *kappa* (κ) (Cohen, 1960), Measure of Agreement on Set-valued Items (MASI) (Passonneau, 2004) and *agr* (Wiebe *et al.*, 2005) metrics were employed for the annotated emotion related components. It is observed that the relaxed agreement schemes like MASI and *agr* are specially considered for fixing the lexical boundaries of emotional expressions and topics in the emotional sentences. The inter annotator agreement of some emotional components such as sentential emotions, holders and topics show satisfactory performance whereas the sentences of mixed emotion and intensities of *medium* and *low* show the disagreement. We observed that a preliminary experiment for the word level emotion classification on a small set of the whole corpus yielded satisfactory results.

In this proposed chapter, we also would like to describe the preparation of the Bengali *WordNet Affect*, an emotion lexicon from its equivalent version already available in English (http://www.cse.unt.edu/~rada/affectivetext/). The collection of the *WordNet Affect* synsets was provided as a resource for the *SemEval*-2007 shared task of "Affective Text." The shared task was focused on text annotation by affective tags not from the whole *WordNet Affect* but a part of it being more fine-grained and re-annotated using six Ekman's emotional classes. Without considering the problems of the lexical affect representation or discussing differences between emotions, cognitive states and affects, the lists were updated with the synsets retrieved from the English *SentiWordNet 3.0* (http://*SentiWordNet*.isti.cnr.it/) to make adequate number of emotion word entries whereas the Part-of-Speech (POS) information for each of the synsets was kept unchanged. Expansion of the English *WordNet Affect* synsets using *SentiWordNet 3.0* has been performed for verifying whether any target emotion word can be produced from a source sentiment word during translation or not. The numbers of entries in the expanded word lists have been increased by 69.77% and 74.60% at synset and word levels, respectively. In addition to that, each verb present in six *WordNet Affect* lists was updated using the retrieved synsets of the *VerbNet* (http://verbs.colorado.edu/~mpalmer/projects/*VerbNet*.html) if any word level match occurs. We have employed a duplicate removal technique that accumulates more emotion bearing words with reduced error from the updated synsets. Finally, the updated lists were automatically translated into Bengali using the synset based English to Bengali bilingual dictionary which is being developed as part of the EILMT project (English to Indian Languages Machine Translation [EILMT] is a TDIL project undertaken by the consortium of different premier institutes and sponsored by MCIT, Govt. of India). The duplicate removal technique was also applied on the translated synsets to reduce the error cases. Human translator translates the non-translated entries containing word combinations, idioms etc. Sense wise separated word groups give a pattern-based similarity clue in Bengali to English bilingual dictionary (http://home.uchicago.edu/~cbs2/banglainstruction.html). The sense disambiguation algorithm based on the similarity clues is applied on the translated Bengali synsets. Two translators carried out the evaluation whereas the inter-translator agreement was measured using a statistical technique, *kappa*. The *kappa* coefficient (k) in case of our agreement measure varies in the range from 0.44 to 0.56 which shows not very high but a moderate result. As there is no drastic difference between the automatic sense disambiguation process and inter-translator agreement results, the fact signifies that our automatic sense disambiguation technique for reducing human effort can be considered as an effective contribution. We have evaluated the coverage of the developed resources by developing a prototype emotion analysis system. Thus, we believe that the proposed chapter would identify and discuss the issues related to the development of emotion analysis resources for other languages as well.

BACKGROUND

Major studies on Opinion Mining and Sentiment Analyses have been attempted with more focused perspectives rather than fine-grained emotions (Quan & Ren, 2009). The majority of subjective analysis methods that are related to sentiment or emotion are based on textual keywords spotting that use specific lexical resources. The emotion-annotated corpora and emotion lexicons are the primary resources to start with.

One of the most well known tasks of annotating the private states in texts is carried out by Wiebe *et al.* (2005). They manually annotated the private states including emotions, opinions, and sentiment in a 10,000-sentence corpus (the MPQA corpus) of news articles. The opinion holder information is also annotated in the MPQA corpus but the topic annotation task was initiated later by Stoyanov and Cardie (2008a).

In other related work, Liu *et al.* (2003) utilized real-world knowledge about affect drawn from a common-sense knowledge base. They attempted to understand the semantics of text to identify emotions at the sentence level and extracted from the knowledgebase those sentences that contain some affective information. This information was utilized in building affective models of text, which were used to label each sentence with a six-tuple that corresponds to Ekman's (1993) six basic emotion classes such as *Anger*, *Disgust*, *Fear*, *Happy*, *Sad*, and *Surprise*.

Alm *et al.*, (2005) considered eight emotion categories (*angry, disgusted, fearful, happy, sad, positively surprised*, and *negatively surprised*) to accomplish the emotion annotation task at sentence level. They manually annotated 1580 sentences extracted from 22 Grimms' tales. The data used in their experiments was manually annotated with emotion information, and is targeted for use in a text-to-speech synthesis system for expressive rendering of stories.

The study of emotions and their expressions in text was conducted within the Appraisal Framework (Martin & White, 2005) using a functional theory of the language that was used for conveying attitudes, judgments and emotions (Whitelaw *et al.*, 2005). Mishne (2005) experimented with mood classification in a blog corpus of 815,494 posts from *Livejournal*, a free Weblog service with a large community.

Mihalcea and Liu (2006) used the same data source for classifying the blog posts into two particular emotions – happiness and sadness. The blog posts are self-annotated by the blog writers with happy and sad mood labels.

Read *et al.* (2007) used a corpus of short stories, manually annotated with sentiment tags, in automatic emotion-based classification of sentences. Their projects focus on the genre of fiction based on only sentence level emotion annotations without identifying the emotion indicators within a sentence. Later, Read and Caroll (2010) reviewed the typology described by appraisal framework and presented a methodology for annotating appraisals on a corpus of book reviews. An inter-annotator agreement study has been discussed within the Appraisal framework. Instances of systematic disagreement has been considered that indicate areas in which appraisal may be refined or clarified.

Neviarouskaya *et al.* (2007) collected 160 sentences from a corpus of online diary-like blog posts and labeled the sentences with one of the nine emotions categories (anger, disgust, fear, guilt, interest, joy, sadness, shame, and surprise) along with the corresponding intensity value. On the other hand, Aman and Szpakowicz (2007) prepared an emotion-annotated corpus with a rich set of emotion information such as class, intensity and word or phrase based expressions.

In contrast to English, the emotion corpora for Japanese have been built for recognizing emotions (Tokuhisa *et al.*, 2008). An available emotion corpus in Chinese is Yahoo!'s Chinese news, which was used for Chinese emotion classification of news readers (Lin *et al.*, 2007). The manual annotation of eight emotional categories (expect, joy, love, surprise, anxiety, sorrow, angry and hate) along with intensity, holder, word/phrase, degree word, negative word, conjunction, rhetoric, punctuation and other linguistic expressions are carried out at sentence, paragraph as well as document level on 1,487 Chinese blog documents (Quan and Ren, 2009).

In case of emotion lexicon generation, the development of the General Inquirer System by Philip Stone (Stone, 1966) in Harvard was probably the first milestone to identify textual sentiment using sentiment lexicon. The extraction and annotation of subjective terms started with machine learning approaches (Hatzivassiloglou and McKeown, 1997). They proposed the log-linear regression model to predict the orientation of conjoined adjectives. The model uses the number of constraints identified from a large corpus and clusters the conjoined adjectives into finite number of groups of different orientations. Finally, the adjectives are labelled as positive or negative.

After a few years, the idea of Thumbs Up and Thumbs Down for positive and negative review classification was attempted by Peter Turney (2002). He devised an algorithm to extract Point-wise Mutual Information (PMI) for consecutive words and their semantic orientation. Pang *et al.*, (2002) suggested the manual development of sentiment lexicon for a domain by involving two annotators independently to choose good indicator words for positive and negative sentiments in movie reviews. The proposed method in (Takamura *et al.*, 2005) extracts sentiment orientations of words from a small number of seed words with high accuracy in the experiments on English as well as Japanese lexicons.

Wiebe and Riloff (2005) have proposed two techniques for automatic generation of lexicon resources for subjectivity analysis of a new target language from the available lexicon resources for English. Two techniques were proposed for the generation of target language lexicon from English subjectivity lexicon. The first technique uses a bilingual dictionary while the second method is a parallel corpus based approach using existing subjectivity analysis tools for English. Andreevskaia and Bergler (2006) present a method for extracting positive or negative sentiment bearing adjectives from *WordNet* using the Sentiment Tag Extraction Program (STEP).

In addition to the above efforts, some well known sentiment lexicons have also been developed, such as subjective adjective list (Baroni and Vegnaduzzo, 2004), English *SentiWordNet* (Esuli et. al., 2006), Taboada's adjective list (Voll and Taboada, 2007), Subjectivity Word List (Banea *et al.*, 2008), etc.

Mohammad *et al.* (2008) proposed a method that helps to measure the relative sentiment score of a word and its antonym. On the other hand, an automatically generated and scored sentiment lexicon, SentiFul (Neviarouskaya *et al.*, 2009) along with its expansion, morphological modifications and distinguishing sentiment features (propagating, reversing, intensifying, and weakening) are significant contributory efforts in developing emotion dictionaries.

In recent trends, the application of mechanical turk for generating emotion lexicon (Mohammad and Turney, 2010) is a promising venue of research. They used an online service from Amazon in order to obtain a large amount of human annotation of emotion lexicon in an efficient and inexpensive manner. But to avoid any monetary investments in developing an emotion lexicon, we prefer the open source, available and accessible resources to achieve our goals.

MAIN FOCUS OF THE CHAPTER

Issues, Controversies, Problems

It is observed that even in English, the crisis of emotion lexicon is still present. The reasons may be that the important aspects that govern the lexical level semantic orientation are natural language context (Pang *et al.*, 2002), language properties (Wiebe and Mihalcea, 2006), domain pragmatic knowledge (Aue and Gamon, 2005), time dimension (Read, 2005), colors and culture (Strapparava and Ozbal, 2010) and so on. Sometimes, a single word may evoke different emotions in different contexts (e.g., the word, "succumb" triggers multiple emotions, fear as well as sad to its reader). Thus, we have proposed a novel method that comprises of two modules; first one is a Fuzzy c-means clustering module that is applied on a lexical network followed by a supervised one that predicts the definite emotion orientations of the words (Das *et al.*, 2012).

But, all of the above mentioned resources are in English and have been used in coarse grained sentiment analysis (e.g., positive, negative or neutral). Similar to the English *WordNet Affect* (Strapparava and Valitutti, 2004), there are a few attempts in other languages such as, Russian and Romanian (Bobicev *et al.*, 2010). Similarly, we have developed the *WordNet Affect* in Japnese (Torii *et al.*, 2011), Hindi and Telugu (Das *et al.*, 2012).

A recent study shows that the non-native English speakers support the growing use of the Internet (http://www.Internetworldstats.com/

stats.htm). This raises the demand of linguistic resources for languages other than English. India is a multilingual country with great cultural diversities. But, the crucial fact is that the Indian languages are resource-constrained and the manual preparation of emotion annotated data is both time consuming and cost intensive. To the best of our knowledge, at present, there is no such corpus or lexicon available for affect analysis in Indian languages especially for Bengali. Bengali, one of the more important Indo-Iranian languages, is the sixth-most popular in the world and spoken by a population that now exceeds 250 million. Geographical Bengali-speaking population percentages are as follows: Bangladesh (over 95%), and the Indian States of Andaman & Nicobar Islands (26%), Assam (28%), Tripura (67%), and West Bengal (85%). The global total includes those who are now in diaspora in Canada, Malawi, Nepal, Pakistan, Saudi Arabia, Singapore, United Arab Emirates, United Kingdom, and United States. The identification of affect or emotion in Indian languages in general and Bengali in particular is difficult and challenging as the language is 1) Inflectional languages providing the richest and most challenging sets of linguistic and statistical features resulting in long and complex word forms, and 2) Relatively free phrase order. Thus, this chapter proposes the techniques and phases for developing the emotion corpus and lexicon in Bengali. We believe that the corpus developed as part of the present work would help the development and evaluation of emotion analysis systems in Bengali.

From the above mentioned discussions, it is observed that several research attempts have been made for developing the emotional resources in English. But, most of the resources were either developed for in-house research experiments or are not available as open source. Thus, one of the major problems of emotion extraction is the lack of appropriately annotated corpora or lexicon. We collected two different types of corpus, a *SemEval 2007* news corpus that is available as open source and a blog corpus that was collected via request to the direct owners/authors of that corpus (Aman and Szpakowicz, 2007).

SOLUTIONS AND RECOMMENDATIONS

Bengali Blog Corpus

Random collection of 123 blog posts containing a total of 12,149 sentences were retrieved from the Bengali Web blog archive (especially from comics, politics, sports and short stories) to prepare the corpus. No prior training was provided to the annotators but they were instructed to annotate each sentence based on some illustrated samples of the annotated sentences. The annotators were free in selecting the text spans for annotating the emotional expressions and topic(s) in the emotional sentences. This annotation scheme is termed as relaxed scheme throughout this chapter. For emotional components, the annotators were instructed to select the annotation tags from some fixed annotation tag sets.

The proposed emotion annotation task in Bengali has been carried out at sentence level. Three annotators manually annotated the Bengali blog sentences retrieved from the Web blog archive1 with Ekman's six basic emotion tags (*anger* (A), *disgust* (D), *fear* (F), *happy* (H), *sad* (Sa) and *surprise* (Su)). The emotional sentences are tagged with three types of intensities such as high, general/medium and low. The sentences of non-emotional (neutral) and multiple (mixed) categories were also identified. The identification of emotional words or phrases and fixing the scopes of different emotional expressions in the sentences were carried out. Each of the emoticons has been considered as an individual emotional expression. The emotion holder and relevant topics associated with the emotional expressions were annotated considering the punctuation marks, conjuncts, rhetorical structures and other discourse information. The knowledge of rhetorical structure helps in removing the subjective discrepancies from the writer's point of view. The annotation scheme was used to annotate 123 blog posts containing 12,149 sentences that include 4,740 emotional sentences having single emotion tag, 322 emotional sentences with mixed emotion tags along with 7087 neutral sentences. Three types of standard agreement measures such as Cohen's kappa (κ) (Cohen, 1960), Measure of Agreement on Set-valued Items (MASI) (Passonneau, 2004) and agr metric (Wiebe *et al.*, 2005) were employed for annotating the emotion related components. The relaxed schemes like MASI and agr were especially considered for fixing the boundaries of emotional expressions and topic spans inside an agreed target span in the emotional sentences. The inter annotator agreement on some emotional components such as sentential emotions, holders, topics have shown satisfactory performance for single emotion sentences while the sentences of mixed emotion and medium and low intensities show the disagreement.

ANNOTATION OF EMOTIONAL COMPONENTS

Emotional Expressions, Sentential Emotions, and Intensity

The identification of emotion or affect affixed in the text segments is a puzzle which can be solved partially using some lexical clues (e.g., discourse markers, punctuation marks (sym), negations (NEG), conjuncts (CONJ) and reduplication (Redup)), structural clues (e.g., rhetoric and syntactic knowledge) and obviously some direct affective clues (e.g., emoticons (*emo_icon*)). The identification of structural clues indeed requires the identification of lexical clues. The rhetoric knowledge plays an important role to identify the emotions expressed from the perspective of a reader or writer.

The Rhetorical Structure Theory (RST) describes the various parts of a text, how they can be arranged and connected to form a whole text (Azar, 1999). The theory maintains that the consecutive discourse elements, termed as text spans, which can be in the form of clauses, sentences, or units larger than sentences, are related by a relatively small set (20–25) of rhetorical relations (Mann and Thompson, 1988). RST distinguishes between the part of a text that realizes the primary goal of the writer, termed as nucleus, and the part that provides the supplementary material, termed as satellite. The separation of nucleus from satellite is usually done based on the punctuation marks (,!@?), emoticons, explicit discourse markers (যেহেতু *jehetu* [as], যেমন *jemon* [e.g.], কারণ *karon* [because], মানে *mane* [means]), connectives (এবং *ebong* [and], কিন্তু *kintu* [but], অথবা *athoba* [or]) and causal verbs (ঘটায় *ghotay* [caused]).

Use of emotion-related words is not the sole means of expressing emotion. Often a sentence, which otherwise may not have an emotional word, may become emotion bearing depending on the context or underlying semantic meaning (Aman and Szpakowicz, 2007) (e.g., "Dreams are in the eyes of the Children"). An empirical analysis of the unstructured Bengali blog texts shows two types of emotional expressions. The first category contains explicitly stated emotion word (EW) or phrases (EP) or the subjective content mentioned in the locus of the nucleus or in the satellite. The other category contains the implicit emotional hints that are identified based on the context or from the metaphoric knowledge of the expressions.

Sometimes, the emotional expressions exist with direct emotion words (EW) (কৌতুক *koutuk* [joke], আনন্দ *ananda* [happy], আশ্চর্য *ashcharjyo* [surprise]), reduplication (সন্দ সন্দ *sanda sanda* [doubt with fear], question words (কি *ki* [what], কবে *kabe* [when]), colloquial words (ক্ষ্যামা *kshy-ama* [pardon]) and foreign words (থ্যাংকু *thanku* [thanks], গোস্যা *gossya* [anger]) etc. On the other hand, the emotional expressions also contain the indirect emotion words, e.g., proverbs or idioms

(তাসের ঘর *taser ghar* [weakly built], গৃহদাহ *grrihadaho* [family disturbance]) or emoticons (☺, ☹, 😐).

It was found that a large number of emoticons (*emo_icon*) present in the Bengali blog texts exist corresponding to various emotional classes. Thus, each of the emoticons was treated as an individual emotional expression and its corresponding intensity was marked based on the image which corresponds to that emoticon. As the emoticons are very much domain specific, the labeling of the emoticons with Ekman's six emotion classes was also verified through the same inter-annotator agreement procedure that was adopted for annotating the emotional expressions.

The intensifiers (*khub* [too/very/much], *anek* [huge/large], *bhishon* [heavy/too much]) associated with the emotional phrases are also taken care of while annotating the sentential intensities. As the intensifiers depend solely on the context, their identification plays an important role during annotation. It was observed that the intensifiers play a crucial role in identifying the intensity of the emotional expressions along with the effects of negations and conjunct words.

Sometimes, the negations না *na* [no], নয় *noy* [not]) and conjuncts freely occur in the sentences and completely change the emotions of those sentences. For that very reason, a crucial analysis of negation and conjuncts was carried out both at intra and inter phrase level for obtaining the sentential emotions and intensities. An example set of the annotated blog corpus is shown in Box 1.

Agreement of Emotional Expressions

Generally, the emotional expressions are the words or string of words that are selected by the annotator and the agreement is carried out between the sets of text spans selected by the two annotators for each of the emotional expressions. As there is no fixed category in this case, we employed two different strategies in addition to kappa (κ) measure while calculating the agreement among the annotators.

First, we have chosen the Measure of Agreement on Set-valued Items (MASI). Secondly, the annotators were asked to annotate different emotional expressions by identifying the responsible text anchors and the agreement was measured using the *agr* metric (Wiebe *et al.*, 2005). The metric *agr* is defined as follows.

If A, B are the sets of anchors annotated by annotators *a* and *b*, respectively, *agr* is a direc-

Box 1. Annotated sample of the blog corpus

<ES_Sa><EW_H> গেদুচাচা: </EW_H> ভাইও <sym>!</sym> <EW_D> বেজার </EW_D> হইছেন? </ES_Sa>

<ES_A><ES_Su> তিনি <EW_Su><EW_Q> কি </EW_Q></EW_Su> বুঝলেন <EW_Su><EW_Q> কে </EW_Q> </EW_Su> জানে <EW_Su>!</EW_Su> <Redup><EW_A> রেগেমেগে </EW_A></Redup> ভিতরে চলে গেলেন । আমাকে <EW_F> বোধহয় </EW_F> চিনতে পারেন <NEG>নি</NEG> । </ES_Su></ES_A>

<ES_H> আপনার <topic> কবিতাটা </topic> পড়তে গিয়া এই <EW_H> কৌতুকটা < /EW_H> মনে পড়ছিলো </ES_H>

EW_Q = Emotion Question Word
EW_X = Sentential Emotion for Emotion Class X where
X € *Anger* (A), *Disgust* (D), *Fear* (F), *Happy* (H), *Sadness* (Sa) and *Surprise* (Su)
ES_X = Sentential Emotion for Emotion Class X
<EW_H> = Emotion Holder
<topic> = Emotion Topic
NEG = Negation Words
Redup = Reduplicated Words
<sym> = Symbols

tional agreement that measures what proportion of a was also marked by b. We specially compute the agreement of b to a as:

$$agr(a \mid\mid b) = \frac{\mid AmatchingB \mid}{\mid A \mid}$$

The *agr (a|| b)* metric corresponds to the recall if *a* is the gold standard and *b* the system, and to precision, if *b* is the gold standard and *a* is the system. The results of the two agreement strategies for each emotion class are shown in Table 1. The annotation agreement of emotional expressions produces slightly less values for both kappa and *agr*. It points to the fact that the relaxed annotation scheme provided for fixing the boundaries of the expressions causes the errors.

Agreement of Sentential Emotions and Intensity

Three annotators identified as A1, A2 and A3 have used an open source graphical tool to carry out the annotation. As the Ekman's emotion classes and intensity types belong to some definite categories, the annotation agreement for the emotions and intensities were measured using the standard Cohen's kappa coefficient (κ). The intensities of mixed emotional sentences were also considered. The agreement results of the emotional, non-emotional and mixed emotional sentences, emoticons along with results for each emotion class and intensity types are shown in Table 1.

It was observed that the sentential emotions with happy, sad or surprise classes produce comparatively higher kappa coefficient than the other emotion classes as the emotional expressions of these types were explicitly specified in the blog texts. On the other hand, the sentences of mixed

Table 1. Inter-annotator agreements for sentential emotions, intensities, emoticons, and emotional expressions

Classes (No. of Sentences/Instances)	Agreement (Pair of Annotators)			
	A1←→A2	A2←→A3	A1←→A3	Average
Emotion/Non-Emotion (5,234/7,087)	0.88	0.83	0.86	0.85
Happy (804)	0.79	0.72	0.83	0.78
Sad (826)	0.82	0.75	0.72	0.76
Anger (765)	0.75	0.71	0.69	0.71
Disgust (766)	0.76	0.69	0.77	0.74
Fear (757)	0.65	0.61	0.65	0.63
Surprise (822)	0.84	0.82	0.85	0.83
Mixed (322)	0.42	0.21	0.53	0.38
High Intensity (2,330)	0.66	0.72	0.68	0.68
Medium/General Intensity (1,765)	0.42	0.46	0.48	0.45
Low Intensity (1345)	0.21	0.34	0.26	0.27
Emoticons for Six Emotion Classes (678)	0.85	0.73	0.84	0.80
Emoticons for three Intensities	0.72	0.66	0.63	0.67
Emotional Expressions (7,588) [*MASI*]	0.64	0.61	0.66	0.63
Emotional Expressions (7,588) [*agr*]	0.67	0.63	0.68	0.66

emotion *class* or general and low type intensity produce poor agreement results as expected. Instead of specifying the agreement results of emoticons for each emotion class, the average results for the three annotation sets are shown in Table 1.

Annotation of Emotion Holder

The source or holder of an emotional expression is the speaker or writer or experiencer. One of the main criteria considered for annotating emotion holders is generally based on the nested source hypothesis as described in (Wiebe *et al.*, 2005).

The structure of Bengali blog corpus (as shown in Box 2) helps in the emotion holder annotation process. Sometimes, the comments of one blogger are annotated by other bloggers in the blog posts. Thus, the holder annotation task in user comments sections was less cumbersome than annotating the holders in the topic section.

Prior work in identification of opinion holders has sometimes identified only a single opinion per sentence (Bethard *et al.*, 2004), and sometimes several opinions (Choi *et al.*, 2005). As the blog corpus has sentence level emotion annotations, the former category, i.e., one emotion per sentence, was adopted. But, it has been observed that long sentences contain more than one emotional expression and hence such sentences associated with multiple emotion holders (EH).

Box 2. General structure of a Bengali blog document

```
-<DOC docid = xyz>
        +<Topic>.... </Topic>
        -<User Comments id=UC1>
                -<U uid=1, tid=t1, secid=UC1>....
                        -<U uid=2, tid=t2, secid=UC1.1>...</U>
                        -<U uid=3, tid=t3, secid=UC1.2>...</U>
                            -<U uid=1, tid=t4, secid=UC1.2.1>...</U>
                    ....
                </U>
         </User Comments>
        +<User Comments id=UC2>
        +<User Comments id=UC3>
          ...
</DOC>
```

All the probable emotion holders of a sentence are stored in an anchoring vector. If multiple emotion holders exist, the successive holders are annotated and placed in the vector according to their order of occurrence in the sentence.

The annotation of emotion holder at sentence level requires the knowledge of two basic constraints (implicit and explicit), separately. The explicit constraints qualify the single prominent emotion holder which is directly involved with the emotional expression whereas the implicit constraints qualify all direct and indirect nested sources as emotion holders.

In Examples 1, 2, and 3 of Bengali sentences, the pattern shown in **bold** face denotes the emotion holder. In the second example, the appositive case (e.g. রামের সুখ (Ram's pleasure)) is also identified and placed in the vector by removing the inflectional suffix (-এর in this case). Example 2 and Example 3 contain the emotion holders রাম (*Ram*) and নাসরিন সুলতানা (*Nasreen Sultana*) based on the implicit constraints.

Agreement of Emotion Holder Annotation

Sometimes, the emotion holders contain multi word Named Entities (NEs) and they are assumed as single emotion holders. As there is no agreement discrepancy in selecting the boundary of the single or multiple emotion holders, we have used the standard metric, Cohen's kappa (κ) for measuring the inter-annotator agreement. Each of the emotion holders in an anchoring vector is treated as a separate emotion holder and the agreement between the two annotators are carried out on each pair of emotion holders from the corresponding anchoring vectors. It has to be mentioned that the anchoring vectors provided by the two annotators may be disjoint. To emphasize the fact, an additional technique has been employed to measure the annotation agreement for emotion holders.

For example, if X is a set of emotion holders selected by the first annotator and Y is a set of

Example 1. EH_Vector: < সায়ণ >

সায়ণ	ভীষণ	আনন্দ	অনুভব	করেছিল
Sayan	*bhishon*	*anondo*	*anubhob*	*korechilo*
Sayan felt very happy.				

Example 2. EH_Vector: < রাশেদ, রাম >

রাশেদ	অনুভব	করেছিল	যে	**রামের**	সুখ	অন্তহীন
Rashed	*anubhob*	*korechilo*	*je*	***Ramer***	*such*	*antohin*
Rashed felt that Ram's pleasure is endless.						

Example 3. EH_Vector: < গেদু চাচা, নাসরিন সুলতানা >

গেদু চাচা	বলে:	না	গো	বোন,	আমি	**নাসরিন সুলতানার**	দুঃখের	কথাতে	কেঁদে	ফেলি।
Gedu ChaCha	*bole:*	*na*	*go*	*bon,*	*ami*	***Nasrin Sultanar***	*dookher*	*kathate*	*kende*	*feli*
Gedu ChaCha says: No my sister, I fall into cry on the sad speech of Nasreen Sultana.										

emotion holders selected by the second annotator for an emotional sentence containing multiple emotion holders, the inter-annotator agreement IAA for that sentence is equal to the quotient of the number of emotion holders in X and Y intersection divided by number of emotion holders in X and Y union:

$$IAA = X \cap Y / X \cup Y$$

Two types of agreement results per emotion class for annotating the emotion holders (EH) are shown in Table 2. Both types of agreement results have been found satisfactory and the difference between the two agreement results was significantly less. The small difference indicates the error involved in the annotation process. It was found that the agreement is highly moderate in case of single emotion holder, but is less in case of multiple holders. The disagreement occurs mostly

Table 2. Inter-annotator agreement for emotion holder annotation

Emotion Class [Sentences, Emotion Holders]	**Agreement between Pair of Annotators (κ) [IAA]**			
	A1←→A2	**A2←→A3**	**A1←→A3**	**Average**
Happy [804, 918]	(0.87) [0.88]	(0.79) [0.81]	(0.76) [0.77]	(0.80) [0.82]
Sad [826, 872]	(0.82) [0.81]	(0.85) [0.83]	(0.78) [0.80]	(0.81) [0.81]
Anger [765,780]	(0.80) [0.79]	(0.75) [0.73]	(0.74) [0.71]	(0.76) [0.74]
Disgust [766, 770]	(0.70) [0.68]	(0.72) [0.69]	(0.83) [0.84]	(0.75) [0.73]
Fear [757, 764]	(0.85) [0.82]	(0.78) [0.77]	(0.79) [0.81]	(0.80) [0.80]
Surprise [822, 851]	(0.78) [0.80]	(0.81) [0.79]	(0.85) [0.83]	(0.81) [0.80]

in the case of identifying the implicit constraints but such issues were resolved by mutual discussion among the annotators.

ANNOTATION OF EMOTION TOPIC

Opinion topic is defined as the real world object, event, or abstract entity that is the primary subject of the opinion as intended by the opinion holder (Stoyanov and Cardie, 2008a). The authors also mentioned that the opinion topic identification is difficult within the single target span of the opinion as there are multiple potential topics, each identified with its own topic span. Though we have used similar definition for annotating the emotion topics, the actual challenge is the identification of target spans that contain one or multiple emotion topics.

Stoyanov and Cardie (2008b) have described that the topic of an opinion depends on the context in which its associated opinion expression occurs. In our case, the text present in the blogs are mostly unstructured from the syntactic point of view but the writer's emotional intentions in a sentence are reflected in the target span by mentioning one or more emotion topics that are related to their corresponding emotional expressions. Though topics are distributed in different text spans of writer's text, they can be distinguished by capturing the rhetorical structure of the text.

In blog texts, it was observed that an emotion topic can occur in the nucleus as well as in the satellite. Thus, the whole sentence was assumed as the scope for the presence of the potential emotion topics. Sometimes, the text spans that contain the emotional expression and emotion holder are also be responsible for being the candidate seeds of target span.

In Example 3, the target span (নাসরিন সুলতানার দুঃখের কথাতে, 'sad speech of Nasreen Sultana') contains the emotion holder (নাসরিন সুলতানার 'Nasreen Sultana') as well as the emotional expression (দুঃখের কথাতে 'sad speech'). For that very reason, the annotators were instructed to consider the whole sentence as their target span and to identify one or more topics related to the emotional expressions in that sentence. As the topics are sometimes multi word components or string of words, the scope of the individual topics inside a target span is hard to identify. Thus, we have not used the standard metrics for measuring the inter-annotator agreement to accomplish the goal. Instead of using Cohen's kappa (κ), we employed MASI and *agr* metric (as mentioned in earlier section) for measuring the agreement of emotion topic annotation.

The emotional sentences containing single emotion topic has shown less disagreement than the sentences that contain multiple emotion topics. It has been observed that the agreement for annotating target span is approximately 0.9 which means the annotation was almost satisfactory. But, the disagreement occurs in the case of topic span annotation. The inter-annotator agreement for emotion topic annotation for each emotion class is shown in Table 3. The selection of emotion topic from other relevant topics causes the disagreement.

EMOTION LEXICON

In case of developing emotion lexicon in Bengali, we have collected the widely used open source English *WordNet Affect* (http://www.cse.unt.edu/~rada/affectivetext/) and *SentiWordNet* (http://SentiWordNet.isti.cnr.it/) for conducting our research experiments. The brief details of these two resources have been described below. In case of Bengali, we have prepared the Bengali *WordNetAffect* as part of the present research work.

English *WordNet Affect*

The English *WordNet Affect*, based on Ekman's six emotion types, is a lexical resource containing information about the emotional words. Compared

Table 3. Inter-annotator agreement for topic annotation

Emotion Class [Sentences, Emotion Topics]	Agreement between Pair of Annotators (MASI) [*agr*]			
	A1←→A2	A2←→A3	A1←→A3	Average
Happy [804, 848]	(0.83) [0.85]	(0.81) [0.83]	(0.79) [0.82]	(0.81) [0.83]
Sad [826, 862]	(0.84) [0.86]	(0.77) [0.79]	(0.81) [0.83]	(0.80) [0.82]
Anger [765,723]	(0.80) [0.78]	(0.81) [0.78]	(0.86) [0.84]	(0.82) [0.80]
Disgust [766, 750]	(0.77) [0.76]	(0.78) [0.74]	(0.72) [0.70]	(0.75) [0.73]
Fear [757, 784]	(0.78) [0.79]	(0.77) [0.80]	(0.79) [0.81]	(0.78) [0.80]
Surprise [822, 810]	(0.90) [0.86]	(0.85) [0.82]	(0.82) [0.80]	(0.85) [0.82]

with the complete English *WordNet* (Miller, 1995), the English *WordNet Affect* is small in size but important for its affective annotation. The collection of the *WordNet Affect* synsets was provided as a resource for the shared task of Affective Text in *SemEval 2007*. The resource is not the whole *WordNet Affect* but a part of it and more fine-grain re-annotated using Ekman's six emotional class labels. It is developed based on WordNet domains where each synset is annotated with at least one domain label, selected from a set of two hundred labels that are arranged hierarchically. In addition to that, *WordNet Affect* includes a hierarchy of the affective domain labels that contain the synsets representing the annotated concepts of affect.

In our present task, we have concentrated on the problem that how the affective meanings are expressed in the natural language using words that describe specific emotions (for example, *joy*, *sad* or *scare*) as well as words that describe mental states, physical or bodily states, personality traits, behaviors, attitudes, and feelings (such as *pleasure* or *pain*), etc.

Bengali *WordNet Affect*

To the best of our knowledge, all the lexical resources that are used in opinion or emotion analysis have been created for English. But, the amount of the text data written in languages other than English is increasing rapidly. Thus, the resource acquisition is one of the most challenging obstacles to work with such resource constrained languages like Bengali. For the very reason, we aimed to develop the *WordNet Affect* lists in Bengali from the *WordNet Affect* lists available in English without considering the problems of the lexical affect representation or the differences between emotions, cognitive states and affects. Our main focus was to develop an equivalent resource in Bengali labelled with six emotions.

The whole data of English *WordNet Affect* was provided in six files named by the six emotions. Each file contains a list of synsets with one synset per one line. An example synset entry from *WordNet Affect* is shown:

a#00117872 angered enraged furious infuriated maddened

The first letter of each line indicates the Part of Speech (POS) and is followed by the synset number. The representation is simple and easy for further processing. There are a large number of word combinations, collocations and idioms. These parts of synsets have shown problems during translation and therefore manual translation was carried out to solve the issues.

Updating Using *SentiWordNet*

It was found that the *WordNet Affect* lists contain fewer emotion word entries. Hence, before translating the lists into Bengali, it was necessary to update the lists with adequate number of emotion words. Thus, the six lists were updated with the synsets retrieved from the English *SentiWordNet* which contains more number of emotion words than *WordNet Affect.* The *SentiWordNet* assigns each synset of the *WordNet* with three sentiment scores, *positive* and *negative* subjective scores and the *objective* score. One example entry in the *SentiWordNet* is shown:

a 1211840.25 0.25 infuriated#a#1 furious#a#2 maddened#a#1 enraged#a#1 angered#a#1

As the *WordNet Affect* and *SentiWordNet* were both developed from the *WordNet* (Miller, 1995), each word of the *WordNet Affect* was easily replaced by the equivalent synsets retrieved from the *SentiWordNet* if the synset contains that emotion word. During the replacement of words by equivalent synsets, some irrelevant synsets were also identified that represent a non appropriate meaning. But, it was observed that in the case of emotion words, this phenomenon is not frequent because the direct emotion words are not very ambiguous. The POS information in the *WordNet Affect* lists was kept unchanged during updating.

In the *WordNet Affect*, there are some synsets (e.g. *huffiness*) that have equivalent synset entries in the *SentiWordNet* without any subjective score (*positive* or *negative*). It was also found that in case of some emotion words (e.g. *offense*), the equivalent synset entries in the *SentiWordNet* may or may not contain any *subjective* score. The examples are shown in Figure 1.

Thus, the subjective score was not considered while replacing the emotion words. It was observed that duplicate emotion words are present in the updated synsets. Thus, we applied duplicate removal technique on the synsets and consequently merged the synsets to form a single synset containing unique emotion words only.

For example, If the words, "A" and "B" appear in an *WordNet Affect* entry "E" and are replaced by the retrieved *SentiWordNet* synsets A' andB' such that A1, A2, A3, B3 ϵ A' and B1, B2, B3, A3 ϵ B', then the updated entry E' = (A' – B') + (B' – A') + (A' ∩ B'). A1, A2 and A3 are the words present in the retrieved synset A' and B1, B2, B3 are the words in the retrieved synset B' as extracted from the *SentiWordNet*. The main objective of the updating was to increase the number of emotion word entries as well as to minimize the number of duplicate entries. As the *SentiWordNet* synsets for an individual entry in a *WordNet Affect* synset are merged during duplicate removal process, the number of synsets remains unchanged but the number of emotion words increases. A *WordNet Affect* synset, the two synsets extracted from the *SentiWordNet* corresponding to the marked words in the *WordNet Affect* synset and the updated synsets are shown in Figure 2. Table 4 shows the number of POS based synsets and words in the six *WordNet Affect* lists before and after updating using *SentiWordNet*.

Figure 1. Equivalent synset entries in SentiWordNet

```
n#05589074 huffiness /* WordNet Affect */
n      7057022  0.0   0.0   huffiness#n#1    /* SentiWordNet */

#05588822 umbrage offense   /* WordNet Affect */
n      7590773    0.0 0.0      offence#n#2 offense#n#4    /* SentiWordNet */
n      1155991    0.125        0.375    offence#n#4 offense#n#1 discourtesy#n#3 offensive_activity#n#1
/* SentiWordNet */
```

Figure 2. Updated synset

/ WordNet Affect Synset */*

n#10337658 fit(A) scene(B) tantrum

/ SentiWordNet Synset for A' */*

tantrum/scene/conniption/fit/burst/fit_out/equip/outfit/tally/jibe/match/correspond/gibe/agree/check/conform_to/meet/set/primed/fit_to/fit_for/convulsion/paroxysm

/ SentiWordNet Synset for B' */*

tantrum/scene/conniption/fit/scenery/view/prospect/vista/panorama/aspect/shot

/ Updated Synset E' */*

tantrum/scene/conniption/fit/burst/fit_out/equip/outfit/tally/jibe/match/correspond/gibe/agree/check/conform_to/meet/set/primed/fit_to/fit_for/convulsion/paroxysm/scenery/view/prospect/vista/panorama/aspect/shot

Table 4. Number of POS based synsets and words in six WordNet Affect lists before and after updating using SentiWordNet

Emotion Classes	*WordNet Affect* Synset (S) and Word (W) [*After SentiWordNet* Updating]							
	N		V		Adj		Adv	
	S	W	S	W	S	W	S	W
Anger	48 [198]	99 [403]	19 [103]	64 [399]	39 [89]	120 [328]	21 [23]	35 [50]
Disgust	3 [17]	6 [21]	6 [21]	22 [62]	6 [38]	34 [230]	4 [5]	10 [19]
Fear	23 [89]	45 [224]	15 [48]	40 [243]	29 [62]	97 [261]	15 [21]	26 [49]
Joy	73 [375]	149 [761]	40 [252]	122 [727]	84 [194]	203 [616]	30 [45]	65 [133]
Sadness	32 [115]	64 [180]	10 [43]	33 [92]	55 [129]	169 [779]	26 [26]	43 [47]
Surprise	5 [31]	8 [28]	7 [42]	28 [205]	12 [33]	41 [164]	4 [6]	13 [28]

Updating Using *VerbNet*

Similar to the updating using *SentiWordNet*, the synset entries for the emotional verbs in the updated lists were again replaced using the English *VerbNet*. The *VerbNet* (VN) (Kipper-Schuler, 2005) is the largest online verb lexicon with explicitly stated syntactic and semantic information based on Levin's verb classification. It associates the semantics of a verb with its syntactic frames and combines traditional lexical semantic information such as thematic roles and semantic predicates, with syntactic frames and selectional restrictions. The verb entries in the same *VerbNet* class share the common syntactic frames, and thus they are believed to have the same syntactic behavior. The class files containing the member verbs with similar sense are stored in a XML format where the member verbs present in a specific class are sense based synonymous verbs. Thus, we collected the synsets that contains similar sensed synonymous verbs as extracted from each of the *VerbNet* classes. Irrespective of other information, a general list containing only the synsets of similar sensed verbs have been prepared by processing all the XML files of the *VerbNet*.

Each word present in the verb synsets (as identified by the "*v*" POS category in the updated *WordNet Affect* lists) is searched in the general list. If a match is found, the word is replaced by its corresponding synsets available in the general list. The results regarding updating of emotion verbs in the *WordNet Affect* lists are shown in Table 5. The number of words before and after updating with the *VerbNet* is shown in the Table 5 for each Emotion Class while the number of synsets before and after updating is shown in brackets. The same duplication removal strategy described in the Section is applied in the verb updating process also.

Table 5. Updating the verbs of WordNet Affect using VerbNet

WordNet Affect Lists	Before Updating	After Updating
Anger	399 [103]	765 [159]
Disgust	62 [21]	195 [46]
Fear	243 [48]	566 [99]
Joy	727 [252]	1824 [321]
Sadness	92 [43]	852 [92]
Surprise	205 [42]	260 [45]

Automatic Translation of Synsets

An English-to-Bengali bilingual synset based dictionary containing approximately 1,02,119 entries was developed using Samsad Bengali to English bilingual dictionary. The dictionary is being developed as part of the EILMT project as mentioned earlier. The synset-based dictionary is being developed from the general domain. We used the English as a source language but have not considered all the word combinations for translation, as they could not be automatically translated. Some words containing suffixes such as "*ness*", "*less*", "*ful*" as well as the adverbs formed using suffix "*ly*" are unlikely to appear in the bilingual dictionaries. Some words were not translated automatically, as our bilingual dictionary is fairly modest. The non-translated entries were filtered from the English synsets after the translation. The percentages of not translated words of the Bengali *WordNet Affect* lists are shown in Table 6. As the total number of non-translated words in the six emotion lists was only 528, it was comprehensible for manual translation. It has been observed that the idioms and the word combinations are not translated automatically and manual effort was therefore applied for translating these non-translated items. It was found that the number of emotion words has increased in all the *WordNet Affect* lists except those corresponding to joy and sadness. But, the duplicate removal technique used in the Section has been used again

Table 6. Number of translated and non-translated synset entries

WordNet Affect Lists	Before Translation: No. of Words (No. of Synsets)	After Translation: Number of Words (No. of Synsets)	Words Not Translated
Anger	1,019 (267)	1,141 (321)	122
Disgust	245 (59)	287 (74)	42
Fear	734 (166)	785 (182)	51
Joy	2,241 (508)	2,344 (567)	103
Sadness	1,128 (205)	1,188 (220)	60
Surprise	322 (66)	472 (125)	150

on the translated Bengali synsets as the translation process also produces the duplicate entries. Thus, before applying the duplicate removal technique, the number of translated Bengali synsets in six *WordNet Affect* lists is shown in Table 6. The example entry of a Bengali translated synset is shown in Box 3.

Automatic Sense Disambiguation

We used an automatic sense disambiguation technique that is similar to the approach adopted for Bengali verb subcategorization frame identification task (Banerjee *et al.*, 2009). The sense disambiguation task of the Bengali translated synsets was carried out by classifying the synsets into groups of synonyms words with similar sense. This process has been introduced not only for clarifying the disambiguation issues but also to minimize the manual effort incorporated during verification process described in the next section. We have introduced an algorithm for disambiguating the words belonging to same as well as different synsets automatically by keeping the total number of emotion words unchanged. The pattern based informative clues present in the Bengali to English bilingual dictionary helps us to accomplish the task. Each word of the Bengali translated synset is searched in the Bengali to English bilingual dictionary to extract their English equivalent synonyms of similar and different senses. The possible example entries present in the Bengali to English bilingual dictionary for the emotional words ক্রুদ্ধ (*kruddha*) and প্রকুপিত (*prakupita*) present in a translated synset are given as follows:

Member Words:

< ক্রুদ্ধ [kruddha] a ***angry; angered, enraged***; wrathful; indignant.>

< প্রকুপিত [prakupita] a ***enraged, angered***, in censed, infuriated; excited. >

<রুষিত, রুষ্ট [ruSita, ruSTa] a ***angered, enraged***; angry.>

In the dictionary, different synonyms of a word with the same sense are separated using "," and different senses are separated using ";". Thus, the synonyms for the different senses of a word are easily extracted from the dictionary. This yields a resulting set called Synonymous Word Set (SWS). For example, the English synonyms (*angered, enraged*) and synonym with another sense (*wrathful* and *indignant*) are retrieved for the Bengali key word "ক্রুদ্ধ" [kruddha] and are categorized as three different SWSs for the Bengali key word. Similarly, two SWSs have been formed for the word "রুষ্ট" [rusta]. The algorithm describes that if two words belong to same or different translated synset, they are to be grouped together to form a new Bengali synset if at least one common English equivalent word (e.g *angered*) is present in any of the SWSs for the words. For example, the two English equivalent classes Cx_b and Cy_b

Box 3. Example of a translated Bengali synset before sense disambiguation

a#00117872 প্রকুপিত #
অগ্নি /অগ্নিকাণ্ড /উন্মত্ত /ক্ষিপ্ত /চণ্ড /প্রচণ্ড /রুদ্র #
উদ্ভ্রান্ত /উন্মদ /উন্মত্ত /ক্ষিপ্ত /খেপা/মত্ত #
কুপিত/ক্রুদ্ধ /খাপ্পা /রুষিত/রুষ্ট #
অমর্ষ /অমর্ষণ /উত্তাপ /কুপিত/ক্রুদ্ধ /খেপা/রুষিত/রুষ্ট #

with respect to the two Bengali words X_b and Y_b are defined as follows,

$Cx_b = \{SWSx_1, SWSx_2, \ldots.., SWSx_q\}$

$Cy_b = \{SWSy_1, SWSy_2, \ldots.., SWSy_p\}$

If for $i = 1$ to $p, j = 1$ to q, $(SWSx_i \cap SWSy_j) \neq \varphi$, or $\exists\, Z_e \mid Z_e \in SWSx_i \cap SWSy_j$, where Z_e is the equivalent English word present in any of the Synonymous Word Sets (SWS) of Cx_b and Cy_b both, then X_b and Y_b form a new Bengali synset containing same sense and the new English equivalent class is formed by merging the SWS_s of both Cx_b and Cy_b. Otherwise, two separate new classes are formed corresponding to X_b and Y_b. The sense based synset classification process continues until any word in the Bengali translated synset remains unclassified. The words (e.g উদ্ভ্রান্ত *(udbhrānta)* and উন্মত্ত *(unmatta)*) are classified into different synsets based on their senses accordingly.

{ < উদ্ভ্রান্ত [udbhrānta] a agitated; confused, embarrassed, perplexed; distracted; ***de mented, maddened***; ***mad***; stupefied; loitering aimlessly or in a disorderly manner.>

< উন্মত্ত [unmatta] a insane, ***mad***; crazy; ***maddened, de mented***, frenzied; excited; impassioned; frantic; furious; unreasonably attached or addicted (to); drunken, extremely in toxicated; bereft of self-possession, beside oneself; delirious.> }

The words containing similar sense are classified to form a synset and the synsets of different senses are separated using "#" symbol for the individual entry. The final separated synsets carrying same sense corresponding to the example entry of Box 3 is given in Box 4.

It has been observed that the total number of words in the Bengali *WordNet Affect* lists remains unchanged after sense disambiguation while the distribution of the translated words into different sense based synsets increases in the translated Bengali *WordNet Affect* lists. The final evaluation of the sense disambiguation process was carried out during the phase of agreement measure. The results related to sense disambiguation for six Bengali *WordNet Affects* are shown in Table 7.

Agreement Measure

We have used the standard metrics for measuring the inter-translator agreement for the emotional words present in the translated Bengali synonym sets. The overall agreement was carried out by two translators for verifying the belongingness of the translated Bengali emotion words to their respective *WordNet Affect* list. The translators consider only binary decision (Yes/No) (Y/N) for finally assigning each emotion word to its corresponding list. The present work shows the agreement values in the range from 0.44 to 0.56 that signifies a moderate agreement value and hence the lists of the Bengali *WordNet Affect* can be considered as an acceptable resource for analyzing emotion related works in Bengali. The inter-translator agreements for the emotion words of each of the emotion lists are shown in Table 8. It has to be mentioned that the inter translator agreement with "Yes-Yes" combination gives the number of emotion words in each of the six lists that are satisfactory. The results of the number of emotion word entries after the sense disambiguation

Box 4. Example of a translated Bengali synset after sense disambiguation

a#00117872 প্রকুপিত / ক্রুদ্ধ / রুষিত / রুষ্ট / কুপিত/# অগ্নি /অগ্নিকাণ্ড /উত্তাপ # ক্ষিপ্ত /চণ্ড /প্রচণ্ড /রুদ্র # উদ্ভ্রান্ত /উন্মাদ /উন্মত্ত /খেপা/মত্ত /খাপ্পা # অমর্ষ /অমর্ষণ

Table 7. Number of synsets after sense disambiguation, manual translation, and agreement measure

WordNet Affect Lists	After Sense Disambiguation: Number of Words (Number of Synsets)	After Manual Translation of Words Not Translated	After Agreement (Y-Y)
Anger	1141 (368)	1263	927
Disgust	287 (110)	329	274
Fear	785 (243)	836	630
Joy	2344 (570)	3047	2488
Sadness	1188 (280)	1248	1110
Surprise	472 (189)	622	426

Table 8. Results of inter-translator agreement

WordNet Affect Lists		Agreement Values		*kappa* (*k*)
		Yes	No	
Anger	Yes	927	110	.47
	No	84	100	
Disgust	Yes	274	16	.53
	No	14	20	
Fear	Yes	630	50	.49
	No	61	71	
Joy	Yes	2,488	562	.44
	No	564	72	
Sadness	Yes	1,110	253	.46
	No	267	68	
Surprise	Yes	426	18	.56
	No	17	25	

process as well as after the agreement measure are shown in Table 7 and the small comparative differences supports the claim for our automatic sense disambiguation process.

FUTURE RESEARCH DIRECTIONS

In case of emotion blog corpus preparation, the future task is to adopt a corpus-driven approach for building a lexicon of emotion words and phrases and extend the emotion analysis tasks in Bengali. In case of Bengali *WordNet Affect*, we are aiming to integrate more other emotion related resources so that the number of emotion word entries in the lists can be increased. The sense disambiguation task needs to be improved further in future attempts by incorporating more number of translators and considering their agreement into account.

CONCLUSION

The present chapter describes the development of emotion corpus and lexicon in Bengali. The Bengali emotion blog corpus addresses the issues of identifying emotional expressions in Bengali blog texts along with the annotation of sentences with emotional components such as intensity, holders, and topics. Nested holders are also considered for annotating the emotion holder information in sentences. The major contribution is the identification and fixing of the text spans that denote emotional expressions and topics in a sentence. It is observed that the preliminary experiments carried out on the small sets of the corpus showed satisfactory performance. On the other hand, the Bengali emotion lexicon, *WordNet Affect* contains six types of emotion words in six separate lists. The automatic way of updating, translation and sense disambiguation task reduces the manual effort. The inter translator agreement is also satisfactory.

REFERENCES

Alm, C. O., Roth, D., & Sproat, R. (2005). Emotions from text: Machine learning for text-based emotion prediction. In Human Language Technology - Empirical Method in Natural Language Processing (pp. 579-586). Academic Press.

Aman, S., & Szpakowicz, S. (2007). Identifying expressions of emotion in text. In Matoušek, V., & Mautner, P. (Eds.), *TSD 2007 (LNAI)* (*Vol. 4629*, pp. 196–205). Berlin: Springer.

Andreevskaia, A., & Bergler, S. (2007). Clac and clac-NB: Knowledge-based and corpus-based approaches to sentiment tagging. In *Proceeding of the 4th SemEval-2007*. ACL.

Aue, A., & Gamon, M. (2005). Customizing sentiment classifiers to new domains: A case study. In *Proceeding of the International Conference on Recent Advances in Natural Language Processing (RANLP-05)*. Borovets, Bulgaria: RANLP.

Azar, M. (1999). Argumentative text as rhetorical structure: An application of rhetorical structure theory. *Argumentation*, *13*, 97–114. doi:10.1023/A:1007794409860.

Banea, C., Mihalcea, R., & Wiebe, J. (2008). A bootstrapping method for building subjectivity lexicons for languages with scarce resources. In *Proceedings of Sixth International Conference on Language Resources and Evaluation (LREC 2008)*. LREC.

Banerjee, S., Das, D., & Bandyopadhyay, S. (2009). Bengali verb subcategorization frame acquisition – A baseline model. In *Proceedings of Asian Language Resources Workshop*. ACL.

Baroni, M., & Vegnaduzzo, S. (2004). *Identifying subjective adjectives through web-based mutual information*. Paper presented at the German Conference on NLP. Berlin.

Bethard, S., Yu, H., Thornton, A., Hatzivassiloglou, V., & Jurafsky, D. (2004). *Automatic Extraction of opinion propositions and their holders*. Paper presented at AAAI Spring Symposium on Exploring Attitude and Affect in Text: Theories and Applications. New York.

Bobicev, V., Maxim, V., Prodan, T., Burciu, N., & Anghelus, V. (2010). Emotions in words: Developing a multilingual WordNet-affect. In *Proceeding of CICLing 2010*. CICLing.

Choi, Y., Cardie, C., Riloff, E., & Patwardhan, S. (2005). *Identifying sources of opinions with conditional random fields and extraction patterns*. Paper presented at the Conference of HLT/EMNLP. New York.

Cohen, J. (1960). A coefficient of agreement for nominal scales. *Educational and Psychological Measurement*, *20*, 37–46. doi:10.1177/001316446002000104.

Das, D., Poria, S., & Bandyopadhyay, S. (2012). A classifier based approach to emotion lexicon construction. In *Proceedings of 17th International conference on Applications of Natural Language Processing to Information Systems*. Springer.

Das, D., Poria, S., Dasari, C. M., & Bandyopadhyay, S. (2012). Building resources for multilingual affect analysis – A case study on Hindi, Bengali and Telugu. In *Proceeding of 4th International Workshop on Corpora for Research on Emotion Sentiment & Social Signals*. LREC.

Ekman, P. (1993). An argument for basic emotions. *Cognition and Emotion*, *6*, 169–200. doi:10.1080/02699939208411068.

Esuli, A., & Sebastiani, F. (2006). Sentiwordnet: A publicly available lexical resource for opinion mining. In Proceedings of Language Resources and Evaluation Campaign. LREC.

Hatzivassiloglou, V., & McKeown, K. (1997). Predicting the semantic orientation of adjectives. In *Proceedings of the 35th Annual Meeting of the ACL and the 8th Conference of the European Chapter of the ACL* (pp. 174–181). Madrid, Spain: ACL.

Kipper-Schuler, K. (2005). *VerbNet: A broad-coverage, comprehensive verb lexicon*. (Ph.D. Thesis). University of Pennsylvania. Philadelphia, PA.

Lin, K. H.-Y., Yang, C., & Chen, H.-H. (2007). What emotions news articles trigger in their readers? In *Proceedings of SIGIR* (pp. 733-734). ACM.

Liu, B. (2010). *Handbook on NLP in sentiment analysis*. Academic Press.

Liu, H., Lieberman, H., & Selker, T. (2003). A model of textual affect sensing using real-world knowledge. In *Proceeding of the International Conference on Intelligent User Interfaces*. Springer.

Mann, W. C., & Thompson, S. A. (1988). Rhetorical structure theory: Toward a functional theory of text organization. *Text*, *8*, 243–281. doi:10.1515/text.1.1988.8.3.243.

Martin, J. R., & White, P. R. R. (2005). *The language of evaluation: Appraisal in English*. London: Palgrave.

Mihalcea, R., & Liu, H. (2006). *A corpus-based approach to finding happiness*. Paper presented at the AAAI Spring Symposium on Computational Approaches to Weblogs. Stanford, CA.

Miller, A. G. (1995). WordNet: A lexical database for English. *Communications of the ACM*, *38*(11), 39–41. doi:10.1145/219717.219748.

Minato, J., David, B., Ren, F., & Kuroiwa, S. (2008). Japanese emotion corpus analysis and its use for automatic emotion word identification. *Engineering Letters*, *16*(1).

Mishne, G. (2005). Emotions from text: Machine learning for text-based emotion prediction. In *Proceeding of SIGIR'05* (pp. 15-19). ACM.

Mohammad, S., Dorr, B., & Hirst, G. (2008). Computing word-pair antonymy. In *Proceeding of the Empirical Methods in Natural Language Processing and Computational Natural Language Learning*. IEEE.

Mohammad, S., & Turney, P. D. (2010). Emotions evoked by common words and phrases: Using mechanical turk to create an emotion lexicon. In *Proceedings of the NAACL-HLT 2010 Workshop on Computational Approaches to Analysis and Generation of Emotion in Text* (pp. 26-34). NAACL.

Myers, D. G. (2004). Theories of emotion. In *Psychology* (7th ed.). New York, NY: Worth Publishers.

Neviarouskaya, A., Prendinger, H., & Ishizuka, M. (2007). Textual affect sensing for social and expressive online communication. In *Proceeding of the 2nd International Conference on Affective Computing and Intelligent Interaction* (pp. 218-229). IEEE.

Neviarouskaya, A., Prendinger, H., & Ishizuka, M. (2009). SentiFul: Generating a reliable lexicon for sentiment analysis. In *Proceeding of the International Conference on Affective Computing and Intelligent Interaction (ACII'09)*. IEEE.

Pang, B., Lee, L., & Vaithyanathan, S. (2002). Thumbs up? Sentiment classification using machine learning techniques. In *Proceedings of the Empirical Methods on Natural Language Processing (EMNLP 2002)* (pp. 79-86). EMNLP.

Passonneau, R. (2004). Computing reliability for coreference annotation. In *Proceeding of the International Conference on Language Resources and Evaluation*. LREC.

Passonneau, R. J. (2006). Measuring agreement on set-valued items (MASI) for semantic and pragmatic annotation. In *Proceeding of the 5th International Conference on Language Resources and Evaluation*. LREC.

Quan, C., & Ren, F. (2009). Construction of a blog emotion corpus for chinese emotional expression analysis. In *Proceeding of the Empirical Method in Natural Language Processing- Association for Computational Linguistics* (pp. 1446-1454). Singapore: ACL.

Quirk, R., Greenbaum, S., Leech, G., & Svartvik, J. (1985). *A comprehensive grammar of the English language*. New York: Longman.

Read, J. (2005). Using emoticons to reduce dependency in machine learning techniques for sentiment classification. In *Proceedings of the Student Research Workshop, ACL 2005* (pp. 43–48). Ann Arbor, MI: ACL.

Read, J., & Carroll, J. (2010). Annotating expressions of appraisal in English. *Language Resources and Evaluation*. doi: doi:10.1007/s10579-010-9135-7.

Read, J., Hope, D., & Carroll, J. (2007). Annotating expressions of appraisal in English. In *Proceeding of the ACL Linguistic Annotation Workshop*. Prague: ACL.

Stone, P. J. (1966). The general inquirer: A computer approach to content analysis. *The MIT Press*. Retrieved from http://www.wjh.harvard.edu/~inquirer/

Stoyanov, V., & Cardie, C. (2008a). Annotating topics of opinions. In *Proceedings of LREC*. LREC.

Stoyanov, V., & Cardie, C. (2008b). Topic identification for fine-grained opinion analysis. In *Proceedings of Coling* (pp. 817–824). Coling. doi:10.3115/1599081.1599184.

Strapparava, C., & Mihalcea, R. (2007). *SemEval-2007 task 14: Affective text*. Paper presented at the 45th Annual Meeting of Association for Computational linguistics. New York, NY.

Strapparava, C., & Ozbal, G. (2010). The color of emotions in texts. In *Proceedings of the 2nd Workshop on Cognitive Aspects of the Lexicon (COGALEX II), COLING 2010* (pp. 28-32). Beijing, China: COLING.

Strapparava, C., & Valitutti, A. (2004). Wordnet-affect: An affective extension of wordnet. In *Proceedings of the 4th International Conference on Language Resources and Evaluation* (pp. 1083-1086). LREC.

Takamura, H., Inui, T., & Okumura, M. (2005). Extracting semantic orientations of words using spin model. In *Proceedings of the 43rd Annual Meeting of the Association for Computational Linguistics (ACL2005)* (pp. 133-140). ACL.

Tokuhisa, R., Inui, K., & Matsumoto, Y. (2008). Emotion classification using massive examples extracted from the web. *Proceedings of COLING, 2008*, 881–888. doi:10.3115/1599081.1599192.

Turney, P. (2002). Thumbs up or thumbs down? Semantic orientation applied to unsupervised classification of reviews. In *Proceeding of the Association for Computational Linguistics (ACL-2002)* (pp. 417-424). Philadelphia, PA: ACL.

Voll, K., & Taboada, M. (2007). Not all words are created equal: Extracting semantic orientation as a function of adjective relevance. In *Proceedings of the 20th Australian Joint Conference on Artificial Intelligence* (pp. 337-346). Gold Coast, Australia: IEEE.

Whitelaw, C., Garg, N., & Argamon, S. (2005). Using appraisal taxonomies for sentiment analysis. In *Proceeding of the 2nd Midwest Computer, Linguistic Colloquium*. Columbus, OH: IEEE.

Wiebe, J., & Mihalcea, R. (2006). Word sense and subjectivity. In *Proceeding of COLING/ACL-06* (pp. 1065-1072). Sydney, Australia:COLING/ACL.

Wiebe, J., & Riloff, E. (2005). Creating subjective and objective sentence classifiers from unannotated texts. In *Proceedings of the 6th International Conference on Intelligent Text Processing and Computational Linguistics (CICLing-2005)* (pp. 475-486). CICLing.

Wiebe, J., Wilson, T., & Cardie, C. (2005). Annotating expressions of opinions and emotions in language. *Language Resources and Evaluation*, *39*, 164–210. doi:10.1007/s10579-005-7880-9.

Zhang, Y., Li, Z., Ren, F., & Kuroiwa, S. (2008). A preliminary research of Chinese emotion classification model. *International Journal of ComputerScience and Network Security*, *8*(11), 127–132.

KEY TERMS AND DEFINITIONS

Bengali Emotion Blog Corpus: A Bengali blog corpus for emotion analysis developed by manual annotators with detailed linguistic expressions such as emotional expressions and intensities, emotion holder, emotion topic and target span and sentential emotion tags.

Bengali *WordNetAffect*: An emotion lexicon in Bengali that consists of six files with respect to Ekman's (1993) six emotion classes (*anger, disgust, fear, happy, sad* and *surprise*). Each of the six files contains synsets of emotional words.

Emotion: *Definition1:* Emotion is a complex psycho-physiological experience of an individual's state of mind as interacting with biochemical (internal) and environmental (external) influences. In humans, emotion fundamentally involves physiological arousal, expressive behaviors and conscious experience (Myers, 2004). *Definition2:* In psychology and common use, emotion is an aspect of a person's mental state of being, normally based in or tied to the person's internal (physical) and external (social) sensory feeling (Zhang *et al.* 2008).

Emotional Expression: Emotions are expressed in natural languages using different language expressions which are termed as emotional expressions in literature. It is said that sentiment or emotion is typically a localized phenomenon that is more appropriately computed at the paragraph, sentence or entity level (Liu, 2010).

Emotion Holder: In linguistics, a grammatical agent or holder is the participant of a situation that carries out the action whereas in computational linguistics, the source of an emotional expression is the speaker or writer or experiencer or the person or organization that expresses the emotions towards a specific topic or event (Liu, 2010).

Emotion Target Span: The text span that covers the syntactic surface form comprising the contents of the emotion (Stoyanov and Cardie, 2008a).

Emotion Topic Span: The real world object, event or an abstract entity that is the primary subject of the emotion as intended by its holder. Emotion topic also depends on the context in which its associated emotional expression occurs (Stoyanov and Cardie, 2008a).

Compilation of References

Abdullah, A. B. M., & Rahman, A. (2003). A survey on script segmentation for Bangla OCR: An implementation perspective. In *Proceedings of 6th International Conference on Computer and Information Technology (ICCIT)*, (pp. 856-860). ICCIT.

Abramson, A. S., Nye, P. W., Henderson, J., & Marshall, C. W. (1981). Vowel height and the perception of consonantal nasality. *The Journal of the Acoustical Society of America*, *70*(2), 329–339. doi:10.1121/1.386781 PMID:7288023.

Abualkishik, A. M., & Omar, K. (2009). Quran vibrations in Braille code. In *Proceedings of the International Conference on Electrical Engineering and Informatics*, (pp. 12-17). Selangor, Malaysia: IEEE.

Adobe. (2008). *OpenType user guide for Adobe fonts*. Retrieved July 16, 2012, from http://www.adobe.com/type/browser/pdfs/OTGuide.pdf

Agbinya, I. (1996). Discrete wavelet transform techniques in speech processing. In *Proceedings of the IEEE Tencon Digital Signal Processing Applications*. IEEE.

Aho, A. V., Sethi, R., & Ullman, J. D. (2002). *Compilers principles, techniques and tools*. New York: Pearson Education.

Akter, N., Hossain, S., Islam, M. T., & Sarwar, H. (2008). An algorithm for segmenting modifiers from Bangla text. In *Proceedings of 11th International Conference on Computer and Information Technology (ICCIT)*, (pp. 177 - 182). Khulna, Bangladesh: ICCIT.

Alam, F., Habib, S. M., & Khan, M. (2008). Acoustic analysis of Bangla consonants. In *Proceedings of Spoken Language Technologies for Under Resourced Language (SLTU'08)*, (Vol 1, pp. 108-113). SLTU.

Alam, F., Nath, P. K., & Khan, M. (2007). Text to speech for Bangla language using festival. In *Proceeding of First International Conference on Digital Communication and Computer Applications (DCCA 2007)*. Irbid, Jordan: DCCA.

Alam, M. M., & Anwer, M. (2005). Feature subset selection using genetic algorithm for Bengali handwritten digit recognition. In *Proceedings of the National Conference on Computer Processing of Bangla*, (pp. 258-263). Independent University.

Alam, S. E. (1995). *Bengali voice synthesis*. (MSs Thesis). University of Dhaka. Bangladesh.

Alam, F., Habib, S. M., & Khan, M. (2008). *Acoustic analysis of Bangla vowel inventory*. Dhaka, Bangladesh: BRAC University.

Alam, M. M., & Kashem, M. A. (2010). A complete Bangla OCR system for printed characters. *International Journal of Computer and Information Technology*, *1*(1), 30–35.

Alam, M. S., Awwal, A. A. S., & Karim, M. A. (1991). Improved correlation discrimination using joint Fourier-transform optical correlator. *Microwave and Optical Technology Letters*, *4*, 103–106. doi:10.1002/mop.4650040305.

Alam, M. S., & Karim, M. A. (1993). Fringe-adjusted joint transform correlation. *Applied Optics*, *32*, 4344–4350. doi:10.1364/AO.32.004344 PMID:20830091.

Ali, A. M. A. (1999). *Auditory-based acoustic-phonetic signal processing for robust continuous speaker independent speech recognition*. (Ph.D. Thesis). University of Pennsylvania. Philadelphia, PA.

Ali, M. G. (1990). *Digital processing of short duration signals and design of digital filters*. (M.Sc. Thesis). Rajshahi University. Rajshahi, Bangladesh.

Ali, M. G., Aziz, M. A., & Sobhan, M. A. (1993). Short-duration voice signal analysis of selected Bangla vowels. *The Rajshahi University Studies, 21*.

Ali, M. N. Y., Das, J. K., Mamun, S. M. A. A., & Choudhury, M. E. H. (2008). Specific features of a converter of web documents from Bengali to universal networking language. In *Proceedings of the International Conference on Computer and Communication Engineering 2008 (ICCCE'08)*, (pp. 726-731). Kuala Lumpur, Malaysia. ICCCE. DOI:10.1109/ICCCE.2008.4580700

Ali, M. N. Y., Das, J. K., Mamun, S. M. A. A., & Nurannabi, A. M. (2008). Morphological analysis of Bangla words for universal networking language. In *Proceedings of the Third International Conference on Digital Information Management (ICDIM 2008)*, (pp. 532-537). London, UK: ICDIM. DOI:10.1109/ICDIM.2008.4746734

Ali, L., Gallagher, T., Goldstein, J., & Daniloff, R. (1971). Perception of coarticulated nasality. *The Journal of the Acoustical Society of America, 49*(2), 538–540. doi:10.1121/1.1912384 PMID:5100276.

Ali, M. N. Y., Ripon, S., & Allayear, S. M. (2012). UNL based Bangla natural text conversion: Predicate preserving parser approach. *International Journal of Computer Science Issues, 9*(3), 259–265.

Alm, C. O., Roth, D., & Sproat, R. (2005). Emotions from text: Machine learning for text-based emotion prediction. In Human Language Technology - Empirical Method in Natural Language Processing (pp. 579-586). Academic Press.

Aman, S., & Szpakowicz, S. (2007). Identifying expressions of emotion in text. In Matoušek, V., & Mautner, P. (Eds.), *TSD 2007 (LNAI) (Vol. 4629*, pp. 196–205). Berlin: Springer.

Amelot, A. (2004). *Etude aérodynamique, fibroscopique, acoustique et perceptive des voyelles nasales du français*. (Ph.D. Dissertation). Université Paris III. Paris.

Andreevskaia, A., & Bergler, S. (2007). Clac and clac-NB: Knowledge-based and corpus-based approaches to sentiment tagging. In *Proceeding of the 4th SemEval-2007*. ACL.

Anwar, M. M., Anwar, M. Z., & Bhuiyan, M. A. A. (2009). Syntax analysis and machine translation of Bangla sentences. *International Journal of Computer Science and Network Security, 9*(8), 317–326.

Anwar, M. M., Shume, N. S., & Bhuiyan, M. A. A. (2010). Structural analysis of Bangla sentences of different tenses for automatic Bangla machine translator. *International Journal of Computer Science and Information Security, 8*(9).

Arai, T. (2004). Formant shifts in nasalization of vowels. *The Journal of the Acoustical Society of America, 115*(5), 2541.

Arai, T. (2005). Comparing tongue positions of vowels in oral and nasal contexts. In *Proceedings of Interspeech*. Lisbon, Portugal: Interspeech.

Asaduzzaman, M. M., & Ali, M. M. (2003). Morphological analysis of Bangla words for automatic machine translation. In *Proceedings of the International Conference on Computer and Information Technology (ICCIT)*, (pp.271-276). ICCIT.

Asaduzzaman, M. (2008). Bangla shdhito prottoy: Punorbuchar. *The Dhaka University Journal of Linguistic, 1*(1), 79–92.

Aue, A., & Gamon, M. (2005). Customizing sentiment classifiers to new domains: A case study. In *Proceeding of the International Conference on Recent Advances in Natural Language Processing (RANLP-05)*. Borovets, Bulgaria: RANLP.

Awwal, A. A. S., Karim, M. A., & Jahan, S. R. (1990). Improved correlation discrimination using an amplitude-modulated phase-only filter. *Applied Optics, 29*, 233–236. doi:10.1364/AO.29.000233 PMID:20556091.

Azad, H. (1994). Bakkotottoy (2nd ed). Dhaka.

Azar, M. (1999). Argumentative text as rhetorical structure: An application of rhetorical structure theory. *Argumentation, 13*, 97–114. doi:10.1023/A:1007794409860.

Bal, K., & Saint-Dizier, P. (2010). Towards building annotated resources for analyzing opinions and argumentation in news editorials. In *Proceedings of LREC 2010*. Valetta, Malta: LREC.

Bandopadhay, A., Mandal, S. D., & Pal, B. (2003). *Effects of pitch contours stylization and time scale modification on natural speech synthesis*. Paper presented at the Workshop on Spoken Language Processing, TIFR. Mumbai.

Bandyopadhyay, A. (2002). *Some important aspects of bengali speech synthesis system*. Paper presented at IEMCT. Pune.

Bandyopadhyay, S., Mondal, T., Naskar, S. K., Ekbal, A., Haque, R., & Godhavarthy, S. R. (2007). Bengali, Hindi and Telugu to English ad-hoc bilingual task at CLEF 2007. In C. Peters, V. Jijkoun, T. Mandl, H. Müller, D. W. Oard, A. Peñas, V. Petras, et al. (Eds.), *Advances in Multilingual and Multimodal Information Retrieval, 8th Workshop of the Cross-Language Evaluation Forum, CLEF 2007, Budapest, Hungary, September 19-21, 2007, Revised Selected Papers* (Vol. 5152, pp. 88–94). Springer.

Banea, C., Mihalcea, R., & Wiebe, J. (2008). A bootstrapping method for building subjectivity lexicons for languages with scarce resources. In *Proceedings of Sixth International Conference on Language Resources and Evaluation (LREC 2008)*. LREC.

Banerjee, R., & Pal, S. (2011). ISM@FIRE-2011: Monoliongual task. In *Proceedings of FIRE 2011, Third workshop of the Forum for Information Retrieval Evaluation*. FIRE.

Banerjee, S., Das, D., & Bandyopadhyay, S. (2009). Bengali verb subcategorization frame acquisition – A baseline model. In *Proceedings of Asian Language Resources Workshop*. ACL.

Baojun, Q., Kang, Z., Prasenjit, M., Dinghao, W., Cornelia, C., & John, Y. ... Kenneth, P. (2011). Get online support, feel better – Sentiment analysis and dynamics in an online cancer survivor community. In *Proceedings of PASSAT* (pp. 274 – 281). PASSAT.

Barman, S., Samanta, A. K., Kim, T., & Bhattacharya, D. (2010). Design of a view based approach for Bengali character recognition. *International Journal of Advanced Science and Technology*, *15*(2), 49–62.

Baroni, M., & Vegnaduzzo, S. (2004). *Identifying subjective adjectives through web-based mutual information*. Paper presented at the German Conference on NLP. Berlin.

Basu, S., Das, N., Sarker, R., Kundu, M., Nasipuri, M., & Kumar, B. D. (2005). Handwritten Bangla alphabet recognition using an MLP based classifier. In *Proceedings of the 2nd National Conference on Computer Processing of Bangla (NCCPB)*, (pp. 285-291). Independent University.

Basu, T., & Warsi, A. H. (2012). *Analysis and synthesis of F0 contours for Bangla readout speech*. Paper presented at the Workshop on Tone and Intonation: Theory, Typology and Computation, WTI, IIT. Guwahati, India.

Basu, J. B., Mitra, T., Mandal, M., & Das, S. K. (2009). Grapheme to phoneme (g2p) conversion for Bangla. In *Proceedings of Oriental COCOSDA*. COCOSDA. doi:10.1109/ICSDA.2009.5278373.

Bazzi, I., & Glass, J. R. (2000). Modeling OOV words for ASR. In *Proceedings of the International Conference on Spoken Language Processing (ICSLP)*. Beijing, China: ICSLP.

Beddor, P. S. (1993). The perception of nasal vowels. In Phonetics and Phonology: Nasals, Nasalization and the Velum (pp. 171–196). Academic Press.

Beddor, P. S., & Hawkins, S. (1990). The influence of spectral prominence on perceived vowel quality. *The Journal of the Acoustical Society of America*, *87*(6), 2684–2704. doi:10.1121/1.399060 PMID:2373803.

Beddor, P. S., & Strange, W. (1982). Cross language study of perception of the oral- nasal distinction. *The Journal of the Acoustical Society of America*, *71*(6), 1551–1561. doi:10.1121/1.387809 PMID:7108030.

Begum, R., Husain, S., Sharma, D. M., & Bai, L. (2008). Developing verb frames for Hindi. In *Proceedings of LREC-2008*. LREC.

Begum, R., Husain, S., Sharma, D. M., Bai, L., & Sangal, R. (2008). Dependency annotation scheme for Indian languages. In *Proceedings of IJCNLP-2008*. IJCNLP.

Bell-Berti, F. (1976). An electromyographic study of velopharyngeal function in speech. *Journal of Speech and Hearing Research*, *19*, 225–240. PMID:979198.

Belousov, S., & Coopery, M. Yonina, Dias, B., Dias, M., Horwitz, F., ... Teves, E. A. (2011). *Study report on disabilities: iSTEP Bangladesh* (Tech. Report CMU-RI-TR-35). Pittsburgh, PA: Carnegie Melon University.

Benguerel, A. P. (1974). Nasal airflow patterns and velar coarticulation in French. *Speech Communication Seminar Proceedings, 2*, 105-112.

Benguerel, A.P., & Hirose, H., S, M., & Ushijima, T. (1977). Velar coarticulation in French: A fiberscopic study. *Journal of Phonetics, 5*(2), 149–158.

Bennett, C., & Black, A. (2006). *The blizzard challenge 2006*. Paper presented at the Blizzard Challenge Workshop. Pittsburgh, PA.

Berger, M. A. (2007). *Measurement of vowel nasalization by multidimensional acoustic analysis*. (M.Sc. Thesis). University of Rochester. Rochester, NY.

Bethard, S., Yu, H., Thornton, A., Hatzivassiloglou, V., & Jurafsky, D. (2004). *Automatic Extraction of opinion propositions and their holders*. Paper presented at AAAI Spring Symposium on Exploring Attitude and Affect in Text: Theories and Applications. New York.

Bethard, S., Yu, H., Thornton, A., Hatzivassiloglou, V., & Jurafsky, D. (2006). Extracting opinion propositions and opinion holders using syntactic and lexical cues. In The Computing Attitude and Affect in Text: Theory and Applications, (pp. 125-141). Academic Press.

Bharati, A., & Sangal, R. (1993). Parsing free word order languages in the paninian framework. In *Proceedings of ACL-1993*. ACL.

Bharati, A., Husain, S., Ambati, B., Jain, S., Sharma, D. M., & Sangal, R. (2008). Two semantic features make all the difference in parsing accuracy. In *Proceedings of the 6th International Conference on Natural Language Processing (ICON-08)*. CDAC.

Bharati, A., Husain, S., Sharma, D. M., & Sangal, R. (2008). A two-stage constraint based dependency parser for free word order languages. In *Proceedings of the International Conference on Asian Language Processing (IALP)*. Chiang Mai, Thailand: IALP.

Bharati, A., Husain, S., Sharma, D. M., & Sangal, R. (2009). Two stage constraint based hybrid approach to free-word order language dependency parsing. In *Proceedings of the 11th International Conference on Parsing Technologies (IWPT09)*. Paris, France: IWPT.

Bharati, A., Husain, S., Vijay, M., Deepak, K., Sharma, D. M., & Sangal, R. (2009). Constraint based hybrid approach to parsing indian languages. In *Proceedings of the 23rd Pacific Asia Conference on Language, Information and Computation (PACLIC 23)*. Hong Kong: PACLIC.

Bharati, A., Chaitanya, V., & Sangal, R. (1995). *Natural language processing: A paninian perspective*. New Delhi: Prentice-Hall of India.

Bharati, A., Sharma, D. M., Husain, S., Bai, L., Begum, R., & Sangal, R. (2009). *AnnCorra: TreeBanks for Indian languages, guideline for annotating Hindi TreeBank v2.0*. Hydearabad, India: IIIT.

Bhaskar, P., Das, A., Pakray, P., & Bandyopadhyay, S. (2010). Theme-based English and Bengali ad-hoc monolingual information retrieval in FIRE 2010. In *Proceedings of Working Notes of the Forum for Information Retrieval Evaluation, 2010*. FIRE.

Bhattacharya, S., Choudhury, M., Sarkar, S., & Basu, A. (2005). Inflectional morphology synthesis for Bengali noun, pronoun and verb systems. In *Proceedings of the National Conference on Computer Processing of Bangla (NCCPB)*, (pp. 34–43). NCCPB.

Bhattacharya, U., Das, T. K., Datta, A., Parui, S. K., & Chaudhuri, B. B. (2002). Recognition of handprinted Bangla numerals using neural network models. In N.R. Pal & M. Sugeno (Eds.), *Proceedings of the 2002 AFSS International Conference on Fuzzy Systems*, (vol. 2275, pp. 228-235). Calcutta: Springer.

Bhattacharya, U., Shridhar, M., & Parui, S. K. (2006). On recognition of handwritten Bangla characters. In *Proceedings of Indian Conference on Computer Vision, Graphics and Image Processing*, (pp. 817–828). IEEE.

Bhattacharya, K. (1993). *Bengali-oriya verb morphology: A contrastive study*. Kolkata, India: Das Gupta & Co. Private Limited.

Bhattacharya, U., Das, T. K., Datta, A., Parui, S. K., & Chaudhuri, B. B. (2002). A hybrid scheme for handprinted numeral recognition based on a self-organizing network and MLP classifiers. *International Journal of Pattern Recognition and Artificial Intelligence, 16*(7), 845–864. doi:10.1142/S0218001402002027.

Bhattachrya, S., Sarker, S., & Basu, A. (2007). Sanyog: A speech enabled communication system for the speech impaired and people with multiple disorders. *Journal of Technology in Human Services*, *25*(1/2).

Bhowmik, T. K., Bhattacharya, U., & Parui, S. K. (2004). Recognition of Bangla handwritten characters using an MLP classifier based on stroke features. In *Proceedings of the International Conference on Neural Information Processing*, (pp. 814-819). Kolkata, India: Springer.

Bhowmik, T. K., Roy, A., & Roy, U. (2005). Character segmentation for handwritten Bangla words using artificial neural network. In *Proceedings of International Workshop on Neural Networks and Learning in Document Analysis and Recognition*, (pp. 28-32). IEEE.

Bitar, N. N. (1997). *Acoustic analysis and modeling of speech based on phonetic features*. (Ph.D. Thesis). Boston University. Boston, MA.

Björk, L. (1961). Velopharyngeal function in connected speech. *Acta Radiologica*, *202*, 1–94.

Blum, A., & Mitchell, T. (1998). Combining labeled and unlabeled data with co-training. In *Proceedings of the Workshop on Computational Learning Theory*. COLT.

Blumstein, S., & Stevens, K. (1979). Acoustic invariance in speech production. *The Journal of the Acoustical Society of America*, *66*, 1001–1017. doi:10.1121/1.383319 PMID:512211.

Bobicev, V., Maxim, V., Prodan, T., Burciu, N., & Anghelus, V. (2010). Emotions in words: Developing a multilingual WordNet-affect. In *Proceeding of CICLing 2010*. CICLing.

Boender, C. G. E., & Rinnooy Kan, A. H. G. (1987). A multinomial Bayesian approach to the estimation of population and vocabulary size. *Biometrika*, *74*(4), 849–856. doi:10.1093/biomet/74.4.849.

Bogaards, P., & Laufer-Dvorkin, B. (2004). *Vocabulary in a second language: Selection, acquisition, and testing*. Amsterdam, Netherlands: John Benjamins Publishing Company.

Bognar, E., & Fujisaki, H. (1986). Analysis, synthesis and perception of French nasal vowels. In *Proceedings of ICASSP*, (pp. 1601–1604). ICASSP.

Boldi, P., & Vigna, S. (2005). MG4J at TREC 2005. In E. M. Voorhees & L. P. Buckland (Eds.), *The Fourteenth Text REtrieval Conference (TREC 2005) Proceedings*. NIST.

Bondopoddaye, H. (2001). *Bongioi shobdokosh*. Calcutta, India: Shahitto Okademy.

Bond, Z. S. (1975). Identification of vowels excerpted from neutral and nasal contexts. *The Journal of the Acoustical Society of America*, *59*(5), 1229–1232. doi:10.1121/1.380988 PMID:956518.

Booch, G. (1993). *Object oriented analysisa and design with applications* (3rd ed.). Boston: Addison-Wesley.

Braschler, M., & Ripplinger, B. (2004). How effective is stemming and decompounding for german text retrieval? *Information Retrieval*, *7*(3/4), 291–316. doi:10.1023/B:INRT.0000011208.60754.a1.

Buckley, C., Salton, G., Allan, J., & Singhal, A. (1994). Automatic query expansion using SMART: TREC 3. In *Proceedings of TREC* (pp. 69–80). NIST.

Bulyko, I., Matsoukas, S., Schwartz, R., Nguyen, L., & Makhoul, J. (2007). Language model adaptation in machine translation from speech. In *Proceedings of the 32nd IEEE International Conference on Acoustics, Speech, and Signal Processing (ICASSP)*. IEEE.

Burwen, M. (2012). *Social media: The end of conventional market research?* Technology Futures.

Bykova, E. M. (1981). *The Bengali language, translation of Bengalskii jazyk, languages of Asia and Africa*. Nauka Publisher.

Cairns, D. A., Hansen, J. H. L., & Kaiser, J. F. (1996). Recent advances in hypernasal speech detection using the nonlinear Teager energy operator. In *Proceedings of ICSLP*, (pp. 780–783). ICSLP.

Cairns, D. A., Hansen, J. H. L., & Riski, J. E. (1994). Detection of hypernasal speech using a nonlinear operator. In *Proceedings of IEEE Conference on Engineering in Medicine and Biology Society*, (pp. 253–254). IEEE.

Cairns, D. A., Hansen, J. H. L., & Riski, J. E. (1996). A noninvasive technique for detecting hypernasal speech using a nonlinear operator. *IEEE Transactions on Bio-Medical Engineering*, *43*(1), 35–45. doi:10.1109/10.477699 PMID:8567004.

Callison-Burch, C. (2002). *Co-training for statistical machine translation.* (Master's Thesis). University of Edinburgh. Edinburgh, UK.

Callison-Burch, C. (2003). *Active learning for statistical machine translation.* (PhD Dissertation). Edinburgh University. Edinburgh, UK.

Callison-Burch, C., Talbot, D., & Osborne, M. (2004). Statistical machine translation with word and sentence-aligned parallel corpora. In *Proceedings of the 42nd Annual Meeting on Association for Computational Linguistics*. Barcelona, Spain: ACL.

Cambria, E., Hussain, A., & Eckl, C. (2011). Taking refuge in your personal sentic corner. In *Proceedings of the Workshop on Sentiment Analysis: Where AI meets Psychology*. IJCNLP.

Carenini, G., Ng, R., & Pauls, A. (2006). Multi-document summarization of evaluative text. In *Proceedings of the European Chapter of the Association for Computational Linguistics*. EACL.

Charles, B., Choi, Y., Steven, S., & Eduardo, X. (2011). Empath: A framework for evaluating entity-level sentiment analysis. In *Proceedings of CEWIT* (pp. 1 – 6). CEWIT.

Chaudhuri, B. B., & Pal, U. (1997). Skew angle detection of digitized Indian script documents. *IEEE Transactions on Pattern Analysis and Machine Intelligence*, *19*(2), 182–186. doi:10.1109/34.574803.

Chaudhuri, B. B., & Pal, U. (1998). A complete printed Bangla OCR system. *Pattern Recognition*, *31*(5), 531–549. doi:10.1016/S0031-3203(97)00078-2.

Chaudhury, F. (1984). *Collected works of Mufazzal Haider Chaudhury (Vol. 3)*. Bangla Academy.

Chen, A., & Gey, F. C. (2002). Building an Arabic stemmer for information retrieval. In *Proceedings of the Eleventh Text REtrieval Conference (TREC 2002)*. NIST.

Chen, M. Y. (1996). *Acoustic correlates of nasality in speech*. (Ph.D. Thesis). MIT. Cambridge, MA.

Chen, A., & Gey, F. C. (2004). Multilingual information retrieval using machine translation, relevance feedback and decompounding. *Information Retrieval*, *7*(1-2), 149–182. doi:10.1023/B:INRT.0000009444.89549.90.

Chen, M. Y. (1995). Acoustic parameters of nasalized vowels in hearing-impaired and normal-hearing speakers. *The Journal of the Acoustical Society of America*, *98*(5), 2443–2453. doi:10.1121/1.414399 PMID:7593928.

Chen, M. Y. (1997). Acoustic correlates of English and French nasalized vowels. *The Journal of the Acoustical Society of America*, *102*(4), 2360–2370. doi:10.1121/1.419620 PMID:9348695.

Chen, M. Y. (2000). Acoustic analysis of simple vowels preceding a nasal in standard Chinese. *Journal of Phonetics*, *28*(1), 43–67. doi:10.1006/jpho.2000.0106.

Chen, M. Y. (2000). Nasal detection module for a knowledge-based speech recognition system. *Proceedings of ICSLP*, *4*, 636–639. Beijing, China: ICSLP..

Cherri, A. K., & Alam, M. S. (2001). Reference phase-encoded fringe-adjusted joint transform correlation. *Applied Optics*, *40*, 1216–1225. doi:10.1364/AO.40.001216 PMID:18357108.

Choi, Y., Cardie, C., Riloff, E., & Patwardhan, S. (2005). Identifying sources of opinions with conditional random fields and extraction patterns. In *Proceedings of the HLT/EMNLP 2005*. HLT/EMNLP.

Choudhury, M. E. H., Ali, M. N. Y., Sarkar, M. Z. H., & Ahsan, R. (2005). Bridging Bangla to universal networking language- A human language neutral meta- language. In *Proceedings of the International Conference on Computer and Information Technology (ICCIT)*, (pp.104-109). ICCIT.

Choudhury, S. Datta, A. K., & Chaudhuri, B. B. (2001). *Concatenative synthesis for a group of languages*. Paper presented at the 17th International Congress on Acoustics. Rome, Italy.

Choudhury, M. E. H., & Ali, M. N. Y. (2008). Framework for synthesis of universal networking language. *East West University Journal*, *1*(2), 28–43.

Chowdhury, N., & Saha, D. (2005). A neural network based text classification method: A possible application for bengali text classification. In *Proceedings of the National Conference on Computer Processing of Bangla*, (pp. 183-188). Independent University.

Chowdhury, N., & Saha, D. (2005). Bengali text classification using Kohonen's self organizing network. In *Proceedings of the National Conference on Computer Processing of Bangla* (pp. 196-200). Independent University.

Chowdhury, S., Datta, A. K., & Chaudhuri, B. B. (2001). Study of intonation patterns for text reading in standard colloquial Bengali. In *Proceedings of the Sixth International Workshop on Recent Trends in Speech, Music and Allied Signal Processing (IWSMSP)*. New Delhi, India: IWSMSP.

Chowdhury, S., Moushumi, G., & Anupam, B. (2005). Partneme as the speech inventory for Bangla text to speech synthesis. In *Proceedings of International Conferences on Computer Processing of Bangla*. Dhaka, Bangladesh: IEEE.

Cleverdon, C. W. (1991). The significance of the Cranfield tests on index languages. In *Proceedings of the 14th Annual International ACM SIGIR Conference on Research and Development in Information Retrieval - SIGIR '91* (pp. 3–12). New York: ACM Press.

Cohen, J. (1960). A coefficient of agreement for nominal scales. *Educational and Psychological Measurement, 20*, 37–46. doi:10.1177/001316446002000104.

Consoli, D. (2009). Textual emotions recognitions with an intelligent software of sentiment analysis. In *Proceedings of the Third International Conference EITM, section Mathematics and Computer Science* (pp. 997-1009). Retrieved November 10, 2012 from http://www.upm.ro/facultati_departamente/stiinte_litere/conferinte/situl_integrare_europeana/Lucrari3/MI/100_consoli_paper.pdf

Cormen, T. H., Leiserson, C. E., Rivest, R. L., & Stein, C. (2009). *PHI learning private limited*. New Delhi: Academic Press.

Daily Prothom Alo. (n.d.). Retrieved from www.prothom-alo.com

Dang, J., & Honda, K. (1996). Acoustic characteristics of the human paranasal sinuses derived from transmission characteristic measurement and morphological observation. *The Journal of the Acoustical Society of America, 100*(5), 3374–3383. doi:10.1121/1.416978 PMID:8914318.

Dang, J., Honda, K., & Suzuki, H. (1994). Morphological and acoustical analysis of the nasal and the paranasal cavities. *The Journal of the Acoustical Society of America, 96*(4), 2088–2100. doi:10.1121/1.410150 PMID:7963023.

Das, A. (2010n). Can we mimic human pragmatics knowledge into computational lexicon? In *Proceedings of the International Conference on Natural Language Processing (ICON 2010)*. ICON.

Das, A., & Bandyopadhyay, S. (2009). Subjectivity detection in English and Bengali: A CRF-based approach. In *Proceeding of ICON*. Macmillan Publishers.

Das, A., & Bandyopadhyay, S. (2009). Subjectivity detection in English and Bengali: A CRF-based approach. In *Proceeding of the International Conference on Natural Language Processing (ICON 2009)*. ICON.

Das, A., & Bandyopadhyay, S. (2009). Theme detection an exploration of opinion subjectivity. In *Proceeding of the Affective Computing & Intelligent Interaction (ACII2009)*. Amsterdam, The Netherlands: ACII.

Das, A., & Bandyopadhyay, S. (2009). Extracting opinion statements from bengali text documents through theme detection. In *Proceeding of the 17th International Conference on Computing (CIC-09)*. GEOS.

Das, A., & Bandyopadhyay, S. (2010). Dr sentiment creates SentiWordNet(s) for Indian languages involving internet population. In *Proceeding of IndoWordNet Workshop*. ICON.

Das, A., & Bandyopadhyay, S. (2010). Towards the global SentiWordNet. In *Proceeding of the Workshop on Model and Measurement of Meaning (M3)*. PACLIC.

Das, A., & Bandyopadhyay, S. (2010). SentiWordNet for Indian languages. In *Proceeding of the 8th Workshop on Asian Language Resources (ALR 8)*. COLING.

Das, A., & Bandyopadhyay, S. (2010). SentiWordNet for Bangla. In *Proceedings of the Knowledge Sharing Event-4: Task 2: Building Electronic Dictionary (KSE4)*. Mysore, India: KSE.

Das, A., & Bandyopadhyay, S. (2010). Subjectivity detection using genetic algorithm. In *Proceeding of the 1st Workshop on Computational Approaches to Subjectivity and Sentiment Analysis (WASSA10)*. ECAI.

Das, A., & Bandyopadhyay, S. (2010). Opinion-polarity identification in Bengali. In *Proceeding of the 23rd International Conference on the Computer Processing of Oriental Languages (ICCPOL 2010)*. KESE.

Das, A., & Bandyopadhyay, S. (2010). Opinion summarization in Bengali: A theme network model. In *Proceeding of the 2nd IEEE International Conference on Social Computing (SocialCom-2010)*. SocialCom.

Das, A., & Bandyopadhyay, S. (2010). Topic-based Bengali opinion summarization. In *Proceeding of the 23rd International Conference on Computational Linguistics (COLING 2010)*. COLING.

Das, A., & Bandyopadhyay, S. (2010). SemanticNet-Perception of human pragmatics. In *Proceeding of the 2nd Workshop on Cognitive Aspects of the Lexicon: Enhancing the Structure and Lookup Mechanisms of Electronic Dictionaries (COGALEX-II)*. COLING.

Das, A., & Bandyopadhyay, S. (2011). Dr sentiment knows everything! In *Proceeding of the 49th Annual Meeting of the Association for Computational Linguistics: Human Language Technologies (ACL/HLT 2011 Demo Session)*, (pp. 50-55). Portland, OR: ACL.

Das, A., & Gambäck, B. (2012). Sentimantics: The conceptual spaces for lexical sentiment polarity representation with contextuality. In *Proceedings of the 3rd Workshop on Computational Approaches to Subjectivity and Sentiment Analysis (WASSA)*. ACL.

Das, A., Gambäck, B., & Bandyopadhyay, S. (2012). The 5W structure for sentiment summarization-visualization-tracking. In *Proceeding of the 13th International Conference on Intelligent Text Processing and Computational Linguistics (CICLING 2012)*. Delhi, India: CICLING.

Das, A., Ghosh, A., & Bandyopadhyay, S. (2010). Semantic role labeling for bengali noun using 5Ws: Who, what, when, where and why. In *Proceeding of the International Conference on Natural Language Processing and Knowledge Engineering (IEEE NLPKE2010)*. IEEE.

Das, D., & Bandyopadhyay, S. (2010). Developing Bengali wordnet affect for analyzing emotion. In *Proceedings of 23rd International Conference on the Computer Processing of Oriental Languages (ICCPOL 2010)*, (pp. 35–40). ICCPOL.

Das, D., Poria, S., & Bandyopadhyay, S. (2012). A classifier based approach to emotion lexicon construction. In *Proceedings of 17th International conference on Applications of Natural Language Processing to Information Systems*. Springer.

Das, D., Poria, S., Dasari, C. M., & Bandyopadhyay, S. (2012). Building resources for multilingual affect analysis – A case study on Hindi, Bengali and Telugu. In *Proceeding of 4th International Workshop on Corpora for Research on Emotion Sentiment & Social Signals*. LREC.

Das, I. (2011). PsychoSentiWordNet. In *Proceeding of the 49th Annual Meeting of the Association for Computational Linguistics: Human Language Technologies (ACL/HLT 2011 Student Session)*. ACL.

Das, S., & Mitra, P. (2011, January). A rule-based approach of stemming for inflectional and derivational words in Bengali. In *Proceedings of IEEE Students' Technology Symposium* (pp. 134-136). Kharagpur: IEEE.

Das, A., & Bandyopadhyay, S. (2010). Phrase-level polarity identification for bengali. *International Journal of Computational Linguistics and Applications*, *1*(2), 169–181.

Das, B., Mandal, S., Mitra, P., & Basu, A. (2012). Effect of aging on speech features and phoneme recognition: A study on Bengali voicing vowels. In *International Journal of Speech Technology*. Springer. doi:10.1007/s10772-012-9147-3.

Das, D. (2011). Analysis and tracking of emotions in English and Bengali Texts: A computational approach. ACM.*Proceedings of WWW*, *2011*, 343–347.

Das, D., Roy, S., & Bandyopadhyay, S. (2012). Emotion tracking on blogs - A case study for Bengali. In Jiang, H. et al. (Eds.), *IEA/AIE 2012, (LNAI)* (*Vol. 7345*, pp. 447–456). Springer. doi:10.1007/978-3-642-31087-4_47.

Dasgupta, S., & Ng, V. (2007). High-performance, language-independent morphological segmentation. In C. L. Sidner, T. Schultz, M. Stone, & C. Zhai (Eds.), *Proceedings of the Human Language Technology Conference of the North American Chapter of the Association of Computational Linguistics, (NAACL HLT 2007), April 22--27, 2007* (pp. 155–163). Rochester, NY: ACL.

Dasgupta, S., & Ng, V. (2009). Topic-wise, sentiment-wise, or otherwise? Identifying the hidden dimension for unsupervised text classification. In *Proceedings of the 2009 Conference on Empirical Methods in Natural Language Processing (EMNLP)* (pp. 580—589). EMNLP.

Dasgupta, S., & Nga, V. (2009). Mine the easy, classify the hard: A semi-supervised approach to automatic sentiment classification. In *Proceedings of the Joint Conference of the 47th Annual Meeting of the Association for Computational Linguistics and the 4th International Joint Conference on Natural Language Processing of the Asian Federation of Natural Language Processing (ACL-IJCNLP)* (pp. 701—709). ACL.

Dasgupta, T., & Basu, A. (2009). Automatic transliteration of indian language text to Braille for the visually challenged in India. *Information Technology in Developing Countries, 19*.

Dasgupta, S., & Ng, V. (2006). Unsupervised morphological parsing of {B}engali. *Language Resources and Evaluation, 40*, 311–330. doi:10.1007/s10579-007-9031-y.

Dash, N.S., & Chaudhuri. (1988). Utterance rules for Bangla words and their computer implementation. In *Proceedings of the International Conference of Computational Linguistics, Speech and Document Processing (ICCLSDP'98)*, (pp. 51-58). ICCLSDP.

DasMandal, S. K., & Pal, B. (2002). *Bengali text-to-speech synthesis system, a novel approach for crossing literacy barrier*. Regional Winner paper in CSI-YITPA(E).

DasMandal, S. K., Saha, A., & Basu, T. (2010). Modeling of sentence medial pauses in bangla readout speech: Occurrence and duration. *Proceedings of Interspeech, 2010*, 1764–1767.

Das, N., Das, B., Sarkar, R., Basu, S., Kundu, M., & Nasipuri, M. (2010). Handwritten Bangla basic and compound character recognition using MLP and SVM classifier. *Journal of Computing*, *2*(2), 109–115.

Das, S. R., & Chen, M. Y. (2007). Yahoo! For Amazon: Sentiment extraction from small talk on the web. *Management Science*, *53*(9), 1375–1388. doi:10.1287/mnsc.1070.0704.

Datta, A. K., Sengupta, R., Dey, N., Banerjee, B. M., & Nag, D. (1998). Perception of nasality in bangali vowels: Role of harmonics between F0, F1. In *Proceedings of International Conferences on Computational Linguistics, Speech and Document Processing*. IEEE.

Datta, A. K., Sengupta, R., Dey, N., Banerjee, B. M., & Nag, D. (1998). Spectral cues of nasality in inherently nasal bengali vowels. In *Proceedings of International Conferences on Computational Linguistics, Speech and Document Processing*. IEEE.

Datta, A. K., Sengupta, R., Dey, N., Banerjee, B. M., & Nag, D. (1998). Speaker Identification using pitch in Bengali. In *Proceedings of International Conferences on Computational Linguistics, Speech and Document Processing*. IEEE.

De Baerdemaeker, J. (2009). *Tibetan typeforms: An historical and visual evaluation of Tibetan typefaces from their inception in 1738 up to 2009*. (Unpublished Doctoral Thesis). University of Reading. Reading, UK.

De, S., Dhar, A., & Garain, U. (2009). Karaka frames and their transformations for Bangla verbs. In *Proceedings of the 31st All-India Conference of Linguists*. Hyderabad, India: AICL.

DeConverter. (2002). *DeConverter specification, Version 2.7*. Tokyo, Japan: UNL Center, UNDL Foundation.

Delattre, P., & Monnot, M. (1968). The role of duration in the identification of french nasal vowels. *International Review of Applied Linguistics*, *6*, 267–288. doi:10.1515/iral.1968.6.1-4.267.

Deller, J. R., & Hansen, J. H. L. (2000). *Discrete-time processing of speech signals*. IEEE Press.

Delvaux, V. (2003). *Contrôle et connaissance phonétique: Le cas des voyelles nasales du français*. (Ph.D. Dissertation). Université Libre de Bruxelles. Brussels, Belgium.

Di Nunzio, G. M., Ferro, N., Mandl, T., & Peters, C. (2008). Advances in multilingual and multimodal information retrieval. In Peters, C., Jijkoun, V., Mandl, T., Müller, H., Oard, D. W., & Peñas, A. et al. (Eds.), *CLEF* (*Vol. 5152*, pp. 13–32). Berlin: Springer.

Diakoumakou, E. (2004). *Coarticulatory vowel nasalization in modern Greek.* (PhD Dissertation). University of Michigan. Ann Arbor, MI.

Dickson, D. R. (1962). Acoustic study of nasality. *Journal of Speech and Hearing Research, 5*(2), 103–111. PMID:13886213.

Diederich, J., & Dillon, D. (2008). Sentiment recognition by rule extraction from support vector machine. In *Proceedings of Computer Games Multimedia & Allied Technology*. IEEE.

Dolamic, L., & Savoy, J. (2008). UniNE at FIRE 2008: Hindi, Bengali, and Marathi IR. In *Proceedings of Working Notes of the Forum for Information Retrieval Evaluation.* Kolkata, India: FIRE.

Dolamic, L., & Savoy, J. (2010). UniNE at FIRE 2010: Hindi, Bengali, and Marathi IR. In *Proceedings of Working Notes of the Forum for Information Retrieval Evaluation, 2010.* FIRE.

Dong, Z., Wejinya, U. C., Zhou, S., Shan, Q., & Li, W. J. (2009). Real-time written-character recognition using MEMS motion sensors: Calibration and experimental results. In *Proceedings of IEEE International Conference on Robotics and Biometrics*, (pp. 687–691). IEEE.

Dorman, M., & Loizou, P. (1996). Relative spectral change and formant transitions as cues to labial an alveolar place of articulation. *The Journal of the Acoustical Society of America, 100,* 3825–3830. doi:10.1121/1.417238 PMID:8969483.

Dugast, D. (1979). *Vocabulaire et stylistique: I théâtre et dialogue: Travaux de linguistique quantitative.* Geneva, Switzerland: Slatkine-Champion.

Dutta, A., & Chaudhury, S. (1993). Bengali alpha-numeric character recognition using curvature features. *Pattern Recognition, 26*(12), 1757–1770. doi:10.1016/0031-3203(93)90174-U.

Eck, M., Vogel, S., & Waibel, A. (2003). Language model adaptation for statistical machine translation based on information retrieval. In *Proceedings of the International Conference on Language Resources and Evaluation (LREC)*, (pp. 327-330). Lisbon, Portugal: LREC.

Eck, M., Vogel, S., & Waibel, A. (2005). Low cost portability for statistical machine translation based in n-gram frequency and tf-idf. In *Proceedings of International Workshop on Spoken Language Translation (IWSLT).* IWSLT.

Ekman, P. (1993). An argument for basic emotions. *Cognition and Emotion, 6,* 169–200. doi:10.1080/02699939208411068.

Ekman, P. (1993). Facial expression and emotion. *The American Psychologist, 48*(4), 384–392. doi:10.1037/0003-066X.48.4.384 PMID:8512154.

EnConverter. (2002). *EnConverter specification, Version 3.3.* Tokyo, Japan: UNL Center/UNDL Foundation.

Esuli, A., & Sebastiani, F. (2005). Determining the semantic orientation of terms through gloss analysis. In *Proceedings of CIKM* (pp. 617–624). CIKM.

Esuli, A., & Sebastiani, F. (2006). A publicly available lexical resource for opinion mining. In *Proceedings of the 5th Conference on Language Resources and Evaluation.* Genova, Italy: ACL.

Esuli, A., & Sebastiani, F. (2006). SentiWordNet: A publicly available lexical resource for opinion mining. In *Proceedings of the International Conference on Language Resources and Evaluation* (LREC-2006), (pp. 417-422). Genoa, Italy: LREC.

Examination Roll. 841. (1997). *A text-to-speech synthesis system for bangla language using concatenative technique.* (MS Thesis). Rajshahi University. Rajshahi, Bangladesh.

Fairhurst, M. C., Rahman, A. F. R., & Rahman, R. (2002). Recognition of handwritten Bengali characters: A novel multistage approach. *Pattern Recognition, 35*(5), 997–1006. doi:10.1016/S0031-3203(01)00089-9.

Fant, G. (1960). *Acoustic theory of speech production.* The Hague, Netherlands: Mouton.

Faridee, A. Z. M., & Tyers, F. M. (2009). Development of a morphological analyzer for Bengali. In *Proceedings of the First International Workshop on Free/Open-Source Rule-Based Machine Translation,* (pp. 43-50). IEEE.

Farnetani, E., & Recasens, D. (1999). *Coarticulation models in recent speech production theories.* Hardcastle.

Fei, Z., Liu, J., & Wu, G. (2004). Sentiment classification using phrase patterns. In *Proceedings of the CIT* (pp. 1147 - 1152). CIT.

Ferguson, C. A., & Choudhury, M. (1960). Phonemes of Bengali: Part I. *Language, 36*(1). doi:10.2307/410622.

Firoj, A., Murtoza, H. S. M., Afroza, S. D., & Mumit, K. (2010). BRAC university institutional repository. *Development of Annotated Bangla Speech Corpora.* Retrieved June 28, 2012, from http://dspace.bracu.ac.bd/handle//10361//633

Fitrianie, S., & Rothkrantz, L. J. M. (2006). Constructing knowledge for automated text-based emotion expressions. In Proceedings of CompSysTech. CompSysTech.

Foster, G., & Kuhn, R. (2007). Mixture model adaptation for SMT. In *Proceedings of the Second Workshop on Statistical Machine Translation*, (pp. 128-135). Prague, Czech Republic: SMT.

Fox, C. (1992). Lexical analysis and stoplists. In *Information Retrieval: Data Structures and Algorithms* (pp. 102–130). New York: Prentice-Hall.

Fujimura, O., & Lindqvist, J. (1971). Sweep tone measurements of vocal tract characteristics. *The Journal of the Acoustical Society of America, 49*, 541–558. doi:10.1121/1.1912385 PMID:5541748.

Fukuhara, T., Nakagawa, H., & Nishida, T. (2007). Understanding sentiment of people from news articles: Temporal sentiment analysis of social events. In *Proceedings of the International Conference on Weblogs and Social Media.* ICWSM.

Furui, S. (2001). *Digital speech processing, synthesis, and recognition* (2nd ed.). Marcel Dekker, Inc..

Gangadharaiah, R., Brown, R. D., & Carbonell, J. (2009). Active learning in example-based machine translation. In *Proceedings of the 17th Nordic Conference of Computational Linguistics, NODALIDA*. NODALIDA.

Ganguly, D., Leveling, J., & Jones, G. J. F. (2010). Exploring sentence level query expansion in the language model. In D. M. Sharma, R. Sangal, & S. Sarkav (Eds.), *Proceedings of ICON-2010: 8th International Conference on Natural Language Processing* (pp. 18–27). Macmillan Publishers.

Gerwirth, L. L., & Blumstein, S. (1984). A reconsideration of acoustic invariance for place of articulation in diffuse stop consonants: Evidence from a cross-language study. *The Journal of the Acoustical Society of America, 76*, 391–404. doi:10.1121/1.391580 PMID:6480990.

Ghosh, A., Das, A., Bhaskar, P., & Bandyopadhyay, S. (2010). *Bengali parsing system.* Paper presented at ICON NLP Tool Contest 2010.

Ghosh, K., Reddy, R. V., Narendra, N. P., Maity, S., Koolagudi, S. G., & Rao, K. S. (2010). *Grapheme to phoneme conversion in bengali for festival based TTS framework.* Paper presented at the 8th International Conference on Natural Language Processing (ICON). New Delhi.

Giménez, J., & Márquez, L. (2004). SVMTool: A general POS tagger generator based on support vector machines. In *Proceedings of the 4th International Conference on Language Resources and Evaluation (LREC'04).* Lisbon, Portugal: LREC.

Giri, L. (2001). *Semantic net like knowledge structure generation from natural languages.* (Unpublished B Tech Dissertation). IIT Bombay. Bombay, India.

Glass, J. R. (1984). *Nasal consonants and nasalised vowels: An acoustical study and recognition experiment.* (Master's Thesis). MIT. Cambridge, MA.

Glass, J. R., & Zue, V. W. (1985). Detection of nasalized vowels in American English. In *Proceedings of ICASSP*, (pp. 1569–1572). ICASSP.

Goldsmith, J. (2001). Unsupervised learning of the morphology of a natural language. *Computational Linguistics, 27*, 153–198. doi:10.1162/089120101750300490.

Graps, A. (2001). An introduction to wavelets. *IEEE Computational Sciences and Engineering*. Retrieved from http://www.amara.com/IEEEwave/IEEEwavelet.html

Grassi, M. (2009). Developing HEO human emotions ontology. In *Proceedings of the 2009 Joint International Conference on Biometric ID management and Multimodal Communication* (LNCS), (vol. 5707, pp. 244–251). Springer.

Grimes, S. (2012). *DeepMR: Market research mines social sentiment.* GreenBook.

Grimm, J. (1822). *Deutsche grammatik* (2nd ed.). Göttingen.

Guiraud, P. (1954). *Les caractères statistiques du vocabulaire*. Paris: Presses Universitaires de France.

Guiraud, P. (1960). *Problèmes et méthodes de la statistique linguistique*. Paris: Presses Universitaires de France.

Haffari, G., & Sarkar, A. (2009). Active learning for multilingual statistical phrase based machine translation. In *Proceedings of the Joint Conference of the 47th Annual Meeting of the Association for Computational Linguistics and the 4th International Joint Conference on Natural Language Processing of the Asian Federation of Natural Language Processing (ACL-IJCNLP)*. ACL-IJCNLP.

Haffari, G., Roy, M., & Sarkar, A. (2009). Active learning for statistical phrase-based machine translation. In *Proceedings of the North American Chapter of the Association for Computational Linguistics - Human Language Technologies (NAACL-HLT)*. NAACL-HLT.

Hai, A. (1985). *Dhvani-vignan o bangla dhvani tattwa*. Mullick Brothers.

Haider, M. R., Islam, M. N., & Alam, M. S. (2006). Enhanced class associative generalized fringe-adjusted joint transform correlation for multiple target detection. *Optical Engineering (Redondo Beach, Calif.)*, *45*(4). doi:10.1117/1.2192471 PMID:20052302.

Haider, M. R., Islam, M. N., Alam, M. S., & Khan, J. F. (2005). Shifted phase-encoded fringe-adjusted joint transform correlation for multiple target detection. *Optics Communications*, *248*, 69–88. doi:10.1016/j.optcom.2004.11.102.

Hai, M. A. (1966). *Bengali language handbook*. Washington, DC: Center for Applied Linguistics.

Hai, M. A. (2000). *Dhani vignan 0 bangla dhvani-tattwa*. Mullick Brothers.

Hajro, N. (2004). *Automated nasal feature detection for the lexical access from features project*. (Master's Thesis). MIT. Cambridge, MA.

Halhed, N. B. (1778). *A grammar of the Bengal language*. Hoogly.

Hamid, M. E. (1993). *Software development for computer processing of bangla speech*. (M.Sc. Thesis). Rajshahi University. Rajshahi, Bangladesh.

Hamid, M. E., Siddique, S. A., Chisty, K. J. A., & Sobhan, M. A. (1995). *Power spectrum analysis of bangla vowels and consonants by windowed short time fourier transforms*. Rajshahi University Studies.

Haque, S. (1997). *Comparative study of extractive features of bangla phonemes with different age and sex groups and synthesis of voiced phonemes with developed software*. (M.Sc. Dissertation). Rajshahi University. Bangladesh.

Haque, S., & Takara, T. (2004). Rule based speech synthesis by cepstral method for standard bangle. In *Proceedings of 18th International Congress on Acoustics, ICA 2004*. Kyoto, Japan: ICA.

Haque, S., & Takara, T. (2006). Nasality perception of vowels in different language background. In *Proceedings of INTERSPEECH 2006 – ICSLP*. Pittsburgh, PA: ICSLP.

Haque, M. N., & Khan, M. (2005). Parsing Bangla using LFG: An introduction. *BRAC University Journal*, *2*(1), 105–110.

Haque, S., & Takara, T. (2011). Bangla oral-nasal vowel pairs: Acoustic categorization and comparative study of feature extraction methods. *Journal of Computing*, *3*(7).

Haque, S., & Takara, T. (2011). Optimal wavelet for bangla vowel synthesis. *International Journal of Scientific and Engineering Research*, *2*(1).

Harman, D. (1991). How effective is suffixing? *Journal of the American Society for Information Science American Society for Information Science*, *42*(1), 7–15. doi:10.1002/(SICI)1097-4571(199101)42:1<7::AID-ASI2>3.0.CO;2-P.

Hasan, K. M. A., Mondal, A., & Saha, A. (2010). A context free grammar and its predictive parser for Bangla grammar recognition. In *Proceedings of International Conference on Computer and Information Technology*, (pp. 87 – 91). IEEE.

Hasan, M. A. M., Alim, M. A., & Islam, M. W. (2005). A new approach to Bangla text extraction and recognition from textual image. In *Proceedings of the 8th International Conference on Computer and Information Technology* (pp. 1 – 5). IEEE.

Hasan, S. M. S., & Adjeroh, D. A. (2011). Proximity-based sentiment analysis. In *Proceedings of ICADIWT* (pp. 106 – 111). ICADIWT.

Hasan, K. M. A., Mahmud, A., Mondal, A., & Saha, A. (2011). Recognizing Bangla grammar using predictive parser. *International Journal of Computer Science & Information Technology*, *3*(6), 61–73. doi:10.5121/ijcsit.2011.3605.

Hasegawa-Johnson, M., Baker, J., Borys, S., Chen, K., Coogan, E., & Greenberg, S. … Wang, T. (2005). Landmark-based speech recognition. In *Proceedings of ICASSP*, (pp. 213–216). ICASSP.

Hasnat, M. A., & Khan, M. (2009). Rule based segmentation of lower modifiers in complex Bangla scripts. In *Proceedings on the Conference on Language and Technology* (pp. 94-101). National University of Computer and Emerging Sciences.

Hasnat, M. A., Habib, S. M. M., & Khan, M. (2008). A high performance domain specific OCR for Bangla script. In Proceedings of Novel Algorithms and Techniques in Telecommunications, Automation and Industrial Electronics, (pp. 174–178). Springer.

Hasnat, M. A., Mowla, J., & Khan, M. (2007). Isolated and continuous Bangla speech recognition: Implementation performance and application perspective. In *Proceedings of International Symposium on Natural Language Processing (SNLP)*. Hanoi, Vietnam: SNLP.

Hassan, F., Kotwal, M. R. A., & Huda, M. N. (2011). Bangla ASR design by suppressing gender factor with gender-independent and gender-based HMM classifiers. In *Proceedings of WICT 2011*. Mumbai, India: WICT.

Hassan, M. R., Nath, B., & Bhuiyan, M. A. (2003). Bengali phoneme recognition: A new approach. In *Proceedings of the 6th International Conference on Computer and Information Technology (ICCIT03)*. Dhaka, Bangladesh: ICCIT.

Hattori, S., Yamamoto, K., & Fujimura, O. (1958). Nasalization of vowels in relation to nasals. *The Journal of the Acoustical Society of America*, *30*(4), 267–274. doi:10.1121/1.1909563.

Hatzivassiloglou, V., & McKeown, K. (1997). Predicting the semantic orientation of adjectives. In *Proceedings of the 35th Annual Meeting of the ACL and the 8th Conference of the European Chapter of the ACL* (pp. 174–181). Madrid, Spain: ACL.

Hawkins, S., & Stevens, K. N. (1985). Acoustic and perceptual correlates of the non- nasal-nasal distinction for vowels. *The Journal of the Acoustical Society of America*, *77*(4), 1560–1575. doi:10.1121/1.391999 PMID:3989111.

Haznedar, B., & Gavruseva, E. (2008). *Current trends in child second language acquisition: A generative perspective*. Amsterdam, Netherlands: John Benjamins Publishing Company.

Heaps, H. S. (1978). *Information retrieval: Computational and theoretical aspects*. Orlando, FL: Academic Press, Inc..

Hedlund, T. (2002). Compounds in dictionary-based cross-language information retrieval. *Information Research, 7*(2).

Hegde, R. M., Murthy, H. A., & Ramana Rao, G. V. (2004). Application of the modified group delay function to speaker identification and discrimination. In *Proceedings of ICASSP*, (pp. 517–520). ICASSP.

Hegde, R. M., Murthy, H. A., & Ramana Rao, G. V. (2005). Speech processing using joint features derived from the modified group delay function. In *Proceedings of ICASSP* (pp. 541–544). ICASSP.

Herdan, G. (1960). *Type-token mathematics: A textbook of mathematical linguistics*. Mouton: Gravenhage.

Herdan, G. (1964). *Quantitative linguistics*. London: Butterworths.

Hess, C. W., Haug, H. T., & Landry, R. G. (1989). The reliability of type-token ratios for the oral language of school age children. *Journal of Speech and Hearing Research*, *32*(3), 536–540. PMID:2779198.

Hiemstra, D. (2000). *Using language models for information retrieval*. Enschede, The Netherlands: Center of Telematics and Information Technology, AE.

Hildebrand, M. S., Eck, M., Vogel, S., & Waibel, A. (2005). Adaptation of the translation model for statistical machine translation based on information retrieval. In *Proceedings of the 10th EAMT Conference Practical Applications of Machine Translation*, (pp. 133-142). EAMT.

Hoemeke, K. A., & Diehl, L. R. (1994). Perception of vowel height: The role of F1-F2 distance. *The Journal of the Acoustical Society of America*, *96*, 661–674. doi:10.1121/1.410305 PMID:7930066.

Holmes, D. (1994). Authorship attribution. *Computers and the Humanities*, *28*, 87–106. doi:10.1007/BF01830689.

Hoover, D. L. (2003). Another perspective on vocabulary richness. *Computers and the Humanities*, *37*(2), 151–178. doi:10.1023/A:1022673822140.

Hopcroft, J. E. (2007). Introduction to automata theory, languages and computation (2nd ed). New York: Prentice Hall.

Hoque, M. M., & Ali, M. M. (2003). A parsing methodology for Bangla natural language sentences. In *Proceedings of International Conference on Computer and Information Technology*, (277-282). IEEE.

Hoque, M. M., & Ali, M. M. (2004). Context-sensitive phrase structure rule for structural representation of Bangla natural language sentences. In *Proceedings of International Conference on Computer and Information Technology*, (pp. 615-620). IEEE.

Hoque, M. M., & Rahman, S. M. F. (2007). Fuzzy features extraction from Bangla handwriten character. In *Proceedings of the International Conference on Information and Communication Technology (ICICT)* (pp. 72-75). Dhaka, Bangladesh: ICICT.

Hoque, M. M., Rahman, M. J., & Dhar, P. K. (2007). Lexical semantics: A New approach to analyze the Bangla sentence with semantic features. In *Proceedings of the International Conference on Information and Communication Technology*, (pp. 87 – 91). IEEE.

Horner, J. L., & Gianino, P. D. (1984). Phase-only matched filtering. *Applied Optics*, *23*, 812–816. doi:10.1364/AO.23.000812 PMID:18204645.

Hossain, S. A. (1991). *Experimental and computer aided analysis of active filters and analog and digital processing of music and bangla speech signals*. (M.Sc. Thesis). Rajshahi University. Rajshahi, Bangladesh.

Hossain, S. A. (2008). *Analysis and synthesis of bangla phonemes for computer speech recognition*. (Ph.D. Dissertation). University of Dhaka. Dhaka, Bangladesh.

Hossain, S. A., & Sobhan, M. A. (1997). Fundamental frequency tracking of bangla voiced speech. In *Proceedings ofNational Conference on Computer and Information Systems (NCCIS)*. Dhaka, Bangladesh: NCCIS.

Hossain, S. A., Rahman, M. L., & Ahmed, F. (2005). A review on bangla phoneme production and perception for computational approaches. In *Proceedings of 7th WSEAS International Conference on Mathematical Methods and Computational Techniques in Electrical Engineering*. Sofia, Bulgaria: IEEE.

Hossain, S. A., Rahman, M. L., & Ahmed, F. (2007). Acoustic classification of bangla vowels. World Academy of Science, Engineering and Technology, 26.

Hossain, S. A., Rahman, M. L., Ahmed, F., & Dewan, M. (2004). Bangla speech synthesis, analysis, and recognition: An overview. In *Proceedings of the National Conference on Computer Processing of Bangla (NCCPB04)*. NCCPB.

Hossain, G., & Asaduzzaman, M.A., Ullah, & Saif Shams, S. M. (2005). Bangla Braille embosser: A tool for Bengali speaking visually impaired people. *Bangladesh Education Journal*, *4*(1), 49–55.

Hossain, S. A., Rahman, M. L., & Ahmed, F. (2007). World academy of science, engineering and technology. *Bangla Vowel Characterization Based on Analysis by Synthesis*, *20*, 327–330.

Hossain, S., Akter, N., Sarwar, H., & Rahman, C. M. (2010). Development of a recognizer for Bangla text: Present status and future challenges. In Mori, M. (Ed.), *Character Recognition* (pp. 83–112). InTech.

Houque, A. K. M. M. (2006). *Bengali segmented speech recognition system*. (Unpublished Undergraduate Thesis). BRAC University. Bangladesh.

House, A. S., & Stevens, K. N. (1956). Analog studies of the nasalization of vowels. *The Journal of Speech and Hearing Disorders*, *21*(2), 218–232. PMID:13320522.

Hu, M., & Liu, B. (2004). Mining and summarizing customer reviews. In *Proceedings of KDD*. ACM.

Huffman, M. K. (1990). The role of f1 amplitude in producing nasal percepts. *The Journal of the Acoustical Society of America*, *88*(S1), S54. doi:10.1121/1.2029054.

Husain, S., Gadde, P., Bharat, A., Sharma, D. M., & Rajeev, R. (2009). A modular cascaded approach to complete parsing. In *Proceedings of the International Conference on Asian Language Processing (IALP)*. Singapore: IALP.

ICON. (2009). *ICON2009 NLP tools contest: Indian language dependency parsing*. Retrieved from http://ltrc.iiit.ac.in/nlptools2009/CR/all-papers-toolscontest.pdf

Iqbal, Z. (2008). *Muktizudher itihash*. Dhaka, Bangladesh: Protity Publisher.

Islam, M. R., Saha, R. S., & Hossain, A. R. (2009). Automatic reading from Bangla PDF document using rule based concatenative synthesis. In *Proceeding of ICCDA*. Singapore: ICCDA.

Islam, M. S. (2009). Research on Bangla language processing in Bangladesh: Progress and challenges. In *Proceedings of the 8th International Language & Development Conference*. Dhaka, Bangladesh: IEEE.

Islam, M. W., Hasan, M. A. M., & Debanath, R. C. (2005). Handwritten Bangla numerical recognition using back-propagation algorithm with and without momentum factor. In *Proceedings of the National Conference on Computer Processing of Bangla* (pp. 177-182). Independent University.

Islam, M. N., & Karim, M. A. (2010). Optical pattern recognition systems and techniques. In Ramakrishnan, S., & El-Omary, I. M. M. (Eds.), *Computational Intelligence Techniques in Handling Image Processing and Pattern Recognition*. Lambert Academic Publishing.

Islam, M. N., Purohit, I. K., Asari, K. V., & Karim, M. A. (2008). Distortion-invariant pattern recognition using synthetic discriminant function-based shifted phase-encoded joint transform correlator. *Optical Engineering (Redondo Beach, Calif.)*, *47*(10), 108201-1–108201-9. doi:10.1117/1.3000589.

Islam, R. (1970). *An introduction to colloquial Bangali*. Dhaka, Bangladesh: Central Board for Development of Bangla.

Javidi, B., & Kuo, C. (1988). Joint transform image correlation using a binary spatial light modulator at the Fourier plane. *Applied Optics*, *27*, 663–665. doi:10.1364/AO.27.000663 PMID:20523656.

Joshi, S. (n.d.). *Selection of grammatical and logical functions in Marathi*. (PhD Thesis). Stanford University. Palo Alto, CA.

Karim, R., Rahman, M. S., & Iqbal, M. Z. (2002). Recognition of spoken letters in Bangla. In *Proceedings of the 5th International Conference on Computer and Information Technology (ICCIT02)*. Dhaka, Bangladesh: ICCIT.

Kato, R. S. M., & Barnard, E. (2007). Statistical translation with scarce resources: A South African case study. *SAIEE Africa Research Journal*, *98*(4), 136–140.

Kawai, Y., Kumamoto, T., & Tanaka, K. (2007). Fair news reader: Recommending news articles with different sentiments based on user preference. In Proceedings of Knowledge-Based Intelligent Information & Engineering Systems (pp. 612-622). KES.

Kawasaki, H. (1986). Phonetic explanation for phonological universals: The case of distinctive vowel nasalization. In *Experimental Phonology*. Academic Press.

Kesavan, B. S. (1985). *History of printing and publishing in India*. New Delhi: National Book Trust.

Keshava, S., & Pitler, E. (2006). A simpler, intuitive approach to morpheme induction. In *Proceedings of the PASCAL Challenge Workshop on Unsupervised Segmentation of Words Into Morphemes - MorphoChallenge 2005*. Venice, Italy: MorphoChallenge.

Kettunnen, K., Paik, J., Pal, D., & Järvelin, K. (2011). Frequent case generation in ad hoc retrieval of the Indian languages. In *Proceedings of FIRE 2011, Third workshop of the Forum for Information Retrieval Evaluation*. FIRE.

Khan, D. O., & Shet, K. C. (2005). A new Architecture for Braille transcription from optically recognized Indian languages. In *Proceedings of International Conference*. London: Academic Press.

Khan, M. H. (1976). *Printing in Bengali characters up to 1866*. (Unpublished Doctoral Thesis). University of London. London.

Kim, S., & Hovy, E. (2006). Identifying and analyzing judgment opinions. In *Proceedings of HLTNAACL*. ACL.

Kim, S.-M., & Hovy, E. (2004). Determining the sentiment of opinions. In *Proceedings of COLING* (pp. 1367-1373). COLING.

King, A. (2001). *Text and Braille computer translation.* (Dissertation). University of Manchester Institute of Science and Technology. Manchester, UK.

Kingston, J., & Macmillan, N. A. (1995). Integrality of nasalization and f1 in vowels in isolation and before oral and nasal consonants: A detection-theoretic application of the garner paradigm. *Journal of the American Society of Acoustics*, *97*, 1261–1285. doi:10.1121/1.412169 PMID:7876447.

Kipper-Schuler, K. (2005). *VerbNet: A broad-coverage, comprehensive verb lexicon.* (Ph.D. Thesis). University of Pennsylvania. Philadelphia, PA.

Kirchhoff, K. (2007). OOV detection by joint word/phone lattice alignment. In *Proceedings of ASRU*. Kyoto, Japan: ASRU.

Kishore, S., Black, A., Kumar, R., & Sangal, R. (2003). *Experiments with unit selection speech databases for Indian languages.* Paper presented at National Seminar on Language Technology Tools: Implementation of Telugu. Hyderabad, India.

Klatt, D. H. (1980). Software for cascade/parallel formant synthesizer. *The Journal of the Acoustical Society of America*, *67*, 971–995. doi:10.1121/1.383940.

Kobayashi, N., Iida, R., Inui, K., & Matsumoto, Y. (2006). Opinion mining as extraction of attribute-value relations. *Lecture Notes in Artificial Intelligence*, *4012*, 470–481.

Koehn, P., & Schroeder, J. (2007). Experiments in domain adaptation for statistical machine translation. In *Proceedings of the ACL Workshop on Statistical Machine Translation*. ACL.

Koehn, P., Hoang, H., Birch, A., Callison-Burch, C., Federico, M., & Bertoldi, N. et al. (2007). *Moses: Open source toolkit for statistical machine translation.* ACL. doi:10.3115/1557769.1557821.

Kornilov, S. A., Rakhlin, N. V., & Grigorenko, E. L. (2012). Morphology and Developmental language disorders: New tools for Russian. *Psychology in Russia: State of the Art*, *5*, 371–387.

Kotwal, M. R. A., Bonik, M., Eity, Q. N., Huda, M. N., Muhammad, G., & Alotaibi, Y. A. (2010). Bangla phoneme recognition for ASR using multilayer neural network. In *Proceedings of the International Conference on Computer and Information Technology (ICCIT10)*. Dhaka, Bangladesh: ICCIT.

Kotwal, M. R. A., Hasan, F., Ahmed, F., Alam, M. S., Daud, S. I., & Huda, M. N. (2011). Incorporation of dynamic parameters in hybrid feature-based Bangla phoneme recognition using multilayer neural networks. In *Proceedings of the International Conference on Computer and Information Technology (ICCIT11)*. Dhaka, Bangladesh: ICCIT.

Kotwal, M. R. A., Hassan, F., Daud, S. I., Alam, M. S., Ahmed, F., & Huda, M. N. (2011). Gender effects suppression in Bangla ASR by designing multiple HMM-based classifiers. In *Proceedings of CICN 2011*. Gwalior, India: CICN.

Krakow, R. A., & Beddor, P. S. (1991). Coarticulation and the perception of nasality. In *Proceedings of The 12th International Congress of Phonetic Sciences*. IEEE.

Krakow, R. A. (1993). Nonsegmental influences on velum movement patterns: Syllables, sentences, stress and speaking rate. In *Phonetics and Phonology: Nasals, Nasalization and The Velum*. Academic Press.

Krakow, R. A., Beddor, P. S., Goldstein, L. M., & Fowler, C. (1988). Coarticulatory influences on the perceived height of nasal vowels. *The Journal of the Acoustical Society of America*, *83*, 1146–1158. doi:10.1121/1.396059 PMID:3356819.

Krovetz, R. (1993). Viewing morphology as an inference process. In R. Korfhage, E. Rasmussen, & P. Willett (Eds.), *Proceedings of the 16th Annual International ACM SIGIR Conference on Research and Development in Information Retrieval* (pp. 191–202). Pittsburg, PA: ACM.

Kshetrimayum, N. (2010). *A comparative study of Meetei Mayek: Form the inscribed letterform to the digital typeface.* (Unpublished Masters Dissertation). University of Reading. Reading, UK.

Ku, L.-W., Lee, L.-Y., Wu, T.-H., & Chen, H.-H. (2005). Major topic detection and its application to opinion summarization. In *Proceedings of the 28th Annual International ACM SIGIR Conference on Research and Development in Information Retrieval,* (pp. 627-628). Salvador, Brazil: ACM.

Kumar, D. C. S. (1999). *Vasha-prokash Bangla vyakaran.* Calcutta, India: Rupa and Company Prokashoni.

Kuntal, D., & Bhattacharyya, P. (2003). Universal networking language based analysis and generation for bengali case structure constructs. In *Proceedings of the International Conference of the Convergence of Knowledge, Culture, Language and Information Technologies.* Alexandria, Egypt: IEEE.

Ladefoged, P. (1982). *A course in phonetics.* New York: Harcourt Brace Jovanovich.

Ladefoged, P., & Maddieson, I. (1996). *The sounds of the world's languages.* Oxford, UK: Blackwell Publishers.

Lahiri, A., Chattopadhyay, S. J., & Basu, A. (2005). A comprehensive Indian languages tool set for the blind. In *Proceedings of the 7th International Conference Conference on Computers and Accessibility.* ACM.

Lahiri, A., & Marslen-Wilson, W. (1991). The mental representation of lexical form: A phonological approach to the recognition lexicon. *Cognition, 38,* 245–294. doi:10.1016/0010-0277(91)90008-R PMID:2060271.

Language, B. (2009). *Wikipedia.* Retrieved May 10, 2009, from http://en.wikipedia.org/wiki/Bengali_language

Larson, K. (2004). *The science of word recognition.* Retrieved July 17, 2012 from http://www.microsoft.com/typography/ctfonts/wordrecognition.aspx

Laufer, B., & Nation, P. (1995). Vocabulary size and use: Lexical richness in L2 written production. *Applied Linguistics, 16*(3), 307–322. doi:10.1093/applin/16.3.307.

Leveling, J. G. J. F. J. (2010). Classifying and filtering blind feedback terms to improve information retrieval effectiveness. In *Proceedings of RIAO'2010: Adaptivity, Personalisation and Fusion of Heterogeneous Information* (pp. 156–163). RIAO.

Leveling, J., Ganguly, D., & Jones, G. J. F. (2010). Term conflation and blind relevance feedback for information retrieval on indian languages. In *Proceedings of Working Notes of the Forum for Information Retrieval Evaluation, 2010.* Gandhinagar, India: FIRE.

Leveling, J., Magdy, W., & Jones, G. J. F. (2011). An investigation of decompounding for cross-language patent search. In W.-Y. Ma, J.-Y. Nie, R. A. Baeza-Yates, T.-S. Chua, & W. B. Croft (Eds.), *Proceeding of the 34th International ACM SIGIR Conference on Research and Development in Information Retrieval, SIGIR 2011,* (pp. 1169–1170). ACM.

Leveling, J., & Jones, G. J. F. (2010). Sub-word indexing and blind relevance feedback for English, Bengali, Hindi, and Marathi IR. *ACM Transactions on Asian Language Information Processing, 9*(3), 1–30. doi:10.1145/1838745.1838749.

Liblouis. (2008). *Google.* Retrieved February 10, 2009, from http://code.google.com/p/liblouis

Lin, K. H.-Y., Yang, C., & Chen, H.-H. (2007). What emotions news articles trigger in their readers? In *Proceedings of SIGIR* (pp. 733-734). ACM.

Lindqvist-Gauffin, J., & Sundberg, J. (1976). Acoustic properties of the nasal tract. *Phonetica, 33,* 161–168. doi:10.1159/000259720 PMID:996111.

Lindsay, R. K., & Gordon, M. D. (1999, May). Literature-based discovery by lexical statistics. *Journal of the American Society for Information Science American Society for Information Science, 50,* 574–587. doi:10.1002/(SICI)1097-4571(1999)50:7<574::AID-ASI3>3.0.CO;2-Q.

Lintz, L. B., & Sherman, D. (1961). Phonetic elements and perception of nasality. *Journal of Speech and Hearing Research, 4,* 381–396. PMID:14465667.

Liu, H., Lieberman, H., & Selker, T. (2003). A model of textual affect sensing using real-world knowledge. In *Proceeding of the International Conference on Intelligent User Interfaces.* Springer.

Liu, B. (2010). *Handbook on NLP in sentiment analysis.* Academic Press.

Liu, B. (2010). Sentiment analysis: A multi-faceted problem. *IEEE Intelligent Systems, 25*(3), 76–80.

Lloyd, L., Kechagias, D., & Skiena, S. (2005). Lydia: A system for large-scale news analysis.LNCS.*Proceedings of String Processing and Information Retrieval, 3772*, 161–166. doi:10.1007/11575832_18.

Loponen, A., Paik, J., & Jarvelin, K. (2010). UTA stemming and lemmatization experiments in the Bengali ad hoc track at FIRE 2010. In *Proceedings of Working Notes of FIRE 2010*. FIRE.

Lu, L., Liu, D., & Zhang, H. (2006). Automatic mood detection and tracking of music audio signals. *IEEE Transactions on Audio. Speech & Language Processing, 14*(1), 5–18. doi:10.1109/TSA.2005.860344.

Maddieson, I. (1984). *Patterns of sounds*. Cambridge University Press. doi:10.1017/CBO9780511753459.

Maeda, S. (1982). A digital simulation method of the vocal-tract system. *Speech Communication, 1*, 199–229. doi:10.1016/0167-6393(82)90017-6.

Maeda, S. (1982). The role of the sinus cavities in the production of nasal vowels. *Proceedings of ICASSP, 2*, 911–914.

Maeda, S. (1982). Acoustic cues for vowel nasalization: A simulation study. *The Journal of the Acoustical Society of America, 72*, S102. doi:10.1121/1.2019690.

Maeda, S. (1993). Acoustics of vowel nasalization and articulatory shifts in french nasal vowels. In *Phonetics and Phonology: Nasals, Nasalization and The Velum*. Academic Press.

Magdy, W., & Jones, G. J. F. (2010). PRES: A score metric for evaluating recall-oriented information retrieval applications.ACM.*Proceedings of SIGIR, 2010*, 611–618.

Magnus, R. (2006). *An introduction to front-end processing and acoustic features for automatic speech recognition*. Swedish National Graduate School of Language Technology.

Mahboob, M. (2009). *TechSpotlight: The power of Bangla*. The Daily Star.

Mahmud, J. U., Raihan, M. F., & Rahman, C. M. (2003). A complete OCR for continuous Bengali characters. In *Proceedings of the IEEE Tencon, Conference on Convergent Technologies for the Asia-Pacific* (pp. 1372-1376). Bangalore, India: IEEE.

Majumdar, A., & Ward, R. K. (2009). Nearest subspace classifier: Application to character recognition. In *Proceedings of the International Conference on Image Processing*. IEEE.

Majumdar, A. (2007). Bangla basic character recognition using digital curvelet transform. *Journal of Pattern Recognition Research, 1*, 17–26.

Majumder, P., Mitra, M., Parui, S. K., Kole, G., Mitra, P., & Datta, K. (2007). YASS: Yet another suffix stripper. *ACM Transactions on Information Systems, 25*(4), 18–20. doi:10.1145/1281485.1281489.

Mandal, D., Gupta, M., Dandapat, S., Banerjee, P., & Sarkar, S. (2007). Bengali and Hindi to English CLIR evaluation. In C. Peters, V. Jijkoun, T. Mandl, H. Müller, D. W. Oard, A. Peñas, V. Petras, et al. (Eds.), *Advances in Multilingual and Multimodal Information Retrieval, 8th Workshop of the Cross-Language Evaluation Forum, CLEF 2007*, (Vol. 5152, pp. 95–102). Springer.

Mandal, S., Das, B., Mitra, P., & Basu, A. (2011). Developing Bengali speech corpus for phone recognizer using optimum text selection technique. In *Proceedings of the International Conference on Asian Language Processing*. Penang, Malaysia: IEEE.

Manning, C. D., Raghavan, P., & Schütze, H. (2009). *An introduction to information retrieval*. Cambridge, UK: Cambridge University Press.

Manning, C. D., & Schütze, H. (1999). *Foundations of statistical natural language processing*. Cambridge, MA: MIT Press.

Mann, W. C., & Thompson, S. A. (1988). Rhetorical structure theory: Toward a functional theory of text organization. *Text, 8*, 243–281. doi:10.1515/text.1.1988.8.3.243.

Mansur, M. (2006). *Analysis of n-gram based text categorization for bangla in a newspaper corpus*. BRAC University.

Martin, J. R., & White, P. R. R. (2005). *The language of evaluation: Appraisal in English*. London: Palgrave.

Maruyama, H. (1990). Structural disambiguation with constraint propagation. In *Proceedings of ACL*. Pittsburgh, PA: ACL.

Masica, C. P. (1993). *The Indo-Aryan languages*. Cambridge, UK: Cambridge University Press.

McNamee, P. (2008). N-gram Tokenization for {I}ndian language text retrieval. In *Proceedings of Working Notes of the Forum for Information Retrieval Evaluation*. Kolkata, India: IEEE.

McNamee, P., Nicholas, C., & Mayfield, J. (2009). Addressing morphological variation in alphabetic languages. In J. Allan, J. A. Aslam, M. Sanderson, C. Zhai, & J. Zobel (Eds.), *Proceedings of the 32nd Annual International ACM SIGIR Conference on Research and Development in Information Retrieval, SIGIR 2009,* (pp. 75–82). Boston, MA: ACM.

Mehedy, L., Arifin, N., & Kaykobad, M. (2003). Bangla syntax analysis: A comprehensive approach. In *Proceedings of International Conference on Computer and Information Technology (ICCIT),* (pp. 287-293). ICCIT.

Mesgarani, N., Slaney, M., & Shamma, S. (2004). Speech discrimination based on multiscale spectrotemporal features. In *Proceedings of ICASSP*. ICASSP.

Michael, S. (2012). Boom or ruin--Does it make a difference? Using text mining and sentiment analysis to support intraday investment decisions. In Proceedings ofHICSS (pp. 1050 – 1059). ACM.

Mihalcea, R., & Liu, H. (2006). *A corpus-based approach to finding happiness*. Paper presented at the AAAI Spring Symposium on Computational Approaches to Weblogs. Stanford, CA.

Miller, A. G. (1995). WordNet: A lexical database for English. *Communications of the ACM, 38*(11), 39–41. doi:10.1145/219717.219748.

Minato, J., David, B., Ren, F., & Kuroiwa, S. (2008). Japanese emotion corpus analysis and its use for automatic emotion word identification. *Engineering Letters, 16*(1).

Minsky, M. (2006). *The emotion machine*. New York: Simon and Schuster.

Miranda-García, A., & Calle-Martín, J. (2005). Yule's characteristic *K* revisited. *Language Resources and Evaluation, 39*(4), 287–294. doi:10.1007/s10579-005-8622-8.

Mishne, G. (2005). Emotions from text: Machine learning for text-based emotion prediction. In *Proceeding of SIGIR'05* (pp. 15-19). ACM.

Mishne, G., & de Rijke, M. (2006). Moodviews: Tools for blog mood analysis. In *Proceedings of the AAAI Symposium on Computational Approaches to Analysing Weblogs* (pp. 153–154). AAAI.

Mohammad, S., & Turney, P. (2010). Emotions evoked by common words and phrases: Using mechanical turk to create an emotion lexicon. In *Proceedings of the Workshop on Computational Approaches to Analysis and Generation of Emotion in Text*. NAACL.

Mohammad, S., Dorr, B., & Hirst, G. (2008). Computing word-pair antonymy. In *Proceeding of the Empirical Methods in Natural Language Processing and Computational Natural Language Learning*. IEEE.

Mohr, B., Wang & W. S.-Y. (1968). Perceptual distance and the specification of phonological features. *Phonetica, 18*, 31–45. doi:10.1159/000258597.

Moilanen, K., Pulman, S., & Zhang, Y. (2010). Packed feelings and ordered sentiments: Sentiment parsing with quasi-compositional polarity sequencing and compression. In *Proceedings of the 1st Workshop on Computational Approaches to Subjectivity and Sentiment Analysis*. ECAI.

Morinaga, S., Yamanishi, K., Tateishi, K., & Fukushima, T. (2002). Mining product reputations on the web. In *Proceedings of the ACM SIGKDD Conference on Knowledge Discovery and Data Mining*. ACM.

Mori, S., Nishida, H., & Yamada, H. (1999). *Optical character recognition*. New York: John Wiley & Sons.

Mridha, M. F., Huda, M. N., Rahman, M. S., & Rahman, C. M. (2010). Structure of dictionary entries of Bangla morphemes for morphological rule generation for universal networking language. In *Proceedings of the International Conference on Computer Information Systems & Industrial Management Applications*. doi:10.1109/CISIM.2010.5643498

Muhammad, G., Alotaibi, Y. A., & Huda, M. N. (2009). Automatic speech recognition for Bangla digits. In *Proceedings of the International Conference on Computer and Information Technology (ICCIT09)*. Dhaka, Bangladesh: ICCIT.

Mukherjee, S., & Das Mandal, S. K. (2012, July). A Bengali speech synthesizer on android. In *Proceedings of The 1st Workshop on Speech and Multimodal Interaction in Assistive Environments, Association for Computational Linguistics*. Jeju, Republic of Korea: ACL.

Mullen, T., & Collier, N. (2004). Sentiment analysis using support vector machines with diverse information sources. In *Proceedings of EMNLP*. EMNLP.

Munteanu, D., & Marcu, D. (2005). Improving machine translation performance by exploiting comparable corpora. *Computational Linguistics*, *31*(4), 477–504. doi:10.1162/089120105775299168.

Murshed, M. M. (1998). Parsing of Bengali natural language sentences. In *Proceedings of International Conference on Computer and Information Technology (ICCIT)*, (pp. 185-189). ICCIT.

Murthy, H. A., & Gadde, V. (2003). The modified group delay function and its application to phoneme recognition. In *Proceedings of ICASSP*. ICASSP.

Myers, D. G. (2004). Theories of emotion. In *Psychology* (7th ed.). New York, NY: Worth Publishers.

Narendra, N. P. K., Rao, K., Ghosh, K., Vempada, R. R., & Maity, S. (2011). Development of syllable-based text to speech synthesis system in bengali. *International Journal of Speech Technology*, *14*, 167–181. doi:10.1007/s10772-011-9094-4.

Nasukawa, T., & Yi, J. (2003). Sentiment analysis: Capturing favorability using natural language processing. In *Proceedings of K-CAP* (pp. 70–77). ACM Press.

Nation, P. (1993). Using dictionaries to estimate vocabulary size: Essential, but rarely followed, procedures. *Language Testing*, *10*(1), 27–40. doi:10.1177/026553229301000102.

Neviarouskaya, A., Prendinger, H., & Ishizuka, M. (2007). Textual affect sensing for social and expressive online communication. In *Proceeding of the 2nd International Conference on Affective Computing and Intelligent Interaction* (pp. 218-229). IEEE.

Neviarouskaya, A., Prendinger, H., & Ishizuka, M. (2009). SentiFul: Generating a reliable lexicon for sentiment analysis. In *Proceeding of the International Conference on Affective Computing and Intelligent Interaction (ACII'09)*. IEEE.

Nitta, T. (1999). Feature extraction for speech recognition based on orthogonal acoustic-feature planes and LDA. *Proceedings of ICASSP*, *99*, 421–424.

Niu, X., Kain, A., & Santen, J. P. H. (2005). *Estimation of the acoustic properties of the nasal tract during the production of nasalized vowels*. Paper presented at Interspeech. Lisbon, Portugal.

Nivre, J., Hall, J., & Nilssion, J. (2006). MaltParser: A data-driven parser-generator for dependency parsing. In *Proceedings of LREC*, (pp. 2216-2219). LREC.

Nomani, M. W. K., Bari, S. M. K., Islam, T. Z., Haider, M. R., & Islam, M. N. (2007). Invariant Bangla character recognition using projection-slice synthetic-discriminant-function based algorithm. *Journal of Electronic and Electrical Engineering*, *7*(2), 403–409.

Och, F. J. (2003). Minimum error rate training in statistical machine translation. In *Proceedings of the 41st Annual Meeting of the ACL*, (pp. 160-167). ACL.

Ohala, J. J. (1971). Monitoring soft palate movements in speech. *The Journal of the Acoustical Society of America*, *50*, 140. doi:10.1121/1.1977664.

Omee, F. Y., Himel, S. S., & Bikas, M. A. N. (2011). A complete workflow for development of Bangla OCR. *International Journal of Computers and Applications*, *21*(9), 1–6. doi:10.5120/2543-3483.

Ono, S., Hamada, Y., & Takagi, Y. (2000). Interactive Japanese-to-Braille translation using case-based knowledge on the web. *PRICAI 2000 Topics in Artificial Intelligence, 1886*, 638-646.

Onsuwan, C. (2005). *Temporal relations between consonants and vowels in Thai syllables*. (PhD Dissertation). University of Michigan. Ann Arbor, MI.

Ordan, N., Itskovich, V., Shlesinger, S., & Kanter, I. (2010). Lexical richness revisited: Blueprint for a more economical measure. *Journal of Quantitative Linguistics*, *17*(1), 55–67. doi:10.1080/09296170903395957.

Paik, J. H., & Parui, S. K. (2008). A simple stemmer for inflectional languages. In *Proceedings of the Working Notes of the Forum for Information Retrieval Evaluation*. Kolkata, India: FIRE.

Pairkh, J., Khot, J., Dave, S., & Bhattacharyya, P. (2004). *Predicate preserving parsing*. Bombay, India: Department of Computer Science and Engineering, Indian Institute of Technology.

Pal, U., & Chaudhuri, B. B. (2000). Automatic recognition of unconstrained off-line Bangla handwritten numerals. In T. Tan, Y. Shi, & W. Gao (Eds.), *International Conference on Multimodal Interfaces* (LNCS), (vol. 1948, pp. 371-378). Springer-Verlag.

Pal, D., Majumder, P., Mitra, M., Mitra, S., & Sen, A. (2006). Issues in searching for Indian language web content. In *Proceedings of iNEWS'08* (pp. 93–94). Napa Valley, CA: ACM.

Pang, B., & Lee, L. (2004). A sentimental education: Sentiment analysis using subjectivity summarization based on minimum cuts. In *Proceedings of the 42nd Annual Meeting on Association for Computational Linguistics*. ACL.

Pang, B., Lee, L., & Vaithyanathan, S. (2002). Thumbs up? Sentiment classification using machine learning techniques. In *Proceedings of the Empirical Methods on Natural Language Processing (EMNLP 2002)* (pp. 79-86). EMNLP.

Papineni, K., Roukos, S., Ward, T., & Zhu, W. (2002). BLEU: A method for automatic evaluation of machine translation. In *Proceedings of the 20th Annual Meeting of the Association for Computational Linguistics*. ACL.

Paramanik, A. K. (1977). *Acoustical study on the vowel structure of Bengali language*. (Doctoral Dissertation). Tohoku University. Japan.

Paramanik, M., & Kido, K. (1976). Bengali speech: Formant structure of single vowels and initial vowels of words. In *Proceedings of the IEEE International Conference on ICASSP*. ICASSP.

Parteek, B., & Sharma, R. K. (2009). Role of punjabi morphology in designing punjabi-UNL enconverter. In *Proceedings of the International Conference on Advances in Computing, Communication and Control (ICAC3'09)*, (pp. 562-566). ICAC3.

Parui, S. K., Guin, K., Bhattacharya, U., & Chaudhuri, B. B. (2008). Online handwritten Bangla character recognition using HMM. In *Proceedings of the 19th International Conference on Pattern Recognition* (pp. 1-4). Tampa, FL: IEEE.

Passonneau, R. (2004). Computing reliability for coreference annotation. In *Proceeding of the International Conference on Language Resources and Evaluation*. LREC.

Passonneau, R. J. (2006). Measuring agreement on set-valued items (MASI) for semantic and pragmatic annotation. In *Proceeding of the 5th International Conference on Language Resources and Evaluation*. LREC.

Pennebaker, J. W., Mehl, M. R., & Niederhoffer, K. (2003). Psychological aspects of natural language use: Our words, our selves. *Annual Review of Psychology*, *54*, 547–577. doi:10.1146/annurev.psych.54.101601.145041 PMID:12185209.

Perez, O., & Karim, M. A. (1989). An efficient implementation of a joint Fourier transform correlator using a modified LCTV. *Microwave and Optical Technology Letters*, *2*, 193–196. doi:10.1002/mop.4650020602.

Picard, R. W. (1997). *Affective computing*. Cambridge, MA: MIT Press.

Picard, R. W., Yzas, V., & Healey, J. (2001). Toward machine emotional intelligence: Analysis of affective physiological state. *IEEE Transactions on Pattern Analysis and Machine Intelligence*, *23*(10), 1175–1191. doi:10.1109/34.954607.

Pickett, J. M. (1980). *The sounds of speech communication*. Austin, TX: Pro-Ed, Inc..

Picone, J. Staples, Kondo, & Arai. (1993). *Processing system of Japanese language*. Japanese Patent No. TIJ-18107. Tokyo: Japanese Patent Office.

Pingali, P., Jagarlamudi, J., & Varma, V. (2006). Webkhoj: Indian language IR from multiple character encodings. In *Proceedings of WWW 2006, May 23--26* (pp. 801–809). Edinburgh, Scotland: ACM.

PJ. (2010). Why Indian languages failed to make a mark online!. *NextBigWhat*.

Ponte, J. M., & Croft, W. B. (1998). A language modeling approach to information retrieval. In *Proceedings of the 21st Annual International ACM SIGIR Conference on Research and Development in Information Retrieval* (pp. 275–281). New York, NY: ACM.

Porter, M. F. (1980). An algorithm for suffix stripping. *Program*, *14*(3), 130–137. doi:10.1108/eb046814.

Pramait & Bangla Braille. (2001). *By blind education and rehabilitation development organisation (BERDO) and Bangladesh blind mission (BBM)*. Dhaka, Bangladesh: Bangla Braille.

Pramanik, K., & Kido, K. (1975). On the formant frequencies of bengali vowels uttered in isolation. *ASJ Trans. of The Com. on Speech Res., S75-02,* 1--8.

Pramanik, K., & Kido, K. (1976). Extraction of, formant frequencies of initial vowels of bengali words. *ASJ Trans. of The Com. on Speech Res., S75-61*, 1—8.

Pramanik, K., & Kido, K. (1977). Auditory experiments of natural and synthesized bengali vowels. *ASJ Trans. of the Com. on Speech Res., S77-22*, 1-7.

Pruthi, T. (2007). *Analysis, vocal-tract modeling and automatic detection of vowel nasalization.* (Ph.D. Dissertation). University of Maryland. College Park, MD.

Quan, C., & Ren, F. (2009). Construction of a blog emotion corpus for chinese emotional expression analysis. In *Proceeding of the Empirical Method in Natural Language Processing- Association for Computational Linguistics* (pp. 1446-1454). Singapore: ACL.

Quatieri, T. F. (2002). *Discrete-time speech signal processing*. New York: Prentice Hall.

Quirk, R., Greenbaum, S., Leech, G., & Svartvik, J. (1985). *A comprehensive grammar of the English language*. New York: Longman.

Rabiner, L. R., & Schafer, R. W. (1978). *Digital processing of speech signal.* New York: Prentice Hall.

Rahman, K. J. Hossain, Das, Islam, & Ali. (2003). Continuous Bangla speech recognition system. In *Proceedings of the 6th International Conference on Computer and Information Technology (ICCIT03)*. Dhaka, Bangladesh: ICCIT.

Rahman, M. (1992). *Power spectrum and formants extraction of bangla speech*. (MSc Thesis). Rajshahi University. Rajshahi, Bangladesh.

Rahman, M. A., & Saddik, A. E. (2007). Modified syntactic method to recognize Bengali handwritten characters. *IEEE Transactions on Instrumentation and Measurement, 56*(6), 2623–2632. doi:10.1109/TIM.2007.907955.

Rajasenathipathi, M., Arthanari, M., & Sivakumar, M. (2010). Conversion of English text to Braille code vibration signal for visually impaired people. *International Journal of Computer Science and Information Security Publication, 8*(5), 59–63.

Rameswar, D. S. (1996, November). Shadharan vasha biggan and bangla vasha. *Pustok Biponi Prokashoni*, 358-377.

Ratkowsky, D. (1988). Review: The travaux de linguistique quantitative. *Computers and the Humanities, 22*(1), 77–81. doi:10.1007/BF00056351.

Ratkowsky, D. A., & Hantrais, L. (1975). Tables for comparing the richness and structure of vocabulary in texts of different lengths. *Computers and the Humanities, 9*(2), 69–75. doi:10.1007/BF02404306.

Read, J. (2005). Using emoticons to reduce dependency in machine learning techniques for sentiment classification. In *Proceedings of the Student Research Workshop, ACL 2005* (pp. 43–48). Ann Arbor, MI: ACL.

Read, J., Hope, D., & Carroll, J. (2007). Annotating expressions of appraisal in English. In *Proceeding of the ACL Linguistic Annotation Workshop*. Prague: ACL.

Read, J., & Carroll, J. (2010). Annotating expressions of appraisal in English. *Language Resources and Evaluation.* doi: doi:10.1007/s10579-010-9135-7.

Riasati, V. R., Banerjee, P. P., Abushagur, M., & Howell, K. B. (2000). Rotation-invariant synthetic discriminant function for optical pattern recognition. *Optical Engineering (Redondo Beach, Calif.), 39*, 1156–1161. doi:10.1117/1.602479.

Richards, B., & Malvern, D. (2000). *Measuring vocabulary richness in teenage learners of French.* Paper presented at the British Educational Research Association Conference. London.

Richards, B. (1987). Type/token ratios: What do they really tell us? *Journal of Child Language, 14*(2), 201–209. doi:10.1017/S0305000900012885 PMID:3611238.

Robertson, S. E., Walker, S., & Beaulieu, M. (1998). Okapi at TREC-7: Automatic ad hoc, filtering, VLC and interactive track. In D. K. Harman (Ed.), *The Seventh Text REtrieval Conference (TREC-7)* (pp. 253–264). Gaithersburg, MD: National Institute of Standards and Technology (NIST).

Robertson, S. E., Walker, S., Jones, S., Hancock-Beaulieu, M. M., & Gatford, M. (1995). Okapi at TREC-3. In D. K. Harman (Ed.), *Overview of the Third Text Retrieval Conference (TREC-3)* (pp. 109–126). Gaithersburg, MD: National Institute of Standards and Technology (NIST).

Robertson, S. E., & Jones, K. S. (1976). Relevance weighting of search terms. *Journal of the American Society for Information Science American Society for Information Science, 27*(3), 129–146. doi:10.1002/asi.4630270302.

Rocchio, J. J. (1971). Relevance feedback in information retrieval. In Salton, G. (Ed.), *The SMART retrieval system -- Experiments in automatic document processing*. Englewood Cliffs, NJ: Prentice Hall.

Ross, F. (2002). An approach to non-Latin type design. In J. Berry (Ed.), Language culture type (pp. 65–75). New York: Association Typographique Internationale (ATypI).

Rossato, S. (2000). *Du son au geste, inversion de la parole: le cas des voyelles nasales*. (PhD Dissertation). INPGrenoble. Grenoble, France.

Ross, F. (1998). Translating non-Latin scripts into type. *Typography Papers, 3*, 75–86.

Ross, F. (1999). *The printed Bengali character and its evolution*. Richmond, VA: Curzon Press.

Ross, F. (2009). *The printed Bengali character and its evolution* (2nd ed.). Kolkata, India: Sishu Sahitya Samsad.

Roy, A., Bhowmik, T. K., Parui, S. K., & Roy, U. (2005). A novel approach to skew detection and character segmentation for handwritten Bangla words. In *Proceedings of the Digital Imaging Computing: Techniques and Applications*. IEEE.

Roy, K. Das, & Ali. (2002). Development of the speech recognition system using artificial neural network. In *Proceedings of the 5th International Conference on Computer and Information Technology (ICCIT02)*. Dhaka, Bangladesh: ICCIT.

Ruhlen, M. (1978). Nasal vowels. In *Universals of Human Language* (pp. 203–242). Stanford University Press.

Saha, G.K. (2006, April). Parsing Bengali text: An intelligent approach. *Magazine Ubiquity*.

Saha, G. K. (2006). Parsing Bengali text: An intelligent approach. *ACM Ubiquity, 7*(13), 1–5. doi:10.1145/1132512.1127026.

Salton, G., Wong, A., & Yang, C. S. (1975). A vector space model for automatic indexing. *Communications of the ACM, 18*(11), 613–620. doi:10.1145/361219.361220.

Sarkar, A., Haffari, G., & Ueffing, N. (2007). Transductive learning for statistical machine translation. In *Proceedings of the Annual Meeting of the Association for Computational Linguistics*. Prague, Czech Republic: ACL.

Sarkar, S., & Bandyopadhyay, S. (2008). Design of a rule-based stemmer for natural language text in Bengali. In *Proceedings of the IJCNLP-08 Workshop on NLP for Less Privileged Languages* (pp. 65-72). Hyderabad, India: IJCNLP.

Sarkar, M. Z. H., Rahman, S., & Mottalib, M. A. (2006). Parsing algorithms for Bengali parser to handle affirmative sentences. *Asian Journal of Information Technology, 5*(5), 504–511.

Sarker, M. Z. H., Ali, M. N. Y., & Das, J. K. (2012). Development of dictionary entries for the Bangla vowel ended roots for universal networking language. *International Journal of Computers and Applications, 52*(19). doi: doi:10.5120/8313-1958.

Sarowar, G., Naser, M. A., Nizamuddin, S. M., Hamid, N. I. B., & Mahmud, A. (2009). Enhancing Bengali character recognition process applying heuristics on neural network. *International Journal of Computer Science and Network Security, 9*(6), 154–158.

Savoy, J. (2006). Light stemming approaches for the French, Portuguese, German and Hungarian languages. In H. Haddad (Ed.), *Proceedings of the 2006 ACM Symposium on Applied Computing (SAC)*, (pp. 1031–1035). ACM.

Sayed, A. Z., Muhammad, A., & Martinz, A. M. (2011). Adjectival phrases as the sentiment carriers in the urdu text. *Journal of American Science, 7*(3), 644–652.

Sebastiani, F. (2002). Machine-learning in automated text categorization. *ACM Computing Surveys, 34*(1), 1–47. doi:10.1145/505282.505283.

Seddiqui, M. H., Azim, M. A., Rahman, M. S., & Iqbal, M. J. (2002). Algorithmic approach to synthesize voice from bangla text. In *Proceeding of 5th ICCIT Conference*. ICCIT.

Seeker, W., Bermingham, A., Foster, J., & Hogan, D. (2009). *Exploiting syntax in sentiment polarity classification*. Dublin: Dublin City University.

Selim, M. R., & Iqbal, M. Z. (1999). Syntax analysis of phrases and different types of sentences in Bangla. In *Proceedings of International Conference on Computer and Information Technology (ICCIT)*, (pp. 175-186). ICCIT.

Sen, A. (2001). *Speech synthesis in indian language*. Paper presented at the Pre-Workshop Tutorial on Speech and Music Signal Processing.

Seneff, S. (2005). A two-pass for strategy handling OOVs in a large vocabulary recognition task. In *Proceedings of Interspeech*. Lisbon, Portugal: Interspeech.

Sengupta, P., & Chaudhuri, B. B. (1997). A delayed syntactic-encoding-based LFG parsing strategy for an Indian language – Bangla. *Computational Linguistics*, *23*(2), 345–351.

Shachi, D., & Bhattacharyya, P. (2001). Knowledge extraction from Hindi text. *Journal of the Institution of Electronics and Telecommunication Engineers*, *18*(4).

Shahidullah, D. M. (2003). *Bangala vyakaran*. Dhaka: Maola Brothers Prokashoni.

Shaikh, M. A. M., Prendinger, H., & Mitsuru, I. (2007). Assessing sentiment of text by semantic dependency and contextual valence analysis. In Paiva, A., Prada, R., & Picard, R. W. (Eds.), *ACII 2007, (LNCS) (Vol. 4738*, pp. 191–202). Springer-Verlag. doi:10.1007/978-3-540-74889-2_18.

Shatil, A. M. S., & Khan, M. (2006). Minimally segmenting high performance Bangla OCR using Kohonen network. In *Proceedings of 9th International Conference on Computer and Information Technology* (pp. 160-164). Dhaka, Bangladesh: IEEE.

Shaw, G. (1981). *Printing in Calcutta to 1800*. London: Bibliographical Society.

Shukla, M. K., Patnaik, T., Tiwari, S., & Singh, D. S. K. (2011). Script segmentation of printed Devnagari and Bangla languages document images OCR. *International Journal of Computer Science and Technology*, *2*(2), 367–370.

Singhal, A., Buckley, C., & Mitra, M. (1996). Pivoted document length normalization. In *Proceedings of the 19th Annual International ACM SIGIR Conference on Research and Development in Information Retrieval - SIGIR '96* (pp. 21–29). New York: ACM Press.

Singh, M., & Vatia, P. (2010). Automated conversion of English and Hindi text to Braille representation. *International Journal of Computers and Applications*, *4*(5), 18–24.

Smith, J. A., & Kelly, C. (2002). Stylistic constancy and change across literary corpora: Using measures of lexical richness to date works. *Computers and the Humanities*, *36*(4), 411–430. doi:10.1023/A:1020201615753.

Stevens, K. N., & Andrade, A., Viana & M. C. (1987). Perception of vowel nasalization in VC contexts: A cross-language study. *The Journal of the Acoustical Society of America*, *82*, S119. doi:10.1121/1.2024621.

Stevens, K. N., Fant, G., & Hawkins, S. (1987). *Some acoustical and perceptual correlates of nasal vowels*. Foris Publications. doi:10.1515/9783110886078.241.

Stolcke, A. (2002). SRILM-An extensible language modeling toolkit. In J. H. L. Hansen & B. Pellom (Eds.), *Proceedings of the ICSLP*, (vol. 2, pp. 901-904). Denver, CO: ICSLP.

Stone, P. J., Dunphy, D. C., Smith, M. S., & Ogilvie, D. M. (1966). *The general inquirer: A computer approach to content analysis*. Boston: The MIT Press.

Stoyanov, V., & Cardie, C. (2008). Annotating topics of opinions. In *Proceedings of LREC*. LREC.

Stoyanov, V., & Cardie, C. (2008). Topic identification for fine-grained opinion analysis. In *Proceedings of Coling* (pp. 817–824). Coling. doi:10.3115/1599081.1599184.

Strapparava, C., & Mihalcea, R. (2007). *SemEval-2007 task 14: Affective text*. Paper presented at the 45th Annual Meeting of Association for Computational linguistics. New York, NY.

Strapparava, C., & Ozbal, G. (2010). The color of emotions in texts. In *Proceedings of the 2nd Workshop on Cognitive Aspects of the Lexicon (COGALEX II), COLING 2010* (pp. 28-32). Beijing, China: COLING.

Strapparava, C., & Valitutti, A. (2004). Wordnet-affect: An affective extension of wordnet. In 4th LREC (pp. 1083-1086). LREC.

Subasic, P., & Huettner, A. (2001). Affect analysis of text using fuzzy semantic typing. *IEEE Transactions on Fuzzy Systems*, *9*(4), 483–496. doi:10.1109/91.940962.

Syrdal, A. K., & Gopal, H. S. (1986). A perceptual model of vowel recognition based on the auditory representation of American English vowels. *The Journal of the Acoustical Society of America*, *79*, 1086–1100. doi:10.1121/1.393381 PMID:3700864.

Takamura, H., Inui, T., & Okumura, M. (2005). Extracting semantic orientations of words using spin model. In *Proceedings of the 43rd Annual Meeting of the Association for Computational Linguistics (ACL2005)* (pp. 133-140). ACL.

Talukder, K. H., Rahman, M. M., & Ahmed, T. (2011). An efficient speech generation method based on character and modifier of bangla pdf document. In *Proceedings of 2nd ICCPB Conference*. Dhaka, Bangladesh: ICCPB.

Talukder, M. M. R. (1992). *Spectral and formant analysis of bangla speech (alphabets)*. (M.Sc. Thesis). Rajshahi University. Rajshahi, Bangladesh.

Tanbeer, S. K., Alam, M. S. E., & Mottalib, M. A. (2000). *Study of phonemes for bangla voice synthesis*. Paper presented at the International Conferences on Computer and Information Technology. Dhaka, Bangladesh.

Tetsuya, N., & Jeonghee, Y. (2003). Sentiment analysis: Capturing favourability using natural language processing. In *Proceedings of K-CAP* (pp. 70-77). K-CAP.

Thomas, D. (2005). *Type-token ratios in one teachers classroom talk: An investigation of lexical complexity*. Academic Press.

Titumir, R. A. M., & Hossain, J. (2005). *Disability in Bangladesh: Prevalence, knowledge, attitudes and practices*. Dhaka, Bangladesh: Unnayan Onneshan.

Tokuhisa, R., Inui, K., & Matsumoto, Y. (2008). Emotion classification using massive examples extracted from the web. *Proceedings of COLING*, *2008*, 881–888. doi:10.3115/1599081.1599192.

Tong, R. M. (2001). An operational system for detecting and tracking opinions in on-line discussions. In *Proceedings of Working Notes from the Workshop on Operational Text Classification*. ACM.

Tracy, W. (1986). *Letters of credit*. London: Gordon Fraser.

Traunmuller, H. (1988). Paralinguistic variation and invariance in the characteristic frequencies of vowels. *Phonetica*, *45*, 1–29. doi:10.1159/000261809 PMID:3237776.

Turney, P. (2002). Thumbs up or thumbs down? Semantic orientation applied to unsupervised classification of reviews. In *Proceeding of the Association for Computational Linguistics (ACL-2002)* (pp. 417-424). Philadelphia, PA: ACL.

Tweedie, F. J., & Baayen, R. H. (1998). How variable may a constant be? Measures of lexical richness in perspective. *Computers and the Humanities*, *32*(5), 323–352. doi:10.1023/A:1001749303137.

Uchida, H., Zhu, M., & Della, S. T. (2000). *UNL: A gift for a millennium*. Geneva: The United Nations University.

Uchida, H., Zhu, M., & Senta, T. C. D. (2005). *Universal networking language*. Geneva, Switzerland: UNDL.

Uddin, M. J. (1993). *Computer aided spectral analysis of bangla phonemes*. (M.Sc. Thesis). Rajshahi University. Rajshahi, Bangladesh.

Uddin, M. J., Sobhan, M. A., & Chisty, K. J. A. (2001). Effect of window length on the formant frequency extraction of bangla phoneme. In *Proceedings of International Conferences on Computer and Information Technology*. Dhaka, Bangladesh: IEEE.

Udupa, R., Jagarlamudi, J., & Saravanan, K. (2008). Microsoft research at FIRE 2008: Hindi-English cross-language information retrieval. In *Proceedings of the Working Notes of the Forum for Information Retrieval Evaluation*. Kolkata, India: FIRE.

Ueffing, N. (2006). Using monolingual source-language data to improve MT performance. In *Proceedings of the IWSLT*. IWSLT.

Ueffing, N., Simard, M., Larkin, S., & Johnson, J. H. (2007). NRC's portage system for WMT 2007. In *Proceedings of the ACL Workshop on SMT*. ACL.

UNDL. (2003). *UNDL foundation: The universal networking language (UNL) specifications version 3.2*. Geneva: UNDL.

Valitutti, A., Strapparava, C., & Stock, O. (2004). Developing affective lexical resources. *PsychNology Journal*, *2*(1), 61–83.

VanderLugt, A. (1964). Signal detection by complex spatial filtering. *IEEE Transactions on Information Theory*, *10*, 139–146. doi:10.1109/TIT.1964.1053650.

Vijayalakshmi, P., & Reddy, M. R. (2005). *Detection of hypernasality using statistical pattern classifiers*. Paper presented at Interspeech. Lisbon, Portugal.

Vijayalakshmi, P., & Reddy, M. R. (2005). *The analysis of band-limited hypernasal speech using group delay based formant extraction technique*. Paper presented at Interspeech. Lisbon, Portugal.

Voll, K., & Taboada, M. (2007). Not all words are created equal: Extracting semantic orientation as a function of adjective relevance. In *Proceedings of the 20th Australian Joint Conference on Artificial Intelligence* (pp. 337-346). Gold Coast, Australia: IEEE.

Warren, D. W., & Dubois, A. B. (1964). A pressure flow technique for measuring velopharyngeal orifice area during continuous speech. *The Cleft Palate Journal*, *1*, 52–71. PMID:14116541.

Weaver, C. S., & Goodman, J. W. (1966). A technique for optically convolving two functions. *Applied Optics*, *5*, 1248–1249. doi:10.1364/AO.5.001248 PMID:20049063.

Weinberg, B., Bosma, J. F., Shanks, J. C., & DeMyer, W. (1968). Myotonic dystrophy initially manifested by speech disability. *Journal of Sport and Health Research*, *33*, 51–59. PMID:5643961.

Weitzman, M. (1971). How useful is the logarithmic type/token ratio? *Journal of Linguistics*, *7*(2), 237–243. doi:10.1017/S0022226700002930.

Whalen, D. H., & Beddor, P. S. (1989). Connections between nasality and vowel duration and height: Elucidation of the eastern algonquian intrusive nasal. *Language*, *65*, 457–486. doi:10.2307/415219.

Whitelaw, C., Garg, N., & Argamon, S. (2005). Using appraisal taxonomies for sentiment analysis. In *Proceeding of the 2nd Midwest Computer, Linguistic Colloquium*. Columbus, OH: IEEE.

Wiebe, J. (1990). *Recognizing subjective sentences: A computational investigation of narrative text*. (Ph.D. Dissertation). SUNY. Buffalo, NY.

Wiebe, J., & Mihalcea, R. (2006). Word sense and subjectivity. In *Proceeding of COLING/ACL-06* (pp. 1065-1072). Sydney, Australia:COLING/ACL.

Wiebe, J., & Riloff, E. (2005). Creating subjective and objective sentence classifiers from unannotated texts. In *Proceedings of the 6th CICLing-2005*, (pp. 475-486). CICLing.

Wiebe, J., Wilson, T., & Cardie, C. (2005). Annotating expressions of opinions and emotions in language. *Language Resources and Evaluation*, *39*(2-3), 165–210. doi:10.1007/s10579-005-7880-9.

Wikipedia. (2012). *Bengali phonology*. Retrieved June 28, 2012, from http://en.wikipedia.org/wiki/Bengali_phonology

Williamson, G. (2009). *Type-token ratio*. Retrieved January 10, 2012, from http://www.speech-therapyinformation-and-resources.com/type-token-ratio.html

Wilson, T., Wiebe, J., & Hoffmann, P. (2005). Recognizing contextual polarity in phrase-level sentiment analysis. In *Proceedings of HLT/EMNLP* (pp. 347–354). ACL.

Witten, I. H., Moffat, A., & Bell, T. C. (1999). *Managing gigabytes: Compressing and indexing documents and images*. San Francisco, CA: Morgan Kaufmann.

Wright, J. T. (1986). The bahavior of nasalized vowels in the perceptual vowel space. In *Experimental Phonology* (pp. 45–67). Academic Press.

Xiao, Z., McEnery, A., Baker, P., & Hardie, A. (2004). Developing Asian language corpora: Standards and practice. In V. Sornlertlamvanich, T. Tokunaga, & C. Huang (Eds.), *Fourth Workshop on Asian Language Resources* (pp. 1–8). Sanya.

Xu, J., & Croft, B. (1998). Corpus-based stemming using co-occurence of word variants. *ACM Transactions on Information Systems*, *16*(1), 61–81. doi:10.1145/267954.267957.

Yarowsky, D. (1995). Unsupervised word sense disambiguation rivaling supervised methods. In *Proceedings of 33rd Annual Meeting of the ACL*, (pp. 189-196). ACL.

Yegnanarayana, B. (1978). Formant extraction from linear-prediction phase spectra. *The Journal of the Acoustical Society of America*, *63*, 1638–1640. doi:10.1121/1.381864.

Yi, J., & Niblack, W. (2005). Sentiment mining in WebFountain. In *Proceedings of the International Conference on Data Engineering*. ICDE.

Yi, J., Nasukawa, T., Bunescu, R., & Niblack, W. (2003). Sentiment analyzer: Extracting sentiments about a given topic using natural language processing techniques. In *Proceedings of the 3rd ICDM*, (pp. 427-434). Washington, DC: ICDM.

Young, S. (2005). *The HTK book*. Cambridge, UK: Cambridge University Engineering Department.

Yousuf, M. A., & Shams, S. M. S. (2007). Bangla Braille information system: An affordable system for the sightless population. *Asian Journal of Information Technology*, *6*(6), 696–699.

Yule, G. U. (1944). *The statistical study of literary vocabulary*. Cambridge, UK: Cambridge University Press.

Zhang, H., Yu, Z., Xu, M., & Shi, Y. (2011). Feature-level sentiment analysis for Chinese product reviews. In *Proceedings of 3rd ICCRD* (pp. 135-140). ICCRD.

Zhang, X., Ortega-Sanchez, C., & Murray, L. (2007). A hardware based Braille note taker. In *Proceedings of the 3rd Southern Conference on Programmable Logic*, (pp. 125-130). Mar del Plata, Argentina.

Zhang, Y., Li, Z., Ren, F., & Kuroiwa, S. (2008). A preliminary research of Chinese emotion classification model. *International Journal of ComputerScience and Network Security*, *8*(11), 127–132.

Zheng, Y., & Hasegawa-Johnson, M. (2004). Formant tracking by mixture state particle filter. In *Proceedings of ICASSP*. ICASSP.

Zhou, L., & Hovy, E. (2006). On the summarization of dynamically introduced information: Online discussions and blogs. In *Proceedings of the AAAI-2006 Spring Symposium on Computational Approaches to Analyzing Weblogs*. Stanford, CA: AAAI.

Zobel, J., & Moffat, A. (1998). Exploring the similarity space. *ACM SIGIR Forum*, *32*(1), 18–34.

About the Contributors

Mohammad Ataul Karim is Provost and Executive Vice Chancellor of Academic and Students Affairs of the University of Massachusetts Dartmouth where he is a professor of electrical and computer engineering with expertise on computing, electro-optical displays and systems, information processing, and pattern recognition. During 2009-2013, he was Vice President for Research of Old Dominion University in Virginia. Professor Karim is an elected fellow of the Institution of Electrical and Electronics Engineers (IEEE), Optical Society of America (OSA), Society of Photo-Instrumentation Engineers (SPIE), the Institute of Physics (InstP), the Institution of Engineering & Technology (IET), and Bangladesh Academy of Sciences. He has authored 18 books, 7 chapters, and over 375 research articles. In addition to being the Editor of *Optics & Laser Technology* and an Associate Editor of the *IEEE Transactions on Education,* he guest-edited to-date 33 journal special issues. Karim received his BS in Physics in 1976 from the University of Dacca, Bangladesh, and MS degrees in both Physics and Electrical Engineering, and a Ph.D. in Electrical Engineering all from the University of Alabama, respectively, in 1978, 1979, and 1981.

Mohammad Kaykobad is Professor of Computer Science and Engineering of Bangladesh University of Engineering & Technology. He received his M.S. (Honors) in Engineering in 1979 from Odessa Maritime University, in Russia, M.Eng. degree in 1982 from the Asian Institute of Technology in Thailand, and completed PhD in 1986 from the Flinders University of South Australia. Elected a fellow of the Bangladesh Academy of Sciences, he is known for his leadership role in pushing forward the higher education agenda of Bangladesh, in particular, in science, mathematics, and information technology. He has authored 15 books, over 45 refereed journal articles, and over 200 opinion pieces in leading dailies. Recognized as the Outstanding Coach in 2002, he has been leading BUET team to participate in the World Finals of Association for Computing Machinery (ACM) ICPC since 1998. He has also played a pioneering role in introducing Bangladeshi school/college students to International Olympiad in Informatics (IOI).

Manzur Murshed is an Associate Professor and Head of Gippsland School of Information Technology, Monash University, Australia, with major research interests in the fields of Video Technology, Wireless Communications, Information Theory, Distributed Coding, and Security and Privacy. He received his B.Sc.Eng. (Hons.) degree in Computer Science and Engineering from Bangladesh University of Engineering and Technology (BUET), Dhaka, Bangladesh, in 1994, and Ph.D. in Computer Science from the

Australian National University, Canberra, Australia, in 1999. He has authored over 160 refereed papers and received more than $1 million nationally competitive research funding including three Australian Research Council Discovery Project grants. He has successfully supervised 16 PhD students and five postdoctoral research fellows. He is an Associate Editor of *IEEE Transactions on Circuits and Systems for Video Technology*, an Editor of *International Journal of Digital Multimedia Broadcasting*, and has had served as a Guest Editor of special issues of *Journal of Multimedia.*

* * *

Farruk Ahmed is a Professor in the School of Engineering and Computer Science, Independent University, Bangladesh (IUB), Dhaka. Previously he worked as Professor and Chair of the Department of Applied Physics, Electronics and Communication Engineering, University of Dhaka, and also of the Department of Electrical Engineering and Computer Science in North South University, Bangladesh. Areas of his teaching and research interests include Digital Signal Processing, Communication Engineering, Microcomputer and Microprocessor based systems, Feedback Control Systems, and Electronic Instrumentation. He is an author or co-author of nearly 180 papers and research articles in various national and international journals and conference proceedings. He holds a PhD degree in Electronic and Electrical Engineering from the University of Salford in Manchester, England. He has been the President of Bangladesh Electronics Society for about 10 years.

Sabrina Ahmed is a Database Specialist in Local Government Engineering Department (LGED), Head Quarter in the PMT (Proxy Means Testing) Project. Sabrina earned her Master of Science in Computer Science and Engineering from United International University (UIU), Dhaka. Her research area covers character recognition and network security.

Nasreen Akter is doing her M.Sc. in Computer Science at St. Francis Xavier University, Antigonish, NS-Canada. She completed her graduation in Computer Science and Engineering from United International University, Dhaka, Bangladesh, in 2012 and under-graduation in CSE from Military Institute of Science and Technology, Dhaka, Bangladesh in 2007. Her research interests are image processing and segmentation.

Al-Mahmud is both a lecturer and post-graduate student of Computer Science and Engineering at Khulna University of Engineering & Technology (KUET), Bangladesh. He received his BSc. Degree in CSE from KUET in 2010. His research interests lies in the area of Soft Computing, Bio-inspired Computing, Natural Language Processing, Graph Theory, Cryptography and Fault Tolerant Systems.

Nawab Yousuf Ali is chair of the Department of Computer Science and Engineering, East West University, Dhaka, Bangladesh. He received MSc. in Computer Engineering from L'vov Polytechnic Institute, Lvov, Ukraine, USSR, in 1992 and PhD in Computer Science and Engineering from Jahangirnagar University, Dhaka, Bangladesh. His research interest includes natural language processing specially Universal Networking Language.

Amitava Das Amitava is a Postdoctoral Scientist at IDI, Norwegian University of Science and Technology (NTNU), Norway. He did his PhD from Jadavpur University, India. His research areas of interest are related with human language, mind and artificial intelligence, Formal Linguistics, Machine Intelligence, and Cognitive Science with a current focus on Sentiment Analysis.

Samiul Azam received his B.Sc. degree in Computer Science and Engineering from Military Institute of Science Technology (MIST), Dhaka, Bangladesh, in 2009, where he has been a Lecturer since 2010. Now he is pursuing M.Sc. program in Computer Science and Engineering at Bangladesh University of Engineering and Technology (BUET), Dhaka, Bangladesh. Areas of his research interests include language processing, image processing, and computational geometry.

Sivaji Bandyopadhyay is Professor of Computer Science and Engineering at Jadavpur University. He received his Ph.D., Master, and Bachelor degrees in Computer Science and Engineering all from Jadavpur University, Kolkata, India, respectively, in 1998, 1987, and 1985. He is engaged with several noteworthy national and international projects involving Cross Lingual Information Access, English to Indian Languages Machine Translation Systems, and Sentiment Analysis. He has had more than 100 publications in conferences and journals and has served in varying capacities with many workshops and conferences.

Anupam Basu is a Professor of Computer Science and Engineering at IIT Kharagpur where from he received his Ph.D. degree in 1984. He is Prof-in-charge of Media Lab Asia – IIT Kharagpur and has received "da Vinci Award" from the Engineering Society of Detroit, USA, and Multiple Scelerosis Society of Michigan, USA (2004), Sir. J. C. Bose Memorial Award for Best Engineering Paper in IETE (2004), and Alexander von Humboldt Fellowship (1997).

Dipankar Das is an Assistant Professor in the Department of Computer Science and Engineering, National Institute of Technology (NIT), Meghalaya, India. In October 2012, he submitted his thesis for the Ph.D. degree in Computer Science and Engineering from Jadavpur University, Kolkata, India. He received his Master of Computer Science and Engineering degree from Jadavpur University in 2009 and B. Tech degree in Computer Science and Engineering from West Bengal University of Technology, Kolkata, in 2005. His research interests are in the areas of Natural Language Processing, Emotion Analysis, Affect Computing, Information Extraction, and Language Generation.

Suprabhat Das has completed his B.Tech degree (in Computer Science) in 2008 from Kalyani Govt. Engineering College, West Bengal and Master of Science (by Research) degree from IIT Kharagpurin 2012. His areas of interest are Information Retrieval, Natural Language Processing, and Machine Learning. He has worked on rule based Bengali stemmer, analysis of lexical richness and stylistic authorship attribution from Bengali literary works.

Sankar De is an Assistant Professor of Computer Application at Gupta College of Technological Sciences, Asansol, West Bengal, India. He completed his Master of Computer Application (MCA) degree in 2000 from Jadavpur University, Kolkata, where he is also a student of M. Tech. in Distributed and Mobile Computing. His research interests are in the field of Natural Language Processing, Wireless Protocols, and Mobile Computing.

Björn Gambäck is Professor of Language Technology at the Department of Computer and Information Science at NTNU, Norwegian University of Science and Technology, Norway, as well as Head of European Collaboration at SICS, Swedish Institute of Computer Science AB, Stockholm, Sweden. He has previously worked at the University of the Saarland, Saarbrücken, Germany; Helsinki University, Finland; the Royal Institute of Technology, Stockholm, Sweden; and Addis Ababa University, Ethiopia. Prof. Gambäck has published over 100 scientific papers on subjects such as conversational agents, spoken dialogue translation, system evaluation, and machine learning.

Debasis Ganguly is a Doctoral student in the School of Computing, Dublin City University (DCU), Ireland. He obtained his Bachelor degree in Computer Science and Engineering from the Kalyani University, India, in 2004, the Masters degree in Computing Science from Indian Statistical Institute in 2008 with first class (Hons.). Before joining DCU, he worked for two years as an R&D engineer on developing tools for logic synthesis of FPGA chips in Synopsys, India. His current research interests include information retrieval, question answering, and navigation and visualization of search results.

Utpal Garain is an Associate Professor of Indian Statistical Institute, Kolkata. His research interest includes Document Image Analysis (DIA), OCRs, handwriting analysis, and document authentication for forensic purposes, etc. Dr. Garain is an associate editor for IJDAR, Springer. For his significant contribution in PR and its applications in language engineering, Dr. Garain received the Young Engineer Award in 2006 from the Indian National Academy of Engineering (INAE). In 2011, he received the Indo-US Research Fellowship in the field of Engineering Sciences.

Shahina Haque is an Assistant Professor of Electronics and Telecommunication Engineering at Daffodil International University in Bangladesh and a Doctoral student of Information Engineering at the University of the Ryukyus, Okinawa, Japan. She received her B.Sc. (Honors) and M.Sc. in Applied Physics and Electronics from Rajshahi University. Her current research interests are speech, image, and bio-medical signal processing.

K. M. Azharul Hasan is with the Department of Computer Science and Engineering, Khulna University of Engineering and Technology (KUET), Bangladesh, since 2001. He received his B.Sc. (Engg.) from Khulna University, Bangladesh, in 1999, and M.E. from Asian Institute of Technology (AIT), Thailand, in 2002, both in Computer Science. He received his Ph.D. from the Graduate School of Engineering, University of Fukui, Japan, in 2006. His research interest lies in the areas of databases and his main research interests include Parallel and distributed databases, Parallel algorithms, Computational Linguistics, Information retrieval, Data warehousing, Multidimensional databases, and Software maintenance.

Foyzul Hassan completed his Bachelor of Science in Computer Science and Engineering (CSE) from Military Institute of Science and Technology (MIST), Dhaka, Bangladesh, in 2006, and Master of Science in CSE Degree from United International University (UIU), Dhaka, Bangladesh, in 2012. His research interests include Speech Recognition, Robotics, and Software Engineering.

Saima Hossain is a Senior Software Engineer in Software Service Division at LEADS Corporation Limited. She completed her post-graduation from United International University (UIU) in 2011 and graduation from Military Institute of Science and Technology (MIST) in the year of 2007. Her interested areas of research are image processing and pattern recognition.

Syed Akhter Hossain is Professor and Head of the Department of Computer Science and Engineering at Daffodil International University. He obtained MSc in Applied Physics and Electronics from Rajshahi University and PhD in Computer Science and Engineering from University of Dhaka. He received Erasmus Mundus postdoctoral fellowship in the area of Informatics and Industrial Engineering for his work with University Lumiere Lyon 2 in France. He has had more than 50 publications/presentations listed in DBLP, IEEE Explore, and other research databases. More details about him can be found at http://syedakhterhossain.blogspot.com/.

Mohammad Nurul Huda is an Associate Professor of Computer Science at the United International University, Dhaka, Bangladesh. He received his B. Sc. and M. Sc. in Computer Science and Engineering degrees from Bangladesh University of Engineering & Technology in 1997 and 2004, respectively. He completed his Ph. D from the Department of Electronics and Information Engineering, Toyohashi University of Technology, Aichi, Japan. His research fields include Phonetics, Automatic Speech Recognition, Neural Networks, Artificial Intelligence, and Algorithms.

Mohammed Nazrul Islam is an Assistant Professor in the Department of Security Systems at the State University of New York at Farmingdale. He received his BS and MS in Electrical and Electronic Engineering from Bangladesh University of Engineering and Technology in 1991 and 1994, respectively, and his PhD from Muroran Institute of Technology, Japan, in 1999. Prior to joining Farmingdale, he worked as a Research Scientist at Old Dominion University, an Associate Professor at Bangladesh University of Engineering and Technology, a Postdoctoral Research Fellow at the University of South Alabama, and as a Visiting Assistant Professor at the University of West Florida. He authored and co-authored more than 120 publications in refereed journals and conference proceedings. His research interests include optical communication, wireless communication, digital image processing and solid state devices. He is a Senior Member of both IEEE and SPIE.

Sajidul Islam completed his B.Sc. degree in Computer Science and Engineering at Khulna University of Engineering & Technology (KUET). His current research interests include Evolutionary Computing, Cloud Computing, Mobile Computing, Artificial Intelligence, and Fuzzy Logic.

Mohammed Navid Izhar completed his B.Sc. Engineering in Computer Science and Engineering from Khulna University of Engineering & Technology (KUET), Bangladesh. He is a programmer in a software company. His areas of research interests are artificial intelligence, networking, game development, Web development, and software marketing.

Gareth J. F. Jones is a Principal Investigator in Centre for Next Generation Localization (CNGL) and Faculty Member of the School of Computing, Dublin City University. He was previously with the Department of Computer Science, University of Exeter, and conducted research at the University of Cambridge, and as a Toshiba Fellow in Japan. He holds B.Eng and PhD degrees from University of Bristol. His research interests are in applications of information retrieval including multilingual and multimedia search technologies. In 2010, he co-founded the MediaEval benchmarking initiative for multimedia evaluation. He is a member of the ACM, ACM SIGIR, IEEE Computer Society, and the steering committee of FIRE (Forum for Information Retrieval Evaluation), India. He has published more than 300 papers including receiving Best Paper Awards at ACM SIGIR and ACM Multimedia.

Ahamad Imtiaz Khan received his B.Sc. degree in Computer Science and Engineering from Military Institute of Science Technology (MIST), Dhaka, Bangladesh, in 2009. Now he is Research Assistant and pursuing M.Phil in the area of Biomedical Physics with Biomedical Physics and Technology Department of University of Dhaka.

Mohammed Rokibul Alam Kotwal completed his Bachelor of Science in Computer Science and Engineering (CSE) Degree from Ahsanullah University of Science and Technology (AUST), in 2007, and Master of Science in CSE Degree from United International University (UIU), in 2010. He is now a graduate assistant at UIU with research interests in Artificial Neural Networks, Natural Language Processing, Speech Recognition, Signal Processing, Fuzzy Logic Systems, Pattern Classification, Algorithms, Data Mining, and Image.

Johannes Leveling is a Research Fellow at Dublin City University where he works on query adaptation for digital content management. His research interests include NLP (Natural Language Processing), IR (Information Retrieval), and QA (Question Answering). He obtained his Diploma on Informatics at the Carl-von-Ossietzky University in Oldenburg, Germany. In 2006, Johannes defended his Doctoral thesis on "Formal Interpretation of User Queries for Natural Language Interfaces Targeting Information Services on the Internet." From 2006 to 2008, he worked at the University of Hagen on natural language processing for question answering, geographic information retrieval, and text readability analysis. Johannes has published more than 60 reviewed papers.

Fakhruddin Muhammad Mahbub ul Islam received his B.Sc. degree in Computer Science and Engineering from Military Institute of Science & Technology (MIST), Bangladesh, in 2009, where he is a Lecturer. He is currently pursuing MSc. degree in Computer Science at St. Francis Xavier University, Canada. His research interests are language processing and real time systems.

G. M. Mashrur-E-Elahi received the B.Sc. Engineering degree (with honors) in Computer Science & Engineering from Khulna University of Engineering & Technology, Bangladesh, in 2009. He is an Assistant Professor in the same department of this university. His current research interests include Computer and wireless mobile networks, Database Systems, Evolutionary computing, Bangla language processing, Distributed computing, and Multi-objective optimization.

Pabitra Mitra is an Associate Professor of Computer Science & Engineering, IIT Kharagpur. He completed his B.Tech degree (in Electrical Engineering) from IIT Kharagpur, 1996, and Ph.D. degree (in Computer Science) from ISI Kolkata in 2003. His area of research interests is Machine Learning, Data Mining, and Information Retrieval. He has won Royal Society Indo-UK Science Network Award (2006), INAE Young Engineer Award (2008), and IBM Faculty Award (2010).

Chowdhury Mofizur Rahman is the Pro Vice Chancellor of United International University (UIU). Before joining UIU he worked as the head of Computer Science & Engineering Department of Bangladesh University of Engineering & Technology. Prof Chowdhury earned his Ph.D from Tokyo Institute of Technology. His research area covers Data Mining, Machine Learning, and Pattern Recognition, and has published more than 100 technical papers in international journals and conferences.

M. Lutfar Rahman is Vice-Chancellor of Daffodil International University, Dhaka, Bangladesh. He was founding Chairman of the Department of Computer Science and Engineering, University of Dhaka. Professor Rahman obtained MSc in Physics in Bangladesh and MSc and PhD in Electronic and Electrical Engineering in England. His teaching and research interests include Microprocessor Applications, Computer Networks, Information Security, and Bangla Language Processing. He has over 100 research papers to his credit and has authored/co-authored sixteen books on Electronics, Communications, and Computer Engineering.

Mohammad Mizanur Rahman is an Assistant Professor of Computer Science and Engineering at Institute of Science and Technology (IST), Dhaka. He earned his M.Sc. and B.Sc. (honors) in Computer Science from Institute of Science and Technology, under National University, Bangladesh. His research area covers character recognition, neural network, network management, congestion control, and QoS at Internetworking platform.

Shamim Ripon is an Assistant Professor in the Department of Computer Science and Engineering, East West University, Dhaka, Bangladesh, where he leads Software Engineering and Formal Method Research Group. Previously, he was a Research Associate in the Department of Computing Science, University of York, UK, and Research Fellow in the Department of Computing Science, University of Glasgow, UK. Ripon holds a B.Sc. in Computer Science and Engineering from Khulna University, MSc in Computer Science from National University of Singapore, and PhD in Computer Science from University of Southampton, UK. His research interests focus on the Requirement Engineering, Software Product Line, Semantic Web, Natural Language Processing. His current research examines the formal representation and verification of knowledge based requirement specification.

Fiona Ross specializes in non-Latin type design and typography, having a background in languages with a PhD in Indian Palaeography (SOAS). From 1978 to 1989, she worked for Linotype Limited (UK), with responsibility for the design of their non-Latin fonts and typesetting schemes. Since 1989 she has worked as a consultant, author, lecturer, and type designer; her recent work as a designer has been in collaboration with Tim Holloway and John Hudson (as Associate Designer at Tiro Typeworks), developing original typeface designs for clients that include Ananda Bazar Patrika, Adobe, Microsoft, and Harvard University Press for the Murty Classical of Library of India. In 2003, Fiona joined the Department of Typography & Graphic Communication at the University of Reading (UK), where she is Reader in Non-Latin Type Design and Curator of the Department's Non-Latin Type Collection.

Maxim Roy received his PhD in Computer Science from Simon Fraser University, Canada. His primary research interests lie in Natural Language Processing (NLP) mainly focused in statistical machine translation, co-reference resolution, and entity extraction techniques. He received his M.Sc. and B.Sc. in Computer Science from the University of Windsor. Currently, he is team lead in the language group at Northside Inc., Canada, where he is involved in R&D of a full NLP pipeline (parsing, reasoning, and generation) for a revolutionary video game technology featuring natural language-based interaction and advanced AI.

Bishnu Sarker received his B.Sc. (Engg.) in Computer Science and Engineering (CSE) from Khulna University of Engineering & Technology (KUET), Bangladesh, in 2011. He is a Lecturer of CSE, KUET since. His research interest includes Evolutionary Computation, Computational Linguistic, Fuzzy Control system, Distributed Computing, and Fault Tolerant Computing.

Hasan Sarwar is a Professor and Head of CSE Department at United International University. He received his PhD from Dept of Applied Physics, Electronics, and Communication Engineering of University of Dhaka in 2006. His research areas of interests are numerical simulation of semiconductor materials and devices, pattern recognition, computer communication and network, telemedicine. He works as a consultant to develop the Research and Education Network of Bangladesh (BDREN).

M. Abdus Sobhan is a Professor in the School of Engineering and Computer Science, Independent University, Bangladesh (IUB), Dhaka. Previously, he was the Executive Director of Bangladesh Computer Council under the Ministry of Science and ICT of the Govt of Bangladesh from 1997 to 2002. He obtained the BSc Hons and MSc degrees in Physics and Applied Physics and Electronics (APE) in 1969 and 1970, respectively, from Rajshahi University (RU), Bangladesh, and his PhD degree in Electronics and Electrical Communication Engineering from Indian Institute of Technology Kharagpur in 1989. He has published over 50 peer-reviewed international journal papers and about 150 International and National level Conference Proceedings papers.

Index

A

B

C

D

N

O

P

Q

R

S

T

U

V

W

Z